WHAT SHOULD POLITICAL THEORY BE NOW?

edited by
John S. Nelson

Essays from the Shambaugh Conference on Political Theory

State University of New York Press
ALBANY

For Lane Davis,

in friendship
and gratitude

Published by
State University of New York Press, Albany

©1983 State University of New York

For information, address State University of New York
Press, State University Plaza, Albany, N.Y., 12246

Library of Congress Cataloging in Publication Data
Main entry under title:

What should political theory be now?

Includes index.
1. Political Science — Addresses, essays, lectures.
I. Nelson, John S., 1950-   . II. Shambaugh
Conference on Political Theory (1981 : University of
Iowa)
JA71.W454   1983   320'.01   82-19167
ISBN 0-87395-694-X
ISBN 0-87395-695-8 (pbk.)

10 9 8 7 6 5 4 3 2 1

What Should Political Theory Be Now?

SUNY Series in Political Theory: Contemporary Issues
John G. Gunnell, EDITOR

PREFACE

What Should Political Theory Be Now? Aside from a somewhat deceptive simplicity, the title pretty well tells the tale of this book. To answer the title question is to address two large, but related issues. First, what is the proper character of theorizing about politics? And second, what are the priority projects for current political theory? In addition, the title question invites reflection on why it is raised now and thus on what has been happening recently in the realms of politics and theory. Accordingly, each essay in this volume is at once an argument about **what is to be done** in political theory and an exemplar of **how to do it.**

Lately, collections of this kind have inclined toward introductions which summarize the arguments of the other contributors -- as though the editor could say nothing better, the main essays could stand the improvement, or the reader could hardly handle them without such help. May this incipient custom be nipped in the bud: its reconstructions seldom aid our understanding, and its repetitions often waste our time and attention. In this respect, the essays to follow speak far better for themselves than any editor could. Instead, this preface aspires only to explain whence the anthology comes and what it attempts to accomplish.

Directly and indirectly, the following essays come out of a research conference held at the University of Iowa in 1981. Sponsored by the Benjamin F. Shambaugh Fund, the conference brought together twenty-one political theorists to consider the topic indicated by the title of this anthology. Participants were chosen for their high quality of work, great diversity of views and ages, and deep capacity of self-reflection. A previous round table at the 1980 Annual Meeting of the American Political Science Association helped to specify issues for the conference and provide an early forum for a few of the arguments later presented at the conference itself. Participants in the Iowa City area warmed up throughout the fall of 1980 with a faculty seminar on the conference topic. After more than three days of discussion, the conferees retired to reconsider and rewrite their contributions in a process of arguing and editing that consumed almost a year. The results are now before you.

Most of these essays were delivered and discussed during the conference. A few were begun for other

occasions, as indicated in acknowledgements made individually by the authors.   But only one has been published previously: the essay by Michael Walzer.   Although not presented   at   the   conference   itself,   the   two   essays   on
"Practices and Principles" were first written and discussed
in preparation for the conference; they are included here in
order to enhance consideration of self-consciously scientific
political   theory,   both   analytical   and   empirical.   Several
other essays were spurred by comments during the conference and were written only after the conference was over.
This   development   has   been   especially   pleasing,   and   the
anthology is much richer for it.

Conferees were invited according to four basic criteria, which accordingly characterize the contributors to the
volume at hand.   Collectively,   its authors are outstanding
practitioners,   excellent critics,   emerging talents,   and diverse representatives of political theory as an academic discipline.   Far from mutually exclusive, several of these virtues are conjoined in each of the political theorists included
here.   Yet these virtues became in turn a basis for special
challenges in composing the conference essays.   Authors
widely acknowledged to produce some of the best political
theory recently written were encouraged to reflect upon the
perspectives which inspire their work, as well as the principles which are implied by it.   Writers known for acute
and provocative considerations of the conception and condition of political theory as an entity were asked to write
about the kinds and priorities of political theory projected
by their previous arguments.   Essayists just beginning the
professional practice of political theory, but already showing significant promise for improving upon previous work,
were mandated to formulate their views on theory and politics with special concern for the prospective or preferable
futures of political theory.   And each contributor was
urged to reflect as comprehensively, critically, and constructively as possible upon the project for political theory
evoked or embodied by the theorist's own work to date.

More generally, contributors were challenged to produce examples of the substantive theorizing which would follow from their positions on the principles, procedures, and
epistemologies appropriate for political theory.   Since these
positions come importantly from consciousness of past shortcomings and needed improvements (in political theory generally and their own projects particularly), this last challenge
has   undoubtedly   been   the   most   difficult.   In   political
theory, at least, to identify errors is far easier than to
remove them, just as to recommend improvements is much
simpler than to make them.   Unsurprisingly, the authors'

success is more scarce and mixed in meeting this challenge than the others. Still, it counts for more than other successes. And in any event, even failures in this regard can tell us much about what political theory should (and should not) be now. Hence the essays to come must be read both as **general arguments about political theory** and as **generic examples of political theory.**

Among political theorists, there is now enormous dissatisfaction with the field and its status, even though most political theorists seem to enjoy their work in an individual way. Much of that unhappiness is still diffuse, but every day more of it becomes pointed at the problems summarized in this preface. Despite their many and deep divisions of position, the theorists producing this anthology are united by a suspicion so widespread and insistent that it borders on a communal conviction. In diverse ways, each suggests that the possibilities and responsibilities of political theory are far from exhausted by its projects in recent years. Something seems to be missing; something appears to have gone wrong; more likely, several things. In this respect, the people writing here seem to be typical of political theorists generally. Almost all share inklings of actual or incipient disasters reaching from politics into theory and vice versa.

Yet contributors to this anthology are typical, too, in feeling that there is enough right with theory and politics for the theorist to be able to say (if not set) them aright. Indeed, most political theorists have ideas about where mistakes are being made in politics; and virtually all have strong convictions about where errors are being committed in their own enterprises of political theory. As might be expected, these ideas are highly disparate; but still they bubble toward the surface, waiting to be stirred by discussion into a more potent potion for political theory. This anthology is devoted to evoking the stories and structures behind these discontents and to provoking the disclosures they permit.

Plainly, the essays to come encompass a large set of themes. This has made for many a difficult choice in ordering the essays into a single volume. Many of the major themes on the minds of recent political theorists are discussed at least indirectly by virtually every essay here. In fact, each essay could be said to concentrate directly on no less than four or five important issues of current politics and theory. In such a situation, no single scheme for ordering these essays can even begin to summarize their main interrelationships. Accordingly, the modes of organization that might have been selected make a fitting finale for these prefatory remarks. Even though they could not be incorporated into the table of contents, such other orders specify principles highly helpful in reading the essays collected here. By contrast, such alternatives also clarify principles embraced by the arrangement finally chosen.

At least six of the essays are centrally concerned with criticism as a project for current political theory. Hence a focus on criticism would produce a single section of arguments by Charles Anderson, Terence Ball, William Connolly, Paul Kress, Allan Megill, and Richard Miller. Their issues of criticism include: what it is, whence it comes, where it leads, what it requires, and why it is needed? More specifically, their essays ask: what especially deserves our criticism, how we should give it, what currently prevents or perverts it, and whether it must or even may be combined with more obviously "constructive" contributions by political theorists? Such issues of criticism connect closely with questions of cultural crisis and political engagement.

If engagement in everyday politics were itself a section of this anthology, then it, too, would include at least seven entries. Essays by Anderson, Booth Fowler, John Gunnell, John Nelson, Ira Strauber, Glenn Tinder, and Michael Walzer would all find a comfortable home in such a grouping. All these essays emphasize dangers in the latter-day disengagement of political theory from politics. All identify difficulties and necessities of returning political theorists to intimate involvement in the actual politics all around them. All propose avenues for moving professional political theory more thoroughly into American politics in particular. Of course, where we find six authors, we must expect to find at least six different diagnoses of current diseases suffered by political theorists due to their distances from ordinary politics. Similarly, we must expect to encounter far more than six different prescriptions for decreasing those distances. What we do find in fact, therefore, is a lively and intricate debate about the sources, strategies, and salves for this present-day divorce of theory from practice. Importantly, the desirability of pushing theorists toward arenas of practical politics is contested vigorously by essays arguing that criticism is the main enterprise now proper to political theory. Thus the six briefs on behalf of greater engagement by theorists in politics are contested in one or another significant respect by the arguments of Ball, Kress, and perhaps Connolly.

Still another major theme of this book is our perplexity within and about history. What is history? What are histories?   How does history relate to politics and theory? How does it relate to science and myth?   How does it relate to us?   How can we live with traditions we make for ourselves?   How can we live without them?   These and other controversies over history are basic to the essays by Richard Ashcraft, Megill, Nelson, Tracy Strong, and Tinder. Such essays are good places to seek junctures between substantive arguments in political theory and epistemological reflections on political theory.   This is because questions of historical crisis and diremption are crucial for strategies of political inquiry and political action alike.   Hence these selections stressing history provide direct debates over some of the assumptions about history which indirectly inform many arguments over other issues arising throughout this book.

Reason is a fourth red skein tying together several of the subsequent essays.   Issues of reason figure prominently in the essays by Connolly, James Glass, Nelson, William Panning, Strauber, Strong, Tinder, and Walzer.   Their essays wonder whether reason is singular or plural, autonomous or conditioned, ruthless or prudent.   They ask if reason is self-expanding, self-limiting, or self-destructive. They consider the wisdom of contrasting reason with emotion, intention, or imagination.   They study the significance of assimilating reason to logic, science, or system.   All these things and more are done in order to weigh the nature of reason in regard to politics and theory.   Since reason is often regarded as the source or medium of criticism, there are interesting ties between the set of essays stressing reason and those emphasizing issues of criticism. Similarly, close connections between essays on reason and essays on history are insured by the hoary conflict over whether to discern reason in and through history or to raise reason above and beyond history.

Many of the essays explore relationships among science, theory, and politics.   How might we conceive and practice a more politically productive study of politics than that of recent years?   What should political inquiry learn from philosophies of inquiry, and vice versa? Are there special theoretical problems posed by the postmodern penetration of science into politics?   Can political theory and political science coexist, converge, or even conjoin?   Should they contest or congratulate one another?   Or are we ill-advised to contrast them at all?   Consideration of these questions is central to the chapters by Anderson, Ball, Fowler, Gunnell, Kress, Nelson, and Panning.   Those essays suggest that old battlelines between political science and political theory have broken down into a creative array of competitions, cooperations, and combinations which defy the classifications of the past.

From these possible patterns, it should be evident that each of these essays has something significant to say in reply to most of the others. Because larger groupings always seemed to exclude some especially pertinent essays, this anthology has found its final arrangement in pairs. As indicated by section headings, each pair highlights a set of issues central to its two component essays. Some pairs are structured to bring out basic conflicts; other pairs are composed to delineate deep agreements. The sections thus formed are arranged as much as possible for the themes, theses, and arguments of the individual essays to progress cogently from the beginning to the end of this book. Even so, thinking back to earlier essays is unavoidably (indeed, desirably) a part of reading any coherent anthology with the careful reflection it deserves; and this collection is no exception.

This preface has sought to provide several perspectives appropriate for putting the particular essays together into a potent whole. But there are bound to be further perspectives also suited to such a task. Carving according to this principle, the book at hand could even include a section devoted directly to this project. Thus contributions by Ashcraft, Fowler, Kress, and Nelson offer histories of recent political theory which give general vantage points for ordering the entire collection of essays. A good next step, then, is into my introductory account of political projects and intellectual perplexities producing the current condition of political theory.

CONTENTS

ACKNOWLEDGEMENTS

Given the project of this book, I must begin by thanking the people primarily responsible for instructing and inducting me into political theory: first, Herbert G. Reid and Ernest J. Yanarella; then Paul F. Kress and W. David Falk; and last, Lane Davis and G. R. Boynton. Each has shared with me his unique perspective in order to encourage me to nurture my own. I know of no greater theoretical gift than that, and I know of no higher professional praise than to acknowledge it.

In preparing this anthology for publication, I have had help from many people. The list includes all who participated in the Shambaugh Conference on Political Theory.

Charles W. Anderson
Political Science
U. of Wisconsin
Madison, WS

Richard Ashcraft
Political Science
U. of California
Los Angeles, CA

Terence Ball
Political Science
U. of Minnesota
Minneapolis, MN

Brian Barry
Political Science
U. of Chicago
Chicago, IL

William E. Connolly
Political Science
U. of Massachusetts
Amherst, MA

Lane Davis
Political Science
U. of Iowa
Iowa City, IA

Paul F. Kress
Political Science
U. of North Carolina
Chapel Hill, NC

Ronald Mason
Political Science
Southern Illinois U.
Carbondale, IL

Allan Megill
History
U. of Iowa
Iowa City, IA

Richard W. Miller
Philosophy
Cornell U.
Ithaca, NY

Hanna Fenichel Pitkin
Political Science
U. of California
Berkeley, CA

John H. Schaar
Politics
U. of California
Santa Cruz, CA

Robert Booth Fowler
Political Science
U. of Wisconsin
Madison, WS

Ira L. Strauber
Political Science
Grinnell College
Grinnell, IA

James M. Glass
Political Science
U. of Maryland
College Park, MD

Tracy B. Strong
Political Science
U. of California
San Diego, CA

John G. Gunnell
Political Science
State U. of New York
Albany, NY

Glenn Tinder
Political Science
U. of Massachusetts
Boston, MA

Mary E. Hawkesworth
Political Science
U. of Louisville
Louisville, KY

Michael Walzer
Social Science
Institute for Advanced Study
Princeton, NJ

Most are represented by essays in the following pages. But even those who are not among the authors have contributed comments and proposals reflected in many of the chapters to come. All the authors join in thanking the other conference participants: Brian Barry, Lane Davis, Mary Hawkesworth, Ronald Mason, Hanna Pitkin, and John Schhar. These six people gave generously of their critical acumen and constructive ideas. Not only the conference, but also this anthology would have been immeasurably poorer without their contributions.

The Shambaugh Conference on Political Theory was made possible by funds provided in memory of Professor Benjamin F. Shambaugh. For forty years, Professor Shambaugh was head of the Department of Political Science of the University of Iowa; and he served as President of the American Political Science Association. The Shambaugh Fund has sponsored a series of lectures by distinguished political scientists visiting the University of Iowa. Shambaugh Lecturers have included: Karl Deutsch, Charles S. Hyneman, Dayton D. McKean, Arnold Rogow, Sheldon Wolin, Herman Finer, Richard Fenno, and John Sprague.

In 1967, the first Shambaugh Conference was held and led to the publication of **Frontiers of Judicial Research** (Wiley, 1969). The second Shambaugh Conference was assembled in 1969 and subsequently produced the publication of **Comparative Legislative Behavior: Frontiers of Research** (Wiley, 1972). The third Shambaugh Conference was staged in 1971 and resulted in the publication of

Legislative Systems in Developing Countries (Duke University Press, 1975). In 1974, the fourth Shambaugh Conference generated publication of **Teaching Political Science: The Professor and the Polity** (Humanities Press, 1977). "The Role of European Parliaments in Managing Social Conflict" was the subject of the fifth Shambaugh Conference, held in 1977. Also in 1977, the sixth Shambaugh Conference assessed "Mathematics in Political Science Instruction," producing materials for instruction which have been published and distributed by the Project on Modules and Monographs in Undergraduate Mathematics and Its Applications. The seventh Shambaugh Conference was convened in 1980 to consider "Biobehavioral Studies of Politics." Papers from that conference have been published as special journal issues on "The Biology of Politics" in **The International Political Science Review** (3, 1, 1982) and on "The Biobehavioral Study of Politics" in **The American Behavioral Scientist** (25, 3, 1982). The collection at hand is based on the 1981 Shambaugh Conference on Political theory, the eighth conference in the series.

Especially, I thank William H. Panning of my own Department of Political Science at the University of Iowa. In order to enhance the book's treatment of scientific theorizing about politics, he has revised a preliminary paper on principles in political science, taking into account discussion at the conference. Like several other departmental colleagues, Bill made valuable contributions to conduct of the conference. I am pleased to be able to share his contributions with you, not only in these acknowledgements, but also in the body of the book.

Similarly, credit should go to members of the University of Iowa Department of Political Science for support at once intellectual, logistical, financial, and moral. I thank Darcy Bisenius, Karen Stewart, Carol Taylor, and Nancy Van Hal for aid in administering the conference and preparing preliminary drafts of the anthology. I appreciate as well the permission of Random House, Inc. for reprinting (as part of Michael Walzer's essay) lines from "Shorts II," originally published in Edward Mendelson, ed., **W. H. Auden: Collected Poems**, 1977. And I am especially grateful to G. R. Boynton, John Kolp, Allan Megill, and Suellen Wenz for assistance with the later stages of manuscript production. Finally, my family helped in many, wonderful ways of its own. Thank you, Connie, Anna, and Aaron.

PART ONE

MYTH AND METHOD

NATURES AND FUTURES FOR POLITICAL THEORY

John S. Nelson

What are the problematics, histories, forms, aims, conditions, methods, and topics proper to political theory? Plainly, these change from one context to another; and yet they may remain stable enough to be prescribed for a curriculum, a lifetime, perhaps even a civilization. In each of these domains, I spin a cocoon of issues for current political theory and thus for the essays to follow. No such scheme should try or pretend to be complete. The one at hand is offered in order to introduce and illuminate some major themes of the chapters to come. Of course, the more you make up your own categories for comprehending those pieces in particular and political theories in general, the more you will be theorizing in your own right: a transcendence of the letter of this introduction which nonetheless would be precisely in its spirit.

PROBLEMATICS

Arguments about priority projects for current political theory can follow in large part from arguments about the proper character of political theorizing, plus claims about the shape of our present situation. Of course, inferences can and sometimes should run in the other direction also. For the moment, however, this interdependence of issues means that quests after futures for political theory can be summarized adequately through questions about natures of political theory. In turn, such questions can be grouped into four basic problematics. These problematics dominate the conduct of recent political theory. Unsurprisingly, they are well represented in the other essays of the anthology at hand. Put briefly, the four problematics concern distinctions and ties between: (1) the humanities and social sciences, (2) theory, (3) politics, and (4) epistemology. Let me present them in this order.

The first problematic involves relationships between **the humanities and social sciences.** Regarded as a field of inquiry, political theory prospers as an oddity within the humanities and social sciences. It persists as an enterprise of the humanities yet makes its home in a discipline of the social sciences. Moreover, in addition to finding its first home in departments of political science, it may be argued to enjoy a second home in departments of philosophy and even a third in departments of history. Thus one continuing concern of current political theory comes out of the tensions and opportunities defined by such a peculiar academic situation. At least implicitly, then, most inquiries into natures and futures for political theory are considerations of past and possible relationships between the humanities and social sciences.

As a prime meeting ground of the two, political theory is bound to be inclined to recurrent, if not necessarily systematic, reflections on such epistemic matters as meaning, method, and communication. Similarly, this strange academic situation encourages and advantages political theory in its long-standing aspirations to synthesis, totality, and universal vision. Like many other self-professed political theorists in the present day, I came and cleaved to the field because it is one of the few places left in academia for the generalist. As an isthmus among more rigorous disciplines and limiting commitments, political theory thrives on eclecticism and protects its practitioners from at least some of the narrowing of mind produced by the more communally constrained inquiries on either side. As a promontory above more restricted studies and specialized research, political theory reaches for horizons and projects its practitioners toward at least some of the broadening of vision traduced by the more strictly academic inquiries on every side.

No doubt, these virtues are not divorced from some of the vices decried in the essays to follow, including my own. Still, they are among the initial and enduring reasons for my joy of joining in political theory. And I know the same to be true of many others in this field, discipline, profession, vocation, vacation: call it what you will. These academic advantages and intellectual glories of political theory must not be lost or forgotten, no matter what else may be done or said about its current condition. Whether in its topics, terms, or even tests, in all its tasks, freedom and ambition are surely among the most important components of what political theory should be now.

The second problematic coalesces around the ambiguity of **theory**. From many angles, the anthology at hand is right to return repeatedly to a multitude of issues about theory. What is a theory? What is a theory of politics? How are we to secure such theories? And what are we to do with them? These questions have received poor attention from political scientists generally, and even from political theorists particularly.   Yet they are not idle issues borrowed from abstract arguments about the logic of knowledge; they are aspects of a problematic crucial for the everyday practice of research in the humanities and social sciences.   Choices about research topics, methods, materials, evidence, conclusions, explanations, and expositions revolve around conceptions of theory.   Indeed, even the premise of the first problematic is controversial when examined from some of the conceptions of theory now popular. In this sense, the second problematic of this collection brings the first one into question.

Increasingly, there are self-professed political theorists who object to the semi-official classification of political theory as one among several fields within the academic discipline of political science.   They are developing many different (and sometimes conflicting) reasons for rejecting "field" conceptions and practices of political theory.   Some push a conception of theory which makes it synonymous with scientific endeavor as a whole.   Thereby, they imply that all properly scientific studies of politics (and nothing else) constitutes political theory.   Others argue that theory is a much broader category, with most academic work seeking its main fruition in theory of some kind.   When all fields of academic inquiry into politics are regarded as properly or potentially theoretical, then segregating political theory into a single field seems impossible or foolish.   Further, at least a few people believe such a starting point almost inevitably supports a perverse academization or professionalization of what should be a richer and more diverse (if also more diffuse) body of study.   And still others contend that treating political theory as a field of inquiry obscures the proper place of political theory in action, in political practice.   This is claimed to hold whether political theory is seen as a field within some larger academic discipline like political science or as a discipline unto itself.   In all these variations and more, some of the subsequent essays discuss how political theory has been, is now, or should be a specific field of study.   Thus this second problematic covers questions about individuated arenas of discourse, academic communities of inquiry, and all other models of enterprises in any sense theoretical.

The third problematic of political theory concerns the ambiguity of **politics**.   Partly, this is a matter of the many ways in which political theorists will always learn new things by battering their heads against different definitions of their subject.   Because a multitude of conceptions of politics, along with extensive sets of political positions and methodologies, have distinguished themselves during the last several decades, challenges of comparison, synthesis, and choice are now unusually acute. By including contributors with a wide variety of views, who are nonetheless eager to learn from one another, this anthology expresses and benefits from the way in which political theory has become a major meeting place for virtually every approach, paradigm, school, worldview, method, and ideology of intellectual life. Hence another part of the third problematic involves facing up to our current (and apparently lasting) **intellectual pluralism.** In turn, that means facing up to the possibility that politics has a certain primacy in most "theoretical" endeavors aimed at human beings: political theory notable (but not exceptional) among them.

Insofar as politics is rhetoric, style, and strategy (or vice versa, as can also be argued), recent intellectual pluralism seems to leave politics as a pivot for much work in the humanities and social sciences. At a minimum, the standard academic splits between theory and practice are called into question by recognizing the difficulty of eliminating politics from even "academic" undertakings. How theorizing **about** politics might or should be theorizing **within** politics now stands as a major issue for political theorists, and hence for the anthology here at hand. Just as the second problematic challenges the first, then, so does the third problematic in turn challenge the second.

Perhaps political theory should cease to be (or pretend to be) "theoretical?" Maybe recent political theory has become insufficiently "political?" Possibly political theory suffers from too little theoretical sensibility and too much political commitment? Can the apparent "politics" of our times be too deficient or corrupt to permit a clear vision (let alone a good practice) of political theory? Indeed, is political theory needed all the more urgently because of the condition of current politics? These kinds of conjectures have become increasingly common in political theory. They insure that all such questions about politics and action must form a third problematic of this volume.

The fourth problematic points to needs and dangers of **epistemology** as part of political theorizing. Our intellectual pluralism requires attention to the "roots" and "grounds" of knowledge and belief. Otherwise, how can we compare, synthesize, and choose among political theories? Plainly, political theorists must strive for adequate conceptions of their projects, just as they must produce suitable sets of standards for self-criticism. Does this not mean that political theorists must keep an eye on epistemology, if not engage continually in it? In fact, is not this collection itself an exercise in epistemological reflection for political theorists?

That it is, obviously; but still any current consideration of political theory must (as this anthology does)
address as well the chronic temptation to substitute metatheory for truly substantive studies of politics, let alone
for politics per se. How can political theory meet its real
epistemological needs without transforming itself into knowledge theory? This task is complicated by the recent political importance of science and language, since their study
leads ineluctably toward epistemological concerns. How to
conceive and practice epistemology while doing truly political theory is bound to be a big issue of this or any other
such web of essays.

In pushing toward continual self-criticism, this fourth
problematic tends to interrupt and even supplant the third
problematic of politics. Epistemology leads political theory
away from immediate concerns of action and political participation. Such reflection seldom avoids some sort of confrontation with the assumptions and aims which guide political
involvement. The obvious danger of the epistemological
problematic as a whole is therefore parallel to the very
problem of epistemology that it engages: how to keep a
legitimate concern for epistemological problems (or even the
problem of epistemology itself) from producing a paralysis
of theory and politics. How can the political theorist prevent epistemological reflections from spinning him into a
steel cocoon of endless self-criticism? How can the very
essays in this volume stop from sliding into sterile abstractions about political theory, when the need is for specific
improvements in political theory?

As far as the book before you is concerned, the
strategy to escape sheer pontificating about epistemology is
simple: balance all arguments about doing political theory
with substantive arguments about politics. Thus this collection contains roughly equal proportions of papers on
political theory and papers in political theory. Moreover,
as much as possible, contributors have tried to integrate
both those projects within each essay. The collection at
hand reveals once again that this is not an easy task. But
making the effort has probably produced better essays,
individually and collectively, than might otherwise have
eventuated.

More generally, the fourth problematic of epistemology
must find limits and criticisms in the other problematics of
political theory, especially the first one of the humanities
and social sciences. By straddling the humanities and
social sciences, political theorists are in an excellent position to reach an unusually diverse and helpful set of

methods, ideas, and audiences in dealing with theoretical tasks.   Indeed, through current projects of substantive theory and ever-available resources of imagination afforded by the peculiar intellectual environs of political theory, every theorist receives a rich variety of reminders that concretely political theory can and must be done.   To tap such resources, wise theorists will attend carefully to the first problematic of the humanities and social sciences, seeking in it a better sense of the potential of political theory.

Brought full circle by these four problematics, I have provided one sort of reasonably succinct summary of issues shared across the essays to come.   But other perspectives on the common contexts and concerns of these essays can be garnered from a brief survey of the recent history of political theory, principally in its American incarnations.   I would shy from this as an exercise in hubris, save for the fact that several other contributors offer their own capsule histories, insuring a decent diversity of views about the sources and structures behind our current situation. Despite a fair degree of agreement about at least some salient facts and factors, these accounts are hardly redundant, for they differ in subtle yet significant respects. And in any case, this historical sketch clarifies some of the concerns which have helped to organize the anthology as a whole.

HISTORIES

The nature and future of political theory have been assessed and reassessed continually since the Second World War.   (After all, these are reflective times.)   Still, the special perspective of the present moment offers several advantages that justify the network of essays presented in this book.   The very possibility of political theory seems no longer in significant doubt, as it once was.   Instead of being preempted by the terrors of twentieth-century politics or the methods of behavioral science, political theory appears all the more necessary for addressing these and other aspects of our current condition.   Moreover, the bare desirability of political theory is much harder to question than several decades ago.   No more need political theorists shrink into sheer speculation, retreat into mere tradition, or fall back into other devices of self-defense.   The days when they felt forced to cluster into small, inwardly directed schools just to protect the very enterprise of political theory seem to be permanently behind us. Now that there has been enough time for a variety of projects to reach some sort of fruition, it is appropriate to reckon achievements and failures, opportunities and needs, complements and conflicts among the many endeavors claiming the mantle of political theory.

This anthology comes from the conviction that a more specific and informed sense of the strengths and weaknesses of different modes of study can and must be attained, at least in some significant measure. It is committed to the idea that a willingness to talk across positions is the key requirement in achieving this aim. Most directly (for the contributors) and only a little less directly (for those who can now read their arguments and reflections), this collection plans to move political theorists a few steps closer to such a condition, taking a good look at the current lay of the land and gaining an even higher ground for future efforts in political theory.

The devastation and degeneracy of the Second World War was disruptive and disillusioning for political theorists. It provoked a time of realism, cynicism, and even despair: both about Western politics and civilization in general and about political theory in particular. Optimists believed that the old political theory had become discredited as romantic, utopian, speculative, evaluative, and inexact. Already it was being supplanted, they hoped, by the new political science. Grand ideological conflicts and programs were no longer needed or welcome in a time of management science and technical adjustments. Pessimists thought that the old political theory had become irrelevant to the new and terrible threats unleashed against public life and private integrity. If Auschwitz rendered poetry passe or perverse, could political theory prove itself any more respectable?

On both sides, of course, there were many different conceptions of "the old political theory." And there continues to be great controversy about the past of political theory (more about that below). But the agreement across these two sides is probably more revealing than the disagreement. On both sides, there was a tendency to blame previous ("traditional") political theorists for the ideas and institutions which had either engendered or ended in the travesties of our times. Furthermore, there was an attempt to celebrate a spirit of pragmatism as the antidote to the poisons of political theorizing. Repeatedly, optimists and pessimists alike fixed upon American institutions and ideologies (although that latter word was seldom used in this connection) as the most resistant to atrocity and disaster in the twentieth century. And equally often, both sides believed that the shrewd genius of the Founders or the deft dynamics of the Constitution and subsequent laws came from a practical (even antitheoretical) turn of mind and deed.

America's relative success in staying above the bloody tides of history was time and again attributed to the American antagonism to abstraction, complication, wishfulness, and all the other features identified with the old political theory. Increasingly, theory was equated with Ideology: in the perversely partisan and arrogantly absolutist sense that Americans have long associated with the Old World and its interminable, irrational conflicts. In popular culture, the animus against theory extended also to politics itself, which has seldom been seen to rise above selfish conniving. The paradoxical task of the post-World War II period was to save or revive an adequate political sensibility, structure political institutions sufficient for the new situation, and yet somehow avoid the presumed problems of political theory. Given that neither optimists nor pessimists seemed to have any significant power or likelihood of future power, however, the only device available for effecting these changes remained that very vehicle of political theory which both sides doubted or even disparaged.

The deepest and fittest irony in all this was that some of the most despairing and compelling indictments of political theory were themselves outstanding works of political theory: Hannah Arendt's **The Origins of Totalitarianism**, Judith Shklar's **After Utopia**, Leo Strauss's **Natural Right and History**, Reinhold Niebuhr's **The Irony of American History**, Eric Voegelin's **The New Science of Politics**, and even (in its rather different way) Sheldon Wolin's **Politics and Vision**.[1] The same could be said of a host of essays by people such as Isaiah Berlin, Alfred Cobban, Ralf Dahrendorf, Robert Dahl, Ernst Cassirer, Hans Morgenthau, and David Easton.[2] To be sure, these and other

----

[1] See: Hannah Arendt, **The Origins of Totalitarianism**, New York, Harcourt Brace Jovanovich, (1951), fourth edition, 1973; Judith N. Shklar, **After Utopia**, Princeton, NJ, Princeton University Press, 1957; Leo Strauss, **Natural Right and History**, Chicago, University of Chicago Press, 1953; Reinhold Niebuhr, **The Irony of American History**, New York, Scribner's, 1952; Eric Voegelin, **The New Science of Politics**, Chicago, University of Chicago Press, 1952; Sheldon S. Wolin, **Politics and Vision**, Boston, Little, Brown, 1960.

theorists had already begun to remake political theory in
many different ways: some subtle and some blatant. Spurred by the arguably unprecedented troubles and treasures
of the twentieth century, they had already begun to turn
out a seemingly unprecedented torrent of writing about politics. They appeared to take for their motto the declaration
of Thomas Mann that "in our time the destiny of man presents its meaning in political terms."

Just as these theorists inclined toward treating politics as the category of totality, analyzing almost anything
and everything in terms of political foundations or implications, so did other writers practice the perspective
expressed in Mann's observation. More than a few of the
novels, poems, and stories written since the Second World
War could be claimed as political theory, albeit expressed
through fictional forms. While American literature of the
last decade or so has offered a strange echo of the pragma-
tist animus against politics (but not theory), portraying
political life in absurdist and dismissive terms, literature
written earlier or elsewhere has been remarkable for its
political insight and intensity. American literature of the
first two postwar decades and much of the notable literature
from other lands has been acutely and astutely political,
worthy of serious attentiion as statements of political
theory. Sophisticated political argument has become common
as well in most of the social sciences, plus several quarters
of journalism. In short, it is clear that earlier announce-
ments of the death of political theory were preludes to its
rebirth rather than its burial.

The plight and flight of a phoenix are easily

----

² See: Isaiah Berlin, "Does Political Theory Still Exist?,"
in Peter Laslett and W. G. Runciman, eds., **Philosophy,
Politics and Society**, Second Series, Oxford, Basil Black-
well, 1962, pp. 1-33; Alfred Cobban, "The Decline of Political Theory," **Political Science Quarterly**, 68, 3, September,
1953, pp. 321-337; Ralf Dahrendorf, "Out of Utopia:
Toward a Reorientation of Social Analysis," **American Journal of Sociology**, 64, 2, September, 1958, pp. 115-127;
Robert A. Dahl, **A Preface to Democratic Theory**, Chicago,
University of Chicago Press, 1956; Ernst Cassirer, **The
Myth of the State**, New Haven, Yale University Press, 1946;
Hans Morgenthau, **Scientific Man versus Power Politics**, Chi-
cago, University of Chicago Press, 1946; David Easton, **The
Political System**, New York, Knopf, (1953), second edition,
1971.

confusing, so that this condition of decrying and doing political theory in the same breath should not be surprising. But beneath these debates about the death of political theory lurk other, less expected peculiarities. Those declaring the old political theory to be dead or dying have talked in terms of a Western tradition of discourse stretching back to ancient Athens. As John Gunnell has argued, however, this tradition may have been more created than cremated in our times. Insofar as there could be said to be such a tradition, it seems to be largely an artifact of twentieth-century attempts both to produce and to resist a postmodern science of politics. In this respect, the history of political theory, both in this century and before, is not only an open question but a crucial issue for any consideration of what political theory should be now. As a category and as a set of practices, political theory is decidedly more ambiguous than the debate about its death would indicate. Furthermore, reminders about the ambiguity of political theory apply with equal force to the next important development to be discussed regarding its recent history.

In short order, the behavioral revolution started and then swept successfully through the American study of politics. A sort of social movement within political studies, behavioralism left behind an academic discipline primarily committed to emulating the rigorous methods and deductive theories taken to characterize the natural sciences. Something of the old political theory was incorporated into this celebration of science, but other projects of the "normative" or "traditional" study of politics were gradually left to a ghetto of the newly restructured discipline of political science. Unfortunately, this internal split has troubled political science ever since.

Behavioralism began an insistence on increasingly sophisticated statistics and quantification. This shows no sign of dying away, even though its earlier militance may be fading as a greater diversity of methods and a better understanding of the foundations of measurement spread throughout political science. The behavioralist requirements of "empirical research," "scientific formation of concepts," "systematic sampling of large populations," and so on have been institutionalized with fair success. Largely lost in its processes of institutionalization, however, has been the single most important part of the revolutionary rhetoric of behavioralism: its commitment to revitalizing the conception and production of political theories. For far too long, American political scientists generally forgot that behavioralism was supposed to supplant the allegedly "barefoot" empiricism of previous decades, even as it was dedicated to turning from speculation and evaluation toward the scientific formulation and testing of truly descriptive theories. The reasons for defaulting on the theoretical promise of behavioralism are too complicated to discuss here. But the important point is that only in the last decade or less have large numbers of political scientists started to think carefully about the requirements of theory and to renew their commitments to reasonably general or otherwise significant explanations of important political events.

While behavioralists were working their way toward the lately proclaimed era of postbehavioralism, political theorists were preoccupied with sorting out solutions to the pseudoproblems of an isolated field of the humanities in a discipline fully dominated by social-scientific commitments. To say "pseudoproblems" is to admit from the outset that not even the reasons for regarding political theory as a field can justify its fairly effective isolation, which was somewhat self-imposed, from the rest of political science. Part of the effort of political theorists was given over to contesting the philosophies of inquiry pushed by behavioralists. Necessary though that was, it nonetheless encouraged a flight from substantive political theorizing into the distinct subject of epistemology. It also left political theory at war with itself, since much of the remainder of the effort of political theorists went to carving out separate projects from those of the behavioralists. These endeavors were to be pursued instead of or (at best) as a complement to the standard projects of other political-science fields, even while the epistemological arguments of political theorists were undermining such separations.

Intellectual history (that is, studying previous political theories, theorists, and their contexts rather than theorizing directly on one's own) became perhaps the biggest activity in the ghetto of political theory. Political theory as intellectual history could shade over into political history in general, since behavioralists were neglecting that subject almost on principle. Because behavioralists emphasized the "empirical" basis of their work, many political theorists accepted or even celebrated the supposedly "normative" basis of the field of political theory. At the same time, the very dichotomy on which this separation was established became less and less respected throughout political science (not to mention philosophy, from whence it first came).

Because behavioralists divided the tasks of science into the empirical (synthetic) and the logical (analytic), many political theorists came to cast their work as conceptual clarification, which presumably could be pursued without bias even as it could be done without the array of methods and statistics thought to be required for the empirical parts of political science. Of course, the analytic/synthetic dichotomy, which was originally borrowed by political scientists from philosophers, was itself under severe philosophical challenge at the time. But almost no one in political science noticed this until the past decade, and real recognition of the objections this implies for most statements of method is still close to nonexistent in the discipline as a whole. Because behavioralists proclaimed science to be restricted to description and prediction, many political theorists saw their avowedly unscientific work in terms of imagination and speculation. With behavioralists stressing the disinterested pursuit of scientific truth, many political theorists promoted political action and commitment. While behavioralists engaged in explanation, many political theorists sought understanding. And as behavioralists attempted to refine the genre of the research report, many political theorists tried to revive the pleasures and practices of literary style and complexity.

Meanwhile, political scientists in fields other than theory were revising their behavioralist assumptions and procedures. They were deciding that, in order to be better social scientists, they would have to face up to the problem and importance of theory. For some, this now means taking the project of deduction seriously for the first time. Self-named "positive" or "analytical" political theorists (the best-known of which are the rational-choice theorists) insist upon the intricacies of axiomatic systems in theorizing. Other formal theorists argue that fairly sophisticated mathematics (previously foreign to political scientists) are needed to produce and express real political theories, given the complexity of political phenomena. For others, this commitment to theory implies a more imaginative political inquiry of mixed methods and daring inferences. Many of these political scientists are edging away from the deductivist conception of theory toward patterning and argumentative models. To complicate the picture still further, there may even be a mild revival of case-study techniques and concomitant conceptions of political theory.

Slow acceptance of the challenges to behavioralist dichotomies has allowed a full-fledged renaissance of public-policy research in political science. Because the old isolation of normative and empirical concerns makes no sense in the study of public policies, political scientists are now scrambling toward revised ideas and practices of objectivity. During this same period, an upswing of ideological debate within the field of political theory has brought into question the standards and defenses of academic objectivity that had previously dominated the writing of political theorists. They had been relying on appeals to presumably transcendental interests argued to characterize political theory in particular and the humanities in general. But an increasing involvement of political theorists in issues of the day leaves the earlier appeals more problematic than before. Even in the academic discipline of philosophy, where the enterprise of political philosophy had been abandoned by analytical professionals as illogical and unempirical, there is now a dramatic return to substantive issues of politics and ethics. Thus in all these settings, renewed attention to public questions of current concern can be cited as both cause and effect of a very real recovery of political controversy and social commitment.

In its years of relative isolation, the academic field of political theory borrowed shamelessly (indeed, almost systematically) from ideas and projects throughout the humanities and social sciences. In assimilating these loans, political theorists have become divided among a multitude of approaches and paradigms. Partly, this reflects the more general phenomenon of academic specialization within disciplines. But it also evidences the tendency of isolation to produce fragmentation of what would have been communities of inquiry into a myriad of small research sects. The gain from reaching out to other fields has up to this point been reduced by the loss from failing to communicate effectively within the field of political theory. And of course, that loss is compounded by poor communication at the theoretical level throughout the discipline of political science. Still, most of the approaches now popular among academic political theorists have been able to develop on their own to the point of tremendous opportunities for mutual instruction and synthesis, as a preparation for broader initiatives in theorizing about politics.

In something approaching this way, the last thirty or forty years have led political scientists and philosophers to a common interest in the nature and future of political theory. The next section elaborates various dimensions of this interest into a direct explanation of current needs for addressing what political theory should be now. And indeed, this anthology offers a fairly extensive sample of the many ways in which such needs might be met.

FORMS

Thus has political theory passed in the last few decades from doubts about its possibility, through virtual segregation as a single subfield of political science, into internal turmoil and tentative outreach toward a variety of projects in the humanities and social sciences. On the whole, this history promotes a particular version of the title question of this book, for we are led to ask: what should political theory be, once the ghetto is gone?

This question is increasingly urgent, not only due to the developments just traced, but also because of recent work within and about political theory. Beyond any doubt, the old walls between political science and political theory have been breached by the simple, but expansive virtuosity of writings from several current political theorists. (These theorists are represented generously in the essays which follow.) Moreover, repeated assaults on the basic justifications of the old partitions have left them with little foundation in fact and even less conviction in principle. (As indicated before, many of the best critics of the earlier assumptions and arrangements are also among the contributors to this volume.) Still further, there are now emerging across a great range of scholars from the social sciences and humanities closely related commitments to reassess the requirements of theorizing, especially as they concern the political needs of the near future. (Advocates of diverse variants of this view are on hand here as well.) Above all, though, this anthology addresses the desire to generate new (or regenerate old) projects of political theory which will speak better to the aspirations and experiences of people in the strange political forms that seem likely to appear in years to come. (Among other things, this accounts for the collection's especially strong contingent of younger theorists.)

In our situation of potentially renewed responsibility for political theory, there must be a sense of priorities for the problems now pressing in upon us. Lest all coherence be lost in an explosion of possibilities, political theory must consider with care its current identities and directions. Its relationships to philosophy, ideology, language, history, myth, science, and especially political action and policy-making must be assessed with sobriety and imagination. The place of politics with regard to the realms of psyche, society, economy, religion, art, technology, and the like must be weighed with tolerance and vision. In the end, the very challenge of coherence must itself be confronted:

whether and in what senses should political theory have a discrete identity and a common core of commitments?

For fending off the confusions of our times, there must be a structure of perspectives to pattern the phenomena now perplexing us. With recent political positions as puzzling as professional ones, political theorists need new histories, concepts, and values to cope with their changing arrangements. More than those, political theorists need new notions of history, analysis, evaluation, and all other aspects of inquiry and action in order to find their bearings in this era. If, as argued elsewhere in this proposal, political theory includes some interesting, perhaps even promising efforts toward these ends, then this book should help to sort through them, as well as imagining others.

In its current condition of substantial opportunity, political theory requires a set of names for the new forms of theorizing now taking shape or soon to come. Political theorists should be seeking to clarify where political theory can, should, or maybe even must go. This means that the essays to follow must examine the tasks, tools, and temptations thrown up by emergent issues and strategies of our times. But it means much beyond that. In addition, these essays must constitute a call for deeper self-consciousness, asking what political theory is now becoming, and why? They must be an invitation to richer imagination, wondering what political theory could become, and how? They must be a challenge to better choice, selecting what political theory should become, and in whom? Most fully, then, they must be an active aid in meeting all these aims and more.

AIMS

Four goals are commonly given for political theory: to comprehend, to conserve, to criticize, and to create. Each project in political theory tends to prize one or two of these ends, ignoring or denigrating the others. At a minimum, reasons are required for celebrating one such purpose and subjugating or castigating another. And that by itself makes useful a better understanding of recent issues regarding each goal. Moreover, there is no general reason for believing that all four must be incompatible. And indeed, every project in political theory tends to produce distinctive ways of pursuing each goal, if only tacitly. Thus inquiry into natures and futures for political theory must ask in what ways these aims are apt, or even urgent, and for whom. In terms of current political theory, each aim evokes at least four further issues. By identifying them, I can clarify the four goals and their challenges to those tackling the title question of this book.

Insofar as political theory is political inquiry, it intends to **comprehend** politics. Since the nineteenth century, the aim of comprehension has been troubled by ambiguity between (scientific) explanation and (humanistic) understanding. From German debates over **Erklaren** and **Verstehen** to Anglo-American dichotomies between the nomothetic and the idiographic, a panoply of distinctions has been deployed and deplored in efforts to resolve disputes about the character of theoretical comprehension. Political theory has been deeply touched by this difficulty. Urgent calls for making the study of politics "more theoretical" persist partly because there is little understanding and less agreement about what this could or should mean.

The other three issues of comprehension coil closely around the first. Controversies of value and method in political theory often turn on the second question of comprehension: how can and should political theory be objective? Differences over what "objectivity" should mean and how it should be effected continue to distinguish many schools of theory from one another. Likewise, political theorists still debate how political theory can and should be a study of totality, if at all. Should theorists seek to see "The Big Picture?" If so, what moves must they make? And how can they stay adequately self-critical in such an aspiration? Of course, answers to these and virtually all other questions, whether of comprehension or other ends of political theory, must depend importantly upon how politics itself is conceived. Hence the fourth issue of comprehension is how "politics" can and should be defined. No collection of essays in political theory could be complete without considerable reflection on that.

As political history of several sorts, political theory seeks to **conserve** both politics and itself. Plainly, the aim of conservation appears in a vast variety of ways. Currently, though, there are four preeminent issues under this heading. First, what is the past of political theory; and how should that past relate to future political theory? Second, should political theory form a tradition (paradigm, universe of discourse, etc.); and if so, what kind? Third, how can perennial issues or other continuing components of political theory best be identified and approached, if at all? And fourth, how can classics of political theory best be identified and addressed? All four questions have lately been the subject of remarkably intense and interesting scrutiny by people with highly disparate positions. As you would expect, this grid of controversies over conservation is easily visible in the essays to come.

Issues of **criticism**, also, are especially prominent in current controversies over natures and futures for political theory. Primarily, the aim of criticism comes into political theory as a matter of political community, although there are other avenues for its appearance. Of late, the poor political prospects of some political theories and theorists have produced a profusion of self-consciously and often self-inclusively critical works. One such species of political writing even brands itself "Critical Theory." Current questions of criticism are numerous and sometimes diffuse, but I find four of them to be truly urgent. Most generally, how have description and prescription been related in political theory; and how should they be related by current and future theorists? Most paradigmatically, how can and should political theory be partisan? Most particularly, how can and should political theory include dystopian visions and degenerative political projections or programs? And most practically, how can and should political theory be political education? In these and other respects, this collection seethes with suggestions about strengths, weaknesses, and strategies of criticism.

Creation is perhaps the main aim of political theory as political action. This purpose of political theory has drawn relatively little attention from Anglo-American political theorists, who have usually worked within and reflected upon the first three aims instead. Very recently, though, there are signs of some challenges and changes for the policy, signs readily discernible in several arguments posed by later chapters. Here the basic question is simply how political theory can and should be political action. But in our times, this points to at least three more specific issues. With the general goal of comprehension in mind, we must wonder how prediction and prophecy have been related in political theory and how they should be related by current and future theorists. Thinking of the broad end of conservation, we must ask how political theory can and should speak to and for the future. And remembering the aim of criticism, we must inquire how political theory can and should include utopian visions and progressive political projections or programs.

Comprehension, conservation, criticism, and creation: all four ends informed the planning and preparation of this book. And all four aims figure mightily in its general object of political theory.

CONDITIONS

No other component of this inquiry into natures and futures for political theory can be understood adequately, unless existing conditions of political inquiry and argument are taken into account. To some extent, of course, this is the province of histories of politics and political theory. Yet a creative concern with futures for political theory keeps the issue of conditions from being covered completely by categories of the past. To our own observations, experiences, hopes, and speculations, as well as to the best available histories, we must put questions about real and desirable situations for political theorizing.

Most personally, we need to know about the real and proper characteristics of those who participate in the enterprises of political theory. What are their forms and contents of political experience: directly and indirectly, actively and vicariously? Are their conditions of inquiry structured by tolerance or persecution, skepticism or activism, alienation or enthusiasm, hope or despair? Are their endeavors primarily matters of scholarship or self-criticism, imagination or resignation, invention or destruction?

Most rhetorically, we should seek to understand the actual and possible features of those who read, listen, and react to the projects of political theory. Audiences differ by size, interest, power, preparation, political experience, composition, opportunities for participation, and so on. Forums and media differ in related ways. Without some sense of such conditions, there is little hope for coming to good terms with any political theory.

Most historically, we must investigate the marks of civilizations, cultures, and subcultures on the pursuits of political theory. Structures of class, myth, aspiration, technology, geography, and the like can be expected to shape the spirits and specifics of all political theories, although seldom in simple, decisive, or deterministic manners. Perhaps the same may be said of all conditions for political theory. But that just makes them all the more intricate and interesting to study.

METHODS

Methods are approaches and techniques of inquiry or argument. In one way or another, virtually every essay in this book carries repercussions for matters of method. How are recent approaches to political theory now to be changed, tested, applied, emphasized, synthesized, supplemented, or ironized? Any good answer to this kind of query must cut across the usual blockade between epistemic and substantive issues. In itself, that is daunting enough. But worse, any decent response to this sort of concern must provide or presume a useful feeling for the field of recent approaches to political theory. Basically, to offer such an orientation is the business of the anthology as a whole; so I make no pretense of giving even an initial sensibility through this introduction. Nonetheless, a supply of labels might be helpful for starters; and that, I can attempt here.

First come the formal theories: most as emigres from economics, but a few from other quarters. Rational-choice (e.g., Anthony Downs) or, more broadly, public-choice (James Buchanan) theories predominate now; but change is in the wind. Axiomatized (Robert Axelrod) and mathematicized (G. R. Boynton) theories of politics are no longer confined to dubious assumptions of individualism, rationalism, and the other substantive postulates of most earlier efforts at formal political theory. Such assumptions have hardly vanished, but they no longer monopolize the market in formal theories of politics. Increasingly, analogies and principles from cybernetics rule this particular roost.

Marxian theories continue to proliferate, even in largely anti-Marxist America. There are so many hybrids with other species of political theory that no short list (and few long ones) can approach completion. Worth such mention (and exemplification) are: the Critical Marxists (the Frankfurt School, including Jurgen Habermas), the Existential Marxists (Jean-Paul Sartre or Maurice Merleau-Ponty), the Freudian Marxists (Herbert Marcuse or Russell Jacoby), the Hegelian Marxists (Georg Lukacs), the Humanist Marxists (Mihailo Markovic or Leszek Kolakowski), the Liberal Marxists (Shlomo Avineri or Michael Harrington), the Phenomenological Marxists (Enzo Paci or Maurice Merleau-Ponty), the Praxical Marxists (Antonio Gramsci), and the Structural Marxists (Louis Althusser), to name a few.

Psychological theories are similarly numerous in branches, if not adherents. Depth psychologies are perhaps the most popular source of political inspiration. They started with Freudian, Jungian, Reichian, Lacanian, and Ego theories; but already others are taking shape. Close on the heels of behaviorist theories (B. F. Skinner) have been those spawned by research on psychophysics and psychophysiology. Then in rapid profusion, there are also cognitive theories (Robert Ornstein), genetic theories (Jean Piaget and Lawrence Kohlberg), gestalt theories (Wolfgang Kohler and Merleau-Ponty again), humanist theories (Abraham Maslow), and learning theories (John Dollard). Political science is reasonably rich with advocates of political theory informed by (and maybe modeled upon) each of these psychologies. But, perhaps appropriately, the political scientists are not nearly as well known as the psychologists who inspire them. Hence I have named the latter rather than the former.

There are many versions of structural and functional theories of politics, including many of the psychological approaches just noted. Beyond them, I might mention: the comparative surveys of Gabriel Almond, Sidney Verba, and so many other political scientists; the symbolic forms of Ernst Cassirer and quite a few casual imitators in political science; and the sociobiologies lately fathered by Edward O. Wilson.

The ranges of interpretive and analytical theory are notably interrelated. The former include: the Hermeticist or Kabbalist theories of Leo Strauss and following, the symbolist theories of Paul Ricoeur and company, the hermeneuticist theories of Hans-Georg Gadamer and others, and the communications theories of Habermas and emulators. Among the latter are: ordinary- and extraordinary-language theories (Ludwig Wittgenstein); speech and action theories (J. L. Austin, John Searle, and Stuart Hampshire); systems theories (Talcott Parsons, David Easton, and Morton Kaplan); and philosophical theories (John Rawls and Robert Nozick). Whether wisely or not, these have recently become real growth areas of political theory, as is evident from the chapters to come.

Less conventional groups of theories may also be identified. These could include distinctively phenomenological, existential, archeological, and practical theories of politics. Of phenomenological theories, there is reason to recognize those which are: eidetic theories (Alfred Schutz), perceptual theories (Merleau-Ponty), interactionist theories (Peter Berger), and frame theories (Erving Goffman). Of existential theories, I would highlight projects of: deic theory (Gabriel Marcel), ontic theory (Martin Heidegger), epic theory (Hannah Arendt), and ironic theory (Soren Kierkegaard). Examples of archeological enterprises span:

idealist theories (Giambattista Vico and G. W. F. Hegel), poetic theories (Friedrich Nietzsche), epistemic theories (Michel Foucault), and deconstructive theories (Jacques Derrida). Finally, there are many, many variants of what I would call practical theories of politics: tactical theories (Hans Morgenthau and Ronald Dworkin), strategic theories (Michael Walzer), polemical theories (George F. Will and Garry Wills), and ethical theories (Willard Gaylin and Richard Sennett).

Of course, such labels and lists help only if you are already fairly familiar with the terrain of current political theory. If so, then you will be pleased to see that the preponderance of these schools and projects appear in the pages ahead. If not, then you can safely ignore these lists for now, confident in the expectation that they will make a good deal more sense once the rest of this book has been read.

TOPICS

After my treatment of methods, you may worry that this last section will attempt a detailed list of every tiny topic touched upon in the entire anthology. Fear not: that is the job of the index, not the introduction. Instead, I end this survey of themes and theses by noting the three main needs served by the book as a whole. For in the largest sense, they are the true topics of this undertaking.

This book is justified by a need to review the recent drift of political theory. It seems unlikely that the disparate directions of intellectual history, conceptual analysis, epistemological abstraction, and ethical clarification deserve equal attention with one another, let alone that they are the only courses capable of being charted for political theory. Furthermore, the aims and methods for these aspects of recent political theory have been appropriated from other enterprises of scholarship, more often than not. Political theorists are only beginning to work through their implications and rework their specifications to fit the distinctive contours of theorizing about politics. Surely there is no reason for political theorists to renounce all involvement in intellectual history, conceptual analysis, or the like. But there is good reason to recognize old reservations and new recommendations with regard to them. More importantly, there is strong reason to remember that each of these endeavors has evidenced a tendency to replace doing original political theory with studying the old political theory of others. And of course, there is every reason to resolve to make any kind of work better than before.

This book is justified also by a need to improve the quantity and quality of discussion across the different schools that have gradually established enclaves in political theory. The present imperative is to produce better dialogue between existentialists and behavioralists, Wittgensteinians and Jungians, Marxists and mathematicians, dramatists and sociobiologists, and so on and on. Thus this collection includes people standing for as many different camps as seemed practicable, while preserving the coherence necessary for substantive and reflective interaction. By no means are all the current schools of political theory represented here. Partly, that is because not even this book is big enough to include so much; and partly, it is due to the limited number of issues which could be considered coherently in one volume. Still, this collection can claim to offer a decent start in confronting the current and future status of political theory.

Finally, this book is justified by a need to remove remaining barriers between political theory as an endeavor of the humanities and political theory as an enterprise of the social sciences. People on both sides need to learn a lot more from one another than they have in the recent past. Far more often than many have wanted to admit, projects limited to either side of the fence have been less valid and successful than if they had been able or encouraged to straddle it. At the least, arguments currently in the air suggest that differences between the two sides have been radically misconceived. Explicitly or implicitly, several of the subsequent essays address what best distinguishes the humanities and social sciences, as well as what accommodation political theory could and should make between them. Similarly, some of the following essays consider what relationships could and should hold among the various academic disciplines sharing projects in political theory: notably, history, philosophy, sociology, psychology, economics, and (of course) political science.

In all these endeavors, this book is neither a beginning nor an end. Better than either, it offers both continuation and innovation along paths of political theory past and present. It provides both the savor of earlier reflections and the vigor of further thoughts on natures and futures for political theory.

IN SEARCH OF THE POLITICAL OBJECT:

BEYOND METHODOLOGY AND TRANSCENDENTALISM

John G. Gunnell

Trees have roots, houses have foundations, and
syllogisms have major premises. Does this tell
us anything at all about knowledge or value?

In the world of science, theories of knowledge
are no substitute for knowledge of theories.

Near the end of his treatise on the human mind,
James Mill stated that he would have preferred to designate
his work a "theory." He hesitated, however, to use the
term, since it had been "perverted" and lost its "original
and literal meaning, that is, viewing or observing" and had
become associated with notions such as supposition and
hypothesis.[1] The history of the concept of theory is complex. But by the nineteenth century, "theory" was associated with a representation of the gap between the world
and the knowing subject, the space into which the activity
of academic epistemology was settling down. Current conceptions of theory are in large measure the legacy of modern epistemology and related philosophical claims about the
foundations of knowledge and value. As a consequence,
political theory has become a thoroughly alienated enterprise. Its identity, apart from its institutional form as a
subfield of political science and its status as a somewhat
loosely defined body of literature, is in crisis if not in
question.

The concept of theory is an abstraction which has
been reified, idolized, and provided with a temporal career.
The idea of the great tradition, from Plato to the present,
gave political theory a past; and aspirations for scientific
and moral certainty have provided it with a future. But as
a concept, activity, and product, political theory is largely
a metatheoretical invention rooted in various doctrines
derived from epistemology, methodology, and a fascination

----

[1] James Mill, **Analysis of the Phenomena of the Human Mind**,
New York, Kelley, 1967, pp. 402-403.

with various forms of philosophical transcendentalism. From the very beginning of political science as an academic discipline and profession, its conceptions of theory have been based on images derived from historical and philosophical interpretations of the canon of classic texts and from philosophy of science. This dependence reached an acute stage during the last three decades as a wide range of political theorists attempted to live out metatheoretical fantasies. Political theory has become a wax musem of philosophical monstrosities.

The alienation of current political theory extends beyond the necessary distancing involved in the relationship between a mode of social inquiry and its universe of discourse on the one hand and its subject matter on the other hand. It even extends beyond what some may feel is the lack of contact with, and relevance to, practical issues. Indeed, it has at least five dimensions.

First, there is alienation from politics. This lies in failures both to make concrete claims about particular configurations of political objects and to attend to the problem of the substantive generic character of these objects. Any relationship of the claims of political theory to actual political things and events is more a matter of assertion than demonstration. Second, there is alienation from the study of politics. As manifested in its literary products, the very activity of political theory has become dependent upon arguments in other disciplines. Much "political theory" consists of little more than imitating work in the philosophies of science and social science, metaethics, history, phenomenology, existentialism, structuralism, critical theory, analytical philosophy and conceptual analysis, psychology, sociobiology, hermeneutics, and the like. The problem is not intercourse with these fields. Rather, when these arguments appear in "political theory," they are seldom critically examined or creatively expanded and deployed; instead, they are merely repeated. These two dimensions of alienation produce a "political theory" caught in a world of secondary and tertiary claims, in a set of problems, analyses, and solutions which involve little more than metatheoretical claims about metatheoretically constituted objects. Continually trying to keep pace with the latest trends in metatheory and paraphilosophy, political theory has become a series of non-claims divorced from any practice except that created by its own inner dialectic.

Third, political theory is alienated from itself in that its self-defined divisions (normative, empirical, formal, historical, critical) are not so much elements of an integrated enterprise as categories drawn from its philosophical preoccupations. Fourth, political theory is alienated from the very species of activity to which it aspires. The ideas of theory and theorizing which guide "political theory" are the residue of various philosophical claims about theory. Finally, political theory is not only alienated from substan- tive study in general and lacking autonomy, but the pro- jects to which it is beholden are themselves products of such alienated enterprises as philosophical epistemology.

There is no doubt that certain elements of this essay are an aspect of the very enterprise that I am criticizing, that is, metatheory. But as Max Weber noted, although methodological arguments seldom contribute anything sub- stantive to the progress of science, they are sometimes nec- essary in order to combat methodological intrusions. Unfor- tunately, however, he was quite correct when he linked this situation to the biblical account of the plague of the frogs.[2] Metatheory begets metatheory, but it is also required in order to deconstruct metatheory. Metatheory is not necessarily pathological. But when it is divorced from substantive theories and the practice of activities which it purports to analyze and yet is simultaneously viewed as their foundation, difficulties begin. And these are the dif- ficulties that have beset political theory.

This essay reflects two basic concerns. The first is to indicate a problem and to suggest how it came about, and the second is to point the way out. No attempt can be made here either to explore fully the various dimensions of the alienation of political theory or to explain their histori- cal evolution. But in the first three sections of this essay I will offer some summary statements on these matters as a preface to suggesting, in the last three sections, a program for the reconstruction of political theory and the dissolution of the metatheoretical dilemmas which have paralyzed it.

THE HISTORY OF "THEORY"

Current notions of theory in social science are for the most part the heritage of rather recent developments in phi- losophy. Mill quite correctly sensed that the classical

----

[2] See: Guy Oakes, "The Verstehen Thesis and the Founda- tions of Max Weber's Methodology," **History and Theory**, 16, 1, 1977, pp. 11-29, on p. 14.

meaning of "theory" was being transformed, and the trend that he noted was even more apparent by the end of the nineteenth century. In Plato's work, for example, "**theorein**" and its cognates are employed exclusively as terms of seeing and ocular imagery. Whether the object is sensible or otherwise, the linguistic constructions are exactly the same. For Plato, seeing is **theoria** whether one is looking at pottery or beauty or whether it is performed by a philosopher or the average Greek on the street. The differences involve the capacities of the person who sees. Translations which make distinctions between contemplation and other types of cognition are inventions of the translators.   Plato also seldom distinguishes between seeing and what is seen, and interpretations of Plato as the quintessential epistemologist who bequeathed to us the subject/object or theory/fact dichotomy (and problem) are retrospective impositions of a distorting framework. My point is not that the "true" meaning of theory can be found in classical philosophy; it is instead that our dilemmas about theory seldom arise as part of the practice of inquiry but rather as problems created within and appropriated from modern philosophy. Earlier notions of theory, however, are in some respects more edifying and actually closer to the understanding of theory in disciplines less affected by epistemology than modern social science.

Despite some sketchy evidence and maybe apocryphal tales about Pythagoras and certain pre-Socratics, the notion of **theoria** as an activity and object of intellectual endeavor has no clear manifestation before Aristotle. In his work, it is associated with the life of the philosopher (**bios theoretikos**). The juxtaposition of theory and practice, or the contrast between the contemplative and active life, constituted a philosophical tradition that reached at least from Aristotle to Marx, but neither in the philosophy nor practice of science was any very systematic meaning attributed to the term "theory."[3] Newton referred to his claims as theories which he pointedly distinguished from hypotheses, but during the seventeenth, eighteenth, and even into the nineteenth century, "theory" increasingly became, often pejoratively, associated with conjecture and speculation. In John Stuart Mill's treatise on logic and science, it is not a special category, and the term scarcely appears. Mill's contemporary Whewell passed off as insignificant what seems to

----

[3] See: Nicholas Lobkowicz, **Theory and Practice**, Notre Dame, University of Notre Dame Press, 1967.

be the emerging question of the relationship between theories and facts.   For Whewell, theories are facts not yet accepted, and facts are confirmed theories. [4]

During the **Methodenstreit** that characterized the emerging social sciences in the late nineteenth and early twentieth centuries, and in the work of individuals such as Weber and Karl Menger, the concept of theory plays no important role.   If this literature had a functionally equivalent idea, it would probably be abstraction; but this says something about the future of "theory" in social science. The "problem" of the nature and function of theories in science and the first systematic use of the term in treatments of the logic and epistemology of science appear in the very late nineteenth and early twentieth centuries, when the history and philosophy of science become distinct academic discplines.   This coincided with, and in part reflected, the contemporary crisis in mechanistic physics and related problems about the reference of certain scientific terms.   In the work of Poincare, Mach, and the founders of logical positivism, the place of theory in science became a definite problem.   Theory was something to be explained (or explained away), since it raised questions about the empirical or observational foundations of scientific knowledge.   Theory was already associated with abstraction, and the philosophical empiricists emphasized the distinction between theory and fact.   Lenin and others who had a stake in certain substantive claims, were understandably upset with this retreat from theoretical realism and the increasing dominance of the instrumental notion of "theory as only a systematization of experience."   He, like Weber, warned against the practice of social inquiry being "led astray by professional philosophy." [5] The philosophy of science originally employed "theory" as an analytical term in the logical analysis of science.   But its arguments increasingly tended to suggest that "theory" referred to an actual aspect or product of the practice of science and to present the problems of theory construction and the relationship between theory and fact as actual scientific problems.   This was the

----

[4] William Whewell, **William Whewell's Theory of Scientific Method**, Robert E. Butts, ed., Pittsburgh, University of Pittsburgh Press, 1968, pp. 58-59, 62, 161-162, 176-177, 275.

[5] V. I. Lenin, **Materialism and Empirio-Criticism**, London, Laurence and Wishart, 1950, pp. 287, 44.

snare awaiting social science.

Social scientists seeking scientific identities and justi-fications for their own endeavors turned to the philosophy of science for instruction and legitimation. They (mis)took philosophical claims about theory as descriptions of scien-tific practices that must be reproduced in both product and activity. Political science as a discipline was born with a subfield of political theory, and this tells us something about the context in which that birth took place. From the very beginning, the idea of political theory was a mutation of the concept of theory in the philosophy of science; but it was also a reflection of nineteenth-century historicism, which was fast giving rise to prototypes of the myth of the tradition.

In the myth of the tradition and in the (initially com-plementary) search for scientific identity via philosophy of science may be found the roots of the modern alienation of political theory. The classic canon of great political books was being "temporalized" and presented as the career of scientific political understanding and the evolution of demo-cratic values. Beginning around the turn of the century, versions of the great tradition created the assumption that the conventional corpus of classic texts constituted the out-put of an actual historical activity or vocation which in turn represented the theoretical dimension of politics. Just as philosophy of science produced the myth of theory in sci-ence, historicism (in German idealism, Marx, Comte, and others) engendered the myth of theory in politics. This was the myth of world-historical actors and texts which, in some mysterious way, supposedly reflected and transformed the thought and action of their ages. They allegedly, for better or worse (usually better until after the Second World War), constituted a tradition that explained the present and was capable of being perpetuated, in some measure, by his-torians of political theory or even political scientists gener-ally.[6]

The remaining true believers who propagate the myth of the tradition are unlikely to enlist much new support, although their myth may be sustained for some time, at least in an attenuated form. Like the hypothetico-deductive myth of science, it is still entrenched in textbooks and uni-versity curricula. But metatheoretical images of theory are

----

[6] For a more detailed analysis of this literature, see: John G. Gunnell, **Political Theory**, Cambridge, MA, Winthrop, 1979.

not dead.   Epistemology thrives and continues to produce alienated forms of theory and method which find homes everywhere from policy analysis to historical interpretation.[7]

EPISTEMOLOGY: APOLOGY AND PATHOLOGY

It is not just, as Paul Kress has urged, that a fascination with the issues and language of epistemology has drawn political scientists away from a concern with political discourse and substantive political problems.[8] It is not simply that there is a fundamental difference between external methodological claims about science (even if correct) and internal methods prescribing how to practice it, so that epistemologies are neither approaches to political inquiry nor theoretical grounds of such inquiry.[9] It is not merely that philosophical representations of the nature of social scientific explanation have been allowed to define a set of issues (such as the problem of the relationship between fact and value) which have been mistakenly assumed to be identical with practical problems of inquiry.   Instead, the problem is epistemology itself.   Traditional epistemology is largely a bankrupt enterprise with no intrinsic legitimacy, let alone the ability to lend legitimacy to other activities.[10]

----

[7] For example, see: John G. Gunnell, "Method, Methodology, and the Search for Traditions in the History of Political Theory," **Annals of Scholarship**, 1, 4, Fall, 1980, pp. 26-56.

[8] Paul F. Kress, "Against Epistemology: Apostate Musings," **Journal of Politics**, 41, 2, May, 1979, pp. 526-542.

[9] See: John G. Gunnell, "Political Science and the Theory of Action: Prolegomena," **Political Theory**, 7, 1, February, 1979, pp. 75-100; Gunnell, "Encounters of a Third Kind: The Alienation of Theory in American Political Science," **American Journal of Political Science**, 25, 3, August, 1981, pp. 440-461.

[10] For recent arguments that call into question the basis and enterprise of traditional epistemology, see: Richard Rorty, **Philosophy and the Mirror of Nature**, Princeton,

It is in fact a kind of philosophical pathology passed on to social science and political theory. Latent in philosophy, the disease becomes active in social science, even spilling over into its relationship with political practice.

Plainly, epistemology can serve ideological functions in politics. It can be employed to justify political values and to underwrite notions of political reality. From Locke's liberal theory of human understanding to positivist legitimations of scientific rationality, this should be apparent. Similarly, philosophy of science can be, and often has been, employed to defend and attack certain practices of inquiry. The debate between behavioralism and its critics in political science is a case in point.

But epistemology can be ideological, apologetic, and rhetorical in a wider, or at least different, sense. This more general role characterized its origins and influenced its subsequent uses. Homer's references to the Muses, Descartes's disquisition on method, Bacon's discussion of induction and observation, and Newton's dismissal of hypothesis: all represent functionally what in retrospect might be termed "epistemology." From Muse to method, all of these claims about the foundations of knowledge were basically and intentionally incontestible. There were no criteria for arguing about them, let alone demonstrating their truth. Nor were they simply incommensurable, like some fundamental claims in science. Epistemology moved on the cusp between science and rival doctrines in theology and metaphysics. It was a means of advancing one position and undercutting contending ones. As they emerged in the context of modern science, epistemology and methodology did not actually reflect the manner in which "knowledge" was obtained, let alone a procedure which others could follow. They were instrumental arguments. They legitimated certain concrete empirical claims and were meaningless when divorced from those claims. Although they were potentially as vulnerable as the most decadent remnants of metaphysics, they eventually (and ironically) gained authority from that which they were designed to authorize: the scientific claims which they supported.

Epistemology often reflected the preferred scientific theories of the time, even after it became the business of philosophy (as with Kant). Yet it became increasingly divorced from substantive claims of knowledge. Science

----

Princeton University Press, 1979; Stanley Cavell, **The Claim of Reason**, New York, Oxford University Press, 1979.

needed ever less justification.   But philosophy needed ever more and turned to a critique of the foundations of knowledge in an attempt to establish, or reestablish, its authority.   That philosophy gave up some of its domain to science is widely noted; that science relinquished some of its province to philosophy is not.   Philosophy took up what science no longer pursued: the search for a methodological legitimating authority.   The foundations of knowledge became the philosophical   problem   of   epistemology,   and   methodology became part of the philosophy of science.   This was the situation in the late nineteenth century, during the formative period of the social sciences.

As a distinct field, epistemology began as sloughed off elements of scientific discourse: arguments without function, substance, or concrete context (except that generated by its own internal churnings).   It had neither the authority to pass judgments on other arguments nor the ability to provide a basis for making them.   It was an alienated enterprise.   Despite pretensions to discovering the foundations of knowledge and the criteria of rationality, it had little to offer practical inquiry in any field until the social sciences came seaching for a scientific image.   They were taken in by the foundations of knowledge scam and believed that scientific method was applied epistemology. As part of academic philosophy, epistemology developed a life of its own, independent of substantive practices of inquiry.   Its relationship with the emerging social sciences was quite evident in the **Methodenstreiten**.   Once we see the difficulties of disembodied epistemology, we can grasp the source of some problems about the meaning and practice of theory in the social sciences.   From the beginning, those problems have been tied to epistemological controversies.

Epistemology sometimes distorts the political object, but mostly it simply directs attention away from it.   This is done on the assumption that the relationship between the knower   and   the   object   is   problematical,   not   the   object itself.   This turns questions about knowledge into pseudopsychological ones and derails substantive theory.   There is no general activity of knowing and no general object (e.g., "the world") toward which it is directed.   At this level, neither metascientific questions nor their generic answers have closure, content, or meaning.   Such epistemology is nothing but alienated commonsense and alienated science. That does not make all epistemology useless.   A "critical" epistemology could inquire whether there are intelligible criteria for knowledge claims in a field such as political science.   An "empirical" epistemology could study the structure   of   such   claims.   As   usually   practiced,   though, epistemology seeks claims independent of the conduct of inquiry. This it cannot do. For even in the form of apology, relevant epistemology is always post hoc and reflects ontology or what I refer to as substantive theory.

Criteria of knowledge are not grounded in a relationship between the subject and the object or in the mental processes of the knowing subject, but rather in the conception of the object. To describe, explain, or evaluate something is to appeal, at least implicitly, to an articulation of what kind of thing it is. This, quite simply, is what I mean by "theory." This is the way "theory" should be used in talking about any mode of inquiry. Theory is embedded in substantive claims. To say this is not to derive a definition of "theory" from some preferred epistemology, but to make a descriptive claim about the practice of inquiry. To say this is to speak in accordance with most established sciences or to talk in terms of what is most common to the various and diverse uses of "theory" in those fields. To say this is also to record what is missing or distorted in political science, to note what has been deferred in favor of epistemological debate or submerged in the unreflective ontology concealed in the everyday language of political discourse. Theories do not explain anything. That is, they are not instruments for understanding given objects. They indicate what is to be explained and provide the criteria of explanation.

THE TRANSCENDENTAL ILLUSION

As it is often now conceived and practiced in political science, political theory is in some respects little more than the residue of philosophical arguments about theory ranging all the way from logical empiricism to critical theory. It is also in part the legacy of transcendentalism. This is another manifestation of the relationship between formal institutional philosophy and social science. There are numerous examples of these transcendental tendencies. Although they often involve a rejection of the methodism characteristic of some aspects of the epistemological turn, they also represent another type of concern with the foundations of knowledge which produces a similar kind of theoretical closure and alienation. But to understand both methodism and transcendentalism requires some further distinctions regarding the meaning of "theory."

Discussions of political theory are often confused,

because the concept exists on two distinct, even if related, levels. Political theory is an object of inquiry in the sense of an ontology and ideology embedded in political action and institutions. It is also an aspect of inquiry into such phenomena. It is important to keep this distinction vivid and to clarify the relationship between the two levels. Logically and historically, their relationship is not unlike that between science and the philosophy of science. Just as much academic philosophy of science and epistemology is an alienated product of scientific discourse, academic or metapolitical theory is an alienated reflection of political discourse and the theory embedded in political life. It has had a career of its own, detached from the political issues which first gave rise to it. Increasingly, it has been governed by problematics generated not only within political theory as an academic field but within other fields such as contemporary philosophy. Just as much philosophy of science relates only remotely to practices of science, much metapolitical theory ties only vaguely to politics. Metapolitical theory need not be transformed into political ideology. But as an element in both understanding and evaluating politics, it can certainly be made more pertinent than it is now. Partly, this is simply a matter of being clear about the distinction between theory in politics and theories **about** politics (metapolitical theory). Making the distinction is the first step in ending pernicious alienation altogether, transforming it into reflective distance.

Conceived as a normative enterprise, political theory is seldom seen now as dependent, in any strict sense, on what happens in politics. It even becomes suspect if associated too closely with some kinds of political ideology. Texts favored in the history of political theory need not have been important politically, just as philosophers tend to get more attention than scientists in philosophy of science. Such texts are often selected for "philosophical" or other academic merits. Even when present, political inspiration or relevance is neglected in many influential interpretations. Many authors of these texts were active in politics and invoked philosophy somewhat instrumentally to generate and justify answers to practical problems. Thus by making the philosophical meaning primary and the political meaning secondary, many a philosophical and historical study of Plato, Machiavelli, Hobbes, Locke, Marx, and others consistently distorts what they were doing. Perhaps it is neither conceivable nor desirable that academic political theory be reintegrated into politics. Yet just as epistemology can be made relevant to actual problems in political inquiry, metapolitical theory must reestablish contact with politics.

Political theory has become detached from political practice. Lacking a concrete concern for that practice, it has become an abstract discussion of concepts such as justice, used less in politics than in talk about politics, and an attempt to give some transcendental meaning to such concepts. In this situation, political theory relates to politics like philosophical explication of concepts such as scientific explanation in terms of freezing radiators and the ubiquity of black ravens relates to science. This search for universal criteria of political judgment is usually based on the latest argument in metaethics or philosophical anthropology. These arguments could conceivably make sense ideologically in the context of practical politics. But like epistemology divorced from scientific discourse, political theory is a disembodied activity, a series of non-claims in a non-context. Such transcendentalism is a symptom of the gap between politics and political theory, but it also serves to perpetuate the gap. Although it may mirror political problems and ideologies to some degree, the reflection is pale.

In many respects, David Easton was quite correct when, in the early 1950s, he criticized political theory for irrelevance to political values and estrangement from empirical analysis of politics. But the next two decades of behavioralist search for scientific political theory did not lead political theory any closer to politics. Behavioralists embraced a particular philosophical image of theory which they tried to actualize (thus inviting criticism in terms of competing ideas derived from philosophy of science), and this philosophical conception of theory (as an instrument for analytically ordering given facts) contributed to the neglect of substantive theory.[11] The behavioral practice and conception of theory provided neither a critical analysis of particular values nor a theory of political values generally. The theory of political systems that did emerge was at once a mere reflection and a gross distortion of politics. To some degree, it did abstract from a particular and somewhat narrowly selected configuration of political experience; but its application to the study of politics reified its analytical system and obscured the actual character of concrete instances of political practice.

----

[11] For a more detailed discussion of the behavioral vision of theory and its relationship to ideas in the philosophy of science, see: John G. Gunnell, **Philosophy, Science, and Political Inquiry**, Morristown, NJ, General Learning Press, 1975.

This analytical transcendentalism and the attack on theory as mere history of political thought precipitated (or encountered) other, but strangely enough, functionally similar forms of transcendentalism.   These included historically immanent myths of the tradition such as Voegelin's account of order in history and Leo Strauss's saga of the decline of natural law.[12] Others such as Herbert Marcuse opposed social scientific methodism by looking for the meaning of politics in Freudian and Marxian visions of human history and human being.   Konrad Lorenz, Robert Ardrey, and Edward Wilson have tried to ground political explanation and judgment in biology; while Isaiah Berlin, H. L. A. Hart, and others have pondered a resurrection of natural law based on notions of the minimal demands of social existence.[13] Still others (J. W. Smith, T. L. Thorson, R. M. Hare) have denied a naturalistic basis to political evaluation and tried to locate logical demands that support certain substantive political values.[14] Finally, Jurgen Habermas has attempted to show that political values are grounded in transcendental demands of knowledge and human interest and that they can be extrapolated from certain conditiions of speech and communicative competence.[15] Various as such arguments have been during the past three decades, they share a retreat from any direct confrontation with politics

----

[12] For a discussion of this literature, see: Gunnell, **Political Theory**, Chapters 2-3.

[13] See: Herbert Marcuse, **Eros and Civilization**, Boston, Beacon Press, 1955; Isaiah Berlin, "Does Political Theory Still Exist?" in Peter Laslett and W. G. Runciman, eds., **Philosophy, Politics and Society**, Second Series, New York, Barnes and Noble, 1962, pp. 1-33; H. L. A. Hart, **The Concept of Law**, Oxford, Clarendon Press, 1961; Konrad Lorenz, **On Aggression**, New York, Harcourt, Brace and World, 1966; Robert Ardrey, African Genesis, New York, Atheneum, 1961; Ardrey, **The Social Contract**, New York, Atheneum, 1970; Edward O. Wilson, **Sociobiology**, Cambridge, MA, Harvard University Press, 1975; Wilson, **On Human Nature**, Cambridge, MA, Harvard University Press, 1978.

[14] See: James Ward Smith, **Theme for Reason**, Princeton, Princeton University Press, 1957; Thomas Landon Thorson, **The Logic of Democracy**, New York, Holt, Rinehart and Winston, 1962; R. M. Hare, **Freedom and Reason**, Oxford,

in favor of a pursuit of transcendental concerns.

They also share a certain "polidolatry." The idea of politics is endowed with a kind of essential quality, and great worth is attributed to it. While much methodological and analytical transcendentalism empties "politics" of substantive meaning and social priority, Wolin and others wrote of "**the** political," its sublimation, and the need for its revival.[16] Just as philosophy of science has always been basically an apology for science, much academic political theory has become an apology for politics. Philosophy of science worships science and attributes transcendental qualities to it as the epitome of human rationality. Similarly, academic political theory often worships the political or public realm. Given its practical origins, this is hardly strange. Since academic political philosophy is in part an alienated form of political discourse, it naturally tends to give political solutions to human problems and to view politics in a messianic manner. The exact source of this transcendental glow is often difficult to locate. For individuals such as Hannah Arendt, nostalgia for the public realm is less for an object in history than for an abstraction conjured up from past ideals. As a result, "the political" has little relationship to the practice of politics. Although an analytical object, it is addressed as if it were an actual activity. This often produces a vacuous normativeness that bears only a grammatical resemblance to substantive political judgment.

Arguments by John Rawls and others about justice or other "political" concepts are seldom related to real political circumstances and events. They are so far removed from actual political discourse that only the faith and isolation of political theorists explain their acceptance as "political" arguments. Because they belong to another realm of discourse, they have about as much hope of guiding politics as metaethics has for influencing the practice of morals.

Oxford University Press, 1963.

[15] See: Jurgen Habermas, **Knowledge and Human Interest**, Boston, Beacon Press, 1963; Habermas, "Toward a Theory of Communicative Competence," in Hans Peter Dreitzel, ed., **Recent Sociology No. 2**, New York, Macmillan, 1970, pp. 115-148.

[16] Sheldon S. Wolin, **Politics and Vision**, Boston, Little, Brown, 1960, p. 8, emphasis added.

Critical theory purports to expose political illusi Popper's critical rationalism influences the practice of science. I do not say "never," only "not often." If political theory really wants to destroy illusion, it should begin with its own illusion of "the political." While this essay emphasizes that there are no transcendental foundations of knowledge, it denies also that there are transcendental foundations of politics. The transcendental mode of theorizing at the metapolitical level must be rejected.

POLITICS AND POLITICAL THEORY

I do not argue that academic or metapolitical theory and politics are, or should be, separated by impermeable membranes. For better or worse, the university certainly provides synanthy. I do not claim that metapolitical theory should be turned into political ideology or forsaken for it. Nor do I suggest that academic political theory can have no important critical and educational role in politics. I insist only that the relationship between politics and political theory is now often confused and falsely conceived. Theory is alienated when it drifts off into realms of discourse not of its own making, when it no longer engages actual problems in political inquiry, or when it becomes absorbed in philosophical methodology and transcendentalism. At the metapolitical level, this alienation contributes to the poverty of substantive political theory and blurs distinctions among epistemology, political inquiry, and politics.

In questions about political theory, there is ambiguity about whether the reference is to a discipline and practice of inquiry or to claims about politics produced by that enterprise. Beyond this, there is difficulty in distinguishing between political theory as metapolitical inquiry (claims about politics within a mode of study) and political theory as claims embedded in political activity and political discourse. The latter distinction is a condition of all cogent discussion about political theory. It is not clear how metapolitical theory does or should relate to political theory as an aspect of political practice. But the first step in dealing with these issues is to recognize the distinction, just as it is necessary to recognize that metapolitical theory and epistemology are different. Simply to concede the existence of such distinctions is to point toward solutions for certain persistent problems or pseudoproblems.

Whatever the merit of work by Thomas Kuhn, Peter

Winch, or Hans-Georg Gadamer, and the like, there is little point to criticisms of it by methodologists, transcendentalists, and rationalists (including Popper, Ernest Gellner and I. C. Jarvie, Carl Hempel, Israel Scheffler, Richard Rudner, Roger Trigg, Karl-Otto Apel, Habermas, Martin Hollis, and Alasdair MacIntyre).[17] The common claim is that it denies either objective knowledge in science or rational bases of critical judgments in morality and politics, thus supporting a kind of relativism, historicism, or subjectivism. Actually, though, the issue is between two contending epistemologies. Only pretension allows Kuhn's critics to suggest that an attack on their position is an attack on science itself, the truth value of scientific claims, or the possibility of critical judgment in philosophy, social science, and political theory, let alone the validity of judgment in society and politics.

There is no doubt that philosophy could influence scientific beliefs or that, for example, anthropology could destroy the beliefs of a primitive society. But these relationships are quite contingent. The point is that epistemology and the criteria of substantive belief are distinct, whatever effect one might have on the other. It is not the duty of philosophy to insure the edifice of science. Nor should philosophy mortgage science (or any substantive

----

[17] For some representative arguments dealing with this issue, see: Peter Winch, The Idea of a Social Science, London, Routledge and Kegan Paul, 1958; Winch, Ethics and Action, London, Routledge and Kegan Paul, 1972; Thomas S. Kuhn, The Structure of Scientific Revolutions, Chicago, University of Chicago Press, 1962; Hans-Georg Gadamer, Truth and Method, Garret Barden and John Cumming, eds. and trans., New York, Seabury Press, 1975; Gadamer, Philosophical Hermeneutics, David E. Linge, ed. and trans., Berkeley, University of California Press, 1979; Richard Rudner, Philosophy of Social Science, Englewood Cliffs, NJ, Prentice-Hall, 1966; Rudner, "Some Essays at Objectivity," Philosophic Exchange, 1, 4, Summer, 1973, pp. 115-135; Karl-Otto Apel, Analytic Philosophy of Language and the Geisteswissenschaften, Harald Holstelilie, trans., New York, Humanities Press, 1967; Israel Scheffler, Science and Subjectivity, Indianapolis, Bobbs-Merrill, 1967; Alasdair C. MacIntyre, Against the Self-Images of the Age, Notre Dame, University of Notre Dame Press, 1971; Bryan R. Wilson, ed., Rationality, Oxford, Oxford University Press, 1970; Karl R. Popper, Objective Knowledge,

enterprise such as political inquiry), anymore than metapolitical theory should rule political judgment. Many charges of relativism stem simply from a failure to distinguish between epistemology and theory, but they also involve attempts by some philosophers to save the authority of philosophy with regard to the foundations of knowledge and to project it as the reflective dimension of practical activities such as science and politics.

When academic political philosophy legislates the just or rational, it often does what logical empiricism does in trying to specify the logical and epistemological grounds of scientific explanation. And to specify what is political tends to involve the same problematic move: attempting to say what is or should be political in a transcendental sense, without sensitivity to the actual units and boundaries of politics. This is exactly like the philosopher of science saying what is scientific, without careful regard for the past and present practice of science. In various forms, transcendentalism lurks behind most "political theory" and its particular descriptive, explanatory, and evaluative claims about politics as well as its notions of the very character of political phenomena. Metapolitical theory must reject such mysticism.

Does this argument relegate political theorists to "underlaborers?" No, for it is is less concerned with what they should not do than with what they are in fact not doing. I am ambivalent about what role they can and should play; but I am not at all ambivalent about what general role they now play and what misconceptions inform it. Until academic political theorists touch concrete political action and discourse more extensively, they will remain underlaborers, no matter what their self-images as instructors or guarantors of political belief and judgment. What

----

Oxford, Oxford University Press, 1972; Imre Lakatos and Alan Musgrave, eds., **Criticism and the Growth of Knowledge**, Cambridge, Cambridge University Press, 1970; I. C. Jarvie, **Concepts and Society**, London, Routledge and Kegan Paul, 1972; Roger Trigg, **Reason and Commitment**, Cambridge, Cambridge University Press, 1973; Trigg, **Reality at Risk**, New York, Barnes and Noble, 1980; Ernest Gellner, "The New Idealism -- Cause and Meaning in the Social Sciences," in Imre Lakatos and Alan Musgrave, eds., **Problems in the Philosophy of Science**, Amsterdam, North-Holland, 1973, pp. 377-406; Martin Hollis, **Models of Man**, Cambridge, Cambridge University Press, 1977.

one recent volume terms the great "upswell of political and social theorizing and speculation in the 1970s" is really not an upswell in thinking **about** (let alone **within**) politics.[18] It is an upswell in alienated political theory.

Political theory today is less a vocation than a philosophical avocation, and its relevance will be muted no matter what its ambitions. Political theorists have launched many charges against orthodox political science, decrying its disengagement from politics and its obfuscation of political reality as a result of methodological preoccupations. But in the past thirty years, it has probably been closer to political objects than most political theory which looked at politics through lenses of philosophy. Behavioralism may have mistaken positivism and methodism for politics, but its opponents in political theory have been lost in the myth of the tradition. Postbehavioralism has only proliferated new philosophical myths for talking about politics and political inquiry, ranging all the way from phenomenology to critical theory. No matter how unreflective, confused, restricted, or incorrect, some mainstream political scientists have at least tried to say something about political things and about what exists politically. It is in saying such things that unalienated political theory lives.

POLITICS AS A CONVENTIONAL OBJECT

To this point, the argument has emphasized that methodological and transcendental concerns divert attention from substantive theory. Such theory is inherent in concrete claims and judgments, and it grounds them in turn. There are no philosophically (that is, metatheoretically) specifiable bases of political knowledge. Criteria of validity for all propositions are ultimately functions of theories: claims and assumptions about the class of objects under investigation. As both a body of literature and a discipline, however, political theory has not only been influenced by epistemology and other metatheoretical literature but has adopted their form. Such "political theory" makes contextless claims about non-objects. Its "politics" is about

----

[18] Peter Laslett and James Fishkin, "Introduction," **Philosophy, Politics and Society**, Fifth Series, New Haven, Yale University Press, 1979, pp. 1-5, on p. 5.

as real, intelligible, and locatable as the "world" constituting the object of traditional epistemology when attempting to specify the conditions and modes of the acquisition of knowledge.

I now turn directly to the question of political objects. My argument is that there are no theoretically constituted political objects and no primarily theoretical criteria for specifying such objects. This is because there there are no intrinsically political objects. Yet from the standpoint of political inquiry, the specification of politics is not arbitrary. Since this agument itself makes theoretical claims about political objects, it must be stated carefully.

There can be no **metapolitical** theory of political objects, because politics is a type, token, or configuration of a certain kind of phenomena. It is a species or subclass of conventional objects. There can, for example, be no theory of political discourse but only a theory of speech and language which political discourse instances. There are political objects, but the fact that they are political is predicational. It is a property, an attribute, or quality attaching to certain instances of conventional objects; and thus there are no phenomena that are essentially or transcendentally political. Politics is a historically and spatially delimited form of conventional action and institutions. Hence there are no generically political objects, except insofar as "politics" refers to various historically connected instances of this form or stipulates certain functional equivalents and family resemblances. There is no other basis for attributing universality to politics.

At this point, the obvious (and theoretically reasonable) question is whether politics is ontological, whether there is a deeper structural or theoretical tie among things conventionally (either internally or externally) designated "political." For example, is politics (in some sense) natural or necessary? Such a claim could be a substantive theory. However specious it might prove in the end, it need not imply a flight of metatheoretical transcendentalism. Reading Marx's historical materialism literally rather than strategically, it could constitute such a claim, as could Freud's theory and certain versions of biopolitics or sociobiology. Such claims deserve to be confronted when they are pursued reflectively and theoretically, but they usually appear as alien imports into the field of political theory and are so flawed that criteria for assessing them cannot be specified.

Much of biopolitics to date does little more than apply a grammar or language game associated with talking about human action to the description of animal behavior.

Sometimes it passes off functional equivalents as theoretical connections, presumes priority for animal behavior, and then reapplies its "findings" to human beings, claiming to present genetic or causal relationships. Similarly, Freudian psychology may be little more than a series of spurious allusions and the transformations of abstracted generalizations into causal principles. But the main point is that such putative explanations of politics are seldom advanced as empirical claims about politics. They care less about the **explanandum** than the **explanans**. "Classical political theorists" were often frustrated political actors; and their academic "successors" are often frustrated philosophers, psychologists, biologists, theologians, and pundits. This accounts in no small way for the alienation of political theory.

Politics is natural in the same sense as a family of natural languages. In other words, politics is irreducibly conventional, and the political object is a species of conventional object. There are only three truly theoretical questions about politics: (1) what is a conventional object? (2) what distinguishes it from other things? and (3) what are its dimensions? This last question asks what phenomena form the class of objects to which the various modes of politics (discourse, action, institution, etc.) belong? Various theoretical claims are relevant to understanding politics; but there can no more be a theory of politics per se than a theory of science, English, or Christianity.

Is this position relativistic, providing little purchase for self-criticism and adjudication of rival claims? If politics has no essence or intrinsic character, if it does not manifest some special feature beyond the general human capacity for conventional behavior, if it is not known in some unique way, then what is the purpose and authority of political theory? To be sure, this worry helps to drive political theory deeper into methodology and transcendentalism. Generating criteria of judgment is a real or practical problem, yet in neither political inquiry nor politics can there be a metatheoretical solution to it. Supratheoretical knowledge is an illusion. The philosophical problem of criteria is abstracted from practice and then, through the medium of methodology or metatheory, comes back to haunt practice. It is the ghost of epistemology past.

In particular, there is no general problem about the critical posture of political inquiry, except that it is not normally part of politics and carries no inherent political authority. But facing this fact seems hard. Actually, the view of politics advanced in this essay can be a powerful instrument of criticism. Politics is often full of transcendental arguments and claims of access to special knowledge; and assuming that political inquiry is parasitic (at least in its origins) in its relationship to politics, it is no wonder that metapolitical theory often reflects this. To show that politics is neither natural nor epiphenomenal, that it is **only** a particular form of conventional objects, is to reveal the emptiness of political transcendentalism and to indicate a potential conflict between the metapolitical and political images of politics.

I call political objects "conventional" rather than "social" because so much of political theory has been concerned about the relationship between society and politics that it is difficult to speak of social objects in a neutral and generic sense. "Social" also suggests a whole range of metatheoretical issues regarding the object of social scientific inquiry which are theoretically irrelevant or at least alienated from any concrete theoretical context. These include the problems defined by such dichotomies as sociologism/psychologism, idealism/materialism, ontological individualism/collectivism, methodological individualism/holism, and historical/nomological. They are not theoretical disputes, even though they are often treated in that manner. Neither do they concern investigatory method, although they are often understood as such. Instead, they are philosophical disputes which may have originated in questions of theory and method but which long ago left the practice of inquiry and found a life of their own in the philosophy of social science. They are now presented to the social sciences in their alienated form as problems to be solved prior to studying substantive issues.

Insisting that social scientists confront such issues is much like telling physicists to address the problem of realism/nominalism before doing physics. But social scientists still struggle with these dichotomies, seeking philosophical authority for their answers. Unless pledged irrevocably to some epistemological persuasion, they usually end up aiming at some metatheoretically inspired mediation. As J. L. Austin noted, most dichotomies cry out for elimination.[19] But the solution is not synthesis. What is required is fission not fusion. This is what theory can do, if extricated from issues in philosophy of social science. This literature (by Peter Winch, A. R. Louch, Charles Taylor, Paul Ricoeur,

----

[19] J. L. Austin, **How to Do Things with Words**, J. O. Urmson, ed., New York, Oxford University Press, 1962, p. 148.

and others) often alienates theoretical into epistemological arguments, usually turning on whether explanation in natural and social science is "symmetrical" or different.[20] A complete reversal of the proper relationship between epistemology and theory, this is the continuing legacy of the nineteenth-century **Methodenstreit.**

Disputes regarding such matters as whether the individual or society is ontologically prior are irrelevant, because conventional objects do not differ from other objects in terms of what instantiates them. Conventional objects, such as linguistic meaning, should be construed as universals which can be predicates of either individuals or groups. Individuals, groups, and events all, in various ways, may be instances of conventional objects. I mention such issues mainly to show how most problems in philosophy of social science make little sense when detached from substantively theoretical claims. For a theory of conventional objects, the reality of groups is neither a theoretical nor a philosophical but a factual (historical) question.

While many Continental philosophers continue to claim ontological priority for collectivities as social actors, Anglo-Saxon philosophers almost always try to salvage priority for the individual. For example, while Anthony Quinton argues that collectivities can be construed as social phenomena and concedes that they are not mere collections of individuals or less than real in their own right, he nevertheless insists on seeing them as logical constructions from individuals which are logically equivalent to the solar system and the Rocky Mountains.[21] This nonsense is engendered by searching for the solution to a metatheoretical problem. As a concept, the solar system belongs to substantive claims about the constitution of the universe. Similarly, the Rocky Mountains are a somewhat arbitrarily circumscribed configuration of physical features. Neither is a logical construction from component entities, any more than persons are logical constructions from cells or actions are logical constructions from bodily movements. Social objects can be either individuals or groups, but the choice

----

[20] For a representative selection of this material, see: Fred R. Dallmayr and Thomas A. McCarthy, eds., **Understanding and Social Inquiry,** Notre Dame, University of Notre Dame Press, 1977.

[21] See: Anthony Quinton, "Social Objects," **Proceedings of the Aristotelian Society,** 76, 1976, pp. 1-27.

is not a metatheoretical one. Social scientists need only know what conventional objects are instantiated by what particular groups or individuals and in what circumstances.

Conventional objects include actions (both linguistic and nonlinguistic), texts, institutions, and other artifacts. They are preconstituted or self-constituted, for (as opposed to natural objects) they are not identified or instantiated by the conventions of inquiry employed in talking about them. (Analogously, the existence of physics as a discipline does not depend on claims in philosophy of science.) Charles Taylor tends to accept a positivist framework for thinking about natural objects. Thus he treats them as given, while maintaining the metatheoretical myth that social facts differ from these "brute facts." Contrary to Taylor's treatment, it must be stressed that conventional objects are just as "brutish" as any other theoretically posited facts.[22] Of course, that they are preconstituted says something about what kinds of things they are and the criteria for distinguishing them. They are not independent of theory; they do not, as May Brodbeck claims, simply "**stand out**, almost begging for names."[23] This is a philosophical version of the old joke about the city dweller who, on first seeing pigs wallowing in farm mud, said that they certainly had been well named. Brute fact, indeed. To ask whether social facts are as objective as natural facts is a metatheoretical diversion.

The first priority for beginning a discussion of political objects is freeing it from categories and issues of the perpetual **Methodenstreit** that repeats itself continually in philosophy of social science. Epistemology does nothing but shortcircuit cogent theoretical arguments. It emphasizes how things are known and how the knower relates to the known; and this leads to the assumption that, once specified, the secret of this relationship can be applied as a method to the act of knowing. Then the thing to be known seems unproblematical or capable of summary treatment. Philosophy of social science emphasizes how something is known and how that knowing compares to other types, and

----

[22] See: Charles Taylor, "Interpretation and the Sciences of Man," **Review of Metaphysics**, 25, 1, September, 1971, pp. 3-51.

[23] May Brodbeck, "Introduction," in Brodbeck, ed., **Philosophy of the Social Sciences**, New York, Macmillan, 1968, p. 3.

this always replays classic battles in epistemology. Whether and how we know something should instead be recognized as largely pragmatic issues, governed by a discipinary matrix and rooted in theoretical claims.

What can instance or bear a conventional object can be no small question (e.g., Washoe the ape or Turing machines). But it is not a theoretical question. Nor can conventional objects be specified by ultimate origins (e.g., human nature or genetic code). I doubt that many recent studies of primate behavior are actually studies of conventional objects, even though that behavior is described (metaphorically) as if it were such an object. But I do not insist that conventional objects are instantiated only by human beings. This issue is too involved to unpack here; but theoretical work on conventional objects requires considerable "regional theory," that is, study of such modes of conventional objects as linguistic and nonlinguistic action. Work on speech seems well advanced, and nonlinguistic action receives increasing attention.[24] The theory of institutions is distinctly less developed.

In metatheoretical discussions of conventional objects, there has been a tendency to confuse modes of these objects with factors in the explanation of such objects. One example is talk about about how thought causes action or how institutions cause thought. This is the root of perpetual controversies in philosophy of social science and historiography, making it a burden borne by much of social science. One particular event or instance of a conventional object might be construed as the cause of another, but one mode does not cause another as such, any more than water explains ice or vice versa. Both are modes of H20. The same is true for thought and action; both are modes of conventional objects. But these categories do not exhaust the modes of conventional objects. Any attempt to understand conventional objects such as political institutions and behavior in terms of some dialectical relationship between thought and action is misguided. In their particular manifestations, speech, thought, action, texts, and institutions are all modes of conventional objects.

The fact that thought is difficult to discuss except as "inner speech" and the like; that distinctions between intentions prior to and part of action or between intentions

----

[24] For example, see: John G. Gunnell, "Political Theory and the Theory of Action," **Western Political Quarterly**, 34, 3, September, 1981, pp. 341-358.

and purposes are needed; that persons can appear to be unaware of their own interests or motives: these are all problems that stem directly from a failure to grasp the modal character of speech, thought, and action. None can be described except by analogy with another, for they are theoretically connected. They relate more like birds and airplanes than famine and birth control; they instance the same theoretical principles, not mere similarities of function. The basic structure of conventional objects is fairly easy to specify. Difficulties arise in elaborating it, connecting its components to a regional theory or analysis of a particular mode, in separating truly theoretical issues from other problems embedded in the conduct of inquiry, and in keeping a firm grasp on differences between theoretical and metatheoretical claims.

The structure of conventional objects consists of three integral but analytically distinct dimensions or levels. The first is their **extension**, which usually is the criteria or sign of the object and which may be manifest in bodily movements, vocal sounds, inscriptions, physical artifacts, and so forth. To qualify as conventional, an object's extension must be significant. This requires that it be recognizable as standing or playing a role within a certain context of conventions (e.g., grammatical, semantic, social). But mere significance does not necessarily individuate, specify, or identify the particular object. That is, it need not reveal the **meaning** which could conceivably be expressed through various significations. For example, political principles can have various institutional manifestations, and it is not always easy to say what political principle is manifested by particular institutions. Meaning is itself conventional; but in turn, it is the dimension of conventionality which identifies particular conventional objects and indicates their specific forces within concrete circumstances. Finally, conventional objects have a dimension of **relationship**. Strictly speaking, it is not a component of their structure but rather involves their contingent (but often conventionally grounded) connection with other things, how they are generated, and what they in turn may generate (as other conventional objects and as events both conventional and physical).

These are the main theoretical characteristics of political objects because political objects are conventional objects. Political objects are political because they express political conventions, because they have political significance and meaning. Political science and theory have recognized political objects as conventional objects but have not thoroughly explored the implications. Regional theory regarding modes of political objects has gone little beyond repeating philosophical claims about the general character of social phenomena and how the study of such phenomena differs from natural science. Not all conceivable objects of political inquiry are conventional objects; and, of course, not all conventional objects are political objects. No particular form of investigation or explanation is entailed by the concept of conventional objects, but it definitely does carry implications for these issues. It is necessary to make a clear distinction between theory (claims about the character of the object under investigation) and the uses or purposes of an investigation (as well as from the particular problems selected for analysis). Confusion about these matters seems implicit, for example, in certain notions of critical theory. Of course, theories are related to such things as scientific purposes. But they are not the same, and the nature of the relationship is not given. Distinctions do not deny relationships and, in fact, make them possible.

Last, let me indicate how engagement in substantive theory can erase some of the metatheoretical images that seem to hold social scientists captive. Instead of elaborating a theory of conventional objects, then, I conclude by demonstrating the need for such theory. This involves suggesting how it can dissolve metatheoretical thromboses in political inquiry and how theory must precede epistemology and methodology. These philosophical blockages include issues about the relationship between fact and value and the problem of what constitutes social-scientific explanation. These questions may have their roots in the practice of inquiry, but when divorced from substantive theory, and posed in an abstract and alienated manner, they emerge as generic, a priori problems for which there are no practical solutions.

THEORETICAL SOLUTIONS TO METATHEORETICAL PROBLEMS

In its various dimensions, the traditional "fact/value" problem reflects the practical importance of distinguishing between specifying (or individuating) a phenomenon and saying various things about it. At least implicitly, the former is a theoretical claim about what kind of thing the phenomenon is; while the latter is a matter of such operations as describing, evaluating, categorizing, or explaining it. Criteria for doing the latter at all, let alone adequately or cogently, are predicated on specification; but they are not the same as specification. Nor is specification a function of these moves. On the one hand, philosophical arguments for dichotomizing fact and value are partly a recognition of this practical difference; but they also try to provide a transcendental or metatheoretical basis for it and to pose the problem outside any practical context. On the other hand, philosophical arguments against such dichotomies are a metatheoretical recognition of the practical interdependence of a class of phenomenon and the various modes of talking about it; but they too pose the problem in a contextless and a priori manner. When theory is absent or when these metatheoretical issues take precedence, the practical relationship is obscured. In both cases, describing and specifying are usually conflated; and questions of the possibility, in principle, of describing without evaluating tend to dominate. Describing, evaluating, and the like are performances within the activity of social science. To distinguish or judge them is to rely on criteria (especially theoretical) within the disciplinary matrix. Although these performances depend on specification, they vary in a way that specification does not. For it states what kind of thing the phenomenon is; and this does not vary with the particular issues posed, as do description, evaluation, and categorization.

In the case of conventional objects, the autonomy of specification has an added dimension. This is why questions of objectivity and value often appear so distressingly difficult in the social sciences. Configurations or historical forms of conventional objects, such as the units and boundaries of politics, are conceptually or symbolically prespecified. They are not merely matters of social scientific stipulation or categorization. Therefore, statements about them in the language of social science sometimes seem inevitably distorting (e.g., value-laden). Social scientists tend to see this as something which either must or cannot be avoided. But it is absolutely necessary to be clear about the difference between specifying a phenomenon and (say) evaluating it. At the same time, it is equally necessary to know that descriptions (for example) always relate to and reflect the concerns of the inquirer. It is necessary, and possible, to make these claims without falling into positivist and antipositivist metatheory. The basis is theoretical.

Explanation is the metatheoretical issue that most needs dissolution. Its existence and persistence within social science is at the heart of the alienation of political theory. There simply is no general problem of explanation that must be confronted and solved prior to explaining

particular things. Social science needs theories which constitute objects to be explained, not theories about the
nature of explanation in social science. If there is a role
for epistemology, it is the explication and criticism of actual
explanations in a field, thereby indicating the theories
involved in that activity. Despite the pretensions of its
practitioners, epistemology is not a master science. To
offer political scientists a choice of naturalistic, hermeneutical, empiricist, or phenomenological approaches to explanation is like offering native speakers a choice among different theories of linguistic meaning. Such choices have no
necessary relevance to practice and are likely to prove
pathological if accepted in the spirit in which they are often
offered.

Theories posit a universe about which many things
can be said and many questions can be asked. The
answers to these questions are explanations. Although
generalizations about the explanations in a field or even a
class of fields (e.g., the social sciences) are possible, they
do not provide principles for the conduct of inquiry. Pervasive belief in the need for and existence of such principles signals a retreat from theory to metatheory. It is a
symptom of the alienation of political theory.

PART TWO

ACTION AND ALIENATION

POLITICAL PHILOSOPHY AND POLITICAL ACTION

Ira L. Strauber

This essay addresses a basic problem for political philosophy: how can recommendations concerning the evaluation and justification of political action follow from philosophical arguments. [1] One of the more vexing dimensions of this problem arises from the fact that there are apparently no necessary connections between philosophical suggestions and ordinary political practice. My interest is in language and argument, and I want to consider the problem of recommending from the angle of the connections (or lack of them) between philosophical arguments about choice or action and ordinary practical arguments. What follows is less a direct answer to the problem of connections than a possible foundation for addressing it. My hope here is to achieve something more than mere stipulation, even as I fall short of a fully justified thesis.

Obviously, there are no necessary connections between philosophical recommendations and those of ordinary political practice. There are many possible accounts of why ordinary political arguments cannot or ought not be held accountable to political philosophy. Indeed, there are probably as many accounts for this as there are ways of describing political philosophy and ordinary language. [2] In

----

[1] In part, this essay is instigated by the distinction between "knowing how" (politics) and "knowing about" (philosophy) that John G. Gunnell uses in "Philosophy and Political Theory," **Government and Opposition**, 14, 2, Spring, 1979, pp. 198-216. I move the issue from "knowing" to "arguing." For an argument that philosophy "cannot provide...the material for political success or political integrity," see: Gordon Graham, "Practical Politics and Philosophical Inquiry," **Philosophical Quarterly**, 28, 112, July, 1978, pp. 234-241, on p. 241.

[2] Although I do not pursue the issue here, I suspect that (social) science relates to politics in the same basic way that philosophy relates to politics. To the extent that this is true, the essay at hand concerns the two main aspects of that fundamental issue of Western political theory: the relationship of theory to practice.

any case, to indicate the gap between philosophy and politics, one prosaic fact is sufficient.   Political philosophy
sometimes considers but rarely turns upon factors crucial
for practical judgments: incomplete information, unforeseen
exigencies, complications of conflict resolution, incommensurability of values, and the like.   Thus, "even if it is
sometimes the case that a philosophical remark is pertinent
in the consideration of a political question, the extent
of...practical involvement will...be bounded by factors over
which the philosopher qua philosopher, has...[no] control...[and probably] no expertise."[3]
    Thus the relationship between philosophical recommen-
dations and ordinary political arguments is highly contingent.   Without necessary connections between philosophical
recommendations and everyday political reasoning, the issue
becomes: how is political philosophy to make itself relevant
to those who make ordinary political choices?   This is no
small difficulty, so that here I narrow the focus to a study
of standards of warrant.   Comparing these standards of
grounding and justification across the domains of philosophy
and politics, I consider how to bridge the gap between
them.

MINIMAL STANDARDS OF WARRANT

    For political philosophers, standards of warrant are
norms for the practice of political philosophy.   To meet
standards of warrant is to explicate an argument's basic
assumptions, its internal structure, and the relevant connections between the philosopher's thoughts and reality.
These norms are minimal standards of warrant.   They limit
the structure of an argument but do not alone determine its
merit.   (They are, for example, insufficient for determining
its normative status.)   Mainly, they insure the compositional
integrity of an argument.   That is, they fix its minimum
clarity of conception, coherence of terminology, logic or
internal consistency of progression, validity of inferences,
and so on.   Because the norms of warrant are "contextual,"
because they are bound by specific philosophical commitments, I treat them here as "formal" categories for

----

[3] Graham, "Practical Politics and Philosophical Inquiry," p.
238.

grounding and justifying an argument.

To a first approximation, philosophical arguments are held to three norms of compositional integrity:

(a) grounding: the nature and plausibility of fundamental or first principles

(b) arguing: the nature and fit of connections among fundamental grounds, intermediate claims, and conclusions

(c) testing: the nature and fit of connections between conclusions and (statements concerning) actual states of affairs or between ends and (statements concerning) means

The practice of political philosophy demands that these three norms of warrant be met. While what satisfies this demand varies contextually, any philosophical argument that fails to be articulated on each dimension of warrant is questionable. A philosophical argument that fails to satisfy its audience at any one level of warrant loses its philosophical power with that audience. Hence these three standards of warrant represent the fundamental, minimal criteria of rationality in philosophical recommending. [4]

Philosophy's reliance upon these minimal standards of warrant greatly contributes to the contingency of its relationship to practical politics. Since the problematical condition of political philosophy cannot be appreciated unless this gap is understood, the main differences between warrant in philosophy and politics must be made manifest. Facing up to these differences is hard, perhaps explaining why they do not receive the attention they deserve.

Clearly, ordinary arguments about politics very rarely are articulated along lines of minimal warrant. Indeed, a political philosopher would have a hard time reconstructing most arguments in political practice to conform to these (philosophical) standards of compositional integrity. But

----

[4] The historical dimensions of rationality may be conceived as standards that a connected series of statements must meet. On one reading, Plato's work points to classical Greek thought as a source of this idea; and Cartesian philosophy certainly encourages this view. If there is a historical tradition of "rationality," then this essay is a modest (or as I later write, "conservative") effort to break with it.

that is not to say that these norms are irrelevant to ordinary political arguments. Since to defend this would require a lengthy digression, let me simply stipulate that the (philosophical) norms of warrant are a more systematic and explicit rendition of connections "in play" whenever we use language.[5] In ordinary arguments, these standards are deeply hidden.[6] Everyday speakers are unaware of the extent to which their arguments depend upon grounding, arguing, and testing in tying together thought, language, and reality. Such ties are embedded in the conventions and habits of ordinary political speech in complex bundles of linguistic and political commitments which are usually beyond recovery by ordinary political speakers.[7]

But if there is a close connection between norms of warrant and making sense of the world, why should we not say that the speech of ordinary political practice is bizarre?[8] The main reason is that philosophy and politics do and should have different interests and thus standards of persuasion. Political actors are in a context of justification which leads them to ignore or reject philosophical warrants, even in the few cases that these norms could be recovered. Whereas philosophers hold arguments to all three standards of warrant, ordinary speakers need not be so strict. Emphasizing the pragmatic and useful, political speakers

----

[5] For an interesting, but complicated, view of the connection between reasons in philosophy and reasons in ordinary practice, see: Joseph Raz, **Practical Reason and Norms**, London, Hutchinson, 1975.

[6] See: Michael Polanyi, **Personal Knowledge**, New York, Harper and Row, second edition, 1964; Polanyi, **The Tacit Dimension**, Garden City, NY, Doubleday, 1966.

[7] See: Philip E. Converse, "The Nature of Belief Systems in Mass Publics," in David Apter, ed., **Ideology and Discontents**, New York, Free Press, 1964, pp. 206-261; Converse, "Public Opinion and Voting Behavior," in Fred I. Greenstein and Nelson W. Polsby, eds., **Handbook of Political Science**, Reading, MA, Addison Wesley, 1975, Volume 4, pp. 75-169. For alternate accounts, see: Norman H. Nie with Kristi Andersen, "Mass Belief Systems Revisited: Political Change and Attitude Structure," **Journal of Politics**, 36, 3, August, 1974, pp. 540-591; John S. Nelson, "The Ideological Connection, I-II," **Theory and Society**, 4, 3-4, Fall-Winter, 1977, pp. 421-448 and 573-590.

tend to presume agreement on first principles (grounding), pass over steps on the way to conclusions (arguing), and concentrate almost exclusively on specifying the relationship of means to ends. Ordinarily, political argument moves from an assumption of shared premises to an articulation of recommended conclusions. Ordinarily, what we want to know is how to get from here to there, politically. Thus ordinary arguments can fail (philosophically) minimal standards of warrant and yet maintain their political power, as long as they appeal to citations of means and ends. What is infelicitous in philosophy is appropriate in politics. Therefore, it is not very surprising that ordinary political actors do not articulate minimally warranted arguments: they have no need to do so.

This brings forward another difference between political philosophy and ordinary argument. For political philosophy, the norms of minimal warrant and the concept of rationality are so closely akin as to be (sometimes) indistinguishable. Philosophically, no argument that lacks compositional integrity could warrant a justification, evaluation, or performance of an action. But this tight connection between compositional integrity and rationality does not hold in ordinary situations. If it did, most political speakers would be irrational: an outrageous and probably even absurd claim for most conditions. If ordinary politics is philosophically irrational, nonetheless ordinary political actors do not speak without reason; nor do they usually (let alone necessarily) act contrary to their conclusions, however ungrounded, unargued, and untested those conclusions may be. In practical speech, compositional integrity is not an indication of irrationality. "All action is for the sake of some end, and the rules of action...must take their whole character and colour from the end to which they are subservient."[9] While ordinary actors do argue nonrationally, out of conformity with (philosophically) minimal standards of warrant, ordinary actors are irrational only when they act contrary to the conclusions of their arguments (about political means and ends). Ignoring the norms of warrant,

----

[8] In the **Leviathan**, Thomas Hobbes comes close to this conclusion in his discussion of the use of reason: "The First Part: Of Man," Michael Oakeshott, ed., New York, Collier, 1962, pp. 21-128.

[9] John Stuart Mill, **Utilitarianism**, Indianapolis, Bobbs-Merrill, 1861, p. 14.

political speech still need not be bizarre.

But for political philosophy, rules of discourse are importantly (although not exclusively) predicated on the idea that the activity would break down if its shared norms of minimal warrant were not practiced. That is why warranted arguments are expected to be either fully explicit or readily explicable. In this sense, failures of reasoning put philosophical arguments in jeopardy. This does not mean that articulation of minimally warranted reasons can always resolve philosophical disputes. But it does mean that such disputes cannot be resolved without adherence to these standards. "Philosophy" is the name for activities which conceive and justify themselves in terms of meeting the norms of minimal warrant. Philosophical speech which fails to ground, argue, or test minimally is irrational or bizarre, giving us good philosophical reasons for rejecting recommendations.

In political discourse, by contrast, we do not expect already or readily articulated grounding, arguing, and testing. This is because politics is predicated on the worry that it will break down **if conflicts are not soon resolved**. Hence in politics, minimal warrant is based upon the necessity of ending political conflicts. In arguments, this mostly means either conquest or compromise. Political disputes are resolved with remarkably little attention to the structure of warrants, at least in the strong philosophical sense. In politics, as in everyday life generally, the ultimate warrant is (of course) practical. Because philosophers claim to know about evaluations and justifications from the norms of warrant, this is **post hoc** to them. But for the most part, ordinary actors assess the warrant of arguments by expectation or (later) realization of (perceived) relationships between events and arguments. Thus, insofar as political argument tells us about means and ends, and insofar as it leads to conquest or compromise, political actors are not irrational to ignore philosophical norms of warrant and recommendations predicated upon them.

Accordingly, the problem of recommending is partly a result of differing conceptions of good reasons. Recently, some political philosophers have argued that the gap between political philosophy and ordinary politics is a problem with epistemology.[10] This thesis takes in a great deal,

----

[10] See: Richard Ashcraft, "On the Problem of Methodology and the Nature of Political Theory," **Political Theory**, 3, 1, February, 1975, pp. 5-25; Paul F. Kress, "Against Epis-

relating to a wide range of descriptions and prescriptions. But its advocates agree that (what they ambiguously call) epistemology can only mislead political philosophy when relied upon for understanding practical political activity. In one sense, my point here is consistent with this thesis; although in more general terms, I reject its conceptions of epistemology and politics.[11] At one level, there is disparity between the epistemology of political philosophy and that of an ordinary activity like politics. The epistemological standards of grounding, arguing, and testing are both ends of philosophy and criteria for what counts as philosophy. Not only are the norms of warrant not ends of politics, but neither they nor conquest and compromise establish what counts as politics. While philosophical recommendation is governed by philosophical epistemology, political recommendation (or action) is governed by the events of the political world. Hence, justification and evaluation of arguments in politics cannot be vulnerable to the political philosopher's charge of "lack of warrant." Clarity and precision are (appropriate) hobgoblins of academicians, not politicians. The corrigibility of political recommendation is found in experience, not in argument.

This problem of recommending points to the problematic position of philosophy. Its norms of warrant are at home in the context of language. Intrinsic to philosophy is the challenge of skepticism: worry that evaluations and justifications are hard to come by and cannot be articulated according to the norms of warrant. The obverse of skepticism is intellectual arrogance: delight in using philosophical warrants to run all arguments (philosophical or not) into

----

temology: Apostate Musings," **Journal of Politics,** 41, 2, May, 1979, pp. 526-542; Gunnell, "Philosophy and Political Theory;" John S. Nelson and Ira L. Strauber, "For Epistemology: Its Importance in Political Theory," unpublished paper.

[11] Thinking in this fashion follows the lead of Ludwig Wittgenstein. Here I am evaluating how we use 'politics' within the grammar and conventions of 'philosophy.' The idea that philosophy has taken a "wrong turn" is explored in a very interesting book by Richard Rorty: **Philosophy and the Mirror of Nature,** Princeton, Princeton University Press, 1979. Rorty's sorts of arguments bear directly on my previous remarks concerning "lines" or "dimensions" of rationality as norms of philosophical inquiry.

the ground. Where philosophy meets politics, there is a clash of contexts and epistemologies, with each mode of argument threatening the other.

Philosophical warrants do not, should not, and cannot apply to political argument, let alone action. Political actors must take much of the political world for granted. Effective political action would be impossible without shared assumptions about purpose and reality. Conquest and compromise could not occur if debate were strictly by the norms of warrant. Skeptical and arrogant debates about politics, like Socrates' attempts to articulate the grounds of others' arguments, can only substitute philosophical epistemology for everyday epistemology, making politics subservient to philosophy. Unless philosophy becomes political, it violates the epistemology of conquest and compromise, destroying the political concern with means and ends. If philosophy is to become political, if it is to recommend to ordinary political actors, then it must face and accept the epistemology of actual, practical politics. This means accepting the preeminence of means and ends, the aims of conquest and compromise, and (most importantly) the priority of nonrational political argument.

Then two questions arise. First, can philosophy cross the gap to politics? Can political philosophy say anything worthwhile to a nonrational activity? Second, how can philosophy cross without destroying itself or politics? How can philosophical warrant and rationality be reconciled with political nonrationality?

I doubt that I can answer the first question, except by answering the second. I do think that philosophers say some important things about connections among thought, language, and political reality. This implies that bridging philosophy and politics would be valuable, because it would clarify our thinking, speaking, perceiving, and choosing. But that is more a matter of "faith" than a foundation for a minimally warranted argument. Besides, its test is in politics, not philosophy. Even so, whatever political arguments are influenced by philosophy must be at least in part nonrational to remain political.

The answer to the second question says it all: to reach toward politics, philosophy must relax or even suspend its norms of warrant. Nonwarranted modes of evaluation and justification must become central components of political philosophy. This is not mostly a use of emotive or symbolic forms to convey philosophically rational recommendations. Nor is it primarily a use of utterly irrational means to manipulate mass publics. Instead, it is a self-conscious effort by political philosophers to make nonwarranted constructions part and parcel of the appraisal of political recommendations.

I know that this is a strange, even threatening, proposal. To recommend that we be "nonrational" is counterintuitive. "Nonwarranted" has negative connotations, suggesting violation of key cognitive principles putatively central to philosophy. At the least, we must wonder in what sense such nonwarranted "political philosophy" remains philosophy. To what extent is this simply a call for "sloppy argument?" Contrary to such suspicions, we need to see how to be "philosophical" (concerned with grounding, arguing, and testing) and yet "political" (concerned with means and ends, conquest and compromise). And thus we need to see how our idea of "political philosophy" is malformed.

Nonetheless, for me this is a conservative enterprise, since the "political philosophy" I recommend seeks to recover politics through a modest limit on philosophy. One does what one understands to be political philosophy but appreciates when to STOP. We stop or (more cautiously) we shade philosophical standards when political matters can no longer accommodate them. With a new sense of purpose, we must relax the philosophical primacy (obsession?) of grounding, arguing, and testing for the sake of recommendations regarding conquest or compromise. Then political philosophy becomes "consequentialist," balancing the philosophically warranted with the politically nonwarranted to engender the political effects sought. [12]

Admittedly, this is vague; but it can be little clarified by further abstractions. Instead, we need a sense of what nonwarranted political philosophy looks like. We need an example of the things that require us to stop, and we need to see how stopping becomes political without altogether rejecting philosophy or making political recommendations sloppy. Let me conclude, then, by pointing us in the direction of nonwarranted political philosophy, the direction

----

[12] Such "balancing" introduces interesting complications. If it is ad hoc, then political philosophy is likely to produce nonrational arguments. On the other hand, if it is principled, then political philosophy is forced into an infinite regress regarding whether the ultimate criterion is rational or nonrational. Either way, political philosophy is challenged to maintain critical validity. Concluding this essay, I make a glancing effort to direct attention toward these problems.

identified in Benjamin Cardozo's description of the common law: when the resources of rationality are exhausted, the final judgment relies on "semi-intuitive apprehensions."[13]

NONRATIONAL POLITICAL RECOMMENDING: MCCULLOCH V. MARYLAND

For political philosophy to recommend, it must incorporate those factors of everyday life which make philosophically warranted argument difficult (if not all but impossible). An example of combining philosophy with political action is Mr. Chief Justice Marshall's opinion in **McCulloch v. Maryland**.[14] It reveals commitment to philosophical warrants as a mechanism for both locating issues and recommending their resolution. It evidences sensitivity to the exigencies of politics and the need to relax the norms of warrant. And it recognizes factors which limit warranted argument (and are potential ammunition for conquest and compromise) in the ambiguity and vagueness of key political concepts.

Political philosophers attempt to transform what is ambiguous and vague about the political world into philosophical forms conducive to the economy and elegance of minimally warranted arguments.[15] In references to "human

----

[13] Benjamin N. Cardozo, **The Nature of the Judicial Process**, New Haven, Yale University Press, 1921, p. 43.

[14] 4, **Wheaton**, U.S., pp. 415-439.

[15] Current political theorists have more trouble with this than did their predecessors. For example, consider Hobbes and Locke. Wheras other readers find their works crippled by "inconsistency," I interpret them as making the accommodations between philosophy warrantability and nonrational necessity that I argue to be required for political recommending. Think of Hobbes on reason, fear, and the contract; or of Locke on consent. As Michael Levin has written of Locke's **Two Treatises**, "perhaps the most brilliant aspect of this work is the high level to which it carries the art of political persuasion. In such an attempt inconsistency might indeed be a merit." See: Levin, "What Makes a Classic in Political Theory?," **Political Science Quarterly**,

nature," "social contracts," "original positions," and the like, this transformation can work well for political philosophy. It reduces that which is vague or ambiguous to a form appropriate for philosophical resolution of political problems, and thus it may tell us something about our vision of the political world. More often than not, though, such reduction is not very helpful for resolving actual political problems, because ordinary political choices must work with the ambiguous and vague **as such**. Marshall's achievement is to recommend a course of political action by working within the limits of the terms, expressions, and values of ordinary political experience.[16] Formally and substantively, his argument recognizes the value of grounding, arguing, and testing. But still, it uses ambiguity and vagueness in a nonwarranted manner for the sake of conquest and compromise. Hence, the philosophically warranted and the politically nonwarranted intersect.

Marshall's opinion does not subordinate the ends of ordinary recommending to philosophical standards of warrant. It exemplifies the political intuition that can exploit possible connections between philosophy and politics. Marshall may not have intended this, yet his efforts in **McCulloch** remain an exemplar of nonwarranted political philosophy. His decision resists the temptation to treat ambiguity and vagueness as diseases to be cured. Instead, it embraces the political appreciation of them as materials to be built into successful recommendations. To a fascinating extent, it obscures and even violates the philosophical standards of warrant (especially those of grounding and testing) in order to generate a political recommendation that works.

The specific question before the Court was the relationship between an act of Congress (establishing the National Bank) and the action of a state (taxing that bank). There were two political and constitutional issues:

88, 3, September, 1973, pp. 462-476, on p. 467.

[16] To anticipate: this does not entail that political philosophy be conservative in epistemology or politics. It implies only that political philosophy must locate its possibilities of criticism and creation within the terms, expressions, and values of the political community. Since such elements are often very vague and ambiguous, political philosophers retain ample room for other epistemologies and politics than those established in that community.

the authority of the Union versus that of the States, and the extent of the power of Congress. The first issue involves a very ambiguous concept: sovereignty. The relationship between popular and state sovereignty was (and is) complicated. The theory and language of the Constitution, the norms and practices of institutions, and the rhetoric of law and politics all seek to reconcile the ultimately irreconcilable tension between these competing notions of political supremacy. The second issue of Congressional power is complicated by these ambiguities and further aggravated by vague constitutional text. By logic, history, custom, and theory, both issues were highly contestable (and combustible). In sum, the very grounds of the dispute push against agreement on any common ground for reconciliation.

Marshall's task was to recommend a course of evaluation and justification that would resolve the issue of sovereignty and specify the power of Congress without altogether antagonizing the conquered party. The results (not just the conclusions) of the whole argument exceeded the sum of its philosophically warranted parts. His arguments are generally accepted to be equivocal and ambiguous, but no less thorough for that. He confronted "a perplexing difficulty in ...legal reconciliation," yet was "persuasive enough to...stand the test of history."[17] It is true that his opinion is based on "a lacuna in principle...supplied by inelegant compromises."[18] But given political exigencies and the need for recommendations, his opinion is an elegant example of nonwarranted political argument. Its compromises maneuver gracefully around and about the issues of political and legal supremacy. The ambiguity of 'sovereignty' required nonwarranted construction of connections between what were otherwise competing, equally legitimate, and irreconcilable political values. Far from inelegant, Marshall's moves are better summarized by Ernst Cassirer's description of myth-making: "all reality, and all events, are projected into [this argument, so that]...they assume a new meaning, one which they [did]...not simply have from the very beginning but which they acquire in this form

----

[17] Robert Kenneth Faulkner, **The Jurisprudence of John Marshall**, Princeton, Princeton University Press, 1968, p. 104; Leonard Baker, **John Marshall, A Life in Law**, New York, Macmillan, 1974, p. 593.

[18] Faulkner, **The Jurisprudence of John Marshall**, p. 104.

[of]...mythical 'illuminations.'"[19] His nonwarranted arguments served to screen out cognitive and emotional elements of the controversy bound to cause resistance, while encouraging political order and obedience. Out of controversy and conflict, Marshall constructed an argument for political consensus and resolution.

Marshall's major innovation makes all this possible. Although acknowledging that the "conflicting powers of the government of the Union and its members" is the central issue, he shifts the issue of power away from the ground of sovereignty.[20] For both parties, the question of the capacity of a particular institution to act depends on whether the institution is part of a political entity that has supremacy. Arguing the Union to be supreme (as the origin of political power), advocates of popular sovereignty then proceed to determine the capacity of Federal institutions; and advocates of state sovereignty use the same logic of supremacy. Neither side can admit the sovereignty of the other without delimiting the power of its institutions, yet both sides have good (warranted) political arguments for sovereignty. Marshall escaped this dilemma by making the foundation of his argument principles of political power concerned with the capacity to act. This is a "lacuna" in terms of the sovereignty issue, because arguments about the capacity to act (although necessary) are not sufficient to determine which political act prevails, which is a question of the origins of political power. This nonwarranted (political) argument is essential to the plausible grounds of objection to Marshall's conclusion for popular sovereignty. Ingeniously, he treated the capacity to act in such a manner that advocates of state sovereignty cannot reject his arguments without undercutting their own position. Although his argument is not minimally warranted, it succeeds in setting the grounds for political conquest and compromise.

Marshall's gambit substitutes the issue of whether "Congress [has the] power to incorporate a bank" as the ground of the controversy.[21] It then appeals to a familiar and generally accepted principle of liberal-democratic

----

[19] Ernst Cassrier, **The Philosophy of Symbolic Forms**, Ralph Manheim, trans., New Haven, Yale University Press, Volume I, 1953, p. 75.

[20] 4, **Wheaton**, p. 418.

[21] **Ibid.**

theory: the positive-law principle that a body's act is
legitimate when promulgated through the established mechanisms:

> The bill incorporating the bank...did not steal
> upon an unsuspecting legislature, and pass
> unobserved. After being resisted, first in the
> fair and open field of debate, and afterwards in
> the executive cabinet...it became law....It
> would require no ordinary share of intrepidity
> to assert that a measure adopted under these
> circumstances was a bold and plain usurpation,
> to which the constitution gave no counte-
> nance. [22]

Of course, according to the principle of state sovereignty,
the positive-law status of the Bank is irrelevant if it is
beyond the sovereign authority of Congress. Yet Marshall's
argument makes it appear that the positive-law principle of
promulgation is the ground for settling the dispute. This
gambit succeeds through an intricate, elliptical, and subtly
deceptive opinion which integrates Marshall's nonrational
opening with warranted arguments.
      Marshall's use of the positive-law principle puts advo-
cates of state sovereignty in a corner more political than
logical. From a philosophical perspective, addressing Congressional power before political supremacy need not rule
out state sovereignty. Logically, a law can be properly
promulgated but still fail to be supreme. Indeed, that was
the fate of the tax. Yet Marshall's appeal to positive-law
grounds does more than detour around the first principle of
sovereignty, for it introduces a new testing warrant as
well. Whereas the test for sovereignty lies in political
theory and defies conclusive evidence in the case at hand,
the test for positive-law legitimacy lies in history and is
easily settled.
      A philosophically warranted connection between first
and intermediate principles would argue from positive-law
authority to a conception of sovereignty. But Marshall was
careful to avoid reintroducing arguments for state sovereignty. Instead, he played on their ambiguity in order to
provide an elliptical defense of the duly (and supremely)
promulgated Bank. He acknowledged that "the counsel for
the State of Maryand have deemed it of some importance, in

----

[22] 4, **Wheaton,** p. 419.

the construction of the constitution, to consider that
instrument not as emanating from the people, but as the act
of sovereign and independent States."[23] Still, the test of
"emanation" is made a matter of history, not of political
theory and the origins of political power. Marshall argued
as if simple events could evidence the validity of the
Union's claim to sovereignty:

> the instrument was submitted to the people...,
> they acted upon it...assembled in their several
> States...and where else should they have
> assembled? No political dreamer was ever wild
> enough to think of breaking down the lines
> which separate the States....Of consequence,
> when they act, they act in their States. But
> the measures they adopt do not, on that
> account cease to be measures of the people
> themselves, or become the measures of the State
> government.[24]

Out of context, these events require a political theory of
sovereignty in order to make them meaningful. In context,
however, skillful scrutiny is required to see through the
apparently logical progression of Marshall's argument, which
proceeds as though the political theory of popular sovereignty and Union supremacy is self-evident and embedded
in the events themselves. His rhetorical flourish against
the "political dreamer" reinforces this commonsensical quality.

Of course, a philosophically warranted argument
would have to explain why ratification has ceased to be an
act of the States, which cannot be done by appeal to the
sheer historical record. Yet in context, Marshall's shift to
"describing" actual events in order to test the legitimacy of
Congressional action makes it difficult to see the issue any
way other than his. Further remarks that "the government
proceeds directly from the people" and that "the constitution...bounds the State sovereignties" compound this effect,
leaving the reader to wonder what the purported argument
about state sovereignty could have concerned.[25] For all

----

[23] Ibid.

[24] 4, Wheaton, p. 420.

[25] Ibid.

intents and purposes, this (nonwarranted) argument defending the Bank on the basis of "facts" establishes the full
legitimacy of the Union's authority.   Although in the
abstract, the state-sovereignty theory remains as strong as
ever, Marshall has made it contextually irrelevant.   State-
sovereignty arguments seem beside the point.

Marshall's gambit worked because state-sovereignty
advocates could not rebut his application of the positive-law
principle to the Bank without risking the political status of
their tax.   To grant positive-law legitimacy to the Bank is
implicitly to warrant the tax, since the same argument
works for both.   This appears to be an innocent, not to
say necessary, compromise.   Nonetheless, proponents of
state sovereignty could not accede even to limited legitimacy
for the Bank, because they needed to discredit Congress as
the Bank's institutional source.   And that was a matter of
political theory, not history.

By conflating positive-law grounds and historical testing, Marshall trapped state-sovereignty advocates in a web
of rational implications generated from the nonwarranted
premise.   To question the limited legitimacy of the Bank on
the grounds articulated by Marshall would be to question
the limited legitimacy of the tax.   Were Marshall's argument
contested directly, state-sovereignty advocates would be
forced into the "self-excepting fallacy."[26] For on Marshall's
first principle, rejecting the Bank meant rejecting the tax.
Hence state-sovereignty advocates were left with a hard
choice: challenge the Bank act and thereby the tax act
with procedural and historical evidence, or accept the tax
act and thereby the Bank act as procedurally legitimate,
thereby acknowledging (at least the limited legitimacy) of
the Bank.   Either way, the Union is supreme over the
States.   Either way, the strong argument for state sovereignty against the legitimacy of the Bank is no longer at
issue in the controversy.   Conquest is well under way.

By shifting grounds and tests, Marshall reduced the
legitimacy of state-sovereignty claims without confronting
their theory directly.   To complete his conquest, Marshall
needed to link this historical defense of the positive-law
status of the Bank with a defense of national supremacy

----

[26] See: Maurice Mandelbaum, "Subjective, Objective, and
Conceptual Relations," **Monist**, 62, 4, October, 1979, pp.
403-428, on p. 405:   "the fallacy of stating a generalization
that purports to hold of all persons but which, inconsis-
tently, is not then applied to oneself."

and the propriety of Congressional power. The specific act that chartered the Bank could meet the postive-law principle of promulgation, but still violate the limits on national sovereignty and Congressional power. Marshall needed to move his argument from an interim claim of limited legitimacy to a conclusion of full legitimacy for the Bank.

By this point, Marshall was ready to take the principle of (popular) sovereignty as the fundamental ground of the issue. In this regard, Marshall's argument should be reconstructed in something like the following form:

(1) The source of political authority is popular sovereignty.

(2) The authority of Congress is limited (from a principle of liberal-democratic political theory) and enumerated in the Constitution (from a principle of constitutionalism).

(3) To understand the Constitution, one must understand its differences from the Articles of Confederation: in the latter, implied or incidental powers were specifically excluded; whereas in the former, no such limiting language exists.

(4) Regarding the Constitution as a whole: "its important objects [are] designated, and the minor ingredients...deduced from the nature of the objects."

(5) Similarly, "a government entrusted with such ample powers must also be entrusted with ample means for their execution."

(6) Further, a "means for carrying into execution all sovereign powers...is a right incidental to the power, and conducive to its beneficial exercise."

(7) Ergo, there exists the "necessary right of the legislature to select the means."

With one eye on the appropriate part of the Constitution, this argument is dazzling. In form, it is so brilliantly warranted that the initial issue of the extent of Congressional power is lost in its glare. While it appears axiomatic and deductive,   its   undefended   first   principle   (popular sovereignty) prejudices the issue, and its connecting claim about "necessity" requires a political substantiation which is not forthcoming.

But Marshall's argument justifies more than the Bank; its general case for extensive authority works for more than Congressional power. Simultaneously, if implicitly, it warrants judicial review by the Supreme Court. Substitute "the Court" for "the Congress," and Marshall's argument slips past constitutional silence on the subject to justify its own authority. Although not philosophically warranted, Marshall's argument appeals to commonsense. It is so convincing that generations have taken it to justify the authority of both Congress and the Court. It works because it sidesteps philosophical standards of warrant in order to satsify political requirements. In this respect, advocates of Congressional authority are the ones cornered. To accept Marshall's sorely needed support for Congressional authority is to accept the Court's authority. Moreover, this offered the Court as protector of the. States, through keeping Congressional power within constitutional limits. Explicitly, the Court's ruling enhanced Congressional power: a conquest over the States. Implicitly, it enhanced the power of the Court: a compromise with Congress. Also implicitly, it promised protection for the textually reserved power of the States: a compromise with the States. Marshall's web was intricate indeed.

SUMMING UP:
REFLECTIONS ON NONRATIONAL RECOMMENDING

McCulloch exemplifies recommending which balances philosophical warrants with nonwarranted needs and devices. Accepting, indeed exploiting, ambiguity and vagueness for the sake of political conquest and compromise does not mean that "anything goes," that philosophical reasoning is abandoned altogether. Marshall's gambit required exquisite philosophical sensibility and political acumen in order to find where the nonrational was needed and how to employ it effectively. To condemn his opinion as (philosophically) nonwarranted is to miss the point. Marshall's argument succeeded politically where a minimally warranted one would fail. A philosophy which fails to recognize the potential and necessity of nonwarranted argument is blind to the exigencies of political practice. Only nonwarranted recommending can provide for political compromise and conquest, yet respect (if sometimes disobey) warrants of compositional integrity.   This does not endorse sloppy or cynical argument.   Marshall's arguments are as well-crafted as those of the most rationalist philosophers.   But Marshall's have the special virtue of integrating nonrational necessities and constructions with respect for rational warrants, making possible recommendations at once political and philosophical.

I cheerfully acknowledge that this essay is only a beginning.   A full treatment of nonwarranted recommending would say more clearly where to stop the norms of warrant; my talk of ambiguity and vagueness is more by way of example than criteria.   A full treatment of political philosophy must address the connections among values in general, standards of reasoning in particular, and uses of nonrational arguments.   Where to draw lines is beyond the scope of this essay, but I suspect that political norms, contextual considerations, and philosophers' obsessions with warrants would be sufficient to limit nonwarranted arguments.   Nonetheless, McCulloch does suggest how to be philosophical without suffering ill political consequences from the constraints of philosophical epistemology or surrendering entirely to the nonrational elements of ordinary political speech.

Finally, a recognition and acceptance of nonwarranted political arguments encourages political philosophers to be political.   To work with the imprecise, inconsistent, and inchoate terms, expressions, and values of ordinary politics.   The philosophical project of politics must remind us that "all things are not permitted."   It permits and perhaps even enforces a constructive civility for political argument as a whole.   Yet the political project of philosophy must remind us that "some things are necessary" for compromise and conquest.   Eventually, political recommending must disrupt mathematized ontologies, formalized language games, and all other philosophical niceties.   Political philosophers must become Machiavellian and "learn how not to be good," how not to be (philosophically) rational.   Philosophy becomes political by facing up to the imprecise, inconsistent, inchoate facts of (political) life.   A political philosophy that recommends recognizes that:

> in politics we are always on volcanic soil.   We must be prepared for abrupt convulsions and eruptions.   In all...moments of man's social life, the rational forces that resist the rise of...mythical [nonwarranted] conceptions are no longer sure of themselves.   In these moments,

the time for myth [nonwarranted political philosophy] has come again.[27]

---

[27] Ernst Cassirer, **An Essay on Man**, New Haven, Yale University Press, 1944, p. 280.

PHILOSOPHY AND DEMOCRACY

Michael Walzer

The prestige of political philosophy is very high these days.[3] It commands the attention of economists and lawyers, the two groups of academics most closely connected to the shaping of public policy, as it has not done in a long time. And it claims the attention of political leaders, bureaucrats and judges, most especially judges, with a new and radical forcefulness. The command and the claim follow not so much from the fact that philosophers are doing creative work, but from the fact that they are doing creative work of a special sort, which raises again, after a long hiatus, the possibility of finding objective truths, "true meaning," "right answers," "the philosopher's stone," and so on. I want to accept this possibility (without saying very much about it) and then ask what it means for democratic politics. What is the standing of the philosopher in a democratic society? This is an old question; there are old tensions at work here: between truth and opinion, reason and will, value and preference, the one and the many. These antipodal pairs differ from one another, and none of them quite matches the pair "philosophy and democracy." But they do hang together; they point to a central problem. The philosopher claims a certain sort of authority for his conclusions; the people claim a different sort of authority for their decisions. What is the relation between the two?

I

I shall begin with a quotation from Wittgenstein that might seem to resolve the problem immediately. "The philosopher," Wittgenstein wrote, "is not a citizen of any community of ideas. That is what makes him into a philoso-

----

[3] A previous version of this chapter by Michael Walzer appeared as "Philosophy and Democracy," **Political Theory**, 9, 3, August, 1981, 379-399, (c) 1981 Sage Publications, Inc. It is reprinted here with permission of the publisher.

pher."[2] This is more than an assertion of detachment in its usual sense, for citizens are surely capable, sometimes, of detached judgments even of their own ideologies, practices, and institutions. Wittgenstein is asserting a more radical detachment. The philosopher is and must be an outsider; he stands apart, not occasionally (in judgment) but systematically (in thought). I don't know whether the philosopher has to be a political outsider. Wittgenstein does say **any** community, and the state (polis, republic, commonwealth, kingdom, or whatever) is certainly a community of ideas. The communities of which the philosopher is most importantly not a citizen may, of course, be larger or smaller than the state. That will depend on what he philosophizes about. But if he is a political philosopher (not what Wittgenstein had in mind), then the state is the most likely community from which he will have to detach himself, not physically, but intellectually and, on a certain view of morality, morally too.

This radical detachment has two forms, and I shall be concerned with only one of them. The first form is contemplative and analytic; those who participate in it take no interest in changing the community whose ideas they study. "Philosophy leaves everything as it is."[3] The second form is heroic. I don't want to deny the heroic possibilities of contemplation and analysis. One can always take pride in wrenching oneself loose from the bonds of community; it isn't easy to do, and many important philosophical achievements (and all the varieties of philosophical arrogance) have their origins in detachment. But I want to focus on a certain tradition of heroic action, alive, it seems, in our own time, where the philosopher detaches himself from the community of ideas in order to found it again: intellectually and then materialy too, for ideas have consequences, and every community of ideas is also a concrete community. He withdraws and returns. He is like the legislators of ancient legend, whose work precludes ordinary citizenship.[4]

----

[2] Ludwig Wittgenstein, **Zettel**, G. E. M. Anscombe and G. H. von Wright, eds., Berkeley, University of California Press, 1967, no. 455.

[3] Ludwig Wittgenstein, **Philosophical Investigations**, G. E. M. Anscombe, trans., New York, Macmillan, third edition, 1958, para. 124.

[4] For an account of this special form of philosophical hero-

In the long history of political thought, there is an alternative to the detachment of philosophers, and that is the engagement of sophists, critics, publicists, and intellectuals. To be sure, the sophists whom Plato attacks were citiless men, itinerant teachers, but they were by no means strangers in the Greek community of ideas. Their teaching drew upon, was radically dependent upon, the resources of a common membership. In this sense, Socrates was a sophist, though it was probably crucial to his own understanding of his mission, as critic and gadfly, that he also be a citizen: the Athenians would have found him less irritating had he not been one of their fellows. But then the citizens killed Socrates, thus demonstrating, it is sometimes said, that engagement and fellowship are not possible for anyone committed to the search for truth. Philosophers can't be sophists. For practical as well as intellectual reasons, the distance that they put between themselves and their fellow citizens must be widened into a breach of fellowhsip. And then, for practical reasons only, it must be narrowed again by deception and secrecy. So that the philosopher emerges, like Descartes in his **Discourse,** as a separatist in thought, a conformist in practice.

He is a conformist, at least, until he finds himself in a position to transform practice into some nearer approximation to the truths of his thought. He cannot be a participant in the rough and tumble politics of the city, but he can be a founder or a legislator, a king, a nocturnal councillor, or a judge; or, more realistically, he can be an advisor to such figures, whispering in the ear of power. Shaped by the very nature of the philosophical project, he has little taste for bargaining and mutual accomodation. Because the truth he knows or claims to know is singular in character, he is likely to think that politics must be the same: a coherent conception, an uncompromising execution. In philosophy as in architecture, and so in politics, wrote Descartes: what has been put together bit by bit, by different masters, is less perfect than the work of a single hand. Thus, "those old places which, beginning as villages, have developed in the course of time into great towns, are generally...ill-proportioned in comparison with those an engineer can design at will in an orderly

----

ism, see: Sheldon S. Wolin, **Hobbes and the Epic Tradition of Political Theory,** Los Angeles, University of California Press, 1970.

fashion".[5] Descartes himself disclaims any interest in the political version of such a project, perhaps because he believes that the only place where he is likely to reign supreme is his own mind.   But there is always the possibility of a partnership between philosophical authority and political power.   Reflecting on that possibility, the philosopher may, like Thomas Hobbes, "recover some hope that one time or other, this writing of mine may fall into the hands of a sovereign, who will...by the exercise of entire sovereignty...convert this truth of speculation into the utility of practice."[6] The crucial words in these quotations from Descartes and Hobbes are "design at will" and "entire sovereignty."   Philosophical founding is an authoritarian business.

II

    A quick comparison may be helpful here.   Poets have their own tradition of withdrawal and engagement, but radical withdrawal is not common among them.   One might plausibly set alongside Wittgenstein's sentences the following lines of C. P. Cavafy, written to comfort a young poet who has managed after great effort to finish only one poem. That, Cavafy says, is a first step, and no small accomplishment:

> To set your foot upon this step
> you must rightfully be a citizen
> of the city of ideas.[7]

Wittenstein writes as if there were (as there are) many communities, while Cavafy seems to suggest that poets inhabit a single, universal city.   But I suspect that the

----

[5] Rene Descartes, **Discourse on Method**, Arthur Wollaston, trans., Hammondsworth, Peguin Books, 1960, pp. 44-45.

[6] Thomas Hobbes, **Leviathan**, Michael Oakeshott, ed., New York, Collier, 1962, part II, ch. 31, end.

[7] C. P. Cavafy, "The First Step," in **The Complete Poems of Cavafy**, Rae Dalven, trans., New York, Harcourt, Brace and World, 1976, p. 6.

Greek poet means in fact to describe a more particular place: the city of Hellenic culture. The poet must prove himself a citizen there; the philosopher must prove that he isn't a citizen anywhere. The poet needs fellow citizens, other poets and readers of poetry, who share with him a background of history and sentiment, who won't demand that everything he writes be explained. Without people like that, his allusions will be lost and his images will echo only in his own mind. But the philosopher fears fellowship, for the ties of history and sentiment corrupt his thinking. He needs to look at the world from a distance, freshly, like a total stranger. His detachment is speculative, willful, always incomplete. I don't doubt that a clever sociologist or historian will detect in his work, readily as in any poem, the signs of its time and place. Still, the philosopher's ambition (in the tradition that I am describing) is extreme. The poet, by contrast, is more modest. As Auden has written:

> A poet's hope:
> to be like some valley cheese
> local, but prized elsewhere. [8]

The poet may be a visionary or a seer; he may seek out exile and trouble; but he cannot, short of madness, cut himself off from the community of ideas. And perhaps for that reason, he also cannot aspire to anything quite like sovereignty over the community. If he hopes to become a "legislator for mankind," it is rather by moving his fellow citizens than by governing them. And even the moving is indirect. "Poetry makes nothing happen." [9] But that is not quite the same thing as saying that it leaves everything as it is. Poetry leaves in the minds of its readers some intimation of the poet's truth. Nothing so coherent as a philosophical statement, nothing so explicit as a legal injunction: a poem is never more than a partial and unsystematic truth, surprising us by its excess, teasing us by its ellipsis, never arguing a case. "I have never yet been able to perceive," wrote Keats, "how anything can be known for truth

----

[8] W. H. Auden, "Shorts II," in **Collected Poems**, Edward Mendelsohn, ed., New York, Random House, 1976, p. 639.

[9] W. H. Auden, "In Memory of W.B. Yeats," in **The English Auden**, Edward Mendelson, ed., New York, Random House, 1977, p. 242.

by consecutive reasoning."[10] The knowledge of the poet is of a different sort, and it leads to truths that can, perhaps, be communicated but never directly implemented.

III

But the truths discovered or worked out by political philosophers can be implemented. They lend themselves readily to legal embodiment. Are these the laws of nature? Enact them. Is this a just scheme of distribution? Establish it. Is this a basic human right? Enforce it. Why else would one want to know about such things? An ideal city is, I suppose, an entirely y proper object of contemplation; and it may be the case that "whether it exists anywhere or ever will exist is no matter": that is, does not affect the truth of the vision. But surely it would be better if the vision were realized. Plato's claim that the ideal city is "the only commonwealth in whose politics [the philosopher] can ever take part" is belied by his own attempt to intervene in the politics of Syracuse when an opportunity arose, or so he thought, for philosophical reformation.[11] Plato never intended, of course, to become a citizen of the city he hoped to reform.

The claim of the philosopher in such a case is that he knows "the pattern set up in the heavens." He knows what ought to be done. He can't just do it himself, however, and so he must look for a political instrument. A pliable prince is, for obvious practical reasons, the best possible instrument. But in principle, any instrument will do; an aristocracy, a vanguard, a civil service, even the people will do, so long as its members are committed to philosophical truth and possessed of sovereign power. But clearly, the people raise the greatest difficulties. If they are not a many-headed monster, they are at least many-headed, difficult to educate and likely to disagree among themselves. Nor can the philosophical instrument be a majority among

----

[10] John Keats, **The Letters of John Keats**, M. B. Forman, ed., London, Oxford University Press, fourth edition, 1952, p. 67.

[11] Plato, **The Republic**, F. M. Cornford, trans., New York, Oxford University Press, 1945, 591A-592B.

the people, for majorities in any genuine democracy are temporary, shifting, unstable. Truth is one, but the people have many opinions; truth is eternal, but the people continually change their minds. Here in its simplest form is the tension between philosophy and democracy.

The people's claim to rule does not rest upon their knowledge of truth (though it may, as in utilitarian thought, rest upon their knowledge of many smaller truths: the account that only they can give of their own pains and pleasures). The claim is most persuasively put, it seems to me, not in terms of what the people know but in terms of who they are. They are the subjects of the law, and if the law is to bind them as free men and women, they must also be its makers. This is Rousseau's argument. I don't propose to defend it here but only to consider some of its consequences. The argument has the effect of making law a function of popular will and not of reason as it had hitherto been understood, the reason of wise men, sages, and judges. The people are the successors of gods and absolutist kings, but not of philosophers. They may not know the right thing to do, but they claim a right to do what they think is right (literally, what pleases them).[12]

Rousseau himself pulled back from this claim, and most contemporary democrats would want to do so too. I can imagine three ways of pulling back and constraining democratic decisions, which I will outline briefly, drawing on Rousseau, but without attempting any explicit analysis of his arguments. First, one might impose a formal constraint on popular willing: the people must will generally.[13] They cannot single out (except in elections for public office) a particular individual or set of individuals from among themselves for special treatment. This is no bar to public assistance programs designed, say, for the sick or the old, for we can all get sick and we all hope to grow old. Its purpose is to rule out discrimination against individuals and groups who have, so to speak, proper names. Second, one

----

[12] Thus an Athenian orator to the assembly: "It is in your power, rightly, to dispose of what belongs to you -- well, or, if you wish, ill." Quoted in: K. J. Dover, **Greek Popular Morality in the Time of Plato and Aristotle**, Berkeley, University of California Press, 1974, pp. 290-291.

[13] Jean-Jacques Rousseau, **The Social Contract**, G. D. H. Cole, trans., New York, Dutton, 1950, book II, chs. iv and vi.

might insist on the inalienability of the popular will and then on the indestructability of those institutions and practices that guarantee the democratic character of the popular will: assembly, debate, elections, and so on. The people cannot renounce now their future right to will (or, no such renunciation can ever be legitimate or morally effective).[14] Nor can they deny to some group among themselves, with or without a proper name, the right to participate in future willing.

Clearly, these first two constraints open the way for some kind of review of popular decision-making, some kind of enforcement, against the people if necessary, of nondiscrimination and democratic rights. Whoever undertakes this review and enforcement will have to make judgments about the discriminatory character of particular pieces of legislation and about the meaning for democratic politics of particular restrictions on free speech, assembly, and so on. But these judgments, though I don't want to underestimate either their importance or their difficulty, will be relatively limited in their effects compared to the sort of thing required by the third constraint. And it is on the third constraint that I want to focus, for I don't believe that philosophers in the heroic tradition can possibly be satisfied with the first two.

Third, then, the people must will what is right. Rousseau says, must will the common good, and goes on to argue that the people will will the common good if they are a true people, a community, and not a mere collection of egoistic individuals and corporate groups.[15] Here the idea seems to be that there exists a single set (though not necessarily an exhaustive set) of correct or just laws that the assembled people, the voters or their representatives, may not get right. Often enough, they get it wrong, and then they require the guidance of a legislator or the restraint of a judge. Rousseau's legislator is simply the philosopher in heroic dress; and though Rousseau denies him the right to coerce the people, he insists on his right to deceive the people. The legislator speaks in the name of God, not of

----

[14] This follows, I think, from the argument that the general will is inalienable, though Rousseu wants to make even more of inalienability than this, as in his attack on representation: **ibid.**, book III, ch. xv.

[15] Ibid., book II, ch. iii and **passim**.

philosophy.[16] One might look for a parallel deception among contemporary judges. In any case, this third constraint surely raises the most serious questions about Rousseau's fundamental argument, that political legitimacy rests on will (consent) and not on reason (rightness).

IV

The fundamental argument can be put in an appropriately paradoxical form: it is a feature of democratic government that the people have a right to act wrongly, in much the same way that they have a right to act stupidly. I should say: they have a right act wrongly within some area (and only, following the first two constraints, if the action is general over the area and doesn't preclude future democratic action within the area). Sovereignty is always sovereignty somewhere and with regard to some things, not everywhere and with regard to everything. The people can rightfully, let's say, enact a redistributive income tax, but they can only redistribute their own incomes, not those of some neighboring nation. What is crucial, however, is that the redistributive pattern they choose is not subject to authoritative correction in accordance with philosophical standards. It is subject to criticism, of course, but insofar as the critic is a democrat he will have to agree that, pending the conversion of the people to his position, the pattern they have chosen ought to be implemented.

Richard Wollheim has argued in a well-known article that democratic theory conceived in this way is not merely paradoxical in some loose sense; it is a strict paradox.[17] He constructs the paradox in three steps:

----

[16] **Ibid.**, book II, ch. vii.

[17] Richard Wollheim, "A Paradox in the Theory of Democracy," in Peter Laslett and W. G. Runicman, eds., **Philosophy, Politics and Society,** Second Series, Oxford, Basil Blackwell, 1962, pp. 71-87. I should stress that the argument here is about implementation, not obedience. What is at issue is how or for what reasons policies should be chosen for the community as a whole. Whether individual citizens should uphold this or that policy once it has been chosen, or assist in carrying it out, is another question.

(1)   As a citizen of a democratic community, I
review the choices available to the community and conclude that A is the policy that
ought to be implemented.

(2)   The people, in their wisdom or their will-
fulness, choose policy B, the very opposite
of A.

(3)   I still think that policy A ought to be
implemented, but now, as a committed democrat, I also think that policy B ought to
be implemented.   Hence, I think that both
policies ought to be implemented.   But this
is incoherent.

The paradox probably depends too much upon its verbal
form.   We might imagine a more modest first person, so that
the first step would go like this:

(1)   I conclude that A is the policy that the
people ought to choose for implementation.

Then there would be nothing incoherent about saying:

(3)   Since the people didn't choose A, but
chose B instead, I now conclude that B
ought to be implemented.

This isn't very interesting; but it is consistent, and I
think it makes sense of the democratic position.
   What underlies Wollheim's version of the first step is
a philosophical, and probably an anti-democratic, argument
that has this form:

(1)   I conclude that A is the right policy, and
that it ought to be implemented **because it
is right**.

But it isn't at all obvious that a policy's rightness is the
right reason for implementing it.   It may only be the right
reason for hoping that it will be implemented and so for
defending it in the assembly.   Suppose that there existed a
pushbutton implementation system, and that the two but-
tons, marked A and B, were on my desk.   Which one
should I push, and for what reasons?   Surely I can't push
A simply because I have decided that A is right.   Who am
I?   As a citizen of a democratic community, I must wait for

the people's decision. And then, if the people choose B, it's not the case that I face an existential choice: where my philosophical arguments point toward A, and my democratic commitments point toward B, and there is no way to decide between them. There is a way to decide.

The distinction that I am trying to draw here, between having a right to decide and knowing the right decision, might be described in terms of procedural and substantive justice. Democrats, it might be said, are committed to procedural justice and can only hope that the outcomes of just procedures will also be substantively just. But I am reluctant to accept that formulation because the line between procedure and substance seems to me less clear than it suggests. What is at stake in discussions about procedural justice is the distribution of power, and that is surely a substantive matter. No procedural arrangement can be defended except by some substantive argument, and every substantive argument (in political philosophy) issues also in some procedural arrangement. Democracy rests, as I have already suggested, on an argument about freedom and political obligation. Hence it is not only the case that the people have a procedural right to make the laws. On the democratic view, it is right that they make the laws, even if they make them wrongly.

Against this view, the heroic philosopher might argue that it can never be right to do wrong (not, at least, once we know or can know what is right). This is also, at least incipiently, an argument about the distribution of political power; and it has two implications: first, that the power of the people ought to be limited by the rightness of what they do; and second, that someone else ought to be empowered to review what the people do and step in when they move beyond those limits. Who else? In principle, I suppose, anyone who knows the truth about rightness. But in practice, in any ongoing political order, some group of people will have to be found who can be presumed to know the truth better or more consistently than do the people as a whole. This group will then be awarded a procedural right to intervene, grounded on a substantive argument about knowledge and moral truth.

Popular legislation might be reviewed democratically: in ancient Athens, for example, citizens concerned about the legitimacy of a particular decision of the assembly could appeal from the assembly as a whole to a smaller group of citizens, selected by lot and empanelled as a jury. The jury literally put the law on trial, with individual citizens acting as prosecutors and defense attorneys; and its verdict took precedence over the legislative act itself.[18] In this case, obviously, no special wisdom was claimed; the same argument or the same sort of argument would justify both the act and the verdict. More often, however, groups of this sort are constituted on aristocratic rather than democratic grounds. The appeal is from popular consciousness, particular interests, selfish or shortsighted policies to the superior understanding of the few: Hegel's corps of civil servants, Lenin's vanguard party, and so on. Ideally, the group to which the appeal is made must be involved in the community of ideas, oriented to action within it, but attuned at the same time to philosophers outside. In, but not wholly in, so as to provide a match for the philosopher's withdrawal and return.

V

In the United States today, it is apparent that the nine judges of the Supreme Court have been assigned something like this role. The assignment is most clearly argued in the work of a group of contemporary law professors, all of whom are philosophers too or, at least, much influenced by political philosophy.[19] Indeed, the revival of political philosophy has had its most dramatic impact in schools of law, and for a reason that is not difficult to make out. In a settled democracy, with no revolution in prospect, judges are the most likely instruments of philosophical reformation. Of course, the conventional role of Supreme Court judges extends no further than the enforcement of a written constitution that itself rests on democratic consent and is subject to democratic amendment. And even when the judges act in ways that go beyond upholding the textual integrity of the constitution, they generally claim no special

----

[18] A. H. M. Jones, **Athenian Democracy**, Oxford, Basil Blackwell, 1960, pp. 122-123.

[19] For example, see: Ronald Dworkin, **Taking Rights Seriously**, Cambridge, MA, Harvard University Press, 1977; Frank Michelman, "In Pursuit of Constitutional Welfare Rights," **University of Pennsylvania Law Review**, 121, 1973, pp. 962-1019; Owen Fiss, "The Forms of Justice," **Harvard Law Review**, 93, 1979, pp. 1-58; Bruce Ackerman, **Social Justice in the Liberal State**, New Haven, Yale University Press, 1980.

understanding of truth and rightness but refer themselves instead to historical precedents, long-established legal principles, or common values. Nevertheless, the place they hold and the power they wield make it possible for them to impose philosophical constraints on democratic choice. And they are readily available (as the people are not) for philosophical instruction as to the nature of those contraints. I am concerned here with judges only insofar as they are in fact instructed, and with philosophers before judges because a number of philosophers seem so ready to provide the instruction. The tension between judicial review and democracy directly parallels the tension between philosophy and democracy. But the second is the deeper tension, for judges are likely to expand upon their constitutional rights or to sustain a program of expansion only when they are in the grip of a philosophical doctrine.

Now, judges and philosophers are (mostly) different sorts of people. One can imagine a philosopher-judge, but the union is uncommon. In an important sense, judges are members of the political community. Most of them have had careers as office-holders, or as political activists, or as advocates of this or that public policy. They have worked in the arena; they have participated in debates. When they are questioned at their confirmation hearings, they are presumed to have opinions of roughly the same sort as their questioners: commonplace opinions, much of the time, else they would never have been nominated. Once confirmed, to be sure, they set themselves at some distance from everyday politics; their special standing in a democracy requires a certain detachment and thoughtfulness. They don the robes of wisdom, and those robes constitute what might be called a philosophical temptation: to love wisdom better than the law. But judges are supposed to be wise in the ways of a particular legal tradition, which they share with their old professional and political associates.

The stance of the philosopher is very different. The truths he commonly seeks are universal and eternal, and it is unlikely that they can be found from the inside of any real and historic community. Hence the philosopher's withdrawal: he must deny himself the assurances of the commonplace. (He doesn't have to be confirmed.) To what sort of a place, then, does he withdraw? Most often, today, he constructs for himself (since he cannot, like Plato, discover for himself) an ideal commonwealth, inhabited by beings who have none of the particular characteristics and none of the opinions or commitments of his former fellow-citizens. He imagines a perfect meeting in an "original position" or "ideal speech situation" where the men and women in attendance are liberated from their own ideologies or subjected to universalizing rules of discourse. And then, he asks what principles, rules, constitutional arrangements these people would choose if they set out to create an actual political order.[20] They are, as it were, the philosophical represenatives of the rest of us, and they legislate on our behalf.

The philosopher himself, however, is the only actual inhabitant of the ideal commonwealth, the only actual participant in the perfect meeting. So the principles, rules, constitutions, with which he emerges are in fact the products of his own thinking, "designed at will in an orderly fashion," subject only to whatever constraints he imposes upon himself. Nor are any other participants required, even when the decision procedure of the ideal commonwealth is conceived in terms of consensus or unanimity. For if there were another person present, either he would be identical to the philosopher, subject to the same constraints and so led to say the same things and move toward the same conclusions, or he would be a particular person with historically derived characteristics and opinions, and then his presence would undermine the universality of the argument.

The philosopher returns from his retreat with conclusions that are different from the conclusions of any actual democratic debate. At least, they have, or he claims for them, a different status. They embody what is right, which is to say for our present purposes that they have been agreed upon by a set of ideal representatives, whereas the conclusions reached through democratic debate are merely agreed upon by the people or by their actual representatives. The people or their representatives might then be invited to revise their own conclusions in the light of the philosopher's work. I suppose that this is an invitation implicitly extended every time a philosopher publishes a book. At the moment of publication, at least, he is a proper democrat: his book is a gift to the people. But the gift is rarely appreciated. In the political arena, the philosopher's truths are likely to be turned into one more set of opinions, tried out, argued about, adopted in part,

----

[20] In this mode of argument, John Rawls is obviously the great pioneer. But the specific use of the new philosophy with which I am concerned is not advocated by him in **A Theory of Justice** (Cambridge, MA, Harvard University Press, 1971) or in any subsequent articles.

repudiated in part, or ignored. Judges, on the other hand, may well be persuaded to give the philosopher a different sort of hearing. Their special role in the democratic community is connected, as I have already said, to their thoughtfulness, and thoughtfulness is a philosophical posture: judicial status can only be enhanced by a little real philosophy. Moreover, judges are admirably placed to mediate between the opinions (temporarily) established in the democratic arena and the truths worked out in the ideal commonwealth. Through the art of interpretation, they can do what Rousseau's legislator does through the art of divination.[21]

VI

Consider the case of "rights." Our ideal representatives, in philosophical seclusion, come up with a list of rights that attach to each individual human being. Let's assume that the list is, as it commonly is among contemporary philosophers, deeply meditated and serious. The enumerated rights form a coherent whole, suggesting what it might mean to recognize in another man or woman the special qualities of moral agency and personality. The philosophical list differs from the list currently established in the law, but it also overlaps with the law and with what we can think of as the suburbs of the law: the cluster of opinions, values, and traditions to which we escape, if we can, whenever we find the inner city of the law constraining. Now the philosopher (the heroic philosopher, the philosopher as founder) invites the judges to attempt a more organized escape, from the law, through the suburbs, to the ideal commonwealth beyond. The invitation is all the more urgent in that rights are at stake. For rights have

----

[21] Like Rousseau's legislator again, the judges have no direct coercive power of their own: in some ultimate sense, they must always look for support among the people or among alternate political elites. Hence the phrase "judicial tyranny," applied to the enforcement of some philosophically but not democratically validated position, is always a piece of hyperbole. On the other hand, there are forms of authority, short of tyranny, that raise problems for democratic government.

this special characteristic: their violation requires immediate relief or reparation.   And judges are not merely the
available, they are also the appropriate instruments of relief
and reparation.[22]

In effect, the philosopher proposes a decision procedure for judges modeled on that of the ideal commonwealth.
This is in part flattery, but it also has a factual rationale.
For the discussions of judges among themselves really do
resemble the arguments that go on in the ideal commonwealth (in the mind of the philosopher) much more closely
than democratic debate can ever do.   And it seems plausible
to say that rights are more likely to be defined correctly
by the reflection of the few than by the votes of the
many.[23] So the philosopher asks the judges to recapitulate
in their chambers the argument he has already worked out
in solitary retreat, and then to give that argument "the
utility of practice," first by locating it in the law or in the
traditions and values that surround the law and then by
deciding cases in its terms.   When necessary, the judges
must preempt or overrule legislative decisions.   This is the
crucial point, for it is here that the tension between philosophy and democracy takes on material form.

The legislature is, if not the reality, then at least
the effective representation of the people assembled to rule

----

[22] The special invitation and the sense of urgency are most
clear in Dworkin's **Taking Rights Seriously**.   But Dworkin
seems to believe that the ideal commonwealth actually exists,
so to speak, in the suburbs.   The set of philosophically
validated rights can also be validated, he argues, in terms
of the constitutional history and the standing legal principles of the United States; and when judges enforce these
rights, they are doing what they ought to be doing, given
the sort of government we have.   For a different reading of
our constitutional history, see: John Hart Ely, **Democracy
and Distrust**, Cambridge, MA, Harvard University Press,
1980.   Ely argues for something very much like the two
contraints that I have defended.   For him, too, the ideal
commonwealth lies somewhere beyond the U. S. Constitution.   It is the proper goal of parties and movements, not
of courts.

[23] For a careful and rather tentative argument to this
effect, see: T. M. Scanlon, "Due Process" in J. Roland
Pennock and John W. Chapman, eds., **Nomos XVIII: Due
Process**, New York, New York University Press, 1977, pp.

themselves. Its members have a right to act within an area. Judicially enforced rights can be understood in two different but complementary ways with regard to this area. First, they are boundaries circumscribing it. From this view, a simple equation follows: the more extensive the list of rights, the wider the range of judicial enforcement, the less room there is for legislative choice. The more rights the judges award to the people as individuals, the less free the people are as a decision-making body. Or, second, rights are principles that structure activities within the area, shaping policies and institutions. Then judges don't merely operate at the boundaries, however wide or narrow the boundaries are. Their judgements represent deep pene- tration raids into the area of legislative decision.[24] Now, all three of the contraints on popular willing that I described earlier can be conceived in either of these ways, as defense or as penetration. But it is clear, I think, that the third constraint simultaneously narrows the boundaries and per- mits deeper raids. As soon as the philosophical list of rights extends beyond the twin bans on legal discrimination and political repression, it invites judicial activity that is radically intrusive on what might be called democratic space.

    But this, it can be objected, is to consider rights only in the formal sense, ignoring their content. And their content may well enhance rather than circumscribe popular choice. Imagine, for example, a philosophically and then judicially recognized right to welfare.[25] The purpose of such a right is plain enough. It would guarantee to each citizen the opportunity to exercise his citizenship, and that is an opportunity he could hardly be said to have, or to have in any meaningful fashion, if he were starving to death or desperately seeking shelter for himself and his family. A defensible right, surely, and yet the argument I have just sketched still holds. For the judicial enforcement of welfare rights would radically reduce the reach of demo- cratic decision. Henceforth, the judges would decide, and as cases accumulated, they would decide in increasing

---

93-125, on pp. 120-21.

[24] Fiss provides some clear examples in "Forms of Justice."

[25] See: Michelman, "Welfare Rights;" Michelman, "On Pro- tecting the Poor Through the Fourteenth Amendment," **Har- vard Law Review**, 83, 1969, pp. 7-59.

detail, what the scope and character of the welfare system should be and what sorts of redistribution it requires. Such decisions would clearly involve significant judicial control of the state budget and, indirectly at least, of the level of taxation: the very issues over which the democratic revolution was originally fought.

This sort of thing would be easier for committed democrats if the expanded list of rights were incorporated into the constitution through a popularly controlled amending process. Then there would exist some democratic basis for the new (undemocratic) power of philosophers and judges. The people would, I think, be ill-advised to agree to such an incorporation and to surrender so large a part of their day-to-day authority. In the modern state, however, that authority is exercised so indirectly, it is so far, in fact, from being day-to-day authority, that they might feel the surrender to be a minor matter. The rights they gain as individuals (in this case, to welfare services from a benevolent bureaucracy) might in their view far outweigh the rights they lose as members. And so it's not implausible to imagine the constitutional establishment of something like, say, Rawls' two principles of justice.[26] Then the entire area of distributive justice would effectively be handed over to the courts. What a range of decisions they would have to make! Imagine a class action suit testing the meaning of the difference principle. The judges would have to decide whether the class represented in the suit was really the most disadvantaged class in the society (or whether all or enough of its members fell within that class). And if it was (or if they did), the judges would than have to decide what rights followed from the difference principle under the material conditions currently prevailing. No doubt, they would be driven to consult experts and officials in making these decisions. It would make little sense for them to consult the legislature, however, for to these questions, if rights are really at issue, there must be a right answer; and this answer is more likely to be known by philosophers, judges, experts, and officials than by ordinary citizens or their political representatives.[27]

----

[26] For a proposal to this effect, see: Amy Gutmann, **Liberal Equality**, New York, Cambridge University Press, 1980, p. 199.

[27] Dworkin, **Taking Rights Seriously**, especially Chapters 4 and 13.

Still, if the people came to feel oppressed by the new authorities that they had established, they could always disestablish them. The amending process would still be available, though it might be the case that the gradual erosion of legislative energy would make it less available in practice than it was in principle.[28] Partly for this reason, and partly for reasons to which I will now turn, I want to argue that philosophers should not be too quick to seek out the judicial (or any other) instrument, and that judges, though they must to some extent be philosophers of the law, should not be too quick to turn themselves into political philosophers. It is a mistake to attempt any extensive incorporation of philosophical principles into the law either by interpretation or amendment. For that is, in either case, to take them out of the political arena where they properly belong. The interventions of philosophers should be limited to the gifts they bring. Else they are like Greeks bringing gifts, of whom the people should beware, for what they have in mind is the capture of the city.

VII

"The philosopher is not a citizen of any community of ideas. That is what makes him into a philosopher." I have taken these sentences to mean that the political philosopher must separate himself from the political community, cut himself loose from affective ties and conventional ideas. Only then can he ask and struggle to answer the deepest questions about the meaning and purpose of political association and the appropriate structure of the community (of every community) and its government. This kind of knowledge, one can have only from the outside. Inside, another kind of knowledge is available, more limited, more particular in character. I shall call it political rather than philosophical knowledge. It answers to the questions: what is the meaning and purpose of **this** association? What is the

----

[28] Judicial interventions on behalf of individual rights broadly understood may also lead to an erosion of popular energies, at least on the left. For a brief argument to this effect, see: Michael Walzer, "The Courts, the Elections, and the People," **Dissent**, 28, 2, Spring, 1981, pp. 153-155.

appropriate structure of our community and government? Even if we assume that there are right answers to these last questions (and it is doubtful that the particular questions have right answers even if the general questions do), it is nevertheless the case that there will be as many right answers as there are communities. Outside the communities, however, there is only one right answer. As there are many caves but only one sun, so political knowing is particular and pluralist in character, while philosophical knowing is universalist and singular.

The political success of philosophers, then, would have the effect of enforcing a singular over a pluralist truth, that is, of reiterating the structure of the ideal commonwealth in every previously particularist community. Imagine not one but a dozen philosopher-kings: their realms would be identically fashioned and identically governed, except for those adjustments required by an ineradicably particularist geography. (If God were a philosopher-king, he would have allocated to each community an identical or equivalent set of geographic conditions.) The case would be the same with a dozen communities founded in the original position: there is only one original position. And it would be the same again with a dozen communities shaped by undistorted communication among an idealized set of members: for it is a feature of undistorted communication, as distinct from ordinary talk, that only a very few things can be said.[29]

Now, we may or may not be ready to asign value to particularism and pluralism. It isn't easy to know how to decide. For pluralism implies a range of instances -- a range of opinions, structures, regimes, policies -- with

----

[29] Even if we were to connect philosophical conclusions to some set of historical circumstances, as Habermas does when he imagines "discursive will-formation" occurring "at a given stage in the development of productive forces," or as Rawls does when he suggests that the principles worked out in the original position apply only to "democratic societies under modern conditions," it remains true that the conclusions are objectively true or right for a range of particular communities, without regard to the actual politics of those communities. See: Jurgen Habermas, **Legitimation Crisis,** Thomas McCarthy, trans., Boston, Beacon Press, 1975, p. 113; Rawls, "Kantian Constructivism in Moral Theory," **Journal of Philosophy,** 77, 9, September, 1980, pp. 515-572, on p. 518.

regard to each of which we are likely to feel differently. We might value the range or the idea of a range and yet be appalled by a large number of the instances, and then search for some principle of exclusion. Most pluralists are in fact constrained pluralists, and the constraints they defend derive from universal principles. Can it still be said that they value pluralism? They merely like variety, perhaps, or they aren't ready yet to make up their minds about every case, or they are tolerant, or indifferent. Or they have an instrumentalist view: many social experiments will lead one day (but that day is far off) to a single truth. All these are philosophical perspectives in the sense that they require a standpoint outside the range. And from that standpoint, I suspect, pluralism will always be an uncertain value at best. But most people stand differently. They are inside their own communities, and they value their own opinions and conventions. They come to pluralism only through an act of empathy and identification, recognizing that other people have feelings like their own. Similarly, the philosopher might come to pluralism by imagining himself a citizen of every community rather than of none. But then he might lose that firm sense of himself and his solitude that makes him a philosopher, and the gifts he brings might be of less value than they are.

I don't mean to underestimate those gifts. But it is important now to suggest that the value of universal truth is as uncertain when seen from inside a particular community as is the value of pluralism when seen from ouside every particular community. Uncertain, I mean to say, not unreal or negligible: for I don't doubt that particular communities improve themselves by aspiring to realize universal truths and by incorporating (particular) features of philosophical doctrine into their own ways of life. And this the citizens also understand. But from their standpoint, it won't always be obvious that the rights, say, of abstract men and women, the inhabitants of some ideal commonwealth, ought to be enforced here and now. They are likely to have two worries about any such enforcement. First, it will involve overriding their own traditions, conventions, and expectations. These are, of course, readily accessible to philosophical criticism; they were not "designed at will in an orderly fashion" by a founder or a sage; they are the result of historical negotiation, intrigue, and struggle. But that is just the point. The products of a shared experience, they are valued by the people over the philosopher's gifts because they belong to the people and the gifts don't: much as I might value some familiar and much-used possession and feel uneasy with a new, more perfect model.

The second worry is more closely connected to demo-cratic principle. It's not only the familiar products of their experience that the people value, but the experience itself, the process through which the products were produced. And they will have some difficulty understanding why the hypothetical experience of abstract men and women should take precedence over their own history. Indeed, the claim of the heroic philosopher must be that the first sort of experience not only takes precedence over but effectively replaces the second. Wherever universal truth has been established, there is no room for negotiation, intrigue, and struggle. Hence, it looks as if the political life of the community is to be permanently interrupted. Within some significant part of the area over which citizens had once moved freely, they are no longer to move at all. Why should they accept that? They might well choose politics over truth; and that choice, if they make it, will make in turn for pluralism. Any historical community whose mem-bers shape their own institutions and laws will necessarily produce a particular and not a universal way of life. That particularity can be overcome only from the outside and only by repressing internal political processes.

But this second worry, which is the more important of the two, is probably exaggerated. For philosophical doc-trine, like the law itself, requires interpretation before it can enforced. Interpretations must be particular in charac-ter, and they invite real and not merely hypothetical argu-ment. Unless the philosopher wins "entire sovereignty" for himself, then, his victory won't in fact interrupt or cut off political activity. If his victory were to take the form that I have been imagining, it would merely shift the focus of political activity from legislatures to courts, from law-mak-ing to litigation. On the other hand, insofar as it is a vic-tory at all, it has to have some universalizing tendencies; at least, it has to impose some constraints on the pluraliz-ing tendencies of a free-wheeling politics. The more the judges are "strict constructionists" of philosophical doc-trine, the more the different communities they rule will look alike and the more the collective choices of the citizens will be confined. So the exaggeration makes a point: the citi-zens have, to whatever degree, lost control over their lives. And then they have no reason, no democratic rea-son, for obeying the decrees of the judges.

VIII

All this might be avoided, of course, if the judges adopted a policy of "judicial restraint," preempting or over-ruling legislative decisions only in rare and extreme cases. But I would suggest that judicial restraint, like judicial intervention, draws its force from some deeper philosophical view. Historically, restraint has been connected with skepticism or relativism.[30] It is of course true that philosophical views change, and judges must be leery of falling in with some passing fashion. But I am inclined to think that judicial restraint is consistent with the strongest claims that philosophers make for the truths they discover or construct. For there is a certain attitude that properly accompanies such claims and has its origin in the ideal commonwealth or the perfect meeting from which the claims derive. This attitude is philosophical restraint, and it is simply the respect that outsiders owe to the decisions that citizens make among themselves and for themselves. The philosopher has withdrawn from the community. It is precisely because the knowledge he seeks can only be found outside this particular place that it yields no rights inside.

At the same time, it has to be said that since the philosopher's withdrawal is speculative only, he loses none of the rights he has as an ordinary citizen. His opinions are worth as much as any other citizen's; he is entitled like anyone else to work for their implementation, to argue, intrigue, struggle, and so on. But when he acts in these ways, he is an engaged philosopher, that is, a sophist, critic, publicist, or intellectual; and he must accept the risks of those social roles. I don't mean that he must accept the risk of death. That will depend upon the conditions of engagement in his community; and philosophers, like other citizens, will hope for something better than civil war and political persecution. I have in mind two different sorts of risks. The first is the risk of defeat; for though the engaged philosopher can still claim to be right, he cannot claim any of the privileges of rightness. He must live with the ordinary odds of democratic politics. The second is the risk of particularism, which is, perhaps, another kind of defeat for philosophy. Engagement always involves a loss (not total but serious enough) of distance, critical

----

[30] For example, see: Ely, **Democracy and Distrust**, pp. 57-59.

perspective, objectivity, and so on. The sophist, critic, publicist, or intellectual must address the concerns of his fellow citizens, try to answer their questions, weave his arguments into the fabric of their history. He must, indeed, make himself a **fellow** citizen in the community of ideas, and then he will be unable to avoid entirely the moral and even the emotional entanglements of citizenship. He may hold fast to the philosophical truths of natural law, distributive justice, or human rights; but his political arguments are most likely to look like some makeshift version of those truths, adapted to the needs of a particular people: from the standpoint of the original position, provincial; from the standpoint of the ideal speech situation, ideological.

Perhaps we should say that, once engaged, naturalized again into the community of ideas, the philosopher is like a political poet: Shelley's legislator, not Rousseau's. Though he still hopes that his arguments reach beyond his own community, he is first of all "local." And so he must be ready to forsake the prerogatives of distance, coherent design and entire sovereignty, and seek instead with "thoughts that breathe and words that burn," to reach and move his own people. And he must give up any more direct means to establish the ideal commonwealth. That surrender is philosophical restraint.

Judicial restraint follows (and so does vanguard restraint and bureaucratic restraint). The judges must hold themselves as closely as they can to the decisions of the democratic asssembly, enforcing first of all the basic political rights that serve to sustain the character of the assembly and protecting its members from discriminatory legislation. They are not to enforce rights beyond these, unless they are authorized to do so by a democratic decision. And it doesn't matter to the judges as judges that a more extensive list of rights can be, or has been, validated elsewhere. Elsewhere doesn't count.

Once again, I don't want to deny that rights can be validated elsewhere. Indeed, the most general truths of politics and morality can only be validated in the philosophical realm; and that realm has its place outside, beyond, separate from every particular community. But philosophical validation and political authorization are two entirely different things. They belong to two entirely distinct spheres of human activity. Authorization is the work of citizens governing themselves among themselves. Validation is the work of the philosopher reasoning alone in a world he inhabits alone or fills with the products of his own speculations. Democracy has no claims in the philosophical realm, and philosophers have no special rights in the political community. In the world of opinion, truth is indeed another opinion, and the philosopher is only another opinion-maker.

PART THREE

CRITICISM AND CONTRADICTION

POLITICAL THEORIZING

IN THE LATE TWENTIETH CENTURY:

FOCI, LOCI, AND AGENDAS

Paul F. Kress

Private existence, in striving to resemble one worthy of man, betrays the latter, since any resemblance is withdrawn from general realization, which yet more than ever before has need of independent thought. There is no way out of entanglement. The only responsible course is to deny oneself the ideological misuse of one's own existence, and for the rest to conduct oneself in private as modestly, unobtrusively and unpretentiously as is required, no longer by good upbringing, but by the shame of still having air to breath, in hell.

Theodor
Adorno[1]

History knows many periods of dark times in which the public realm has been obscured and the world became so dubious that people have ceased to ask anymore of politics than that it show due consideration for their vital interests and personal liberty. Those who have lived in such times and been formed by them have probably always been inclined to despise the world and the public realm, to ignore them as far as possible, or even to overleap them, and, as it were, reach behind them -- as if the world were only a facade behind which people could conceal themselves -- in order to arrive at mutual understandings with their fellow men without regard for the world that lies between them. In such times, if things turn out well, a special kind of humanity develops.

Hannah
Arendt[2]

----

[1] Theodor W. Adorno, Minima Moralia, E. F. N. Jephcott, trans., London, NLB, 1978, pp. 27-28.

PRELIMINARIES

To begin by questioning the title of the anthology in which this essay finds its home would seem to be in dubious taste at best.   To proceed in this fashion is to invite the natural question of why one agreed to participate in the first place.   Beyond that, to presume to present an argument to one's peers is at least tacitly to claim something to say, whereas to commence with apparently negative reflections upon the agenda scarcely seems a promising start. Nonetheless, I shall take the risk, less in a spirit of negativism than in the hope of settling my later remarks in a firmer context.   Put differently, I shall say some things about what the title of this book means to me, including some of the questions it raises in my mind.

"What Should Political Theory Be Now?" suggests minimally that there is an intelligible and and identifiable entity, a literature, an activity which can be said to "be" and that this state of being is accessible to reasoned discourse.   A number of familiar and unresolved questions come immediately to mind.   We will wonder whether political theory is thus unitary or monolithic, whether there are (ontologically speaking) political "things" (as the late Leo Strauss sometimes suggested), or whether the enterprise can be said to constitute a "tradition" in the sense of exhibiting diverse responses to recurrent problems such as liberty and authority (as Sheldon Wolin has maintained). We may worry further about the boundary problem posed by overlapping academic disciplines such as philosophy, intellectual history, political sociology, or even literary criticism.   Such questions are frustrating, not simply because they often prove so recalcitrant, but because efforts to resolve them lapse, almost as frequently, into scholastic thickets wherein the ingenuity of distinction far outstrips its utility.   It is at times such as these that we are tempted to deemphasize political theory as an entity and to view it as an activity: what political theorists do.   Of course, the difficulty here is that, if we are to escape tautology (consider the question of whether Montaigne is properly considered a political thinker), we must find another way to ground the adjective; and at this juncture, recourse to the sociological demension recommends itself.   I shall return to

----

[2] Hannah Arendt, **Men in Dark Times**, New York, Harcourt, Brace and World, 1968, pp. 11-12.

this point below.

We need to ask what an appropriate response to the title question would look like. In turn, this suggests that we need to specify a context in which both question and answer may be made meaningful. Perhaps we can agree to an initial, if somewhat soft, distinction between the writing or "doing" of political theory and the study of political theory or thought itself. By the latter, I intend the historical analysis of classic or current texts. Let me set this second activity aside for the moment; for while there may be worry over identifying the political element in intellectual history, and there is now surely much dispute over proper historiographic technique, what the history of political thought should intend seems relatively uncontroversial.

If we then focus on the activity of "original" political theorizing, it seems plain that we are engaged in an agenda-setting exercise. But what might be its applications? Such an enterprise or exercise does not, in imagination, appear appropriate in the context or practice of so-called "epic theory" as illustrated by the **Republic**, the **Discourses**, or the **Leviathan**. This is precisely because those works **set** agendas by generating compelling visions to transcend and transform the cognitive universe of the politics of their times.[3] In any event, it seems absurd, if only from hindsight, to contemplate instructing a Machiavelli in the proper mode of political theorizing. For the very point of

----

[3] "Agenda setting" is one of the functions assigned to paradigm works by Thomas Kuhn. For an explicit application of Kuhn's constructions to epic political theories, see: Sheldon S. Wolin, "Paradigms and Political Theories," in Preston King and Bhikhu Parekh, eds., **Politics and Experience**, New York, Cambridge University Press, 1968, pp. 125-152. In this respect, while contending political theories explicitly dispute various subject matters, they implicitly offer rival conceptions of problems and their relative priorities. I make no effort here to use the term "paradigm" in any closely specified sense. Margaret Masterman has shown that Kuhn's usage in the first edition of **The Structure of Scientific Revolutions** (Chicago, University of Chicago Press, 1962) was quite ambiguous. Though he made an effort to clarify his meaning in the second, revised edition (1970), much ambiguity remains. See: Margaret Masterman, "The Nature of a Paradigm," in Imre Lakatos and Alan Musgrave, eds., **Criticism and the Growth of Knowledge**, New York, Cambridge University Press, 1970, pp. 59-89.

his writing, as that of so many other giants, was to illustrate the inadequacy of his predecessors. Such theorists
are properly seen as tradition-breakers and agenda-setters.
Indeed, the view of men such as Plato, Machiavelli, and
Hobbes as inconclasts rests upon their radicalism in the
realm of **ideas**, their break with intellectual traditions.

But I have thus far been speaking of the works of
the epic theorists themselves and not of the "schools" which
they spawned. That such collectivities not only existed but
were often intentionally created is clear. Plato and Aristotle established their respective academies, and Thomas
Hobbes hinted in **Leviathan** that his new science of politics
might one day become part of a university curriculum. If
we consider such historical antecedents as the forerunners
of our contemporary academic discipline of political science,
then the question which frames this anthology finds a much
more direct application, for it can be addressed to the
activities of a body of practitioners who are presumably
concerned with roughly similar phenomena and share to
some extent a similar language and culture.[4]

Still, such an application immediately encounters a
formidable obstacle: our lack of an epic theory to "contain"
or direct our efforts, to set our agenda. Indeed, as John
Gunnell has suggested, there is something in that congeries
of ideas and institutions which we call liberal constitutionalism that may militate against epic theory and almost surely
militates against heroism as an ideal for either thought or
action.[5] Further, as many students of Thomas Kuhn have
pointed out, the condition of current political science is
best described, not as a field lacking a paradigm work, but
rather as one in which alternate, often incommensurable
models proliferate. In his 1953 book, **The Political System**,
David Easton put the point squarely when he wrote that the
version of systems theory he recommended was offered as a
framework within which research results might be organized
and reported. It may well be that he hoped for more: for
example, that systems theory might serve such other paradigm functions as itself constituting a substantive, exemplar

----

[4] In Kuhn's terms, such schools practice the "normal science" of their respective theories.

[5] See: John G. Gunnell, **Political Theory**, Cambridge, MA,
Winthrop, 1979, pp. 131-163; Kirk Thompson, "Constitutional Theory and Political Action," **Journal of Politics**, 31,
3, August, 1969, pp. 655-681.

work or providing an agenda of researchable questions. If so, the fate of systems analysis over the last fifteen years has surely disappointed that hope. Easton's example is but one of many comparable efforts in our field which have shared the fate of decline after enjoying an initial enthusiasm.

Thus the question which needs to be asked is how the title question can be made meaningful to an enterprise presently without an epic work or "dominant paradigm?" To what agencies or sources ought we repair to find imperatives?[6] A brief, contrasting glance at the condition of the natural sciences may be helpful at this point.

It is often observed that these disciplines differ from the social sciences in that they enjoy the benefits of dominant paradigms. Although I am inclined to think that their degree of unity or concensus is somewhat exaggerated, it is certainly greater than that of political science. Here, however, I invoke the example of the natural sciences for a somewhat different reason. In Kuhn's listing of paradigm functions, one of the most important is agenda-setting: providing research imperatives.

Unfortunately, Kuhn sometimes writes as if natural scientists operate within a closed intellectual universe: as if their sole imperatives emanated from the state of their art and not to any significant extent from the wider culture. Today we do not lack for evidence of the interpenetration of science and culture: through technological applications in general, wartime exigency such as that which accelerated development of atomic and later nuclear energy, as well as the subtler alterations in personality formation and social value occasioned by the spread of what has been called "technological rationality." In terms of sheer magnitude of trained personnel and institutional budgets, the burgeoning of natural science is staggering. As James Conant was fond of reminding lecture audiences, more "scientists" were

----

[6] We should not forget that such direction may come from exogenous as well as endogenous sources. That is, we may feel impelled by urgent problems or dangers in "the real world" to alter priorities favored by the "intellectual" or internal agenda of a discipline. See: Jerome Ravetz, **Scientific Knowledge and Its Social Problems**, New York, Oxford University Press, 1971. To investigate the impact of extrinsic or exogenous factors in directing any specific enterprise would be to engage in the sociology of knowledge, as distinct from "pure" history of ideas.

alive and at work in 1950 than had lived in the previous two centuries or perhaps all recorded history. But our recent awareness of the gigantism of contemporary science should not occasion us to forget that, while the classical Greeks may have distinguished between **techne** and **sophrosyne** or even **phronesis** as modes of knowing, the seventeenth-century adventurers were much less cautious. Certainly if such Baconian works as **The New Atlantis** and **The Advancement of Learning** are taken as at all representative of their time, the phenomenon or movement we now call "modern science" was at its core "political," not to say utopian. The apparent, but perhaps superficial, difference in our time of liberal democracy and **wert-frei** science is that our rhetoric insists upon the primacy of political decision over the internal imperatives of the scientific agenda. The relationship of politics and science is, of course, much more complex and interactive than the previous sentence suggests; but I entertain the simplification in order to draw some parallels and contrasts to the condition of current political thoery.

This digression into the state of natural sciences illustrates the contrasting position of social science and particularly of political science and theory. With the possible exception of some areas of micro-economic theory, the sciences of man are not disciplines with dominant paradigms, in any reasonable sense of that designation. Indeed, despite the ritual of replication, it is questionable whether research is more than rarely cumulative, even within specialized subfields (in political science: voting behavior, socialization, decision or preference theory, etc.). However difficult to define, certainly that work which we consider "theory" can make no such claim to embrace a unified agenda **within the academy and the discipline**. But what of the relationship of the study of politics to the society and culture at large? This, I think, is a much more promising avenue along which to approach the title question. Yet again I digress to draw another contrast: this time between political science and other social sciences.

All teachers of political science have had the experience of offering undergraduate majors or graduate students who seek nonacademic careers advice on alternate opportunities. The fact is that federal, state, and local governments often find themselves in need of economists, psychologists, sociologists, and accountants. But rarely do they recognize a need for students of government itself. With the exception of persons trained in such specialities as public administration, the generalist and surely the theorist finds himself no more in demand than the hapless humanist or the

occasional anthropologist. (To be sure, there is now a profusion of schools and programs of "policy analysis;" but
even if they become flesh as subfields and achieve some
recognition from an external clientel, their present intellectual thrust will remain borrowed from variants of cost-benefit analysis and their practitioners will more likely be
trained in economics than political science.) Why should
this condition or circumstance obtain, let alone to the dramatic degree which it does? There are two major reasons
(or perhaps only one, differently emphasized), and some
reflection upon them may bring our concern with political
theorizing into sharper focus.

Practitioners widely assume though seldom say that
the division of labor among the social or behavioral sciences
is or should ideally be hierarchical. As the foundation discipline, we might envision an experimental psychology
well-grounded in physiology (which could, in the strongest
of scenerios, link further or more "basically" to chemistry
and ultimately to particle physics). From this would arise
the specialized studies of the economy and polity, while the
totality of interactions within a specified space would
become the province of sociology. To anthroplogy would be
assigned the most inclusive task of all: to study the envel-
oping culture. At its "upper" and "lower" conceptual
boundaries, each discipline would establish a set of "linking
concepts" and a language which could presumably "carry"
the investigator over into its adjoining province. The contribution envisioned of philosophy, understood as logic of
inquiry or epistemology, has never been very clearly articulated. Presumably, the philosopher would perform what
Peter Winch has called an "under-laborer's" task of establishing the rules of validation or even investigation for
enterprises seeking legitimation as sciences: a role not
unlike that dreamed by Otto Neurath and Rudolf Carnap in
their days of compiling the encyclopedia of "unified science."[7]

The   influential   Harvard   seminar   of   the   1950s

----

[7] See: Peter Winch, **The Idea of a Social Science, and Its
Relation to Philosophy**, London, Routledge and Kegan Paul,
1958. There are, of course, many ways in which a hier-
archy of the sciences might be constructed. Apart from
text examples, see: John Gillin, ed., **For a Science of
Social Man**, New York, Macmillan, 1954; Roy R. Grinker,
Sr., ed., **Toward a Unified Theory of Human Behavior**,
New York, Basic Books, second edition, 1967.

expressed something like this idea, not in the image of hierarchy, but rather that of concentric circles. Psychology (the relations of ego and alter) occupied the core, and cultural studies composed the outer or most inclusive ring.[8] The point of special interest to us in the charming if rather innocent report of these meetings is the discomfiture of the participants in accommodating those disciplines which claim to study a distinctive subject matter or dimension of "sociation": namely, economics and politics. Significantly, that discomfort was recorded in a footnote. In the lead essay, psychologist Richard C. Sheldon distinguishes between economics and politics by noting that economics has succeeded in developing a body of predictive theory based upon a relatively few variables nested within an identifiable institution (the market), while political science exhibits a more "diffuse" character. Sheldon concludes, albeit it in an unenthusiastic tone, that students of politics should rest content with this residual character of their discipline.[9]

Sheldon's remark prompts several observations. First, should we explain to Aristotle the meaning of "diffuseness," we might suppose him to be in accord with Sheldon's characterization of the study of politics. We may further suppose the Philosopher to be at least receptive to the idea of a hierarchy of the sciences. And yet, Aristotle valued the study of politics very differently from our contemporaries. To Aristotle, the fact that the **practice** of politics involves managing heterogeneous "variables" and setting society-wide imperatives exalted the role of the

----

[8] See: Talcott Parsons and Edward Shils, eds., **Toward a General Theory of Action**, Cambridge, MA, Harvard University Press, 1959.

[9] See: Richard C. Sheldon, "Some Observations on Theory in the Social Sciences," in **ibid.**, pp. 28-29. Sheldon wisely refrained from pursuing the beguiling chimera of "modeling" political studies after the example of economics. One might, for example, analogize votes to dollars and elections to markets. Parsons himself has not always been deaf to this siren song. For an older attempt to build a rigorously deductive political science upon the concept of power, see: George E. G. Catlin, **A Study of the Principles of Politics**, New York, Macmillan, 1930. The deductivist work best known to political scientists is probably: Harold Lasswell and Abraham Kaplan, **Power and Society**, New Haven, Yale University Press, 1950.

stateman and elevated the study of politics to the status of master science. Conversely, current political scientists lament the diffuse nature of their subject matter, envy more "fundamental" disciplines, and commonly expend remarkable energies in "retooling" themselves as "political" psychologists, economists, sociologists, and so on. It is instructive to contrast this view with Hannah Arendt's conception of the statesman's task as one of "seeing" through the eyes of disparate persons and groups, while yet preserving a vision of the general welfare.

What I describe is, of course, but one consequence of the differing conceptions of the nature of political knowledge. For Aristotle, it approximated our idea of **wisdom** and was inescapably evaluative; for us it is, or ought to be, predictive and value free. This contrast is too well known to require elaboration; my interest lies less in a rehearsal of these historical differences than in a consideration of their consequences. Thus one reason that the services of political scientists or theorists are not in greater demand by governments is that their "expertise" is diffuse (at least, in contrast to that of economists and psychologists). It does not readily lend itself to instrumental application. This might be called the "negative qualification" of the political scientist: i.e., what his disciplinary training lacks.

There is yet a second and more interesting source of disqualification, this of a more "positive" nature. Again, it is useful to return to a contrast with the Classics. For the ancient Greeks, to **have** knowledge about something is to hold a certain ascendancy over that subject, whether the "knowing" relationship obtained between sentient and non-sentient or adult and child. To them, the crucial element in that ascendancy was superior consciousness, which could be attained through contemplation. To achieve such "power," it was not necessary to manipulate or somehow act upon the object, as it was to become to the men of the seventeenth century. Even if contemplative, possession of superior knowledge of an object justified (if it did not demand) that the knower adopt a critical, even directive, posture. Plato's ideal forms might be transcendent and Aristotle's immanent, but both opened a critical distance between knowing and being. Of course, this should remind us that neither would have imagined our fact/value dichotomy to hold for genuine knowledge. But it also suggests that we should be wary of drawing too sharp a historical dichotomy between these respective times or of taking the protestations of our colleagues at face value. Probing only a bit beneath the surface of current social science, it is apparent that a rigorously "non-valuative" stance is no more attractive today than it was in the fifth and fourth centuries B.C.

Consider the appreciable attention accorded the idea of "rationality" in recent decades, in psycholanalysis as well as economics and political science. Rational behavior functions as a norm from which "deviations" are noted and measured. While those who employ such a criterion usually protest that they do not "prescribe" the rational posture, their position seems disingenuous when "rationality" is typically defined as providing "more extended knowledge" of an action's consequences.[10] If such judgments can in fact be made, do they **truly** constitute **no** claim whatever to superiority over those of "less extended knowledge?" To persist in this claim seems bizarre; but beyond that, it appears to undermine justifications for the pursuit of knowledge itself, such as benefitting one's fellows. At the very least in a culture such as that shared by the industrial nations , with their specific norm of instrumental rationality, to label a person, group, or action as "other than rational" is effectively to dismiss any claims it may make, even to raise questions of mental competence or good will.

In a condensed and partial way, I am only reiterating the indictments of industrial society articulated by critics on both right and left. Still, I hope to approach the title question more closely by accepting (rather than arguing) that the evaluative function which Classical theory performed explicitly on the basis of knowledge **proclaimed** (not "acknowledged") to be "normative" is today practiced implicitly. To be sure, it now employs forms of knowledge purporting to be value-neutral. This is possible, its proponents claim, because its imperatives flow from a social concensus, **not** the science itself. In contrast, I contend that current theory written by social scientists is actively complicit in maintaining, if not in forming, this alleged consensus. For in one sense, the manifestos of the late 1950s were correct, at least in their view of the state of social science. Debate over the great alternatives **had** largely absented that arena, to be replaced by a preoccupation with relatively minor adjustments in the management and administration of established policies. The emergence of the social-science expert could thus serve the ideological function of masking the political content of the substructure.

----

[10] See: Talcott Parsons, **The Structure of Social Action**, Glencoe, IL, Free Press, 1949.

Where the analyses of Daniel Bell, Robert Dahl, Charles Lindlbom, and others went awry was in their assessment of the strength and stability of the underlying consensus, as the events of the 1960s were to demonstrate.

To this point, I have distinguished between the study of historical texts and attempts to write what I have rather inadequately called "original" political theory. I have noted that epic theorists not infrequently (indeed, more or less intentionally and institutionally) generated "schools" which can be considered spiritual, if not historical, ancestors of current disciplines based in universities. Invoking Thomas Kuhn, I have remarked on the absence of disciplinary consenus within social science and especially political science, suggesting that the latter seems to occupy a unique and anomalous position. To those who sought a unified science of man, the claim of political studies to have isolated a distinctive dimension of human behavior is implausible: an indigestible lump in the intellectual intestine. Economics, to the extent that it laid similar claims to a distinctive subject matter, provides a similar discomforture; yet its disciplinary identity and agenda is rescued not, as is sometimes said, by its powerfully predictive theory, but by its relationship to an extra-academic institution: the market. While undergraduate students of economics do earn academic degrees, they may also anticipate employment in the "real world" institutions which their training **sympathetically** presents to them. This is to say that the relationship between academic economics and careers in brokerage houses is not an adversarial one, while political scientists and theorists learn an expertise that cannot but make them critics or even competitors of their own "shadow" group and subject matter: politicians and government.

The point is important enough to underscore. Unique among the social sciences, economics and political science claim to take as their province a distinctive (and presumably more or less identifiable) set of behaviors. In the case of the former, however, academic experience qualifies one to enter the object world and "practice" (as in the case of law or medicine). Yet in the latter, an adversarial and competitive relationship obtains. If reached by a somewhat more pertinent route, this conclusion is familiar to those who regard economics as a "vocational degree." More deeply, this account is a gloss on Gunnell's speculation that liberal constitutionalism is hostile to epic theory precisely because that they are rival bases for legitimacy. To argue this way is to return to Plato, albeit in the mode of sociology rather than philosophy.

From these diverse preliminaries, I turn now to some

suggestions ("conclusions" would be too strong a word) for the current conduct of political theorizing. I want more to delineate **postures** (strategies, goals, and foci) than to detail an agenda for our enterprise. In addition, I am interested in the loci, the institutional matrices, that house us.

ORIENTATIONS

As noted above, this essay is little concerned with interpreting historical texts, whether considered as a coherent and specialized set of recurrent concepts and issues (a "tradition") or more properly seen as a skein woven into the tapestry of intellectual history in general. I do not denigrate either the intrinsic worth or the utility of such research and instruction. Most theorists would probably agree that study of the past has pragmatic value, plus the more elusive function we speak of as the "cultivation" of mind. There are significant intellectual issues within the conduct of interpretation, and these controversies will likely persist.[11] Given that the history and analysis of political events and ideas will remain a distinct subfield within political science, I now direct attention outward from our familiar grove toward external reference systems.[12]

It is helpful to set out, necessarily in summary form, some perspectives and assumptions which inform what follows. About fifteen years ago, in a paper entitled "Paradigms and Political Theories," Sheldon Wolin suggested that the institutions and culture of a society might be considered paradigm articulations of epic theories. A few years earlier, Norman Jacobson had reminded us that theories serve a general function of political education in addition to whatever epistemological, utopian, or truth claims they may

----

[11] For an overview of current disputes in this area, see: John Gunnell, **Political Theory.**

[12] Here, as in remarks that follow, I touch on the concerns of Booth Fowler's essay in this anthology. But my approach to the subject of the status of political theory within the academy is different from his, and we do seem to differ significantly in our responses to the title question.

advance.[13] There are difficulties with both views, perhaps especially with the former, but both emphasize an important point often overlooked by academic political science: that political theories have a self-fulfilling aspect. To Marxists, theories have a praxial dimension; to Michael Oakeshott, they express and transfer the accumulated political wisdom of a culture.[14] Some three decades ago, Alfred Cobban announced a decline of political theory which he attributed to a retreat of the enterprise to the academy and a loss of connection to the practice or **craft** of politics.[15] Again, although there are objections to his conclusion, it points toward important changes in relations between the study and practice of politics in this century. It is in these changes, complex and profound as they have been, that we should seek a response to the title question.

At this point, I advance a very large claim which will likely occasion vigorous dissent from some, especially since I can in no way demonstrate it, but only urge its plausibility. Specifically, I suggest that the most profound political (social and cultural) process of the twentieth century has been that which Max Weber called the "rationalization" of Western civilization. (He also used the more somber phrase "**die Entzauberung der Welt**," or disenchantment with the world. This he believed to accompany, if not constitute, the process.) It is not completely clear to me whether Weber regarded this process of rationalization as an irreversible historical current or a moment in a recurrent cyclical pattern; there seems evidence for each view. But plainly, he was profoundly ambivalent toward it, with pessimism dominating his later years.[16]

----

[13] See: Wolin, "Paradigms and Political Theories"; Norman Jacobson, "Political Science and Political Education," **American Political Science Review**, 57, 3, September, 1963, pp. 561-569.

[14] See: Michael Oakeshott, **Rationalism in Politics**, New York, Basic Books, 1962.

[15] See: Alfred Cobban, "The Decline of Political Theory," **Political Science Quarterly**, 68, 3, September, 1953, pp. 321-337.

[16] For consideration of this question within the context of Weber's methodology, specifically his use of typologies, see: Reinhard Bendix, Max **Weber**, Garden City, NY, Doubleday,

The specifics of his diagnosis are too well known to require more than summary statement. The more important include: the hegemony of rational-legal forms of domination and their institutionalization in hierarchical bureaucracies, the rise of experts to policy-making prominence (and the consequent decline of the "amateur" elected politician), the cultural dominance of a means-ends conception of rationality, and the exile of choice of "ultimate" values to the realm of faith. In short, one should think of all those lineaments of a society Weber likened to the famous "iron cage," in which we enter the "icy night of polar darkness and hardness." Thus one of his darker prophecies, which he applied to the **novus homo** of his age, but which might well be taken to characterize the age itself, gloomily anticipated "specialists without spirit, sensualists without soul."[17]

This has surely been an apocalyptic and powerful, if not uncontested vision. Despite significant differences, subsequent theorists have accepted very much of it. The Critical Theorists of both prior and current generations have added a new emphasis on the role of natural science and found a greater need for depth psychology. The Catholic sociologist Jacques Ellul, numerous American ecologists and historians, and the philosopher William Barrett have contributed fresh awareness of the power of technology or technique to shape industrial society. With characteristic audacity, Herbert Marcuse indicted Western culture as a whole, from principles of income distribution to seductive shop girls, for its "one-dimensional" repression. Further illustrations could be elaborated in wearisome detail.

What I find worthy of attention is that Weber's idea of rationalization, although seriously incomplete by current standards of formulation, still commands such respect and illuminates so many of our discontents.[18] My concern here is neither with Weber's accuracy in depicting bureaucracy

----

1962, especially pp. 298-328.

[17] See: Max Weber, "Politics as a Vocation," in **From Max Weber**, H. H. Gerth and C. Wright Mills, eds., trans., New York, Oxford University Press, 1946, pp. 77-128.

[18] G. R. Boynton has reminded me that many current students of bureaucracies have found Weber's model seriously flawed; see his unpublished essays on: "Max Weber's Vehicle for Assigning Blame," "The Freedom Machine," and "About Systems that Reproduce Themselves."

as an institution (the principle of instrumental rationality made flesh) nor with the "hardware" aspects of technology (even though the machine is a ubiquitous metaphor in recent political theory). Instead, borrowing words from Manfred Stanley, I would stress Weber's "metaphorical dominance" of our **culture**. The result has been a "technicism" which "encompasses two acts and their consequences. The first act is ignoring, within science, the need to pay attention to the **discontinuities** between the human world and other worlds that are also the objects of scientific attention. The second act is ignoring the epistemological limits of science relative to other modes of reflection and action."[19]

This establishes a context for my three main recommendations for political theory. The first urges that political theorists adopt a posture of relentless **criticism** of contemporary politics and society. By this injunction, I intend nothing esoteric nor sectarian. It would be satisfied by Marx's demand for deep, general, and sustained analysis of the dynamics of control, of the constraints upon human liberation. Thus Marcuse's advocacy (at least during the 1960s) of the "great refusal" would do as well Camus' "No!" or the writings of genuinely conservative critics of corporate society. It is the posture or animating spirit which matters more than the substance. I have little patience with centrist cant which recognizes only "constructive" criticism as legitimate. Instead, it appears to me that the

----

[19] Manfred Stanley, **The Technological Conscience**, New York, Free Press, 1978, p. 13. Writing in a similar vein, though employing a somewhat different terminology, is William Barrett; see: **The Illusion of Technique**, Garden City, NY, Doubleday, 1978, especially pp. 20-29. Not the least virtue of Stanley's book is its attempt to bring some order to the protean dimensionality of the critique of "Technicism" from Lewis Mumford's **Technics and Civilization** (New York, Harcourt, Brace and World, 1934) to Langdon Winner's **Autonomous Technology** (Cambridge, MA, M. I. T. Press, 1977). It is a major conceptual task to disentangle purely technological or "hardware" factors from such institutional elements as bureaucracy, from socio-political variables such as the emergence of the expert, from problems generated by sheer scale, and from such grand cultural and philosophical themes as the dominance of instrumental rationality. Of course, all these dimensions cohere as part of the "critique of modernity." My focus here on Weber is but a necessary economy.

forces of domination are today so powerful and persuasive as to endanger the very habit and practice of critique. As someone has pithily observed, even Hercules was not asked to fill the Augean stables. It must, of course, be kept in mind that significant political critique can scarcely ever be devoid of a "constructive" dimension. Thus the very categories and logic of Marx's analysis of domination provide intimations of his conception of a liberated society. Still, he specifically (and in my view, correctly) declined to offer "blueprints" of a communist order. Terence Ball's contribution to the volume at hand may be read with profit on this point.

My second recommendation is to meet our need for criticism of **culture**, not simply of economics and politics conventionally understood. With the collapse of the industrial proletariat as a reasonably hopeful source of liberation (if, indeed, it is even identifiable as a class), radicals have found no material or social actors to conduct revolutionary praxis, though they have exhausted virtually every group which might imaginably be considered a candidate. Blacks, gays, women, "the young," "the external proletariat," and even the performer-entrepreneurs of rock and roll have had their "auditions" and been found wanting. But the importance of the analysis of culture is not exhausted by the disappearance of agents of social change, economically and politically defined. For as Critical Theorists, and notably Marcuse, have argued persuasively, the texture, content, and values of current culture comprise a powerful if subtle engine of domination. Indeed, with Weber in mind, we might say that no analysis of so protean an idea as rationalization could be conducted without a cultural dimension. Thus some of our more stimulating recent works of social criticism have included Richard Sennett's study of public etiquette, Christopher Lasch's analysis of the family's disintegration before encroachments of sociological and psychological "counselling" services, Gary Wills' dissection of the personality and career of Richard Nixon, and Daniel Bell's description of the disjunction among political, economic, and cultural systems.[20]

----

[20] See: Richard Sennett, **The Fall of Public Man**, New York, Random House, 1978; Christopher Lasch, **The Culture of Narcissism**, New York, Norton, 1978; Garry Wills, **Nixon Agonistes**, New York, New American Library, 1969; Daniel Bell, **The Cultural Contradictions of Capitalism**, New York, Basic Books, 1976.

These first two recommendations have surfaced several times before in this essay. But there remains a third, only implicit in my prior arguments and now deserving direct statement. It is no more original than the others; but like them, it is no less important for that. We must confront the alleged failure of liberalism. This proposal implies a more specific diagnosis of our current **political** malaise: the decline and crisis of our main political ideology. Prognoses and therapies for this condition diverge as widely as diagnoses and etiologies, and I will not weary readers with one more review of the exhaustion of the political imagination. Still, the subject cannot be ignored altogether. Etiologies aside, there are good reasons to think that a set of largely Anglo-American ideas formulated in the eighteenth century and assuming institutional shape in the nineteenth are now unable to cope with tensions induced by rationalization and their own internal contradictions. In such diverse areas as political (non)participation, (non)functioning of key institutions, decreasing public levels of confidence in the future, and increasing doubts about government legitimacy, the indicators of danger are manifest if not yet conclusive.

Assessing the advent of the Reagan Presidency, Sheldon Wolin writes that such aspects of rationalization as the managed economy and welfare bureaucracies have sharply diminished the sphere in which **political** action, by either elites or mass publics, can be effective. Complex and technical issues, sluggish and unresponsive institutions, the extensive "lead time" necessary to realize research and development programs, increased militancy in third-world peoples, and sheer scale have induced a sense of powerlessness in both leaders and publics. To a considerable extent, a vibrant and participatory civic life is incompatible with the needs of what he calls the "political economy" (what in Europe might be termed the "state"). Though the decline of "self rule" to periodic elections following irrelevant campaigns is a considerable diminution of the more elevated hopes of democratic theorists, it may at least offer stability, provided that the political economy does not itself experience severe and prolonged crises such as "stagflation," destabilizing levels of unemployment, and the collapse of major industries. At such times, the legitimacy of the managers will be seriously challenged precisely because "consent" is so narrowly construed and "mandate" so empty of substance. Worse, all of this can hold even without deliberate and skillful use of manipulative techniques to which a desperate or malign elite might turn. In short, the liberal state faces a dilemma: it cannot tolerate the strains of participatory democracy, but the limited self-rule which it can accomodate will likely prove an insufficient source of legitimacy precisely when it is most urgently needed. If such an analysis has merit, it raises the most serious questions, not simply for champions of more vibrant democratic regimes, but also for those satisfied with stable plebiscitary orders.[21]

WHAT IS TO BE DONE?

This final section might more appropriately, if less magisterially, be entitled "What CAN be done?" -- especially by persons so bereft of both constituency and power as political theorists. Surely even brief reflection on the magnitude of the issues delineated above can scarcely inspire optimism as to their ultimate tractability. There is, perhaps, some reason for hope in the thought that seldom have political theorists enjoyed positions of great authority; and as in the examples of Plato and Machiavelli, rarely has that experience long endured or happily concluded. The preceding section identified three general foci or questions and sought to suggest postures and attitudes which would usefully inform their investigation. In concluding these somewhat disparate remarks, I hope to be more concrete, to speak more directly to the level of praxis, and yet to avoid offering a laundry list.

There is, first of all, the matter of audience. As professional communicators situated largely though not exclusively in the academy, the natural clients of our writing and teaching are students, peers, and extra-academic elites; and such audiences are unlikely to be either large or homogeneous. There is, of course, the alternative of seeking to reach a **large** popular audience. But given

----

[21] See: Sheldon S. Wolin, "Reagan Country," **New York Review of Books**, 27, 20, December 18, 1980, pp. 9-12. This general interpretation is expanded by Wolin, Lasch, and others in a symposium on "The Current Crisis" in: **Democracy**, 1, 1, January, 1981. For a similarly oriented critique from a quite different tradition, see: Jurgen Habermas, **Legitimation Crisis**, Thomas McCarthy, trans., Boston, Beacon Press, 1975. William Connolly's contribution to this volume is yet another variation in the theme.

conglomerate control of the media, the prospect is not an encouraging one; and few of us are Tom Paines in either skill or temperament.   Still, before any of these audiences can become targets, we must set about providing disciplinary legitimacy to publication in journals of opinion often considered either irrelevant or damaging to professional advancement and reputation.   Our colleagues in sociology seem to have been more successful in widening their professionally legitimated outlets to include **Commentary, Dissent, Partisan Review,** and **The New York Review of Books.**   We should become more sensitive to this issue and to its obverse: the extending of an academic imprimatur to writers located essentially outside the discipline.   And undoubtedly our culture would profit from greater exchange among elites than can be accomplished within the triangle of Boston, New York, and Washington.

Having opened the issue of our vocation and university location, it may be appropriate to mention some related matters.   We should, I think, try to make departments and universities safe for the students and faculties who inhabit them.[22]   What I have in mind here is the fact that academia is not especially resistant to the pressures and blandishments of rationalization used by Exxon or its governmental counterparts.   These pressures are especially strong within what Jerome Ravetz, in his splendid book, **Scientific Knowledge and Its Social Problems,** calls the "immature or ineffectual" sciences, a category to which he consigns virtually all of the sciences of man.[23]   The temptation to substitute the trappings of more robust sciences for our relative lack of substantive success and to impose an orthodoxy, usually of methodology, on its practitioners is too familiar to require documentation.   But it needs to be resisted nonetheless, along with such corollary forces as disciplinary self-images or goals which project achievement of cumulative knowledge.

According to Alvin Gouldner, a paradigm instance of the former occurred within sociology.   The antagonists were the "Parsonian" or establishment wing (prominently housed at Columbia) and the critical or dissenting sociology (practiced primarily at the University of Chicago).   To the former, sociology was or should become a **profession** on the

----

[22] Here again I touch upon matters also discussed in Booth Fowler's contribution to this volume.

[23] See: Ravetz, **Scientific Knowledge and Its Social Problems,** especially chapter 14.

model of medicine. Replying for the latter, Everett Hughes presented a view of the discipline as a learned society of intellectuals with a shared interest in the critical analysis of society.[24] The differences transcend verbal fencing. As should now be apparent, my view of the agenda of political theory is much more sympathetic to the critical view. It should also be clear that I regard the disciplinary value of cumulation as dubious at best. In no circumstance should it or any other such value become a disciplinary norm. As a footnote to Gouldner's anecdote, it should be remembered that he was among the insurgents who joined the Society for the Study of Social Problems (an activist association as its title suggests) and served, if memory is reliable, as one of its early presidents.

I have here reviewed a few of the issues on the internal or vocational agenda: the task of putting our house in order. In making the university "safe," I may be committing myself to a pluralism or at least a polycentrism with which I am not entirely comfortable. Still, I am more concerned to promote a spirit of critical inquiry and an environment which at least does not actively inhibit intellectual risk-taking and a sense of adventure. Again, it is important to remember that achievement of these goals is an institutional as well as an intellectual task. We need, for example, to provide more and more varied outlets for writing out of the mainstream. That might be accomplished by founding of additional problem- or subject-oriented journals such as **Philosophy and Public Affairs** and **Political Theory**, rather than following our traditional pattern of establishing regional **American Political Science Reviews**. There is a congeries of other vocational issues, such as policies of promotion and tenure, which merit the concern of political theorists, not less because they involve ourselves. But to pursue such particulars would distract from my main point. We need to recall that political theorists are or can be (albeit in circumscribed contexts) actors as well as scholars. It is to these possibilities I now turn. turn.[25]

----

[24] See: Alvin W. Gouldner, "Anti-Minotaur: The Myth of a Value-Free Sociology," in Irving Louis Horowitz, ed., **The New Sociology**, New York, Oxford University Press, 1964, pp. 196-217.

[25] My own critics might assert that (to this point, at least) I have proposed a conception of political commentary which is elitist in terms of its practitioners and which defends an

Given my injunction that political theorists practice a persistent and radical critique of corporate society, plus my rejection of vocational images of political knowledge, careers within private or public bureaucracies can hardly be recommended. Nor is it my belief that conventional partisan politics offers hopeful possibilities for significant change. Doubtless there will be dissent from my judgment. I will not press the point, but instead consider more marginal forms of praxis: first, utopianism.

While frankly utopian literature has declined, if not vanished, in our century (with the possible exception of science fiction), the genre lives on through its mirror image: dystopian creations. We should not forget the intimate historical and conceptual linkages between the utopian and critical projects, and there seems no reason to suppose that it does not obtain at least as strongly between dystopia and critique. Both utopian and dystopian impulses permit exploitation of satire, parody, and irony: devices so useful to creation of the psychic and narrative **distancing** necessary to critique. And who can forget the use Marx makes of them in his more savage polemics? These uses of utopian speculation stand apart from the more muted and implicit critiques of the comparatively "straight" literatures of alternative futurists.

But utopianism may also constitute a praxis. Despite Marx's ridicule of Robert Owen's version, utopianism has not lost its attraction to dissidents and marginals.[26] Moreover, a recent development in utopian experimentation

----

enterprise esoteric and even "ornamental." I doubt that these are either necessary or desirable attributes of my position. Still, serious political thinking has many parallels to musical and other artistic creation: all make demands on practitioners and audiences which are unlikely to be met by large numbers of persons. Moreover, the university as an institutional locus imposes many constraints upon praxis, as activists of the 1960s discovered. See: Paul F. Kress, "Reply to Commentaries on 'Against Epistemology'," **Journal of Politics**, 42, 4, November, 1980, pp. 1168-1169.

[26] Utopian construction is not a device available only to those marginal in a **sociological** sense. For surely neither Plato nor More, to cite only the most obvious examples, could be so described. My argument here encompasses those intellectually or spiritually uncomfortable with their times.

should be noted.   To my knowledge, virtually all such experiments, at least those of the last two centuries, have been energized by and organized according to either the principles of some explicit social or political theory (a general but powerful idea such as anarchism or the latest therapy to emerge in Big Sur) or the creed of some sort of religious faith (in the broad sense).   We are now witnessing the formation of alternative communities founded on ecological and environmental concerns.   It is true that in a sociological sense they do not differ functionally from their predecessors.   Their members share a vision, often apocalyptic; they study "sacred" texts; they "follow" gurus.   Usually, members share general attitudes toward such matters as authority, education, and community.   (One current example is: "Small is beautiful!") In the future, this broader consensus may well become explicitly articulated.   But my interest lies elsewhere: specifically, in the ways that such "secular utopias" are forms of critical praxis.

A specific example may prove both illustrative and economical.   My former colleague, David Orr, recently departed the academy to establish in the Ozark mountains a self-sustaining community with the arcadian name of the Meadowbrook Project.   It intends to demonstrate the feasibility of the "soft energy path" programs of Amory Lovins and Dennis Hayes.[27] Meadowbrook's developers anticipate that the project will serve the Owenite purpose of teaching through example, eventually becoming parent to similar progeny, but will also provide an alternate **locus** for those writers, organizers and critics who share its visiion.

Another strategy for critical praxis, and the last I consider here, stands somewhere between the academy and the utopian community.   The English historian and philosopher of science Jerome Ravetz has reviewed the vast physical, moral, and political damage wrought through many applications of natural and social science by corporations and governments.   This has led him to recommend that we promote what he calls "critical science," a program or movement he believes to be already under way.   Though his description is drawn primarily from disciplines in natural science, the operant principles have broader application.

----

[27] See: Amory B. Lovins, **Soft Energy Paths**, Cambridge, MA, Ballinger, 1977; Dennis Hayes, **Rays of Hope**, New York, Norton, 1977; David W. Orr, "U. S. Energy Policy and the Political Economy of Participation," **Journal of Politics**, 41, 4, November, 1979, pp. 1027-1056.

> The reponse to this peril is rapidly creating a new sort of science: critical science. Instead of isolated individuals sacrificing their leisure and interrupting their regular research for engagement in practical problems, we now see the emergence of scientific schools of a new sort. In them collaborative research of the highest quality is done, as part of practical projects involving the discovery, analysis and criticism of the different sorts of damage inflicted on man and nature by runaway technology, followed by their public exposure and campaigns for their abolition.[28]

As examples of critical science, Ravetz cites individuals such as Barry Commoner, journals such as **Environment,** and associations such as The Society for Social Responsibility in Science. They practice rather more conventional politics than the kinds which have received attention in these pages, but the idea of a critical science need not remain so confined.

CONCLUSION

After distinguishing the study of the history of ideas from the practice of theory, I have argued that Weber's diagnosis of the rationalization process is **the** political phenomenon of our time. Further, I have characterized that process, at least in its present manifestation, quite negatively; and I have urged its need for sustained critique. Without specifying the styles or targets of such critique, I have suggested that current tension between the study and the practice of politics should lead us to challenge the vocational conceptions of political knowledge which now dominate the academy. I have tried to show the possibility and desirability of this through a review of praxial alternatives open to the political theorist who would be thus critical.

A contributor to this volume, Michael Walzer, has perceptively observed in another essay that we should be less concerned with the abolition of the state than with its

----

[28] Ravetz, **Scientific Knowledge and Its Social Problems,** p. 424.

"hollowing out." If I understand him, this extends the recommendations of his previous works that the values of participation, loyalty, and community must be realized through a strengthening of primary and small secondary group life.[29] Such creation and nurturance of "human sized" associations is vital to shelter people from our Weberian world. (It is in this sense that I earlier urged making the universities safe for their inhabitants.) But this enterprise complements, rather than contradicts, political theorists' contributions of critique. Indeed, the two projects may require one another. Critique without **Gemeinschaft** may produce only alienation; communitarianism without a cutting intellectual edge, as we have recently and sadly learned, ends in futility and a rejection of reason by anyone's definition. Love, perhaps unhappily, is not all that we need.

However variously we may view it, the issue which animates this anthology is vulnerable to the error of isolating some presumably special role or obligation of the political theorist. When it comes to hollowing out the state, we may well not be the peers of, for example, community organizers. But such questions should probably not be determined a priori. Nor, as the spirit of this essay testifies, do I find much utility in exclusionary definitions of our field and the practitioners within it. If we are to find ways, even a way out of the iron cage, then we will need all the allies and resources we can command.

I wish that I might be more sanguine at our prospects.

----

[29] At this point, of course, "participatory democracy" is often advocated. Hannah Arendt somewhere commented that the demand for popular participation in some form is always made and always defeated in revolutionary movements after the fifteenth century, but such considerations are beyond the scope of this essay.

CONTRADICTION AND CRITIQUE

IN POLITICAL THEORY

Terence Ball

Every sleeper has numbered himself among the elect, but the concepts he has acquired in sleep are themselves of course only the wares of sleep.

G. W. F. Hegel[1]

The question I am asked to address here is: What should political theory be now? I am sorely tempted to sermonize upon a subject about which I have many strong feelings and even some settled convictions. But because I should hate to conform to the caricature of the "normative" theorist, I shall do my best to resist this temptation. My plan, accordingly, is to begin by formulating a controversial thesis regarding the relation between political theory and practice. My statement of this thesis must of necessity be brief, and my defense scarcely more than an argument-sketch to be filled in at a later date. Here I am concerned, in the main, with the implications that my thesis has for the opening question. This question itself requires reformulation. Political theory is not a product but a process, not a finished achievement but an ongoing **activity**. We need, therefore, to ask: What should political theorists be **doing** now? My answer is that political theorists should nowadays be doing what political theorists have always done: namely, criticize other theorists' theories. That this is itself a **political** activity, and not some academic parlor-game, can be more clearly seen once we view the relation

----

[1] G. W. F. Hegel, **Philosophy of Right**, T. M. Knox, trans., Oxford, Oxford University Press, 1967, p. 5. I am indebted to Brian Barry, James Farr, Stephen Leonard, and John Nelson for criticizing an earlier version of this essay. None is of course responsible for any errors (grievous, innocuous, or otherwise) which, despite their good counsel, still remain. The author teaches political science at the University of Minnesota in Minneapolis.

between political theory and practice in the way that I propose.

In making out my case, I begin by briefly stating what I mean by "theory" and how I understand its relation to practice. My thesis is that the relation of theory to practice is not a contingent or instrumental one but is, rather, a conceptual and constitutive relation between belief and action. The claims advanced in section I derive not only from the modern philosophy of action but, perhaps surprisingly, from Marx's conception of contradiction and critique. My reasons for claiming this particular pedigree are spelled out in section II. In section III, I contend that the Marxian critique of philosophy and political economy needs nowadays to be extended to the naturalistic social and "policy" sciences, the concepts and categories of which are increasingly constitutive of a technocratic social and political reality. To criticize these scientistic self-understandings is to reflect critically upon the relations between science and society, theory and practice.

I

A "theory," in my sense, is a more or less systematically interrelated set of beliefs about man and society.[2] If you prefer to call this an "ideology," I shall not object; for I agree with Quentin Skinner that the history of political theory, properly understood, is the history of political ideologies.[3] At any rate, a person's beliefs do not stand in a contingent relation to his behavior. For an agent's behavior cannot be identified and described apart from his beliefs.[4] Or, to put the point in the now-familiar idiom of

----

[2] Here I follow Alasdair MacIntyre's suggestion. See: "Ideology, Social Science, and Revolution," **Comparative Politics**, 5, 2, April, 1973, pp. 321-342, on p. 326.

[3] See: Quentin Skinner, **The Foundations of Modern Political Thought**, Cambridge, Cambridge University Press, in two volumes, 1978, v. I, pp. xi-xiii.

[4] For example, self-interested behavior is constituted by and rendered intelligible by reference to the agent's beliefs about what is and is not good for him, i.e., "in his inter-

the philosophy of action, "behavior" is not reducible without remainder to physical or bodily movement. For example, in signing a letter, a check, and an autograph I make identical movements; but in so doing I perform three quite different actions, each constituted according to different beliefs, intentions, and conventions. If you set out to explain my behavior, you must first know what it is that I am doing; and this in turn presupposes your knowing something about my beliefs. Yet these beliefs are not, and indeed cannot be, mine alone; they are, of necessity, shared by others: for example, by the person who asks for my autograph, who accepts my checks, and the like. Now these public or shared beliefs are conceived in, learned through, and communicated by the concepts and categories of the language I share with my fellows. One need only consider the type and range of beliefs to which an agent must subscribe (and to which the observer must have access) before he can be said to conceive and execute any sort of political act. To take a rather dramatic example, we might ask what is required to identify, describe, and explain an act of tyrannicide. Before one can perform such an action, one must be able to conceive of it, which of course requires that certain criteria, categories, and concepts be available to the agent. He must, for example, know (or have certain beliefs about) what a tyrant is, what counts as tyrannical behavior, how it differs from legitimate rule, and so on. He must, minimally, have a stock of political beliefs, which is to say that he must, in short, subscribe to a political "theory." It is in this sense that all political agents may be said to be political theorists. [5]

A theory consists, at a minimum, of various types of propositions, some of which will characterize its object's properties or potentialities. In the case of social or

----

est." From this, it follows that his interests cannot figure as contingent Humean causes of his behavior. For a fuller elaboration and defense of these claims, see: Terence Ball, "Interest-Explanations," **Polity**, 12, 2, Winter, 1979, pp. 187-201.

[5] See: Alasdair MacIntyre, "Is a Science of Comparative Politics Possible?" in **Against the Self-Images of the Age**, Notre Dame, University of Notre Dame Press, 1978, pp. 260-279; MacIntyre, **After Virtue**, Notre Dame, University of Notre Dame Press, 1981, especially p. 58; MacIntyre, "Ideology, Social Science, and Revolution."

political theories, these will characteristically include true descriptions of particular practices and beliefs. These propositions may nevertheless prove, upon closer critical examination, to be mutually inconsistent, i.e., contradictory. But since social reality is socially constructed or structured (i.e., constituted by people's shared beliefs) then we may fairly say that such contradictions are not merely logical ones: they are in fact social-structural contradictions. Social and political reality itself may be contradictory, as I argue in the section following. The exposure and criticism of these contradictions I take to be one of the key tasks of a critical political theory. For to recognize and rectify theoretical contradictions entails the alteration of theoretically constituted social arrangements, practices, and institutions. Although this set of claims is by no means specifically or uniquely "Marxist," it is nevertheless true that their clearest and most controversial defense was first supplied by Karl Marx.

But before turning to Marx's conception of contradiction and critique, and its relation to his version of critical theory, it might be well to say a few words about "logic" and contradiction. In stressing their importance for any properly critical political theory, Marxist or otherwise, I am not denying that people's utterances often are contradictory; nor am I suggesting that contradiction and inconsistency are evils that can, and should, be forever banished; nor do I mean to play the part of the pedant bent, as was Goethe's Mephisto (though with tongue firmly in cheek), upon shackling the human spirit:

> My friend, I shall be pedagogic,
> and say you ought to start with Logic.
> For thus your mind is trained and braced,
> In Spanish boots it will be laced,
> That on the road of thought maybe
> It henceforth creep more thoughtfully,
> And does not crisscross here and there,
> Will-o'-the-wisping through the air.[6]

For poets and playwrights, the pedantic logician is a stock figure of fun. (One thinks, for example, of le logicien in Ionesco's Rhinocerous). Yet logic need not be the province of pedants. Attention to such matters as

----

[6] J. W. von Goethe, **Faust**, Walter Kaufmann, trans., Garden City, NY, Doubleday, 1961, p. 199.

consistency, identity, entailment, and contradiction, far from being the pastime of professional logicians, is to some degree an essential activity for communicative creatures like ourselves. For our ability and determination to detect and correct errors and inconsistencies is a practical requirement of social life: it answers to a practical interest in mutual understanding.[7] Having this capacity is a necessary, though of course scarcely a sufficient, condition of rationality or, to speak in the linguistic idiom of Chomsky and Habermas, of "communicative competence."[8] The "strain toward consistency," understood psychologistically by cognitive consistency theorists a few years back, is not a narrowly psychological phenomenon.[9] It is, rather, characteristic of social creatures trying to communicate with their fellows and to make themselves understood.[10] That is why one need only be a layman and not a professional logician to detect errors in logic, and contradictions in particular. As Locke, arguing against the Schoolmen of his day, quipped: "God was not so sparing to men to make them barely two-legged creatures, and left it to Aristotle to make them rational."[11]

For language-using creatures like ourselves, then, logic and life are inextricably intertwined. It is because we speak a language that we **can** hold mutually contradictory

----

[7] This notion of a communicatively constituted "practical interest" is borrowed from: Jurgen Habermas, **Knowledge and Human Interests**, Jeremy J. Shapiro, trans., Boston, Beacon Press, 1971. I should add, though, that I am exceedingly skeptical of the quasi-transcendental status which he claims for it. For reservations much like my own, see: Richard J. Bernstein, **The Restructuring of Social and Political Theory**, New York, Harcourt Brace Jovanovich, 1976, pp. 219-225, 260 (fn. 30); Paul Thomas, "The Language of Real Life: Jurgen Habermas and the Distortion of Karl Marx," **Discourse**, 1, Fall, 1979, pp. 59-85.

[8] See: Jurgen Habermas, "Toward a Theory of Communicative Competence," in Hans Peter Dreitzel, ed., **Recent Sociology No. 2**, New York, Macmillan, 1970, pp. 115-148; Habermas, "What Is Universal Pragmatics?" in **Communication and the Evolution of Society**, Thomas McCarthy, trans., Boston, Beacon Press 1979, especially chapter 1.

[9] I have in mind especially the work of Leon Festinger and his associates: **When Prophecy Fails**, Minneapolis, Univer-

beliefs, utter contradictory statements, and the rest of it. These must, however, be the exception rather than the rule. For, to paraphrase Wittgenstein, though it is possible for some of us to contradict ourselves some of the time, it is quite impossible for all of us to contradict ourselves all of the time. Otherwise, the concept of contradiction, and indeed of communication, would have lost its point.[12] A society whose members told only lies, or whose every utterance was contradictory, is unconceivable; it would, in Alasdair MacIntyre's apt phrase, be incapable of social embodiment.[13]

    Still, there are societies (and ours is one) whose members' beliefs, aims, desires, and aspirations are often contradictory. Indeed it may well be true (though I shall not argue the point here) that one of the key characteristics of modern, morally anomalous, and technologically complex societies like our own is their increasingly self-divided or "contradictory" character. One of the functions of uncritical, socially embodied theories (ideologies, if you will) is to mask or, failing that, to rationalize these contradictions.[14] By contrast, the aim of a critical theory like Marx's (but quite unlike what passes for "Marxism" in the Soviet Union) is to unveil illusions and to expose real social contradictions by exposing theoretical ones. It is to Marx's

----

sity of Minnesota Press, 1956; **A Theory of Cognitive Dissonance**, Stanford, Stanford University Press, 1957. Among psychologists, cognitive dissonance theory has fallen out of favor. For a retrospective critique and summary of the shortcomings of cognitive dissonance theory in its various psychologistic versions, see: William J. McGuire, "The Current States of Cognitive Consistency Theories," in Martin Fishbein, ed., **Attitude Theory and Measurement**, New York, Wiley, 1967, pp. 401-421. As best I understand this twisting, turning debate, it centers on whether human beings are rational and consistent, or not. With some reluctance, I have concluded that Wittgenstein was right: "The confusion and barrenness of psychology is not to be explained by calling it a 'young science'; its state is not comparable with that of physics in its beginnings....In psychology there are experimental methods and **conceptual confusion.**" (**Philosophical Investigations**, G. E. M. Anscombe, trans., Oxford, Basil Blackwell, 1958, p. 232.) I hasten to add, however, that psychology is no less confused than the other social-science disciplines, political science in particular.

much-maligned and oft-misunderstood conception of contradiction and critique that I now turn.

II

Considerable confusion still surrounds the well-worn Marxian notion of "contradiction."[15] Yet this confusion owes less to Marx himself than to later Marxists' misuse and abuse of the concept, particularly by prefixing that obfuscating adjective, "dialectical." Marxists still remember with embarrassment and non-Marxists with amusement Stalin's Delphic pronouncement: "We stand for the withering away of the state. At the same time we stand for the strengthening of the dictatorship of the proletariat, which is the mightiest and strongest state power that has ever existed....Is this 'contradictory'? Yes, it is contradictory. But this contradiction is bound up with life, and it fully reflects Marx's dialectics."[16] Stalin thus succeeded in showing that nonsense is nonsense, even (or perhaps especially) when outfitted in "dialectical" dress.

It seems likely that Marx would have been less

----

[10] Ralph Waldo Emerson certainly understood this, though he was not worried overmuch by mere contradiction. "A foolish consistency," said he, "is the hobgoblin of little minds, adored by little statesmen and philosophers and divines. With consistency a great soul has simply nothing to do." Not surprisingly, a great soul, presumably like himself, will "be sure to be misunderstood." "To be great," he concluded, "is to be misunderstood." (**Essays,** Boston, Houghton Mifflin, 1883, pp. 58-59.) By these lights, Emerson was surely among the greatest thinkers of his, or any other, age.

[11] John Locke, **Essay Concerning Human Understanding,** A. D. Woozley, ed., New York, New American Library, 1974, p. 418.

[12] Wittgenstein, **Philosophical Investigations,** remarks 142, 345. Kant had of course made much the same point about telling the truth and keeping promises. The gist of his argument is that one can intelligibly universalize such maxims as "Tell the truth!" and "Keep your promises!" -- as

amused than appalled by all the doublespeak and logical confusions that have too often passed for "Marxian" or "dialectical" analysis. Small wonder, then, that Marx himself denied that he was a Marxist.[17] Small wonder, too, that the concept of "contradiction" has fallen into disrepute. Even among Marxists, it seems vaguely suspect (or maybe simply vague) to speak of "contradictions." Such suspicion is justified to the extent that the concept keeps strange company these days. On the infantile far-left, the Red Brigades launch terrorist attacks in hopes of "sharpening the contradictions"; while on the academic near-right, some social scientists speak solemnly of the contradictions afflicting modern capitalism. Surely the confusion is very nearly complete when Daniel Bell writes about **The Cultural Contradictions of us. Capitalism.**[18] A perusal of that work suggests that Bell is none too clear about what constitutes a contradiction, "cultural" or otherwise, and that he uses the term more for alliterative than for analytical purposes.[19]

The notion of "contradiction" plays a useful, indeed indispensable, role in analysis and criticism within political theory, Marxist or otherwise. My purpose here is to clarify the meaning of this crucially important concept in one particular theory, Marxism, and in so doing to rescue and rehabilitate it.

----

one cannot universalize the contrary maxims. Since universalizability constituted for Kant the essential difference between moral and nonmoral utterances, beliefs, principles, or practices, the former maxims are shown to be not merely moral, but valid truths to which all rational agents must assent. Although Kant's logical point is well taken, the practical-moral inference he draws is exceedingly problematic and notoriously difficult to defend.

[13] MacIntyre, **After Virtue**, p. 22.

[14] This, I hasten to add, is **not** a distinctly Marxian conception of the functions of ideology. See: Francis X. Sutton, **et al.**, **The American Business Creed**, Cambridge, MA, Harvard University Press, 1956, especially chapter 1.

[15] The second section of this essay is adapted from "Marx on Contradiction and Critique," which I presented at the 1978 Annual Meeting of the American Political Science Association in New York City. I thank fellow panelists Nancy Hartsock and Bertell Ollman for their criticisms and sugges-

Marx conceived his task as a theorist to be one of "relentless criticism." To all his major writings, from the youthful **Critique of Hegel's "Philosophy of Right"** through his mature masterwork, **Capital**, Marx affixed the label "critique." "Criticism," Marx wrote, "does not remain within itself, but proceeds on to tasks for whose solution there is only one means -- **praxis**." Revolution without criticism is blind; criticism without revolutionary **praxis** is impotent. If the working class is to emancipate itself it must have in its arsenal "the weapon of criticism."[20] Only by having at its disposal a genuinely **critical** theory can the proletariat, in abolishing itself as a class, thereby abolish class society: "the proletariat cannot be abolished without the actualization of philosophy."[21]

Although I cannot delineate all of its features here, I can at least focus upon a central feature of Marx's conception of critique. By "critique," Marx means (among other things) the detection and exposure of **contradictions**. The method is critical, but the intention is practical: only by first exposing contradictions, by bringing their existence and import to a level of **conscious** awareness, can they be rationally resolved or overcome. The only sense in which contradictions "develop" is through being exposed **as** contradictions.

----

tions. I was at that time unaware of Jon Elster's very similar interpretation of Marx in: **Logic and Society**, New York, Wiley, 1978, chapters 4-5.

[16] Joseph Stalin, **Selected Works**, Moscow, Progress Publishers, 1965, v. 12, p. 381.

[17] See: David McLellan, **Karl Marx**, London, Macmillan, 1973, p. 443.

[18] Daniel Bell, **The Cultural Contradictions of Capitalism**, New York, Basic Books, 1976, especially pp. 14-16, 36-37.

[19] Indeed, Bell prefers to speak not of contradictions, but of some more ethereal "disjunction of realms." For an incisive critique, see: Peter Steinfels, **The Neo-Conservatives**, New York, Simon and Schuster, 1978, pp. 167-174.

[20] Karl Marx, **Critique of Hegel's "Philosophy of Right"**, A. Jolin and J. O'Malley, trans., Cambridge, Cambridge University Press, 1970, p. 137.

We must of course remember that Marx never used the English word "contradiction" but the German term **Widerspruch**. To translate **Widerspruch** as "contradiction" may not, at first sight, seem entirely satisfactory. The English term is generally used in a narrowly **logical** sense: a "contradiction" can obtain only between two or more statements, propositions, or utterances. The meaning of **Widerspruch**, by contrast, is not similarly restricted: it can, to be sure, mean "contradiction" in the narrowly logical sense; but it can also mean "opposition," "disagreement," and "conflict." Although Marx's conception of "contradiction" sometimes appears to encompass all these meanings, its primary sense is, for Marx, the strictly and straightforwardly **logical** one.

Although Marx does not do so explicitly, we can draw (and later withdraw) a provisional distinction between two kinds of contradictions. The first sort of contradiction is **structural**, the second **ideological**. Marx's discussion of the "fundamental contradiction" of capitalist production, between changes taking place in the **material forces** of production and the **social relations** of production, refers to a particularly crucial **structural** contradiction.[22] A structural contradiction might not appear, at first sight, to be a contradiction in the narrow logical (or propositional) sense; in this instance, **Widerspruch** might better be rendered as "opposition" or "conflict." As the adjective suggests, **ideological** contradictions, by contrast, have to do with the logic of our socio-political ideas, beliefs, and self-understandings. Moreover, these can be stated in propositional form as descriptions of states of affairs or assertions concerning what is true or believed to be true. Ideological propositions can, therefore, be shown to be contradictory in a rather strict and narrow logical sense. Thus an ideological contradiction is a logical contradiction existing between action (or belief) descriptions.

It is just this latter sort of contradiction that Marx finds in Hegel's **Philosophy of Right**. For instance, Hegel maintains, on the one hand, that the basis of family life is love (or "particular altruism") and, on the other, that primogeniture is a rationally defensible institution. Yet Hegel cannot have it both ways, for there is a logical

----

[21] Ibid., p. 142.

[22] See: Gary Young, "The Fundamental Contradiction of Capitalist Production," **Philosophy and Public Affairs**, 5, 2, Winter, 1976, pp. 196-234.

contradiction at the very center of his description and defense of these social institutions or practices. Primogeniture prohibits the parents' "passing on to the children whom they love equally" equal parcels of land, all of which goes upon their deaths to the eldest son. No one has any choice in the matter: the land, in effect, inherits the man. The private ownership of property in such a system is thus "independent even of the smallest society, the natural society, the family." Yet, as Marx continues, "Hegel declared...[that] family life would be [the] basis, the principle, the spirit of family life." But love is impartial, and primogeniture partial. Thus in civil society as described by Hegel, "the principle of private property contradicts the principle of the family."[23]

Note, however, that Hegel's is no **mere** logical contradiction. That is, it is not the sort of contradiction that can be resolved or set right simply by amending one of the relevant propositions. For since these statements are in fact true descriptions of shared social beliefs, arrangements, practices, and self-understandings, they are not open to logical or verbal amendment-by-fiat. On the contrary, changing the descriptions entails changing the referents, that is, the social arrangements themselves. As Marx noted, Hegel did indeed offer in his **Philosophy of Right** a true description of a contradictory social reality. Because Hegel correctly described an "inverted" or "topsy-turvy" (**umgestellt**) reality, his account of that reality harbors a number of contradictions. In exposing the **(ideo)logical** contradictions in Hegel's account, Marx thereby exposed the **structural** contradictions inhering in the society whose arrangements and self-understandings Hegel correctly described. We can now see why Marx draws no hard-and-fast distinction between ideological and structural contradictions. For the critical exposure of ideological contradictions is simultaneously the exposure and analysis of structural contradictions. That, after all, is why Marx's later critique of capitalism takes the form of a critique of political economy; for that theory embodies, albeit in supposedly scientific form, the self-understandings of the newly dominant class.

Thus in Marx's view, it is not only revolutionary but also conservative and even reactionary theory that takes on the character of a "material force once it grips the masses."

----

[23] Marx, **Critique of Hegel's "Philosophy of Right"**, pp. 98-100.

Social structure and participants' self-understandings do not exist independently of one another; they are, as it were, two sides of the same coin. Distorted self-understandings are themselves constitutive of alienated social relations and dehumanizing social structures. Because structural contradictions are reflected in ideological contradictions, they can be revealed through critical reflection. And only if they are first revealed, can they be overcome. We can more easily tolerate contradictions if we are ignorant or unaware of them; by bringing them to a level of conscious awareness, by showing a supposed consistency to be spurious, we reveal a rupture in reality itself: a contradictory social reality constituted and maintained by these contradictory beliefs. The exposure and criticism of contradictions that are at once structural and ideological is in this sense a radical activity. "To be **radical**," says Marx, "is to grasp matters at the root. But for man the root is man himself."[24] To transcend our present situation, to alleviate our suffering and overcome our alienation, requires critical reassessment of our self-understandings: our beliefs about who we are and what we do and why we do it, how we are (or might be) related to others, and so on. Such inquiries, going as they do to the root of our socially shared human existence, are necessarily radical and, inasmuch as they touch and transform our common practices, "practical" as well.

To this partial reconstruction of Marx's methods and intentions, I can anticipate two kinds of objections. The first is well made by Karl Popper, the second by Louis Althusser. Let me raise and reply to each in turn.

Virtually all of Marx's critics, Popper perhaps foremost among them, maintain that "contradictions" can exist only in theoretical **account** of reality, **not** in reality itself. Contradictions exist in theories, not in the phenomena conceptualized, described, and explained by those theories. The discovery of such a contradiction becomes, for the natural scientist, a reason for modifying or, failing that, abandoning the theory. Theoretical and conceptual change is brought about by criticism; and "all criticism," says Popper, "consists in pointing out contradictions." It is not these contradictions themselves that are "progressive," but our determination to expose and resolve them; for "criticism, i.e., the pointing out of contradictions, induces us to change our theories, and thereby to progress."

----

[24] **Ibid.**, p. 137.

Contradictions are not to be **accepted** as normal, natural, or (historically) inevitable but **criticized** and **overcome**.[25] On this much, at least, Popper and Marx would surely agree. Where they disagree profoundly is over Marx's further contention that there may be **real** contradictions, i.e., contradictions in social and political reality itself and not (merely) in our social and political theories.

Now as Popper rightly notes, no reputable natural scientist would defend an internally contradictory physical theory by claiming that the reality it depicts is itself contradictory. Yet this is precisely the claim that Marx makes about social and political reality. He never claims that, for example, Hegel's theory of the state or the theories articulated and advanced by the political economists are mistaken **simpliciter** because they contain contradictions. On the contrary, he holds that these theories are contradictory **and** that they do in certain crucial respects correctly describe and depict the reality of capitalist society. The contradictions are not merely in the theories but in the reality for which they claim to account. In a word, contradictions can be real. This view, according to Popper, is utterly mistaken, if not nonsensical.[26] Marx, he maintains, failed to understand the character of scientific theory and its fallible and contingent relation to reality.

Though very critical of positivism, Popper is nevertheless enough of a positivist (or methodological naturalist) to subscribe to two characteristically positivist theses. The first is that physical reality exists independently of our theories, the second that explanation in the physical or natural sciences constitutes something of a paradigm for the social and political sciences. The upshot of these combined theses is that the social scientist or political theorist is no

----

[25] Karl Popper, "What Is Dialectic?" in **Conjectures and Refutations**, New York, Harper and Row, 1968, pp. 312-335, especially pp. 316-319, 329. This aspect of Popper's critique of "dialectical" logic and contradiction is right on target, although the target hit is not the one aimed for. Popper scores a bull's-eye not against Marx but against Stalin and other "dialectical materialists" who hold that contradictions afflicting Soviet and other "socialist" societies must simply be accepted without dissent or criticism.

[26] See: H. B. Acton, **The Illusion of the Epoch**, London, Cohen and West, 1955, pp. 95-96; Popper, "What Is Dialectic?"

more warranted in claiming that socio-political contradictions are "real," than a physicist would be in claiming physical reality to be contradictory. Insofar as he insists that contradictions exist not (merely) in social theories but in social reality, Marx stands exposed as a pseudoscientist.

Yet Popper's position is defensible only if it is true that social and political theories resemble those of the natural sciences in standing in a purely contingent (as opposed to constitutive) relation to reality. This is almost certainly false, at least as a description of the relation of political theory to political institutions and practices. If I am right in arguing that, for agents and observers alike, theories (or at least the socially embodied theories we call ideologies) may themselves be partially **constitutive** of reality, then Popper's objection is without foundation. If, unlike natural-scientific theory, social and political theory can at least partially constitute its object, then Marx was not speaking nonsense in claiming that social contradictions could be real enough.[27] To criticize the theory is **pari passu** to criticize the reality to which it stands, not in a contingent, but in an epistemically symbiotic relationship.

Another objection comes from a rather different quarter. The disciples (if that is not too strong a term) of Louis Althusser would no doubt accuse me of focusing on the "young" or "humanist" left-Hegelian ideology critic and, in consequence, of neglecting the "mature" Marx who, turning away from philosophy in general and Hegelianism in particular, devoted his middle and later years to the study of political economy.[28] Leaving aside my view that such a distinction is entirely bogus, it seems to me that such a rejoinder rather badly misses and misconstrues Marx's aims, intentions, and method. For from the beginning, Marx viewed his task -- a task at once theoretical and practical -- as a "critical" one. It was necessary to criticize Hegel's **Philosophy of Right** precisely because it captured and

----

[27] See: Jean Hyppolite, "La conception hegellienne de l'Etat et sa critique par Karl Marx," in **Etudes sur Marx et Hegel**, Paris, Marcel Riviere et Cie, 1955, p. 120; Shlomo Avineri, **The Social and Political Thought of Karl Marx**, Cambridge, Cambridge University Press, 1970, pp. 16-17; Elster, **Logic and Society**.

[28] In particular, see: Louis Althusser, **For Marx**, Ben Brewster, trans., New York, Random House, 1969, especially chapters 2, 5, 7.

distilled the self-understanding, not of a solitary closet-philosopher but of a society and an age. Everyone, says Hegel, "is a child of his age; so philosophy too is its own time apprehended in thoughts. It is just as absurd to fancy that a philosophy can transcend its contemporary world as it is to fancy that an individual can overleap his own age, jump over Rhodes." Moreover, by Hegel's own admission, philosophy cannot be "pursued in private...but has an existence in the open, in contact with the public, and especially, or even only, in the service of the state."[29] With this, Marx entirely agreed. Philosophers are men; and "man is no abstract being squatting outside the world. Man is the world of man, the state, society." To criticize the philosopher's inverted categories and concepts is to criticize the "inverted world" which he and his fellows inhabit together.[30]

Much the same could be said of the then-new science of political economy. Political economists, no less than philosophers, are children of their age. Originally, the concepts and categories of their science (wages, prices, profits, etc.) were not exclusively scientific but also **social** ones; constituting the participants' own self-understandings, they partially constituted a particular social formation in a particular epoch. The critic's task is not only to expose as spurious their claim to universal validity but to reveal their political and ideological content. In short, the critic of political economy exposes the ideological function of a supposedly value-neutral, non-historical, metaphysically presuppositionless and universally valid "science." Such criticism is made all the more necessary by political economy's penchant for borrowing from, and subsequently refining and reinforcing, the concepts and categories constitutive of capitalist society's own self-understandings. In this way are the social relations characterized by these shared concepts effectively hypostatized: "definite social relations between men assume the fantastic form of relations between things."[31]

Such hypostatized categories, concepts, and relations are apt to appear to participants as normal, natural, and

----

[29] Hegel, **Philosophy of Right**, pp. 11, 7.

[30] Marx, **Critique of Hegel's "Philosophy of Right"**, p. 131.

[31] Karl Marx, **Capital I**, New York, International Publishers, 1967, p. 72.

eternal. The existence of different classes, of rich and poor, of patently unequal life-chances, and the rest are, when viewed through the categories of political economy, rendered natural and necessary.[32] This uncritical and ahis- torical view was ratified and reinforced by the new science of political economy. The older mystifications of religion were being rapidly supplemented (or even supplanted) by the scientistic mystifications of the political economists. Hence the need, Marx thought, for a critique of political economy: a critique that differed only in its object, not in its method or intent, from the "young" Marx's critique of Hegel.

It hardly needs saying that much of what Marx said has since proved to be muddled, mistaken, misguided, or false. He was an eminently fallible human being. Yet it is nevertheless with Marxian theory, with Marx's concepts, categories, and above all his critical method, that Marxists and non-Marxists alike must still contend. For as Sartre rightly remarked, Marxism "remains the philosophy of our time. We cannot go beyond it because we have not gone beyond the circumstances which engendered it."[33] Those circumstances include not only the demise of feudalism and the rise of capitalism but the newly emergent theory of human nature which served to pave the way for, and jus- tify, this new social order. Marx believed that this new kind of society required a radically new method of analysis and criticism. And it is indeed his critical-methodological legacy, more than his eminently fallible and time-bound substantive theory, which constitutes Marx's most distinc- tive and valuable bequest to social and political theory.[34]

To Marx's methodological bequest, one should add a Socratic supplement. The criticism of theories (pace Popper and Marx) surely involves more than the exposure of con- tradictions: it involves the discovery of dilemmas, conund- rums, and paradoxes in explanatory and justificatory argu- ments. It is therefore "dialectical" in the original Socratic

----

[32] **Ibid.**, chapter 1, section 4.

[33] Jean-Paul Sartre, **Search for a Method**, Hazel Barnes, trans., New York, Knopf, 1967, p. 30.

[34] See: Georg Lukacs, **History and Class Consciousness**, Rodney Livingstone, trans., London, Merlin Press, 1971, pp. 1-4; Terrell Carver, "Marxism as Method," in Terence Ball and James Farr, ed., **After Marx**, forthcoming.

sense.   The contradictions, conundrums, dilemmas, and
paradoxes thus exposed are, as both Marx and John Stuart
Mill recognized, not merely those of formal logic but of life,
not merely of abstract thought but of action as well.[35] Our
thoughts and beliefs stand in an intimate, indeed constitutive, relation to actions and social structures; our theory-
laden thoughts and our institutions, practices, and actions
are not several things, but one.   And for better or worse,
the theories which inform our beliefs and thoughts today
come increasingly from the social sciences.

III

The ideological function of political economy in Marx's
day has subsequently been supplemented by a wider array
of social-scientific disciplines.   Ranging from sociology and
political science to sociobiology (whose stock appears to be
rising on the academic exchange), these sciences share several features in common.   Two of these features are worthy
of special note.   The first is that they are apt to share the
naturalist (or "positivist," if you prefer) view of social-scientific inquiry and explanation.   This requires, among
other things, that they discover (or at least purport to
provide) general laws governing social structure and political change.[36] The second feature of a naturalistic social
science is its instrumentalist conception of theoretical
knowledge.   Assuming that such a science could discover
and give unambiguous formulation to laws, then they would

----

[35] It should not be forgotten that J. S. Mill's **System of
Logic** had the avowed **political** purpose of exposing and
combatting the "intellectual support of false doctrines and
bad institutions" which was supplied by rival systems of
logic, Whewell's in particular.   See: John Stuart Mill,
Autobiography, New York, Columbia University Press, 1924,
p. 158.

[36] Whether such laws have been or can be discovered is of
course open to question.   See: John S. Nelson, "Acci-
dents, Laws, and Philosophic Flaws: Behavioral Explanation
in Dahl and Dahrendorf," **Comparative Politics**, 7, 2, April,
1975, pp. 435-457; MacIntyre, "Is a Science of Comparative
Politics Possible?"

permit not only the explanation but the **prediction** and **control** of human behavior.[37] For by specifying the factors or conditions necessary to produce or prevent certain outcomes, these laws would yield knowledge of a kind that readily lends itslf to manipulation and control.[38]

Given this second feature of a naturalistic social science, it is hardly surprising that social scientists aspire to become the soothsayers of our age. The authority of social planners, managers, and bureaucrats relies increasingly upon the authority of the "empirical" social sciences. Modern social reality is man-made in a double sense. First, it is partly the product of supposedly scientific policy-making (**vide** the emergence of the "policy sciences").[39] Second, as already suggested, it is partially constituted by the concepts, categories, and beliefs of social agents. Now at least some of these agents are, in the course of their education, exposed to social-scientific modes of thought and analysis. Training in social-scientific thinking has itself become part of the "socialization" of the citizenry. This involves, among other things, learning how **not** to think about certain issues. Consider, for example, the orthodox view that social disruption, discontinuity, and change (not stability and continuity) stand in need of social-scientific explanation. As Barrington Moore observes:

> The assumption of inertia, that cultural and social continuity do not require explanation, obliterates the fact that both have to be recreated anew in each generation, often with great pain and suffering. To maintain and transmit a value system, human beings are punched, bullied, sent to jail, thrown into concentration

----

[37] Recall Auguste Comte's aphorism: "From science comes prediction (**prevision**); from prediction comes control." See: **Auguste Comte and Positivism**, Gertrud Lenzer, ed., New York, Harper and Row, 1975, pp. 56-57, 88, 222-224.

[38] See: Brian Fay, **Social Theory and Political Practice**, London, Allen and Unwin, 1975, especially chapters 2-3; Sheldon S. Wolin, "The Politics of the Study of Revolution," **Comparative Politics**, 5, 2, April, 1973, pp. 343-358.

[39] See: Lawrence Tribe, "Policy Science: Analysis or Ideology?", **Philosophy and Public Affairs**, 2, 1, Fall, 1972, 66-110; Fay, **Social Theory and Political Practice**.

> camps, cajoled, bribed, made into heroes,
> encouraged to read newspapers, stood up
> against a wall and shot, and sometimes even
> taught sociology.[40]

Or political science, psychology, sociobiology, and so on.

In any case, that portion of the populace educated on the street and in the ghettos, not having been initiated into the sublimities of the social sciences, will presumably require pummeling and punching by the police. Their more fortunate, formally educated fellow citizens will in the meantime learn how to define and solve "social problems." As Michael Walzer observes:

> We live in societies that produce extraordinarily
> large numbers of educated men and women and
> that increasingly need their authority and deci-
> sion-making skills....[They] are the more spe-
> cialized seers of a secular age: masters of
> ideology and technical experts. Ideologists and
> experts don't claim to rule because of their
> birth or blood or land or wealth, but solely
> because of their insight. They penetrate the
> complexity of modern economies and technolo-
> gies; they have a grip on the historical pro-
> cess; they make predictions about the future.
> Theirs is a new legitimacy, one not easy to
> challenge. Insofar as the modern state is com-
> mitted to planning, welfare, and redistribution,
> it plainly requires a vast civil service of edu-
> cated people; intellectuals are its natural rul-
> ers....Here then are our new masters:
> bureaucrats, technocrats, scientists, and their
> professional allies, doctors, lawyers, teachers,
> and social workers.[41]

Might Walzer be mistaken in claiming that the authority and legitimacy of this new class is exceedingly difficult to challenge? For consider: insofar as this class's authority rests upon such intellectual grounds as possession of

----

[40] Barrington Moore, Jr., **Social Origins of Dictatorship and Democracy**, Boston, Beacon Press, 1966, p. 486.

[41] Michael Walzer, "The New Masters," **New York Review of Books**, 27, 4, March 20, 1980, pp. 37-39, on p. 37.

superior knowledge, expertise, or intelligence, then to that degree it would be particularly vulnerable to criticisms couched in such terms. To show that members of this class subscribe to mistaken beliefs (about, e.g., the value-neutral character of social-scientific theories, techniques, and technologies) or cling to contradictory assumptions and beliefs (e.g., that "equality of opportunity" is a coherent and internally consistent doctrine) could prove especially damaging to its authority.[42]

Such Panglossian optimism is, I fear, unfounded. For it fails to consider what happens when power and knowledge join forces. Each develops a vested interest in the other. This is perhaps especially true of knowledge that claims the mantle of science. Consider again the case of the social sciences. Our new class's claim to recognition and respect rests upon the practical efficacy of knowledge derived in no small part from the "behavioral" or "policy" sciences. Therefore, they have a vested (indeed, perhaps a class) interest in the practical efficacy of their theories. From this, it follows that they have an interest in ever-increasing rationalization and routinization, which both **result from** and are **required for** these sciences. A naturalistic social science applies best to a world in which behavior is predictable. With our world increasingly constituted through social-scientific categories and concepts, our behavior becomes ever more open to manipulation, control, and hence, presumably, to prediction.[43]

Even so, the "laws" of the behavioral sciences, far from being genuinely lawlike, are apt to be artifacts of man-made arrangements, practices, and institutions. Instead of being "theoretical statements [which] grasp invariant regularities of social action as such," says

----

[42] I take this to be the basis of Alvin Gouldner's optimism; see: **The Future of Intellectuals and the Rise of the New Class**, New York, Seabury Press, 1979, especially pp. 28-43.

[43] Alasdair MacIntyre has devised an arresting argument to the contrary. (**After Virtue**, chapter 8.) He argues that there are essential and ineliminable sources of unpredictability in human affairs, that these render any notion of "total control" incoherent, and that totalitarianism of the Orwellian variety is in consequence impossible in the long run. This optimism is rather clouded by Keynes' reminder that, in the long run, we are all dead.

Habermas, these laws may well turn out to "express ideologically frozen relations of dependence that can in principle
be transformed."[44] But, to the extent that these ideologically frozen relations might be rationally transformed
through critical self-reflection, a naturalistic social science
has a vested interest in the unreflective and uncritical
character of its objects. Or to be more precise, it has an
interest in the widespread, pervasive, and uncritical
deployment of its own concepts and categories. Hence
there is, in this and in other respects, a contradiction
between its professed value-neutrality and its normative
biases. It is worth saying something, if only briefly, about
the social sources, character, and consequences of this particular contradiction.

The biases of the social sciences are not necessarily
so much the social scientists' own as they are those of the
civilization of productivity.[45] An ahistorical and uncritical
social science takes its cues and ideological coloration from
the particular society in which it is situated institutionally
and financially. In our society, unsurprisingly, the social
sciences are often put in the service of production; and
this is as true of the "pure" as of the applied behavioral
sciences, whose practitioners have generally been well paid
for their services. Indeed, so dependent have the social
sciences become upon foundation and government grants
that many of their practitioners have, as MacIntyre quips,
come to expect research grants in much the same way as
Melanesian cargo-cultists expect cargo.[46] That they could
long remain indifferent, "neutral," or entirely "objective"
with regard to such a feeding hand seems unlikely. Yet
social scientists persist, rather implausibly, in professing
the unbiased and value-neutral character of their enterprise. At any rate, so much is true of their introductory
textbooks and methodological treatises.

But their more recent public pleas and pronouncements are quite another matter. As I write this, the Reagan

----

[44] Habermas, **Knowledge and Human Interests**, p. 310.

[45] I have purloined this pithy phrase from William Connolly;
see: **Appearance and Reality in Politics**, Cambridge, Cambridge University Press, 1981; "The Dilemma of Legitimacy," in this volume.

[46] MacIntyre, "Ideology, Social Science, and Revolution,"
p. 332.

administration and the Congress have just exempted the social sciences from the sweeping budget cuts with which they were threatened short months ago. This backpedaling comes in the wake of dire warnings by prominent social scientists, who stressed not their disciplines' value-neutrality but its partiality, and in particular their service to the civilization of productivity. This threatened withdrawal of support, reported **The New York Times**, has "enraged leaders in psychology, economics and other disciplines, who have begun a campaign to preserve their grants by stressing their importance to economic productivity, national defense and other current concerns." The American Psychological Association, for one, "argues that improved American competition against Japan depends not on better technology but better understanding of organizations and worker behavior."[47]

The social sciences' instrumental character, and their partiality to productivity, is further underscored by Professor Robert Lucas, a University of Chicago economist. He writes that the social sciences have "provided most of the scientific underpinning of the revolution in managerial methods that has been going on in the United States since World War II." Scientific management involves "organizing collections of people and other resources so as to attain certain outcomes. The better this largely intellectual task is executed, the more productive is the managed enterprise and the society of which it is a part." Such managerial expertise "is a kind of capital, as intimately related to productivity as is tangible capital like machines and structures." The immediate source of this intellectual capital is the modern business school, but the real source is to be found in the various social science disciplines. Indeed, "the best business schools have become institutions of applied social science. The ideas one hears being debated in their halls and classrooms are social science ideas." American society, Lucas concludes, "has reaped enormous productivity gains from modest subsidies to basic social science research."[48] Weber's "iron cage" is evidently still in place; but what ever happened to the social sciences' much-vaunted value-neutrality?

Their leading practitioners' professions of partiality

----

[47] **New York Times**, April 21, 1981, pp. 15, 17.

[48] Robert E. Lucas, Jr., "Incentives for Ideas," **New York Times**, April 13, 1981, p. 12.

have exposed, more deftly and surely than any purely philosophical argument ever could, the falsity of the social sciences' ritualistic incantations of ideological neutrality.
Those whose services are for hire can hardly be indifferent
to the interests of their employers.[49] And this contradiction
between profession and practice sheds some light upon the
present predicament of the political theorist. For the theorist, as critic, calls attention to this and to other contradictions. For those whose business is to supply instrumentally useful knowledge to political decision-makers and to
lend an aura of scientific legitimacy to both, this is not a
welcome reminder. The thankless vocation of political
theory is not, within the context of the civilization of productivity, irrelevant or useless: it may prove dysfunc-
tional, if not indeed dangerous. It poses, at least potentially, a genuinely political threat. Little wonder, then,
that political theory, thus understood, should be the black
sheep of the contemporary academy, half of whose members
pride themselves upon utter apolitical Olympian detachment,
half upon their **Realpolitische** relevance.

This goes some way toward explaining the frustration
and discontent of some of my fellow contributors. Booth
Fowler laments the unpopularity of political theorists, which
he traces in part to the fact that ours is a historically
minded branch of an ahistorical discipline.[50] In this, I
believe that he is essentially correct. But this does not
mean that we should seek to become "relevant" by becoming
similarly ahistorical. For the critical character of our
enterprise consists, not only in exposing and calling attention to contradictions, but in our persistent remembrance
and recollection of other nobler or more coherent ways of
life. To resurrect and keep alive the memory of the Greek
polis, the Roman republic, or the Digger or Paris communes
is not a purely perverse or antiquarian exercise. On the

----

[49] It strikes me as exceedingly odd that self-described
political realists should nevertheless turn a blind (or at any
rate, complacent) eye to this phenomenon. For example,
see: Robert A. Dahl, "The Behavioral Approach in Political
Science," **American Political Science Review**, 55, 4, December, 1961, pp. 763-772, on p. 765; Marian D. Irish, **Political Science**, Englewood Cliffs, NJ, Prentice-Hall, 1968, p.
16.

[50] Robert Booth Fowler, "Does Political Theory Have a
Future?" in this volume.

contrary, it supplies a source of alternative visions of the good society and an invaluable conceptual, moral, and critical distance from our present-day civilization of productivity. These supply us and, more importantly, our students with a sense that political forms and social formations are not forever fixed and final: the present is history, and this too shall pass.

To expose and criticize the paradoxes, dilemmas, and contradictions in the social-scientific construction of contemporary reality is one of political theory's most pressing tasks. The critique of political economy in Marx's day has been superseded by the critique of social science in our own. A truly critical social science can only emerge from the sustained and systematic critique of the presuppositions, claims, and consequences of an uncritical and ofttimes contradictory (not to say, conceptually confused and occasionally paradoxical) social science. This would at the same time be nothing less than the exposure, critique, and supersession of the contradictory social reality represented, indeed partially constituted, by the self-understandings of this science's proponents and practitioners. By means of such a critique, we can at least begin to awaken ourselves and our fellows from our dogmatic slumbers.

PART FOUR

PERSONS AND PUBLICS

WHAT SHOULD POLITICAL THEORY BE NOW?

Glenn Tinder

Political theory traditionally has been the result of an effort to delineate the principles of good order or justice. Most of the great political thinkers have either explicitly described an ideal society or have set forth norms which could be cast in terms of such an ideal. I grant exceptions. Augustine's conception of history, for example, appears to be logically independent of any principles of good order; and Machiavelli's principal contributions to political theory do not concern justice or ends of any kind. It is fair to say, nevertheless, that from the time of Plato and Aristotle to that of Herbert Marcuse and Hannah Arendt the main question asked by political thinkers has been how society and the state should be structured and that political doctrines throughout history can be construed largely as answers to this question.

I

So firmly established is this way of thinking that for many it seems natural and inevitable. It is not, however. It arises from certain assumptions.

These assumptions concern the nature of the world, of human beings, of history, and of the relationship of the individual to history. They may, at the risk of over simplification, be reduced to the following four propositions.

1. An ideal of good order can be unequivocally defined. Plato's **Republic**, as customarily interpreted in the past, reflects this assumption as clearly as any great work of political theory. According to this assumption, the fundamental principles of good order are logically harmonious. In Plato, for example, the principle of philosophic rule was not in conflict with that of equality, since the latter was not among Plato's commitments. In the nature of things, however, it would be possible to believe that some considerations dictate absolute authority and others equality and that these norms cannot be reconciled. No coherent and comprehensive ideal could in that case be framed.

2. Human beings have the capacity to build and sustain an ideal order or at least an approximation thereto. If

the first assumption concerns the constitution of reality, the second concerns the ability of human beings to understand and deal with reality.   Plato believed that the intellectual and political capacities of some human beings were such that the principles of good order had practical relevance.

3. The human capacities for constructing and maintaining a good society are represented in identifiable historical entities, such as Plato's philosophers or Marx's proletariat.   Such entities may be diffuse in reality and vaguely defined theoretically; an example would be the middle classes to which Aristotle and a number of modern thinkers have appealed.   But even a thinker like John Stuart Mill, who counted heavily on human capacities assumed to be diverse and scattered, believed that these capacities could be encouraged and effectively channeled through particular institutions, such as proportional representation.

4. Any individual with ability can make a significant contribution to the realization of the ideal order.   For some thinkers, of course, the requisite ability is found only among a few.   The idea that each one among those few, in a properly ordered state, would weigh appreciably in the conduct of public business was plausible.   It has come to be widely thought, however, that almost everyone has the ability to participate in public affairs; and this more generous appraisal has not nullified the assumption that each individual participant can make a practical difference.   Even with great multitudes involved in political affairs, any serious and energetic participant can help appreciably in the task of establishing and upholding good order.   This is perhaps more popular attitude than political theory, but it has not been seriously challenged by political theory.

For the sake of convenience, let me call these assumptions "hellenic."   Although the designation is only roughly accurate, it still can serve to signal the major origin and general character of the outlook underlying traditional political theory.   The first two assumptions reflect powerfully, the second two partially, attitudes we have inherited from the ancient Greeks.

1. Thus the assumption that an ideal order can be unequivocally defined manifests an ontological rationalism that is present in almost every ancient thinker.   The universe is a cosmos, a harmonious order; it lends itself to intelligent understanding; and it provides principles on the basis of which a well-ordered polity can be constructed.

2. The second assumption, that humans beings have the capacity to build and sustain an ideal order, manifests a psychological rationalism which arises naturally, if not

logically and inevitably, from ontological rationalism.   Man is at home in a rational universe.   His powers of reason enable him both to understand the order of nature and to govern his own life, including his collective life, according to his understanding.

3. The third assumption, that the human capacity for constructing and maintaining an ideal order is represented in identifiable historical entities is clearly reflected, not only in Plato but in Aristotle as well, in the idea that those of modest means, neither rich nor poor, bring a saving prudence and moderation into political counsels.   If this assumption is less distinctively Hellenic than the first two, that is only because it has been more strikingly manifest in modern times, in the modern tendency to exalt a particular nation, class, race, or party.   But I suggest that this tendency is only an idolatrous expression (arising perhaps from tensions inherent in the rise of atheistic humanism and the corresponding crisis of Christian faith) of a way of thought inherited from antiquity.

4. The fourth assumption, that any individual with ability can make a significant contribution to the realization of the ideal order, is perhaps the most distinctively modern of the four assumptions because of its association with democracy.   Every citizen, it is widely held, should take an interest and a part in public affairs.   To support that demand, we feel compelled to assert that every that every citizen can have a practical impact.   But the participatory ideal traces its lineage back to the practices of ancient Athens; and as restricted as the citizen-body of Athens was, the notion that every citizen counts had a reality in the city-states which it has never had in the giant nations of modern times.

I am suggesting, in short, that Western political theory has a specific structure and that this structure was given its foundations and general form in ancient Greece. Not everything, of course, fits within the structure.   The main source of alien elements has undoubtedly been Christianity, with Augustine's theory of history a case in point. But it may be said that Christianity has been hellenized in its politics as well as in other ways.   The best-known example of this process is probably the thought of Thomas Aquinas (where an ideal order comes to the fore and the Augustinian philosophy of history fades into the background).   The modern world has been more whole-heartedly hellenic than the Middle Ages and readier to recast Christian insights in hellenic terms.   Would it not be roughly accurate to say that Hegel hellenized Augustine?

All of this implies that our habitual ways of thinking

politically are not the only possible ways and may not be the best ways. Today, I believe, we are in a good position to reflect on these facts. In the course of this century a new perspective has become readily available: a perspective of which political theorists have not yet very fully availed themselves.

II

What has happened is that hellenic attitudes have been seriously shaken. This has taken place not only in the minds of philosophers but in the attitudes of almost everyone. Through the gates opened by Kant, philosophers of various persuasions have left the precincts of hellenism and have argued the "mystery," or "absurdity," or in some other way the unintelligibility, of being. That this route has not been followed by philosophers alone is indicated by phenomena such as the increasing popularity of far-Eastern religions. Psychological rationalism has been shaken not just by intellectual developments, such as the rise of psychoanalysis due to the influence of Freud and his followers, or the resurgence of the doctrine of original sin in Karl Barth, Reinhold Niebuhr, and others. It has been shaken by a series of historical events, beginning in 1914, which mock man's supposed reasonableness. These events have affected the third assumption as well. Idealized historical entities (nations, races, parties) have been discredited by occurrences which show that they are not merely fallible but potentially demonic. Finally, the single individual in history has been reduced to the proportions and state of a grain of sand swept along in the currents of a river. Politics has become an affair of distant authorities and giant bureaucracies, influenced by ordinary people only when combined in such vast numbers that one person is of infinitesimal weight.

It would be going much too far to claim that our hellenic assumptions have collapsed or become indefensible. They may, however, be more vulnerable, by virtue both of apparent philosophical weakness and of declining appeal, than they have been for several hundred years. It is easy now to look at the political world from the standpoint of very different assumptions. Again risking oversimplification, these may be stated in the following way.

1. No ideal order can be defined. For example, over a period of several generations some have argued that

private property constitutes an ideal arrangement, whereas others have argued unqualifiedly for public ownership. At present, the most plausible argument by far is that both private and public ownership involve drawbacks and that no ideal property arrangement is possible. Similar comments could easily be made concerning other issues, such as authority versus equality. The point is not that we always fall short of the ideal but that the ideal is inherently defective. In support of this proposition, one might apeal to the critical philosophy of Kant. In contrast with hellenic reverence for the cosmos, Kant argues that the natural order and the moral order are distinct and incongruous. The implication (not, I admit, emphasized in Kant's own moral and political writings) is that moral and political principles which take into account natural possibilities are almost certain to conflict with one another.

2. A social and political order is almost invariably worse than is necessitated by our ontological situation. Human beings do not fail only where tragic moral conflicts make failure inevitable. They fail gratuitously and even defiantly. It is strange that the neo-orthodox reassertion of the doctrine of original sin has aroused such impassioned opposition, for it can hardly be seen as merely an effort to refurbish a dusty and outmoded theological antique. In view of the incompetence and malice pervading the politics of our time, probably no other conception of human nature is so plausible.

3. All historical entities are untrustworthy, and some of them are treacherous. The Communist Party is not the only god that has failed. So powerful and constant is our yearning to find some august, visible thing on which to rely absolutely, thus giving the world around us a less hazardous appearance, that the search for mortal gods goes on. But it is hard in our day to resist a consciousness of the vanity of the effort. If this consciousness is not allowed to settle into mere lethargic cynicism, it can develop into an awareness that no authority (not even expert or scientific authority), no political system, no social or political organization of any kind, can assure our collective safety or success. That awareness might call forth a more realistic kind of civil courage.

4. The power of the single individual is negligible. Hence even if an ideal order could be defined, and human beings had the capacity to establish it, what I in particular think and do is historically irrelevant. I have no more effect on history than on the stars. Of course, civic organizations continually dispute this manifest truth. They are able to do so with a measure of credibility only because

the yearning to believe in one's historical signigicance is so strong; it is not less strong, probably, than the yearning to find an absolutely reliable historical power. It is unpleasant to feel that the course of affairs is absolutely indifferent to my personal wishes and desires. No one heedful of reality in an age of mass politics, however, can doubt that it is.

It would be beyond the scope of an essay of this kind to try to show that these assumptions are valid. Perhaps in any case, it would be inappropriate. The first three are of an order of magnitude that argumentation cannot match. They involve the premises on which argumentation is based and must therefore be accepted or rejected on transrational grounds. The fourth assumption seems to me undeniable. It is contested only when it is unclear. What I shall try to do here, then, is to see what effect the adoption of all four assumptions has on political theory.

III

Good order (or justice) can no longer be the main subject of political theory. This appears to be the primary consequence of adopting the perspective offered by the new assumptions. I do not mean to suggest that the principles of good order lose all interest whatever for political theorists. I shall try to show the kind of interest they necessarily retain. Nevertheless, a significant shift of attention necessarily occurs. Good order is no longer the focal point of reflection. The subject which replaces it is the individual, alone in history.

It is the plight of the individual, in the light of the new assumptions, that brings about this refocussing. Old connections are cut or, rather, found to be tenuous. I can no longer relate myself to others through the image, or through activities guided by the image, of an ideal society. Those who devote themselves with others to a goal like socialism or reestablishment of a pious, family-centered society base their activities and relationships on a chimera. Much less can I expect to inhabit a good society in actuality. The conservative rejoinder to revolution (that what is vainly sought in common aspiration can be found, at least in measure, in old and established institutions) is barred along with radical hope. Nor can I identify a set of leaders, or a nation, or a class, which I can trust to set valid historical directions. There is no reliable authority of any kind. Finally, underlying all other considerations is a divestiture of personal responsibility imposed by the immensity of everything that influences history. What I do personally will have no bearing on the course of events.

To put things in a dangerously simple way, our times make us feel a political alienation which places in question the hellenic preoccupations of traditional political theory. Questions not concerned with justice or good order force themseleves upon us. The following four questions, for example, correspond more or less to the altered assumptions stated above.

1. How are one's political purposes to be defined, given the impossibility of defining an ideal order? At present, we mark out political positions primarily in terms of allegiance to one or another conception of good order: that represented by a socialist, liberal, or traditional society. Such designations have been meaningful largely because of the nearly universal assumption that one or another order of society really is best. That assumption, however, is not inescapable and is not, from every point of view, even sensible. I do not want to overstate my argument. Perhaps a particular order of society is preferable although it is not ideal. Perhaps, accordingly, the old political designations retain some meaning. However, a political commitment having to do only with defective ends, and separated from other commitments only by degrees of value, cannot serve very well to characterize a personal stance; too much of the person is omitted. A political theorist is forced to wonder whether a better way of defining political commitments and convictions can be devised. Or must we give up trying to define and occupy stable political positions?

2. How is moral integrity to be maintained within the more or less degraded social and political order one is bound to inhabit? Silently to acquiesce is to be an accomplice in injustice. To engage in revolution not only imposes sacrifices and demands few are able to accept; but where revolution is not a matter of tragic and irresistible necessity, it usually has catastrophic consequences. The obvious solution, it may seem, is to stand for gradual, peaceful change. This is the solution commonly adopted by liberals in the industrialized constitutional democracies. Is it, however, really a solution? Peaceful change is often illusory, as exemplified in the slight effects that a generation of reform has had on the distribution of income in the United States. And it may be subtly treacherous, reaching intended goals but bringing far less happiness than was anticipated. The tepid and uncertain satisfactions of socialism in the Scandinavian countries exemplify this. In any

case, we are speaking of countries in which conditions are exceptionally favorable to gradualism. In many countries, even in most countries, such conditions do not prevail and standing for peaceful reform is not an available political position. The ideal of consensual social development is in its most prevalent forms a product of assumptions such as psychological rationalism and historical optimism. It is practicable only in societies built on these assumptions. It cannot for everyone resolve the moral dilemmas inherent in living in a degraded social order. It is not absolutely certain that it can do this for anyone.

3. An allied question is this: how, in the absence of reliably constructive historical entities, can one avoid either irresponsible inaction or compromising alliances? One can grant, with Emmanuel Mounier, that we are never engaged except in dubious causes. For all its wisdom, however, Mounier's observation does not help one to decide when a cause is too dubious to justify the moral compromises it requires. Nor does it help one to know what to do when no legitimate causes are at hand. The individual thus is alone in history, not only by virtue of the ambiguity of all shared ideas and the imperfection of every existing society, but also because any authority or cause he accepts is bound to be questionable.

4. More daunting than any other question, finally, is the one presented by the powerlessness of the single person. What standards are to guide individual action in view of the ineffectiveness of every individual action? Should individuals act by purely moral, as distinguished from expediential, criteria? Action is an effort to produce certain consequences and is therefore essentially expediential. But the political actions of the average individual have no consequences, no appreciable consequences with respect to history. It seems to be everywhere assumed that an individual should act as though he were representing all, or a given class of, individuals. Perhaps this is so. But why? And how is it to be decided whom one ought to represent? Political theorists have accorded remarkably little attention to these puzzling questions.

Hence, asked what political theory should be now, I would say that it should be a discipline which accords serious attention to questions bearing on the political responsibility of individuals living in a state of historical abandonment. The four questions I set forth have a certain primacy because of their corrspondence with the four nonhellenic attitudes our experiences in the twentieth century have encouraged. But I noted the risks of oversimplification in laying out those four assumptions, and I would not want to claim systematic completeness for the questions based on them. They are designed mainly to illustrate the kind of issues I think political theorists should be facing.

If I were to try to characterize these issues in general, I would say that they are far more personal than those usually addressed by theorists working on hellenic premises. A political theory centered on them would be more personalist than traditional theory. The new assumptions, as I suggested, bring to the forefront of attention the individual, divested of connections, alone in history. Without the guidance of any unambiguous ideal of good order, inhabiting a more or less degraded society, offered alliances only with dubious causes, and in any case politically powerless, what should one do? This question is a condensation of the four questions asked above. It suggests other questions as well. By glancing at a few of these, we may be able to see more clearly the kind of political theory I am advancing.

Traditional theory asks: what is justice? Political theory now must ask, in one way or another: why one should care? What concern has the individual with the overall social order? It can be taken for granted that everyone wishes to avoid pain and humiliation. But so long as I personally am able to do this, why should I give any further thought to politics or justice? This question was taken seriously by Plato, and with the downfall of the city-state it became so pressing that for a time it seemed unanswerable. The Epicurean and early Stoic doctrine of withdrawal was the consequence. The question has been less urgent, however, during most periods of history. Again I want to emphasize that the difference I am discussing is one of degree. In defining justice, traditional theorists have necessarily written of its significance for the individual. I maintain only that the relatively impersonal question of what good order is has had priority over the more personal question as to why one should care. The possibility that one might legitimately be indifferent to the character of society and the polity has been slighted. Political theorists have not felt as threatened as they should have by the doctrine of withdrawal.

A closely allied issue concerns social reform. It is ordinarily assumed by reformers that everyone is or ought to be on the side of political actions and movements that promise progress. Why should they be? The issue here is not quite the same as that of why one should care about justice. Reformers and revolutionaries have almost wholly neglected the highly personal question of death. Why should a mortal being care anything about social changes the fruition of which he will not live to profit from or even to see? The limitations of Marx's thought can be seen in the complete absence of any attention to this question.

Finally, political theory concerned with personal issues such as death is bound to be concerned as well with the question of God. By referring to God as a question, I mean to make it clear that I have no intention of saying that political theory must be religious. But it cannot be casually irreligious, as a good deal of modern political theory has been. Both John Stuart Mill and Karl Marx, for example, although opposed on many basic issues, were casually irreligious. Both had provocative things to say about religion, but neither entered fully enough into the plight of the individual alone in history to consider issues of faith with anything like the profundity of, say, Kierkegaard and Nietzsche. The result was that both created theories which were in important ways, for all of their brilliance, superficial.

What I am suggesting, in short, is that political theory ought to be focused not on just order in itself but on the relationship of just order and the particular person. Clearly, the old question of the nature of the best order must continue to be asked. This is not a question that can ever be unimportant. But the ways in which it is important, in view of the situation of the individual in history, need to be examined and clarified as they never have been. In other words, what I am arguing for is not the abandonment of traditional concerns but rather their incorporation within a wider, personalist context. One of the implications of this argument is that the history of political theory is still an important subject of study; the issues it deals with have not become matters of indifference. If those issues are to be put in an altered context, however, then the history of political theory needs to be read in a somewhat different fashion than is usual. I shall deal with this subject in the following section.

IV

Perhaps the most penetrating of all commentaries on Hegel is Kierkegaard's **Concluding Unscientific Postscript.** Kierkegaard's approach to Hegel is defined by a small and simple question: what does the Hegelian system mean for the existing individual? The existing individual, in Kierkegaard's mind, was not man in general (an immortal abstraction) but the concrete and mortal "I." The existing individual knows, not just that every man is mortal, but that he in particular is going to die. He also knows that the meaning of this event is beyond the reach of reason yet has to be decided; since how he lives, whether for the sake of eternal or worldly happiness, has to be decided and that requires an interpretation of death. It followed, for Kierkegaard, that the existing individual has little interest in universal history but a great deal of interest in his own personal destiny. Looking at Hegel from the standpoint of personal destiny, Kierkegaard argued that the system he constructed was a splendid, but uninhabitable, palace. It might accomodate man in general but not any particular human being.

Kierkegaard had little interest in politics. His example, however, might easily and profitably be followed in the study of past political theories. This would require that we ask of every ideal order: what does it mean for the existing individual? In some cases, it would be found that the designer of the order was not unprepared for the question. Plato, for example, was not oblivious of the existing individual, even though his ideal polity seems in many ways designed deliberately to suppress unique and personal being. In other cases, it might be found that thinkers revered for their profundity had neglected some of the elemental conditions of human life. Karl Marx, for instance, for all of his attention to the outrages suffered by workers in his time, was arguably insensitive to the fundamental concerns of human existence. Anyone familiar with Kierkegaard's confrontation with Hegel in the **Concluding Unscientific Postscript** is apt to wish that there could have been a comparable confrontation between Kierkegaard and Marx. It is not part of my point that Kierkegaard's understanding of existence must be accepted. It can be held that Kierkegaard overemphasized death and neglected other ordeals of existence, such as loneliness and poverty; it can be held that he overemphasized the ordeals and neglected the joys of existence. What I am suggesting is merely that students of the history of political theory relate the ideal polities of the past to clear and reasonable conceptions of personal existence and that they do this more explicitly and carefully than is customary among either political thinkers or intellectual historians.

Were this done, the historical narrative might be considerably altered. Not only, as the preceding paragraph suggests, might some of the great figures be enhanced and others diminished. Figures hitherto scarcely noticed by historians of political theory might be accorded significant roles. For example, the slight attention given Dostoevsky in the history of nineteenth century political thought can scarcely be justified by the fact that Dostoevsky was a novelist. He was also a political thinker, and he set forth ideas as profound and original as any of the standard figures in the history of political thought. It is strange that academic political theorists have created an intellectual setting in which it is respectable to know little of Dostoevsky but in which one is expected to be well-acquainted with so limited a mind as Jeremy Bentham. A personalistic reading of the history of political thought would tend to reshape the intellectual past and to eliminate such disproportions.

Can it be legitimate, however, to blur the distinction between philosophy and fiction? I suggest that it is not only legitimate but imperative, for the concrete individual tends to diappear from philosophy but to come to life in fiction. It is true that a student of political theory is interested primarily in political ideas, and hence is interested necessarily in all good political philosophy, but not in all good political fiction. Not all good fiction deals with ideas. But some fiction does; and, as others have noted, the dialogues of Plato, which we unhesitatingly include in the canon of political theory, probably have as much in common with philosophical fiction such as Dostoevsky's as with works of formal theory such as Hegel's.

In summary, my argument is that the principles of good order ought still to be investigated not only through philosophical reflection but also through study of the history of political theory. These principles, however, ought to be related at every point to concrete existence as distinguished from generic humanity. Doing this would reshape significantly the narrative that constitutes the history of political theory.

To summarize more comprehensively, the view I am advancing is affirmative regarding the individual but negative regarding institutions. It is respectful of the person and suspicious of society. This is to speak very roughly, but it is to indicate why the state of the individual in history is seen as one of solitude and vulnerability. As political theorists hardly need to be told, however, a negative attitude toward institutions and society has its dangers. These dangers consist primarily in political demoralization, and they impose on political theory a task which so far has not been noted in this paper. To describe that task will be the subject of the following, and final, section of this essay.

V

Political demoralization is apt to occur among those who believe that all societies are equally degraded and that all institutions are radically imperfect. Under such conditions, it may be assumed, there is no such thing as a good society and no point in efforts at social reform. Moreover, if all institutions are radically imperfect, there can be no spiritual power such as the medieval church and no representative institution such as the modern parliament with the moral authority to impose constitutional limitations on government. Political absolutism of some kind becomes inevitable. This describes roughly the viewpoint of both Paul and Luther: spiritually individualistic; socially pessimistic; politically authoritarian.

It must be noted relative to the second of these points that the position outlined in this paper, although socially pessimistic, implies no unqualified condemnation of society. To say that all societies are degraded is not to say that they are equally degraded. To argue that no institution or historical entity is perfect enough to be counted upon to bring an ideal society into existence is not to imply that no institution can be fit or able to impose constitutional limits. To question whether human beings have the capacity for realizing an ideal society or for achieving justice through a reform movement is not to suggest that all political efforts are doomed by crime and incompetence. Hence the position I have taken is not quite so perilous as the one represented by Paul and Luther.

That position, nevertheless, is too similar to the one held by Paul and Luther to be perfectly safe. It presupposes that every human being possesses an inherent dignity, whereas societies and particular institutions possess nothing of the kind and are, moreover, bound by their very nature both in thought and action to objectify, thus betraying the humanity of, their members. These are the underlying princiles of this essay. It must be admitted, accordingly, that the argument set forth could contribute to political demoralization and could in that way be hostile to constitutionalism, social justice, and various other decencies. The danger would be particularly great were the argument to affect the attitudes of very many people. However esoteric political theory may normally be, a theorist who is not willing to tell the public "noble lies" must acknowledge that the truths he tries to formulate are truths for all human beings. He must hold himself responsible for that most unlikely of eventualities: their widespread acceptance. If the social and political pessimism expressed in this paper became widespread, it would not be suprising if political demoralization, and in turn various adverse consequences for the social and political world, were to ensue. This would not have to happen, however, and preventive measures are within the capacity of political theory.

I suggest that the task of political theory is, not only to pursue such questions as those discussed in this paper, but also to work out the standards and methodology of a critique of institutions and societies that would aid in distinguishing between the good and evil in view of human possibilities. Such a critique could serve as a barrier between pessimism and despair. It could guide efforts to define, achieve, and maintain the social and political decencies that are historically possible. It also could logically accompany reflection on the basic questions of political theory, questions of the kind which it has been the major task of this essay to outline. Reflection on the basic questions aims to enable individuals, in their historical alienation, to achieve a wise political orientation. Developing the standards and methodology of an institutional and social critique should help individuals to render that orientation politically responsible and practical.

The standards of such a critique would have to be a good deal more subtle and complex than those normally employed by intellectuals in the present-day political world. Liberals, radicals, and conservatives alike often judge the political phenomena about them quite ideologically, and in this way simplistically. Societies and movements are condemned or endorsed wholly on the basis of whether or not they conform (or, surprisingly often, whether or not they claim to conform) to a certain prior ideal. Thus, for example, Spain under Franco was uniformly and unqualifiedly condemned by most radicals and liberals, while the Soviet Union was blindly anathematized by most conservatives. One can make comparable statements concerning many other regimes. The realities, of course, are far more ambiguous in most cases than such judgments presuppose. Political theorists may not be so ideological. Many of them, however, are; and their efforts to define universally valid standards of good order may encourage ideological judgments. The critique of institutions I am suggesting would take into account the impossibility of enacting a comprehensive and systematic set of ideals. Although concerned with norms such as freedom and equality, it would pay close attention to the problematic relationship between one norm and another and between norms and concrete circumstances. In judging institutions and societies and in assessing possibilities of reform, it would be sensitive to the moral incongruities that are inherent in political action. People versed in a critique of institutions would be a good deal less predictable in their political judgments than are most people today.

Subtle and complex standards would also be necessary if due consideration were given the needs of the concrete individual, with care being taken not to oversimplify in the interests of a universal ideal.   Although the arguments supporting a particular conception of justice may be intricate and delicately shaded, the conception itself is apt to be simple: fundamentally egalitarian, for example, or elitist.   One may say the same of the ideal of good order. On the other hand, the needs of the concrete individual are numerous.   Simone Weil lists fourteen of them: order, liberty, obedience, responsibility, equality, hierarchism, honor, punishment, freedom of opinion, security, risk, private property, collective property, and truth.   It is easy to think of others, such as food, comradeship, and stability.   Developing an institutional and social critique based on a determination not to forget any genuine needs would constitute a demanding intellectual task.

The importance of the task is that it bears on the preservation, or recovery, of political morale.   Its aim would be to provide a basis for political responsibility in place of the ideal order which, I have argued, ought to have a less dominant role in political theory than it has hitherto had.   Its aim would be the kind of civility that becomes possible when people divest themselves of simple and definite ideas as to how the world should be organized. For not only is the pessimism in which ideals are given up dangerous, so are ideals.   They encourage self-righteousness and judgments of the dehumanizing kind condemned by Jesus.   Removing ideals from the center of our minds may heighten our sensitivity to the complicated and enigmatic character of political realities.   If we can learn to tolerate and intelligently to deal with such realities, which a personalistic critique of institutions and society is designed to help us do, our humanity will be enhanced.

That an enhancement of humanity is among the possibilities presented by the approach I have outlined may be worth a concluding note of emphasis.   Very simply, I have suggested that the foucs of political theory be shifted from justice to the person.   It would be idle to claim that there is not danger involved when we begin giving less thought to justice.   It can be argued, however, that the principal intuition of the Western moral consciousness is not justice but the sanctity of every person.   This suggests that in giving less thought to justice but giving more thought to the person we create an occasion for hope.

POLITICAL THEORY AS POLITICAL RHETORIC

John S. Nelson

Let us begin in burlesque. But how, then, shall we end?

What follows is part inquiry, part polemic, part con-
fession, and more.[2] In all these modes, I mean to encourage
wider and better practice of political theory as political
rhetoric. (What I mean by the contentious categories of
political theory and political rhetoric should become clearer,
if hardly less controversial, with each step in the ensuing
dance of arguments.)

As inquirer, I experiment with the notion of a tradition of political theory counter to the Western concerns and
categories more often carved from history. This device
allows me to identify at least three general lines of political
theory which now deserve far more appeciation and practice
than they have received for some time in Anglo-American
circles of academia. Each treats political theory as political
rhetoric, in ways importantly distinct from and yet intimately tied to the others. Emphasizing their interrelationships, I explore them as a joint Rhetorical tradition.

My purpose is not to persuade you to turn Rhetorical. Not myself entirely sure what to make of this counter-
tradition, I evoke it (and somewhat playfully at that) in
order to generate some sense of where it might take us.
Its principles and practices certainly deserve our attention
but may not in the end command even my allegiance. In
other words, I am confident that we should take the Rhetorical tradition seriously; but I am not fully decided what it
should mean to do so. In the original sense of the word,
this is an **essay** in the Rhetorical tradition, rather than an
argument for it. Here I seek to sketch its contours,

----

[2] At various points in its progress, this essay has learned
(and I hope benefitted) from being discussed by colleagues
at the Shambaugh Conference on Political Theory, the University of Iowa Rhetoric Seminar, the Philosophy Colloquium
of Virginia Commonwealth University, and the Irregular Colloquium On Politics, Etc. of the University of Iowa. Most
especially, I thank Booth Fowler and Michael McGee for
detailed commentaries on earlier drafts.

constraints, and complaints against more familiar modes of political theory. And hence I invite you to join me in a genuine inquiry into political theory as political rhetoric.

Why should you do so? What has convinced me that the Rhetorical tradition is worth exploring? Of course, my best answer is this essay as a whole. Yet let me caution that even its presentation of the Rhetorical tradition must remain programmatic and incomplete, so large is the territory to be covered. If for no other reason, though, I urge you to tour the Rhetorical tradition because it easily and readily recognizes much excellent political theory by ways and people insufficiently credited in academic political theory. Thus a signal virtue of political theory reconstituted on Rhetorical principles would be its ability to accommodate and even celebrate endeavors now often excluded from political theory proper.

Also let me tempt your attention further by noting that figures of the Rhetorical tradition try desperately to face up to the greatest needs and dangers of our day. (How well they succeed is the question I would have us investigate.) Some Rhetorical alternatives would involve big departures from current tendencies in political theory; some would not. Here I focus on the former, in order to strike a sharp initial contrast with conceptions of political theory prevalent now and in the recent past. There can be plenty of opportunity on other occasions for emphasizing comparisons, compromises, qualifications, and costs: all of which would be elicited by a more complete accounting than is appropriate for a first attempt. Here I propose simply to come to an understanding of some of the Rhetorical tradition's basic principles. (One basic principle of political theory as political rhetoric is that every practice prompts not only its own dangers, but also its own dissolutions; another is that its proponents need not dwell on them initially.)

As polemist, I summarize Rhetorical accusations against Western political theory. In this capacity, I decry several established tendencies in our theorizing about politics. True to form, I bestow complimentary titles upon them: academism, rationalism, ideologism, and ironism for the four main classes of mistakes castigated here. These inclinations are assessed on the assumption that they account for much, if far from all, that now passes as political theory. In fact, I take these tendencies to be sufficiently familiar to us that there is no need to dwell on any demonstration of their presence or even their importance in recent political theory. Instead, I concentrate on explaining what is wrong with each Western inclination when

considered according to Rhetorical standards. (These inclinations can be defended in some degree, of course, but I
leave that task to their practitioners.)

As confessor, I admit to sharing some of the sins of
my cotheorists. Like too many of you, I have pretended
that good political theory could be wholly reduced to
(instead of partly pursued through) such merely academic
efforts as: understanding earlier theories, analyzing political concepts, producing models and analogies, collecting
facts and data, assessing previous theories, arguing about
grounds of inquiry, and addressing various other enterprises that are at most now marginally political (but more
often almost utterly unpolitical). No more than many of
you, have I wanted to endorse these reductions and detours
in principle or face up to practicing them myself. Nor have
I gone all the way with any one of these mistakes, let alone
made them all at once. But just as many of you, I have
committed such errors often before and remain much too
susceptible to them still. (From time to time, I have even
flirted with the common, if collosal, mistake of finding
improvement in some program for doing all kinds of reductions and detours together; but I trust that this is not a
defect of the proposal to practice political theory as political
rhetoric.)

RHETORIC

Dialectic, which is the parent of logic, came
itself from rhetoric. Rhetoric is in turn the
child of the myths and poetry of ancient
Greece. That is so historically, and that is so
by any application of common sense.

Robert
Pirsig[2]

Perhaps there is some hypocrisy in our situation,
both because political theorists of virtually every stripe
expend extravagant energies in violating their own rules
about theorizing and because most of us make the mistakes

----

[2] Robert M. Pirsig, **Zen and the Art of Motorcycle Maintenance**, New York, Bantam Books, 1974, p. 385.

just mentioned almost as much as we condemn them on the part of others. Perhaps also there is some shortfall of ambition or self-confidence among present-day political theorists. What John Gunnell deplores as "the myth of the tradition" surely has one source in the recurrent compulsion to see ourselves as stunted children of those heroic giants who strode political theory past.[3]

Yet the deeper problem is the sheer difficulty of doing good political theory. Leaving aside any complications peculiar to our politics and times, we would do well to remember that high quality is seldom easy to achieve and that it is especially hard to generate in goods as exacting and complex as the stock in trade of political theorists. This is why we must avoid unnecessary difficulties and distractions. Until impulses toward academism, rationalism, ideologism, and ironism are at least domesticated (if not entirely transcended), good work in political theory gets unduly discouraged (and discouraging). Theorists misconceive what to do, make it many times tougher than before, and then excuse failures or accept substitutes far faster than is defensible.

On the whole, it is not surprising that the many different practices of political theory today share a depressing range of deficiencies. I attempt no direct demonstration of this claim here, but it is worth stating and even elaborating so that some of the sources of the Rhetorical alternative may be better understood. For example, most of the projects now proclaiming themselves to be political theory are terribly derivative of developments in other fields. Such borrowing is not bad in itself, even though inspiration is better than borrowing in political (not to mention intellectual) affairs. Nonetheless, this pattern of borrowing must raise doubts about all academic ideas of political theory: not only those advanced within any particular "subfield" so labeled, but also those pushed generally in political philosophy and political science. This pattern probably points to an unconscious exodus from much that deserves to be termed political theory. Few recent borrowings are fully suited to the provinces and purposes of political theory, which generally gets adjusted to them rather than the other

----

[3] See: John G. Gunnell, **Political Theory**, Cambridge, MA, Winthrop, 1979. Do not forget, though, that this move is sometimes part of a strategy for freedom. See: Harold Bloom, **The Anxiety of Influence**, New York, Oxford University Press, 1973.

way around. Predictably, few of these "new" projects are pursued with the skill and subtlety marking truly good work, even in terms of the standards implicit within each such project. Worse, this borrowing has fragmented a field in which practitioners need broad learning and broader discourse in order to produce good positions and persuasive arguments for them.

All this implies a pervasive poverty of political imagination and perhaps even intelligence. Many political theorists of apparent academic talent shy away from conceiving, let alone confronting, the troubles and opportunities of our politics. Topics are defended in terms of preparing for further studies, filling a hole in the research literature, or permitting a demonstration of some new method. Statistics are substituted for argument, and then positions are expressed in terms as distant as possible from those current in politics or otherwise comprehensible. Correlations are counted as theories, with all too little correspondence in any case between data deployed and claims made. These and other dodges from the responsibilities of political rhetoric have been identified and condemned across the board, for practically every project in recent political theory. Thus academic theorizing about politics is now too seldom significant for politics, too often unpersuasive in argument, and almost always alienated from its initial premises and promises.

Perhaps the conditions of political theory have been worse in various periods of the past, but the point here is that there are better directions possible for political theory in the present and future. At least some of the needed improvements can be provided through a Sophistic correction of current political theory. To political theorists who would practice the philosophical discourse created by Plato and Aristotle, the historical discourse created by Hegel and Mannheim, or the scientific discourse created by Hobbes and Weber, the latter-day Sophist responds with reminders that the basis and burden of their academic endeavors must remain rhetorical and political. Like all who proclaim new programs, I can at present convey only a slight sense of the nature and future of political theory as political rhetoric. And even that is more by way of saying negatively what this Sophistic correction is not than through specifying positively what it is. At least, articulating Rhetorical alternatives to recent political theory should provide a better sense of needed improvements. At most, it could provide the improvements themselves. (In turning now to a brief evocation of the Rhetorical tradition and its corrections for current political theory, let us all hope for somewhat more than the minimum.)

The practice of political theory as political rhetoric can be traced back at least as far as the ancient Sophists.[4] Although typically assigned to some terribly minor or outright insulting roles, it has stayed on the scene ever since. Indeed, it has even enjoyed an occasional chance at the lead: as, for example, in the Humanism of the Italian Renaissance.[5] Rhetorical conceptions of political theory were early reviled by Plato and Aristotle, setting the stage for the academic, if not political, subjugation of rhetoric to philosophy (i.e., dialectic).[6]

With the rise of Modern science, rhetoric was again cast low as the foe of reasoned discourse and inquiry.[7] This led to the Enlightenment parody of rhetoric as verbal decoration and cynical deception.[8] And much the same complex of attitudes stimulated the nineteenth- and twentieth-century turn toward formal logic and technical language as protections against the notorious perversion of argument and imagination by rhetoric.[9] These negative notions of rhetoric continue to dominate politics, academia, and everyday life in most of the West.[10] In fact, the strong association of rhetoric with politics in particular probably accounts in part for the low repute of politics among most Americans.

No matter how negative conceptions of rhetoric have

----

[4] W. K. C. Guthrie, **The Sophists**, Cambridge, Cambridge University Press, 1971.

[5] See: Jerrold E. Seigel, **Rhetoric and Philosophy in Renaissance Humanism**, Princeton, Princeton University Press, 1968; Albert William Levi, **Humanism and Politics**, Bloomington, Indiana University Press, 1969; Ernesto Grassi, "Can Rhetoric Provide a New Basis for Philosophizing? The Humanist Tradition, Parts I and II," **Philosophy and Rhetoric**, 11, 1-2, Winter-Spring, 1978, pp. 1-18, 75-97; Grassi, "Italian Humanism and Heidegger's Thesis of the End of Philosophy," John **Michael Krois, trans.**, Philosophy and Rhetoric, **13, 2, Spring, 1980**, pp. 79-98. Plainly, Grassi is someone whose thinking runs along lines of the Rhetorical tradition as sketched here.

[6] See: Paul Ricoeur, **The Rule of Metaphor**, Robert Czerny, trans., Toronto, University of Toronto Press, 1977.

[7] See: Paolo Rossi, **Francis Bacon**, Sacha Rabinovitch,

become, however, the study of rhetoric has never ceased, if only because such a formidable and enduring enemy must be known well in order to be fought effectively. Furthermore, as the aspiration to purge rhetoric from human communication waned after the Second World War, the study of rhetoric once again came to be pursued positively. It has risen to a new renaissance of its own, right along with theorizing about language, literature, speech acts, and action generally. (These nominally separate fields of inquiry may as well be taken together, since they share many commitments, questions, and findings.)

But a still more significant source of knowledge about rhetoric is a series of dissenters from the dominant desire to replace rhetoric with dialectic and logic. Strung across the history of the West is a sparse scattering of people like Giambattista Vico and Friedrich Nietzsche. They could be said to comprise a Sophistic tradition of sorts, seeking to reestablish the academic and practical prestige of rhetoric and insisting on its actual supremacy in all human affairs. Such counter-Western writers have emphasized the dependence of dialectic and logic (and hence of philosophy and science) upon rhetoric. Apart from a few inept attempts to deny this dependence, the usual Western strategy has been to ignore the primacy of rhetoric, in hopes that it can somehow be circumvented. As a result, this counter-tradition has been almost the only locus of sustained efforts to identify and come to terms with the deeper implications of the fact that all speech (oral or written) is rhetorical. And

----

trans., Chicago, University of Chicago Press, 1968; Karl R. Wallace, **Francis Bacon on Communication and Rhetoric**, Chapel Hill, University of North Carolina Press, 1943; Paul N. Campbell, "Poetic-Rhetorical, Philosophical, and Scientific Discourse," **Philosophy and Rhetoric**, 6, 1, Winter, 1973, pp. 1-29.

[8] See: Peter Gay, **The Enlightenment**, New York, Random House, 1966.

[9] See: Stephen Toulmin, **The Uses of Argument**, New York, Cambridge University Press, 1964.

[10] See: Wayne C. Booth, **Now Don't Try to Reason with Me**, Chicago, University of Chicago Press, 1970; Booth, **Modern Dogmas and the Rhetoric of Assent**, Chicago, University of Chicago Press, 1974.

accordingly, it is this Rhetorical tradition which inspires much of what I write here.

SOPHISTIC

> This is philosophy not as thought, but as thea-
> ter: a theater of mime with multiple, fugitive,
> and instantaneous scenes in which blind ges-
> tures signal to each other. This is the theater
> where the explosive laughter of the Sophists
> tears through the mask of Socrates...
>
> Michel
> Foucault[11]

One feature of this Rhetorical tradition must be mentioned immediately: its concentration of membership in the
years since Nietzsche. After the ancient Sophists but prior
to Nietzsche, its members might include a few Classical
rhetoricians and a cluster of men from the Italian Renaissance, but very few others. Aside from Vico, coming up
with members from the middle of the Modern Age is very
hard; maybe Jean-Jacques Rousseau might qualify. In the
nineteenth century, toward the end of the Modern Age,
straddling the divide between Western tradition and Rhetorical counter-tradition became increasingly common.
Either/or classifications would box Hegel, Marx, and Mill
with the Westerners; but there would remain strong reasons
for recognizing their kinship with the Sophists. With the
Postmodern Period, however, the problem of membership in
the Rhetorical counter-tradition becomes the profusion of
candidates. Any such list would surely include: Sigmund
Freud, Ludwig Wittgenstein, Martin Heidegger, Hannah
Arendt, Kenneth Burke, Marshall McLuhan, Michel Foucault,
Jacques Derrida, Hayden White, Stanley Cavell, and many
others. (I do not mean that the Sophistic tradition should
be proud of every such member, let alone that it should
prize each to the same degree; still, they must be admitted

----

[11] Michel Foucault, **Language, Counter-Memory, Practice,**
Donald F. Bouchard, ed., Donald F. Bouchard and Sherry
Simon, trans., Ithaca, NY, Cornell University Press, 1977,
p. 196.

as members.)

Plainly, one important question is why the Sophistic tradition is much more amply represented in the last century or so. At least two answers, or two ways of putting the same answer, come quickly to mind. The former involves sorting through three strands of the Rhetorical tradition as a whole; the latter involves appreciating the special importance of the third strand.

Before the Enlightenment, most of what is now identified as "political theory" was written by men of public affairs. And it was written as part of their public endeavor, their political action. Academies, monasteries, and universities were not widely available to cloister the politically interested or inclined.[12] Nor were the aspirations to philosophize, scientize, romanticize, or otherwise transcend the perspectives of practical politics generally attractive to people who reflected on the fundaments of worldly affairs.[13] Only in the wake of the Enlightenment have "engaged" participants like politicians and rhetoricians come to be contrasted with "objective" spectators like philosophers and scientists. The last century contributes more obviously and numerously to the Rhetorical tradition because its conditions, concerns, and categories allow (indeed, almost require) becoming acutely self-conscious about rhetorical principles and problems.

----

[12] Note, however, that the household was then available to cloister the political theorist. For example, Machiavelli and (in a way) Thucydides effectively retired in later life to theorize from their households. Interestingly, the tacit relationships of households to political affairs were peculiarly intricate and repressed by comparison with those typically obtaining between academies, monasteries, or universities and politics. On one side, this topic ties to the problematic of public/private distinctions. On another, it intersects the subject of women as political theorists, since they were often relegated to theorizing from the household or such extensions of it as the salon.

[13] At least one (partial) exception in this regard would be the recurrent Western impulse to escape (historically contingent) politics. This surfaces in such "formal" theorists as Plato and Hobbes, as well as in such "utopian" theorists as Comte and Marx. See: John G. Gunnell, **Political Philosophy and Time**, Middletown, CT, Wesleyan University Press, 1968.

Cicero, More, Machiavelli, Locke, Burke, and the like strove directly and primarily for effects in the everyday politics of their times. Even their most abstract and uninvolved contributions to "political theory" were largely intended (and, in their own eras, received) as important aspects of their political activities. Such "political theorists" wrote unacademically and unself-consciously as rhetoricians. For the most part, they had neither the need nor the opportunity to seek a self-consciously "rhetorical" stance. This is why many of the standard classics of Medieval and Modern "political theory" are so easily and often read to support important principles of the Rhetorical tradition, even as they are so fairly and officially read as part of the Western tradition of philosophy and science. Perhaps as late as Karl Marx, practicing political theory as political rhetoric was not particularly unusual.

In this sense, there has been (or was once) an unself-consciously Rhetorical tradition, notwithstanding the Western animus against rhetoric (and maybe even enabled by it). Read as the rhetoric of political actors, many classics in the academic canon of political theory can come strangely alive, even after decades of being scientized or philosophized. (At best, ere objectivisms out and rhetoric is reinterred in History, the "New Historians of Political Thought" reveal this latent rhetorical life of many Western works.) To be sure, the unself-conscious tradition has been deeply troubled for at least two centuries. But the simultaneous trouble of the Western tradition is no coincidence. It implies that excoriating rhetoric was the Western strategy for staying simply rhetorical, which is to say, unaware that its fabric was rhetoric. It also suggests the possibility of seeing the Western tradition as the unself-consciously Rhetorical tradition.

Whatever the merit of that interpretation, though, trouble for unreflective Rhetoric often calls forth contributions to the conscious tradition of Rhetoric. We hear from this second strand of the Rhetorical tradition on two kinds of occasions: when theorizing is troubled in its own terms and when theorizing is troubled by extreme distance from politics. Quarrels about the proper character of theorizing tend in the end to produce revivals of attention to rhetorical techniques and conceptions of political theory. Indeed, this is now happening in some quarters of political science, where we are urged to attend carefully tools and requirements in order to theorize more adequately.[14] To solve problems of theory, invoke solutions from rhetoric.

The former kind of conscious Rhetorician treats the great goal of political theory as academic argument or scientific persuasion. The latter kind pushes the preeminent aim of political theory toward political persuasion, supplanting standard academic ends such as understanding. Then we are told to make political studies more political, addressing more directly and skillfully the topics and participants of ordinary politics. This is to practice political theory on the model of political rhetoric. And it, too, has adherents among current members of the profession.[15]

After the fashion of the ancient Sophists, this latter side of the second lineage of the Rhetorical tradition prizes political practice and the kinds of theorizing (that is, rhetoric) suited to effective engagement in political affairs. Here the main problematic is how to move from theory to rhetoric. Rhetorical concern with constructing arguments and shaping them to particular audiences is what our inquiry requires. But what of the relationship between rhetoric and politics? And what if we have reason to worry about the condition of rhetoric itself? In the conscious tradition, these questions arise seldom and never severely. Neither getting from (good) rhetoric to (good) politics nor

----

[14] For example, see: Hayward R. Alker, Jr., "The Dialectical Logic of Thucydides' Melian Dialogue" and "Logic, Dialectics, Politics: Some Recent Controveries," both project working papers, M.I.T. Center for International Studies, 1980; G. R. Boynton, "On Getting from Here to There: Reflections on Two Paragraphs and Other Things," in Elinor Ostrom, ed., **Strategies of Political Inquiry**, Beverly Hills, Sage, 1982, pp. 29-68; Boynton, Sage, 1982, pp. 29-68; Boynton, "Linking Problem Definition and Research Activities: Using Formal Languages," in Judy Gillespie, ed., **Missing Elements in Political Inquiry, Beverly Hills, Sage, 1982, forthcoming**; George J. Graham, Jr., "The Role of the Humanities in Public Policy Evaluation," **Soundings**, 64, 2, Summer, 1981, pp. 150-169; Graham, "Values and Rhetoric in Politics and Political Studies," paper presented to the Biannual Meeting of the Philosophy of Science Association, Toronto, October 17-19, 1980.

[15] For example, see this book's essays by Michael Walzer and Ira L. Strauber. Sometimes John Gunnell sounds a part of this project; sometimes not.

securing the integrity of rhetoric is a real concern to the conscious Rhetorician, who merely learns rhetorics and applies them without serious complication to politics. In the conscious tradition, political theory as political rhetoric is political persuasion, which is primarily a matter of making good arguments about and within politics.

But this does not always seem possible, especially when established rhetorics cannot be relied upon. Either alienations of theory from practice appear too great to be attacked head-on, antagonisms within politics seem too great to be subdued directly, or corruptions of politics loom too great to be tackled rhetorically. In reaction to such situations, the West has turned to philosophy and science in order to subdue or supplant rhetoric. Reacting to these same circumstances and also to resulting attacks on rhetoric, the third thread of the Rhetorical tradition spins into existence. It turns to the renewal of rhetoric itself, as a roundabout road to reaching and improving politics. Moreover, it takes the tie of rhetoric to politics to be problematical. Thus the third tradition is the self-conscious tradition, acutely concerned with rhetoric: not only with using and understanding it, but also with setting it aright and even revelling in it. This, in the strict sense, is the Sophistic tradition.

In unself-conscious Rhetoricians, this project is only potential; in conscious Rhetoricians, mostly implicit; in self-conscious Rhetoricians, almost explosive. Therefore, there are **three** Rhetorical traditions to be identified. On the same basis, however, there are three Rhetorical traditions to be **identified**. All three lead in the same general direction, even though the first two lack the drama and daring of the third. (By compensation, they lack also its desperation and danger.) What follows is dominated by inquiry into the specifically Sophistic tradition. But by this route, there is much to learned about the Rhetorical tradition as a whole. (That tradition teaches the uses of inquiry through exaggeration.)

A second reason for the relative profusion of self-conscious Rhetoricians in recent times is foreshadowed by my description of the Sophistic tradition as counter-Western, for it opposes many (but far from all) of the main commitments of (what it regards as) the dominant Western tradition. Academic and intellectual circles of the past hundred years have generated a recurring ethos of cultural decay and apocalypse. This ethos has made conditions favorable for thinking in large historical terms and seeking fundamental alternatives to existing arrangements.

Moreover, just as the political and intellectual

pluralisms of our times leave some people yearning after restoration of what they imagine to have been more coherent and unified ways of living and thinking, so they prompt others to conceive a need or possibility of greater freedom and fulfillment. This is conceived to occur in a new world where rules are seldom general, often remakable, and almost always contestible. Some in the Rhetorical tradition cele- brate pluralism, whereas others simply insist on accepting it as a current and foreseeable fact. Still, the sense that the cultural unity or even coherence of the West has been slip- ping decisively away accounts for the recent concentration of figures in the Sophistic tradition.

Thus most recent figures in the Sophistic tradition could be counted as "crisis theorists," who argue that some vast civilizational shift or cataclysm is nearly or already upon us. That the classics of "political theory" have almost always been generated by times of crisis is a commonplace among current political theorists. Accordingly, I must emphasize that the diremptions and irruptions discerned by recent "crisis theorists" are decidedly more radical (or, significantly the same, more historical) than those discov- ered by most classic writers of the Western tradition (excepting perhaps Plato, the Stoics, and very few others). The end of the Modern Age and the onset of our Postmo- dern Period of atrocities and disasters have been seen to sunder us so severely from commonsense judgments and practical politics that our times, if not all times, are declared radically evil, dismally impotent, or simply absurd. No standard statesmen or strategies or institutions can save us; no ordinary deeds can make a decisive difference.

Hence theorists can be right to retire to the academy or other protected place. There they can produce the words which may help, not as a part of everyday or even radical politics, but as a protest against the pathetic choices that conditions now appear to impose upon us. Then their words may do what their deeds cannot: topple, trample, and trod beyond the old tradition. This psycho- logical and perhaps cultural situation encourages the divi- sions of thought and lifestyle which sustain the Sophistic tradition. In neither writing nor acting are the skills and sensibilities suited to unself-consciously rhetorical conduct either routinely practiced or readily available. For the past century, those who would tap not only the linguistic but also the ethical and political resources of rhetoric have found themselves on a road toward the concious and self- concious traditions of political rhetoric. Once on this road at one point or another, many have still turned back or off; but recently, more have been motivated to go all the

way. They have become the acutely self-conscious rhetoricians who suit the Sophistic tradition.

At this point, there is no reason to agonize over the
propriety of this talk about "traditions" and "the West."
For one thing, this is a topic to which I return repeatedly
in sections to follow. For another, few groups are more
aware of the ways in which traditions are retrospectively
constructed than are the Sophists. By the paradox standard in such oppositions, this counter-tradition has played
a major role in defining the meaning and reality of such
categories as culture, tradition, and the West, even as it
has sought (with some success) to challenge, discredit, or
bury them. The issue here is less whether there has been
some "objective" historical entity termed "the Western tradition" than what its self-professed challengers have noted,
approved, and opposed about various patterns of life. Virtually every person in the Sophistic tradition has intended
to reject some basic commitments ascribed to Western culture, realizing all the while that this rejection somehow
derives from Western culture and must be expressed in
terms of Western discourse or inspiration.

As Hannah Arendt explained this situation, the Rhetorical rejection of Western culture can only be effected by
a "turning operation" in which the terms of the Western
tradition are twisted toward new meanings and uses, including attempts to discredit the original tradition. Significantly, Arendt argued that such turning operations mark
out the West itself. In Arendt's version, the West begins
in the turning operation of Plato and ends in the
(attempted?) reversals of Kierkegaard, Marx, and Nietzsche
(or of Heidegger and his student, Arendt herself?).[16] As
should be expected, the anti-rhetorical West turns out to be
rooted in its own rhetorical reversal of Sophistry in particular and prephilosophical Greek culture in general. As one
way of establishing the priority of rhetoric over dialectic
and logic, and thereby establishing the propriety of "theorizing" and living in ways different from those dominant in
the West, this gambit is common in the Sophistic tradition.
(Since on most accounts the category of "theorizing" has its
origin in the rhetorical turn with which the West began, I
have invoked quotation marks to recognize the qualms that
some might have about its use in this context.)

The Rhetorical tradition is no more and no less

----

[16] See: Hannah Arendt, **Between Past and Future**, New
York, Viking Press, second edition, 1968, pp. 35-40.

compatible with Western culture than Sophistry was with the ways of life and mind promoted by Plato and Aristotle. The ambiguity of this declaration is meant to reflect the ambiguity of our political and intellectual situation, as well as the ambiguity intrinsic to talk of traditions (especially as my Postmodern, perhaps Postwestern, Sophists tend to understand them both).

To be sure, severe limits on our knowledge of ancient Sophists makes interpreting their stances as much akin to reading Rorschacht patterns as to reading the works of Plato or understanding Caesar's decision to cross the Rubicon. Partly, deciding to construct the Rhetorical tradition in terms of Sophistry is justified by the unusual attention and admiration that my latter-day Sophists have bestowed upon the original Sophists and other Presocratics. More interestingly, this tie is appropriate because the ironical sensibility embodied by self-conscious Rhetoricians encourages the playful, mythic possibilities of finding inspiration in such an ambiguous source. Mostly, though, the idea of a Sophistic tradition reaching into the twentieth century is supported by the sharing of principles and proclivities among the diverse people identified as its contributors.

In one way or another, each of the defining principles of the Rhetorical tradition could be said to articulate its basic insistence that rhetoric is more fundamental than dialectic, logic, or method; in other words, that rhetoric is the realm of learning or inquiry itself. As such, rhetoric is conceived to include or draw upon the resources of meaning, imagination, and expression typically attributed to poetry and myth. Hence the Aristotelian sundering of rhetoric from poetic was unknown to the first Sophists and has generally been ignored throughout the rest of the Rhetorical tradition.

Furthermore, as the ancient Sophists would remind us, rhetoric is also seen as specifically political inquiry: in fact, as the first and foremost political science. This is to say that the Rhetorical tradition regards inquiry per se as "politics," by which it mainly means inspired and directed by human interests as embodied in people interacting with one another. (Remember: man is the measure!) This is to say as well that the Rhetorical tradition regards politics per se as "inquiry," by which it mainly means created and comprised by communal efforts at understanding and affecting reality. Incidentally, if this latter thesis seems odd or incredible, let me call your attention to its eloquent defense by Glenn Tinder.[17]

According to the Rhetorical tradition, then, inquiry undercuts, crosscuts, incorporates, or transcends (however you prefer to put it) the Classical trinity of the true, the good, and the beautiful. Similarly, it reconceives the Modern splits among the empirical (or synthetic), the normative (or aesthetic), and the logical (or analytic). Nietzsche's "transvaluation of values" is relevant in this respect, as are Pirsig's presentation of rhetoric as inquiry into "Quality," Freud's identification of inquiry with the dynamics of desire and self-deception, White's format for "prefiguration of the phenomenal field," and so on.

More specifically, the Sophistic tradition rejects Western reliance on rhetorics of di- and tri-chotomy. Working in terms of simple splits into twos and threes, the mainstream of Western analysis has proved overly vulnerable to hypostatizing categories and missing complications. Dualisms run rampant in the dichotomous culture of the West, and not even appeal to trinitarian rhetorics has been able to infuse Western consciousness with a suitable sense or capacity of self-criticism. The Aristotelian and Hegelian transformations of Plato's di-alectic have retained its apparent incapacity for circling back to reassess first principles, and this deep deficiency is reflected in various Western institutions. Thus the Sophistic tradition would fault Hegel's three dialectical moments (simple positivity, negation, and the negation of the negation) for failing to including a fourth (ironical) moment in which the whole notion of di- or tri-alectic could be brought into question.

Indeed, insofar as many latter-day Sophists self-consciously choose an apparently formal four-thinking, they can be seen to ironize uncritical formalism (here representative of a broader rationalism) as a repeated problem in Western culture. By emphasizing the fourth (deconstructive) moment, of course, the Sophistic tradition turns toward the very ironisms which it observes to plague the West. Here again, the ambiguity of relationships between traditions and counter-traditions is evident in the Rhetorical critique of Western commitments. Perhaps the interesting thing in this regard is that such complications cannot discredit the critique itself, which in its resistance to (or play with) simple logics of contradiction is something that the

--------------------   .

[17] Glenn Tinder, **Community**, Baton Rouge, Louisiana State University Press, 1980.

Sophistic tradition is able to appreciate.[18]

One standard Sophistic strategy is to proliferate distinctions, playing them off one another in order to communicate and criticize with a subtlety and accuracy that sheer di- or tri-chotomizing can seldom match. This strategy is hardly absent from the Western tradition, of course, but it is seldom deployed with anything approaching the same self-consciousness and skill toward which the Sophistic tradition strives. Naturally, there are many situations suited to two-splits and three-splits expressed sans qualification. The able, self-conscious rhetorician recognizes this, while remembering not to project what fits one situation into an iron platform for addressing all similar concerns. Over the long haul, this results in different personal conceptions, which in turn translates into different political problems, solutions, dissolutions, and achievements. Presumably, the advantage of the Sophistic tradition is its commitment to revealing the limitations of any particular rhetoric or perspective by assessing it from other stances. Reverberations of this theme are familiar from recent theories of inquiry by Thomas Kuhn, Paul Feyerabend, and many others.[19]

Another common Sophistic strategy is to proliferate particulars, resisting the Western drive to order them in

----

[18] See: Roberto Mangabeira Unger, **Knowledge and Politics**, New York, Free Press, 1975. For a taste of the ambiguity inherent in such categorizing, compare: Hayden White, **Metahistory**, Baltimore, Johns Hopkins University Press, 1973; John S. Nelson, "Review Essay," **History and Theory**, 14, 1, 1975, pp. 74-91.

[19] See: Hannah Arendt, "Thinking and Moral Considerations," **Social Research**, 38, 3, Autumn, 1971, pp. 417-446, on pp. 420-421; Arendt, "A Reply," **Review of Politics**, 15, 1, January, 1953, pp. 76-85, on pp. 80-83; Arendt, **Between Past and Future**, pp. 95ff; Thomas S. Kuhn, **The Structure of Scientific Revolutions**, Chicago, University of Chicago Press, second edition, 1970; Paul K. Feyerabend, **Against Method**, Atlantic Highlands, NJ, Humanities Press, 1975. Ellen Meiksins Wood identifies two components of Western rationalism: the metaphysical and the dialectical. She discusses what amounts to a rhetorical dissolution of these rationalisms through extensive use of oppositions which cut across standard Western splits such as subject/object and individual/society. See: **Mind and Politics**,

grand classifications. A first reflection of this strategy can be seen in Sophists' hostility for Hegelian and other systems. I think immediately of Kierkegaard and Nietzsche in this context, but you may have your own favorite examples. Here the vast diversity of life is celebrated in all its detail, which no simple system can capture. Of course, categories must be used to capture the particulars in rich descriptions; but the Sophist insists that any categorization must be incomplete and every system of categories must be inconsistent. Indeed, the Sophist is inclined to celebrate this as a protection of possibilities for human freedom and as an escape from the iron cage of Weberian (Western) rationalization.

A second species of this strategy is apparent in the ironical or playful (but still somehow serious) use of such abstract systems by candidates for inclusion in the rhetorical tradition. Perhaps the most familiar exemplar of this strategy in recent American political theory is Henry Kariel, with his open systems.[20]

A third way to proliferate particulars is shown by various styles of form-al investigation, sometimes inspired by Wittgenstein's philosophy of language games and forms of life. Most such styles resist establishing vast, abstract compartments for sorting the smaller concepts and creations of our world. Thus J. L. Austin and John Gunnell rebut advocates of a grand dichotomy between facts and values by pointing out the multitude of concepts which have to be crammed into each of these two containers and showing how silly it is to think that all the distinctions involved amount to pretty much the same split in every context. And once that grand dichotomy is dissolved, then many other dichotomies dear to recent political theory can be washed away

----

Berkeley, University of California Press, 1972. As a first step, this tends to produce four-pole fields or grids to ironize the usual dualisms of the West. See: William Irwin Thompson, **At the Edge of History**, New York, Harper and Row, 1971.

[20] See: Henry S. Kariel, **The Promise of Politics**, Englewood Cliffs, NJ, Prentice-Hall, 1966; Kariel, **Open Systems**, Itasca, IL, F. E. Peacock, 1969; Kariel, **Saving Appearances**, Belmont, CA, Duxbury Press, 1972; Kariel, **Beyond Liberalism, Where Relations Grow**, San Francisco, Chandler and Sharp, 1977.

with it.[21]

A fourth proliferation of particulars could even be identified in the "New History of Political Theory," where there is now cultivated an admirable insistence upon facing up to the past in its actual, if sometimes daunting, detail. Once again, this has the effect of challenging the Western proclivity to eliminate incidental particulars in pursuit of impregnable orders of thinking and living. While the Sophistic tradition might worry about other aspects of this historiographic endeavor, it can certainly applaud and include such commitment to detail.[22]

From these considerations, it follows that talk of "the defining principles" of the Rhetorical tradition is not meant to call to mind categories of necessary and sufficient conditions. To be sure, such a logic of definition would remain available as one rhetorical strategy among many. But the Rhetorical tradition recognizes that there are many strategies of definition, with the situation and interests at hand playing an important part in making some strategies more appropriate than others.

In the current context, individuating and distinguishing between the Sophistic and Western traditions is undoubtedly done best through a combination of several strategies. Thus my definitions here are done partly by family

----

[21] See: J. L. Austin, **How to Do Things with Words**, J. O. Urmson, ed., New York, Oxford University Press, 1962; John G. Gunnell, **Philosophy, Science, and Political Inquiry**, Morristown, NJ, General Learning Press, 1975, pp. 231-298. Also see Gunnell's essay in this volume.

[22] See this book's essay by Richard Ashcraft. Also see: John Dunn, "The Identity of the History of Ideas," in Peter Laslett, W. G. Runciman, and Quentin Skinner, eds., **Philosophy, Politics and Society**, Fourth Series, Oxford, Basil Blackwell, 1972, pp. 158-173; J. G. A. Pocock, "The History of Political Thought: A Methodological Enquiry," in Peter Laslett and W. G. Runciman, eds., **Philosophy, Politics and Society**, Second Series, Oxford, Basil Blackwell, 1962, pp. 183-202; Quentin Skinner, "Meaning and Understanding in the History of Ideas," **History and Theory**, 8, 1, 1969, pp. 3-53; Skinner, "'Social Meaning' and the Explanation of Social Action," in Laslett, Runciman, and Skinner, eds, **Philosophy, Politics and Society**, Fourth Series, pp. 136-157; Skinner, "Some Problems in the Analysis of Political Thought and Action," **Political Theory**, 2, 3,

resemblance (i.e., by parameters, with clear cores and fuzzy boundaries), partly by limits (i.e., by perimeters, with fuzzy cores and clear boundaries), partly by purposes, partly by examples, and partly by images or symbols. As you might expect, this particular combination of strategies is itself fairly typical of definition within the Sophistic tradition, which usually relies as well upon definition by "imaginative etymology."[23] Moreover, members of the Sophistic tradition are especially apt to turn to such a combination of strategies in seeking a self-definition.

One signal of this looser (but at least in this kind of case, arguably more accurate) approach to definition is the appeal to principles rather than rules. Like aphorisms, principles state a heart of the matter. They project a perspective which is valid and important, but which is understood to be hedged in by other perspectives which can conflict with it. Principles are adamant enough, and they seldom try to include the self-qualifications necessary for literalistic precision. Yet they come in complexes; with interaction among principles in a set, let alone among whole sets, capable of keeping them admirably limited and flexible.[24]

By contrast, the Western tradition relies more on rules, which offer greater rigidity and apparent precision.

August, 1974, pp. 277-303.

[23] Hannah Arendt's treatment of "authority" is a good example of the rhetorical strategy of defining by imaginative etymology. See: Arendt, **Between Past and Future**, pp. 91-141.

[24] See: Hannah Arendt, **On Revolution**, New York, Viking Press, 1973, pp. 85, 93-94, 213-214; Arendt, **Between Past and Future**, pp. 152-153, 248-249; Alasdair MacIntyre, **After Virtue**, Notre Dame, University of Notre Dame Press, 1981, pp. 84-102. Please note that this distinction between principles and rules differs from that of Ronald Dworkin; see: **Taking Rights Seriously**, Cambridge, MA, Harvard University Press, 1977, pp. 14-80. Also note that my use of "principles" departs dramatically from that of Stephen Toulmin. Indeed, you need only to substitute "rules" for "principles" in order to see that Toulmin's treatment of ethics reverberates with Sophistic lessons of the sort I am summarizing here; see: "The Tyranny of Principles: Regaining the Ethics of Discretion," **Hastings Center**

The Sophistic preference for principles reminds actors of the inevitability of interpretation and application, plus the broad ranges of discretion and conflict which accompany them. Accordingly, the predominance of principles is meant to remind people more emphatically of personal responsibilities for action than is encouraged by the Western ethos of rules and order, even allowing for the morality of personal responsibility attached to Western individualisms. The high incidence of existentialisms among latter-day Sophists connects with this consideration. (But that is a point to elaborate in talking about the ideologism of recent Western political theory.)

In defending the Western tradition, Alasdair MacIntyre argues that its emphasis on rules is a recent atavism, symptomatic of a modern rejection of the Aristotelian appreciation of virtues. Just as persuasively, however, some Postmodern Sophists have presented the recently emergent dominance of rules as a natural, if not inevitable, outgrowth of Western rationalism: the culmination rather than the renunciation of the Aristotelian project.

More generally, MacIntyre maintains that the Western features which draw the fire of the Sophists result from an Enlightenment rejection of the previous tradition of virtues epitomized by Aristotle. Admittedly, MacIntyre makes a more than decent case for this disjunction. Yet, from one Sophistic standpoint, the continuities between the Aristotelian and Modern Ages are more impressive than the discontinuities. MacIntyre recognizes Nietzsche, perhaps the premier Sophist of the Postmodern Period, as his main nemesis. Not unfairly, MacIntyre endorses the mainstream verdict that, despite himself, Nietzsche was unable to avoid nihilism. Of course, nihilism (along with nostalgism and radical relativism) is a standard charge brought against the Rhetorical tradition in general and Postmodern Sophists in particular by defenders of the West in general and Modern rationalism in particular.[25]

In these terms, though, the confrontation between MacIntyre and Nietzsche is highly ambiguous, if not downright misleading. Initially, this is because MacIntyre's

----

Report, 11, 6, December, 1981, pp. 31-39.

[25] See: MacIntyre, **After Virtue**, pp. 103-113; White, **Metahistory**, pp. 331-374; Tracy B. Strong, **Friedrich Nietzsche and the Politics of Transformation**, Berkeley, University of California Press, 1975.

alternative to rationalism (and the rest of the Enlightenment list of perversities) stands sans anything like the suggestion of efficacy and timeliness needed to save it from nostalgism.   More interestingly, this is because MacIntyre's alternative is itself easily seen as a species of Sophism. Far more than not, in both spirit and specifics, MacIntyre and Nietzsche share indictments and diagnoses of our current predicaments.   Despite significant differences, even their prescriptions for treating our Postmodern diseases share important features.

Indeed, contrasting MacIntyre and Nietzsche expresses another major divide in Postmodern Sophism: over whether to trace current troubles mainly to the Modern Age (begun by the Renaissance and the Reformation; epitomized by the Enlightenment) or to follow them as far back as the Classical Age (begun by the Attic migration; epitomized by the Greek polis and the Roman empire).   This issue relates directly to many other issues debated among Postmodern Sophists, setting up one of the characteristic cleavages in that tradition.   (There are, though, at least several more divisions of equal significance: over kinds of causes sought for current predicaments, over styles and forms of persuasion, over hopeful signs at present, and so on.)

If the Sophistic tradition is at all correct, then the West's writers and actors are all rhetoricians, inevitably and sometimes despite themselves.   Yet they flee at first opportunity into dreams of dialectical, logical, or methodological purity.   The limits embraced thereby are supposed to encourage substantive or political objectivity, but generally have a poor record because they cannot substitute for and yet do sometimes impede what William Connolly has called "theoretical self-consciousness," which is celebrated and cultivated by the Sophistic tradition.[26] (I do not, however, want to denigrate what gains in objectivity and understanding can and, to a much lesser degree, have been generated through the many methods of Postmodern social science. Although often exceeded by related reductions in the quality of inquiry and argument, these gains have been far from negligible.)

The Rhetorical tradition conceives objectivity in terms

----

[26] See: William E. Connolly, "Theoretical Self-Consciousness," **Polity**, 6, 1, Fall, 1973, pp. 5-35; Connolly, **Appearance and Reality**, Cambridge, Cambridge University Press, 1981.

of careful criticism within and across conscientious, but not necessarily academic, communities of inquiry. Just as it works through proliferation of distinctions in qualification of one another, it prizes proliferation of paradigms in communication with one another.[27] The principle of the primacy of rhetoric implies that dialectic and logic are rhetorically created and sustained; in other words, that they are rhetorical constructs. Self-conscious Rhetoricians revel in displaying the covert rhetorical strategies (and mistakes) employed (consciously or not) in reaching for various Western ideals of The Dialectic, The Logic, or, The Method. (Of course, proponents seldom spell these ideals with the capital letters I have used, for from their perspectives that would be rhetorically uncouth or otherwise unwise; nonetheless, their vocalizations give them away.)

In interaction with its recognition of rhetoric as politics and inquiry, the Rhetorical tradition also realizes that rhetoric is style, not centrally in the trivial sense of empty embellishments or the sinister sense of amoral manipulations, but in the substantive sense of personal and communal patterns of life.[28] As elaborated in the section on rationalism, the first virtue of this principle is its facility for slipping past the Scylla and Charybdis of Western culture: the impossible (and unnecessary) choice between absolutism and relativism. As explained in the section on ideologism, the second virtue of this principle is its appreciation for genres or forms of communication and action. As elucidated in the section on academism, the third virtue of this principle is its encouragement for conceiving politics and inquiry themselves in terms of style. And as explicated in the section on ironism, the fourth virtue of this principle is its possibility for a politics that is principled but flexible in the face of Fortuna.

There is one last principle of the Rhetorical tradition

----

[27] See: John S. Nelson, "Tropal History and the Social Sciences," **History and Theory**, 19, 4, 1980, pp. 80-101, on pp. 91-92.

[28] See: A. L. Kroeber, **Style and Civilizations**, Berkeley, University of California Press, 1957; John Murray Cuddihy, **The Ordeal of Civility**, New York, Dell, 1974; Peter Gay, **Style in History**, New York, Basic Books, 1974; Robert Nisbet, **Sociology as an Art Form**, New York, Oxford University Press, 1976; Berel Lang, ed., **The Concept of Style**, Philadelphia, University of Pennsylvania Press, 1979.

that requires statement before plunging into a Rhetorical critique of current political theory.   For the Rhetorician, the study and practice of rhetoric form one and the same domain.   This is why the word "rhetoric" regularly and simultaneously means: "what is communicated," "how it is communicated," "the study of its specific communication," and "the theory of communication generally."   Seeing how insistently these categories slip into one another, the Rhetorical tradition tends to avoid perplexities that recent linguistic theorists have produced by their abstract and emphatic splits (for example, among signs, signifieds, and signifiers).   The same goes for trichotomies of analytical philosophy (for example, among the empirical, the theoretical, and the normative; or knowing how, knowing that, and knowing why).   This is one more way in which the Rhetorical tradition seeks to heal the wounds of analysis run wild within Western categorical order.[29]

The Rhetorical strategies spun off this principle show further the Sophistic resistance to some of the fundamental dichotomies through which so much Western discourse is structured.   About as well as anyone, Sophists recognize the impossibility of pushing very far or fruitfully with many of the bifurcations common to academia these days.   With depth psychologists, Sophists see the nonsense in static separations between case studies and general theories. With activist epistemologists, Sophists concede the elusiveness of deep divisions between metatheory and theory. With praxiologists, Sophists repudiate the standard Western sundering of theory from practice or thought from action. With Wittgensteinians, Sophists are suspicious of thoroughgoing gaps between thought and language.   Let me emphasize that the Sophistic tradition is seldom in the business of denying all such distinctions regardless of context. Rather, it typically stresses the abstract multiplicity of possible splits, while warding off the Western impulse to collapse them all into a few gigantic dualisms (or even trinities).

As implied by these challenges to the categorical order of Western culture, the Sophistic tradition restricts neither its criticisms nor its remedies to discourse alone, for it is extremely sensitive to the ways in which conceptual

----

[29] See: Owen Barfield, **Saving the Appearances,** New York, Harcourt, Brace and World, n.d.; C. S. Lewis, **The Abolition of Man,** New York, Macmillan, 1947; Pirsig, **Zen and the Art of Motorcycle Maintenance.**

commitments   constitute   political   constraints.   Sophists
scramble scramble beyond the spell of Western categorical
order precisely in order to escape the iron cage of rationalization which worried Max Weber.   They are bursting with
evocations of the banal routine and chilling rigor with which
the West subtly systematizes the speech and restructures
the politics of other cultures to fit its own imperatives.
Thus incorporated, the alien ways are reduced to a
repressed remainder, surviving as the shadowsides that
sometimes serve to inspire the Sophistic tradition itself.
Consciously and unconsciously, then, the West wields its
rationalistic rhetoric as an instrument of domination.   And
this means in turn that the alternate rhetorics of the
Sophistic tradition can be both the instrument and the
attainment of significant liberation.

Thus what may seem to unsophisticated Western ears
and eyes as merely verbal challenges to Western ways can
at least hope for fully institutional effects.   Indeed, were
political theorists more prone to Sophistic self-conceptions
and styles, their capacities for active involvement and for
cogent criticism could improve together.   This is not to say
that most Sophistic theorists would actually plunge into
ordinary politics or become unqualified critics of same, but
simply that the Sophistic repertoire of stances puts either
move on better footing.   To see why, let us examine the
Rhetorical rejection of Western rationalism, especially with
respect to recent political theory.

RATIONALISM

The rhetoricians of ancient Greece were the
first teachers in the history of the Western
world.   Plato vilified them in all his works to
grind an axe of his own and since what we
know about them is almost entirely from Plato
they're unique in that they've stood condemned
throughout history without ever having their
side of the story told.   The Church of Reason...was founded on their graves.   It's supported today by their graves.   And when you
dig deep into its foundation you come across
ghosts.

Robert
Pirsig[30]

There is reason to locate the decisive beginning of the Western tradition, not in Socrates' daemon of dialectical ignorance, but in Plato's sundering of the soul (and polity) into three parts. For only with support from the separation and elevation of reason over appetite and will, was dialectic able to distance itself definitively from rhetoric and myth. Thereafter, the Western tradition is a story of similar splits and ever more extreme celebrations of reason. In this sense, G. W. F. Hegel was right to see himself as the culmination of Western (if not World) History, since he is the epitome of the Western ambition to free reason from dependence upon other human (or in Hegel's case, Historical) faculties. To unitize, autonomize, universalize, and hegemonize reason as Reason, freed from human and historical limitations, has been a defining ideal of the West.

Perhaps there is poetic justice (and certainly there are ironies and reversals aplenty) in the way the West has come to its end by Sophistic accounts. Paradoxically, there is reason to locate the definitive demise of the Western tradition in Freud's decision to split the psyche into three parts (rather than two). For this move made manifest the implicit message of Freud's earlier work with the dynamics of symbolism and desire: reason could no longer be distinguished decisively from other human faculties like memory, emotion, imagination, morality, or will, let alone could reason be seen as Sovereign over the person or society. Almost despite himself, Freud demonstrated that faculties akin to Plato's original tripartition must remain utterly interdependent.

Of course, Freud's efforts hardly stand alone in discrediting the Western worship of Reason. Reinforcing Freud's studies, Postmodern inquiries into virtually every aspect of culture converge on the same conclusion: that neither actually, potentially, or properly is reason fully separate from the rest of our attributes, let alone fully sovereign over them. Increasingly, we find ourselves forced to concede and even cultivate a plurality of reasons (indeed, a plurality of rationalities). This connects with grudging concessions to such academically awkward phenomena as nationalism and patriotism. Accordingly, and most importantly, the main events and experiences of the Postmodern Period lean unmistakably toward this relativizing of reason.[31]

----

[30] Ibid., p. 166.

A telling symptom of the times is that the critique of reason spreads far beyond the confines of any Rhetorical tradition. But the Sophistic tradition in particular is distinguished (and advantaged) by its avoidance of the usual Western dilemma of relativized reason: the impossible choice between absolutism and (radical) relativism. Many advocates of Western ideals and institutions have felt forced into their approval by apocalyptic challenges to intelligent life implicit in the only alternatives they were able to conceive: relativisms either passive and self-refuting (skepticisms) or active and self-destroying (nihilisms). Some brave (if foolish?) people have bucked the Western tide by embracing one or both of these radical relativisms, giving rise to counter-traditions often confused (and a bit overlapping) with Sophistic alternatives to Western culture. And I must admit that at least a few Sophists have strayed into skepticism or nihilism from time to time, even as most of them have recognized these denials of reason to be even more dangerous than Western idolizations of same.

How, when successful, have Sophists side-stepped this terrible choice between rationalism and relativism? By turning its terms against itself. That the Western tradition produces this dilemma is taken as decisive evidence against Western conceptions of coherence in general and of reason in particular. As an increasingly impressive array of (post?)philosophers are recognizing, this impossible decision is an artifact of Western commitments which are themselves far from wise, let alone unavoidable.[32] Once an abstract

----

[31] On the end of the West or at least its Modern Age, see: Roderick Seidenberg, **Post-Historic Man**, Chapel Hill, University of North Carolina Press, 1950; Arendt, **Between Past and Future**, pp. 17-40; Romano Guardini, **The End of the Modern World**, New York, Sheed and Ward, 1956; Glenn Tinder, **The Crisis of Political Imagination**, New York, Scribners, 1964; John Lukacs, **The Passing of the Modern Age, New York, Harper and** Row, 1970; Allen Wheelis, **The End of the Modern Age**, New York, Basic Books, 1971; MacIntyre, **After Virtue**, pp. 210-226. On relativism, skepticism, and nihilism, see: Michael Polanyi, **Beyond Nihilism**, Cambridge, Cambridge University Press, 1960; Stanley Rosen, **Nihilism**, New Haven, Yale University Press, 1969; **The Monist**, 60, 4, October, 1977, **passim**. Also see this volume's essays by Tracy B. Strong and Allan Megill.

[32] See: Stanley Cavell, **The Claim of Reason**, New York,

standard of Reason or Philosophy or Science is intimated to rule all (or any?) of life, the necessary particularity and plurality of humanity is imperiled. The mistake lies in accepting the Western aspiration to a single, universal standard of coherence and defensibility. As the Rhetorical tradition insists, reasons and reasonings are plural. No one rhetoric rules all others, not even some "rhetoric of rhetoric," which is recognized by Sophists to be incapable of rising in rigorous solitude over the battles of substantive styles and decisions at the heart of human existence.

Turning reason upon itself discloses how intimately and inevitably it is entwined with memory, emotion, imagination, morality, will, and the all the rest. As Postmodern social sciences have shown in an amazing variety of ways, we explain reason internally in terms of these other faculties and externally in terms of their historical embodiments in cultural ethoi and institutions. One way to recognize different rationalities is by their distinctive networks of interest, motivation, feeling, perception, recollection, symbolization, extrapolation, and so on. Another is to tease them from the different practices they indwell, inform, and invade. Then their circumstances and repercussions can be compared in order to elicit their characteristics. One way or another, social scientists are thus coming (slowly) to terms with the absence and apparent impossibility of any single Rationality for human affairs. As they do so, rhetorical topics like language, symbol, story, community, and communication become ever more important for their work.

Beyond this, reasoning about reason (instead of idolizing it) reveals how much **reason is argument is rhetoric is style**. And even though Westerners have doubted the rationality of style, they have seldom doubted its plurality. This is to say that "reason" is a collective noun, concealing plurality within its singular form. Properly and practically, "reason" means "reasons." For this Rhetorical thesis, too, the social sciences lend sturdy and extensive support. The psychologies of cognitive style, the sociologies of knowledge, the anthropologies of cultural difference and development: all these skeins and more testify to the rhetorical plurality of reason and truth. Even the economies of rational choice evidence this Rhetorical proposition, if mostly by their current condition of theoretical confusion

----

Oxford University Press, 1979; Richard Rorty, **Philosophy and the Mirror of Nature**, Princeton, NJ, Princeton University Press, 1979.

and practical collapse. Thus, Postmodern Sophists are able
to show with increasing clarity that there are good reasons
to present choices among styles in terms of reasons (and
choices among reasons in terms of styles). This is at least
one way in which current, Western political theory needs a
Sophistic correction in order to survive in vigor and worth.

A Sophistic correction of current political theory
would concentrate on rooting out the commitments which
compose or embody recent rationalisms. At a minimum,
these include: objectivism, literalism, methodism, and formalism. Since Sophists say that these doctrines instigate
much of the trouble now encountered by the would-be prac-
titioner of political theory, they deserve deeper discussion
than they receive here. But the least I can do is devote a
brief paragraph to each of these ills.

Objectivism is the doctrine of the positivist (or passi-
vist) epistemologist. It contends that there is a single,
exhaustive, and ineradicable separation between subject and
object. Often, this is associated with an ontology of atomism, such that the world is claimed to consist of elemental
particles (objects) individuated prior to and apart from any
intervention by subjects. At any rate, the objectivist is
convinced that the world (of objects) is simply there
(somewhere), utterly independent of his activities in investigation of it. The issue of objectivity then becomes the
problem of keeping subjectivity out of inquiry; in other
words, of saving the appearances while also saving the
sanctity of beings (objects).[33]

Given trust in the appearances, of course, this seems
no problem at all. Appearances are then taken as fully
faithful and transparent media through which we can see
objects inviolate. To be sure, this move (dependent as it
is upon the dubious idea of transparent media) does call for
at least one additional doctrine: **literalism**. This states
that languages (media) can give neutral, stable, and precise expressions of (objective) observations. In other
words, language can be an utterly transparent medium of
relationship to (objective) reality. Such language simply
and specifically refers its users to objects already (and
absolutely?) there, in no way constituted by the creation

----

[33] See: Michael Polanyi, **Personal Knowledge**, New York,
Harper and Row, second edition, 1964; Thomas A. Spra-
gens, Jr., **The Dilemma of Contemporary Political Theory**,
New York, Dunellen, 1973; Spragens, **The Irony of Liberal
Reason**, Chicago, University of Chicago Press, 1981.

and use of language itself. Rational discourse is that which lets the order of reality shine through (objectively) without hindrance or distortion. Thus there is a further Western dichotomy between literal and figurative language. Literal language is the realm of dialectic, logic, and method; whereas figurative language is the realm of poetry, myth, and rhetoric. Literalism declares that literal language can and should stand completely clear of figurative language. Moreover, literalism declares that we should rely on literal language: it is what really counts.[34]

But Westerners are too realistic and consistent to make things so deceptively easy on themselves. For of course, the categorical commitments already mentioned bind them to a distrust of appearances. By crossing the subject/object split with the dichotomy between being and appearance, they insured themselves a vast array of epistemological problems. Of course, they then proceeded to pack every imaginable problem of inquiry into The Problem of Epistemology: how can we infer from appearance to being in fully objective (utterly unsubjective) fashion? So abstract a problem could only be "solved" with something equally (or even more extremely?) abstract: Method.

Thus was born the doctrine that objectivity is guaranteed by exact adherence to procedural rules of inquiry: **methodism** (or methodolatry) for short. So much has recently been written about mistakes of methodism that there is no need to repeat details here.[35] Suffice it to say that methodism produces its own epistemological problems, since someone is bound to ask whether The Method is an object. If so, then how can we subjects get to know it (objectively) without already knowing it? (Remember that The Method is said to be our only way of really reaching the realm of objects in the first place.) If not, then what is it? (Remember that objectivism allows us only "subject" or "object" in answer to this question. If The Method is not objective, then it must be subjective; but the subjective

----

[34] See: Hayden White, **Tropics of Discourse**, Baltimore, Johns Hopkins University Press, 1978; Nelson, "Tropal History and the Social Sciences."

[35] See: Hans-Georg Gadamer, **Truth and Method**, Garrett Barden and John Cumming, eds., trans. from the 1965 second edition, New York, Seabury Press, 1975; Sheldon S. Wolin, "Political Theory as a Vocation," **American Political Science Review**, 63, 4, December, 1969, pp. 1062-1082.

is never objective. Thus The Method is neither neutral nor certain in inquiry, as it must be to satisfy the requirements of objectivism. In short, The Method cannot be The Method.)

From the standpoint of this dilemma, the Sophist's sober acceptance of plurality and inconsistency (not to say, utter incoherence) may be looking more attractive than ever. But the Western rationalist proposes to dissolve the dilemma through the doctrine of **formalism**. He answers that The Method is subjective, so that we subjects can possess it prior to inquiry into objects. Yet it is neutral or certain precisely because its subjectivity is unalloyed. This makes it transparently accessible to us as subjects (which no object of inquiry can be).

Since the Western rationalist started by seeking scientific excellence in the object (objectivism), it is somewhat surprising to see this turn toward the subject (subjectivism). Thus there have been several different strategies for effecting and defending this turn as truly Western, truly rationalist. But there is really no getting around the fact that this move twists rationalism in a most remarkable way. What has been faith in the inherent coherence and utter knowability of a reality fully independent of the knower becomes faith in the knower's ability to produce a reality (or route to reality) fully coherent and yet somehow objectively independent of the knower. Method is to be logic, and logic is to be either tautology or otherwise empty of objective content. Neutrally, form is to show us (subjects) The Way to content (objects).

This remarkable move shook the Western tradition to its foundations. Its repercussions led Vico to reinvent the Rhetorical counter-tradition. But still, it did not cause anything approaching an immediate collapse of Western culture, with its rationalism. Why? In my view, the resilience of Western rationalism can be explained mostly by the practical success of the active, institutional side of such rationalism. By this, I mean the **instrumentalism** which has become so dominant that it is virtually the whole of Weber's notion of rationalization.

Although neither necessitated nor especially encouraged by the contemplative beginnings of Western culture, the Modern production of instrumentalism from rationalism probably saved the day for the West. One way or another, instrumentalism shared the scene with the West's great technological success and even came to claim credit for it. Any dependence upon subjects (that is, people) for rationalizing a recalcitrant reality could be tolerated when the Westerners seemed able to create and control instruments for ordering the world in all its important aspects: natural and human.

As we have discovered with horror, however, a "rationalism" at once subjectivist and instrumentalist is actually an irrationalism of potent proportions and destructive propensities. I will not harp on the atrocities and disasters of the past century. Others have elsewhere recited them more cogently and completely than I could hope to do here. Nor will I claim that the deeper past reveals sweeter times, for the Sophist's case need not and cannot rest on this kind of comparison. But our recent skepticism and nihilism suggest strongly that the West is ending, with skirmishes already begun among its possible replacements. Since traditions (like people) form their own alternatives, the issue is which of the counter-traditions of the West will take its place: Skepticism, Nihilism, Sophism, or something else? I, at least, find Rhetorical alternatives to rationalism to be especially worth exploring.

In place of objectivism, the Sophist puts **perspectivism**. Because it projects neither truth nor reality as singular and universal, perspectivism protects itself against the dilemma of rationalism versus relativism. Instead of repressing or suppressing our plurality, perspectivism seeks to nurture it in communal practices of inquiry designed to improve realities "intersubjectively sustained." Thus does it substitute argument for method as our main modality of inquiry. (Although perspectivism is interested in methods of argument, it pursues them more as styles than rules. Thus does it resist methodizing argument after the fashion of Modern textbooks of rhetoric, Postmodern research reports, or the like.) And when argument is saved from shortcircuiting into dialectic-logic-method, the inevitability and advantage of figuration for persuasive discourse is easily evident. Moreover, the insufficiency of argument alone becomes readily apparent, leading to its completion in myriad other forms of persuasion, expression, and thought.[36]

Although admittedly some Sophists have made mistakes at this point, it is not that we should or even could eliminate literality as stabilized meaning and ready, reliable

----

[36] See: Kenneth Burke, **A Grammar of Motives**, Berkeley, University of California Press, 1945; Burke, **A Rhetoric of Motives**, Berkeley, University of California Press, 1950; Richard M. Weaver, **The Ethics of Rhetoric**, Chicago, Henry Regnery, 1953.

reference.   After all, without literality, figuration would make no sense.   It is rather that we should refuse to abso-lutize literality.   This would open many different directions to us.   Some Sophists turn to imagery and aphorism, others to word-play and poetry, still others to irony and story-telling.   Whatever the trope or genre, the point is to exploit **the plurality of literality**, instead of denying or debasing it; that is, to find in the interdependence of liter-ality and figuration a new freedom, rather than an old order.   Or, to put the point differently, we must overcome the old dichotomy which pits the literal against the figura-tive.   We should substitute richer separations among many kinds of language (and thought) which straddle this stan-dard divide.   Inquiry into tropes of discourse may meet this test, but there are bound to be other ways of passing it as well.   Whatever the way, when we cease to idolize lit-erality, then persuasion, expression, and inquiry should all prosper.

In an interesting sense, this option is a revised and ironized formalism: a fairly critical, sober, and self-con-scious playing with forms.   Far from the absolutism and neutralism of the late-Western notion of form, however, this perspectivist notion celebrates the interdependence of form and content (style and substance).   Perhaps the most important implication of this principle of interdependence is the impossibility of radical dichotomies between means and ends.   For this implication stands in steady criticism of Western instrumentalism.   And it carries the corollary that reliance upon strict means/ends calculation is generally (especially politically) inadvisable in the dying night of Western civilization now upon us.[37]

Another implication is worth mentioning here.   In denying that form and content can be completely separated, the Rhetorical tradition denies that there can be absolute, supracontextual standards of argument, let alone judgment.

----

[37] See: Max Horkheimer, **Eclipse of Reason**, New York, Seabury Press, 1947; Hannah Arendt, "History and Immor-tality," **Partisan Review**, 24, 1, Winter, 1957, pp. 11-35, on pp. 23-26; Arendt, **The Human Condition**, Garden City, NY, Doubleday, 1958, pp. 82-83, 125-134, 204-213; Arendt, **Crises of the Republic**, New York, Harcourt Brace Jovano-vich, 1972, **pp. 150-151; Lon L. Fuller**, The Principles of Social Order, **Kenneth I.** Winston, ed., Durham, NC, Duke University Press, 1981; MacIntyre, **After Virtue**, pp. 92-95, 139-141, 175-186.

Neither science nor philosophy is able to rise above rhetoric into some utterly pure, unbiased, uncompromising arena of Rationality. Without some absolute and implausible bifurcation of reason from emotion or will, such (typically formalist) attempts to reduce argument to deduction cannot get off the ground. Instead, they simply sweep the meat of argument under the rug thrown over controversial translations of substantive matters into some particular form. This hardly means that there are no significant differences in the patterns of rhetoric characteristic of philosophy, science, management, architecture, engineering, and so forth. But no enterprise is abstractly superior to the others in its fidelity to Rationality, if only because Rationality is nonexistent in human affairs. To pretend otherwise is to participate in deception of oneself or others.

There are many rationalities (although in principle not as many as rhetorics). One might say that each field is bounded by its special rationality. But this is obviously not correct as far as conventional academic disciplines or fields are concerned, since each includes at least several rationalities. The same seems true of nonacademic enterprises such as business, law, art, and politics. One might go farther with the claim that each field is defined by a special rationality, characteristic and concentrated there even if identifiable elsewhere. But that thesis, too, would require refinements. In any event, the formalist standard of Rationality is itself a rhetorical gambit, even though far from all its users seem to understand that.

In particular, all too many recent political theorists succumb to the Rationality scam. This is too common in "Rational-Choice" and other formal theorizing about politics to merit more than a mention. Let me emphasize, though, that this is neither a necessary nor a universal mistake in formal political theory; as one strategy and genre among many others, formal theory is sometimes deployed to achieve and convey very good work.[38] Less obviously, this scam surfaces in conceptual analysis: for example, when the analyst claims to establish the true or best meaning of some concept or locution virtually regardless of context. The Rationality scam even shows up in historical and textual interpretation, although objective ambiguity in particular

----

[38] See: G. R. Boynton, **Mathematical Thinking about Politics**, New York, Longman, 1979; Robert Axelrod, "The Emergence of Cooperation among Egoists," **American Political Science Review**, 75, 2, June, 1981, pp. 306-318.

and rhetorical consciousness in general might be thought to prevent it for the most part.

Perhaps the most common occurrence of rationalist interpretation (and also a chronic shortcoming of "ideology critique") is the attempt to parse some "classic of political theory" according to purportedly timeless (or ideologically insured) standards of philosophy (or political rectitude). Thus "rationally reconstructed" into a caricature allegedly bereft of rhetorical clutter, the classic can then suffer dialectical praise or condemnation with no qualms concerning its displacement from the original rhetorical context to whatever rationalist setting serves the interests of the interpreter or critic. Given the pathetically limited range of apprehension allowed by most of the pseudocontexts used in rationalist interpretation, the issue of interpretation tends to devolve into whether some arbitrary standard of rationality is met ("consistency") or flouted ("contradiction").

Usually, this rationalist technique of interpretation prevents appreciation of precisely the political and rhetorical achievement of the classic under "study." Written mostly to contemporary philosophers, John Locke's **Essay on Human Understanding** has at least managed a minimal respect through its subsequent rationalizations, even though it has suffered many accusations of "inconsistency." But Locke's **Two Treatises of Government**, written principally to people of public affairs, may well have received more rationalist abuse than any other classic in the canon of political theory. Importantly, although of course not exclusively, this has been because its pointed rhetorical commitment to the political arena leaves it vulnerable to all sorts of rationalist deconstructions. Accordingly, most commentary has been dedicated to demonstrating Locke's (worse, Liberalism's) alleged "contradictions." And yet, as Michael Levin remarks, "perhaps the most brilliant aspect of this work is the high level to which it carries the art of political persuasion. In such an attempt inconsistency might indeed be a merit."[39]

More emphatically, my claim is that "inconsistency" in this rationalist sense is a necessity in such an attempt. This hardly means that there are no senses and ways in which a work can be criticized for inconsistency or even

----

[39] Michael Levin, "What Makes a Classic in Political Theory?," **Political Science Quarterly**, 88, 3, September, 1973, pp. 462-476, on p. 467.

irrationality. Nor does it imply any other general repuda-
tion of rationality. Instead, it entails a general resistance
to fetishizing or otherwise absolutizing rationality. It
means that commentary and criticism should be rhetorically
sophisticated and self-conscious, recognizing the need for
attention to appropriate contexts in informing a particular
interpretation. Sometimes (more often than now, we may
hope) this will require serious historical research. But it
should not always follow the same paths, since there are
many potentially legitimate modes of historiography. (This
is where the "New History of Political Theory" often goes
wrong.) And even then, there is no general primacy of
historical research as an indispensable requirement of
defensible interpretation. Propriety of contexts is no more
a merely historical matter than it is a sheerly rational one.
This is evident from the second standard sin of recent
political theorists: ideologism.

IDEOLOGISM

> Do the traditions of understanding politics
> which have been developed in Europe over the
> last two and a half millennia possess any real
> residual capacity to direct us in the face of the
> world which now confronts us? Do they still
> exert any real imaginative or moral purchase
> upon this world which we, as a species, have
> remade so drastically? Or are they simpy
> crazed myths clashing meaninglessly in a night
> which they can neither understand nor illumi-
> nate?
>
> John
> Dunn[40]

     Recent political theory has been hung up within Mod-
ern ideologies. In form and content, they dominate the
apprehensions, attachments, and antagonisms apparent these

----

[40] John Dunn, **Western Political Theory in the Face of the
Future**, Cambridge, Cambridge University Press, 1979, p.
vii.

days in theorizing about politics. By "Modern ideologies," I mostly mean the four obvious examples of liberalism, socialism, conservatism, and anarchism, although others could perhaps be identified. To be sure, Modern institutions continue to structure important parts of our lives. Hence, there are reasons to be concerned with Modern ideologies. But current political theory seems mesmerized by the terms, issues, and answers of these ideologies, even though little of our everyday experience and less of our political environment could (or would want to) claim any compelling connection with them. Bewitched theorists have accordingly had quite a struggle on their minds in trying to cram recent developments into these old systems of belief.

The single most important point about this ideologism is that its spell spans not only the contents, but also the forms of current political theory. I suppose that a fully convincing demonstration of this claim would amount to a hefty book or more. More likely, not even that would be enough to snap the spell by which many political theorists remain bound. Luckily, there have already been many persuasive presentations of this argument or its components. Briefly, let me review just a few of them, beginning with the contents of current political theory, particularly in Anglo-American circles.

John Dunn answers his own set of questions by sketching "some of the central anomalies of our political understanding today."[41] To my eye, these current perplexities about democracy, liberalism, nationalism, and revolution run so deep in recent theory and yet reflect so much of importance in current politics that it is almost impossible to conclude that political theorists have been doing a decent job. Significantly, Dunn explains these defects in such a manner as to make unmistakable their connection to (and probably their cause by) a general inability to step past the obsolescent standpoint of Modern ideologism. His presentation strongly implies that the dominance of old ideological debates bedevils our attempts to address the specific actualities of our own (very different) political and cultural situations.

Still, Dunn's indictment is far from comprehensive and can be supplemented by many other demonstrations of ideologism and its dangers. Socialists that they profess to be, Michael Walzer and Hugh Stretton nonetheless seem to me to end up showing that no Modern ideology (socialism

----

[41] Ibid.

included) can come to grips with Postmodern projects of liberation and ecology, without bending itself out of shape.[42]
Peter Berger does the same for the Postmodern problems of
bureaucracy and third-world development, evidently despite
his self-identification with conservatism.[43] These very theorists suggest that not even the late-Modern simplification of
politics into Left and Right retains much to recommend it
for our political theorizing. Nor is this the only dichotomy
of Modern ideology to bite the Postmodern dust.

Take the Modern bifurcation of public from private
affairs. One of the main achievements of the Modern Age is
its proliferation of institutions and enterprises which either
straddle such splits or evade them altogether. Not even
academics can avoid direct, everyday experience of the
obvious obsolescence of public/private dichotomies: witness
the shifting sense of speaking in terms of "public" and
"private" universities. Can anyone read Charles Lindblom
on **Politics and Markets** and fail to find public/private
dichotomies inadequate for coming to terms with business
and politics in the United States?[44] Can anyone read Grant
McConnell on **Private Power and American Democracy** or
Theodore Lowi on **The End of Liberalism** and still find any
Modern split between public and private affairs systematically applicable to recent American life?[45] Can anyone read
Christopher Lasch on the **Haven in a Heartless World** or
The Culture of Narcissism and yet regard the family as a
plainly "private" institution?[46]

----

[42] See: Hugh Stretton, **Capitalism, Socialism and the Environment**, Cambridge, Cambridge University Press, 1976;
Michael Walzer, **Radical Principles**, New York, Basic Books,
1980.

[43] See: Peter L. Berger, Brigitte Berger, and Hansfried
Kellner, **The Homeless Mind**, New York, Random House,
1973; Peter L. Berger, **Pyramids of Sacrifice**, New York,
Basic Books, 1974.

[44] See: Charles Lindblom, **Politics and Markets**, New York,
Basic Books, 1977.

[45] See: Grant McConnell, **Private Power and American
Democracy**, New York, Random House, 1966; Theodore J.
Lowi, **The End of Liberalism**, New York, Norton, second
edition, 1979.

Actually, of course, I know that many people (even political theorists) can and do continue to make such moves. But the Rhetorical question is whether there are reasons in each case to merit such appeals to public/private splits? Insofar as a general answer can be given in the context of American politics and theorizing about politics, I doubt it. A far more precise and persuasive approach surely must be to recognize the great diversity of meanings and uses such a simple split has incorporated by now, spinning them off into a respectable profusion of verbal distinctions with real political relevance and bite.[47]

Another favorite example of mine (since it indicts not only Modern ideologism, but also Western rationalism) is the bizarre inclination of recent political theorists to cling to simple Modern bifurcations of individual from society or some other "collective" entity (economy, polity, culture, institution, etc.). Probably, political theorists who are uncritically committed to the unfortunate "universes of discourse" constituted by Modern ideological debates feel that there is no other way to protect people from Weberian rationalization into roles, totalitarian bureaucratization into automatons, authoritarian domestication of people into dependents and consumers, or similar eradications of personality. In defense of reasonably free and responsible selves, however, this strategy leaves a lot to be desired.

Postmodern inquiry into selfhood and the situation of the individual has repeatedly revealed the inextricable intertwining of person and society. In socialization research, depth psychology, anthropological field studies, and a variety of other projects, the interdependence of

----

[46] See: Christopher Lasch, **Haven in a Heartless World**, New York, Basic Books, 1977; Lasch, **The Culture of Narcissism**, New York, Norton, 1979.

[47] See: J. Roland Pennock and John W. Chapman, eds., **Nomos XIII: Privacy**, New York, Atherton Press, 1971; Herman van Gunsteren, "Public and Private," **Social Research**, 46, 2, Summer, 1979, pp. 255-271; Hanna Fenichel Pitkin, "Justice: On Relating Private and Public," **Political Theory**, 9, 3, August, 1981, pp. 327-352; Daniel Callahan, "Minimalist Ethics: On the Pacification of Morality," **Hastings Center Report**, 11, 5, October, 1981, pp. 19-25, on pp. 22-24; Jean Bethke Elshtain, **Public Man, Private Woman**, Princeton, NJ, Princeton University Press, 1981.

individual and institution has generated a host of distinctions loosely (but in the end, misleadingly) collectable under this old dichotomy. I dare say that many of us experience daily the need for departures from the simplism of Modern-ideological divisions between human beings and cultures. Indeed, this may explain in part our (admittedly sometimes abstract) craving for enhanced communities of one kind or another. Recognizing the diversity of distinctions to be drawn in support (and criticism) of selfhood (and individualism) can generate more realistic and effective rhetorics for confronting current conditions.

This kind of dogged or desperate grasp on categories incapable of coming to terms with the world in which we live could be illustrated with almost endless instances, including in one way or another the entire conceptual content of Modern ideologism. Some additional examples were mentioned earlier, among them: empirical/normative, analytic/synthetic, rational/rhetorical, and means/ends. Still other examples include: mental/physical, idealistic/realistic, centralized/decentralized, and political/economic. It is telling that ideologism's main defense against the complaints registered here is an attempt to distinguish stringently (and rationalistically) between philosophy or science and ideology. But how much longer can political theorists rely on such implausible dichotomies, when ordinary academic and political experience often scoffs at them and even Western common sense can seldom credit them?

In turn, these considerations raise a larger, extra-conceptual question of content: how relevant to present politics and culture are the perspectives of Modern times, as embodied in Modern ideologies? There are at least two ways of addressing this question, shy of a full-fledged treatment of Postmodern politics and culture.

One is to reckon with the series of atrocities and disasters of the past century, noting their tendency to defy explanation or even decent description on the basis of liberalism and the like. The same goes for many of the triumphs of twentieth-century existence. Some political theorists have felt driven to new concepts in order to come to terms with these events and experiences; and a few have tried to follow through with the Postmodern, postideological theorizing about politics that this should call forth. But the common response of political theorists has been for advocates of one ideology to attempt to blame the troubles of our times on the foolishness and perversity of other ideologies. The rhetorical trap here is that, if I am at all right about the obsolescence of socialism and so on, there is plenty of such blame to go around. Clinging to a particular ideology and refusing to face its fundamental defects, any political theorists can occupy a lifetime in criticizing obvious (let alone subtle or even invented) problems with the positions of other ideologies.

The result has been a body of political theorizing directed ad nauseum to tacitly or explicitly socialist criticisms of liberalism, conservatism, and anarchism; tacitly or explicitly liberal criticisms of socialism, conservatism, and anarchism; etc.   And yet even now, some basically sensible people are calling for more political, cultural, economic, aesthetic, and other kinds of criticisms of one or more of these ideologies.[48] Why? Surely the burden of argument should be on them to show that this sort of project deserves high priority in current theorizing about politics. Undoubtedly we can still learn many things from "studies" of this sort; but what evidence is there that urgent lessons remain to be discovered through ideological critique? What credibility can we assign to the ideologies informing these critiques? And what hope have we that they can take us beyond the debilitating nexus of Modern ideologies, that they can produce categories better able to comprehend current practice, that they can prompt rhetorics more able to affect it?

The few who address these questions half-way adequately are mostly political theorists who have made some remarkable changes in what they identify as the one Modern ideology worth further development and enactment.   Thus the second standard move is to make whatever modifications seem desirable in the ideology with which one starts, in order to accommodate the phenomena of Postmodern politics. This is often accomplished with admirable grace and political acumen, up to a point.   And that point is the theorist's inability to give up the ethos and label of whatever ideology is judged best.

Accordingly, the "anarchisms" of Paul Goodman and Robert Paul Wolff would hardly be recognized by that label without their urgings.   The "conservatisms" of the neoconservatives have often been remarked to be suspiciously close to disillusioned "liberalisms."   The "socialisms" of Walzer, Stretton, and almost innumerable academics have travelled so far from what previous centuries might have

----

[48] See: Richard Ashcraft, "Political Theory and the Problem of Ideology," **Journal of Politics**, 42, 3, August, 1980, pp. 687-705. Also see this book's essays by Terence Ball and Paul F. Kress.

understood by that category as to run afoul of the truth-in-advertising laws. Perhaps aside from the neoconservatives, the defenders of "liberalism" have "developed" its doctrines so extensively in so many different directions that it retains little, if any, **ideological** coherence. The "Marxisms" of Michael Harrington, Jurgen Habermas, and so many others look like an attempt to merge liberalism and socialism. And so it goes: Modern ideologies can make just as little sense of current political theorizing worth careful study as they can make of current political realities worth active concern.

But after all, what's in a name? Why shouldn't Walzer identify his arguments with "socialism," Berger with "conservatism," Paul Feyerabend with "anarchism," etc.? Even though such labeling obscures the impressive agreements and important disagreements among such theorists, isn't there something to be said for continuity with the past? And wouldn't pointed mislabeling be part of the rhetorician's bag of tricks? Perhaps; yet I hope that we will ask what the point is here. For if Sophists are right that the two main points are to understand our conditions and affect them favorably, then even the best ideologists are failing the rhetorical test on both points. They limit unduly their abilities to face up to obvious facts and find out the nonobvious ones, thus failing the "theoretical" test. But they also limit unduly their abilities to affect the (American?) facts, thus failing the "political" test, too.

That there might be momentary tactical advantage in presenting one's political arguments in terms of "conservatism" could be true these days in the United States, although I doubt it. But what political advantage is there now (or will there be anytime ahead) in addressing other Americans as proponents of "socialism," "liberalism," or "anarchism?" I know there are several different defenses of these practices, but I have yet to come across one which does not revive millennarian (and destructive) dreams or defeatist (and destructive) nightmares. Can either of those be openly defended?

This political incapacity of Modern ideologies slides over into their formal obsolescence. As a specifically (and originally) Modern category, "ideology" designates a programmatic (and usually comprehensive) System of thought. It is a Science of (or as) Ideas. In other words, "ideology" is virtually defined in terms of Enlightenment rationalism. This is not some etymological fluke, for major exponents of every Modern ideology (perhaps excepting "conservatism") have insisted upon the (Truly) scientific basis of their visions and recommendations. "Conservatism" has been at a severe rhetorical disadvantage, of course, because when standards of argument are rationalist, then (in order to gain persuasive power) an antirationalist world view is apt to suffer rational recontruction, thereby becoming rationalist in its own way. Or, it is apt to seem backward-looking and unconvincing. This suggests that recent revivals of "conservatism" draw some strength from the revised rhetorical context of Postmodernity, in which rationalism is no longer de rigure.

Thus these Modern "sciences of society" (as many ideologies have regarded themselves) are fairly immediate ancestors of the Postmodern social sciences. Insofar as the latter receive blame for serving Postmodern problems more than solutions, the same charge is easily expanded to include Modern ideologies. Insofar as the social sciences receive credit for serving Postmodern solutions more than problems, we have to suspect that their achievements are tied to their presumed advances over Modern ideologies.

In any event, every Modern ideology is so intimately tied to twentieth-century troubles that the very form of Modern ideology may be faulted. To think, speak, write, or act ideologically is to reach for a systematic scheme to rationalize reality (or at least human beings). Yet we should know that this courts totalitarianism. Ideological politics are large-scale, both because ideological visions tend to be comprehensive (something I myself recommend, incidentally) and because ideological programs try to engineer highly specific plans of rationality into existence. Even the incrementalist examples contain such ambitions. Yet we should see that our Postmodern condition enjoins a more sober sense of scale and a more determined recognition of decent limits.

In short, there is a single style of thought, persuasion, and action extending in common across the divergent contents of Modern ideologies.[49] Moreover, this style is distinctive to ideologies, which are distinctive to the Modern age. (To try to fit the positions of Plato, Occam, or even Machiavelli into the confines of "ideology" in this sense is to invite frustration and confusion.) The contents appropriate to Postmodern beliefs and deeds are deeply at odds

----

[49] See: Dante Germino, **Beyond Ideology**, New York, Harper and Row, 1967; Glenn Tinder, **Tolerance**, Amherst, University of Massachusetts Press, 1980; Tinder, **Community**; John S. Nelson, "Ashcraft's Problem of Ideology," **Journal of Politics**, 42, 3, August, 1980, pp. 709-715.

with this ideological style. And therefore, current political theorists should stop trying to force new ideas, issues, and inquiries into a shape that can neither receive nor communicate them without changing them in subtle but significant ways.

Many other senses and uses of "ideology" are legitimate, of course, even in regard to lists like the one I have invoked here. Thus I can accept much that is urged nowadays under the rubrics of "ideology critique" and "theory of ideology." But the basic point ought not to be abandoned. Think of the many things that the category of existentialism can call to mind. Ideological style surely should not be one of them. Nor could the contents standard for Modern ideologies be well represented in any such specification. For existentialists have given us excellent examples of what I would mean by "nonideological" political theory. Some shy away from systematic assessments of the human condition; virtually all avoid projects for fully re-engineering political reality, let alone for "rationalizing" it. To treat existentialism as an ideology is typically to distort it. The same should be said of Sophism or any other rhetorical pattern recommended to Postmodern people.

This means that political theorists should give more attention to forms and genres of politics. In this respect, there is much greater choice than recent political theorists have presumed, just as the consequences of choice are much more profound than presumed. To recognize this is to raise the rhetorical consciousness of Postmodern political theory. And it is to open theorists to far better appreciation of colleagues working in forms normally neglected or suspected by social scientists especially, but even by academics at large. In the same way that rhetoricians of inquiry should prize the poems of Wallace Stevens or the chautauquas of Robert Pirsig, so rhetoricians of politics should esteem the novels of V. S. Naipaul and Gabriel Garcia Marquez or (my personal predeliction) the science fictions of Frank Herbert, Ursula Le Guin, and Samuel Delany.

Finally, this formal self-consciousness should shed a somewhat different light on recent debates about political theorizing. What have been presented exclusively as conflicts of method can, when recast as squabbles of style, be appreciated as partially (sometimes primarily) differences of genre.

Take the most obvious case of intellectual history. Some disparage it as merely the study of the political theories of others, failing to qualify as political theory on its own. And some criticize it for depending upon the political

positions of the intellectual historian, whose methods somehow never satisfy us that their products comprise the
objective past, merely described or explained rather than
constituted by the historian. Together, however, these two
complaints almost correct one another. Together, they
suggest that intellectual history can be one among many
possible genres of political theory.

The same sort of presentation could be made for genres like conceptual analysis, philosophy of political inquiry,
empirical or normative theory, and so on. Nor should we
neglect more obvious candidates at somewhat different levels
of genre: utopias, dystopias, ideologies, essays, research
reports, etc. Such forms are not mutually exclusive; they
can be combined. Moreover, new forms can be conceived.
When there is little sophistication about selection and use of
forms, then rhetorical errors run rampant, which is how
both criticisms of intellectual histories of political theory
can justifiably apply at once. These errors are no mere
errors of form, though, for as recent debates about intellectual history reveal: **errors of form are errors of content**. Thus the substantive political claims and commitments
of intellectual history have been damaged by lack of rhetorical knowledge and self-consciousness.

Let me be clear that identifying some categories as
forms or genres is not claiming that everything intended by
those categories should be regarded as a form or genre,
either in general or in any given case. Similarly, not all
political or theoretical categories should ever be so considered. One must look and see. The last thing the Rhetorician would want is a general reduction of "ideology" to
"mere genre."

Still, a large part of the point is that, although form
is not fully destiny, it remains very important rhetorically
(and hence politically). If nothing else, ideologism in political theory now produces all sorts of practical, political inc-
apacities. Fitting present-day points into foreign forms,
current ideologists are almost forced into jargons and other
styles (of language, action, strategy, and the like) that
guarantee political alienation and impotence. Aside from the
significant fact that labels like socialism, anarchism, and
marxism are themselves anathema to most Americans, how
can anyone expect to produce politically effective rhetorics
out of the academese we practice daily? Indeed, I wonder
how anyone could expect to produce even theoretically
potent rhetorics in ways recently relied upon. (And yes, I
know all too well that I offend this very principle. If nothing else, trying to improve rhetorically continues to teach
me about the immense minefield between most academics and

decent rhetorics.) In short, this quick survey of ideologism should serve to show that political theorists must attend more intelligently and imaginatively to their forms.

ACADEMISM

One chooses dialectics only when one has no other expedient. One knows that dialectics inspire mistrust, that they are not very convincing. Nothing is easier to expunge than the effect of a dialectician, as is proved by the experience of every speech-making assembly. Dialectics can be only a last-ditch weapon in the hands of those who have no other weapon left.

Friedrich
Nietzsche[50]

Through a variety of devices, recent political theorists have retreated to academia. This has been motivated in part by the professional desire to protect (rationalist) standards of inquiry and discourse from pollution by political and rhetorical influences. Brief examination of some modes of academism in recent political theory should make some of the rhetorical corrections needed by current theory easy to present. Four modes come to mind immediately in this connection, political theory as: history, science, interpretation, and philosophy. Each mode embodies distinctive aspects of the drift of political theory away from its properly rhetorical penetration into political practice.

HISTORY

There are at least two reasons that historical studies of politics and political theories past can make a key contribution to current political theory. On the one hand, there is the blatant presentism of political science particularly and

----

[50] Friedrich Nietzsche, **Twilight of the Idols** (with **The Anti-Christ**), R. J. Hollingdale, trans., Baltimore, Penguin Books, 1968, pp. 31-32.

the social sciences generally. For no good reasons (but plenty of obvious ones), political science since the Second World War has been dedicated to leaving behind both its own past and that of politics. Just about every style of political science has been guilty of such historiocide, including virtually every project in the "subfield" of theory (except, of course, intellectual history). These considerations suggest that academic theorizing about politics needs almost all the history it can handle. On the other hand, there is the hunger for history apparently characteristic of America particularly and rapidly changing cultures generally. And that takes somewhat more explaining.[51]

Our hunger for history is hardly antiquarian, except for the few who truly wish to lose themselves in the past. Even for them, the project is far more likely to be nostalgic than antiquarian. That is, it is more often interested in certain imaginative potentials of the past than the past per se. Nor is the common hunger for history satisfied by what Friedrich Nietzsche termed "critical history" (or what I might call "objectivist history"), which provides mostly arguments purported to describe and debunk the past. Instead, our hunger for history seeks some personal and public significance in the past. This may extend slightly beyond Nietzsche's notion of "monumental history," but that category is close enough to serve as a general summary of the sort of history sought.[52]

----

[51] See: Allan Megill, "Foucault, Structuralism, and the Ends of History," **Journal of Modern History**, 51, 3, September, 1979, pp. 451-503, on pp. 500-503; Anthony Brandt, "A Short Natural History of Nostalgia," **Atlantic**, 242, 6, December, 1978, pp. 58-63; John Lukacs, "The Future of Historical Thinking," Salmagundi, 30, Summer, 1975, pp. 93-106; John Lukacs, "Professional History as Myth," **Salmagundi**, 37, Spring, 1977, pp. 155-160; Lukacs, "Obsolete Historians," **Harper's**, 261, 1566, November, 1980, pp. 80-84; George Steiner, "The Cleric of Treason," **New Yorker**, 56, 42, December 8, 1980, pp. 158-195, on pp. 183-185; Theodore Roszak, "In Search of the Miraculous," **Harper's**, 262, 1568, January, 1981, pp. 54-62.

[52] See: Friedrich Nietzsche, **The Use and Abuse of History**, Adrian Collins, trans., Indianapolis, Bobbs-Merrill, revised edition, 1957, pp. 12-17; Judith N. Shklar, "Rethinking the Past," **Social Research**, 44, 1, Spring, 1977, pp. 80-90.

This hunger for history is discernible in a variety of phenomena. Genealogically and culturally, the search for "roots" is an expression of a hunger for personal and familial context. The explosion in popularity of museums, old styles and techniques of living (think of the **Foxfire** books), history book clubs, and "outdoor historical dramas" is testimony to strong drives to establish touch with the past. The preservation movement reflects attempts to build a temporally and culturally richer environment by retaining past buildings and other objects of (potential) public and personal significance. In the wake of the West, movements to institute programs in Women's Studies and Black Studies can be viewed as efforts to create and sustain new cultural traditions for and about people dispossessed of significant or detailed pasts. (In this sense, such programs stand in comprehensive opposition to most of the rest of university programs in the humanities and social sciences, virtually all of which express the Western tradition. To a lesser extent, university programs in African Studies, Asian Studies, and the like can embody the same project.) The recitation of similar projects could continue indefinitely.[53]

Some of the reasons behind this hunger for history are also worth summarizing here. Western rationalism has little place for the past, except as raw material to be

----

[53] The usual reason cited for opposing such programs is their plainly political import. Yet most disciplines in the humanities and social sciences that are institutionalized today in American universities have almost equally, if differently, political origins. That these sources were quickly forgotten is testimony to the peculiar politics of Western objectivism in its attempt to enforce formal separations of thought from action, fact from value, and so forth. Beyond this, though, academics imbued with Western categories and calculi often sense, albeit vaguely, that Women's Studies, Black Studies, and the like can constitute a radical challenge to scholarly subordination of rhetoric to dialectic. Such projects illustrate ways in which the West has generated some of its own most fundamental, if not yet fully effective, criticisms and counter-traditions. Somewhat sadly, they also show repeatedly how counter-Western movements are betrayed by insistence on developing them within Western concepts and institutions. For example, I take this mistake to trouble: Charlotte Bunch, ed., **Building Feminist Theory**, New York, Longman, 1981. Somewhat more sensitive to deep differences between current feminism

rationalized and as a source of tools to spread such rationalization. For Western culture, the questions have always been about the uses of the past: whether there are any; and if so, what they are? But one may as well ask about the uses of the truth or the uses of identity (personal, institutional, moral, political, or whatever). To treat these only as instruments is to misunderstand and thus misuse them. Accommodating not only such instrumentalization of history, but also Modern and Postmodern accelerations of technical and cultural change, has often demanded an extreme and warping flexibility. Other times, it has meant an equally severe and dehumanizing routinization. Both conditions generate a craving for some sense of significance, some strategy and mode of connection to one's deeper self and to others.

Much popular culture not only fails to fulfill these desires, but actually aggravates them. The dominant inclination of American mass media is disconnection, rather than connection. Thus it can be argued that television is the context of no-context, seeking significance only in the image of the moment. Or it can be claimed that popular reading (e.g., murder mysteries, gothic romances, fantasies, science fictions) offer pseudocontexts of escape. No doubt at least some of these indictments distort more than they report. But even so, is there much doubt that the turn to history should be explained in important part by what it has to offer that these other resources do not?[54]

Perhaps the crucial contribution of history is an encounter with what is other and objective, even within oneself. Without confronting what is alien, we cannot learn

----

and traditional Western commitments are: Elshtain, **Public Man, Private Woman**; Susan Moller Okin, **Women in Western Political Thought**, Princeton, NJ, Princeton University Press, 1979. Notice that none of my co-contributors to this volume seems to recognize in any way that feminism, nationalism, environmentalism, or any of the other movements with anti- or non-Western impulses pose significant difficulties for political theory as a primarily Western project and phenomenon. Is this a sign of complacency or cunning?

[54] See: Ursula K. Le Guin, "Escape Routes," in **The Language of the Night**, Susan Wood, ed., New York, Putnam's, 1979, pp. 201-206; George W. S. Trow, Jr., "The Decline of Adulthood: Within the Context of No-Context," **New Yorker**, 56, 39, November 17, 1980, pp. 63-171.

and improve. The cognitive or emotional estrangement possible in meeting projections of ourselves is unduly limited,
although still valuable. Even for self-discovery, let alone
for the greater project of self-development, ability to face
the other is essential. Sometimes, the other turns out to
be reflected in the self; and that discovery might not be
made without the aid of an objective association. Sometimes, the other turns out to be fully foreign; and that
discovery both clarifies personal limits or identities and
allows us to develop true worlds.

More than a few recent attempts have been made to
invent traditions and histories for those dispossessed of
pasts.[55] By comparison with historiographical efforts to
compose and present the past, merely fictional endeavors
suffer the disadvantage of deficient extension beyond ourselves as we know them. Sheerly fictional evocations of
context are typically too idiosyncratic to satisfy our craving
for connections to the reality of others. And that is
because of the deeper disadvantage of insufficient objectivity. In other words, what we prize and hunger for in history is a sense of context, a sense of contact with what we
have not created and cannot alter, and yet which has
helped to create us. When it is said that the past is our
present, this is part of what is meant. And this is how
history can help us to know both ourselves and others.
(In these respects, significantly, myth is on the side of
history far more than fiction.)

In times of transition, the hunger for history, context, and tradition is easy to understand. But what about
the acute awareness that such times (at least, our times)
tend to have of the constitution of the past by people in
the present? If we yearn for patterns to tie present to
past because we need contact with what creates us (as well
as what we create), then how can patterns we compose meet
that longing? Retrospective construction of traditions and
histories implies not only their pluralism, but also their
perspectivism. Can that satisfy our need for a sense of
objective context?

One answer is simply that the alternative is either
ignorance of the past or ignorance of our rhetorical presentation of it. Retrospective construction of traditions and
histories is not identical with creation of "pasts" utterly out
of nothing (except ourselves). This is why John Gunnell

----

[55] See: Sally Helgesen, "Instant Tradition," **Harper's**, 262,
1568, January, 1981, pp. 81-82.

and Larry Spence can argue effectively against Leo
Strauss, Sheldon Wolin, and so many others that there has
been no "Western tradition of political theory" in the sense
of a continuing debate among academics addressing basically
common questions and one another through aspiring to write
"classics."[56] It is not hard to tell that Aristotle, Augustine, Machiavelli, Rousseau, and company had little, if anything, in the way of such self-conceptions or intentions.
In fact, the rhetorician can claim this as one more reason to
attend historically to questions of intent, context, audience,
strategy, and so on. Moreover, the rhetorician is able to
portray many of the daily activities and textual specifics of
"the past greats of political theory" precisely according to
his principles of praxis, genre, science, and so forth.
        Why, then, would I have written repeatedly of "the
Western tradition," since this implies that some of its more
distinguished members are part of a Sophistic tradition, if
indeed there is any ground for parsing the past into traditions at all? What separates the Western tradition from its
Sophistic counter-tradition is primarily the set of ambitions
and self-conceptions which I have summarized in terms of
rationalism. If the Sophists are right on this point, then,
as I explained before, members of the Western tradition are
(despite themselves) bound to be rhetorical (rather than
"Rational" in special Western senses). And this signals a
second, more subtle reason that retrospective construction
of traditions can satisfy a hunger for objective history.
        The Rhetorical tradition has been exquisitely sensitive
to "the social construction of reality."[57] Sophists, especially, rely on a variety of distinctions designed to explain
that objectivity need not (and cannot) be attained through
objectivism. Even so, they recognize that there is little
advantage in substituting a dichotomy between objectivity
and objectivism for the Western dichotomy between subjectivity and objectivity, which is the 'ground of objectivism.
Sophists seek instead an enterprise capable of expressing

----

[56] See: Gunnell, **Political Theory**; Larry Spence, "Political
Theory as a Vacation," **Polity**, 12, 4, Summer, 1980, pp.
697-710.

[57] See: Peter L. Berger and Thomas Luckmann, **The Social
Construction of Reality**, Garden City, NY, Doubleday, 1966;
W. Lance Bennett and Martha S. Feldman, **Reconstructing
Reality in the Courtroom**, New Brunswick, NJ, Rutgers
University Press, 1981.

how we question and constitute the past, even as it creates and consternates us. Hence they turn instead to overtly interpretive historiography, which professional historians denounce as either merely popularized or sheerly speculative history.

The latter is disparaged by historians and philosophers alike as "speculative philosophy of history." ("Critical philosophy of history," that branch of analytical philosophy concerned with the epistemology of historiography, is prized by philosophers and ignored by historians.) Rhetorically, this reeks of objectivism. As Hayden White and others have shown, the distinction between historiography and philosophy of history (either "critical" or "speculative") is more a distinction of genre than of method, epistemology, or even substance.[58] Insofar as "speculative philosophers of history" speak for the meaning of history, then no historian can avoid being one almost all the time (and vice versa). Albeit in a difference sense, much the same could be said of distinctions between popular and professional historiography. Insofar as "popular historians" strive to manifest the significances of history in strikingly public or personal terms, then few historians produce important work without being at once popular and professional in their standards.

Protected by rhetorical principles, we can seek the histories we need. Dedicated to drawing out meanings for our lives generally and our politics particularly, these histories are highly theoretical, no matter how tacitly and unself-consciously so. The "New Historians of Political Thought" often appear to add to the objectivist pull away from speculative philosophy of history. But a Sophistic correction of current political theory would push toward that project. For we need that great meeting ground of theory and history in order to grow understandings adequate to our hunger for history.

SCIENCE

This consideration of philosophy of history as a rhetorical bridge between political theory and practice turns easily into a treatment of rhetorical ties between political science and policy. In Rhetorical critique, Modern science comes out as covertly (but no less determinedly)

----

[58] See: White, **Metahistory**, pp. 426-434.

technological.   The Modern dichotomy between science and
technology is shown to celebrate small differences at the
expense of large commonalities, and thus science is seen to
strive for effective intervention into reality rather than
passive comprehension of it.

Nonetheless,   the   rhetoric   of   Modern   science   is
accepted uncritically by many people and enterprises, political science among them.   Out of objectivism (as well as a
more admirable humility), most political scientists (including
self-professed "theorists") stay away from direct, self-conscious connection between their academic endeavors and
their political efforts (if any).   This projects a wall
between political science and political policy.   Paradoxically,
it is supported in part by a diffuse and simplistic democra-
tism, which pretends to reserve political inferences to the
people and their elected officials.   It is further sanctified
by the theoretical ambition of political scientists, who presume that applications of theory can and should be strictly
separate from theorizing itself.

A more complete presentation of the Rhetorical tradition would have to consider its responses to the democratist
defense of this dichotomy between political science and political decision.   Here, however, a consideration of the bifurcation between theoretician and politician should suffice.
The Rhetorical tradition disputes this simple split by insisting that both political theory and political decision (policy-
making) are political argument: that is, political rhetoric in
some of the most obvious senses.   And this holds no matter
how scientific the political theory.

Epistemological efforts to discredit objectivism have
generated a rhetorical conception of theories in science (and
other enterprises).   Theories are neither sacks of independent generalizations about "empirical reality" nor "deductive
nexes" of definitions, axioms, laws, theorems, corollaries,
and so on.   If we must picture them (and picturing is a
time-honored rhetorical strategm in the West), then "theories" are not walls being built or pyramids being tested.
Instead, they are webs of arguments, strung together into
wholes that are testable and coherent.   Theories are
always arguable and open to change, always striving to
make good sense of something, yet neither necessarily nor
fully deductive.   Every theory either lays out its own language or depends upon that of another theory, yet every
theory is committed to some communication across such language barriers.   The symbols and images intrinsic to language and argument are irremovable from theories.   In

sum, theories are (living) bodies of argument.[59]

Presumably, then, political theories are webs of political argument. Thus political theorists are political arguers: that is, political rhetoricians. Does anyone dispute that politicians are political rhetoricians? And does this mean that there are no significant differences between political theorists and politicians, between political theory and politics? No, there are many differences in principle and (perhaps unfortunately) somewhat more in fact. But Sophists would insist that those differences do not have to do with whether political theorists should embrace (or could avoid if they wanted to) the address of current policy issues in the political realm. Certainly, there are differences in genre and strategy, as well as in purpose, in their respective considerations of political affairs. Still, both theoretician and politician are held to rhetorical standards of truth; and although in somewhat different respects, both do poorly when this is forgotten.

There are too many possibilities of involvement in policy decisions to try to discuss all the theorist's options here. It is significant that recent political science has (rather incoherently) leaned ever further into the realm of public policy. And the same is true of recent political philosophy, as is evident in such journals as **The Hastings Center Report, Philosophy and Public Affairs, Social Theory and Practice,** and **Ethics.** With more than a few possibilities under active exploration these days, some substantial changes in old academic reserves could be forthcoming.

Probably the single most important point about political scientists and philosophers working on public-policy issues, though, is that they are tempted to forget their real rhetorical footing. Clinging to rationalist standards, little can be said within and about politics that makes good sense.[60] Standing by rationalist shibboleths, little can be done within and about politics that avoids disaster. When

----

[59] See: Paul F. Kress, "The Web and the Tree: Metaphors of Reason and Value," **Midwest Journal of Political Science**, 13, 3, August, 1969, pp. 395-414; John S. Nelson, "The Ideological Connection: Or, Smuggling in the Goods, I-II," **Theory and Society**, 4, 3-4, Fall-Winter, 1977, pp. 421-448, 573-590. Also see the Panning essay in this collection.

[60] See the essays by Ira L. Strauber and Michael Walzer in this collection.

political scientists start offering "statistical demonstrations" that some policy or another has succeeded or failed, reasoned arguments have a way of being the farthest things from their minds. More bureaucratic dictates of that kind, no democracy needs. And when political philosophers begin handing down declarations of rights from on high, disingenuous dialectics have a way of suphocating any real reasoning.

Champions of "the scientific study of politics" tend to portray "traditional" political theory as either radically limited or deeply defective in argument. As practitioners of the humanities (instead of the social sciences), political theorists are credited at most with strictly normative, analytical, and historical arguments: refining values, concepts, and interpretations (of the past). More often, political theorists are dismissed as mere imaginers or sheer speculators: failing utterly to produce decent evidence for their claims. The (sometimes) covert contempt of Political Scientists for "traditional" political theory even extends to lumping it with what their realism leads them to assess as the dreary idealism or corrupt utterance of politicians, who see and say out of self- rather than scientific-interest. In any event, the field of political theory is said to be "unscientific" precisely because it does not now and perhaps cannot ever achieve sound specifications and arguments for its "empirical" claims about present and future politics.

This accusation is strange enough for its source, since twentieth-century attempts at Political Science tend to slight political argumentation in favor of frame-working, method-making, and fact-finding. Only a skilled avoidance of substantive argument could achieve the major mismatches of data to hypotheses suffered uncritically by many recent political scientists. Moreover, such scientifically crucial steps as selecting problems, choosing among statistics, assessing models for fit, and interpreting results rely primarily upon the same dynamics of informal inference derisively attributed to humanities-style "theorists." In other words, "political sensibility," "background knowledge," "immersion in the issue," "feel for the subject," and "capacity to project into alien situations" are the sorts of things that allow understanding of the more obviously "objective" data of political scientists. Without this political understanding, argumentative development of data into evidence is impossible in any straightforward, let alone systematic, fashion.

By no means does this discount the kinds of data to which political scientists are now prone to appeal. On the contrary, "traditional" political theorists can often be faulted for failing to take such data into account when making their arguments. Nonetheless, "objectivist" data can seldom stand alone in support of claims about significant political phenomena or choices. Nor could anyone clearly conscious of the rhetorical necessity of argument to inquiry long neglect "the data of the humanities" when marshaling evidence for important political contentions.

Yet for the motley field of political theory, the truly troubling thing is that "traditional" theorists now tend to accept their dubious distinction as unscientific students of politics, instead of insisting on their proper argumentative credentials and dedication. If there were any intellectual principle expressed in the largely social and political splits between political theory and the rest of political science, it would involve a difference over preferred kinds of evidence (and hence over methods for generating, evaluating, and using it). I say "preferred" because, even though there can be no general reason for elevating one kind of evidence over another regardless of context, there is room for different styles of inquiry and persuasion, with each style emphasizing special sorts of data and characteristic strategies of inference. Most projects in the field of political theory are "unscientific" when compared with projects in other fields of political science only if "science" is thus a matter of style.

Or, to put the point in still another way, the difference is not nearly so much over whether as it is over how to be "rigorous," "empirical," or (in sum) "scientific." Good theories of politics can no more manage without the styles of data and argument typical of "traditional" political theory than without the forms of evidence and persuasion dominant in "behavioral" and "postbehavioral" political science. In this way, to treat political theory as political rhetoric is to undermine the standard split between the social sciences and the humanities. Historically, it is to treat the social sciences as sets of projects in the humanities.

Similarly, to regard political theory as political rhetoric is to cut across the supposed separation of academia from action. It is to insist that no academic abode for political scientists and philosophers can ever remove them thoroughly from politics. According to the Rhetorical tradition, all argumentation and inquiry is latently or prospectively "political" in some potentially important respect, although the precise sense may vary from one circumstance to the next. On one side, this means that political theorists should not shy away from their own political commitments. On another, it suggests that political theorists can learn much of general import for politics by examining the politics within and around them everyday in academic institutions and inquiries, family affairs, and other social situations.

I suspect that the academic endeavor most satisfactory from the Sophistic standpoint is best termed "political education."[61] Later in this book, I say more about political education. For the moment, then, let me make only two points of particular importance to the Rhetorical tradition.

If political theorists were to seek political education more than academic prestige, they would work hard to address audiences beyond their own disciplines. One notable implication of this would be more attention to publication in places outside the standard scholarly outlets. Another would be more recognition for theorists who neither speak nor write from the usual university or college campus.[62] And if pursuing political education as Postmodern Sophists, political theorists would combine expert advice to elites with political counsel to their constituencies. Partly, this could push political theorists toward more direct contributions to public policy-making; but it could also incline them toward more active opposition to some publics and policies.

Similarly, this could spur political theorists to better respect for their most obvious, least prestigious, yet best practiced project of political education: introducing children and adults to political action. Taking political education truly seriously would entail that political theorists better exploit their opportunities (and acquit their responsibilities) close to home, recognizing a certain superiority of classroom instruction over scholarly publication as an arena for arete. Thus would the project of political education turn theorists more emphatically toward education in and about political affairs: learning to teach and teaching to learn.

----

[61] See: Joseph Tussman, **Obligation and the Body Politic,** New York, Oxford University Press, 1960; Tussman, **Government and the Mind,** New York, Oxford University Press, 1977; Michael Oakeshott, **Rationalism and Politics,** New York, Basic Books, 1962; Norman Jacobson, "Political Science and Political Education," **American Political Science Review,** 57, 3, September, 1963, pp. 561-569.

[62] On both implications, see this book's essays by Paul F. Kress and Robert Booth Fowler.

INTERPRETATION

In recent political theory, political interpretation has usually been difficult to distinguish from political history. Typically, these projects are treated as though they were necessarily the same. This is symptomatic of our confused conception and conduct of both enterprises. To be sure, substantial interdependence, not to say intersection, is inevitable and desirable between interpretation and history of politics. Yet we should no more collapse or conflate these endeavors than other projects of political theory. (All are interrelated and partly overlapping, if only by virtue of sharing the field as a whole.)

Political interpretation should be the project of seeing and saying what occurs politically so as to affect favorably the perceptions and actions of others (as well as oneself). That is, political interpretation should be the single project of academic political theory which most directly contacts political practice. In a few capable hands, of course, it still is. By various devices and from diverse viewpoints, political interpretation continues to be practiced with distinction by such "theorists" as Daniel Bell, James Fallows, Andrew Hacker, Irving Howe, Christopher Lasch, Max Lerner, Nathan Glazer, Thomas Schelling, Michael Walzer, George Will, Garry Wills, James Q. Wilson, and Sheldon Wolin.

One or two of these names may seem a little far afield, which is why I indcate that my use above of "theorists" may be thought somewhat unconventional. Were I to list as well such people as Marshall Frady, Jeff Greenfield, Meg Greenfield, Charles Peters, and Roger Starr, then some would insist on changing the category from "political theory" to "journalism," an epithet evidently more dismissive in their ears than mine. (These days, dare political theorists feel superior to any other profession, let alone ones which engage actual politics more fully, if less critically, than our own?)

Stubbornly, then, I maintain that such people and their efforts at political interpretation are to be prized parts of political theory past, present, and (we may hope) future. Thus I recommend such academically questionable (or in some cases, uncouth) publications as **The Atlantic Monthly, Democracy, Dissent, Harper's, The Nation, The New Republic, The New York Review of Books, The New Yorker, The Progressive, The Public Interest, The Washington Monthly,** and **Working Papers.** (I cannot bring myself to count **The American Spectator,** though others might.) These purveyors of political interpretation produce useful material for almost every kind of undergraduate instruction in political theory, perhaps save historical surveys of "the great tradition." On balance, these are more ample sources of good texts for undergraduate teaching than even the best "professional" journals of political theory.

Furthermore, that should tell us something about the drift of our academic field. Like many other political Theorists, I have argued for years that the gigantic disjunction of materials and topics between undergraduate and graduate education in political Science should show its practitioners that they are turning too far away from pointedly political issues and events. Can practitioners of political Theory infer otherwise of themselves?

The objects proper to political commentary include not just "traditional" political theories but political writings and activities generally. In too much recent political theory as political interpretation, commentary on "classic works" in political theory crowds out other objects.[63] The "New History of Political Thought" may restore attention to works and writers of less individual importance and familiarity. (Still, this school tends to treat them as linguistic and historical contexts for the classics, rather than as objects of commentary in their own right or in pursuit of our own politics.)

By all odds, though, academic political theory has tried least and failed most at commentary on current politics and culture. Few academics attempt it, few of their attempts succeed, and few professional journals publish even the successes. For reasons easy to extrapolate from this essay, such practical commentary is discouraged and disrupted by recent rationalism, ideologism, and ironism. I suspect that to get past these inhibitions is to cast off the academism which keeps political interpretation turned toward the same small set of dated actors and texts.

In a strict sense, political commentary is our attempt "to come to terms" with politics. Thus interpretation of classics is neither all nor perhaps most of what should be counted and conducted as political commentary. And ironically, insofar as commentary on classics becomes a mode of

----

[63] For a stirring call to political commentary, but one still reluctant to reach past the classics, see: Deborah Baumgold, "Political Commentary on the History of Political Theory," **American Political Science Review**, 75, 4, December, 1981, pp. 928-940.

commentary on current politics, it is done better on the model of that master rhetorician Machiavelli than of those more recent movements in hermeneutics. As political preparation and participation, the point of commentary is to develop (partly through a kind of vicarious experience) those capacities of judgment, motivation, and imagination which Machiavelli called **virtu**. Social scientists seldom overcome their "craving for generality" sufficiently to approach political practice skillfully through political commentary. Similarly, hermeneuticists scarcely raise their gaze from the text enough to engage political practice directly through political commentary. To be sure, untoward textuality is no more inherent in hermeneutics than untoward generality is necessary in social science. (Otherwise, current academic conditions could hardly allow much hope for turning political commentary more toward political practice.)

If and when political interpretation better treats political practice, a signal result should be more stress on political style. Many who comment regularly on contemporary politics soon develop distinctive styles of perception and expression. Indeed, commentators are more readily identifiable by style than by any other feature of their interpretations of politics. Knowing this, some commentators have described themselves as striving first and foremost for a special style of thinking and writing.

As literary critics appreciate, these styles are not only favorite standards of judgment and evaluation, not just distinctive types of rhetorical tropes and tricks of the trade, not merely identifying features of interest and imagination, not simply special sets of political questions and positions, not even personal predelictions of inference and extrapolation. Styles of political interpretation are all these; nonetheless, such styles more subtle and pervasive than any short, discrete selection of analytical elements can convey. Style is the main political mark of commentators, amounting to their distinctive stamps on our languages, perspectives, paradigms, and practices.

If political interpretation is closer than other academic projects of political theory to political practice, and if style is especially central to political interpretation, then we might infer that style is especially important in politics per se. Perhaps it is more a comment on the peculiar pluralisms of our times than on politics generally, but this inference is hard to resist.[64] At a minimum, it seems to follow for the historical moment that political theory as political interpretation should concentrate on studying politics as style and style as politics.

Style is apt for appreciating the diffuse (but potent) packaging of units like languages, perspectives, paradigms, and practices. Increasingly, these are the analytical tools and cultural realities upon which theorists rely in interpreting political acts, texts, and institutions.[65] We can no longer find in standard ideologies, nor even in the sheer form of ideology, enough of the general shapes of our own politics to account for evident cleavages, possible alliances, or obvious occurrences. Seeing politics as style encourages us to recognize how styles of speech, action, and life sometimes constitute and often contribute to arrays of agreements, disagreements, and events which configure our political affairs.

In addition, by reorienting attention to questions of political form, criticisms of ideologism converge with criticisms of means/ends dichotomies. For once we refuse to relegate means to merely instrumental goods, we can recognize that means are not empty forms for achieving contents in the end. In turn, we can celebrate participation and performance as meaningful contents of our action and potential goods in themselves. Few may want to go as far as Hannah Arendt, who found the sole essence of politics in performance, in styles of action (rather than and to the exclusion of its effects).[66] Yet Sophists, especially, do want to make more room for virtues of performance than has been allowed by Western instrumentalisms. What we need,

----

[64] See: Nelson, "Tropal History and the Social Sciences," p. 85.

[65] See: John Danford, **Wittgenstein and Political Philosophy**, Chicago, University of Chicago Press, 1978, pp. 1-120; MacIntyre, **After Virtue**, pp. 6-34, 76-102; Hanna Fenichel Pitkin, **Wittgenstein and Justice**, Berkeley, University of California Press, 1972, pp. 140-168; Tracy B. Strong, **Friedrich Nietzsche and the Politics of Transformation**, Berkeley, University of California Press, 1975, pp. 53-86.

[66] See: John S. Nelson, "Politics and Truth: Arendt's Problematic," **American Journal of Political Science**, 22, 2, May, 1978, pp. 270-301, on pp. 287-292.

then, is a way of resisting reductions of politics to pure performance, while still celebrating participation and performance for their considerable worth. Seeing how politics is style encourages us to appreciate that performance is a crucial component of politics.

Similarly, seeing how style is politics encourages us to recognize the importance in politics of other substantive aspects of action: conditions, aims, instruments, effects, etc. As politics, style is both an arena and an object of political struggle or (more broadly) action. When no longer regarded as mere ornamentation, style matters politically. It ceases to be sheer form, utterly alien and indifferent to contents. It becomes part of the substance of politics, blending with other components of action. All these (analytical) aspects of action limit, relate, and lead to one another so intimately and completely that specifically political splits among them can only be posed contextually and pragmatically. Accordingly, styles of action can be characterized only along with their conditions, aims, instruments, effects, and the like. That is, actions can be performed only with conditions, aims, instruments, effects, and so on. To treat style as politics is to emphasize that these "substantive" concerns enter into style and hence performance. It is to show that not even defining politics as action as performance can keep out the concerns of "society" and "economy" which Arendt sought to confine to subpolitical activities of "making" and "labor." (This is not to deny Arendt ample justification and credit for her arguments, considering their contextual, pragmatic, rhetorical force.)

In sum, political commentary should attend to political actions, actors, and institutions, as well as texts. Especially by emphasizing political style, political interpretation should reach around and through classic texts into current politics. Thereby, it can overcome at least one aspect of the academism which has alienated political theory from politics and can become in its own right an important part of political practice.

PHILOSOPHY

For more than a century, (Anglo-American) philosophy has made itself the main academic base of rationalism. This was accomplished through the virtual self-definition of philosophy as rationalist efforts to find foundations for knowledge and to fathom operations of language. As a result, some assumed that philosophy could have nothing to do with (non- or even ir-rational) politics. Although conceding that there could be no philosophy of politics, others presumed that any science of politics must depend on philosophy for methodology and conceptual clarity.

These positions led many political theorists to turn away from philosophy toward history, science, and interpretation (as just discussed). But others were spurred into philosophy: either to bring back methods of inquiry and conceptual clarification, to criticize some of those methods and meanings in favor of others, to dispute the very separation of philosophy from politics, or even to escape the convolutions and uncertainties of politics. Almost despite itself, academist philosophy has drawn in an impressive portion of self-professed political theorists.

As indicated by my criticisms of rationalism, foundational and linguistic philosophy has been, on balance, a bad home for political theory. Academist philosophy alienates political theory from political practice by replacing political with philosophical languages, styles, tasks, actors, actions, and institutions. It imposes abstract criteria of philosophers on concrete decisions for political scientists. It even substitutes analytical stipulations for historical investigations of political realities. These complaints have been made often and vehemently enough elsewhere not to require further rehearsal here.[67]

But this is not to say that philosophical studies of knowledge and language have nothing to contribute to political studies. On the contrary, these two topics converge on a singularly significant focus for political theory: the symbol. Again, this is something I discuss in my later essay on political education; so again, I settle here for a few points of interest in regard to the Rhetorical tradition.

Rationalism tends to treat symbols as mere signs, sloughing off the rhetorical richness of one-to-many and many-to-many relationships in favor of strict and simple one-to-one mappings. Gradually, academist philosophy itself has helped to show how symbols cannot be supplanted by signs, which are fated to fail in comprehending human affairs. Hence we should hardly be surprised to find that emphasis on the symbol is becoming increasingly common in philosophical epistemology and linguistics, so that they may be starting to slide past rationalism toward more generally and self-consciously rhetorical stances. Of course, the need to fathom the full implications and possibilities of

----

[67] This claim is ably argued by John Gunnell in his essay for this book.

symbolism has long been a central tenet and impetus of the Sophistic tradition.

Perhaps the main project promoted by proper appreciation of symbols should be generation of adequately rhetorical or political epistemologies. The need for rhetorically and politically sophisticated epistemologies is not confined to political inquiry, but political theorists can make a special contribution to their conception and practice. Such Sophistic epistemology aims at avoiding the doomed choice of Modern, philosophical theories of knowledge: between foundationalism (on the one side) and skepticism or relativism (on the other side).

These days, the defects of foundationalism in epistemology are being demonstrated almost everywhere: in philosophy by Stanley Cavell and Richard Rorty, in hermeneutics by Hans-Georg Gadamer and Paul Ricoeur, in rhetoric by too many to mention individually, and in political theory by John Gunnell and Paul Kress.[68] There can be no supracontextual, transcendental criteria of knowledge or methods of inquiry. To seek them is to conjure some single, neutral, transparent set of signs for observation or metatheory. But all we can have, and what we actually need, are the shifting, purposeful, partly opaque strata of symbols for our actual multitude of meanings and uses.

To Sophists, transcendental epistemology is antipolitical. If achieved, its avowed singularity and neutrality would keep it from comprehending politics, which is just as irreducibly symbolical as other human affairs. Because it cannot be achieved, the principles claimed for it must always carry covert and sometimes unself-conscious contents, which discourage the scrutiny and choice important to intelligent and free politics. Since many of its main issues are predicated on false premises, it produces

----

[68] See: Cavell, **The Claim of Reason**, pp. 129-243; Rorty, **Philosophy and the Mirror of Nature**, pp. 315-394; Hans-Georg Gadamer, **Philosophical Hermeneutics**, David E. Linge, trans., Berkeley, University of California Press, 1976; Paul Ricoeur, **Interpretation Theory**, Fort Worth, Texas Christian University Press, 1976; Michael C. Leff, "In Search of Ariadne's Thread: A Review of Recent Literature on Rhetorical Theory," **Central States Speech Journal**, 29, 2, Summer, 1978, pp. 73-91; Gunnell, **Philosophy, Science, and Political Inquiry**, passim; Paul F. Kress, "Against Epistemology: Apostate Musings," **Journal of Politics**, 41, 2, May, 1979, pp. 526-542.

intractable pseudoproblems, which distract theorists from substantive issues of politics. Finally, due to its implicit vision of a world with basic controversies settled by philosophical fiat, foundational epistemology is a standing invitation to escape from politics altogether. Hence political epistemology is urgently needed, if only to defend the integrity of politics and political studies from the depredations of transcendental epistemology.

In many senses, the specters of skepticism and relativism are mere artifacts of foundational epistemology: two of the pseudoproblems which are substituted for issues of actual politics.[69] Still, there is at least one sense in which skepticism and relativism now pose real trouble for epistemology and politics. Without transcendental standards of knowledge, how are political actors and inquirers to judge politics? And most pointedly, how are they to criticize themselves? That this is a current, sometimes acute, issue for our politics is partly because foundational epistemology has been a real political force in our times. (Score one for political epistemology, since transcendentalists typically deny that epistemology involves politics in any way like this.) Other factors include the political importance of science and technology in Modern times and the degeneration of Modern ideologies already discussed under the heading of ideologism.[70] For the moment, though, such sources are less important than sheer recognition that there is trouble with skepticism and relativism.

The point is that politics and political theory now have pressing need of nonfoundational principles and practices of political inquiry. More specifically, politics and political theory are challenged to produce and apply imminent criteria of self-criticism. Figuring out how to do this is the defining task of rhetorical or political epistemology. To some extent, this is a matter of discerning how we have

----

[69] In addition to Richard Ashcraft's essay in this volume, see: Cavell, **The Claim of Reason**, pp. 129-243, 329-496; Rorty, **Philosophy and the Mirror of Nature**, pp. 306-311.

[70] For example, see: Jane Flax, "Why Epistemology Matters: A Reply to Kress," **Journal of Politics**, 43, 4, November, 1981, pp. 1006-1024; John Barth, "The Literature of Replenishment: Postmodernist Fiction," **Atlantic**, 245, 1, January, 1980, pp. 65-71; Annie Dillard, "Is Art All There Is?," **Harper's**, 261, 1563, August, 1980, pp. 61-66.

done this in the past.   After all, the very impossibility of transcendentalism implies that we have been relying all along on distorted or unacknowledged criteria of this kind. Studies of science by Wilfrid Sellars, Thomas Kuhn, and Paul Feyerabend seem to confirm such a conjecture.[71] To some extent, this is a matter of incorporating the lessons already generated in philosophy and history of science.   To them, add insights by sociologists of knowledge and science, principles of learning and communication conceived by cyberneticists and students of artificial intelligence, and accounts of why "rhetoric is epistemic" by rhetoricians (who else?).

To a large extent, however, this challenge remains to be met with the sophisticated political knowledge to which political theorists aspire.   Enough other work has been done to show that imminent standards of self-criticism are importantly political.   Now political theorists need to address the task of making epistemology more directly and overtly political.   The new epistemology needs to learn a lot about politics, but many of the lessons are likely to be new to political theory as well.   Its contributions should stretch from the politics of decision and organization to the politics of symbols, language, and communication: in short, the politics of rhetoric.[72] Accordingly, the Rhetorical project of political epistemology promises further insight into how political theory could and should be practiced as political rhetoric.

----

[71] See: Paul K. Feyerabend, **Science in a Free Society**, London, NLB, 1978; Thomas S. Kuhn, **The Essential Tension**, Chicago, University of Chicago Press, 1977; Wilfrid Sellars, **Science, Perception and Reality**, New York, Oxford University Press, 1963.

[72] See: David V. J. Bell, **Power, Influence and Authority**, New York, Oxford University Press, 1973; William E. Connolly, **The Terms of Political Discourse**, Lexington, MA, D. C. Heath, 1974; Claus Mueller, **The Politics of Communication**, New York, Oxford University Press, 1973.

IRONISM

> Instead of regretting the end of the great tra-
> dition or pretending that it is still alive or that
> something like it is just around the corner, one
> might just as well face up to the pluralism of
> political ideas that do not individually or
> together constitute a political philosophy.
>
> Judith
> Shklar[73]

How does, how should political theory face up to the
intellectual pluralism of our times?   The Rhetorical tradition
evoked earlier in this essay is predicated on a certain
desirability, even inevitability of intellectual pluralism.   The
whole book at hand is replete with evidence that we now
experience such pluralism, particularly where political
theory is concerned.   But what does it mean to face up to
our intellectual pluralism?   Should we simply see it as our
condition, fight it as our nemesis, or celebrate it as our
achievement?   Indeed, how is any of these stances actually
to be taken, in detail?   This is a major challenge for current political theory.
    Although there may be many acceptable responses to
this challenge, I am impressed with how seldom political
theorists recognize our intellectual pluralism, let alone take
some self-conscious stance toward it.   Few political theorists
explicitly deny its existence, but most simply ignore it,
implicitly doubting the necessity or propriety of some
resonse.   Rationalists tend to treat our intellectual pluralism
as a temporary condition of cooperative disagreement, on
the way to a Rational resolution of differences at some
future date.   Inclined to imagine away our intellectual pluralism in the long run, they fail to take it seriously in the
short run.   Ideologists sometimes pretend to accept intellectual pluralism, only to shoe-horn all ideas into either Right
and Left or Right and Wrong.   Through such ideological
reduction, our multiplicity of positions is transformed into a
dichotomy of the correct view (and its variants) versus the
corrupt (and erroneous) ones, which can be explained

----

[73] Judith N. Shklar, "Facing Up to Intellectual Pluralism,"
in David Spitz, ed., **Political Theory and Social Change**,
New York, Atherton Press, 1967, pp. 275-295, on p. 293.

(away) by the favored view. Academists retreat into a superficial celebration of intellectual pluralism as somehow synonymous with "academic freedom." This ready device keeps them from seeing how seriously our intellectual pluralism can conflict with conditions and missions previously thought important or even imperative for academia. Thus do these postures miscarry in current political theory. Perhaps they seem to face up to our intellectual pluralism, but actually they avoid its challenge instead.

In at least some important respects, these three avoidances fall into the family of "ironism."[74] Ironism is a suspicion of (almost) all commitments, unto absoluteness or absolution. It derives from conditions of highly motivated and accomplished ability to criticize options of (almost) all kinds. Such conditions are certainly encouraged by and may be virtually definitive of our intellectual pluralism, especially in the study of politics. (Considerations noted in connection with the recent resurgence of the Rhetorical tradition surely support this claim.)

The unconscious ironist backs into avoidance of intellectual and other commitments, mostly through fear of unpleasant controversies. (Still, the relatively pervasive critical acumen of the age plays a large part, by subjecting a wide variety of positions to severe doubt.) The conscious ironist adopts such avoidance as a set of tactics for dealing with a situation of great (intellectual) uncertainty, but fails to discern (let alone defend) the overall implications of this strategy. In relatively full recognition of these implications, the self-conscious ironist acts unceasingly to question, criticize, and avoid (almost) all convictions. Defended as last-ditch resistance to (intellectual) imperialism or oppression, self-conscious ironism is celebrated for its capacity to endure what are taken to be permanent threats to (intellectual) autonomy and responsibility. By contrast, the self-transcendent ironist seizes this strategy as the way to survive ironism and the transient conditions requiring it for a while. Yet even to the self-transcendent ironist, how ironism can climb beyond itself must remain unclear until it has done so.[75] (By analogy, are

----

[74] See: John S. Nelson, **Ironic Politics**, doctoral dissertation, Chapel Hill, University of North Carolina Department of Political Science, 1977, pp. 14-43 (on rationalism), 788-795 (on ideologism).

[75] See: **ibid.**, pp. 844-847.

there self-transcendent Rhetoricians?)

By this measure, many theorists who refuse to recognize our intellectual pluralism slip toward unconscious ironisms. And at least some who do try to face up to it lean toward the other three brands of ironism. This is especially true of the more outrageous Rhetoricians among us, since resistance to the Western tradition makes them aware of how hard sustained dissent can be and since acceptance of intellectual pluralism is easily detoured or reduced to celebration of intellectual play. Thus can unremitting criticism (often of self) become unrestricted indulgence (often of self).

As students of politics, our tastes and talents for ironism trace partly to lack of political interest, conviction, and involvement; and I come back to these factors in the next section. Otherwise, our penchant for ironism stems from an unreserved bent for "the culture of critical discourse."[76] For ironism, this is the intellectualist milieu par excellence. Significantly, ironism is shared across the divide between political Science and political Theory, precisely because of self-uncertainties produced through criticism of each camp by the other.

Conversation and observation reveal more than a few political Scientists suspended in ironism between old urges toward objectivism and recent recognition of the impossibility of that goal. One obvious dimension involves their reluctant acceptance of criticisms lodged against the previous generation's project of "value-free" or "value-neutral" political science. Of course, these criticisms were made mostly in order to move political scientists more self-consciously and -consistently into concrete political commitments. But whispered aspirations to some political science which would stay out of politics have not really been abandoned by many who mouth admissions that "value-freedom" is an impossible aim. As a result, some political Scientists now hold back from professional political commitments even more stringently than before. To make matters worse, accomplishing this appears to require not only that they stay far away from politics but also that they hedge commitments to their own (professional) work. From moment to moment, they really believe in what they are doing, and yet they really doubt it too much to defend (let alone assert)

----

[76] See: Alvin W. Gouldner, "The New Class Project, Parts I-II," **Theory and Society**, 6, 2-3, September-November, 1978, pp. 153-203, 343-389.

it. The self, not the work, is the object of their defense. But in an odd turn typical of ironism, the main mode of self-defense is anticipatory self-criticism so extreme that would-be critics will be too embarrassed to proceed.

Too many political Theorists adopt similar strategies with similar results. Under attack for failing to use approved methods and "empirical evidence," some political Theorists implicitly seek to placate their accusers by accepting the premises of attack. What are we to make of "defenses" which confine political Theory to mere normativeness, strict semantics, or sheer speculation? For these are the results of restricting political Theory to arguments bereft of sufficient "empirical" content or support to be put on a par with political Science. The political compass of such "political theory" includes only arguments about political values, concepts, and visions. To keep these arguments from being ill-supported or insignificant, some theorists then wander altogether away from politics toward projects of philosophy, biology, and the like. Yet we already know that such ventures into epistemology, meta-ethics, sociobiology, and so on have often (but not necessarily) turned meta- or even anti-political, producing "theories" which are scarcely "political" at all.

But as with political Science, many who talk this game for political Theory actually retain ambitions to address politics more directly, comprehensively, and convincingly than their official postures could imply. Such Theorists cannot quite believe ambitions to epic theory, public policymaking, conceptual legislation, and the like; but they cannot quite accept humiliations at the hands of empiricists, either. So they shuttle in ironism between endeavors with arrogant goals but inadequate tools and projects with modest aims yet adventurous means and implications. Thereby, they too attempt to domesticate our intellectual pluralism by corporatist tolerance of some differences and ironist retreat from even their real repercussions.

As a result, little professional commitment is left on either side of the great divide, save reminders to the beleaguered researcher of the life-style advantages of academia. But the price is high. Substantive standards are sacrificed, for how can people pretend to say that specific research is good, bad, mediocre, or otherwise? Between political studies and a resigned relativism stand little more than a shaky sense of professional self-worth, an ordinary impulse toward conservation of the status quo, and a practical knowledge of departmental politics. Backs turned and noses held, then, academic students of politics too often accept a limited intellectual pluralism, without really weighing substantive implications of the pluralism of political ideas in our times.   Do not criticize my work (face-to-face), and I shall not criticize yours, especially since we must coexist in the same department.   Through institutionalization, this pluralism has passed into modest departmental and disciplinary corporatisms.   In turn, these produce fields and methods which have little to do with actual inquiry in the past and present, let alone the pro- spective future.

POLYSCIENCE AND POLYTICS

There may be an important sense in which the open society and political theory are incompati- ble.

John
Gunnell[77]

How does, how should political theory face up to the political pluralism of our times?   This question identifies two distinct, but related, difficulties in deciding what political theory should be now.   One worry is that political theory is historically (even inherently) heroic and visionary, while the very virtues of present (or proper) politics leave little need and less room for such a venture.   How, then, can political theory face up to pluralism in politics?   Another worry is that political theory lacks any discrete subject matter, since politics is conventional.   Lacking any essence, boundaries, or set criteria for counting candidates in or out of "politics," claims to politics and kinds of politics can eas- ily multiply.   How, then, should political theory face up to pluralism of politics?

Political theorists are often tempted to define away our political pluralism.   But this misses its real challenge. To the extent that political theory now does face up to these two issues of political pluralism, too little is done to defend the choices made, which is to say that these ques- tions are skirted, not faced squarely.   Of course, this book is meant to shape up and add to such defenses as have been offered.   Still, that must be less by way of answering

---

[77] Gunnell, **Political Theory**, p. 160.

these questions than of posing them more cogently than before.

And I would say the same of the essay at hand. Were it to have a single basic point (as it does not), that would be the need for political theory to face up to our **political** pluralism. Exploring the Rhetorical tradition is meant as one move toward meeting that need. Ours is an ample pluralism of political theories, ranging from the Western to the Sophistic and then some. And ours is an odd pluralism of politics, sprawling across and beyond Modern ideologies. It combines the incremental and the revolutionary, the elitist and the participatory, the pedestrian and the heroic, the democratic and the oligarchic. In the face of our intertwined pluralisms, it may be neither wise nor possible to specify, in one precise way, what politics or even political theory should be now. But whatever the answers, we must learn to question our purposes and plans continually, even as we act upon them. So taught Socrates, the greatest Sophist. **Political theory is the art of political questioning, of others and of ourselves.** Let us, then, end in openness.

PART FIVE

HIATUS AND HISTORY

NIHILISM AND POLITICAL THEORY

Tracy B. Strong

I speak as a white male Westerner who is a political theorist.[1] Any political theorist with our history may, in reflecting upon that history, find that he is required to respond to it on two apparently separate and untouching planes. On the one hand, the political events of the century compel address to the general framework of what is called "Western Civilization." Fascism, certain aspects of what is called Stalinism, the rationalization of everyday life do not seem to me to be easily dismissable as aberrant dead ends. They are integral, if not necessary, developments of Western politics and culture. On the other hand, I am constantly faced with the reminders of the importance of moral and political judgments in the everyday minutiae of life. I seek in this essay to explore this disjuncture and to suggest a way of addressing it which does not simply repeat it.

The first demand, that of the world historical crisis, is succinctly summarized in a passage written by Hannah Arendt.

> We can no longer afford to take that which was good in the past and simply call it our heritage, to discard the bad and think of it as a dead load which by itself time will bury in oblivion. The subterranean stream of Western tradition has finally come to the surface and usurped the dignity of our tradition. This is the reality in which we live. And this is why all efforts to escape from the grimness of the present into nostalgia for a still intact past, or into the anticipated oblivion of a still better future, are vain.[2]

----

[1] I thank John Nelson for organizing the Shambaugh Conference on Political Theory, and I thank him and the other conference participants for their comments and criticisms. Not all of their objections and suggestions have been met to their satisfaction, I am sure, but nonetheless this essay has been improved by their advice.

These words concluded Arendt's 1951 book on **The Origins of Totalitarianism.** Its mood is Heideggerian, filled with consciousness that the Second World War signified a turn in human events and marked the end of a long era of human affairs. If, as Ezra Pound had written, men had died in the First World War for "an old bitch, gone in the teeth," the Second War had revealed that humans had achieved forms of social organization so total that human beings could commit the worst sorts of atrocities and not find themselves called to the bar of their consciences. Radical evil, as much an inheritance of our tradition as the goodness of intentions, had come to the surface; and it was increasingly difficult, Arendt felt, to find a natural common ground for moral virtue and human activity. Arendt's view of totalitarianism informed all of her subsequent work. It reflected a vision of human history as having come to an impasse. Though the experience of the Jews in the Second War was central for Arendt, the Holocaust was not alone in prompting her to write about the origins of a new form of politics. Equally important was the fact that the destruction of European Jewry had been made possible by this new form of politics and a new moral problem which it posed. For Arendt, the war had not been an aberration, but a possible genealogical result of dynamics inherent in the Western world. The war was an unavoidable sign that we must confront troubles for which our moral logic had only difficult solutions. Increasingly, all cases would be hard ones. [3]

Associated with this somewhat apocalyptic vision was an understanding that the modern age is not one in which governing and politics take place in a "normal" fashion. In criticism of a famous book of political science, Arendt herself once remarked that this may not be the time to ask "who governs?" If, in fact, the values on which humans had rested their activity in the past had now revealed themselves as flawed and dangerous ("the subterranean stream...has finally come to the surface"), then traditional

----

[2] Hannah Arendt, **The Origins of Totalitarianism,** New York, Harcourt Brace Jovanovich, fourth edition, 1973, p. 381.

[3] This is the central thrust of the last part of her book on Eichmann; see: Hannah Arendt, **Eichmann in Jerusalem,** New York, Viking Press, revised edition, 1974, especially pp. 272-279.

justifications for political choices must themselves be seen as flawed, ineffective, and ultimately as ideological rational- izations of self-serving positions.   And so, it would also not be a time for political theory, at least not as that had been understood, but rather for deeper, more ultimate inquiries.   Once more, Heidegger had proclaimed in **An Introduction to** Metaphysics, it was possible or even neces- sary to raise the question of Being.

One of the sources, then, for the attempts at writing political theory in this century has been consciousness that the human race stands at some kind of turning point in its development.   At least, this is so for the portion of human- ity which is white, Western, industrialized (and male?).   In writers such as Arendt and Heidegger, as well as in much of the continental tradition (which includes twentieth-cen- tury developments of Marxism), the sense of not knowing one's way about is very strong.   All questions here are big questions.   Ontology, rather than epistemology, is the queen of the sciences; we ask what it would mean to have meaning, rather than how it is possible.

Yet from another perspective, Arendt's vision and others like it seem overly dramatized and even dangerous. One wants to say: people still kill each other; people can still refrain from killing each other; humans are still capa- ble of moral reasoning and of the application of thought to action.   Every day a thousand major and minor injustices cross our paths, no matter who we are or where we sit.   It is possible to think coherently about these questions; it is possible to make coherent judgments about abortion, affir- mative action programs, racial discrimination, minimum wages, and hiring policies.   Do we not lose sight of all this, if we are to be concerned about the fate of Western Civilization and Platonic epistemology?   As such, we are faced with a changing set of **problems**.   Our moral integrity is always in need of repair and supervision; for we know at least when something is wrong, even if we do not know what The Good would be.

Those who would practice political theory thus seem to move in two directions.   We must admit that our moral (not to mention, physical) security is threatened when, as Orwell wrote, "highly civilized men are flying over my head, trying to kill me."[4] That a human being can carry

----

[4] George Orwell, "England, your England," in **A Collection of Essays by George Orwell**, Garden City, NY, Doubleday, 1954, pp. 256-283, on p. 256.

around all the cultural baggage that I do, share or espouse the same values that I do, and still find this almost no obstacle to trying to exterminate me threatens any claim that there is a relationship between what people know and what they do to each other. On the other hand, there is something wrong with bombing civilians as a matter of policy.

I do not think that this disjuncture is due solely or even primarily to insufficient or faulty moral vision. Not only the various experiments on obedience to authority, but also the facts of our century show that human beings cannot be counted on to act consistently on their moral intuition and training when in largely supervised environments.[5] This disjuncture cannot be accounted for by insufficient moral sensibility on the part of those who commit atrocities. We must face the fact that we do not now know what might prevent people from engaging in atrocities. After all, it has been known since Socrates that no one **purposely** does a **known** evil. Yet part of our past attraction to morality and practical moralizing in philosophy came from our persuasion that the good would always, **in the end**, win out.[6]

It is thus not without reason that we are wont to say that there is some kind of crisis, a sort of rupture in our moral epistemology, which has been unveiled by the events of the past century.[7] To a great degree, we have lost the faith that human understanding will, because of what it is, ultimately be able to come to an understanding of the world as we are now experiencing it. On the other hand, it is equally true that life is not a series of timeless moments: epistemological rupture or not, it remains a fact that men and women are born, fornicate, read newspapers, fail to be

----

[5] See: Stanley Milgram, **Obedience to Authority**, New York, Harper and Row, 1969, especially pp. 123-124; Erving Goffman, **Asylums**, Garden City, NY, Doubleday, 1961, pp. 1-124.

[6] See: Stanley Cavell, "The Dandy," in **The World Viewed**, New York, Viking Press, 1971, pp. 55-60; Cavell, **The Claim of Reason**, New York, Oxford University Press, 1979, pp. 313-328.

[7] For a most sensitive treatment of the terrible paradoxes inherent to the modern relationship between culture and politics, see: George Steiner, **After Babel**, New York, Oxford University Press, 1975.

happy, and die. Any political thought which ignores this simply treads water.

Both experiences have a claim on us: it is as if experience of our place in history were completely separate from experience of our everyday life. We can make little sense of the movement of our times, even if we can and do make many decisions in the immediate present. More for us than our forebearers, the ultimate purpose or justification seems lacking in any clear sense. To be sure, not all our actions could or should be imbued with world-historical significance. Still, human beings want to feel their actions as meaningful, as important beyond immediate performance. This desire has been recognized at least since Thomas Hobbes described the state of nature as one in which humans could not be sure that tomorrow would be like today and that their actions would carry consequences beyond the here and now. By saying that both experiences have a claim on us, I am asserting that, though we may find meaning in particular actions, few (if any) relates us to a larger process. The end of each activity appears to be only and precisely the end of that activity. Everything is a new beginning.

This is, I believe, the meaning of the passage in **Science as a Vocation,** where Max Weber wrote that it "is not accidental that our greatest art is intimate and not monumental" and that it is only in "pianissimo" that something corresponds to the "**pneuma** which in former times swept through the great communities like a firebrand, welding them together."[8] If political theory is a sufficiently complex set of metaphors which extends familiar language into new realms, then we are no longer able to make our words carry us into worlds which we have not already exhausted. Our anxiety is not of the unknown, but of the familiar: the nauseated repetition of all that has already been.[9] Clifford Geertz, in a well-known article, has discussed the cultural

----

[8] Max Weber, "Science as a Vocation," in **From Max Weber,** H. H. Gerth and C. Wright Mills, eds., New York, Oxford University Press, 1946, pp. 77-128, on p. 155.

[9] I believe this to be the state evoked by Nietzsche in **Die Froehliche Wissenschaft,** where he wrote about experiencing everything as if it had been experienced before. This seems to revise and extend the similar condition which Hegel described phenomenologically as "Absolute Freedom and Terror" and logically as "bad infinity."

system of ideology.[10] He sees it as the process by which people come to understand the world in new ways. If the view which I have associated with Hannah Arendt is true, it would imply that metaphorical bridges for extending political discourse are no longer available. It is as though we had reached the edge of our mesa on all sides and thrown out a rope to that beyond, simply to see it fall limply along the edge of the cliff before us. Indeed, it is as though we had known our situation only because there seemed nowhere to go from where we were.

This may perhaps appear to be a position of unrelieved pessimism, but it does not suffer this liability, which was common in academic circles during the 1950s and 1960s. My point is that political theory consists in effectuating metaphorical links between the everyday and the "more generally meaningful," to use a necessarily infelicitous phrase. These links endow everyday life with coherence, significance, and even validity. Our current inability to make such links is due, at least in part, to the fact that the main meaning left in the "more generally meaningful" is that of crisis in our sources of meaning.[11]

Thus I am not wailing yet another version of the thesis that political theory is dead. When David Easton and others announced what was to them a timely demise of political theory, they meant that it was no longer able to pretend to give true answers to the subjects for which it provided the questions. My claim here, however, is that our crisis comes at the level of the questions. If we are not simply journalists, political theory is no longer a (fully) viable form of discourse, because it can no longer presume to ask questions which would provide answers beyond the immediate.[12]

----

[10] See: Clifford Geertz, "Ideology as a Cultural System," in **The Interpretation of Cultures**, New York, Basic Books, 1973, pp. 193-233; Eugene F. Miller, "Metaphor and Political Knowledge," **American Political Science Review**, 73, 1, March, 1979, pp. 155-170.

[11] I believe this to be the position diagnosed sometime ago by Judith N. Shklar; see: "Facing Up to Intellectual Pluralism," in David Spitz, ed., **Political Theory and Social Change**, New York, Atherton Press, 1967, pp. 275-295. If Shklar does not actually celebrate the abyss, she certainly seems more comfortable with it than am I.

For such reasons, some have recently attacked the idea of a "tradition" in political theory.[13] They argue that political theory falsely transforms itself into epic by the assumption that it provides an ongoing thread of meaning to Western social life. By and large, these critics reject the notion that political theorists have sought to do otherwise than address the world as it confronts them. Yet this means that those who say political theory should emphasize the practical problems of everyday life share an assumption of those who talk of The Tradition of Political Theory. Both parties presume that the general questions and problems for political theory are given perennially. To some degree, they are right to remind us that many problems we confront still do have answers, at least in principle. Accordingly, they keep us from the despair, now all too fashionable, that there is "nothing we can do about it all." They also impede the impulse, so often a spectacle in the daily papers and ordinary existence, to retreat from public life.

To live after "the tradition" has played itself out is not necessarily to encounter troubles. After all, the claim behind positivist criticisms of political theory and the "behavioral revolution" was precisely that such theorizing is not needed (any more?). The positivists would be right, at least in part, if there were in fact no new problems. So the question is whether there are new problems for political theorists. The theoretical structures from which Michael Walzer works, for example, are fundamentally those of the tradition. Ingeniously, brilliantly, Walzer has been able to adapt traditional structures to current problems. For Walzer, we do not confront anything **morally new**, merely new circumstances in which to recognize and apply old truths.[14]

----

[12] This situation is similar to what Imre Lakatos termed a "decaying research programme." See: "Falsification and the Methodology of Scientific Research Programmes," in Lakatos and Alan Musgrave, eds., **Criticism and the Growth of Knowledge**, Cambridge, Cambridge University Press, 1970, pp. 91-195.

[13] See: John G. Gunnell, **Political Theory**, Cambridge, MA, Winthrop, 1979. Also see: J. G. A. Pocock, "Review," **Political Theory**, 8, 4, November, 1980, pp. 563-567.

[14] See: Michael Walzer, **Just and Unjust Wars**, New York,

But I believe that both Arendt and Walzer are importantly correct. Therefore, I suspect that their conflicting imperatives bind political theorists to perform two tasks, ordinarily intertwining and yet now oddly divorced. On the one hand, we need to address the position to which history has brought us; on the other, we must discuss the many particular problems which cry out for application of morally serious intelligence.

There is no reason not to continue investigating the kinds of problems which confront us daily. Moreover, our moral integrity demands that we do this. Nonetheless, there is also a need to confront seriously our historical position's demands for general meaningfulness. In a sense, there is a "crisis of the understanding," to take over the phrase by which Maurice Merleau-Ponty described the work of Max Weber.[15] Indeed, were there no such crisis in our capacity to make meaningful statements about our (political) world, then we would be thrust toward despair that our intelligence could ever again be of more than casuistical use. If there is a crisis of the political understanding, it comes from the fact that people now find themselves acting willy-nilly in a world in which justifications of their actions (and inactions) are withheld from them until some later and unspecified time. Until about 1950, for instance, one might claim with some credibility to be acting in the name of history. Such was Merleau-Ponty's Pascalian wager on the historically progressive. When **Humanism and Terror** was written, this could pretend to be a viable position, if only

----

Basic Books, 1977. This leaves me troubled. Walzer insists on the applicability of more or less traditional standards of morality to current sorts of warfare situations: terrorism, nuclear combat, etc. Might this somehow be beside the point? The answer is not clear, because the point is not clear. Perhaps Walzer is comfortable with casuistry, with going case by case, precisely because he knows the impossibility of defining once and for all the meaning of what one does. In this, he seems to evidence the theoretical perspective which he once identified in Calvin: God is **absconditus**, only "posterior signs" are known; yet all the same, one keeps working away at life.

[15] Maurice Merleau-Ponty, "The Crisis of Understanding," in **Adventures of the Dialectic**, Joseph J. Bien, trans., Evanston, IL, Northwestern University Press, 1973, pp. 9-29.

to one as honest and as tortured by that honesty as was
Merleau-Ponty. By now, however, we realize that history
is less kind to persons than even Hegel had told us. History now gives us new problems, but no language in which
to address (or sometimes, even recognize) them.

A better phrasing for this problem would be: to
what degree are political theorists forced to take the question of history seriously? Martin Heidegger claimed that
"the unchanging unity of the underlying determinations of
Being [is] only an illusion under whose protection metaphysics occurs as the history of Being." In agreement, Richard Rorty writes that "the really fundamental 'split' in contemporary philosophy...is between those (like Dewey,
Heidegger, Cavell, Kuhn, Feyerabend and Habermas) who
take Hegel and history seriously, and those who see 'recurring philosophical problems' being discussed by everyone
from the Greeks to the authors of the latest journal articles."[16] I take Heidegger to be right in declaring that "the
historical is the natural."[17] That is to say, what confronts
us cannot be understood except in terms of its specific historicity.

We have several options. With analytical philosophers, we can simply assert or act as if we believe that our
problems are fundamentally the same as those since philosophy "began," making our main task to weed false issues
from true. Then we would not attend to the notion that
philosophy might have had a beginning. Instead, we would
proceed as though our questions are basically those of Plato
and virtually everyone thereafter. (Of course, we may
pose them more clearly and answer them more compellingly,
at least for us.) Not only could these questions be listed,
but, as Kant showed in founding the profession of philosophy, they could be subsumed under the single issue of
relating universals to particulars. Thus would the history
of philosophy culminate neatly in the problematics of the
First Critique, rendering full comprehension of the **Critique**
a prerequisite for all further work in philosophy. Or so we
would think were we to travel the analytical trail.

Should this position appear unduly disrespectful of

----

[16] Richard Rorty, "Overcoming the Tradition: Heidegger
and Dewey," **Review of Metaphysics**, 30, 2, December,
1976, pp. 280-305, on p. 283, fn. 7.

[17] Martin Heidegger, **What Is a Thing?**, Chicago, Henry
Regnery, 1967, p. 39.

doubts about the analytical coherence of our moral and political condition, we could instead attempt to extend "the tradition." This effort is exemplified by the theorizing of Leo Strauss (and his followers), Sheldon Wolin (at least in his early work), and Hannah Arendt (throughout her life). It presumes that at least the main set of questions, the grammar of inquiry, for political theorists was laid down in the early days of political philosophy. It further presumes that the beacon then lit has continued to illuminate human endeavors up to and including those of our times. Study may show that we no longer mean much the same thing as the ancient Greeks by "politics" and other key categories, as Arendt so often reminded us. Still, such reminders are not simple exercises in nostalgia. They show how our lives have become less than possible, less than when the **bios politikos** enriched our activities. In this vision, political theory consists at least in reminding us of what might be, since it was once.

Here there are profound differences between those like Arendt or Wolin and those like Strauss. The former give us a genealogy of modern politics, an account of its relationship between continuity and change. The latter, however, see the world of political theory as a great cosmic battleground where the forces of true politics are at war with those of anti-politics. This explains (or purports to) why modern political thought is merely evidence of a disease tracing back to a break with the classics. Thus the prophets and analysts of modernity must be rejected, no matter what perspective they take. Admittedly, this insistence can produce insights, such as Strauss's brilliant display of the close family relationship between positivism and historicism, allowing him to dismiss them by the same argument.[18] He thereby discerned some important connections, even if we need not follow the prescriptions he derived from them.

Let us ask seriously if there are **new** problems in political theory. "New problems" arise when traditional language does not make sense of event configurations for us. Then we learn nothing from (we are not changed by) what we understand. In **Ecce Homo**, Nietzsche wrote of occurrences and understandings which lie "altogether beyond the range of human experience." He noted that "in this case since nothing is heard, it will be assumed that nothing is

----

[18] Leo Strauss, **What Is Political Philosophy?**, Chicago, University of Chicago Press, 1961, pp. 25ff.

there."[19] On such occasions, we are unable to apprehend
what is happening because it is incommensurable with the
world we have known to this point. Thus if we insist that
"history makes a difference" and that our age poses radically new problems, so new that we may not yet even
known them as problems, we will be forced to revise radically our notion of the knowing subject.

From Plato onward, political theory has presumed that
some part of the self or aspect of its construction is more
real, authentic, permanent, or foundational than the others.[20] So for Plato, a person should seek in the self what
can transcend becoming; for Augustine, what is cut off
from God; for Machiavelli, what allows energetic action in
the world; for Hobbes, what fears violent death; and for
Locke, what enables mixing energy with nature and recognizing the result as a personal possession. Each theorist
presumes that something of the self endures. To take history seriously is to abandon the idea that philosophy should
or could provide us with a secure ground for knowledge,
whether in science, morality, or politics. It is to give up
the notion that the knowing subject can reach into a realm,
material or otherwise, which can be known indefeasibly and
foundationally. It is to understand the self, not as a unity
to which all that is knowledge can be related, but as a multiplicity through which one is capable of mutual incompatibil-
ities. Thus we must acknowledge a self which not only
wields the tools of the anthropologist but is in fact anthro-
pologically grounded. Not only do I "contain multitudes,"
but I am a multitude in myself.

As a political theorist, then, I need to address the
relationship of the self and history. This raises questions
which, in our times, I believe to be questions of nihilism.
This topic has begun to receive fruitful consideration. It
spurs significant criticisms of the past and present practices of political theory, and it provides at least some indication of directions for escaping from the chalk circles of
our times.

Philosophy and the Mirror of Nature culminates Richard Rorty's work within and attempt to escape from the

----

[19] Friedrich Nietzsche, "Why I Write Such Excellent Books,"
in **Ecce Homo**, R. J. Hollingdale, trans., Baltimore, Penguin
Books, 1979, pp. 69-77.

[20] See: Tracy B. Strong, "Texts and Pretexts: Nietzsche
on Perspectivism," **Nietzsche Studien**, forthcoming.

Anglo-American tradition in philosophy.   He intends a radical attack on the notion of the subject as philosophically
conceived, since at least Descartes and possibly since Plato.
He argues that this subject asks philosophy to do what
religion did earlier: provide a touchstone of certainty for
the self.   The Western subject must be shored up as a
structure for certainty; that is, it requires (in principle) a
knowledge not affected or infected by the fact that a subject "has" it.   Epistemology is our tool for grounding
knowledge in certainty, so Rorty directs his general attack
against epistemology.   In so doing, he traces its ties to
traditional philosophy of mind and the Western problem of
mind and body.
     Rorty maintains that we in the West have assumed
that a particular part or entity of human beings, most often
called the "mental," is distinguished from other parts or
entities by its special kinds of experience.   The "mental" is
that "portion" of the person thought to be especially, specifically, uniquely human (as opposed to animal, organic, or
even nonorganic).   Intentional and phenomenal experiences
have been thought to characterize the "mental."   Phenomenal experiences span "having a pain" and "seeing a tree."
Plainly, they are seldom treated as limited to people.   But
presumably, only people can have intentions, such experiences as "having a belief" about something.   Rorty insists
that the "mental" is a peculiar and probably objectionable
category precisely because it links the phenomenal and the
intentional for obscure and likely bogus reasons.   Through
historical inquiry, Rorty infers that these two types of
experience became analytically connected as determinant
signs of the "mental" because, at least since Descartes, we
have assumed them to be "incorrigibly known."   In other
words, we presume for them a certain privileged status in
reports we make of experience: "you can't tell me that I
don't have a pain; I KNOW."
     From this beginning, Rorty moves to an analysis of
the incorrigible as a mark of the mental and to a general
critique of the notion that any "portion" of the self is privileged in the claims that it can ultimately make about itself.
He attacks all epistemological dualisms: the idea that we
try to read off what is "out there" (one or another complicated form of empiricism), the view that we "make" the
world which we experience (one or another complicated combination of Kant and romanticism), and the like.   Drawing
instead on work by Wittgenstein, Quine, and Sellars, Rorty
disputes the atttitude that it is the task of philosophy to

discover "the right method of seeking truth."[21] He argues instead that there is no framework of inquiry is neutral toward the outcome of inquiry.

Rorty clearly finds matter for his work from Heidegger's vein. He rejects previous philosophical problems as wheelspinning, for now if not for all times. "The word knowledge would not seem worth fighting for, if it were not for the Kantian tradition that to be a philosopher is to have a 'theory of knowledge' and the Platonic tradition that action not based on the knowledge of the truth of propositions is 'irrational.'"[22] Presumably, Rorty tries to espouse the converse of these Kantian and Platonic propositions: first, that we need no general theory of knowledge, which may in any event be impossible; and second, that we can behave reasonably, even rationally, without worrying whether the fundamental propositions which ground our behavior are "true." Rorty hints that worries about the truth of such propositions are foolish and misguided. Thereby, Rorty might be said to stand positivism on its head or, following Marx's example, to turn it from its former headstand right-side-up onto its historical feet.

How, then, does Rorty treat the activity of knowing the world? Toward the end of his book, Rorty alludes to Michael Oakeshott's view of philosophy as part of the conversation of humankind. "If we see knowing as not having an essence...but rather as a right, by current standards, to believe, then we are well on our way to seeing conversation as the ultimate context within which knowledge is to be understood." Thus for Rorty, **truth is what one is entitled to**: a "right...to believe" by "current standards."[23] To rest the question of truth on entitlement has strong implications. Apparently as Rorty intends, it moves him close to Heidegger, who asserted in **Sein und Zeit** that the "authentic" individual receives self-understanding in relationship to his own **Volk**, to the linguistic and historical community which enables personal existence in the world.[24]

----

[21] **Richard Rorty**, Philosophy and the Mirror of Nature, **Princeton**, Princeton University Press, 1979, p. 211.

[22] **Ibid.**, p. 356.

[23] **Ibid.**, p. 389.

[24] Martin Heidegger, **Sein und Zeit**, Frankfurt am Main, Vittorio Kostermann, 1977, p. 384. Also see: Karsten

This implies that philosophy, like everything else, is irreducibly historical. Thus political theorists should accept the historicity of their own work. But then the question becomes why we want political theory to provide solutions to problems, why we should ask it to give enforceable or even certain answers to political questions? What kinds of things do we desire to know about abortion, income redistribution, multinational corporations, and so on? From Rorty's perspective, political theory from Plato to the present has mistakenly required and unnecessarily sought permanent, neutral, "objective" answers susceptible to translation and application for any particular problem which we might encounter, no matter how or where. With Michel Foucault, Rorty claims that this is an impossible project, to be abandoned in favor of introducing "chance, discontinuity, and materiality" into history.[25] If Rorty is right that thought can no longer expect ever to become sure of itself, and he has identified many features consistent with such a fact, then nothing viable can emerge from insisting that we continue a search for the right answers to particular political problems. To ask what I (with emphasis on the pronoun) am entitled to believe and say about abortion is very different from asking what it is right (in some unspecified, general sense) to believe and say about abortion.

When we insist that there are answers at once general, definite, and precise for questions quite particular, then we stumble toward nihilism. For most of us, nihilism is conceived as something encountered most memorably in long-haired characters which could have (and perhaps sometimes did) come from Russian novels. Or we think of death camps and orgies of material destruction. Historically, nihilism has recently seemed a characteristic affliction of late adolescence. If we read political theorists, we might also think of nihilism as the denouement of historicism, since Leo Strauss assured us that our world faces the choice between the true, natural values of The Tradition and the disastrous complex of historicism, relativism, and nihilism. Strauss warned that the belief in history leads to the bankrupt conviction that history is meaningless: such is the course of nihilism. As Kirsanov remarks in **Fathers and**

Harries, "Heidegger as a Political Thinker," **Review of Metaphysics**, 29, 4, June, 1976, pp. 642-669.

[25] Rorty, **Philosophy and the Mirror of Nature**, p. 391, fn. 29.

Sons, "there used to be Hegelians, and now there are nihilists."

What might this mean? At least since Socrates, people have apppreciated that the essence of the moral and
examined life is to be able, even if not always to be willing, to give reasons for behavior. "What do you mean
when you say..?" is the basis of moral discourse (not **just**
moral) and testifies to reciprocity between human beings.
To be able to ask that question is to recognize a nexus of
sense between some people, a nexus beyond individual
choice. Moral behavior rests on the recognition that making
sense is a kind of compulsion or condemnation. From this
perspective, nihilism is an insistence that sense must, but
cannot, be made.[26] Importantly, this imperative behind nihilism is a fundamentally moral imperative. It is an insistence
on making full or final sense of the world in ways which
are impossible or call sense-making itself into radical question.

Nihilism is thus a set of ways of doing things: what
one might call a culture, a "web of significance" which people spin and within which they are suspended (as Geertz
has defined the term). As the ways in which humans make
sense of the world into which they are thrown, cultures
provide people with their categories of sense, from the
minutiae of everyday life to the most extraordinary
events.[27] By this understanding, nihilism considered as a
cultural form is in fact a way of preserving the world, not
of repudiating or losing it.

Such considerations are developed by Johannes
Goudsblom in **Nihilism and Culture.** Fruitfully, Goudsblom
suggests that the nihilistic imperative which some feel in
modern society traces to the imperatives of modernity.[28]
Following Norbert Elias, Goudsblom claims that the result of
what he calls, "the civilizing process" has been historically
specific rather than universal. That is, it has not moved
Westerners closer to cultures and comprehensions which are
truly human, applying generally to all human beings.
Instead, it has led us to mistake our modes of life and

----

[26] See: Tracy B. Strong, "Language and Nihilism,"
Theory and Society, 3, 2, Summer, 1976, pp. 239-263.

[27] Geertz, **The Interpretation of Culture,** p. 5.

[28] See: Johannes Goudsblom, **Nihilism and Culture,**
Oxford, Basil Blackwell, 1980, p. 98.

thought for ideals of universal validity. Central to this process has been the development of what Goudsblom calls the "reflective attitude," the search for reasons and the desire to ground activity in truth. Modern science is only its latest and most pervasive manifestation. The Western civilizing process has spawned groups specializing in exploration and fulfillment of the demands of Western cultures. This point is inspired by Nietzsche, since those who promote the imperatives of culture are, of course, the "ascetic priests" of the third essay of On the Genealogy of Morals. The main imperative of our civilization has been the search for truth, conceived to progress through refutation of errors. Unsurprisingly, by the turn of the last century, no claim could be made so indefeasible that it would not fall to someone's criticism.

Goudsblom argues that social and political developments of the last hundred years have diffused the nihilistic problematic throughout advanced Western cultures, whereas it had previously been the province of a few intellectuals. "On the one hand, the humanist tradition was democratized, which made the cultural property of an elite accessible to all; on the other, there was greater freedom of intellectual movement for the individual, which made the choice of a philosophy of life more and more a personal matter. Both developments encouraged the free play of ideological forces, one of which was the nihilist problematic."[29] For a cultural leftist of the sixties, Goudblom's brushstrokes are broad and peculiarly reminiscent of Durkheim. Goudblom contends that the unreflective ties earlier linking individuals to each other and to communities have been broken in favor of more abstract and universalistic norms. A tendency inherent in the Western process of civilization has thus been transformed into the goal of that process.[30]

Goudsblom's work is confused in some respects. He waivers over whether the nihilistic problematic is a cultural imperative or a mere invention. If the former, then the nihilistic problematic has been somehow inevitable for the West. If the latter, then we have been taken in by some intellectuals, alienated from their own cultures, floating messages on the skiff of social democratization. Goudsblom

----

[29] Ibid., p. 179.

[30] Ibid., p. 154. On p. 199, Goudsblom cites Redfield to support an argument that "the process is only fatal, if one begins to distrust one's own cultural commands."

comes very close to saying that we should remain content with the truths of our "own" cultures, so that our danger is one of "surrender" to nihilism through a weakness of will. At book's end, he even suggests that the very "truth imperative" which has produced our present straits will nevertheless now take us out of them: this by turning on nihilism itself to effect what would have to be an **Aufhebung** of the present. (I feel here the same suspicion of slight-of-hand as when I watch Hegel liberating the **Geist** from "Absolute Freedom and Terror," a state which resembles nihilism in its thoroughgoing solipsism of the understanding.[31] Goudsblom shares more with Hegel than he perhaps realizes.)

Even so, Goudsblom manages to clarify and produce evidence (sociologically) for the claim that nihilism is a project of our civilization, not (as Strauss would have it) a deviation precipitated by Machiavelli and company. Nihilism is rather a potentiality with us from the beginning and only now emerging. By making the "truth imperative" an unfortunate consequences of listening too closely to mongerers of cultural imperatives, however, Goudsblom fails to say precisely why nihilism has such appeal to us. He does not explain a common occurrence in political theory classes, where students admit easily and often that "nothing is (really) true," and where they respond to all kinds of counterarguments with: "well, that's MY opinion."

Exploring the sources of this temptation is the central concern of Stanley Cavell's book on the interplay between the claims rationality makes of us and those we make of rationality. **The Claim of Reason** is not exactly **about** philosophy, except as that topic arises in the performance of philosophy. It is rather a demonstration of what it means to make oneself available **to** philosophy, to take existence in the world seriously and meaningfully. Knowledge of this book is therefore to knowledge of the other two books something like what knowledge of Paris is to knowledge of the height of Mont Blanc.

Here I cannot begin to exhaust the complexity of this book. But together, two of Cavell's passages join the everyday and the world-historical, indicating how to span their gap by bridges of human meaning. At ground level, Cavell argues that serious skepticism, the problem of other minds, and what I have been calling nihilism are exemplars of the same pattern. In each case, the trouble is that one

----

[31] See: **ibid.**, p. 181.

person is unable or unwilling to accept or acknowledge another as a person. Despite an insistent desire for knowledge of the other, one always finds oneself falling short of "real," "true" knowledge of that entity. One is never (completely) sure that there is anything, let alone anyone, "out there" at all, for there must always remain doubts which call any assurances into serious question. Each of these three closely related positions is what Cavell calls a denial of "justice," a refusal to see an entity for who or what it is.

After Cavell, let us take an issue to relate to this analysis of skepticism and nihilism: are human embryos human beings? This way, abortion becomes a problem about personal knowledge of others. Why do some deny but others insist that human embryos are human beings? Cavell argues that some are tempted to see a parallel between thinking about embryos and thinking about slaves: those who deny the humanity of slaves think in the same manner as those who deny the humanity of embryos. Yet, according to Cavell, this parallel misleads us because people might have gone to war to acquire slaves (implying that their humanity is not problematical), whereas people would never have had intercourse in order to have an abortion.

Since permissability of abortion can in our times no longer rest on an argument about the risk to the safety of another, those opposing abortion now argue that "a human embryo is a human being." Cavell maintains that these words are not and cannot be meant seriously. Instead, people opposed to abortion use such words to emphasize that a human embryo is human (not, say, feline) and thereby to generate in us feelings of abhorrence forceful enough to turn us against abortion. Cavell denies, however, that any one aspect of human beings, even that they are human in embryo, is sufficient ground for turning ahborrence into principle. In our times, being a human being also includes: unjust laws that discriminate against the poor, difficulties faced by adopted children, the shame of bastardy, dangers of contraception, difficulties for male parents in having time to care for their children, fears and dangers of childbirth and pregnancy. Were there no such complications, Cavell and the rest of us could oppose abortion purely and simply; but not now, not knowing these things. "Voluntary abortion is less bad than its criminalization; but it is therefore not all right. The more terrible one takes it to be, the more terrible one should take its indictment of society to be. It is a mark of social failure, not unlike the existence of prisons."[32]

Cavell's point appears to be that **historical realities** determine what we are entitled to regard as moral and immoral in specific circumstances. This does not make morality utterly dependent upon or relative to history, but it does mean that moral decisions are formed by history. Remembering Heidegger's self-defense against the accusation of historical relativism, we might say that Cavell portrays historical circumstances as **disclosures** of human beings. To acknowledge human beings and human beings, which is justice, we must understand them historically. No **single** feature defines being a human being, especially if this means some predicate which transcends the historical and contingent. Yet the nihilist has soughtsuch a predicate. Again, Heidegger noted in **What Is a Thing**, "the historical is always the natural."[33] There are human beings all about us, but there is no single thing which qualifies them as such. With Rorty, Cavell decries all attempts to require a physical or mental account of the phenomenology of being a human being. Neither do we need nor do we require some version of Cartesian self.[34]

Now let us generalize the previous issue, asking what is the **validity** of morality? Most moral philosophers, Cavell argues, have assumed that morality is measured and justified by its applicability to any conceivable situation, that it is to our practical life what epistemology is to our knowing life. But this implies the claim that any and every issue (at least of behavior) is a moral issue, a claim for which we have **no reason**. This "moralization of moral theory," says Cavell, "has done to moral philosophy and the concept of morality what the events of the modern world have often done to the moral life itself: made it a matter of academic question."[35]

To do this is to universalize morality and, in effect, to deny that morality is of and about human beings. Like the epistemology rejected by Rorty, this would require a

----

[32] Cavell, **The Claim of Reason**, pp. 374-375.

[33] Heidegger, **What Is a Thing?**, p. 39.

[34] See Rorty's comments on "What Is It Like to Be a Bat?" by Thomas Nagel: **Philosophy and the Mirror of Nature**, p. 28, fn. 4.

[35] Cavell, **The Claim of Reason**, pp. 269-270.

final (moral) answer, one pretending to escape from the contingencies of our human world. (In his commentary on Hegel, Marx rightly termed such demands "perverse.") Contrary to this inclination, we must be able to ask **who is to say** what is and isn't moral? Similarly, we must accept that some behavior is best understood without the "foundation" of moral discourse. In **Ethics and Language**, Charles Stevenson wrote that when an "oversexed emotionally independent adolescent" and one who is "undersexed [and] dependent" argue about the desirability of free love, their controversy may be "permanently" irresolvable. Appropriately, Cavell responds that "it makes a difference whether the argument is conducted by an oversexed emotionally dependent adult like D. H. Lawrence or an undersexed, sublimated, emotionally independent adult like Freud; and that difference is part of the subject that not every opinion has the same weight nor every disagreement the same significance."[36] Moreover, when Cavell says "it makes a difference," he means it. All moral decisions start parochially; and some must leave the limits of moral discourse to become part of love, religion, politics, or another of the many voices in the conversation of humankind.[37]

In the end, the demand that all decisions remain in the realm of the moral is a refusal to acknowledge others for who they are. It is an insistence on what Rorty calls a "glassy essence", on pretending that there is some thing which a human being **is**. If we accept Rorty's and Cavell's arguments against this requirement, then the key question is Goudsblom's: why do human beings **need** to insist that there is something which they **are**? Or alternately, why does our political theory start from the premise that there are solutions to problems?[38]

----

[36] Ibid., p. 270.

[37] Cavell does not cite Oakeshott in this connection, but see: Hanna Fenichel Pitkin, **Wittgenstein and Justice**, Berkeley, University of California Press, 1972, pp. 51-54, 141-142.

[38] I should say: not **all** our political theory. Henry Kariel has been trying to impress this point upon us for years; and so, occasionally, have J. G. A. Pocock and others. Also see: Tracy B. Strong, "'Hold On to Your Brains': An Essay in Meta-theory," in Philip Green and Sanford Levinson, eds., **Power and Community**, New York, Random

I cannot, of course, manage a complete answer to this kind of question. Still, let me say that the starting point for political theory should now be the second of Marx's theses on Feuerbach. "The question whether objective truth can be attributed to human thinking is not a question of theory but is a **practical** question. Man must prove the truth, i.e., the reality and the power, the this-sidedness of his thinking in practice."[39] One implication is that political theory should not rest its arguments on claims about "human psychology," "human nature," or "human needs." Such concepts are historically relative and transient, yet their appearance prompts us to take them as foundational or even transcendental. A further implication is that political theory should criticize what keeps human beings from standing with each other in justice, from acknowledging others as they are. And a final implication is that political theory should discard its simple oppositions of individuals to communities. We should stop insisting that communities are built up of unit individuals; instead, we should learn to see individuals as communities already, as multiplicities in conjunction and coterminality with other such multiplicities. It is precisely because neither of us is a **One** that we understand each other.[40]

House, 1969, pp. 328-356, especially pp. 349-351. But this should be revised in light of Cavell's treatment of knowing and acknowledging.

[39] Karl Marx, "Theses on Feuerbach," in **Karl Marx**, David McLellan, ed., Oxford, Oxford University Press, 1977, pp. 156-158, on p. 156.

[40] See: Morton Schoolman, **The Imaginary Witness**, New York, Basic Books, 1980; Benjamin R. Barber, **Strong Democracy**, forthcoming. I think that a dim perception of this point has recently led Barber to defend Joseph de Maistre and many from the movements of the sixties to be interested in Durkheim and the like. On the other hand, the absence of this perception in Herbert Marcuse's work prevents my position from adhering more closely to his.

MARTIN HEIDEGGER

AND THE METAPOLITICS OF CRISIS

Allan Megill

In this essay, I address an idea that has played an important role in the political theory of our century. This is the idea that a radical break or crisis has occurred in Western consciousness. In the minds of crisis theorists, this event is absolutely the most compelling reality in modern history, and perhaps in all history since Plato and Aristotle. This notion of a crisis of belief or authority (the "death of God," to use Nietzsche's formulation) is central to the works of such noted political theorists as Hannah Arendt, Leo Strauss, and Eric Voegelin. It makes an appearance in the writings of many others as well. Not surprisingly, the specter of crisis haunts this anthology's essays by Tinder, Kress, and Nelson, and strikes the major theme for Strong.

Here I suggest that the crisis idea is both misleading and dangerous. I trace its danger to the fact that it is rarely subjected to critical examination. Most theorists of the crisis consider it as something almost self-evident, its reality utterly beyond debate. In consequence, its somewhat questionable foundations are seldom made explicit. My aim is less a direct discrediting of crisis theory than a demonstration of how dubious its basic assumptions are.

Obviously, even this theme is too immense and significant to be treated adequately in a single essay. To make it more manageable, I focus on one of its foremost propagators: Martin Heidegger. More specifically, I analyze Heidegger's political writings, an emphasis that seems triply determined. First, this anthology's concern with political theory makes appropriate the study of Heidegger's own political pronouncements. Second, Heidegger's crisis theme first surfaces in them. Third, they are associated with Heidegger's political involvement, which exemplifies the most formidable dangers of crisis theory. Looking to the past, I show how convoluted and questionable are the assumptions beneath Heidegger's crisis theory, plus how much they are shared by his commentators. Looking to the present, I call attention to the presence of the same unargued assumptions in some current political theory. What should political theory be now? Certainly not what recently it has all too often been: crisis theory.

I

Richard Rorty has lately proposed that Heidegger's project is, in one of its aspects, an attempt to liberate Western thought from the visual or "ocular" metaphor of understanding that has dominated it from the time of the ancient Greeks.[1] "Ocular" knowledge depends on dividing the viewer from the viewed.   Rorty argues that this split generates a whole series of subsidiary dualisms that have pervaded Western thought: subject/object, theory/practice, fact/value.   It also generates an image of the mind as a "mirror of nature" containing "representations" of the world that are either accurate or inaccurate, correct or incorrect. As Rorty puts it, "without the notion of the mind as mir- ror, the notion of knowledge as accuracy of representation would not have suggested itself."[2] Finally, it generates the notion of foundations: that the function of philosophy is to establish a kind of global basis for our understanding of the world.   The point of this attack is not, according to Rorty, the setting up of a new, contrary way of thinking. Rather, like Dewey and Wittgenstein, whom Rorty also sees as important in attacking the ocular metaphor of under- standing, Heidegger wanted us to question what too long has remained unquestioned, to free us from encumbered, rigidified ways of thinking by showing that these are simply ways of thinking and not reality itself.   In Rorty's words, the work of these three thinkers is "therapeutic rather than constructive, edifying rather than systematic, designed to make the reader question his motives for philosophizing rather than to supply him with a new philosophical pro- gram."[3]

One commentator on Heidegger, Reiner Schürmann, has recently claimed that "Heidegger's writings on the phe- nomenological Destruction of the history of ontology have

----

[1] On the general prevalence of the "ocular" metaphor, see: Richard Rorty, **Philosophy and the Mirror of Nature**, Princeton, Princeton University Press, 1979, pp. 11, 13, 38-39, and 60 (fn. 32).   Though Rorty has not here attempted an interpretation of Heidegger's philosophy, it is addressed on: pp. 162-163, 371.

[2] **Ibid.**, p. 12.

[3] **Ibid.**, pp. 5-6.

been said to be harmful for public life since they deprive political action of its ground." This is said to be because, in Heidegger's view, political action cannot rely on "any extrinsic, foundational, unquestionable ground from which to borrow its credentials."[4] To the contrary, I argue that the "danger" of Heidegger's thought for public life lies, not in this presumably therapeutic deprivation of ground, but in Heidegger's failure to carry his therapy far enough. Rorty has suggested something of this failure in an article in which he compares and mutually criticizes Heidegger and Dewey. He finds particularly questionable Heidegger's adherence to a "myth of the tradition." As he points out, Heidegger pursued a peculiarly idealist form of historicism in which a sequence of "great dead philosophers" are seen as offering us "words of Being."[5] I concentrate here not on Heidegger's historicism but rather on another aspect of his thought that is perhaps the mirror image of this historicism: namely, his commitment to a notion of absolute cultural crisis.

Shifting the focus in this manner, I point away from Rorty's trio of Heidegger, Wittgenstein, and Dewey toward another and rather more apocalyptic trio of Nietzsche, Heidegger, and Foucault. For though Nietzsche and Foucault are hardly mentioned in **Philosophy and the Mirror of Nature**, both thinkers fit astonishingly well into Rorty's schema of therapeutic, anti-ocular thought. Think of Nietzsche's attack on "theoretical man" and his attempt to undercut the formalistic and (though this is often missed) the visualistic Apollonianism which he saw as dominating modern science. Think, too, of Foucault's move from the visual metaphoric dominant in **The Order of Things**, through the parodistic attack on "method" and "theory" in **The Archaeology of Knowledge**, to the explicitly

----

[4] Reiner Schürmann, "Principles Precarious: On the Origin of the Political in Heidegger," in Thomas Sheehan, ed., **Heidegger**, Chicago, Precedent, 1981, pp. 245-256, on p. 245.

[5] Richard Rorty, "Overcoming the Tradition: Heidegger and Dewey," in Michael Murray, ed., **Heidegger and Modern Philosophy**, New Haven, Yale University Press, 1978, pp. 239-258, especially on pp. 250-252, 256-258. The notion of a "myth of the tradition" is John Gunnell's; see: **Political Theory**, Cambridge, MA, Winthrop, 1979, especially pp. 65ff.

antitheoretical and antivisual perspective of the writings after 1969.[6] What distinguishes my trio of Nietzsche, Heidegger, and Foucault from Rorty's trio of Heidegger, Wittgenstein, and Dewey is that the members of my trio are all explicitly thinkers of crisis. This relates importantly to their attempts to function as cultural therapists.

Heidegger's political writings all date from the one period in his life when he became directly involved in political events. In May 1933, shortly after the Nazi seizure of power, he agreed to serve as rector of Freiburg University. He joined the Nazi party and in public pronouncements vehemently supported the new direction that Germany seemed to be taking. At the same time, he disagreed with some of the actions taken by the Nazi arbiters of education. He forbade antisemitic posters within the precincts of the university and sought to avoid dismissing several Social Democratic professors. But he soon came to realize that he could do little against the authorities; and in February 1934, he resigned the rectorship.[7]

The basic facts of Heidegger's political intervention, then, are simple. But to interpret them is difficult. What led Heidegger to cast his lot with the Nazis in the first place? What significance ought we to see in his apparent "inner emigration" of the years 1934-45? Why, after 1945,

----

[6] On this attack on the "metaphoric of light" in Nietzsche and the turning away from such a metaphoric in Foucault, see: Allan Megill, "Foucault, Structuralism, and the Ends of History," **Journal of Modern History**, 51, 3, September, 1979, pp. 451-503, especially on pp. 472-473 and passim. Derrida fits into this anti-ocular scheme as well, though in my view he escapes from the kind of criticism that I shall be directing against Heidegger (and by extension, against Nietzsche and Foucault). Richard Rorty has recently turned his attention to Foucault; see: "Beyond Nietzsche and Marx," **London Review of Books**, February 19-March 4, 1981, pp. 5-6.

[7] For a brief account, see: George Steiner, **Heidegger**, London, Fontana, 1978, pp. 112-113. Despite what Steiner says, however, I know of no evidence that Heidegger left the Party in 1934. Presumably, his membership simply lapsed or was cancelled, without any action on his part. So far as I know, the most detailed factual survey of Heidegger's involvement with the Nazis is contained in an unpublished doctoral dissertation (available from University

did he remain so silent? And why, on the few occasions when he broke that silence, did he speak with ambiguous, self-serving words? To a considerable extent, the answers to these questions lie beyond our ken, though this has not prevented the emergence of a large and growing literature concerned with accounting for and judging Heidegger's behavior in this period.[8] Fortunately, my concern in the present essay is not with the actions of Heidegger the man, but rather with the presuppositions and implications of his thought. Though the two cannot be entirely kept apart, they can legitimately be distinguished. Such a distinction allows us to omit assigning precise degrees of guilt or inno-cence to Heidegger the man, focusing instead on a question much more easily answered by extant texts: namely, what is the relation of Heidegger's political writings of 1933-34 to those other writings which establish him as one of the most important of modern thinkers?

Among Heidegger's more sympathetic commentators, some have simply ignored his political involvement of 1933-34, viewing it as a personal matter having no relation to his enterprise as a philosopher. It is striking that Otto Pöggeler makes no mention of the events of 1933-34 in his 1963 book **Der Denkweg Martin Heideggers**, the most com-prehensive study of Heidegger in German and (in some

----

Microfilms): Karl A. Moehling, **Martin Heidegger and the Nazi Party**, Department of History, Northern Illinois Uni-versity, 1972. Moehling includes transcriptions of several documents that do not seem to be available elsewhere. Unfortunately, he is deaf to the moral equivocacy of many of Heidegger's pronouncements of 1933-34. Still, this does not invalidate his assemblage of facts. Moehling summarizes his findings in: "Heidegger and the Nazis," in Sheehan, ed., **Heidegger**, pp. 31-43.

[8] For an admirably brief and sensitive discussion, see: Steiner, **Heidegger**, pp. 111-121. At the end of his book, Steiner lists some of the more interesting literature on Heidegger's involvement with the Nazis; see: pp. 155-156. For a more extensive, though less current listing, see: Winfried Franzen, **Martin Heidegger**, Stuttgart, Metzlersche, 1976, pp. 78-85. Articles and interviews by Maurice de Gandillac, Alfred de Towarnicki, Karl Löwith, Alphonse de Waehlens, and Eric Weil which appeared in **Les Temps mod-ernes** in 1946-1947 represent the first outbreak of the con-troversy over the depth of Heidegger's implication in the

ways) a quite useful and intelligent work.[9] Equally striking is the fact that, in his long exegesis of Heidegger's writings (**Heidegger: Through Phenomenology to Thought**, also published in 1963), William J. Richardson relegates the Nazi episode to a single footnote.   There he tells us that the controversy over Heidegger's involvement with the Nazis "has no place within the scope of the present work," which runs to more than 760 pages.[10] The notion that Heidegger's political involvement had nothing whatever to do with his philosophy becomes explicit in a more recent, semipopular book, Walter Biemel's **Martin Heidegger: An Illustrated Study** (first published in German in 1973).   Biemel says in defense of Heidegger that "the political error of 1933 was of short duration....It is superficial to pounce on it in order to discredit Heidegger.   Had the error been a result of his philosophical thought, this thinking itself would have come to an end with the correction of the error.   What actually happened was just the opposite."[11] It is hard to understand Biemel's argument here.   Biemel is saying that because Heidegger continued to do philosophy after 1934, his political error of 1933-34 could not have been a result of his philosophy.   But this simply does not follow.   Logically speaking, the question of the relationship between Heidegger's political involvement of 1933-34 and his philosophy is quite

----

Nazi debacle.   They are still worth reading.   So, too, are such more recent contributions as: Stanley Rosen, **Nihilism**, New Haven, Yale University Press, 1969, pp. 119ff; Henry Pachter, "Heidegger and Hitler: The Incompatibility of Geist and Politics," **Boston University Journal**, 24, 3, 1976, pp. 47-55; Karsten Harries, "Heidegger as a Political Thinker," in Murray, ed., **Heidegger and Modern Philosophy**, pp. 304-328.   The recent book by Mark Blitz, **Heidegger's Being and Time and the Possibility of Political Philosophy** (Ithaca, NY, Cornell University Press, 1981), is disappointing.   Blitz discusses Heidegger's involvement with the Nazis on pp. 210-222.

[9] Otto Pöggeler, **Der Denkweg Martin Heideggers**, Pfullingen, Neske, 1963.   Note, however, that Pöggeler has more recently turned to the question of Heidegger's politics; see: **Philosophie und Politik bei Heidegger**, 2. Auflage, Freiburg, Karl Alber, 1972.

[10] William J. Richardson, **Heidegger**, The Hague, Martinus Nijhoff, 1963, p. 255.

independent of the question of what Heidegger did or did not do after 1934.

Rather more attuned to the problems raised by Heidegger's political involvement are those of his sympathizers who argue that this involvement was indeed a consequence of his thought, but one that induced him to come to grips with the limitations of his earlier philosophical position and to embark upon a new and quite different thinking. Such is the position adopted by Hannah Arendt. On Arendt's view, the Heidegger of 1933 fell victim to the temptation to leave his true residence, that of "thought," and "get involved in the world of human affairs." But fortunately, according to Arendt, Heidegger was "still young enough to learn from the shock of the collision, which after ten short hectic months thirty-seven years ago drove him back to his residence, and to settle in his thinking what he had experienced." From this collision with the brute reality of Nazism, there emerged a new and radically different thinking that is clearly separated from the thinking to which Heidegger adhered in 1933-34. [12]

Below I return to Arendt's reading of Heidegger. For the moment, suffice it to say that I share Arendt's insistence on an important connection between Heidegger's political and philosophical careers. Against Arendt, however, I argue that Heidegger's later thought is closely tied to his position of 1933. Indeed, these political writings in some ways mark the first public appearance of "the later Heidegger." This is not to say that Heidegger's position of 1933 corresponds in all respects to his position of 1947 or 1966, for there is a very important shift of emphasis in the period after 1933. But one theme remains constant: namely, Heidegger's notion that the modern world is beset by a radical crisis of spirit. Throughout, Heidegger believed "nihilism" to be mankind's most pressing problem. There are foreshadows of this in **Being and Time** and "What is Metaphysics?" (1929), but his political writings

----

[11] Walter Biemel, **Martin Heidegger**, J. L. Mehta, trans., New York, Harcourt Brace Jovanovich, 1976, p. xii.

[12] Hannah Arendt, "Martin Heidegger at Eighty," in Murray, ed., **Heidegger and Modern Philosophy**, pp. 301-303. Earlier, in the immediate wake of World War I, Arendt's view of Heidegger had been very negative; see: "What Is Existenz Philosophy?," **Partisan Review**, 13, 1, Winter, 1946, pp. 34-56, especially on p. 47.

constitute the first published texts in which Heidegger specifies nihilism as our problem. Diagnosing nihilism, Heidegger persistently **responded** with nostalgia: looking back to a mythic (and unattainable) past.[13] Diffusely, **Being and Time** embodies a similar orientation; but after 1932, Heidegger's writings express a highly specific nostalgia, articulated within the context of our presumed crisis.

Many of those commenting on Heidegger's political writings have pointed out their prevalent tenor of crisis.[14] It is hardly surprising that in 1933 Heidegger believed Germany to stand in a state of extreme political and social crisis. But the **tone** of Heidegger's evocations of crisis is unexpected, for they seem intended to accentuate and glorify the crisis and thus the "movement" which was to master the situation, to "take charge." Extreme situations demand extreme responses. The old order is about to give way to the new, but the time is nonetheless one of great danger. Courageous action and hard sacrifice are required if the German nation is to fulfil its destiny. Such was the language of Heidegger in 1933.

In a message to "German students," published in the **Freiburger Studentenzeitung** for November 3, 1933, he declared that:

> the National Socialist Revolution brings a complete transformation in our German existence. Under these circumstances it is up to you always to remain eager and at the ready, perseverant and continuing to develop

----

[13] I borrow the notion of nostalgia from: R. N. Berki, **On Political Realism**, London, Dent, 1981. I am likewise indebted to Berki for the contrasting notion of a future-oriented "imagination," explained below.

[14] For example, see: Steiner, **Heidegger**, p. 117; Pachter, "Heidegger and Hitler," pp. 52, 55; Harries, "Heidegger as a Political Thinker," p. 327; Karl Löwith, "Les Implications politiques de la philosophie de l'existence chez Martin Heidegger," Joseph Rovan, trans., **Les Temps modernes**, 14, November, 1946, pp. 358-359. As argued below, however, these and other commentators underestimate the extent to which Heidegger's preoccupation with the notion of crisis postdates 1927. In consequence, they tend to overestimate the continuity between **Being and Time** and Heidegger's words and actions of 1933-34.

> yourselves....Doctrines and 'ideas' shall no
> longer be the rule of your Being. The Führer,
> he and he alone, is the present and future
> German reality and its law. Learn this ever
> more deeply: From now on each and every
> thing demands decision and each and every act
> reponsibility. Heil Hitler![15]

These themes recur in a speech to representatives of the
German professoriate in Dresden on November 11, 1933, the
eve of the plebiscite in which Hitler asked the German people to ratify withdrawal from the League of Nations.

> German teachers and comrades! German compa-
> triots! The German people is called by the
> Führer to a choice....Tomorrow the people will
> choose nothing less than its own future. This
> choice cannot be compared to any previous
> choice. The unique quality of this choice is
> the simple grandeur of the decision to be taken
> in it. The inexorability of the simple and of
> the last allows no delay. This final decision
> reaches out to the uttermost boundaries of the
> existence of our **Volk**...[16]

And on January 22, 1934, six hundred formerly unemployed
workers were marched to the largest lecture hall in the
university to hear Heidegger proclaim that:

> there is a new, common will to throw up a liv-
> ing bridge between the worker of the hand and
> the worker of the brain. This will to bridge-
> building is no longer a hopeless dream -- and
> why not? Because through the National Social-
> ist state our entire German reality has been
> altered, and this has as its consequence that all
> previous ideas and thinking must also change

----

[15] Martin Heidegger, "Deutsche Studenten," in **Nachlese zu
Heidegger**, Guido Schneeberger, ed., Bern, privately
printed, 1962, pp. 135-136.

[16] Martin Heidegger, "Bekenntnis zu Adolf Hitler und dem
nationalsozialistischen Staat," **Nachlese zu Heidegger**, pp.
148-150, on p. 148.

into something else.[17]

Heidegger's rhetoric of crisis is not confined, however, to his observations on the political situation of Germany in 1933. For he was convinced that the political crisis was merely one manifestation of a wider and much more significant crisis in philosophy or thought. This is evident in what is by far the most important of his political texts: **The Self-Assertion of the German University**, given as his **Rektoratsrede** before the students and faculty of Freiburg University in May, 1933. In **Being and Time**, he had referred to alleged crises in mathematics, physics, biology, the **Geisteswissenschaften**, and theology. Indeed, he had asserted (without argument) that "a science's level of development is determined by the extent to which it is capable of a crisis in its basic concepts."[18] He took up the theme again in "What is Metaphysics?", pointing to the fragmentation of disciplines as evidence for crisis in science as a whole.[19] In **The Self-Assertion of the German University**, he then extended this notion of crisis to all of Western culture.

According to Heidegger, the crisis has been caused by our departure from the essence of science: that is, from its Greek beginnings. In his words, "we do not at all experience the essence of science in its innermost necessity so long as we merely contest...the independence and presuppositionlessness of an all-too-contemporary science." We

----

[17] Martin Heidegger, "Nationalsocialistische Wissensschulung," in Schneeberger, ed., **Nachlese zu Heidegger**, pp. 198-202, on p. 200.

[18] Martin Heidegger, **Being and Time**, John Macquarrie and Edward Robinson, trans., New York, Harper and Row, 1962, pp. 9-10. I use the pagination of the later German editions of **Being and Time**. These are indicated in the margins of both the Macquarrie and Robinson translation and the edition published in the **Gesamtausgabe**: Martin Heidegger, **Sein und Zeit**, Frankfurt am Main, Vittorio Klostermann, 1977.

[19] Martin Heidegger, "Was ist Metaphysik?" in **Wegmarken**, Frankfurt am Main, Vittorio Klostermann, 1976, pp. 103-122, on p. 104; English trans. in Martin Heidegger, **Basic Writings**, David Farrell Krell, ed., New York, Harper and Row, 1977, pp. 95-112, on p. 96.

need instead to cast our eyes back, for we can grasp the
essence of science only if "we place ourselves again under
the power of the beginning of our spiritual-historical existence."

> This beginning is the awakening of Greek phi-
> losophy. Therein Western man, out of a **Volk**
> heritage that he possesses by virtue of his lan-
> guage, for the first time stands up against
> that-which-is as a whole and questions and
> grasps it as the being that it is. All science is
> philosophy, whether it knows and wishes it or
> not. All science remains bound up with that
> beginning of philosophy. Out of it, it creates
> the power of its essence, assuming that it re-
> mains at all equal to this beginning.[20]

He declared that we are now separated by 2500 years from
the Greek beginnings of science. Between us and those
beginnings stand both the "Christian-theological world
interpretation" and the "mathematical-technological thinking
of the modern age."[21] Indeed, for the first time in any of
his published writings, he evoked the crisis statement of
"the passionately God-seeking last German philosopher,

----

[20] Martin Heidegger, **Die Selbstbehauptung der deutschen
Universität**, Breslau, Korn, 1933, pp. 7-8: "Das Wesen der
Wissenschaft erfahren wir allerdings nicht in seiner inner-
sten Notwendigkeit, solange wir nur -- vom neuen Wissen-
schaftsbegriff redend -- einer allzu heutigen Wissenschaft
die Eigenständigkeit und Voraussetzungslosigkeit be-
streiten....soll Wissenschaft aber sein und soll sie für uns
und durch uns sein, unter welcher Bedingung kann sie
dann wahrhaft bestehen?...Nur dann, wenn wir uns wieder
unter die Macht des Anfangs unseres geistig-geschichtlichen
Daseins stellen. Dieser Anfang ist der Aufbruch der grie-
schischen Philosophie. Darin steht der abendländische
Mensch aus einem Volkstum kraft seiner Sprache erstmals
auf gegen das Seiende im Ganzen und befragt und begreift
es als das Seiende, das es ist. Alle Wissenschaft ist Philosophie, mag sie es wissen und wollen -- oder nicht. Alle
Wissenschaft bleibt jenem Anfang der Philosophie verhaftet.
Aus ihm schöpft sie die Kraft ihres Wesens, gesetzt, dass
sie diesem Anfang überhaupt noch gewachsen bleibt."

[21] Ibid., pp. 10-11.

Friedrich Nietzsche," linking Nietzsche's "death of God" with his own developing notion of "the abandonment of present-day man in the midst of beings."[22] But if God is dead and Being forgotten, Heidegger nonetheless saw the possibility of a transformation: one taking the form of a return to the origin. "The beginning is yet to be. It does not lie behind us as something long past, but on the contrary stands before us....The beginning has fallen into our future, it stands there as the distant decree over us, to bring again its greatness."[23]

   Very noticeable in the **Self-Assertion** speech is the ease with which Heidegger moved back and forth between two quite different levels of concern: on the one hand, the immediate political condition of Germany (which finds itself, in 1933, in a state of crisis); on the other hand, the condition of Western thought (which **also** finds itself, after Nietzsche, in a state of crisis). An elevated and highly abstract consideration of the essence of science blurs into a more down-to-earth, but equally abstract consideration of the destiny of the German **Volk**. "German students are on the march."[24] But we never quite learn whether they are on the march toward a true understanding of the essence of science or toward the complete overthrow of the Treaty of Versailles. At the end of the speech, Heidegger told his audience that "we only fully understand the glory and greatness of this awakening [**Aufbruch**] when we carry

----

[22] **Ibid.**, p. 12: "Und wenn gar unser eigenstes Dasein selbst vor einer grossen Wandlung steht, wenn es wahr ist, was der leidenschaftlich den Gott suchende letzte deutsche Philosoph, Friedrich Nietzsche, sagte: 'Gott ist tot' -- wenn wir Ernst machen müssen mit dieser Verlassenheit des heutigen Menschen inmitten des Seienden, wie steht es dann mit der Wissenschaft?"

[23] **Ibid.**, p. 11: "Der Anfang ist noch. Er liegt nicht hinter uns als das längst Gewesene, sondern er steht vor uns....Der Anfang ist in unsere Zukunft eingefallen, er steht dort als die ferne Verfügung über uns, seine Grösse wieder einzuholen."

[24] **Ibid.**, p. 14: "Die deutsche Studentenschaft ist auf dem Marsch." Note also the words on a poster to be seen at bookburnings in 1933: "Deutsche Studenten marschieren wider den undeutschen Geist." (photograph, **Der Spiegel**, 30, 23, May 31, 1976, p. 196.

within us that deep and wide reflection, out of which ancient Greek wisdom spoke the words "**ta...megala panta episphale**: All that is great stands in the storm."[25] But which **Aufbruch** did Heidegger have in mind: the **Aufbruch** of Greek philosophy or the **Aufbruch** heralded by Hitler's accession to power? Does **Sturm** refer to the difficulties with which a return to Greek philosophy is fraught or to the task of creating an entirely "coordinated" German nation?

Karl Löwith captured the flavor of this when he remarked, in his **Temps modernes** articles of 1946, that Heidegger's listeners didn't quite know whether they ought to turn to the study of the Presocratics or join the storm troopers.[26] Heidegger never resolved the ambiguity; in this sense, his language is, by the standards of **Being and Time**, "inauthentic."[27] In effect, he had it both ways; hence he could later claim, without fear of textual disconfirmation, that he had **intended** only the more elevated meaning. In his letter of self-justification of November 4, 1945, written to the incumbent rector of Freiburg University, he noted of 1933 that "I was at that time...convinced that through the independent, collaborative work of men of learning [**Geistigen**] many essential beginnings of the 'Nazi Movement' could be deepened and transformed, in order to place the Movement in such a position as to be able in its own way to help to overcome the confused situation of Europe and the crisis of the Western spirit."[28] But it seems

----

[25] **Ibid.**, p. 22: "Die Herrlichkeit aber und die Grösse dieses Aufbruchs verstehen wir dann erst ganz, wenn wir in uns jene tiefe und weite Besonnenheit tragen, aus der die alte griechische Weisheit das Wort gesprochen: ta...megala panta episphale...'Alles Grosse steht im Sturm'." Heidegger here quoted the **Republic**, 497d, 9; the passage is more conventionally rendered as "all great undertakings are risky." See: Plato, **Republic**, H. D. P. Lee, trans., Baltimore, Penguin Books, 1955, p. 260.

[26] Löwith, "Les Implications politiques de la philosophie de l'existence chez Martin Heidegger," p. 351.

[27] See: Heidegger, **Sein und Zeit**, section 37, pp. 173-175.

[28] Heidegger's letter is given in full in: Moehling, "Martin Heidegger and the Nazi Party," pp. 263-268, on p. 263 (my translation).

clear that many of Heidegger's listeners could only have taken his words in their "lower" sense. These words thus lent an aura of high intellectual and moral purpose to the "Nazi Movement": that is, to the movement that actually existed, as distinguished from the hypothetical movement existing only in the mind of Martin Heidegger.[29]

One prominent aspect of Heidegger's political writings, then, is their persistent reference to a crisis of society, politics, culture, intellect, or spirit, with no great effort to distinguish between different types or levels of crisis. Heidegger responded nostalgically to the supposed crisis. He held that its resolution can only come through a return, a going **back**, whether to an ideal past or to an extant but as yet unrealized possibility. In fact, this nostalgic motif predated Heidegger's conviction that the modern world is confronted by nihilism, that is, by the reality of crisis. Like Heidegger's later works, **Being and Time** is pervaded by a metaphoric of return. Heidegger perpetually proposed to go back, to return, to go home again to some more primal, more immediate, less articulate, but definitely more authentic condition.

For the most part, those who have commented on **Being and Time** have ignored this aspect of the work.[30] Yet Heidegger's predilection for a metaphoric of return is more important for understanding what is going on in that work than is its structure of arguments, which repeatedly seem simply not to follow, even granting Heidegger his explicit presuppositions. Indeed, one reason why philosophers in the analytical tradition have found it so difficult to come to grips with **Being and Time** is that they focus on its logic. They fail to see its really compelling part: its metaphorical bias, the peculiar direction of its rhetoric.

----

[29] Moehling writes of the "veracity" of Heidegger's comments in this letter, in another letter of 1945 to the de-Nazification Committee at Freiburg University, and in his 1966 interview with the German newsmagazine **Der Spiegel**: "Heidegger and the Nazis," p. 32. But the "veracity" of these comments is sustained only if one ignores the ambiguity of Heidegger's words of 1933.

[30] One notable exception is Theodor W. Adorno, who shrewdly pointed out the existence in **Being and Time** of "the mental posture of a permanent 'back to'." (**Negative Dialectics**, E. B. Ashton, trans., New York, Seabury Press, 1973, p. 62.)

Since this essay mainly concerns the later writings, I can deal only briefly with **Being and Time**. But perhaps a few reminders will suffice. Heidegger's predilection for "going back" is most obvious in the ontological aspect of **Being and Time**, where his concern with the "meaning of Being" is paramount. Note that Heidegger was concerned, not simply with **asking** what Being means, but with **recovering** a question that "has today been forgotten," a question that "provided a stimulus for the researches of Plato and Aristotle, only to subside from then on **as a theme for actual investigation**."[31] In short, Heidegger wanted us to find our way **back** to the question of the meaning of Being. The same motif of return also pervades his existential analytic, where the notion of a "going back" is almost obsessive. Thus, the "call of conscience" is a call "from afar unto afar" that "reaches him who wants to be brought back."[32] In resoluteness (**Entschlossenheit**), **Dasein** "comes toward itself futurally in such a way that it comes **back**."[33] In the state of anxiety, **Dasein** is "taken all the way back to its naked uncanniness [**Unheimlichkeit**] and becomes fascinated by it."[34] At the same time but on a more general plane, the characterization of **Dasein**, in its "thrownness," as "Being-ahead-of-itself" has the implication that it is perpetually trying to find its way back to its "ownmost potentiality-for-Being."[35]

The nostalgic motif is equally present in the political texts; indeed, it is both extended and intensified there. We have seen how, in response to the alleged intellectual crisis in our time, Heidegger advised a return to the original Greek essence of science, a recommendation in keeping with the nostalgia of **Being and Time**. Entirely new, however, is the appearance of a specifically social nostalgia, looking back to an earlier and allegedly more authentic

----

[31] Heidegger, **Being and Time**, p. 2.

[32] **Ibid.**, p. 271. I am well aware how questionable is any attempt to make a rigid distinction between the "ontological" and "existential" aspects of **Being and Time**. Here I entertain the distinction only for purposes of presentation.

[33] **Ibid.**, p. 326.

[34] **Ibid.**, p. 344.

[35] **Ibid.**, pp. 191-192.

social order. To be sure, some commentators, especially Marxists, have seen a social dimension in **Being and Time**; the classic example of such a reading is that of Georg Lukacs in **The Destruction of Reason.**[36] Generally, such commentators have tied the existential analytic to "the anonymous and depersonalized subject of the modern industrial city."[37] Yet Heidegger clearly did not intend this analysis in any such socially specific way. On the contrary, the anonymous "they" (**das Man**) of **Being and Time** can appear in a close-knit village as well as in an anonymous city. It is something that exists wherever Being-with-one-another comes into play, which is to say, at every moment of **Dasein**'s existence.

Different, however, are the writings of 1933-34, where Heidegger did stigmatize the city and correspondingly glorified the supposedly simple life of peasants. This comes out most clearly in his radio address of early March, 1934, entitled "Why Do We Stay in the Provinces?" Here he explained why he had turned down calls to the more prestigious universities of Munich and Berlin, preferring instead to remain at Freiburg: near his birthplace, near the Black Forest, near the Alps. He told his listeners that he carried out his philosophical work in a small ski hut in a wide valley of the southern Black Forest. And why here? As he explained it:

> philosophical work does not take its course as the aloof business of a man apart. It belongs in the midst of the work of peasants. When the young peasant drags his heavy sledge up the slope, and then guides it, piled high with beech logs, down the dangerous descent to his house, when the herdsman, lost in thought and slow of step, drives his cattle up the slope, when the peasant in his shed gets the countless shingles ready for his roof -- then is my work of the same kind. It is ultimately rooted in and related to the life of the peasants.

----

[36] Georg Lukács, **The Destruction of Reason**, Peter Palmer, trans., Atlantic Highlands, NJ, Humanities Press, 1981, pp. 498ff.

[37] Fredric Jameson, **Fables of Aggression**, Berkeley, University of California Press, 1979, p. 128.

Heidegger lauded the thoughtfulness and sense of remembrance that prevail in peasant life. Moreover, he regretted that "the world of the city runs the risk of falling into a destructive error," for a "very loud and very pushy and very fashionable obtrusiveness" is abroad, passing itself off as "concern for the world and existence of the peasant." But precisely this threatens to destroy the peasants' world. The peasant, Heidegger declared, must be left alone; he does not want this "citified officiousness," but rather "a quiet reserve with regard to his own way of being and its independence." Finally, Heidegger noted how, after receiving his second call to Berlin, he withdrew from the city and returned to his hut. "I listened to what the mountains and the forest and the farms said. I came to my old friend, a 75-year-old peasant. He had read about the call to Berlin in the newspaper. What would he say? Slowly he fixed the sure gaze of his clear eyes on mine, and keeping his mouth tightly shut, he placed his true and considerate hand on my shoulder -- ever so slightly, he shook his head. That meant -- absolutely no!"[38]

What, then, explains Heidegger's susceptibility to the Nazi appeal? The answer, I think, is clear. Firstly, Heidegger's rhetoric of crisis finds an echo in the political language of the Nazis. Secondly, Heidegger's stance of nostalgia is repeated in the political posture of the Nazis. Those disturbed by "the crisis of the European spirit" could move in either a "nostalgic" or an "imaginative" direction. That is to say, they could respond to the presumed dereliction of the present by looking toward either a mythic past or a mythic future.[39] In the wake of World War I, many Germans opted for the former. There was much in German thought and society to incline people this way. One set of comparative statistics is perhaps worth citing: in 1871, 5% of the German population lived in cities of 100,000 or more; by 1925, the proportion had grown to

----

[38] Heidegger, **Nachlese zu Heidegger**, pp. 216-218. For the most part, I have followed the translation by Thomas Sheehan in his **Heidegger**, pp. 27-30.

[39] Again, I owe this contrast to: Berki, **On Political Realism**, especially pp. 192ff. As Berki points out on p. 222, a past-oriented nostalgia very easily turns into a future-oriented imagination. Though Heidegger remained primarily nostalgic, traces of an imaginative orientation are also, not surprisingly, to be found in his work.

27%.[40] Inevitably, many looked back to the serene and joyful, but (alas) largely imaginary period before the city had taken over. Indeed, the whole idea of the **Volk**, which in its more extreme versions idealized the primeval world of the ancient Germans, was nostalgic in bearing.[41]

In view of the political and social factors also at work, it is not surprising that in the 1920s Germany saw a flowering of neo-conservative thought: a "conservative revolutionism" that proclaimed the bankruptcy of middle-class humanism and that strove to create, by vaguely defined revolutionary means, one or another variety of nostalgic utopia.[42] Heidegger's affinities with this strand of thought are too striking to be ignored. Like Oswald Spengler, Moeller van den Bruck, and Ernst Jünger, Heidegger believed that the West stood in a state of crisis. If his interpretation of that crisis differed (sometimes quite radically) from these thinkers, he still shared much in common with them. Nazism, too, shared many of these same prejudices: idealization of the German past, ideological fondness for the peasant, suspicion of rootless cosmopolitans, and (above all) commitment to the notion of crisis. The Nazis were not always ideologically consistent, but they were coherent enough in espousing and exploiting these themes for Heidegger to take them, for a time, as a vessel for his ontological hopes.

----

[40] David Schoenbaum, **Hitler's Social Revolution**, Garden City, NY, Doubleday, 1966, p. 3.

[41] For an illuminating account of **völkisch** notions, see: George L. Mosse, **The Crisis of German Ideology**, New York, Grosset and Dunlap, 1964, especially pp. 1-87.

[42] On neoconservatism, see: Klemens von Klemperer, **Germany's New Conservatism**, Princeton, Princeton University Press, 1957, especially pp. 117ff, 153-226. Also see: Moehling, "Martin Heidegger and the Nazi Party," pp. 131ff.

II

I now turn to the broader question of the place of Heidegger's political writings within his corpus as a whole. Of course, in the eyes of many, philosophers and nonphilosophers alike, Heidegger's involvement with the Nazis utterly discredited him; he was a "Nazi philosopher" and hence undeserving of serious treatment. This is unjustified. Not only did Heidegger quickly pull back from the Nazis, but he soon came under attack from a true Nazi philosopher, the now-forgotten Ernst Krieck.[43] Moreover, while biography may help us to understand an author's texts, their validity is a separate issue. Past the notion that Heidegger's philosophy is disqualified due to his association with the Nazis, there remains the question of connecting his political and unpolitical texts. Here I challenge two answers to this question which, whether wittingly or not, "sanitize" Heidegger's work by associating the political texts of 1933-34 with a philosophy that he soon abandoned.

One interpretation links the political writings back to the notion of "destiny" (**das Geschick**) on which Heidegger laid considerable emphasis in the later chapters of **Being and Time**. To emphasize "destiny" need by no means clash with my stress on "crisis," for the two notions are closely connected. Thus those who see "destiny" as fundamental for explaining Heidegger's susceptibility to Nazism also allude to "crisis." Karsten Harries notes that Heidegger's thought was "born of a widely shared sense of crisis."[44] George Steiner observes that Heidegger and Nazism share with "so much of German thought after Nietzsche and Spengler" the "presumption of...a nearing apocalypse, of so deep a crisis in human affairs that the norms of personal and institutional morality must be, shall inevitably be,

----

[43] On Krieck, see: Jean-Michel Palmier, ed., **Les Écrits politiques de Heidegger**, Paris, L'Herne, 1968, pp. 95ff, 297-331. But lest the fact that Heidegger came under attack from such hundred percent Nazis as Krieck seem to turn him into an anti-Nazi, see: Jean-Pierre Faye, "Attaques nazies contre Heidegger," **Médiations**, 5, 1962, pp. 137-151, on p. 145ff. There we learn of the "enigmatic affinities" linking Heidegger to Krieck.

[44] Harries, "Heidegger as a Political Thinker," p. 327; also p. 313.

brushed aside."[45] Still, both Harries and Steiner specify "destiny" as decisive for Heidegger's political involvement. Harries portrays Heidegger as committed to freedom, understood as autonomy: that is, as giving law to oneself. But unlike Kant, he was unable to ground freedom in the authority of pure reason, since for obvious reasons this authority was no longer available to him. In order to give content to "autonomy," he had to appeal elsewhere; and he chose "history." If the individual is to understand what his essence commands, he "has to understand also the origin of that essence and the destiny which ties him to others, to his people."[46]

More interesting on this point, because somewhat more copious and explicit, is Steiner. He ties the political writings specifically to the second half of **Being and Time**, which tries to show that **Dasein** is ineluctably temporal. Especially important in this regard are the last two chapters of **Being and Time**, which discuss history. Here **Dasein** is placed within a historical community, because accepting **Dasein**, in all its temporality, requires accepting one's historical inheritance. And hence the resolve displayed in **Dasein** must be rooted in an inherited past. Since one shares this inheritance with others, "Dasein's fateful destiny in and with its 'generation' goes to make up the full authentic historizing of Dasein."[47] Obviously, this gives an opening for National Socialism's urging that Germans grasp the decisive moment, seeking resolutely to fulfill their destiny as a people. These are the precise terms of Heidegger's political writings, which Steiner thus sees as having an "organic" connection with Part II of **Being and Time**.[48]

----

[45] Steiner, **Heidegger**, p. 117.

[46] Harries, "Heidegger as a Political Thinker," pp. 312-313. In support of this interpretation, Harries appeals to: Heidegger, **Die Selbstbehauptung der deutschen Universität**, p. 15; Heidegger, **Being and Time**, p. 384.

[47] Ibid., pp. 384-385.

[48] Steiner, **Heidegger**, pp. 114, 98, 107-109. In fact, Steiner refers to "Part III" of **Being and Time**, but this seems to be a misprint, since no "Part III" ever appeared. Moreover, Steiner refers to "Parts" whereas the Macquarrie and Robinson translation refers (correctly) to "Divisions" (**Abschnitte**). Here I follow Steiner, but let me emphasize

As far as it goes, Steiner's argument is plausible and even correct; but it nonetheless suffers from two serious difficulties. Firstly, it tends to diffuse and undercut the very relationship that it seeks to posit: namely, that between **Being and Time** and the political writings.   To claim an "organic" connection between the political writings and only Part II of **Being and Time** is to imply that the same does **not** hold for Part I.   This accords with the often-expressed view that Part II (with its investigation of the tie between **Dasein** and temporality) is a palpable decline from Part I (which offers a "Preparatory Fundamental Analysis of Dasein").   But are not these two parts themselves "organically" connected?   After all, **both** parts are concerned, implicitly and explicitly, with temporality. As Steiner notes, Heidegger's conception of time has affinities with such previous, eschatological thinkers as Augustine.   Heidegger differed from such predecessors as Plato and Descartes, who thought of reality in terms of the fixed eternity of geometrical space, where time is irrelevant to truth.[49] Thus Heidegger's temporal, as opposed to spatial, focus (which plainly connects with Rorty's notion of an attack on the "ocular" metaphor of understanding) is absolutely fundamental to the entirety of **Being and Time**, not alone to Part II.   The title of the work well indicates its central, driving theme.

Of course, one could still attempt to make a division between the "good" and the "bad" parts of **Being and Time**, perhaps singling out for condemnation the last two chapters.   But surely Heidegger was **obliged** to make this final turn to history and thus to work out his notions for grasping history: heritage, fate, and destiny.   What if Heidegger had **not** sought to root **Dasein** within a historical community?   Then there would have threatened a solipsism far worse than that facing Cartesian subjectivism, for Heidegger has denied the possibility of appealing to a universal reason.   Hence, if the political writings tie at all to **Being and Time**, surely they connect to the whole, not to some defective and potentially dispensable part.

Still, I do not want to place too much weight on this

----

that by Parts I and II, I mean Divisions 1 and 2 of Part One.   Part One was to be followed by Part Two, which Heidegger never published.   (See his plan for the whole, unfinished work: **Being and Time**, pp. 39-40.)

[49] Steiner, **Heidegger**, p. 99.

first argument. A "destiny" which roots individuals within a historical people is important for the political writings, and it does trace back to **Being and Time**. To this extent, Steiner, Harries, and others are entirely right. But **Being and Time** is separated from the writings of 1933-34 by a crucial break in Heidegger's thought. In consequence, the affinities that bridge the break are less important than the differences which constitute it. To argue this is, of course, to evoke what Heidegger himself called the **Kehre**: the "turn" or "reversal."[50] When, exactly, the "turn" occurred is extremely significant for the place of Heidegger's political writings in his corpus as a whole. If it came before 1933-34, there must be some important sense in which the political and subsequent writings remain within the ambit of the "error" of 1933; if it came after 1933-34, there must be some significant sense in which the later writings abandoned the philosophical territory within which the error was committed and transcended the error itself. (Obviously, I reject the view that Heidegger's error had nothing to do with his philosophy.)

Hence my second argument challenges another interpretation of the tie between Heidegger's political and unpolitical texts. In "Martin Heidegger at Eighty" and again, in more detail, in her posthumously published **Life of the Mind**, Hannah Arendt located Heidegger's "turn" in the period 1936-1940. This turn entailed Heidegger's shift from willing to nonwilling. In Arendt's words, "what the reversal originally turns against is primarily the will-to-power." The significance of this for the problem of Heidegger's politics is clear. As Arendt put it, "in Heidegger's understanding, the will to rule and to dominate is a kind of original sin, of which he found himself guilty when he tried to come to terms with his brief part in the Nazi movement." In Arendt's view, the turn took two stages. Originally, it was against "the self-assertion of man," as proclaimed in the **Rektoratsrede**. The symbol of this self-assertion is Prometheus, "the first philosopher," who is mentioned in the **Rektoratsrede** and nowhere else in Heidegger's works. Later, it was also against "the alleged subjectivism of **Being and Time** and the book's primary concern with man's

----

[50] Heidegger's first published reference to the "turn" occurs in his "Letter on Humanism," **Wegmarken**, pp. 327-328; English trans. in Heidegger, **Basic Writings**, pp. 207-208. Also see his discussion of the turn in his preface to Richardson's **Heidegger**, pp. xvi-xvii.

existence, his mode of being." This rejection of subjectivism entailed, too, a rejection of politics and a return by
Heidegger to his proper abode: thought, not practical
affairs.[51]   Thus   on   Arendt's   interpretation,   Heidegger
became an entirely unpolitical thinker.

Arendt was certainly right to point out the importance
of "nonwilling" in the later thought of Heidegger.   Yet I
disagree   with   her   characterization   of   its   significance.
There is indeed a crucial difference in Heidegger's writings
between 1933 and 1940 (let alone 1966), a difference well
summarized in Arendt's contrast between willing and nonwilling.   Heidegger's political writings clearly claim that human
will   can   have   an   impact   on   the   course   of   history.   For
example,   in   the   peroration   to   **The Self-Assertion of the
German University**,   Heidegger   insisted   that   the   spiritual
fate of the West hangs on "whether we as a historical and
spiritual **Volk** still and again **will** ourselves -- or whether
we no longer will ourselves.   Every single individual con-
currently makes his decision on this, even when -- especially when -- he avoids this decision."[52]   By way of contrast,   Heidegger's   later   writings   show   a   deep   sense   of
regretfulness and loss, elegaic in its intensity.   Thus in an
interview for the German newsmagazine **Der Spiegel**, given
in 1966 though not published until after his death in 1976,
Heidegger held that:

> philosophy will not be able to effect an immedi-
> ate transformation of the present condition of

----

[51] Hannah Arendt, **The Life of the Mind**, New York, Harcourt Brace Jovanovich, two volumes, 1978; **Volume 2:   Willing**, p. 173.   Also see: Arendt, "Martin Heidegger at
Eighty," pp. 302-303.

[52] Heidegger, **Die Selbstbehauptung der deutschen Universität**, p. 22:   "Aber niemand wird uns auch fragen, ob wir
wollen   oder   nicht   wollen,   wenn   die   geistige   Kraft   des
Abendlandes versagt und dieses in seinen Fugen kracht,
wenn die abgelebte Scheinkultur in sich zusammenstürtz und
alle Kräfte in die Verwirrung reisst und im Wahnsinn er-
sticken lässt.   Ob solches geschieht oder nicht geschieht,
das hängt allein daran, ob wir als geschichtlich-geistiges
Volk uns selbst noch und wieder wollen -- oder ob wir uns
nicht mehr wollen.   Jeder einzelne entscheidet darüber mit,
auch dann und gerade dann, wenn er vor dieser Entscheid-
ung ausweicht."

the world.   This is not only true of philosophy,
but of all merely human thought and endeavor.
Only a god can save us.   The sole possibility
that is left for us is to prepare a readiness,
through thinking [Denken] and poetic creation
[Dichten], for the appearance of the god or for
the absence of the god in the time of founder-
ing [Untergang], for in the face of the god
who is absent, we founder.[53]

Or, as he put it in "Conversation on a Country Path about
Thinking" (based on notes of 1944-45, published in 1959),
"We are to do nothing but wait."[54]
    Still, this shift, though genuine, is less momentous
than Arendt suggested.` To see this, let us consider the
origins and persistence in Heidegger's thought of the notion
of crisis, which I have already shown to be important for
his political writings.   The "problem of nihilism" -- the
allegedly oppressed and alienated condition of "modern
man," who finds himself forced to live in a world lacking
the security of absolute values -- does not exist in Being
and Time.   But in Heidegger's later writings, "nihilism" is
our most serious problem.   For example, his Letter on
Humanism (1947) is clear about this: "Homelessness is coming to be the destiny of the world.   Hence it is necessary
to think that destiny in terms of the history of Being.
What Marx recognized in an essential and significant sense,
though derived from Hegel, as the estrangement of man has
its roots in the homelessness of modern man."   Here Heidegger wrote also of "the modern age," "the present stage of
world history," and "the present world crisis" (die jetzige

----

[53] Martin Heidegger, "Only a God Can Save Us: Der Spiegel's Interview with Martin Heidegger," Maria P. Alter and
John D. Caputo, trans., Philosophy Today, 20, 4, Winter,
1976, pp. 267-284, on p. 277, translation altered.   Another
translation, by William J. Richardson, appears in: Sheehan, ed., Heidegger, pp. 45-67.

[54] Martin Heidegger, "Zur Erörterung der Gelassenheit:
Aus einem Feldweggesprach über das Denken," in Gelassen-
heit, Pfullingen, Neske, 1959, p. 37; English trans. by
John M. Anderson and E. Hans Freund in: Heidegger,
Discourse on Thinking, New York, Harper and Row, 1966,
p. 62.

Weltnot).[55]

Nothing of this sort appears in **Being and Time,** where concern with **Dasein** is as unspecific historically as it is socially. If **Being and Time** hints that somehow, before Plato and Aristotle, humans had a greater affinity with Being than now, it merely hints and fails to work this out in historical terms. **Dasein**'s propensity for falling away from "authentic potentiality for Being its Self" should not be interpreted historically.[56] Every **Dasein** manifests such fallenness at **all** times. There is no notion of an "age of anxiety." Heidegger did not hold that the "existential-onto-logical" situation portrayed in **Being and Time** is peculiar to "modern man." Only in the later writings does that tormented soul, "modern man," make his appearance; only then is an attempt made to situate alienation within a specifically modern context. In short, only in the later writings is there the notion that the modern age is beset by crisis, a crisis prompted by (or identical with) the advent of nihilism.

Precisely when, and under what auspices, did this concern with nihilism enter Heidegger's thought? The question is crucial, because here (and not in the shift from willing to nonwilling) is Heidegger's basic "break." To be sure, Heidegger's "turn" is not **exhausted** by his taking up the problem of nihilism. Though this essay cannot develop the idea, I would argue that there are ways in which Heidegger's new concern with nihilism merely set the stage for other important alterations in his thought. The most important was his shift from the "conceptual" language and thinking of **Being and Time** to what his later writings champion as "a thinking more rigorous than the conceptual."[57] Still, nihilism remained Heidegger's decisive preoccupation, underpinning the whole of his later thought.

Plainly, nihilism was a problem for Heidegger in 1933. His evocations in **The Self-Assertion of the German University** of Nietzsche's notion of the "death of God" and of "the abandonment of present-day man in the midst of beings"

----

[55] Martin Heidegger, "Brief über den 'Humanismus'," in **Wegmarken,** pp. 339, 317, 351, 364; English trans. in Heidegger, **Basic Writings,** pp. 219, 197, 230, 242.

[56] Heidegger, **Being and Time,** p. 175.

[57] Heidegger, "Brief über den 'Humanismus'," p. 357; English trans. in Heidegger, **Basic Writings,** pp. 235-236.

testify to that.[58] Nietzsche's name is decisive in this connection. **Being and Time** cites him only three times. Only
one of these citations, to **The Use and Disadvantage of His-**
tory, is significant.[59] Yet Heidegger later lectured and
wrote extensively on Nietzsche, even producing a two-vol-
ume study of his predecessor. Published only in 1961, it
was based on lectures given between 1936 and 1940.
Indeed, Arendt located the "turn" as "a concrete autobio-
graphical event" between these two volumes.[60]

Obviously, sometime between 1927 and 1933, Heidegger "discovered" Nietzsche. More precisely, he "discovered" Nietzsche's theme of ontological crisis in the modern
world: a theme absent from **Being and Time**, but emphatically present in the political writings. Unfortunately, most
of Heidegger's post-1927 writings appeared in print only
long after their first composition. Thus they must pru-
dently be regarded as at least partly the products of later
revision. Indeed, Heidegger published virtually nothing
between 1929 and 1941. This makes the political writings
more important for understanding his intellectual career
than they might otherwise be.[61]

There is some reason to believe that Nietzsche and
the problem of nihilism entered Heidegger's thought about
1930. In **Philosophie und Politik bei Heidegger**, Otto Pöggeler writes that "ever since 1929/30, when Nietzsche
became a matter of 'decision' for him, his new starting point
for thinking the truth of Being was dominated by the all-

----

[58] Heidegger, **Die Selbstbehauptung der deutschen Univer-**
sität, p. 12.

[59] Heidegger, **Being and Time**, pp. 264, 272 (fn. vi), 396.

[60] Martin Heidegger, **Nietzsche**, Pfullingen, Neske, two volumes, 1961; Arendt, **Willing**, p. 173.

[61] To be specific, Heidegger published three writings in
1929: "What is Metaphysics?," "On the Essence of Reasons," and **Kant and the Problem of Metaphysics**. In 1941,
he published "Hölderlin's Hymn, 'Wie wenn am Feier-
tage...'." Between these two dates, the only nonpolitical
writing of Heidegger's to appear was "Hölderlin and the
Essence of Poetry," published in 1936. Heidegger's political
writings were entirely confined to the period between May,
1933 and March, 1934.

determining presupposition that God is 'dead.'"[62] In the
Foreword to **Nietzsche,** Heidegger himself expressed the
hope that these volumes would grant readers "a glance at
the way I have gone from 1930 to the 'Letter on Humanism'
(1947)."[63] And in his 1964 lecture on "The End of Philosophy and the Task of Thinking," he referred to his "attempt
undertaken again and again ever since 1930 to shape the
question of **Being and Time** in a more primordial
[presumably more Nietzschean] way."[64]

Especially significant in this regard is Heidegger's
essay on "Plato's Doctrine of Truth," which he traced to a
lecture course of 1930-31, though it first appeared in print
only in 1942. There he described Nietzsche as the thinker
in whom "the history of metaphysics has begun its uncondi-
tional completion." He epitomized Nietzsche's time (and
ours) as "the epoch in which the completion of the modern
age begins."[65] This theme is developed at great length in
Heidegger's **Nietzsche,** which portrays ours as the age of
the completion of metaphysics and the appearance of nihilism, with "Being" forgotten in the face of "beings," in the
face of "that-which-is."[66] Of course, this echoes **Being and
Time** a bit, for nihilism turns out to involve the "forgetfulness of Being" (the **Seinsvergessenheit**) so central to the
earlier work. But this forgetfulness is now presented much

----

[62] Otto Pöggeler, **Philosophie und Politik bei Heidegger,** p.
25.

[63] Heidegger, **Nietzsche,** v. I, p. 10; English trans. by
David Farrell Krell, **Nietzsche, I: The Will to Power as
Art,** New York, Harper and Row, 1979, p. xvi.

[64] Martin Heidegger, "Das Ende der Philosophie und die
Aufgabe des Denkens," in **Zur Sache des Denkens,** Tübingen, Niemeyer, 1969, p. 61; English trans. by Joan Stambaugh in: Heidegger, **Basic Writings,** p. 373.

[65] Martin Heidegger, "Platons Lehre von der Wahrheit," in
Wegmarken, pp. 233, 237; English trans. by John Barlow
in: William Barrett and Henry D. Aiken, eds., **Philosophy
in the Twentieth Century,** New York, Random House, three
volumes, 1962, v. III, pp. 267, 269, translation altered.
Regarding the composition of this essay, Heidegger said in
Wegmarken, p. 483, that "Der Gedankengang geht zürück
auf die Freiburger Vorlesung im Wintersemester 1930/31
'Vom Wesen der Wahrheit.' Der Text wurde 1940 zusammen-

more pointedly as a historical event: one which produces
the present crisis.   In short, nihilism is not an explicit
problem in **Being and Time**, whereas it troubles all of Heidegger's works after 1930, when it became absolutely the
most important problem we face.

This means that the intellectual orbit of 1933 is
already the orbit of Heidegger's later thought.   His "break"
occurred before, not after, involvement with the Nazis.
Richardson's recently published "summary" of Heidegger's
intellectual career (read and approved, we are told, by
Heidegger himself) is convincing on this point.   According
to Richardson, the "turn" occurred circa 1930, with the
"main lines" of Heidegger's new position firmly drawn in **An
Introduction to Metaphysics**, given as a lecture course in
the summer of 1935 (but published only in 1953).[67]

Undeniably, in the late 1930s Arendt's shift from willing to waiting also occurred.   Indeed, in his 1962 letter
which prefaces the Richardson volume, the ever sly philosopher declared that "the matter thought in the term 'reversal' was already at work in my thinking ten years prior to
1947," thus placing his "turn" in the period suggested by
Arendt.[68] But just how significant is the shift from willing
to waiting?   Heidegger's apologists habitually portray this
shift as a turning away from the arrogant, subjectivist conception of the will to power.   Yet the shift does not beto-
ken a rejection of Nietzsche's problematic of crisis; it only
signals a new stance **within** that problematic.

Following a pregnant suggestion in R. N. Berki's **On
Political Realism**, I have already noted two responses to
situations of radical crisis.   When the present is perceived

----

gestellt und erschien zuerst in [1942]." There is room for
doubt about Heidegger's dating here, since the plan for
Heidegger's **Gesamtausgabe** (Wegmarken, p. 489) attributes
the course "Vom Wesen der Wahrheit" to Winter Semester
1931-32, as does Heidegger's listing of his courses in Richardson, **Heidegger**, p. 667.

[66] Especially see the long essay on "Der europäische Nihil-
ismus" (1940) in: Heidegger, **Nietzsche**, v. II, pp. 3-256.

[67] William J. Richardson, "Heidegger's Way Through Phenomenology to the Thinking of Being," in Sheehan, ed.,
Heidegger, pp. 79-93, on pp. 88ff.

[68] Richardson, **Heidegger**, pp. xvi-xvii.

to be absolutely derelict, one can move in either a nostalgic
or an imaginative direction, opting for either a mythic past
or a mythic future. In Nietzsche's terms, this comes down
to an opposition between the "nostalgic" notion of eternal
return and the "imaginative" ideas of the will to power and
the superman. For all his nostalgic attraction to the past,
in 1933 Heidegger was equally caught up in the lure of
active willing, a notion which plainly points away from the
past, as Heidegger himself noted in his study of Nietzsche.[69] In contrast, such later writings as "Conversation
on a Country Path about Thinking" show Heidegger to be
consistently nostalgic, utterly rejecting the will. Still, this
is not a rejection of Nietzsche's problematic. Quite the contrary, it is a working out, with greater consistency and
rigor than Nietzsche himself managed, of the nostalgia in
this project.[70]

III

Heidegger's writings pose a "danger" for political
thought, not because they "deprive political action of its
ground," but because they fail to carry their therapy far
enough. For they fail to treat what is most in need of
therapy: the notion of crisis itself. I touch here on a
range of thought and sensibility far beyond Heidegger's
own important, if limited territory. For the notion of a
radical crisis in the affairs of men is the great cliche of
modernist and postmodernist writings. Modernism and
postmodernism are absolute in their conviction of the reality
of crisis. This notion is fundamental for their various
world views and approaches to life. Here I can do little
more than point out the crisis motif in these productive
strands of twentieth-century aesthetic and intellectual life,

----

[69] Heidegger, **Nietzsche**, v. II, p. 468.

[70] For his part, Heidegger denied any such affinity with
Nietzsche. But for a work that emphasizes "the important
formal identity" between Heidegger and Nietzsche, see:
Harold Alderman, **Nietzsche's Gift**, Athens, Ohio University
Press, 1977, especially pp. 164-173. To my mind, Alderman
manages to give a genuinely Heideggerian interpretation of
Nietzsche, where Heidegger himself did not.

leaving to the reader the specific connections without which
my gesture may seem entirely empty.

An astonishing number of twentieth-century artists
and thinkers have been preoccupied by crisis, break, rupture, discontinuity, separation. This holds for modernism
and postmodernism in their strictly literary and artistic
senses.[71] But it holds also for existentialism, structuralism,
poststructuralism, and the more radical postpositivistic philosophies of science. Beyond Nietzsche, Heidegger, and
Foucault, such figures as Yeats, Pound, Eliot, Tzara,
Cioran, Pynchon, Barth, Barthelme, Lévi-Strauss, Althusser, Barthes, Kuhn, and Feyerabend come to mind. Obviously, this sweep is too wide for the present essay, where
I confine myself to political theory. Here Hannah Arendt
has perhaps been the most prominent thinker of crisis.
The notion of a radical crisis in Western history is already
evident in her **Origins of Totalitarianism**; in her later
works, this crisis is explicitly portrayed as a crisis of tradition, authority, values, and belief.[72] I note, too, the
writing of Leo Strauss, who sees the "crisis of our time" as
the consequence of a crisis in political philosophy, and the
works of Eric Voegelin, who sees this crisis as the consequence of a misdirected, gnostic attempt to immanentize the
Christian eschaton.[73]

However different their perspectives, this is a sensibility shared by Nietzsche, Heidegger, and Foucault: all
quintessentially thinkers of crisis. Heidegger's proclama-
tions of crisis have already been sampled in this essay.
But one thinks as well of Nietzsche's: in **The Gay Science**
evoking the "death of God" and in the section of **Ecce Homo**

----

[71] For an illuminating treatment of the crisis theme in this
sphere, see: Alan Wilde, **Horizons of Assent**, Baltimore,
Johns Hopkins University Press, 1981, pp. 19ff.

[72] See: Hannah Arendt, **The Origins of Totalitarianism**,
New York, Harcourt Brace Jovanovich, fourth edition, 1973,
pp. 460ff; Arendt, **Between Past and Future**, New York,
Viking Press, second edition, 1968, pp. 10-11, 26, 34, 89,
91, 141, 173, and **passim**; Arendt, **Willing**, pp. 9ff.

[73] See: Leo Strauss, "The Crisis of Our Time," in Harold
J. Spaeth, ed., **The Predicament of Modern Politics**,
Detroit, University of Detroit Press, 1964, pp. 41-54; Eric
Voegelin, **The New Science of Politics**, Chicago, University
of Chicago Press, 1952, especially pp. 121ff.

entitled "Why I am a Destiny" declaring that "one day my name will be associated with the memory of something tremendous -- a crisis without equal on earth, the most profound collision of conscience, a decision that was conjured up **against** everything that had been believed, demanded, hallowed so far. I am no man, I am dynamite."[74] And one thinks, too, of Foucault's various attempts to demonstrate that history is beset by "mutations" which utterly eradicate the thought of the preceding period. Derrida was right to observe of **History of Madness**, Foucault's first important book, that "nowhere else and never before has the concept of **crisis** been able to enrich and reassemble all its potentialities, all the energy of its meaning."[75]

This is not, however, the only affinity among the three, for all show deep interest in "history," albeit in a special sense. At least superficially, this interest is most evident in Foucault, who claims emphatically to be a historian and who, in such works as **The Archaeology of Knowledge** and the important essay on "Nietzsche, Genealogy, History," has engaged in a theoretical (or antitheoretical?) reflection on the meaning of historiography as an enterprise.[76] It appears, too, in Nietzsche's own reflection on **The Use and Disadvantage of History** and his persistent criticism of "modern historiography" for claiming to be a

----

[74] Friedrich Nietzsche, **The Gay Science**, Walter Kaufmann, trans., New York, Random House, 1974, section 125, pp. 181-182; Nietzsche, **Ecce Homo**, "Why I am a Destiny," section 8, in **Basic Writings**, Walter Kaufmann, ed., New York, Random House, 1968, p. 789.

[75] So pervasive is the crisis theme in Foucault that I am at a loss in deciding what passages to cite. But perhaps one could do little better than to read: **The Order of Things**, New York, Random House, 1970, pp. 306-307, 384-387; **The Archaeology of Knowledge**, Alan Sheridan, trans., New York, Pantheon, 1972, pp. 22ff. Derrida's comments on the crisis notion in Foucault appear in: "Cogito and the History of Madness," in **Writing and Difference**, Alan Bass, trans., Chicago, University of Chicago Press, 1978, pp. 31-63, on p. 62.

[76] Michel Foucault, "Nietzsche, Genealogy, History," in **Language, Counter-Memory, Practice**, Donald F. Bouchard, ed., Donald F. Bouchard and Sherry Simon, trans., Ithaca, NY, Cornell University Press, 1977, pp. 139-164.

"mirror" of events: being subject to "the dangerous old conceptual fiction" of a "pure, will-less, painless, timeless knowing subject."[77] And it shows also in Heidegger's emphasis toward the end of **Being and Time** on "historicity" (**Geschichtlichkeit**), as well as his later and repeated attacks on conventional, "representational" historiography.[78]

Why is this preoccupation with history and its perception shared by these writers?   Is this not strange, for shouldn't their commitments to the notion of a break with the past lead them to remain utterly indifferent to history, let alone historiography?   How does this preoccupation connect with their similarly shared notion of crisis?

Here I focus on Heidegger, for his connection of crisis to "history" is especially clear.   (But I believe that the same argument holds for Nietzsche and Foucault as well.) The answer starts with Hegel, to whom Heidegger attributed immense significance.   (Nietzsche and Foucault also evoke Hegel.[79] But because Heidegger was more deeply imbedded in the German philosophical tradition, Hegel has a more obvious role in his writings than in those of his fellow prophets of extremity.)   Heidegger meant to "take Nietzsche seriously as a thinker."[80] And after 1930, this is certainly what   he   attempted   to   do.   Perhaps   no   other

----

[77] See: Friedrich Nietzsche, **The Use and Abuse of History**, Adrian   Collins,   trans.,   Indianapolis,   Bobbs-Merrill, 1949; Nietzsche, **On the Genealogy of Morals**, Walter Kaufmann and R. J. Hollingdale, trans., in **Basic Writings**, sections 12, 16, pp. 593, 555.

[78] See: Heidegger, **Being and Time**, pp. 372ff.   Among other places, Heidegger attacked conventional historiography in: "Überwindung der Metaphysik," in **Vorträge und Aufsätze**, Pfullingen, Neske, 1974, p. 80; English trans. by Joan Stambaugh, "Overcoming Metaphysics," in Heidegger, **The End of Philosophy**, New York, Harper and Row, 1973, p. 93.   This is also a theme of: "Der Spruch des Anaximander," in Heidegger, **Holzwege**, Frankfurt am Main, Vittorio Kolstermann, 1977, pp. 326, 372; English trans. by David Farrell Krell and Frank A. Capuzzi, "The Anaximander Fragment," in Heidegger, **Early Greek Thinking**, New York, Harper and Row, 1975, pp. 17, 57.

[79] See: Nietzsche, **The Use and Abuse of History**, chapter 8; Michel Foucault, **L'Ordre du discours**, Paris, Gallimard,

twentieth-century thinker has taken Nietzsche so seriously. Still, it is clear that he took Hegel with equal seriousness. As Stanley Rosen remarks, "beneath the Nietzschean surfaces of Heidegger's thought we may detect a continuing Hegelian resonance."[81] In **An Introduction to Metaphysics**, Heidegger wrote of the 1840s' German turn away from "idealist" (that is to say, Hegelian) philosophy: "it was then that occurred what is popularly and succinctly called the 'collapse of German idealism'....It was not German idealism that collapsed; rather, the age was no longer strong enough to stand up to the greatness, breadth, and originality of that spiritual world, i.e., truly to realize it..."[82] And in "Overcoming Metaphysics," he stated that "in spite of the superficial talk about the breakdown of Hegelian philosophy, one thing remains true: Only this philosophy determined reality in the nineteenth century, although not in the external form of a doctrine followed, but rather as metaphysics, as the dominance of beingness in the sense of certainty. The countermovements in this metaphysics belong **to** it. Ever since Hegel's death (1831), everything is merely a countermovement, not only in Germany, but also in Europe."[83]

Note the radically idealist character of Heidegger's evocation of Hegel and his view of history. Whatever his

----

1971, pp. 74ff. On the Hegelian presence in **History of Madness**, see Derrida's shrewd comments in: "Cogito and the History of Madness," p. 36.

[80] Martin Heidegger, "Nietzsches Wort 'Gott ist tot'," in **Holzwege**, p. 210; English trans. "The Word of Nietzsche: 'God is Dead'," in Heidegger, **The Question concerning Technology, and Other Essays**, William Lovitt, trans., New York, Harper and Row, 1977, pp. 54-55.

[81] Rosen, **Nihilism**, pp. 127-128. Also see: Hans-Georg Gadamer, "Heidegger and the Language of Metaphysics," in **Philosophical Hermeneutics**, David E. Linge, ed. and trans., Berkeley, University of California Press, 1976, pp. 230-231: "Heidegger's thought has revolved around Hegel until the present day in ever new attempts at delineation."

[82] Martin Heidegger, **Einführung in die Metaphysik**, Tübingen, Niemeyer, 1953, pp. 34-35; English trans. by Ralph Manheim as **An Introduction to Metaphysics**, New Haven, Yale University Press, 1959, p. 45.

"idealism," Hegel himself was also a "realist," eager to confront the manifold complexity of the social, political, intellectual, and cultural world.[84] This is clear from such works as the **Philosophy of Right**, the **Philosophy of History**, and the **Lectures on Aesthetics**, which taken together indicate well the breadth of Hegel's vision of human history. Heidegger chose to ignore the full range of Hegel's project. Instead, he treated Hegel as if the **History of Philosophy** were the whole of his view of history. Heidegger found attractive the side of Hegel which suggests, or at any rate seems to suggest, that the ideas of philosophers play the governing role in world history. Notwithstanding incessant talk of "technology," Heidegger's later writings repeatedly see **spiritual** phenomena as making up the whole of the historical process. **An Introduction to Metaphysics** identifies "the whole spiritual history of the West," with "its history pure and simple."[85] Similarly, "The Age of the World Picture" proclaims that "metaphysics grounds an age, in that through a specific interpretation of what is and through a specific comprehension of truth it gives to that age the basis upon which it is essentially formed. This basis holds complete dominion over all the phenomena that distinguish the age."[86] Hence it is no surprise to see, in "Overcoming Metaphysics," that "the 'world wars' and their character of 'totality' are...a consequence of the abandonment of Being."[87]

Nowhere did Heidegger seek to justify his attribution of such tremendous significance to the realm of "spirit." It remains a matter of simple faith, a part of Heidegger's own "myth of the tradition." Presumably, Heidegger's immersion in a "traditional" set of philosophical texts did not allow him

----

[83] Heidegger, "Überwindung der Metaphysik," p. 76; English trans. in Heidegger, **The End of Philosophy**, p. 89.

[84] See: Berki, **On Political Realism**, pp. 67-69 and **passim**.

[85] Heidegger, **Einführung in die Metaphysik**, p. 105; English trans. in **An Introduction to Metaphysics**, p. 137.

[86] Heidegger, "Die Zeit des Weltbildes," in **Holzwege**, p. 75; English trans. in **The Question concerning Technology**, p. 115.

[87] Heidegger, "Überwindung der Metaphysik," p. 92; English trans. in **The End of Philosophy**, p. 103.

to see how problematic this is. Yet unless one accepts his conviction of the pivotal historical importance of the German idealist tradition in particular and philosophy or metaphysics in general, there is no reason to take Heidegger's speculations on the destiny of the modern world with anything like the seriousness he intended.

Even so, conceptions of history similar to Heidegger's **are** taken seriously in political theory and elsewhere. I propose to take as my text two sentences that epitomize the perception of political reality to which I am objecting. To be sure, the context is but a review article dealing with some recent books on politics. But it so well sums up the notion of an apocalypse of ideas that I cannot resist using it. This text embodies a view which has widespread currency, if seldom such a clear and unequivocal articulation.

> If the very notion of political authority is called into question, then the politics **of our time** may properly be seen as institutionalized violence, as Weber noted. Hannah Arendt once remarked that this may not be the time to ask 'Who governs?'; the question tells us not just something about politics but rather about the phenomenology of politics for those who live after the death of God and the eradication of moral horizons, for those who live in absolute freedom and terror.[88]

This begs to be torn apart. First, we are told that the politics "of our time" may be seen as "institutionalized violence." Surely this is true. But why imply, as this does, that politics has not **always** been institutionalized violence? I simply do not believe that any such time ever existed; in any case, its existence has not yet been demonstrated. Why, then, refer to "our time" (Heidegger's "modern age") at all? To be sure, in our era of ICBMs, **the scale** of violence, real or potential, is vastly increased. But what evidence would tie this in any way to the supposed fact that political authority has been "called into question"? I see none whatever. Indeed, it would be far more plausible to attribute our increased scale of violence to other factors which may relate to the supposed decline in

----

[88] Tracy B. Strong, "On Revolution, Politics, and Learning from the Past," **Polity**, 12, 2, Winter, 1979, pp. 303-317, on p. 316.

authority of political belief systems, but do not connect with "the death of God and the eradication of moral horizons." More likely, our increased scale of violence is partly attributable to the fact that modern political authority has been called into question little, if at all, so that states remain relatively unhindered in the exercise of power.

Second, we are said to have experienced "the death of God and the eradication of moral horizons." This notion is important not only for Heidegger and Nietzsche but also for Foucault. For example, Foucault writes in a 1963 essay that "the death of God is not merely an 'event' that gave shape to contemporary experience as we now know it: it continues tracing indefinitely its great skeletal outline."[89] The contention is that the "death of God" (understood in its broadest sense, as the dissolution of authoritative moral standards) is absolutely the most compelling reality in modern history. Although Heidegger and Foucault have had lots of company in claiming this, neither they nor others have presented evidence to this effect. Thinking for the moment of recent American politics alone (a provincial sphere, perhaps, but still an important one), it seems clear that the "death of God" theorists have not flipped their television dials to the Christian Broadcasting Network or bothered to follow election campaigns. How these phenomena can be reconciled with a Nietzschean reading of history is difficult to see. But suppose that the "death of God" had actually or soon will have occurred; imagine there to be a global move away from commonly accepted values and authoritative moral standards. Why should this be considered an important event? To a pastor's son, a sexton's son, or someone making a career as a theologian, it might indeed be important. But why it should be important for anyone else is not clear.

Third, we are claimed to live "in absolute freedom and terror." Though this reference is intended to evoke Hegel, the canonical text is clearly Dostoevsky's (and Nietzsche's) suggestion that if there is no belief in God or immortality, "everything is permitted."[90] But how does it

----

[89] Michel Foucault, **Language, Counter-Memory, Practice**, p. 32.

[90] See: Georg Wilhelm Friedrich Hegel, **Phenomenology of Spirit**, A. V. Miller, trans., London, Oxford University Press, 1977, pp. 355-363; Fyodor Dostoyevsky, **The Broth-**

follow that "everything is permitted?" How does it follow from a collapse of authoritative moral standards that people live in "absolute freedom?" This inference seems absolutely false, for there are both natural and social limits to human behavior, even in the absence of authoritative moral standards. How many modern individuals can be said to live in "absolute freedom?" I would wager very few: the constraints of earning a living, raising a family, pursuing a career, and the like are powerful and compelling; and no evidence I know suggests that these are on the way out. As for "terror," here, too, the claim seems highly questionable. Many of us may live in terror some of the time; perhaps some of us do most of the time. But this has nothing whatever to do with "the death of God and the eradication of moral horizons." Where is the terror "of our time?" People live in terror because they cannot feed themselves, because they might be fired, because they are lonely. They live in terror, too, because they know that thermonuclear warfare and other similar, if more limited, catastrophes are possible. But to trace their terror to eradication of their moral horizons is a highly elevated form of claptrap. It has all the authority of Nietzsche behind it; but it is claptrap nonetheless.

In my view, there is yet another reason why Nietzsche's notion of crisis, since aped by so many other theorists, ultimately collapses. Underlying this notion is a residual historicism. In his magisterial **History, Man, and Reason**, Maurice Mandelbaum defines "historicism" as "the belief that an adequate understanding of the nature of any phenomenon and an adequate assessment of its value are to be gained through considering it in terms of the place which it occupied and the role which it played within a process of development."[91] In a sense akin to, but much broader than Mandelbaum's, I here use "historicism" to denote any attribution of directionality to history. In its original and still decisive meaning, "crisis" denotes a

----

ers **Karamazov**, Constance Garnett, trans., New York, Random House, 1964, pp. 69, 273, 663, 688, and **passim**; Friedrich Nietzsche, **Thus Spoke Zarathustra**, R. J. Hollingdale, trans., Baltimore, Penguin Books, 1961, especially Part IV, "The Shadow," p. 283. (Nietzsche's version is: "Nothing is true, everything is permitted.")

[91] Maurice Mandelbaum, **History, Man, and Reason**, Baltimore, Johns Hopkins University Press, 1971, p. 42.

turning, a point of decision. It was initially applied to the
course of a disease, denoting its turning-point, at which
"an important development or change takes place which is
decisive for recovery or death."[92] Unless history has a
direction of some sort to change or continue or lose in aim-
less wandering, it cannot have a "crisis" or "turning." Yet
the notion that history **has** directionality (or even **is** directionality) seems extremely odd. I am not even sure that
such a metaphor (which it clearly is) could be coherent.

Nonetheless, this historicist metaphor has often
attracted wide allegiance. As Mandelbaum makes clear, it
was especially influential in the nineteenth century, when
historicism (in his sense, but also by extension in my
sense) was the closest thing to a unifying notion beneath
the diverse schools of thought in this period.[93] As Mandelbaum also points out, historicism has lost its grip on more
recent thought. This is partly because of purely intellectual developments, such as the emergence of the view that
laws simply **describe** events rather than **govern** them, a
shift implying that there was "no longer reason to suppose
that history necessarily followed a definite, determined
course." The decline of historicism is also attributable to
historical events, especially World War I and subsequent
social and political upheavals. These undermined the nineteenth-century faith in progress and thus destroyed what
had become, by late in that century, a crucial underpinning
of historicist doctrine.[94]

Thus we confront a paradox. Historicism has disappeared from the mainstream of current thought; yet modernism and postmodernism are centrally defined by adherence
to a notion that itself makes sense only if historicism is
true. As a matter of historical fact, the notion of crisis to
which our prophets of extremity adhere was the product of
a brilliant intellectual move by Nietzsche. Historicism
rejected the concept of absolute value but retained its own
absolute: namely, the historical process itself, in terms of
which all particular values were to be understood and
judged. Nietzsche de-absolutized this absolute by using
against it the same intellectual solvent that historicism had

----

[92] Oxford English Dictionary, Volume 2, "crisis."

[93] See: Mandelbaum, **History, Man, and Reason**, especially
pp. 41-138.

[94] Ibid., pp. 369-370.

applied to all other realities. History disappeared into history, into moment-by-moment experience. Thus Nietzsche
saw history not as "an organic adaptation to new conditions" but as a (largely arbitrary) set of breaks, leaps,
and compulsions: in a word, of crises.[95] Yet all this
depends on the existence of something to be broken, leapt
over, and compelled: that is, something ordinary to be
disordered or reordered through human action. Accordingly, there is a close (organic?) relation between taking
Hegel seriously and taking Nietzsche seriously. For
whether and to what extent Hegel was an idealist, he was
undeniably a historicist. In fact, his relationship to the
historicist tradition is paradigmatic.[96]

This suggests in turn what we can establish more
directly: that the notion of crisis is essentially **reactive** in
character.[97] In its postulation of various breaks, leaps,
mutations, and divine deaths, it reacts against an implied
assumption of development (or at least, of continuity) over
time. Heidegger could suggest that we are "latecomers in a
history now racing towards its end" only insofar as he was
still under the spell of historicism.[98] We can see the logic
in the observation of one of Turgenev's characters, that
the Hegelians have now been succeeded by the nihilists.[99]
But in attacking assumptions of development or continuity,
such theories of radical or chronic crisis must destroy their
very own grounds. The more successful their attacks, the
more completely their own reasons for existing are undermined.

And here I arrive at the crux of my argument. I
take it as given that, insofar as creative art and thought

----

[95] Nietzsche, **On the Genealogy of Morals**, Second Essay,
section 17, p. 522.

[96] See: Mandelbaum, **History, Man, and Reason**, pp.
59-60.

[97] On the "reactive" character of edifying, hermeneutical
thought in general, see: Rorty, **Philosophy and the Mirror
of Nature**, pp. 365-366.

[98] Heidegger, "Der Spruch des Anaximander," p. 325; English trans. in **Early Greek Thinking**, p. 16.

[99] Ivan Turgenev, **Fathers and Sons**, Constance Garnett,
trans., New York, Airmont, 1967, p. 27.

are concerned, we live in a posthistoricist age.   In this sense, Nietzsche and his successors have done their work well.   But if we are posthistoricist, we ought to be postcritical as well, dropping the metaphor of crisis entirely.   And yet, if crisis theory is not a call to critical consciousness, it is nothing.   This, then, is the paradox or perhaps even the self-defeating contradiction of crisis theory.   It is the insoluble problem and interminable oscillation of Nietzsche, Heidegger, Arendt, Foucault, Derrida, and so many other theorists of recent years.

In a brilliant book, Robert Pirsig wrote that he "would like not to cut any new channels of consciousness but simply dig deeper into old ones that have become silted in with the debris of thoughts grown stale and platitudes too often repeated."[100] My point is that the invocation of crisis has grown stale; it has become a platitude too often repeated.   It now obscures more layers of reality, more aspects of experience, than it reveals.   Nietzsche, Heidegger, Foucault, and company are profoundly therapeutic thinkers; but to take their therapeutic pronouncements literally is to open the way to new concealments, not new powers of criticism.

Note the title of this essay: "Martin Heidegger and the Metapolitics of Crisis."   I write of "metapolitics" because political theories like Heidegger's are radically out of touch with political reality.   They are "beyond" that reality, and this is their true danger.   For Nietzsche, son of a pastor, and Heidegger, the son of a sexton, the "death of God" was a profoundly disturbing event.   So too was the collapse of the "two-worlds" theory of morality for philosophers within "the tradition."[101] But for most people, and particularly for us, these events are nothing.   For historicists like Nietzsche and Heidegger, breaking the continuity was both exciting and terrifying.   But those days are gone.   We have no such continuity; for us, such breaks are nothing.   Those who have never believed are not afraid of unbelief.   Professors are being mugged in Manhattan, reliable household help is hard to find, and the world generally is in a sorry state.   But these facts have little and quite possibly nothing to do with the death of God, the

----

[100] Robert M. Pirsig, **Zen and the Art of Motorcycle Maintenance**, New York, Bantam Books, 1974, p. 8.

[101] See: Arendt, **The Life of the Mind; Volume I: Thinking**, pp. 10-11.

crisis of values, the eclipse of authority, or the breaking of the tradition. Nor should we fall victim to any view that leads us to believe they do. We can read Heidegger and his ilk as ironic commentators on a cultural reality that may never have existed. But to read them literally is a serious error. Heidegger and similar prophets of extremity are dangerous, not because they deprive political action of its ground, but because their very sophistication tempts us into neither seeing nor feeling what our politics is about.

And so I would argue that political theorists would be more successful in helping us to understand our current situation were they to cast a skeptical eye on all manifestations of crisis theory. Crisis theorists claim to be illuminating the most profound aspects of contemporary life. They contend that the possibilities of being mugged, the loneliness of experience, the threat of war, and the like are all traceable to the moral and intellectual crisis. But the connections they adduce between these realities and the alleged crisis turn out to be peculiarly empty and abstract. Crisis theorists are often accused of an elitist orientation, but this misses the point. It is rather their strangely academic conception of the relationship between moral codes and human action that leads them astray. Crisis theorists hold that, without the crumbling of these codes, the atrocities committed in our century would not have been possible and would perhaps not even have been imaginable. This over-estimates the effect that those codes had when they were operative, as if "Thou shalt not kill" meant that murder did not exist, and under-estimates the remarkable power of human imagination. It probably also exaggerates the extent to which such codes have actually crumbled. Beyond this, we need to ask what consequences follow from the exercise of tracing our manifold difficulties back to some crisis of belief. Perhaps in some instances, no consequences at all would follow: itself a devastating indictment. More likely, however, is concealment of the proximate causes of those difficulties and hence the loss of whatever opportunity we have to avert their worsening.

PART SIX

CONCEALMENT AND CONTROL

THE DILEMMA OF LEGITIMACY

William E. Connolly

> In our times we can neither endure our faults
> nor the means of correcting them.
>
> Livy

In a highly structured order, people tend to be pulled simultaneously by one wish to identify with established norms and another to evade or resist onerous claims made upon them. Some are drawn exclusively toward one of these poles, but many others are torn between them. The latter will endorse law and order belligerently and cheat on their income taxes, or express anarchistic impulses and raise their children to be lawyers, or insist that the government get off the backs of the people and support policies which extend surveillance over marginal constituencies. The tensions here are not merely psychological; they embody attempts to meet the claims of the self and the claims of order in a setting which makes it difficult to do both.

The classical doctrine of liberalism projected a vision of social life which honored both sets of claims. Endorsing a general set of constitutional rules which all citizens were to obey, it entrusted a broad range of conduct to the impersonal control of the market and placed the remainder within a private sphere beyond the normal reach of direct public control. The liberal ideal never harmonized closely with the actual organization of private and public life, but the fit was close enough to allow its supporters to help define the form and limits of operative public authority.

The attraction of the liberal doctrine resided largely in its desire to acknowledge together the claims of public authority and private prerogative. But, as its conceptual resources have lagged behind changes in the structure of modern life, this attraction has faded. The web of social life is now too tightly drawn to sustain this picture of public authority and private refuge. The current proclivity to characterize behavior once thought to be eccentric as mental illness in need of medical care presents merely one sign of the penetration of public-private bureaucracies into the inner citadels of private life. Put another way, a broad range of private activities and social practices must today be coordinated (to use a neutral term) by public means;

and a large number of people unable or unwilling to comply voluntarily with official expectations are now subjected to legal controls, therapeutic counsel, and incentive systems to bring their conduct in line with the limits of the order.

As the web of social discipline has tightened, other familiar doctrines of the nineteenth and twentieth centuries have also begun to seem vaguely disconnected from our current condition. Critics who appeal to a communitarian ideal of life or gesture toward anarchism illuminate features of our life otherwise left in the shadows, but the counter-ideals they pose lack specificity and credibility. Pressed very hard by communitarians or anarchists, most of us retreat toward liberal standards of citizenship, freedom, and privacy. And yet when the liberal, inflated by success in piercing these pretensions, attempts to woo us back to the liberal camp, we discern even more poignantly how the doctrine draws a veil of ignorance across the most disturbing features of contemporary life.

This condition can be generalized across the entire landscape of contemporary theoretical discourse. Dissident perspectives demystify features of the established order, but then condense into a light mist of lofty ideals; and the operative ideals, which retain some ability to set limits to the morally tolerable in the existing order, rest on assumptions and perceptions increasingly at odds with established realities. Political theorists thus find themselves wandering through the debris of old doctrines, searching for stray material from which to construct new understandings. These features of current political theory, I contend, are themselves symptoms of the dilemma of legitimacy which is beginning to emerge in our civilization.

How should we try to pick our way through this field? My own effort is informed by the following judgment: the categories supplied by a collectivist theory of legitimacy provide the most refined instruments with which to probe subterranean developments in our civilization, but these instruments themselves must be redesigned once that excavation is finished, once we begin digging our way out. In defending this perspective, I first delineate a collectivist conception of legitimacy which transcends the thin conception governing much current social theory, next define the contours of a dilemma of legitimacy which is beginning to take shape in American politics, then examine briefly two theories which are themselves symptoms of this development, and last confront an alternate perspective which might allow us to correct the repressive tendencies implicit within the collectivist problematic of legitimacy.

THE QUESTION OF LEGITIMACY

A thin theory of legitimacy continues to inform most accounts of current politics. It assumes: that allegiance to the order is intact unless there is overt, widespread, and well-articulated opposition to it; that belief in the legitimacy of the order is equivalent to the order's legitimacy; that the beliefs most pivotal to the question of legitimacy are those concerning the constitutive principles of the political process; and that since the ends governing our civilization are inherently rational they could not themselves become illegitimate. Few theorists accept all of these provisions today. But a variety of recent theorists, representing diverse ideological positions, adopt one or more of them when posing questions about the legitimacy of the order.[1]

The thin conception of legitimacy misconstrues the way in which social relations and institutions are constituted. Misreading the constitutive dimensions of social life, it may be able to detect certain symptoms of a withdrawal of allegiance from the order, but it lacks the conceptual resources to comprehend its internal structure or to assess its potential import.

A healthy order, from the vantage point of its participants, is a way of life which promotes the good we share in common; the limits it imposes are tolerable to most because they are thought to be necessary to the common good it fosters. To participate in such a way of life is to carry an enormous load of pre-judgments embodied in the common language and solidified in institutional practices. One's personal identity is intimately bound up with the larger way of life: it provides one with the density needed to maintain social relations, to form practical judgments, and to criticize specific features of the common life.

This is an incomplete picture of any way of life. (For instance, its structural dimension has been ignored.) But it is complete enough to allow us to relocate the question of

----

[1] See: Daniel Bell, **The Cultural Contradictions of Capitalism**, New York, Basic Books, 1976; James O'Connor, **The Fiscal Crisis of the State**, New York, St. Martin's Press, 1973; Theordore Lowi, **The End of Liberalism**, New York, W.W. Norton, 1968; George Kateb, "On the 'Legitimation Crisis'," **Social Research**, 46, 4, Winter, 1979, pp. 695-727, and Erik Olin Wright, **Class, Crisis and the State**, London, New Left Books, 1978.

legitimacy.   First,   if   the   pre-understandings   implicit   in social relations seriously misconstrue the range of possibilities inherent in the order, expressions of allegiance at one moment   will   rest   upon   a   series   of   illusions   which   may become apparent at a future moment.   The historical course of development actually open to the order may ensure that future generations will become disenchanted with it.

Second, a widespread commitment to the constitutional principles of the political order may be matched by distantiation from the role imperatives governing everyday life.   In a highly structured order, the withdrawal of allegiance in this second sphere will carry profound implications for the performance of the economy, the tax levels required by the state,   the   scope   of   the   state's   police   functions,   and   the ability of the state to bear the burdens imposed upon it. It may, in short, impair the state's ability to play its legitimate role in the current order of things.

Third, the ends and purposes fostered by an order can   themselves   become   objects   of   disaffection.   Hegel explored instances when a set of priorities which once gripped a populace lose their credibility as the negative dimensions in them become more fully visible to later generations. Such a contradictory tendency embodies a historical dimension   whereby   abstract   goals   inspire   a   populace   at   one moment but decline in their ability to secure reflective allegience once their actual content becomes clear through cumulative experience.   If the institutional complex sustaining these purposes has solidified, we might expect expressions of disaffection to be more symptomatic than articulate and more covert than overt.   The lack of any sense of credible alternatives operates to limit the political definition of the new sense of disenchantment, but its emergence nonetheless affects the performance of the institutional complex.

But why such an emphasis on the symptomatic, the covert, the indirect, and the unarticulated when pursuing the question of legitimacy?   Because, fourth, the identities of the participants are bound up with the institutions in which they are implicated.   The modern individual, possessing the capacity for self-consciousness, is never exhausted by any particular set of roles.   But one's sense of dignity, of   self-identity,   is   intimately   linked   to   one's   ability   to endorse the way of life one actually lives.

This relation between personal identity and institutional practice complicates the question of legitimacy.   To become severely disaffected from that which one is called upon to do in work, family, and consumption is also to become disaffected from the self one has become.   When the distance between what one is and what one does is great, one is likely to hold oneself in contempt. For one must now either appear to be unfree (acting only under duress) or appear deceitful (pretending to endorse roles experienced as hateful). In either case, one feels cast off from onself, anxious and demoralized.

The situation is not helped if the experience is joined to the conviction that little can be done to remedy it through politics. One way to save appearances in such a setting is to reconnect rhetorically that which is disconnected in practice. Some politicians understand how difficult circumstances can foster collective self-deception or, better described, the careful cultivation of a shared innocence about the historical course a people is on. "They want to believe, that is the point isn't it?" So Nixon whispered to Haldeman and the tape recorder when they were assessing his chances of overcoming the mass of evidence piling up against him. He understood the close relation between the quest for personal identity and the will to believe that all is right with the world.

Because these connections can be so intimate, a theory of legitimacy must probe the implicit, the unacknowledged, and the symptomatic as well as that which is acknowledged and articulated. And because it must do so, any particular account is bound to be controversial and problematic in some respects. This result resides more in the character of the object of inquiry than in the defective design of the theoretical perspective governing inquiry into it. The philosophical recognition of this feature of modern life carries political implications. It provides, as it were, philosophical space for politics. It identifies politics as the sphere of the unsettled, as the mode of social relations which properly emerges when issues require resolution and the available resources of reason and evidence are insufficient to settle them.

The question of legitimacy is important to us because we wish to live, to the extent possible in any complex, modern society, as free agents in an order which deserves our allegiance and is responsive to our deepest grievances and criticisms. It is also important because we sense that politics, in the best sense of that term, requires a background of public allegiance to the most basic principles governing the order. The thin conception of legitimacy appears to avoid a series of perplexing issues posed by acceptance of the alternate perspective. That is also its defect. It converts the concern behind the question of legitimacy into a set of more manageable and trivial questions.

PRODUCTIVITY AND LEGITIMACY

Two fundamental sets of priorities have governed the American civilization.[2] It seeks to sustain an economy of growth so that each generation can be more prosperous, secure, and confortable than its predecessor. And it seeks to support a constitutional democracy in which the state is accountable to its citizens and the citizens have rights against the state. The first priority is expressed in the organization of work, profit, property, and consumption which typifies the society. These practices are constituted in part by the standards of efficiency, cost effectiveness, productivity, punctuality, and consumer satisfaction inherent in them. The second priority is reflected in our concern with human rights, freedom, the entitlements of citizenship, and competitive elections. Its constitution involves the readiness of participants to see themselves as citizens and to carry out the prerogatives of citizenship.

The legitimacy of the entire order involves, first, the ability of each set of priorities to retain the reflective allegiance of most citizens and, second, the continued ability of each priority to exist in harmony with the other.

I believe that the first set of institutions and priorities, the civilization of productivity, is progressively losing its credibility as its imperatives become more deeply entrenched. The decline in credibility involves a process of disillusionment in which the institutional pursuit of a set of ends once thought to be self-evident begins to appear more and more as self-defeating to new generations. In turn, the disillusionment adversely affects the ability of the institutions to promote these ends by non-coercive means. Since the institutional forms which constitute the order are now solidified, since they now form an interdependent structure in which none can be reconstituted very thoroughly without corollary shifts in the constitution of the others, this disaffection is not likely to find clear political

----

[2] This section includes a radically abbreviated and modestly revised version of arguments I develop more fully in: **Appearance and Reality in Politics**, Cambridge, Cambridge University Press, 1981. That text was not available when this paper was initially composed, and I think that this summary of its argument is still needed to set the stage for the new themes pursued in the remainder of the essay at hand.

expression. Its political articulation tends to be displaced. The disaffection does, though, take its toll in the civilization of productivity. It also increases the burdens imposed upon the welfare state, the one institution which is accountable to the electorate. The long term effect strains the ability of the state to retain democratic accountability. The erosion of legitimacy in the one sphere eventually contaminates the legitimacy of the other.

What, more concretely, is involved in this experience of disillusionment? First, it becomes more apparent to consumers that the pursuit of universal private affluence, full of promise during its early stages, eventually generates a self-defeating dialectic. The economy may produce riches, but the good life contained within the ideal of "affluence" seems to recede constantly into the horizon. Goods introduced initially as luxuries or conveniences later become necessary objects of consumption, and much of their initial charm is lost.

This conversion process is propelled partly by the changes in the social infrastructure of consumption which must accompany each significant change in the social composition of consumption goods.[3] The automobile, for example, brings with it an expensive public highway system, a complex apparatus for acquiring and refining oil, a military establishment to secure a steady supply of oil, changes in the location of stores, shopping centers, factories, recreational areas, and the entire redesign of cities. These changes in the infrastructure of consumption convert the initial luxury into an expensive necessity of consumption, they tend to reduce pleasure in the use of the vehicle, and they impose heavy costs of maintenance and support upon the state. Moreover, many of the paradigmatic goods of the affluent society, because they are built around the assumption of **private** consumption, decline in value as they are extended to more people. Private resorts, technical education, suburban living, and (again) the automobile decline in value as they are universalized, partly because much of their initial value resided in the exclusivity of their

----

[3] This argument is most cogently developed in: Fred Hirsch, **The Social Limits to Growth**, London, Routledge and Kegan Paul, 1977. An earlier version, more attuned to the implications for politics and less precise with respect to the self-defeating character of the universalization of affluence, can be found in: Michael Best and William Connnolly, **The Politicized Economy**, Lexington, D. C. Heath, 1976.

possession and partly because the setting in which they are consumed normally deteriorates as they are universalized. If these goods (representing the paradigm goods of the affluent society) were to be restricted, the end of universal affluence which helps to legitimate the civilization of productivity would be jeopardized. But if they were indeed extended to everyone, the achievement of "affluence" itself would contradict the hopes which inspired earlier generations to pursue it.

If the universalization of affluence is one of the ends which legitimize the role imperatives governing the civilization of productivity, and if that end is now seen by many to contain illusory expectations, everyday allegiance to role assigments will deteriorate. The reaction, experienced as growing skepticism about the system's ability to universalize the good life it pursues, does not expunge the desire for consumption goods, for to opt out of the expansionary process is to worsen one's own comparative position. But it does weaken the willingness to impose disciplines upon oneself at work, home, and school.

Suspicions arise in other areas as well. Institutions, standards, and norms which once seemed conducive to private welfare and public good now present a more ambiguous appearance. It begins to appear that the system of labor mobility, which promises to improve the standard of living for many each generation, also operates over the long term to damage cherished ties of kinship and neighborhood; that the stratification system needed to motivate people to fill the lowliest positions also operates persistently to close some segments of the society out of its paradigmatic rewards; that the massive exploitation of natural resources needed to fuel the economy of growth deepens the nation's dependence on resources located in foreign lands; that the established forms of investment, production, and work which generate abundance also render the natural environment less hospitable to future human habitation; that the pace of occupational change required to propel perpetual economic growth also renders each generation of workers obsolete just when it reaches the point in the life cycle where its members are most in need of the respect and dignity bestowed on those functionally important to the society; and that the intensification of managerial controls over the work process to increase productivity drains these role assignments of dignity and social significance. The suspicion forms that these are not dispensable "side effects" to a common pursuit which can be carried out without them; rather they are intrinsic to the historical development of the civilization of productivty. They are part of its success, and any sustained effort to eliminate them would undermine the principal aims which the civilization of productivity can promote.

Other civilizations, of course, have faced difficulties in promoting the material welfare of their populations. But that is not the point here. For not many of them were constructed around the promise to universalize private affluence. I am not contending, either, that most people today have a "lower standard of living" than people had two or three generations ago. The contention is rather that the orientation to the future is undergoing significant change. Nostalgia refers less to a past which is thought to have been richer and more secure and more to one which could believe in the future it was building. The nostalgia of today embodies a loss of innocence about the future we are building. As the feeling grows that the fulfillment of the American dream must always recede into the horizon, as it becomes clear that it might even become a nightmare for future generations, identification with the disciplines and sacrifices required to sustain the civilization of productivity is placed under severe strains. These strains in turn weaken the performance of the defining institutions of the civilization.

The relation between the state and the system of productivity works to deflect political articulation of this disillusionment, to increase the burdens imposed upon the state, to deplete the civic resources the state can draw upon in bearing these burdens, and to set up the welfare apparatus of the state as the screen upon which the disaffection is displaced. The welfare state looks in two directions at the same time. It is the agency of public accountability through competitive elections, and it is dependent upon the successful performance of the privately incorporated system of productivity. This dual accountability of the state discourages political articulation of the disillusionment with the civilization of productivity. For it must foster private productivity to generate tax revenues, and its successful accountability to the electorate depends upon its ability to generate those revenues.

The state is caught in a bind which its citizens actively help to create. Our cherished view of ourselves as free citizens depends upon the belief that the state, as the one institution of public accountability, has sufficient resources to promote common ends and purposes. Its capacity to act effectively is closely bound up with my understanding of myself as a free agent. I see myself as free if the roles I play are congruent with the principles and purposes I adopt upon reflection. If those rules or the purposes they serve were experienced as onerous and oppressive, and if individuals were unsuccessful in defining new ones, their sense of personal freedom would then depend on the ability of the state to reconstitute these established forms. If it could not act even if we wished it to and we were thoroughly disaffected from the drift of our private and public life, then we would have to see ourselves as unfree, as governed more by fate and necessity than by reason and decision. And our collective unfreedom would eventually become the unfreedom of particular individuals as well.

One way to preseve the desired appearance of collective and personal freedom is to define the troubles which grip us to fit within the range of options effectively available to the state in the current order. Victims of inflation, therefore, unable to alter the consumption priorities, shoddy products, expensive style changes, and price mark-ups in the corporate sector, demand what the state can give them: cuts in school budgets and welfare expenditures. They attack those proximate sources of inflation which are subject to public control. Workers in depressed areas, unable to stop runaway companies, call upon the state to expand unemployment benefits and to stimulate the production of new jobs. Citizens, unable to curb the processes which weaken kinship ties, call upon the state to care for the victims of this process (the elderly, the infirm, the mentally ill, and delinquents), even though state agencies cannot care for these dependent constituencies with the dignity needed.

The bind in which the corporate system and its citizens place the state is this: if state policies undermine economic expansion, it loses its economic basis for action; if it acts within these constraints, it increasingly absorbs the dependent constituencies and unprofitable tasks closed out of the privately incorporated economy. It is then unable to meet the standards of efficiency and profitability operative in the private economy or to hold its budget levels down; and it is held responsible for the failure to live up to these expectations.

The state is seen as accountable to the degree that it is seen to be capable of responding to our grievances in the established order. We see ourselves as free, free as a people, to the extent that we define our grievances to fall within the range of its capacity for action. The welfare state thus emerges from this historical process as a depository for clientele closed out of the system of productivity and programs unable to resolve the troubles which it generated. The bloated welfare state is thus set up to be the visible target of public disaffection more deeply rooted in the priorities and practices of the civilization of productivity.

We publically call upon the state to promote growth, eliminate superfluous public programs, control inflation, and discipline those who siphon off public resources; and we resist privately the specific sacrifices it would impose upon us. The point in calling upon it in general to take those actions is that they fall within its orbit of legitimate action. The point in resisting the specific application of state policies to one's particular constituency flows from the conviction that the roles we bear in the civilization of productivity already constitute sacrifice enough. Anything more becomes unacceptable and unbearable. The cumulative result is a decline in allegiance to the **welfare** state and an increasing tolerance of state programs designed to intimidate, control, and suppress its former clients. The decline in the legitimacy of the welfare state is joined to allegiance to an abstract idea of the American state in the civilization of productivity. The logic supporting such a combination is this: we are potentially free as long as the existing state bureaucracy is unnecessarily inept; it can be seen as unnecessarily inept as long as we can identify new courses of state action in the prevailing order which promise to transcend the policies of the discredited welfare state. This combination secures the appearance of collective freedom, but it does so by masking a deeper and rational disaffection from the institutional imperatives and priorities of the civilization of productivity.

The preceding summary leaves out themes which would have to be developed in a more complete presentation, but a more complete account would not prove convincing if this brief outline now appears incredible. The framework, I hope, is sufficiently clear to allow me to formulate the crucial elements in the dilemma (or perhaps dilemmas) of legitimacy.

First, the ends fostered by the civilizations of productivity no longer can command reflective allegiance of many who are implicated in those institutions, while the consolidation of these institutions into a structure of interdependencies makes it extremely difficult to recast the ends to be pursued. The institutional complex declines in its ability to secure the allegiance of its role bearers once its actual achievements have been experienced; but the practices of work, profit, international trade, consumption, and stratification have solidified into an interdependent structure resistant to serious reconstitution.

Second, it will become increasingly difficult to

maintain the performance of the system of productivity, and the policies required to do so will further erode operational allegiance to its roles and priorities. These barriers emerge on two fronts. On the one side, the investment funds, disciplinary controls, and resources needed to promote the required rate of growth in an unfavorable environment will be generated by the imposition of austerity on large segments of the populace (if they are generated) and by a further retreat from environmental policies designed to protect the health of the populace. Maintenance of the system of productivity in adverse circumstances thus requires contraction of the paradigmatic benefits it promises to dispense. These selective reductions in affluence, security, and health will further deplete the allegiance of many who are expected to carry out role assignments within the system. On the other side, resistance to these impositions by those without effective market or political leverage (e.g., welfare recipients, workers in the market sector, low and middle level public employees, the mentally ill, delinquents, criminals) will encourage an extension of private and public modes of disciplinary control. The deterioration in the performance of the system of productivity, combined with the pressures to mobilize additional resources to maintain its performance, operates eventually to squeeze the space for democratic politics.

Third, if, as I claim, disenchantment with the civilization of productivity is based upon a growing experiential knowledge of illusions inside those pursuits, it is pertinent to ask: what constellation of ends, limits, imperatives, and priorities could a modern populace endorse today as worthy of its allegiance? If a reconstitution of the defining institutions were possible, what direction should the evolutionary changes take? What could replace or temper the ends of the civilization of productivity? The failure to answer this question, even at the level of theory, contributes to the gap between the covert symptoms of disaffection and the overt insistence on supporting established political priorities.[4] In the absence of credible alternatives, there is a certain rationality in holding onto illusions with which we are already familiar. One of the best ways to accomplish that is to cultivate a studied innocence about the historical

----

[4] I am assuming that a shared commitment to constitutional democracy, while part of the answer, could not in principle provide a sufficient answer. I argue this point in chapter four of **Appearance and Reality in Politics**.

course we are on.

The first two ingredients in the dilemma of legitimacy press most heavily on those who pretend that democracy and productivity can continue to cohere without undue strain. The third presses critics who believe that the future of democracy requires a reconstitution of the ends and imperatives governing the system of productivity. In what follows, I try to indicate how recent shifts within a variety of theoretical orientations provide indirect acknowledgement of the dilemma posed here; and I use the opportunity to ascertain how each orientation can, though not always intentionally, deepen our understanding of the character of this dilemmma.

THE BIFURCATION OF LIBERALISM

Current liberalism cannot be defined merely through its commitment to freedom, rights, dissent, and justice. It must be understood, as well, through the institutional arrangements it endorses. Its unity grows out of the congruence between these ideals and their institutional supports. If the first principle of liberalism is liberty, the second is practicality. Liberal practicality involves the wish to support policies which appear attainable within the current order; it is the desire to be part of the action, to be "in the middle" of things, to propose policies today which might be instituted tomorrow.

The priorities of liberty and practicality can be united as long as it is possible to believe that the welfare state in the privately incorporated economy of growth can be the vehicle of liberty and justice. Liberalism, so constituted, avoids the dilemma of legitimacy. But if such a dilemma is beginning to shake the ground underneath its feet, we should expect its proponents to acknowledge these shifts somehow, if only indirectly. I think this is happening. Liberalism is increasingly divided against itself. One constellation of liberals subordinates the commitment to practicality to preserve liberal ideals, and the other submerges the ideals to preserve practicality. Neither side acknowledges the dilemma of legitimacy. But the new division is a symptom of its emergence. The bifurcation of liberalism and the dilemma of legitimacy unfold together.

The first constellation, the beautiful souls of our day, strive to find space in the current order where the ideals of virtuous action, freedom, and justice can be preserved. Sometimes following the lead of Hannah Arendt, they strive to close the instrumentalities of labor, interest, profit, and consumption out of the political sphere. These practices and priorities are not to be treated as the materials of politics, properly understood. But because the virtues the new liberals support are increasingly at odds with the way of the world, and because they evade (treat as subordinate and secondary) the deep intrusion of these worldly concerns into political life, the commitment to liberal principles is increasingly matched by the disengagement from practical issues. The principles themselves tend to become more abstract, more difficult to articulate specifically or to link to particular questions.[5]

The gradual retreat from practicality is principled; the abstract voice of virtue does help to set the limits of the morally tolerable in the existing order. Its voice is not, therefore, to be demeaned or ridiculed. But this principled liberalism is neither at home in the civilization of productivity nor prepared to challenge its hegemony. Its protection of liberal principles, combined with the residual commitment to productivity, requires a retreat from practicality.

The other side of liberalism retains the commitment to practicality by sliding toward a technocratic conception of

----

[5] A good example of this principled liberalism can be found in: Ronald Dworkin, "Liberalism," in Stuart Hampshire, ed., **Public and Private Morality**, Cambridge, Cambridge University Press, 1978, pp. 113-143. The essence of liberalism, says Dworkin, is not some particular conception of the good life or commitment to some particular set of institutional practices. It is to "treat all its citizens with equal concern and respect." This principle requires government to "be neutral on what might be called the question of the good life." But to conclude that established institutions meet this requirement, Dworkin is implicitly required to narrow the variety of "conceptions of the good life" to those which fall within the range of tolerance of the established system of productivity. And if its tolerance becomes more restricted, his conceptions are likely to become more abstrct. Similar tendencies can be found in George Kateb's challenging essay "On the 'Legitimation Crisis," cited above. Kateb wants to preserve the open, exploratory conception of self encouraged by representative democracy. (That's the interesting part.) But he thinks the concentration on "economic" issues tends to lose sight of that dimen-

politics. It acknowledges indirectly the dilemma of legitimacy by insisting that significant areas of social life must be regulated increasingly through an elaborate set of incentives and coercive devices. Since these controls are thought only to do more consciously and coherently what traditional guides to conduct did unconsciously and unevenly, it can be concluded that they represent no real threat to liberty or democracy. By treating, first, widespread resistance to role expectations as a universal condition, second, the ends of the civilization as inherently rational, and, third, the enlarged sphere of social life in need of conscious coordination as merely a function of the greater complexity of the system of productivity, the technocrats retain both practicality and the semblance of concern for liberal freedoms. When the order is understood in this way, it is not an unjust infringement of freedom to do what is necessary to promote rational ends.

Charles Schultze, the last liberal intellectual to hold a position of importance in the government, represents this perspective when he reverses the traditional rationale for the market. If it was once thought to price goods rationally, to promote personal freedom, and to limit the effective hegemony of the state, it is now to become an instrument of state control. The idea is to introduce a system of incentives into the market so that it becomes more in the self-interest of workers, owners, and consumers to promote the imperatives of the civilization of productivity. This politicization of the market will work because it does not depend upon civic resources that are in scarce supply: it "reduces the need for compassion, patriotism, brotherly love, and cultural solidarity as motivating forces behind social improvements."[6]

This particular version of the theory contains serious defects. The introduction of these incentives will merely provide new motives and possibilities for evasion, unless

----

sion of political life. I contend that we must politicize our understanding of economic life and seek ways to infuse these "instrumentalities" with space for the open self. Failing that, the instrumentalities are likely to overwhelm the political sphere, as that sphere is understood by the beautiful souls. To them I must appear as an ugly duckling.

[6] Charles Schultze, **The Public Use of Private Interest**, Washington, D. C., The Brookings Institute, 1977, pp. 17-18.

the purposes they serve and the sacrifices they impose speak to the convictions of large segments of the populace. They enhance the space, for instance, for the growth of the "underground economy." Failing to understand the logic of this reaction, Schultze will be drawn into a negative dialectic whereby each new set of evasions must be met by a new set of incentives and controls. The dialectic of social dissolution thus moves in tandem with a corollary dialectic of regimentation. This, then is the version of the dilemma of legitimacy which emerges in the Schultzean theory, but it is not clearly recognized within the theory itself.

Schultze does faintly discern its outlines. For while he finds it unrealistic to promote public purposes without the institution of private incentives, he does ask how those incentives could be equitably introduced by democratic means? Confronting this issue, Schultze is forced to end "rather lamely." When we move from the regulation of private conduct to the question of forming the public will to establish those regulations, there turns out to "be no instrumental solution to the dilemma."[7] Exactly.

Schultze refuses to consider the next step. It is likely to be considered, though, by those technocrats who are no longer haunted by the ghost of liberal principles. The recent attraction of former liberals to the new theory of "reindustrialization" is one index of how far the commitment to practicality can pull many proponents away from democratic convictions as the imperatives of the civilization of productivity make themselves felt more powerfully.[8] The

----

[7] Ibid.

[8] **Business Week** of June 30, 1980 is devoted to "The Reindustrialization of America." Amitai Etzioni claims to be one of the principal authors of this thesis. On page 84, he claims that we ask too much of the American system of political system of political economy; we ask it to "support an ever rising standard of living, create endless jobs; provide education, medical care, and housing for everyone; abolish poverty; rebuild the cities; restore the environment; satisfy the demands of Blacks, Hispanics, women, and other groups." I would have thought those were among the defining ends and promises of the civilization of productivity, but they are now interpreted as excessive expectations on its behalf. To reindustrialize, we supposedly must give up these high expectations. We must: (1) shift from an

dilemma of legitimacy produces a bifurcation in contemporary liberalism. When the two sides are brought into juxtaposition, we can see the dilemma at work in the background. For either liberal practicality or the belief in liberal ideals must be sacrificed by those who refuse to reconsider the priorities and standards governing the civilization of productivty.

THE RETREAT OF CRITICAL THEORY

The interpretation of the declining allegiance to the civilization of productivity advanced in this essay owes a considerable debt to the theories of "legitimacy" and "motivation" crisis developed earlier by Jurgen Habermas.[9] Habermas explores the ways in which the evolution of "advanced capitalism" undermines its preconditions of healthy existence, depletes the motives needed to carry out the dictates of production, forces the state into the role of subsidizer and supporter of private production, and imposes new limits on the state's ability to meet the needs of con-

----

emphasis on consumption to one on savings and investment; (2) shift within investment away from "quality of life improvements" toward the "production of capital goods"; (3) increase state subsidies to business; (4) form a new social contract in which workers give "management more help in improving productivity" and agree as well to decrease the rate of pay increases; (5) shift to coal and relax environmental constraints on its use; (6) introduce tax reforms to allow much higher depreciation allowances for business; (7) deregulate business to reduce impediments to growth and business costs of compliance; (8) increase military expenditures massively. With this in mind, my disagreement with the beautiful souls can be articulated more specifically. The reindustrializationists are approximately correct about what it would take to get the civilization of productivity rolling again: a progressive withdrawal from cherished liberal principles. Liberal principles are threatened if the system of productivity does not meet these imperatives, and they are thretened if it does. This "deconstruction" of the beautiful soul is designed to bring out a certain beauty in its retreat and to open it to the stituencies to whom it is formally accountable.[10]

The theory deepens our comprehension of the problem of legitimacy in modern society. It helps us to understand why a range of practices which previously appeared to be coordinated through the impersonal market and unreflective tradition are now necessarily and visibly objects of conscious coordination by the state or private bureaucracies. Arrangements which previously appeared to be left to the market, such as income distribution, employment levels, comparative rates of development in different parts of the country, and the protection of the environment, are now the visible objects of political contestation; and those which previously appeared to be governed by unreflective tradition, such as the sexual division of labor, the treatment of old people, the composition of the school curriculum, the relations between parents and children, are now the visible objects of state policy. This means that the scope of policies and practices which must be legitimated explicitly to the citizenry has expanded. The question of legitimacy now encompasses an enlarged ensemble of social relations.

Habermas also shows us why it is no longer possible to aspire either to a democratic society in which citizens unreflectively identify with the way of life they share in common (the classic idea of civic virtue) or to one in which

----

possibility of reconsidering its residual commitment to the civilization of productivity.

[9] See: Jurgen Habermas, **Legitimation Crisis**, Boston, Beacon Press, 1973. My debt to and differences from Habermas are formulated in: "Review Essay [on **The Critical Theory of Jurgen Habermas** by Thomas McCarthy]," **History and Theory**, 18, 3, 1979, pp. 397-417.

[10] I prefer the (no doubt awkward) term "civilization of productivity" for a variety of reasons. First, it refers to the fact that existing socialist societies are also mobilized around the priorities of economic growth, rendering them inappropriate as contrast models. Second, it signals a refusal to organize a critique around the labor theory of value, thereby rejecting the idea that one technical analysis of the order can be supplanted by another. Third, it refers to the intersubjective dimension within the modes of work, consumption, and bureacratic control constituting the system of productivity without losing sight of the ways in which those institutions form a complex structure. Fourth,

the citizenry has become highly privatized (the idea of civil liberty without civic virtue). Democratic politics today requires a combination of citizen self-consciousness and civic virtue. A relentless attempt to restore unreflective tradition today must issue in fascist control; and the attempt to secure democratic order without civic virtue must founder against the imperative to coordinate by conscious means a wide variety of social practices and activities. To accept these two themes, though, is to establish both the primacy of the question of legitimacy and the difficulties in responding to it democratically.

Habermas does not seem to me to confront this last issue directly enough. Rather he acknowledges it indirectly by retreating to a metatheoretical question. He does not ask what reforms and new priorities could hope to be instituted and to attract the reflective allegiance of the populace. He asks instead how in principle could we decide whether a particular complex of understandings and practices is valid. The current question of legitimacy is translated into a universal problem of knowledge. The consensus theory of truth and morality emerge as the answer.

The theory can be criticized, even at the abstract level at which it is pitched. For example, if the conditions of ideal speech (e.g., the symmetrical distribution of chances to enter into dialogue, the effective opportunity to call any presupposition of established discourse into question, the suspension of all motives except the wish to reach the correct conclusion) are loosely defined, there is no assurance that one result could emerge from the discourse. And if the conditions are closely specified, it is always possible to claim that the specification itself is not neutral between alternate theoretical perspectives. The problem is that the expressive theory of language and discourse Habermas draws upon to construct his ideal of pure discourse contains within it the expectation that a discourse is unlikely to achieve the practical concensus to which

----

it suggests the possibility that the priorities of productivity could overwhelm the practice of democracy. The squeeze on democratic politics could occur if the priorities are not met (i.e., intensified contestation over the limited economic pie could cast the democracy of compromise and equity into disarray); and it could occur if the priorities are met (i.e., forceful imposition of sacrifices on those without strategic market or political resources could close many out of effective citizenship).

Habermas aspires.   Any consensus capable of generating
specific courses of action will be based upon some set of
pre-judgments which cannot be called into question during
that discourse.   Some set of pre-judgments must form the
unreflective background of discourse while others are called
into question, or the discourse will lack sufficient density
to generate a conclusion.   And if inquiry into a broader
range of pre-judgments is encouraged, no free consensus is
likely to emerge.

There is something apolitical in this ideal of a perfect
consensus, even if it is situated outside the realm of historical probability.   It understates the extent to which our limited resources of reason and evidence unavoidably generate
a plurality of reasonable answers to perplexing practical
questions.   It thus fails to appreciate the creative role for
politics in those persisting situations where public action
must be taken and the resources of knowledge are insufficient to generate a single result.   As an ideal, it aspires to
take the heat out of the cauldron of contested interpretations and orientations to action.   It is in this sense closer
to a collectivization of administration than to the democratization of politics.   In asking too much from legitimacy, it
takes too much away from politics.

Yet apprehended from another angle, the construction
of the ideal speech situation (and other versions of the
consensus theory of practical judgment) can be seen to
carry a political message.   It is a symbol as well as a construct.   It expresses the anxiety that the potential dilemma
of legitimacy actually may be realized in history.   It con-
veys the fear that the space for democratic discourse may
become squeezed increasingly by the imperatives of the
political economy.   As a "limiting case," unintended for full
achievement, it helps to insulate thought from a world
which threatens to become less hospitable to democratic
ideals; it is an intellectual retreat which protects the idea
of democracy by placing it beyond the reach of practical
imperatives.   The Habermas doctrine, failing as a theory of
truth, succeeds as a symbol of the dilemma of legitimacy.

THE FOUCAULDIAN REVERSAL

Foucault would be unsurprised by the critique of the
discourse theory of truth briefly outlined here.   It is

authorized by the "episteme" governing modern discourse.[11]
Whether defined as the implicit, the unconscious, the sedi-
mented, the in-itself, the horizon, or the intersubjective
background, theoretical discourse since the nineteenth century has been haunted by the unthought which provides
the ground for its vaunted celebration of reflexivity or
self-consciousness.   Every   philosophy   which   celebrates
reflexivity also makes the material it works upon recede
constantly into the darkness. Modern "man" (as Foucault
describes us) is endlessly pursued by a "double," by "the
other that is not only a brother, but a twin," by an
unshakable shadow "both exterior to him and indispensable
to him."[12]
        This eternal regress in the relation between the
thought and the unthought, between the subject and its
other, makes reflexivity possible at the expense of rendering a valid political consensus impossible. It is always possible to dissent from any new interpretation of the previously unthought. "For modern thought, no morality is
possible....As soon as [thought] functions it offends or
reconciles, attracts or repels, breaks, dissociates, unites or
reunites; it cannot help but liberate and enslave."[13] My
critique of Habermas, then, operates within the episteme
which authorizes it.   But it does not, Foucault would

----

[11] The episteme, as I understand it, is constituted by the
relations between a theory of language, a conception of the
subject, a notion of knowledge, and the like, all of which
are available to theorists at a particular time.   Each component enables and restricts the space in which the others
can move. Together they form a complex, an episteme.
The episteme does **not** produce the hegemony of one discourse (ideology) over all others; it does produce the space
in which alternative discourses can function. The episteme
enables and confines theoretical discourse.   It renders
inoperative today, for instance, the theory of words as
signs residing within the world conveying an eternal meaning to be interpreted by commentators; and it thereby renders the Renaissance comprehension of madness as a meaningful text to be deciphered inoperative. A "discursive
practice" functions inside the space provided by the episteme; it is a set of concepts, instruments, architectural
structures, regulations, credentials, and rules of evidence
which operate at a practical level.   Penology and psychiatry
are operative disciplines; prisons and asylums are among
the media in which they function; delinquents, criminals,

insist, pursue its own line to the limits. It fails to enunci-
ate how the very problematic of legitimacy, with its associated concepts of the subject, freedom, reflexivity, allegiance, responsibility, and consent, is the juridical twin of
the problematic of disciplinary order. The former is not,
as it sees itself, the alternative to the latter; the two function together to produce the modern subject and to subject
it to the dictates of the order. The critique, in Foucauldian terms, sets the stage for the reversal of the problematic of legitimacy.

In a perfectly legitimate order, the imperative
becomes the indicative: the "you must" assumes the form
of "we will." All seems smooth and unruffled, but the
voice of body can still be detected beneath the whine of the
socially produced soul. To extrapolate slightly, we might
apply Foucault's documentary studies to an account of the
relation between the theoretical perspective of Jean-Jacques
Rousseau and the Marquis de Sade. For Sade is not merely
the adversary of Rousseau; the theorist of illicit desire is
the double of the theorist of civic virtue. Rousseau's legitimate order invokes the free acceptance of self-restraint,
the communal endorsement of self-censorship, the production of chaste, subordinate women. And the Sadean counter-order, perfect in its own way, treats these limits as
invitations to transgressions: restraints are produced to
the broken; censorship intensifies the will to pornography;
and the women of virtue become the perfect objects of deg-
radation.

----

and a variety of mental patients are the objects they constitute and treat. These elements together form the discursive practices of criminology and psychiatry. The modern
episteme allows these, but it does not uniquely determine
them. It forecloses punishment as spectacle, for instance,
because we cannot now think of the torture-confession complex as a **sign** of truth; but it allows the juridical conception of crime (rational agents who are responsible and
guilty) to function alongside the treatment model. The
shift in emphasis in the Foucauldain texts from archeology
to genealogy would need to be treated in a thorough discussion of his thought. I will not attempt that here.

[12] Michel Foucault, **The Order of Things**, New York, Random House, 1970, p. 326.

[13] **Ibid.**, p. 328.

By demanding self-restraint in pursuit of virtue, Rousseau's polity loads the counter-self with illicit desires. It doubles pleasure by adding the pleasure of transgression to the original desire, and the world of virtue produces perfect human objects for the realization of its intensified pleasures. Rousseau's vision of order through virtue thus contains virtue **and** an underground world of illicit desire. He articulates one side of this polity, and Sade articulates the other. Without the presence of the other to oppose and to provide the contrast against which virtue is defined, virtue could not emerge as an achievement; without the other embodied in specific figures of vice, virtue could not fend off the other in itself. But an order which constitutes vice in this way assures that the other will appear in a more aggressive form: it appears as those who take special pleasure in violating virtue. The struggle between vice and virtue is thus loaded in favor of vice, and the virtuous order thereby generates internal pressures to convert the other from the classical figure of vice into the modern object of medical treatment. The classical idea (or this version of it) sets up the modern order which medicalizes insanity, delinquency, sexual perversity, and abnormality. The new order subjects these newly defined figures to treatment; it strives thereby to dampen the pleasures that classical vice had experienced in its struggle with virtue. The old ideal prepares us for modern modes of treatment and discipline.

Individualization is the process by which the modern disciplinary self is produced. One part of the self endorses the rules of the order; it is the free, rational, responsible agent, worthy of punishment for breaking norms to which it freely consents. The second part represents the other which individuals seek to expunge in themselves and to treat when others manifest it in criminality, delinquency, madness, or perverse sexuality. The juridical apparatus and the disciplinary apparatus together constitute the subject and its other.

> In a system of discipline, the child is more individualized than the adult, the patient more than the healthy man, the madman and the delinquent more than the normal and non-delinquent. In each case, it is towards the first of these pairs that all the individualizing mechanisms are turned in our civilization; and when one wishes to individualize the healthy, moral and law-abiding adult, it is always by asking how much of the child he has in him, what

> fundamental crime he has dreamt of commit-
> ting....All the sciences, analyses or practices
> employing the root "psycho-" have their origin
> in this historical reversal of the procedures of
> individualization.[14]

Foucault's texts seek to document the multiple ways in which modern attempts to liberate sexuality, madness, and criminality from arbitrary and repressive controls entangle the self in a web of more insidious controls. The politics of liberation, in its radical and liberal guises, actually helps to produce the subject and to subjugate those other parts of the self which do not fit into this production. The reforms typically **medicalize** sexuality, delinquency, mental "illness." They enclose the objects of treatment in a web of "insidious leniencies."

Critical legitimists, of whom I am one, are generally eager to shrug off Foucault. We seek not to subjugate people in this order, but to imagine a counter-order which is worthy of their allegiance. But Foucault seems to iden-tify us with our adversaries, and that could not be quite right. Besides, his vocabulary is inflated, and we speak more carefully.

But I do not think we (I) can be let off the hook so easily. Foucault's detailed archeologies remind us how the dictates of a particular order and the conceptual resources of a particular episteme can soon appear barbaric to its successor (e.g., the way the ships of fools and torture as instruments of truth appear to us today). The history of unreason indirectly challenges the contemporary constitution of reason. Moreover, if Foucault's metaphors seem inflated to us, they challenge us to justify the mellow metaphors through which we characterize either the existing order or the one we would bring into being. In substituting "sur-veillance" for "observation," "interrogate" for "question," "interrupt" for "pause," and "production" for "emergence" he at once challenges the transparency of the mellow meta-phors we adopt and claims to detect hidden violence within the discourse of the legitimist. In elaborating the micro-physics of the modern subject as a disciplinary production, he is unmasking the denial of the body and how that denial functions. Legitimists are treated as participants in the cover-up. Our metaphors, slipped silently into our

----

[14] Michel Foucault, **Discipline and Punish**, Alan Sheridan, trans., New York, Random House, 1977, p. 193.

discourse, provide the medium through which our potential violence is disguised.

After Foucault, we can understand more clearly why Habermas struggled so valiantly to validate the principle of a free and rational consensus. For that would be a consensus which did not enslave while it liberated; it would create unity without subjugating the other. We can also understand why Foucault must read the project as a counter-tyranny of insidious leniency. For it constantly insists on assimilating material into its categories which can only be made to fit by force. It practices denial in the name of free discourse.

A case can be made, I think, in favor of the legitimist, particularly the dissident type, **accepting** Foucault as a double. The quest for legitimacy must open itself to the voice of the other; it must review itself from the vantage point of conceptualizations it finds alien, questions it tends to ignore, and answers it tends to exclude. It must confront three questions. What is to be done to, with, or "for" the other which does not fit into the actual or ideal order? What is the justification for doing it? And what is the ground of the justification?

But can Foucault demand more? Must the quest for legitimacy itself be expunged because **any** answer given to it must tyrannize and subjugate? I think not. For Foucault is entagled in his own version of the dilemma of legitimacy. Consider the political strategy open to Foucault after the strategies of technocratic control, liberal reform, and radical liberation have been rejected. In his early work, Foucault sought to allow the "voice of unreason" to speak for itself by historicizing the various relations to the other imposed by historical variations in the constitution of reason. His more recent stance is more overtly political; he now supports "the insurrection of subjugated knowledges," and he is now more confident in his belief that the attempt to "understand" the other within any established framework amounts to the attempt to control the other by insidious leniency.[15]

----

[15] Michel Foucault, **Power/Knowledge**, Brighton, Sussex, Harvester Press, 1980, p. 81. My reading of the earlier texts is supported on page 108 of this more recent essay: "it is not through recourse to sovereignty against discipline that the effects of disciplinary power can be limited because sovereignty and disciplinary mechanisms are two absolutely integral constituents of the general mechanisms of power in

Yet Foucault is not, as he would characterize it, a naive anarchist of the nineteenth century. He does not seem to believe that an anarchistic order could be established. Order is unavoidable for social life; and any order, particularly any order in the modern world, necessarily implies limits.[16] Thus to oppose in principle the quest for legitimacy is to deny one postulate in the Foucauldian problematic. It is to subjugate one dimension of Foucauldian knowledge in the interest (the political interest) of allowing the other dimension to flourish. "To imagine another system," Foucault contends, "is to extend our participation in the present system...; the 'whole of society' is precisely that which should not be considered except as something to be destroyed."[17]

But if I am right, the exclusion of political imagination and affirmation emerges as the Foucauldian denial. Strategic considerations lead him to mask a dimension of his own theory, and the denial is fraught with political consequences dangerous to his own objectives. The release of subjugated knowledges may illuminate political imagination, but it does not release us from the enterprise. Because order implies limits, we must seek a set of limits which could deserve our allegiance. The dilemma of legitimacy inside Foucault's theory thus emerges starkly. It becomes

----

our society."

[16] Will the new episteme which is now beginning to tremble beneath our feet break this relation between life, order, and limits? We cannot now know. But it seems likely that the Foucaldian strategy of proliferating resistance and oppositions without affirmations rests upon a faith in the unknown possibilities residing in the next "break." The strategy seems designed to hasten its arrival. The insistence that radical breaks or ruptures divide the Renaissance from the classical age and the classical from the modern age (with its two giant regimes) is governed by this political intent. If those breaks were complete, maybe the next one will be too. I agree that the Left needs a break, but there is no ground for such a faith. The strategy, in the order we now know, promises to tighten and extend reactive forces. A complete account would need to discuss this theory of breaks (it is exaggerated) and the reversal of the theory of the subject associated with it. Another defense of Foucauldian strategy rests upon the view that, since the forces of order are always with us, we need a

a dilemma of order: social life requires order, but the order which does receive the allegiance of its subjects subjugates them, while the one which does not subjugates them too.[18]

The way to loosen the hold of this dilemma, at least at the level of theory, is to show that the circle of reflexivity is not as closed as Foucault pretends it must be. We may concede that the assimilation of the other to established dualities of reason/unreason, virtue/vice, sanity/insanity, and normality/abnormality always contains the elements of a political conquest. For Foucault's documentary histories do support the conclusion that standards and judgments which possessed hegemony at one historic moment appear arbitrary and closed from the perspective of another; and we can therefore suspect that those categories which now govern our thought and practice will assume such an appearance at a later date. Thus the view of reflexivity which assumes that we can listen to the other through our categories or that we can now broaden them enough to draw the other into their orbit without arbitrariness must now appear to be too narrow; the circle in which it moves is too tightly drawn. But what about a mode of reflexivity which profits from Foucault's histories of madness, criminality, and perversity and which acknowledges that it now lacks the

----

counter-force unconfined by the need to affirm and, thereby, unconfined by the need to limit itself. But a reversal of the reversal is needed here: since the voice of order is always with us, we need to legitimize oppositional efforts through counter-affirmations to gain leverage. My position depends on qualifying the theory of breaks, the reversal of the subject, and the denial of affirmation; and I think that advances in one of these areas will promote success in the others. At any rate, the Foucauldian schema itself is too mired in the present to authorize a strategy based upon faith in the break to come. Foucault says as much in the last paragraph (p. 387) of **The Order of Things**. "If those arrangements were to disappear as they appeared, if some event of which we can at the moment do no more than sense the possibility -- without knowing either what its form will be or what it promises -- were to cause them to crumble, as the ground of Classical thought did, at the end of the eighteenth century, then one can certainly wager that man could be ereased, like a face drawn in sand at the edge of the sea."

resources to comprehend the other? What about a mode which reflexively acknowledges the limits to reflexive assimilation of the other? Such a view warrants a different response: it encourages us to find space for the other to live and speak on the ground that **we** know enough to know that we cannot comprehend it. It supports, I want to say, an ideal of social order which can sustain itself without having to draw so much of the self into the orbit of social control.

This theoretic response contains implications for political conduct. If ours is an order which has "dirt denying" tendencies; if we tend to sweep that which is out of place under the rug by pretending that we can assimilate it to established categories of rationality and treatment; if we medicalize, confine, and exclude the others who do not fit into the existing order of things: there have been other societies with a loose enough texture to be more "dirt affirming."[19] They could acknowledge the dirt that they themselves produce and thereby (though imperfectly or ambiguously) confront the limits of their own conceptual and political orders.

Tribal festivals of reversal had this quality. Seasonal festivals were enacted in which that which was forbidden was allowed and those who were normally subordinated (because their order necessitated it) were temporarily placed in a superior position. In these festivals, that which was officially circumscribed or denied was temporarily allowed and affirmed. The participants were able to glimpse the injustices implicit in their own necessities; they were encouraged to live these necessities with more humanity

----

[17] Michel Foucault, **Language, Counter Memory, Practice,** Oxford, Basil Blackwell, 1977, pp. 230, 233. It is possible, more than possible, that underlying the bravado about breaks and implicit in the restriction of oppositional discourse to resistance is the sense that the current order is beyond the reach of serious reconstitution.

[18] On page 96 of **Power/Knowledge,** Foucault declares: "Right should be viewed, I believe, not in terms of a legitimacy to be established, but in terms of the methods of subjugation it instigates."

[19] The terms are borrowed from Mary Douglas (who borrowed them from William James). See: **Purity and Danger,** Baltimore, Penguin Books, 1966.

during the normal periods of the year. They acknowledged that some features of their own order, some of the dirt they produced, was mysterious to them. The reins of social coordination were not so tightly drawn that they had to pretend that they possessed sufficient categories to comprehend and eliminate the dirt in their order.

One criterion of comparative legitimacy suggested by the Foucauldian forays into the logic of unreason speaks to the differential capacity of regimes to acknowledge the dirt, the matter out of place, they themselves produce. The civilization of productivity, if its actual trajectory fits the course projected earlier in this essay, will be too constrained by the drive to mobilize its populace around the simultaneous pursuit of growth and austerity to nourish this capacity. To challenge the interdependent complexes of consumption, production, profit, and resource dependency which generate these imperatives is thus to challenge the preconditions of closure in the order. A margin of success on this terrain could help to maintain space for political dialogue. If, for instance, the infrastructure of consumption were reconstituted so that the intensification of consumption demands (or pleas) was not fueled by the perpetual expansion of consumption needs, the imperative to impose growth and austerity together could be relaxed.[20] The effect would be the provision of needed slack in the order, allowing political engagement to be the medium through which we probe the ambiguities and cope with the limits of modern social life.

By "slack in the order," I mean an order which does not have to coordinate so many aspects of our lives and

----

[20] To change the infrastructure of consumption, it is necessary to revise also the modes of investment, profit, work, and state expenditures. These themes are developed in: Best and Connolly, **The Politicized Economy**. I think the alternatives reduce to three: (1) refusing to support the imperatives of the system of productivity without modifying the institutions which produce them; (2) successfully imposing austerity on politically weakened constituencies to provide the basis for "reindustrialization"; (3) reconstituting the established mode of consumption, etc., to curtail imperatives. Each of these strategies would face resistance, opposition, limits, setbacks, and so forth. But only one of them contains the promise to preserve space for democratic politics. That is also the one (3) which is unexplored within the established terms of political discourse.

relations to maintain itself; an order which can afford to let some forms of conduct be; an order which is not compelled by its own imperatives of coordination to convert eccentric, odd, strange behavior into the categories of vice, delinquency, or abnormality.   Such an order would require virtue among its citizens, but the space virtue must cover would not extend too broadly; A residual space would flourish in which neither the control of virtue nor coercion would be necessary.   The provision of that space would itself allow virtue to displace coercive discipline in those areas where the order did require coordination to sustain itself.

This, at least, is the vision which seems to me to contain the most promise for responding to the dilemma of legitimacy.   But slack in the order can only be produced if we can find ways to tame or relax the new imperatives which are generated by the civilization of productivity. And (again I express only an intuition) the relaxation of those imperatives can best be achieved if we reconstitute the infrastructure of consumption to reduce those consumption needs which now impel citizens to validate through the political process social disciplines and sacrifice which they themselves find onerous.

Perhaps there are other or better ways to promote slack in the order, but here I want to concentrate on the importance of the end rather than on the most appropriate means to it.   For when the legitimist introduces the conception of slack into the problematic of legitimacy, we can hear the echo of an earlier liberal doctrine in the background. A theory which has been inspired by the wish to leave liberal notions of privacy, rights, tolerance, and diversity behind now redefines and reinstitutes them.   The irony in this new vision contains the seeds of a renewed dialogue between liberals and radicals.   For although the liberal appreciation of private space is acknowledged in this vision, it sees that established liberal programs and priorities now erode both that space and the implicit allegiance of the populace to the order.   Similarly, the radical appreciation of virtue is now endorsed as well as the understanding that an order must produce a double dialectic of regimentation and corruption when it loses the ability to sustain the affective allegiance of its participants.   But the radical image is then modified by the admission that the ideal of virtue and legitimacy requires the provision of slack in the order.   Slack is both a precondition of and limit to virtue in a modern polity.

Such a perspective is too abstract to resolve the dilemma of legitimacy.   It does not define a common good which could at once reorient the priorities of the civilization of productivity, maintain contact with unavoidable parameters of modern life, and provide the slack needed for politics to flourish.   Still, it does acknowledge the dilemma of legitimacy; and it establishes a direction to pursue in striving to loosen its grip.

POLITICAL THEORY

AND THE INTERNAL STRUCTURES OF THE SELF:

REFLECTIONS ON WHERE POLITICAL THEORY

SHOULD BE NOW

James M. Glass

I am not sure there can be an "answer" to "where should political theory should be now?" Of course, it should be timely; it should look at the classical issues of authority, participation, the meaning of action, community, and the like. (For example, modern themes of community might include identity, boundary, generation, and disintegration.) Political theory should be where it always has been: an activity of theoretical construction that tries to say something meaningful about how individuals organize their lives. It is therefore an activity, a process, a conversation that situates the observing or theoretical self within a matrix of influences, each of which involves speculation and some separation from the ongoing processes of political life. Current academic or professional theorists are dominated by paradigms of study that presume a measure of separation from the political process, from first-order experiences generating theory. They are primarily observers of political life, placing considerable importance on "history," philosophy, and historical patterns of knowing. They are involved in the historical task of reminding students (who are their primary audience) that the concept of the political is more than a name for corrupt and jingoistic politicians.

In my view, political theory "should" be an activity that focuses on the relationship between self and political life. I am not saying that this should be the only or even primary aim of political theorists. This is, however, a critical issue for me and one that lies at the heart of much in the historical tradition of political thought. The "self" is a reality; it exists; it is there. It is not a fiction, any more than the psychological operations by which individuals orient action and perception in the world are fictions. To argue that there is no such entity as "human nature" or "self" would be to dispense with the meaning of dreams, slips of the tongue, erratic or unusual behavior, sexuality, the flows of appetite, desire. Not only does the concept of self situate the individual in a social and economic matrix, but it infuses modes of knowing and perception which form the core of ethical and philosophical systems. Political theory often has been a response to what the theorist conceives of as the energy of the self, the direction of that psychic energy, and ways to contain or embody it in political form.

Take for example the Republic and its representation of the relationship between character and polity. "Recall the general likeness between the city and the man and then observe in turn what happens to each them," we are directed. Tyranny appears through imbalanced "souls" and psyches ravaged by desire: "the tyrant is...filled with multitudinous and manifold terrors and appetites...convulsions and pains."[1] Or look at Aristotle's view of the good man and the good citizen: his underlying assumptions about psyche in knowing how to rule and how to be ruled. And notice the modern obsession with conceptions of the natural man, the state of nature, and the natural condition as fictions for describing human nature in contact theory. Or mark the impact of Marx's theory on conceiving the relationship between human need and the distribution of human products.

As political theorists, should we not be concerned with what is interior to the self, what is "inside," what psychlogical dynamics propel people into participatory relationships, into effective citizenship? If individuals lack "internality," or if talk of "inside" and "outside" distorts human action, then whether political theorists take seriously the idea of the unconscious, of hidden or inaccessible parts of the self, makes little difference. If the self is fully manifest in what appears to be, then there is no value in such concepts as the unconscious, the intrapsychic, and the splitting of the ego.

I accept the proposition that feelings derive from complex interactions between intrapsychic events and external "objects." Thus I believe the human self to be a bundle of defenses that may inhibit or interfere with the creation of relationships or the sense of connectedness. "Psychoanalytic exploration of character pathology" means locating one arena of political struggle in what Otto Kernberg defines as "the intrapsychic relationship that arises between the patient's ego and superego."[2] From this

---

[1] Plato, **The Republic**, Francis MacDonald Cornford, trans., New York, Oxford University Press, 1945, par. 804, 806.

perspective, the nature of character or self depends on events that happen "inside" and on the ways in which "past pathogenic internalized object relations (representing a particular conflict) have become 'frozen' into a character pattern." Further, the outcomes of these interactions are often "forgotten," repressed and inaccessible to consciousness. Hence to bring to consciousness what has been forgotten is to uncover or recover what is unconscious in the self.

This implies that the self possesses a "history," written in each stage of development through events being acted out in an internal field. This process may be summarized as three dynamics: the "internalization of interpersonal relations" beginning from birth, the "contribution" of such relations to "normal and pathological ego and superego developments," and the reciprocal effect or "mutual influences of intrapsychic and interpersonal object relations."[3] The ego is subjected to great stress and trauma throughout its growth. Certain feelings that threaten its stability, its ability to survive or hold itself together, may be split off and repressed. In the form of affect, these become "recognitions" that may later come back to haunt the self through strange or unusual behavior, thoughts, and sensations. Serious disruptions within the stages of development, particularly the earliest ones (in the first two or three years of life), provoke schizophrenic or psychotic behavior: loss of identity, dissolution of ego, confusion over boundaries or gender, and withdrawal into fantasized object relations (signaled by delusional symbologies).

Why are current political theorists reluctant to look at methodologies, terminologies, and perspectives directed toward understanding and analyzing internal, psychological states? Why are theorists now so skeptical and often hostile toward the theoretical implications of psychoanalytic methodology? For me, these are crucial questions about the current condition of political theory.

In an intellectual sense, such reluctance derives primarily from two sources. On the one hand, political theory has become the study of political thought, so that (even in its philosophical projects) it is now dominated paradigmatically by historical methods of analysis. On the other hand,

----

[2] Otto Kernberg, **Object-Relations Theory and Clinical Psychoanalysis**, New York, Jason Aronson, 1976, p. 79.

[3] Ibid., p. 57.

political theorists assume that it is somehow "unphilosophical" to assimilate a clinical language to theoretical discourse.[4]

Mainly, historians of political theory object to psychoanalytic methodology because its clinical language is thought
to distort the "meaning" of history and the language environment in which theorists should work. How, they ask,
can we reach toward "intentions" in political theory, if we
must continually "translate" from one language game (of the
texts and contexts studied) to another (of psychoanalytic
methods of study)? They worry that differences in assumptions, values, traditions, and intellectual habits make it
highly unlikely that the "gestalt" of any current methodology (with psychoanalysis but one example) can fit or
respond well to perceptions generating meaning, value, and
choice in earlier environments. Clinical languages not only
distort the theorist's intention, but also obscure the historical foundation and matrix of any act of theory construction. For historians of political theory, what matters is
accuracy of description and attribution of meaning. And
they doubt that any depth-psychological theory can be an
adequate tool for discovering meaning.

The clinical literature itself, however, suggests that
psychoanalytic methodology is sensitive precisely to "history." Psychoanalysis studies the generation of meaning
structures in a particular past. Sympathetic to psychoanalytic method, the philosopher Paul Ricoeur notes that, in
this psychoanalytic process, "the patient is both the actor
and the critic of a history which he is at first unable to
recount."[5] I do not argue that historians of political theory
are intolerant of nonhistorical languages of analysis. At
issue is whether clinical languages can penetrate intentionality and recover "historical" meaning. The debate centers
on how to approach intentions, how to make sense out of
the relation between an idea and its historical field. For
the psychoanalyst, "history" is meaningful in two forms: in
its capacity to produce symbolic manifestations of meaning
(symptoms) and in its constitution as a relationship between

----

[4] See: James M. Glass, "The Language of Analysis:
Theory as Defense against the Internal," **Polity**, 12, 1,
Fall, 1979, pp. 129-141.

[5] Paul Ricoeur, "The Question of Proof in Freud's Psychoanalytic Writings," **Journal of American Psychoanalytical
Association**, 25, 4, 1977, pp. 835-873, on p. 862.

the content of symptoms and the order of "reasons" that motivate incapacitating mental acts.

Psychoanalytic method directs itself toward recovering the sources of intention. It is an investigative or hermeneutic activity committed to uncovering a historical truth: the knowledge of processes and structures that give rise to psychological events. In looking at a political theory, therefore, psychoanalytic method is far from insensitive to intentions. Indeed, what motivates the psychoanalytic technique is an extraordinary sensitivity to the meaning and structure which provoke the self's historically identifiable behaviors. For the psychoanalyst, the true meaning of intentionality lies hidden; it is a product of the unconscious. Moreover, intentions lead us to truth not so much through the symptoms themselves (which may be defenses, protections from recognizing the truth), but through the pathways that symptoms provide to the largely inaccessible areas of the psyche. For the psychoanalyst, history is the reason for the therapeutic dialectic. But history disguises, dissembles, hides. Therefore, analytic activity must view history as two-sided: both as the conscious formation of meaning (symptom) and as the dissembler of meaning.

In the latter respect, the conscious and recognizable history of the self can be seen as a mask for the order of unconscious "reasons" which embodies the self's historical truth. And on this basis, the psychoanalyst argues that the true objectivity of the self lies in what is hidden: the unconscious. Cannot the same argument be made about political theory?

If theory is approached as symbolization, then the search for intention in the history of political theory is much like the search for meaning in psychoanalysis. What is true about intentionality is not what is immediately visible. There may be unconscious states in political theory much as there are in individuals. Reaching an understanding of these unconscious states means assuming that the theoretical statement or formulation represents or symbolizes psychological states. It also means adopting a methodology compatible with this assumption. Theoretical concepts such as the Hobbesian natural condition then become ways of speaking about "unconscious" contents of the theory itself. Thus theoretical constructions are to be studied as symbolizations of psychological states. Such states are accessible through a modern language that "translates" classical statements into an interpretive environment. This is done in an attempt to discover the common tie between the theory as symbolic representations of mind (e.g., the Hobbesian natural condition of mankind as narcissistic pathology) and the implications of such a "reading" of those theoretical symbols for a contemporary audience. This is an analysis of meaning, but it treats theoretical symbolizations much like the analyst would treat "symptoms" in the patient. It is what Ricoeur calls an "interrogation of the text." But here the text is seen not as some historical fact or historians' debate, but as a psychological production that moves on an unconscious level.

For example, what is important about the concept of pathological narcissism is not only its clinical background, but its usefulness in drawing out implications of an important statement in the political tradition. It helps to show how narcissistic states relate to demands for political order, control, and dominance. It tries to translate Hobbesian theory into a modern context.[6] It forges a connection between internal states and politically destructive behavior. This is not to deny the importance of understanding or pursuing political theory as a historical investigation of meaning and cause. It is rather to add another dimension to that meaning. Hobbes demonstrated that narcissistic pathologies motivate conceptions of political rule, choice, and power. He provided theoretical evidence of the importance of intrapsychic states in recommending structures for political rule. It is therefore appropriate to look at Hobbes, a theorist placing tremendous importance on the self conceived as an isolated monad locked into its own needs and "secret thoughts," through the perspective established by psychoanalysis in dealing with similar psychological structures. Thus what psychoanalytic theory calls "pathological narcissism" has a history and meaning for political philosophy.

Now I should address a few remarks to the objection that clinical languages are unphilosophical. Psychoanalytic theory consists of more than techniques for dealing with specific character disorders. It gives a philosophical justification for conceptions of mind that posit unconscious or hidden layers. It is metapsychological in providing frameworks or points of view that move beyond strictly clinical issues. One obvious example is Freud's analysis of the relationship between human "happiness" and the interests of civilization on the one side and struggles among sexuality, instinct, and demands for order on the other. **The Future**

----

[6] See: James M. Glass, "Hobbes and Narcissism: Pathology in the State of Nature," **Political Theory**, 8, 3, August, 1980, pp. 335-363.

of Illusion, Civilization and Its Discontents, Moses and Monotheism: all attend to philosophical, cultural, and political questions that move beyond a clinical focus. [7]

It is not unusual in recent times to see considerable philosophical interest directed toward Freudian assumptions. Examples abound in works by Paul Ricoeur, Jacques Lacan, Geza Roheim, Harold Lasswell, Herbert Marcuse, Max Horkheimer, Theodor Adorno, Jurgen Habermas, and Alexander Mitscherlich. [8] Philosophical and clinical projects move along many common lines: interpreting perceptual structures, analyzing influences on the "self," evaluating connections between emotion and action.   Freud and Nietzsche are frequently noted to have had a great deal in common; and there is some evidence in the minutes of the Vienna Psychoanalytic Association that Freud was made aware of his affinity with Nietzsche.   In addition, psychoanalytic theory raises issues of considerable interest to political theory, issues which have never in the past been central objects of inquiry within political theory.   (One example is the theme of the 1981 International Congress of Psychoanalysis: sex and language.)

To argue that psychoanalytic theory is unphilosophical not only distorts its origins (in nineteenth-century dialogues over the meaning of mind), but also neglects its

----

[7] See: Sigmund Freud, **The Future of an Illusion**, W. D. Robson-Scott, trans., James Strachey, ed., Garden City, NY, Doubleday, 1964; Freud, **Civilization and Its Discontents**, James Strachey, trans. and ed., New York, Norton, 1961; Freud, **Moses and Monotheism**, Katherine Jones, trans., New York, Knopf, 1939.

[8] See: Paul Ricoeur, **Freud and Philosophy**, Denis Savage, trans., New Haven, Yale University Press, 1970; Jacques Lacan, **The Language of the Self**, Anthony Wilden, trans., Baltimore, Johns Hopkins University Press, 1968; Geza Roheim, **The Origin and Function of Culture**, Garden City, NY, Doubleday, 1943; Harold Lasswell, **Psychopathology and Politics**, New York, Viking Press, 1930; Herbert Marcuse, **Eros and Civilization**, New York, Random House, 1955; Max Horkheimer and Theodor Adorno, **Dialectic of Enlightenment**, John Cumming, trans., New York, Herder and Herder, 1944; Jurgen Habermas, **Knowledge and Human Interests**, Jeremy J. Shapiro, trans., Boston, Beacon Press, 1971; and Alexander Mitscherlich, **Society Without the Father**, Eric Mosbacher, trans., New York, Schocken Books, 1963.

metapsychological impact (especially on reevaluation of traditional political concepts).   To look at mind as an outgrowth only of purely rational processes and historical modes of generating understanding is to construct a judgment as to what mind is.   It makes just as much sense to study mind as a function of symbolic, metaphoric, repressed, and irrational psychological states.   What mind is remains an open question, and therefore psychoanalytic theory can at least contribute to alternate conceptions of it.

If postulations of an unconscious are denied, then mind indeed becomes an extension of strictly rational processes.   If distinctions between rational and irrational are discredited, then the very concept of human nature is banished or reduced to mere processes, reactions, imputs, and energies unlimited and unenlightened by any sense of ethics.   This would be nihilism.   Then any human act reflecting passionate feeling or desire would have to be conceived as coming from random impulses.   Identity would come not from a "self," but from past psychophysiological events, such as the mobilization of defenses.   We could only say that identity "is" because it happens, that we "are" whatever specific situational influences happen to affect us.   This "self" is like a sieve: experience runs right through it, never retained; only an empty vessel remains.   There is nothing stored up; there are no layers, no sediments of the self; there is no human archeology.   Identity is stark energy emodied only through what it encounters in chance meetings, in randomness.   This "human nature" could be comprehended only through a theory of indeterminacy.

In this view, the self is a monad: not a Hobbesian monad, because at least Hobbes granted an autonomy to the "secret thoughts that run over all things without praise or blame," but an alienated monad without dimension.   It is human energy without meaning, purpose, choice, or commitment.   It is the individual as raw material to be shaped by whatever dynamic situation confronts it.   To do away with any sense of a "buried" self (an unconscious) is to eradicate the very concept of human nature, if only because the unconscious self is that aspect of the human being neither fully outside nor fully inside, neither fully determining nor fully determined.   It is the abiding structure of human nature, bridging effective humanity and affective being.   To posit an unconscious is to posit that human experience encompasses a generativity or creativity not subject to the molding influence of social reality, environment, or historical tradition.   It seems to me very difficult to construct a theory of liberty without a conception of human nature (and the purposes of human impulses).   What is Freud speaking about if not the liberty of the self?   Are not individuals as incapacitated by emotional disorders as they are by external threats?   Are not "introjects" (tormenting ego formations) as painful in restricting freedom as unjust laws?   Should not political theorists be sensitive to the forms in which the self is enchained though internal sources of tyranny?

If there is no human nature, then we exist as "monads" traveling around in the existential universe, mirrors for the datum of consciousness.   We therefore have no "insides," no "interior," no psychological past, no forgotten memories.   To dispense with the notion of an "interior" self means to accept that we ourselves are either (1) completely determined beings, thoroughly conditioned by behavioral forces, (2) "systems" distinguished by inputs and outputs, or (3) transcendent energies unbound by anything other than the facticity of the will to power (a kind of reconstituted **Ubermensch**).

I find these three alternatives unacceptable.   The first two reduce the individual to a cipher of external influences;   the third glorifies narcissistic grandiosity.   To release the self from a psychological past is to do away with the need for any limitation.   The struggle between the unconscious and the conscious creates limits: the need and potential for ethics as a restraint on impulse.   Without the unconscious, there is no superego, no sense of conscience;   or at best, there is a perverted and overly restrictive superego that comes back to haunt and torment the self.   To do away with the superego altogether is exceedingly dangerous, for it is to live without any sense of limitation, to inhabit a nihilistic emptiness.   To deny the unconscious is to deny not only the ego, leaving the self no reflection in the world, but also the conscience, encircling the self in meaninglessness.

As Otto Rank suggests through the concept of psychical reality, "truth" and "reality" depend on internal modes of knowing.   Thus the psychological interior is a "place": it constructs, creates, and projects life.   Structures of meaning and value originate inside the self.   Inside is the world of affect, desire, and feeling.   Rank should be taken seriously when he declares that affect defines what is true.   "The only trueness in terms of actual psychic reality is found in emotion, not in thinking, which at best denies or rationalizes truth, and not necessarily in action unless it flows from feeling and is in harmony with it."   Truth is recovered through inward movement, not through intellectual abstraction or romantic projection.   Similarly, will is not just "there."   Rather, "our own act of will" derives from the self's interior.   It is the consequence of the "inner pressure after truth."[9] In Rank's view, there is little sense in knowing facticity ("the data") without mediating that material through the inner sources of will; will is perceptual energy. In turn, this conception depends on the generative sources of an unconscious, on the "truth" of the self. For Rank, then, knowledge of will is knowledge of the unconscious.

From this perspective, it is inevitable that individuals impose on their worlds a conception of reality that comes from unconscious sources. At an extreme, this is exemplified by the delusional symbology of schizophrenics. Indeed, it is even unclear to what extent a consensual universe is affected by unconscious sources of knowing. The following case indicates the extent to which truth involves the psychological operations of projection. A clinically diagnosed schizophrenic believes that all "machines" want to have "sex" with her; all mechanical devices (coke machines in the hospital, lawnmowers on the hospital grounds, refrigerators in the hospital kitchen) desire her sexually. She is terribly frightened of these machines when they are operating, when they are producing noise (the medium for communicating messages about sexuality). These feelings (and the attribution of sexual desire and will to machines) are not random utterances; nor is the patient responding randomly to her confusion. Hers is not utterance produced without meaning or purpose. Her thoughts are intended and, in their own context, logical.

Her belief in machine sexuality is part of a complex inner epistemology which regulates her self-consciousness and action. This patient constructs a symbology, of which machine sexuality is only a part. That symbology represents a hidden, internal, inaccessible causality. Her asserations create her reality, and what she speaks mirrors a "will" that assimilates the external world through powerfully expressed fears of penetration by machines. Such messages do not come from a socially constructed or historically defined universe. Her utterance is "ordinary" language, but her frame of reference differs radically from the traditional, conventional, and social.[10] What she means and infers in her language is the product not of convention or

----

[9] Otto Rank, **Truth and Reality**, New York, Norton, 1978, pp. 40, 12.

[10] See: Harry Stack Sullivan, **Schizophrenia as a Human Process**, New York, Norton, 1962.

history, but of truth buried deeply within herself. Her symbology includes communicating with alien spaceships, turning into a cat, and experiencing her lover as a mechanical force, as an airplane descending. Such symbols convey information about the self's interiority: its conception of desire and the relationship of desire to thought. They portray the structure of unconscious thought.

This kind of discourse, with its many variations, is relevant to the study of political life. Inner dialogues, the language of delusion, internal epistemologies: all can be seen to raise philosophical questions about the origins of ethics, conceptions of good and bad, structures of power and perception, judgments of fact, and (most importantly) relationships between the meaning of "truth" and unconscious sources of knowledge.[11] Thus a knowledge of internal states may illuminate value assumptions and psychological forces underlying the historical construction of political theory.

Clinical language can offer new and useful information to political theorists. But even more, it can give them new and enlightening questions. Here the political theory of exclusion is but one example. Why, in a great many political theories, are certain groups included and others excluded from participation in political life? Why did Aristotle banish "beasts" and "gods" from his polity? What is the political form of such types; what do they represent? How might psychological models be used to discover or demonstrate the dynamics of inclusion and exclusion? Is it that "beasts" and "gods" threaten to break through limits, through the political identity established by the golden mean? Was Aristotle writing about the disruptive effects of passion and other psychological states on the boundaries, and thus on the identity, of the polity? Or do "beasts" and "gods" threaten the philosophic ego, the philosopher's claim to knowledge, insight, control, and power? Are Aristotelian and psychoanalytic "truth" common, convergent, or incompatible? What kind of ego did Aristotle create for his polity; what are its conditions; and how more generally did Aristotle conceive the self? Did he give sufficient consideration to the effects of making polities the primary source of self-identity for the creation of psychologically healthy

----

[11] See: James M. Glass, "Facts and Meaning: From the Perspective of Schizophrenic Internay," Contemporary Psychoanalysis, forthcoming; James M. Glass, "Schizophrenia and Language," **Ethics**, forthcoming.

people?   Or did he formulate a conception of rule that depends on internalizing assumptions, values, and preferences in the form of superego domination?

Through psychoanalytic languages, new and important questions may be asked of Aristotelian political theory, questions that historical languages ignore or even deny. A psychoanalytic approach to political theory claims that the contexts of clinical languages are useful for examining Aristotelian conceptions of the beast, the mean, rationality, knowledge, and the dual capacity to rule and be ruled. These clinical contexts permit analysis of Aristotelian and other political theories against the backdrop of symptom and the expression of desire.

The desires generated by unknown forms of psychic energy, the possibilities that such desires might break through boundaries, the dynamism and violence of a self lacking political identity: all these themes are central to the theoretical tradition and the interests of political philosophy.   For example, how might Plato's cave be understood as a metaphor for unconscious states of being; or the Aristotelian beast as a symbol of human experiences of seduction, overpowering desire, hostility to control through a political ego?   We might ask whether the Aristotelian fear of extremes is a reaction against what Otto Rank has described as "self tormenting introspection," a state of mind that turns the self away from the polity (with its administrative apparatus, activity, and values) as the preeminent touchstone for personal identity?   Does knowledge of truth as a function of psychological interiority (consider the "cave" Plato refuses to show us as the abode of unconscious knowledge) diminish the impact and even place of "politics" or "the political" as a set of standards to guide consciousness and behavior?

Perhaps psychoanalytic theory is Aristotelian in its belief in friendship, trust, balance, limitation, and reason. But for the most part, it does not share Aristotle's hostility toward passion or feeling as a source of knowledge.   Nor, even though the dyadic exchange of psychoanalytic therapy involves political considerations, is it as intolerant of extreme expressions of passion and desire, which Aristotle and most political theorists since have reckoned as anti-political impulses.   To be sure, most current psychoanalytic methods derive from Aristotelian premises concerning reason and logic.   But it is one thing to argue matters of method and quite another to penetrate the meaning of specific theoretical constructs in Aristotelian thought.   As commentaries on political types, tendencies, and needs, Aristotle's writings show an obvious fear of a certain type of passion:

what might be called "precivil" or "nonsocial" passion.
Aristotle (not to mention many theorists since) could fairly
be said to assume that such drives and feelings threaten
the underlying cohesion of a well-ordered polity.[12] Yet
what is to prevent any one group of rulers, no matter how
possessed of such an abstraction as "virtue," from naming
others as the possessors of dangerous passions which
require that they be excluded from the benefits of civility
and citizenship? Then is it simply that "virtue" becomes
synonymous with "power?" Or is it that the powerful
define "virtue?" Usually, we might think it more accurate
to say that the powerful in society decide what groups are
to be named "dangerous," so that those can "legitimately"
be banished from politics, excluded from participating as
full citizens.

     For the rest of the essay, I concentrate on the ways
in which clinical languages point up the facticity of what
theorists historically have called "human nature." From
this perspective, where political theory should be now is
shown by connecting historical and current expressions of
human nature. How, for example, is a political theorist to
enter "human nature," to "listen" to what Rousseau called
the "languages of the heart?"[13] Or to put it another way,
what are the properties of language and utterance that
might allow the political theorist an "empirical" experience
of what is designated by the concept of human nature?
What would constitute first-order evidence of the existence
of a "human nature" that precedes civil and social forms of
knowing, interaction, and identity? Where should political
theorists look for confirmation and specification of a concept
like human nature; might a psychoanalytically informed language, using notions like conscious and unconscious, ego
and super ego, provide more coherence and better definition for a term so important in the history of political
thought?

     In a psychoanalytic sense, language embodies the
unconscious; utterance makes unconscious conflict and

----

[12] See: James M. Glass, "The Schizophrenic and Primitive
Thought: The Implicit and Unconscious Nature of Psychological Rebellion," **Politics and Society**, 6, 3, 1976, pp.
327-345.

[13] See: James M. Glass, "Political Philosophy as Therapy:
Rousseau and the Pre-Social Origins of Consciousness,"
Political Theory, 4, 2, May, 1976, pp. 163-184.

struggle visible, placing feeling in a public context.   It
therefore makes sense to look for the facticity of human
nature in language: indeed, in a peculiar kind of language, with a frame of reference that sharpens the distinction between conscious and unconscious forms of knowledge.
This distinction is characteristic of delusional symbology.
It represents long-buried unconscious conflicts and desires
in an imagery that, to be sure, possesses a "logic," but
one organized according to terms of unconscious knowledge.
Delusion generally is a property of schizophrenic utterance,
which society excludes from its common fund of meaning.
The language posseses no functional or technical significance; it is not heard.   And when it becomes too obtrusive
or intrusive, its speakers are either locked up in family cel-
lars (to avoid embarrassment) or turned over to mental
hospitals (agents socially designed for handling excluded
speech).

Such language is not seen to possess any ontological
significance; political theorists and philosophers ignore it.
In everyday life, we have pejorative words for such utterance: "crazy," "lunatic," "mad."   But there are technical
words too: "asyndetic speech," "concrete thinking,"
"word-salad," and so on.   It is not pretty or soothing language; it is not comforting; the emotions are neither uplift-
ing nor regenerative.   It is the language of despair, hope-
lessness, and (at times) death.   Most importantly, it is
language that represents a period of human development
prior to the acquisition of formal linguistic structures.   It
expresses the trauma, fear, and anxiety of the infant; the
first two years of human life emerge in symbology through
what the schizophrenic speaks.

The preverbal or presocial origin of schizophrenia
still needs to be argued; for now, it remains one argument
in one theory among many.   Yet given the considerable
research done by psychoanalysts on preverbal emotional
states, this argument seems to me persuasive.[14]   For the
time being, I treat it as a partly tested hypothesis and
potential "fact" (in an empirical sense).   There is now, and
I suspect always will be, great controversy over what schizophrenia is and how it comes to be (its "etiology").   This

----

[14] See: Margaret S. Mahler, **On Human Symbiosis and The
Vissitudes of Individuation, Volume I: Infantile Psychosis,**
New York, International Universities Press, 1968; Rene
Arpad Spitz, **The First Year of Life,** New York, Interna-
tional Universities Press, 1965.

essay cannot possibly consider all the different psychological theories of schizophrenic etiology, let alone the physiological, genetic, and chemical theories. I sometimes doubt that the etiological issue will ever be resolved. It is bound up with the politics of interpretation in schizophrenia research itself, with continuing battles between psychodynamic schools and those medical psychiatrists who are strongly committed to a physical cause (whether it be in the schizophrenic's genes, body chemistry, brain structure, or other physiological malfunction).

Whatever the etiological explanation of the condition, though, the issue here is that condition itself (its qualities as experienced from inside and outside) and what it can tell us about political actions, institutions, and texts. Schizophrenics stand apart from what is understood as "civil" society. They experience themselves as nonpersons: without rights, denied any meaning or significance in the world. They are seen by agents of society as possessors of (or possessed by) what Michel Foucault has called "unreason."[15] They are regarded as the modern representatives of what the eighteenth century had named "animal nature." In Platonic terms, schizophrenics live in the cave, in the shadows, in darkness. Theirs is not a happy state; to be a schizophrenic is not desirable; it is not a pathway to redemption. But it is a condition that testifies amply for the existence of a human nature which precedes social and civil form. In particular, the language of schizophrenics provides empirical evidence for Rousseau's concept of the languages of the heart and the human nature from which they arise.

Schizophrenic languages are primarily delusional languages; and in that form, they present themselves as theories of knowledge. Delusional symbologies are different ways of thinking about the world and experience. They are "real" in the sense that their symbols embody thought processes and feelings which arise in the human self prior to the acquisition of language. They are evidence of "intrapsychic" events in infants; they chronicle the extent to which infantile consciousness can be traumatized by intrapsychic experience. Such symbologies, including their stories or tales, are complex intellectual structures with an

----

[15] See: Michel Foucault, **Madness and Civilization**, Richard Howard, trans., New York, Random House, 1961; Foucault, **Mental Illness and Psychology**, Alan Sheridan, trans., New York, Harper and Row, 1976.

epistemological foundation. They demonstrate primitive feelings: undefined emotional reactions, global reactions that
recognize no limitation in any social or consensual sense.
If anything, schizophrenic utterance confirms the existence
of structures of a primary narcissism in the development of
the human ego. From this point of view, infantile, emotional reality is not pure "id," pure impulse and need.
Instead, gratification or lack of it through external (and
internal) objects initiates clusters of feeling that become
part of an unintegrated ego structure.

Unintegrated aspects of the ego emerge in schizophrenic language as symbologies of grandiosity, power, and
victimization. Schizophrenic utterances "possess" reality,
but theirs are "possessions" motivated or provoked by an
epistemology which originates in internal, emotional structures rather than what society certifies as external, rational
reality. In these utterances, knowledge is the product of
interiority. Significantly, this interior form of knowledge is
obsessed with political concepts: boundary, identity,
power, good and evil, domination, violence, justice. As
language expressing the self's earliest emotional and psychological experience, as symbols prior to the acquisition of
formal linguistic structures, schizophrenic symbology is
precivil or presocial thought and reality. Thus schizophrenics may be said to recover an ontogenetic past
through their production of language.

If the utterances of schizophrenics are any indication,
the natural inclination of human nature lies in narcissistic
gratification. The first-order, most intimately charged
'knowledge' appears in a narcissistic framework that remains
(although repressed) in the human self. Further, in listening to the stories of schizophrenics (the fables, the "delusional possessions" of reality), it is not at all clear that
impuses toward sociality are stronger than more regressive,
narcissistic dynamics. Narcissistic structures remain within
the self throughout development; and it may be that all
forms of maturation and individuation depend on a persistent struggle between the interests of sociality (plus the
forces of socialization and routinization) and the more
underlying or unconscious narcissistic energies that periodi-
cally achieve prominence in the internal life of the self or
psyche. Schizophrenics vividly exemplify the power of
regressive dynamics in the ego. Grandiosity and omnipotence appear frequently in delusional imagery. Moreover,
especially destructive aspects of narcissism are also visible
in individuals who would not normally be classified as "psy-

chotic" or "schizophrenic."[16]

Many of the concerns of schizophrenic epistemologies mirror themes in the history of political thought. Boundary, identity, power, reason and its uses: all are thematic structures of political thought. I do not say that theoretical statements in the tradition are schizophrenic or that they reflect or represent schizoid dynamics, although there may be interest in looking at certain aspects of political theory from such points of view. I do argue, however, that the stories, fables and "theories" implicit in schizophrenic delusions reflect ideas that historically have been of concern to political theory. For example, is not the Republic a treatise on identity, on the meaning of passion and desire, on the nature and organization of power? Although not the same sort of statement on identity as the schizophrenic's "possession" of reality, the **Republic** is still similar in being a story, a tale, a fable: it takes place as an imaginative construction. The point is not that delusional symbology should be compared to theoretical imagination, but that political theorizing may be occasioned by many of the same issues and motivated by many of the same forces which unconsciously preoccupy schizophrenics. Of course, the two remain distinguished by their separate kinds of intellectual production. The political philosopher is certainly better able to express contents and structures of identity (both personal and political), boundary (what constitutes human nature, what separates individuals, what feelings or needs hold communities together, how "reason" provides or takes away from a sense of boundary), and power (images of grandiosity and omnipotence, agents designated with transforming political historical life, actors of great presence of mind and will).

To conclude, let us look briefly at another issue which spans the worlds of schizophrenia and political theory: therapy and the role of therapists. Those who work with schizophrenic patients (not manage them), who believe in the potential of verbal communication, accomplish on an intimate level what political theorists discuss in collective or historical terms. Psychodynamic psychotherapy works on issues of boundary, identity, and self. Therapists emphasize interaction of the intrapsychic and the

----

[16] See: Otto Kernberg, **Borderline Conditions and Pathological Narcissism**, New York, Jason Aronson, 1976; James F. Masterson, **Psychotherapy of the Borderline Adult**, New York, Brunner/Mazel, 1976.

interpersonal. Their task involves reflecting on human nature, understanding the self, and appreciating injuries to the self through unsympathetic "introjects."

The psychotherapist shares the role of what Rousseau termed "the Legislator." The Legislator takes the precivil or presocial self as a solitary wanderer without direction or meaning and situates it within a community, from which it "receives...life and being." The Legislator tries to help the person substitute a "partial and moral existence for the physical and independent existence nature has conferred on us all."[17] And the psychotherapist does something similar. Schizophrenics are selves without meaning or significance mirrored through others. They are human beings isolated and withdrawn, solitaries functioning by private knowledge. The psychotherapist tries to help such selves become "whole," connected to something other than the narcissistic internality that has produced their isolation, pain, and lack of what Rousseau called "moral existence." The psycho-therapist attempts to lead them to lives defined by their sociality, their consensual bases. In this sense, there are important parallels between Rousseau's contrast of precivil to social selves and Harry Stack Sullivan's distinction of consensual from delusional (or parataxic) reality.[18] The Legislator's purpose is to create a political ego; the psycho-therapist's purpose is to integrate an ego so fractured that the person has no normally recognizable identity. Legisla-tor and therapist alike work to found self-sustaining and responsible identities. Both seek to break down identities built on nonconsensual modes of reality; both seek to estab-lish selves within some form of community or civility. For the Legislator, the aim is political civility; for the psycho-therapist, the goal is civility premised on dyadic relation-ship and a sense of trust. Then eventually, they depart.[19]

What is the therapeutic function, if not ridding the "body politic" of the diseased self, the self tormented and

----

[17] See: James M. Glass, "Rousseau's Emile and Sade's Eugenie: Action, Nature and the Presence of Moral Struc-ture," **Philosophical Forum**, 7, 1, Fall, 1975, pp. 38-55.

[18] See: Sullivan, **Schizophrenia as a Human Process**.

[19] See: James M. Glass, "The Philosopher and the Shaman: The Political Vision as Incantation," **Political Theory**, 2, 2, May, 1974, pp. 181-196.

persecuted by its own introjects? Therapy is an activity, an **intervention**, that legislates movement toward the foundation of ego structures. Ideally, the newly integrated ego differentiates and decides through "political" exchanges, at least in an ethical environment. Ideally, the newly integrated ego develops sensitivity to justice and trust, belief in ties among human beings, awareness of limitation and possibility in authority, and appreciation of the forms in which authority exercises its rights.

Like Rousseau's natural self, schizophrenics lack these structures of political consciousness in their psychological "state of nature." Aware of the depths and costs of their alienation and withdrawal, schizophrenics experience intense isolation and exclusion. The idea and "affect" of connection with a larger, participatory community of human beings holds little comfort or promise for them. Re-entering community, rediscovering sociality, renewing trust, and learning how to become part of what Rousseau would call a greater "whole" require critical political recognitions. These trace to issues arising out of interaction with the psychotherapist: the therapist's autonomy, the nature of "power" in the delusional imagery, the therapists's own "power," the patient's emerging sense of cooperation and justice, the self's discovery of boundaries. Let me add that the creation of identity is vital in therapy with schizophrenics, as it is in "therapy" with wounded polities. In some ways, it is the central issue of therapy, since the schizophrenic is terribly confused about what the self contains and means in relation to others. Even sexual identity (which in a psychodynamic sense is considered fundamental) is often in doubt.

It is not uncommon to find patients who feel possessed by alien spirits, believe that something inside is tearing the self apart, know the body to be inhabited by forces beyond control, and see the therapist as an Other to rescue them from torment. This echoes such introjects as Plato's drones, Machiavelli's condotierri, Rousseau's particular wills, and Marx's capitalists, all driving the community (and the self) toward death and disintegration. Also, this suggests that the political theorist and the psychotherapist fight historical forms of identity and impositions of given histories on the "body," whether it be the body politic or the individual psyche. For both the political theorist and the psychotherapist, the function of therapy is to restore "health" to bodies ravaged by the effects of historical time. For both, the objective of therapy is to integrate ego structures and provide a sense of identity that represents the self in its totality, its wholeness. This is what Machiavelli called "regeneration."[20] In the case of the political state, it is history understood as collective identity; in the case of the schizophrenic, it is history understood as the psycho-physiological past of the self.

Where, then, should political theory be now? It is naive in these times even to imagine "grand" theory emerging. Still, it is necessary to do theory that asks questions of our institutions and that looks at the past to see what messages make sense for our own age. Yet it is also important for political theorists to remember that their activities derive inspiration from realities, experiences, and expectations situated in feelings, needs, and desires. Political theory studies individuals: living, sentient presences that breathe, eat, engage in sexual relations, and experience friendship, disappointment, pain, and sorrow. We should not lose sight of the human basis of political theory. We should not forget that even to think about politics as a word is to imagine people acting and interacting in all their rationality and irrationality, with thoughts formed and directed through the pathways of desire.

---

[20] See: James M. Glass, "Machiavelli's Prince and Alchemical Transformation: Action and the Archetype of Regeneration," **Polity**, 8, 4, Summer, 1976, pp. 503-528.

PART SEVEN

POWER AND PRAGMATISM

QUESTIONS OF POWER IN POLITICAL THEORY

Richard W. Miller

A central task of political theory has traditionally been to discover where political power lies. This tradition will continue to be reasonable so long as people want to change things (or to prevent change) and so long as what government does affects their success. There are, however, not one but many questions about a society that might be expressed in the words: where does political power lie? Here political theorists need not feel inferior to natural scientists, who would not dream of abolishing all but one specification of "energy," "wave," or "information-storage in the brain." The danger, rather, is that investigators will ignore the differences between different versions of the question of political power and lose track of an intelligible, important question as a consequence. My purpose is to show that this danger is real. This is part of a broader project of showing how methodology has been abused through definitions, research methods, and criteria of scientific status which exclude from consideration theories and perspectives that deserve empirical investigation investigation.[1]

The questions of political power that dominate the study of politics today are (very roughly): to what extent do various people get what they want out of government? by what mechanisms, institutional or informal, do various social groups influence government? what makes government effective and stable? The question that is missing is (again, very roughly): whose interests does government serve? I hope to show how utterly different the neglected question is from the questions that are pursued and to suggest that its neglect depends on overly rigid methodologies and on practical political assumptions that political theory should question, not presuppose.

----

[1] I have pursued other aspects of this project in: "Reason and Commitment in the Social Sciences," **Philosophy and Public Affairs**, 8, 3, Spring, 1979, pp. 241-266; "Methodological Individualism and Social Explanation," **Philosophy of Science**, 45, 3, September, 1978, pp. 387-414; "Fact and Method in the Social Sciences," in Jerald Wallulis and Donald Sabia, eds., **Changing Social Science**, forthcoming.

The investigation of these questions of political power is especially urgent in the current state of academic political theory. Few are satisfied any longer with obsessive methodological disputes with behavioralism or a total retreat into the history of political thought. At the same time, if political theory is not to become a minor league of moral philosophy, it ought to bear some special relation to the empirical investigation of political reality. One solution is renewed concern with claims about the distribution of political power that are general enough to regulate the interpretation of particular bits of historical and behavioral data, but sufficiently empirical that their ultimate warrant is superior capacity to explain historical episodes and typical patterns of behavior. Concern with such middle-range generalities, in between pure conceptual analysis and particular empirical findings, is, after all, characteristic of most of the classics, from Aristotle to Marx. I hope that this essay will show that the imagination and thorough analysis which are encouraged in political theory can clarify and advance general but empirical claims about the distribution of political power that have been submerged in the current practice of piecemeal empirical research.

My subsequent arguments are also meant to serve two other, more specific goals. One is to describe a radical conception of political dominance which is abstract and flexible enough to be plausible, dynamic enough to be relevant to historical research and to political activism, and specific enough to be falsifiable. By falsifiability, I do not have in mind the goal of definitive testing by one or a few case studies or experiments. That goal is never reached in the natural sciences, much less in political science. But it should be possible to decide whether the central thesis about political power does a better job than its rivals of explaining relevant bits of history and behavior.

The other goal is to help place the Behavioral Revolution in historical perspective. Political theorists often assume that the positivist methodology of behavioralists was mainly responsible for the neglect of basic questions about politics. My arguments will suggest that this blame is largely misplaced. The crucial question of political power and social interests has been neglected not just by behavioral-minded pluralists, but by their critics (including some who have been influenced by critical theory), by those who investigate power structures and elites, and by partisans of a structural-functional approach to politics. The common feature of these extremely diverse approaches is a failure to provide a substantial, rational basis for deciding whether to work for change through activities that confront government in illegal and disruptive ways. This suggests (but only suggests) that social forces of a conservative kind, not positivist methodology, are the most important source of limitations on questions of political power.

THE QUESTION OF INTERESTS

The dangerously neglected question about political power and social interests needs to be made more specific, since the mere words "Whose interests does government serve?" are in their turn a label for a cluster of questions. At one extreme, one might be inquiring after the truth of a conspiracy theory or some other hypothesis in which government officials consciously dedicate themselves to helping one social group, in spite of any conflict with the interests of others. For most modern societies, including the United States, these hypotheses are sufficiently far-fetched that failure to investigate them is not dangerous. At another extreme, the question of interests might be understood as a request for a tabulation of the actual costs and benefits of particular government actions for various social groups, without attention to the causal processes linking what government does to what social groups need. At least in policy studies, this question is not ignored.

The question I advocate lies between these extremes. It might be stated as the question of the extent to which the role of government in society fits a certain model: to what extent is there a ruling class, in a sense I will now describe? (Instead of "ruling class," a more neutral phrase, "politically dominant social group," with no implications of personal, almost monarchic intervention, might be more apt. But that phrase is clumsy and dull. Besides, the interpretation of Marx is meant to be an implicit issue in what follows.)

The claim that there is a ruling class, as I use the phrase, is a thesis with three parts. These three claims exhaust the intended meaning of the phrase, which has, no doubt, been used to express conspiracy theories that ought to be neglected. To begin with, the thesis that there is a ruling class states that, in the social setting in question, government acts in a way which serves the interests of a social group or a coalition of groups, even though those interests do not coincide with those of the rest of society. This is not to say that government never does something that benefits a subordinate group and is, taken by itself, a cost to the dominant group. However, in effect, if not intention, such government activity must be a means of coping with problems of acquiescence or cooperation that government did not create, problems from the standpoint of the dominant group.

Often, of course, it is hard to tell whether a course of action is, in effect, a concession helping a dominant group to cope with a less than ideal world or a result of the less than total dominance of the interests of that group. Did New Deal policies represent the end of a tendency for the Federal government to do what served the interests of big business or a continuation of that tendency in a new situation of economic, social, and international disorder? To answer such questions, a political theorist must become a political economist (studying the impact of government action on social interests), an economist (since it may be a matter of economic controversy whether policies were apt to help or hurt relevant economic groups), and a historian (asking which hypothesis about interests best explains the actual course of history). The investigation of history will be especially important. Because of rival accounts of what social groups are coherent, how institutions affect their well-being, and what members of these groups want or need, a finding as to whether a benefit to an allegedly subordinate group reflects the need for acquiescence of a dominant one is typically subject to dispute. It can rarely be read off of uncontroversial facts through an uncontroversial interpretation. A claim that such a policy is, in effect, a concession usually requires a complex historical argument that such a characterization is part of the best explanation of government activities in the period in question. Indeed, as we shall see, the question of the extent to which there is a ruling class interacts with historical explanation in so many ways as to make political theory virtually continuous with political history.

Not only must we appreciate that circumstances may be less than ideal for a ruling class, making concessions to other groups in their interests, we must take it into account that political leaders will not be ideally smart and well-informed. We are inquiring as to whether, in a certain period, the over-all course of government action serves the best interests of the dominant group as well as can be expected, given the limit of skills and knowledge in general and at the time. Roosevelt's attempts to balance the budget may have been a disaster for all dominant social groups. If they reflected prevailing economic ignorance, these effects do not challenge a ruling-class hypothesis. Nonetheless, in assessing a ruling-class hypothesis, the appeal to human

weakness must not be abused.   If alleged mistakes imply an
implausible level of stupidity or fall into a pattern suggesting the influence of competing interests, we have grounds
for supposing that these episodes reflect an independent
tendency to fulfill the interests of other groups, apart from
the supposed ruling class.

The second aspect of the existence of a ruling class
concerns the nature of the connection between government
actions and the interests of the dominant group.   This connection is not an accident, if that group is a ruling class.
At any given time, a variety of definite mechanisms work to
maintain this connection.   Moreover, unless there is a major
shift of extra-governmental resources away from the dominant group, new mechanisms will replace old ones if the latter become inadequate to maintain the connection between
government action and dominant social interests.   By way of
illustration, campaign contributions and campaign expenditures would constitute one, quite nonconspiratorial mechanism to which a Marxist would appeal in arguing that big
business is the ruling class in the United States today.   An
example of a shift in mechanisms in response to crisis might
be the dramatic change in mechanisms of government in
Chile, when parliamentary democracy no longer suited the
interests of a coalition of mine-owners, bankers, manufacturers, and large land-owners.

No doubt, some theorists might label a dominant
group a ruling class at a given time, even though it lacks
the capacity to use its resources to initiate new rules of the
political game in response to crisis.   But as we shall see,
an important practical motivation for singlng out the question of the existence of a ruling class would, then, be missing: testing the limits of "going through channels" as a
means to social change.   Moreover, classical arguments in
favor of ruling-class hypotheses would be unavailable, on
this alternate reading of the phrase.   The hypothesis of a
ruling class is often attractive on account of its power to
suggest historical explanations of changes in governmental
institutions, as responses to new challenges to the dominant
social group.   Finally, by requiring continuity of political
dominance throughout relevant periods of crisis, we can
test the scope of the dominant group or coalition, perhaps
making it relatively exclusive and, hence, relatively deter-
minate in its collective interests.   For example, if old-style
political leaders are replaced when they cease in times of
crisis to serve dominant extra-governmental interests, that
is a basis for supposing that politicians are not themselves
a part of the ruling class.   In general, we determine which
elites are dominant by looking at periods of crisis when the

interests of elites seriously conflict. The capacity for continued dominance in these situations of conflict is evidence
for the underlying order of dominance in normal times.

Finally, the claim that there is a ruling class is concerned with the **strength** of the connection between what
government does and the interests of the dominant group.
If that connection can be ended by activities that government would encourage, protect, or, in any case, permit,
then there is no ruling class. **Ruling-class** dominance can
be ended only by a major shift in extra-governmental
resources which must be brought about by "going outside
of channels," as those channels would be defined by government responses to discontent. Consider, by way of contrast, one picture of political power in the United States at
the turn of the nineteenth century. On this conception,
government was serving the interests of big business as a
consequence of a variety of mechanisms, shifting in
response to changing social circumstances. But the electorate could have changed this situation, through electoral
processes protected by government; and in the subsequent
decades, it did. If politics at the turn of the nineteenth
century had this as-yet latent potential for change, then it
would be wrong to say that big business was a ruling class
politically. At any rate, this is not the usage of those
theorists most attracted to ruling-class hypotheses. Moreover, if it were adopted, a powerful practical motivation for
investigating such hypotheses would be lost, as we shall
see.

Understood in this way, the thesis that there is a
ruling class in society seems to be intelligible. It is intelligible, even plausible, that a coalition of large land-owners,
big merchants, and manufacturers were the ruling class in
eighteenth-century England. So it ought to be at least
intelligible (whether true or false) to say that there is a
ruling class in the United States today. Moreover, a social
group can approach the status of a ruling class on all three
dimensions. So it seems an interesting question **to what
extent**, say, big business is a ruling class in the United
States today.

Finally, we can investigate some single part of the
three-part question: to what extent is there a ruling
class. In the course of this paper, I present a variety of
reasons, theoretical and practical, for studying the whole,
undissected question. But the parts have independent
interest, too. One outcome of my subsequent arguments is
that the questions of political power that now dominate political theory are inadequate to investigate any one of the
three parts. None sheds any light on the relevant question

about government actions and social interests. If the question of mechanisms of influence is raised at all, it is raised in a way that neglects the dynamic aspect of the question, the adjustment of mechanisms to changing circumstances. The questions of militance, repression, and entrenchment raised by the third sub-thesis tend simply to be ignored.

As I have defined it, the question "to what extent is there a ruling class?" is quite complex and, often, very hard to answer.   Yet it is central to a great many frameworks for inquiry that have generated important historical explanations. Some examples are: Marx on nineteenth-century French history; Neumann on twentieth-century German history; Hill on the English Civil War; Genovese on the United States Civil War; Hilton on English feudalism; Bowles and Gintis on United States educational systems; Lenin, Hilferding, and Hobson on imperialism and the background for World War I; Williams on United States diplomatic history; recent explanations of the persistence of racism in the twentieth-century United States; and recent explanations of the Vietnam War as a defense of United States corporate hegemony.[2] I am not dogmatically proposing that these explanations are valid. But they are worth taking seriously. And all depend on the thesis that certain social groups have been a ruling class or have approached the status of one in large part and to a high degree.

Why is the complex, difficult question "To what extent is there a ruling class?" so important in the pursuit of social explanations? In part, because of its explanatory power, as revealed in the writings to which I have alluded. In part, because of its practical importance, when certain interests in change are prominent.   Suppose you want to bring about a major change in society.   To the extent to which there is a ruling class, with interests opposed to such change, there are grounds for pessimism about any strategy based on the expectation that government will tolerate, perhaps even protect, crucial activities for change, until they are successful. If, for example, big business is a ruling class or something like one, many of us have grounds for pessimism about the prospects of bringing

----

[2] For recent explanations of the persistence of racism, see: David Gordon, ed., **Problems in Political Economy**, Lexington, MA, D. C. Heath, second edition, 1977, especially the essays by Robert Cherry and Michael Reich. On Vietnam, see: Harry Magdoff, **The Age of Imperialism**, New York, Monthly Review Press, 1969.

about major change by voting, by becoming activists within the major parties, by appealing to the consciences or interests of politicians, or by confining agitation to means that police and courts respect. The mechanisms of rule will tend to thwart these efforts, where the interests of big business are involved. Government will tend to take back gains initially won, in ways we are ill-prepared to resist if we only work through channels. By the same token, not to ask to what extent there is a ruling class is to avoid systematic investigation of the issue: how far outside of channels would activists have to go?   "Revolution" and "Nowhere" are not the only answers here. Others include such diverse activities as civil disobedience, illegal or disruptive demonstrations, wildcat strikes, sitdowns, ghetto rebellions, and mutinies.

It is important for my subsequent argument that there be some group in the United States today to which something approaching ruling-class status can be attributed with at least some plausibility. By this well-hedged claim, I simply mean that some hypothesis of ruling-class or near-ruling-class status should be worthy of further investigation and refinement, not outright dismissal. After all, the analysis of the present-day United States and similar societies has, understandably, been the central pursuit of political studies in the United States. If there is no plausible candidate for anything approaching ruling-class status in this country, then the neglect of the notion of a ruling class is just a reasonable economy. In any case, for exposition's sake, a specific example of a putative ruling class will be needed to illustrate subsequent discussions of how confusions between different questions of power might obscure the existence of a ruling class.

I would propose that at least one group is such a candidate for something approaching ruling-class status in the United States: families whose wealth is a source of significant influence on the policies of major corporations. High-level executives in these businesses and in major corporate law firms are typically led by their situations to make common cause with these wealthiest few. For present purposes, they may all be counted as part of the same group, which I shall label "big business." Whatever the importance for the internal dynamics of corporate life (in my view, overrated) of potential splits between managers and dominant owners, the basic solidarity of actual interests is the important fact for the study of political power.

A number of facts suggest the need to take seriously the possibility that big business may approach the status of a ruling class as I have defined it. In the United States, a mere one-fifth of one percent of the spending units own two-thirds of the individually held corporate stock. Senatorial races, much less Presidential ones, frequently cost over a million dollars each. Since World War II, peaceful and successful initiatives for major shifts in national policy have almost always begun with proposals from groups sponsored by big business, for example, the Council on Foreign Relations, the Committee on Economic Development, the Rockefeller Brothers Fund, the Urban Land Institute, and the Trilateral Commission. Periods of reform which have bettered the situations of large groups of working people have almost always been preceded by related outbreaks of illegal violence, including the uprisings of urban workers and of sharecroppers in the 1890s, the general strikes, sit-down strikes, and violent labor-management confrontations between the World Wars, and the ghetto rebellions of the 1960s. If reform has been one response, repression has been another, including the use of the National Guard and support for the Klan and Pinkertons in the 1890s, Wilson's Red Scare, Roosevelt's jailings of Communist Party leaders, Truman's leadership of the post-War anti-communist campaign, and police and National Guard violence in the 1960s. These facts do not, remotely, demonstrate that big business is a ruling class. They do make it dangerously hasty simply to dismiss the question of whether big business approaches this status.

There are other candidates for ruling-class status, for example, a triumvirate of stable leadership groups dominating major business firms, national politics, and the military. In concentrating on the option of big business dominance, I do not mean to dismiss these alternatives. It should be clear, in what follows, that the ways in which the hypothesis that big business approaches ruling-class status has been obscured correspond to ways in which the alternate ruling-class hypotheses would be obscured as well. Though space requires emphasis on one of these alternatives, the goal of these discussion is to show that the broad category of ruling-class hypotheses has, as a whole, been neglected in illegitimate ways.

PLURALISM AND ITS DISCONTENTS

Despite its great importance, theoretical and practical, the question "Is there a ruling class?" is a hidden question in the study of politics today. Political scientists

do ask where political power lies. Moreover, an enduring
legacy of Marx, they do not presuppose that real political
power is located at the top of official government hierar-
chies.   But the meanings they attach to the question
"where does political power lie?" do not shed much light on
the question of whether and to what extent there is a ruling class.   This is true, moreover, not just of the pluralist
mainstream and their structural-functionalist allies but of
most dissenters as well.

Many theorists take the question of political power to
be "to what extent do various people currently get what
they want out of government in the face of opposing interests, where relevant particular issues are concerned?" For
pluralists, getting what you want, here, means getting the
outcome you **actually** voted for, either literally or figura-
tively by investing time or money in influencing the political
process. Peter Bachrach and Morton Baratz, in their influential criticism of pluralism, in effect propose a different
understanding of getting what you want: getting the outcome you **would** have voted for if appropriate alternatives
were on the agenda. They are, however, unwilling to
depart too far from the situation of explicit choice that the
pluralists favor. If you would have voted for an alternative, then its existence is a token of your power, even if
your choice would have resulted, in turn, from manipulations of your information or preferences.[3] Critics from the
left, Steven Lukes among them, have suggested that the
real basis for an assessment of power should be the choice
that would be made with adequate information and undistorted deliberations.[4] On the basis of such distinctions
between actual inclinations and real interests, political theorists sometimes take the question of political power to be
the question of whether government does what various

----

[3] See: Peter Bachrach and Morton S. Baratz, **Power and
Poverty**, New York, Oxford University Press, 1970, p. 49:
"suppose...there appears to be universal acquiescence in
the status quo. Is it possible, in such circumstances, to
determine whether the consensus is genuine or instead has
been enforced through nondecision-making? The answer
must be negative. Analysis of this problem is beyond the
reach of a political analyst and perhaps can only be fruitfully analyzed by a philosopher."

[4] See: Steven Lukes, **Power**, New York, Macmillan, 1974,
pp. 23ff.

people would have wanted if their information were the best available and if their insight into their own needs were clear.

On any of these understandings of the question of political power, the basic thesis of Robert Dahl's **Who Governs?** is converted into a truism. Political power is dispersed throughout society, though different bases for political power are differently and unequally dispersed.[5] As Dahl used the term at the time, we live in a polyarchy.[6] In particular, major businesspeople don't always get either the outcomes they vote for, the ones they would vote for if those alternatives were on the agenda, or the ones they would vote for if they were perfectly informed and rational. This resolution of the question of political power does not matter one way or another so far as the existence of a ruling class is concerned. Of course, there will be polyarchy is there is no ruling class. But the existence of polyarchy, in the indicated sense, is also a consequence of the most plausible ruling-class hypotheses concerning our society.

In general, the best arrangement for a ruling class is one in which government takes on the job of adjusting that class's short-term interests on particular questions to its long-term interest in stability and acquiescence. Big

----

[5] See: Robert A. Dahl, **Who Governs?**, New Haven, Yale University Press, 1961, p. 228.

[6] See: Robert A. Dahl, **Modern Political Analysis**, Englewood Cliffs, NJ, Prentice-Hall, 1963, p. 73: "'polyarchy' (rule by many)" is a political system "in which power over state officials is widely, though by no means equally shared." Subsequently, both in official definitions and in practice, there is a shift in usage from the description of power relations to the description of governmental institutions. See: Dahl, **Polyarchy**, New Haven, Yale University Press, 1971, pp. 2-9; Dahl, **After the Revolution?**, New Haven, Yale University Press, 1970, p. 78. "Polyarchy" is defined as government with a system of elections involving broad suffrage and competition for offices. In the earlier usage, it is open to question, to put it mildly, whether India, Venezuela, and Pakistan in the 1950s were polyarchies. In the later usage, they obviously are. Yet formal polyarchy continues to be treated as if it has the same tendencies to fulfill social needs and moral demands as substantive polyarchy. Below I suggest that this shift signals

business might have an isolated, short-term interest, if a small one, in my not giving a lecture sympathetic to Marxism. But here (if not in Chile or South Africa), it is now against its long-term interest for a policeman to stop me. The resultant uproar would not be worth the gain. In advanced industrial societies in normal times, the best arrangement for adjusting the interest in short-term gains with the long-term interest in stability is one in which political leaders are elected and are not usually businesspeople. In such a setting, the most effective ruling-class arrangement is one in which businesspeople often agitate for measures more pro-business in immediate terms than government leaders will accept. The typical major businessperson acknowledges the crucial distinction between institutional interests and issue-by-issue preferences when he says that he is a lifelong Republican and declares that he would be appalled if the Democratic Party were to disappear.

At least three important needs usually would be served by this political division of labor, if big business is a ruling class. (Similar factors would point in similar directions, where other dominant groups are concerned.) In an industrial capitalist society, it is an extremely important source of stability if most people believe that elections are a means of counterbalancing the obvious influence on society created by the obvious concentration of economic power in the largest firms. This belief would not last for long if a typical Presidential election pitted the Chairman of the Board of Citicorp against the Chief Executive Officer of General Electric. In the second place, big business is routinely divided into competing factions, with conflicting interests which might be crucially affected by government policies. Eastern Establishment versus the Southern Rim, Rockefeller interests versus Morgan interests, manufacturers versus large-scale merchants versus plantation-owners are a few historical examples. If the common interests of big business are not to be submerged in these rivalries, it is desirable that corporate factions not typically face the risk that political leadership will be held by an active member of a rival faction. (Correspondingly, a President such as Nixon who tilts too far toward one side or another poses a significant threat to stability.) Finally, though major businesspeople are fairly good judges of what corporate

----

a tendency to convert earlier explicit claims about power into unstated, undefended, but highly influential assumptions.

policies benefit their firms, they are not good judges of most people's attitudes and likely responses to government policies. Nor are they good creators of public opinion. Mistakes along these political dimensions may carry a heavy price in social disorder. Yet nothing in the career or situation of a typical leader of big business nourishes the needed talents. There is a need, then, for political leadership to be exercised by people who have succeeded in distinctively political careers, the career politicians who are the prime ingredients in Max Weber's recipe for a strong, expansionist, capitalist nation-state.[7] Given this official leadership by career politicians, specially sensitive to social costs in discontent and disorder, business leaders are free to advocate policies more blatantly pro-business than their long-term interests permit. For example, when in 1973 the Committee on Economic Development called for the virtual dismantling of liberal arts education for young working-class people, instantaneous implementation would have produced pervasive discontent, hardly worth the savings. In context, this proposal was a rational policy initiative, which became a reality in due time, under the ultimate guidance of career politicians.[8]

Given the division of labor between business leaders and political leaders, businesspeople will lose many votes. After all, in this system, the votes of businesspeople will tend to underestimate their own need for acquiescence and cooperation in society at large. Moreover, the political interests of particular firms or factions will sometimes depart from the interests of big business as a whole. As a result, there is a wide dispersal of wins and losses in votes over public policy issues. And this dispersal does not depend on fixed agendas or misinformation. So, counting

----

[7] Max Weber, "Politics as a Vocation," in **From Max Weber,** H. H. Gerth and C. Wright Mills, eds., New York, Oxford University Press, 1946, pp. 77-128.

[8] See: G. William Domhoff, **Who Really Rules?,** New Brunswick, Transaction Books, 1978. This reanalysis of Dahl's New Haven data is an extremely detailed and persuasive account of the interaction between business initiatives in major policy shifts and the special sensitivities and talents of political and media leaders. Without contradicting Dahl's finding that big business often lost votes over officially contested issues, Domhoff displays the real (and nonconspiratorial) dominance underlying this particular polyarchy.

vote by vote, people in many social groups often "get what they want out of government" and often fail to do so, on all the standard readings of the phrase, not just the pluralists'. There is polyarchy **because** there is a ruling class, with government acting as its long-term interests require.

One reason why the question "to what extent do people get what they want from government?" may be unilluminating is that it does not discriminate between two kinds of government responsiveness to social interests. Government may respond to the interests of one group of people, but only to the extent to which another group needs its cooperation, acquiescence, or obedience. In this sense, the government of the United States is often responsive to the interests of the Politburo of the U. S. S. R. On the other hand, government may respond to the interests of one group beyond the point at which such concern is of value to any other group. The question "to what extent is there a ruling class?" is concerned with whether government attends to interests outside the dominant group only on the first basis or on the second as well. Despite ferocious disputes between partisans of the three different readings, the question "to what extent do people get what they want from government?" does not discriminate between these two bases for getting what you want.

The need to disentangle the two bases for responsiveness is one reason why political theorists need to be political and social historians, choosing among explanations of government responses to crisis. One way to distinguish between the two bases is to look at what government does when it creates or alters institutions affecting the interests of groups outside an alleged ruling class. In the times of crisis in which such changes are made, the conflicts between rival social interests are relatively acute. The extent to which alternate courses of government action would advance or defeat a group's interests are, though far from transparent, clearer than in more placid times. Inertia or mere shrewdness in political maneuvering is no longer a plausible explanation of the effective choices of dominant political leaders. Do political changes in times of crisis correspond to the changing needs of the dominant group when faced with new challenges? Or do they represent unnecessary, even dangerous, concessions from the standpoint of that group? It is often through such debates over history that the two sorts of responsiveness are disentangled. The claim that big business is the ruling class in the United States implies, for example, that Federal protection of union organizing was, in form and timing, the best way of reducing the militancy and unpredictability of unregulated organizing; that the welfare programs of the sixties were a response to urban unrest, not urban needs as such; and that the current shift from welfare spending to defense spending reflects new challenges to the world-wide power of United States corporations. If, on the other hand, the question of whether there is a ruling class is divorced from the relatively familiar and coherent debates over such claims, it may seem unanswerable.

The other reason why the question "Who gets what he wants out of government?" sheds little light on the exis-tence of a ruling class is that it fails to take account of the enormous difference that the existence of certain kinds of political institutions can make to the content of rational, informed political preferences. In a parliamentary democ-racy, major businesspeople often advocate measures the immediate adoption of which would not be feasible or would create unacceptable turmoil. In this respect, their votes do not reflect their real interests, but not because of any manipulation of agendas, information, or preferences. Rather, beyond a point, it is not their job but the job of the political system to take feasibility and acquiescence into account. If the Taft-Hartley Act had been enacted in 1945, without a campaign against labor unrest and communists in the unions, the results would probably have been disas-trous for big business. It would have been equally disas-trous not to press for such changes before they were feasi-ble.

In sum, the questions of political power which I have examined are limited in scope because they are, in a way, apolitical. The distinctive function of government is to cre-ate a stable framework for reasonably efficient and peaceful interactions. Because government, by its nature, must be concerned with cooperation, acquiescence, and obedience, the questions posed by pluralists and many of their critics cannot tell us whom government is serving. They cannot distinguish between interests that are of primary concern and interests which are problems for coordination, between losing votes that reflect a lack of power and losing votes that reflect the distinctive role of government in maintaining social power.

My point is to distinguish different questions, not to eliminate any. There are important practical concerns that dictate special attention to the question of the extent to which various people get what they want out of govern-ment. People engaged in electoral politics, lobbying (including the most benevolent "citizens' lobbying"), or simply trying to persuade the powerful of what morality or reason dictate will want to know where the powerful people

are and will find this question their best guide. Similarly,
the question of who gets what he wants is a central one for
the social critic wondering which people bear individual
moral responsibility for the mess we are in. In this context
of moral judgment, it may be irrelevant, even misleading, to
argue that Presidents and generals are not part of the ruling class. But these are not the only political concerns
that ought to be based on rational political inquiry. Knowing to what extent various people get what they want out of
government will not help someone wondering to what extent
the government must actively be resisted for social change
to be produced. Thus, it is a pun to say that questions of
political power involve the impact of government on interests. In content, some of these questions should ask how
government action is connected to group interests. In
addition, from context to context, investigator's interests in
politics will dictate which question of power they ought to
pursue.

It might seem that I have been unfair to Bachrach,
Baratz, Lukes, and other critics of pluralism, through neglect of their emphasis on the exercise **of power** over **someone else.** Thus in **defining power, Bachrach and** Baratz
propose that a power relation exists between A and B when
B acts as A wishes, when he otherwise wouldn't, out of
fear that A will deprive him of something.[9] Lukes says, in
summary of his view of power, "I have defined the concept
of power by saying that A exercises power over B when A
affects B in a manner contrary to B's interests."[10] It is
above all because notions of power are presented through
descriptions of relations of dominance that these writings
have such a different tone from Dahl's **Who Governs?** and
other pluralist classics.

However, if we are asking "where does political power
lie?", these differences turn out to be more matters of style
than of substance. In measuring the distribution of power,
pluralists have always acknowledged that power means getting what you want in the face of opposition. For their
part, when Bachrach, Baratz, and Lukes are asking, not
whether power is exercized in a particular interaction of A
with B, but how power is distributed in a society, their
crucial comparisons also concern tendencies to get what one
wants in the face of opposition. The significant differences

----

[9] Bachrach and Baratz, **Power and Poverty,** p. 24.

[10] Lukes, **Power,** p. 34.

among these theorists concern the role of manipulated agendas, information, and preferences. These differences, we found, will not close the gap between the assessment of the question of polyarchy and the assessment of the extent to which there is a ruling class.

How can discussions so concerned with domination tell us so little about the existence of a ruling class? The answer, once again, is their apolitical nature. Knowledge of whether the various As have exercised power over the various Bs may tell us little about political power, power depending on the operation of political institutions. In the Bachrach-Baratz-Lukes conception, blue-collar workers exercise power over businesspeople whenever they produce a concession through a threat to strike. Unless we know the role of government in such interactions, this tells us nothing about political power. Of course, we can also ask who has the most power over political leaders: businespeople or blue-collar workers? But here, the results are apt to be positively misleading, if we want to know to what extent there is a ruling class. If big business is a rulng class, one would expect the interests of politicians and businesspeople generally to coincide. Indeed, I argue that this congruence is essential to a psychologically plausible ruling-class hypothesis. Thus the conflicts of interest presupposed by the Bachrach-Baratz-Lukes conception of power will be rare, and will often reflect nothing more than the arrogance or rigidity of individual politicians. On the other hand, if big business is a ruling class, it will be relatively common for political leaders to be roused to an uncomfortable or risky level of activity by the rebelliousness of workers or a new threat of rebelliousness. The course of life which is preferable, given a politician's personal interests, will be disturbed. If we extend concepts of dominance appropriate to one-on-one interactions to the study of politics in society at large, we may find that workers have more power over government than bankers do, precisely when big business is the ruling class.

Lukes insists that "the point...of locating power is to fix responsibility for consequences held to flow from the action or inaction of certain specifiable agents".[11] A similar concern for fixing individual responsibility sometimes seems to underlie the insistence by Bachrach and Baratz on the importance of agenda-fixing, as against forthright debate, as a basis for power. No doubt, this is a point that

----

[11] **Ibid.**, p. 56.

locating power may have, and one best served by asking who is getting what he wants in the face of opposition. I hope that I have shown that it is not **the** point, either of all theorizing or of all important strategic discussions bearing on the question of locating power.

THE FATE OF PLURALISM: A DIGRESSION

Pluralists believe that no social group or minority coalition of social groups dominates government in the United States. Political power, in their view, is more dispersed. This is the substantive issue that pluralists try to settle. I have argued that this substantive question must be begged, despite pluralists' intentions to the contrary, if the investigation is regulated by the general conceptions of political power which pluralists recommend.

Many political theorists now believe that such arguments with pluralism are antiquarian. In their view, pluralism has passed away. Most are influenced in this judgment by the leftward trend in the views of some pluralists, especially Robert Dahl, the most widely read and one of the most persuasive pluralist writers of the early sixties. Most are influenced, as well, by the new, more pessimistic tendency of mainstream political scientists to analyze failures of government in the United States and other Western democracies. Often, these investigators attribute those failures to distorting effects of interest-group politics. Because of all these changes, the danger that inappropriate understandings of questions about power will lead to an unjustified preference for pluralism may seem irrelevant to current concerns.

At the cost of digression, I shall offer some evidence that pluralism is, if anything, more entrenched now than it was twenty years ago. In the early sixties, pluralists were at least compelled to make their methodology explicit and to marshal arguments for their beliefs about the distribution of political power. Now the belief in the wide dispersal of political power is more apt to be a tacit assumption, a framework within which conservative, liberal, and even leftwing alternatives are advanced and debated. If mainstream political scientists less frequently advance pluralist definitions of political power in defending their views, that is largely because they assume the truth of pluralism without defending it. My initial treatment of ruling-class hypotheses will clarify, by way of contrast, the continued presence of the underlying pluralist doctrines.

In the heyday of pluralism as an explicit and explicitly defended theory, defenders identified the general thesis at issue as the claim that government policy is the outcome of a system of widely dispersed resources for influencing government officials, interacting with the preferences and talents of officials who are not wholly constrained by these influences. Each kind of political resource may be unequally distributed. But dominance of one kind of resource would, at most, enable a social group to dominate a few areas of government policy. In particular, the concentration of wealth is not decisive, since universal suffrage makes the weight of numbers an important resource for the nonwealthy majority. The dispersal of different kinds of political resources often gives a political leader considerable options for successful initiatives in support of policies that would not otherwise be proposed as an outcome of bargaining among various social groups. Of course, political leaders may play a more passive role, based on circumstances, self-interest, or personal style. [12]

Within this broad framework, important variations are possible, especially along two dimensions. First, the extent and moral significance of inequalities in different kinds of resources might be variously assessed. Second, the extent to which political leaders passively reflect the interplay of different influences, and the extent to which they should do so, might be variously judged. One can imagine an extremely conservative pluralism which holds that the bundles of resources on which political influence depends do not differ much (on balance) from person to person, that the inequalities which exist are not pressing moral problems, that major political figures passively reflect the balance of forces among competing groups, and that they should do so. The view that pluralism is passe reflects the fact that few, if any academic theorists are now committed to this extremely conservative version.

The identification of pluralism with this version of it is historically inaccurate and theoretically misleading. There was never a pluralist consensus of this kind. For example, in **Who Governs?**, the official six-point statement of the pluralist view of government has (as its second clause) the thesis that, "With few exceptions these [political] resources are unequally distributed."[13] Dahl is

----

[12] See: Dahl, **Who Governs?**, p. 228.

never so naive as to suppose that the average citizen of New Haven has a bundle of political resources about as weighty as the Chairman of the Board of the First New Haven Bank. Only weight of numbers, through the medium of universal suffrage, balances the resource of wealth. Though Dahl is largely silent, he is certainly not smug about the moral importance of interpersonal inequalities. Finally, far from being a celebration of "interest-group politics," **Who Governs?** describes how the more passive politics of Mayor Celentano were replaced by the aggressive and independent initiatives of Mayor Lee, a leader portrayed as virtually obsessed with the moral importance of urban renewal, sensibly aware of the distribution of political influence, but concerned to put these facts of political life to the service of a larger vision.

More important than historical accuracy, forgetting the options open to pluralism has meant ignoring its persistence as an unstated, undefended background for important arguments about American politics. This entrenchment of pluralism is illustrated by two books which are leading documents used to support the verdict that pluralism is passe: Dahl's **After the Revolution?** and Theodore Lowi's **The End of Liberalism.**

In **After the Revolution?**, Dahl acknowledges that there are enormous differences in politically effective resources from person to person in the United States and advocates their redistribution. He recognizes the powerlessness of employees in large corporations and calls for internal control of corporate policies by employees, combined with external control, where appropriate, by government bodies subject to the more equal distribution of political resources. Nothing here is incompatible with early-sixties pluralism. Of course, nothing here is incompatible with the hypothesis that big business is something like a ruling class. What discriminates between these outlooks is Dahl's conception of how the recommended changes could be brought about.

Here, pluralist assumptions are crucial. The best means to a radical redistribution of effective political resources are said to be the use of universal suffrage for social change pioneered in European countries.[14] There is no discussion, in this context, of the role of such

----

[13] Ibid.

[14] Dahl, **After the Revolution?**, pp. 105-110.

nonelectoral factors as general strikes, sitdowns, popular uprisings, and mutinies in these European processes.   The evidence that a major redistribution of resources and influ- ence resulted is confined to the fact that income (not wealth) is distributed more unequally in the United States than in Britain, Norway, and other advanced countries.[15] We are told that the recommended democratization of indus- trial firms would deprive present business leaders of most of their economic power.   But we are also told that, "although sentimentalists on the Left may find the idea too repugnant to stomach, quite possibly workers and trade unions are the greatest barriers at present to any profound reconstruction of economic enterprise in the country."[16] The only evidence cited is a study arguing for the preva- lence of consumption-oriented, family-centered attitudes among affluent workers in England.

It would be very unfair to criticize **After the Revolu- tion?** for failing to marshal substantial evidence in support of an underlying view of the power relations within which change is pursued.   The book is avowedly speculative.   My point is rather that a general view of political power in the United States is presupposed, without substantial argument. It is the same as the one which was explicitly stated and defended in **Who Governs?** nine years before.

Lowi's **The End of Liberalism** is influential and typical of books attributing the failures of United States govern- ment since World War II to the substitution of interest- group politics for presidential leadership based on moral appeals to common interests and the creation of well-defined statutes and unified bureaucracies.   The book often seems a vigorous critique of pluralism.   "Interest-group liberalism," the villain, is said to be the result of transforming plural- ism from a political theory into an ideology.[17]   Since United States politics allegedly did not conform to this ideology before World War II and will not do so if present failures are corrected in time, the enduring validity of pluralist theory seems cast in doubt as well.

The link between "interest-group liberalism" and real pluralist theory is, in fact, tenuous at best.   Lowi's ideal

----

[15] **Ibid.**, p. 112, fn. 1.

[16] **Ibid.**, p. 134.

[17] Theodore Lowi, **The End of Liberalism**, New York, Nor- ton, second edition, 1979, p. 36.

President is not very different from Mayor Richard Lee of
Who Governs? writ large. More important, the main strategy of argument in Lowi's book depends on the assumed
validity of pluralist theory, as it really was.

The general thesis of The End of Liberalism is hardly
obvious. In public statements, Johnson and Nixon, the
alleged epitomes of interest-group liberalism, made moral
appeals to the common interest so sanctimonious that some
of us felt vaguely sick. Proceeding policy area by policy
area, Lowi adopts the following strategy for showing that
an ideology of interest-groups had triumphed nonetheless.
He points to failures in the pursuit of stated goals, for
example, a drastic reduction in poverty and an effective yet
humane foreign policy. He describes a proliferation of governmental and quasi-governmental agencies, often tied to
particular interest groups, officially controlled by representatives of interest groups, or justified on the grounds that
interest groups should participate more directly in government. This dispersal of authority is said to be the best
explanation of the consistent failure to achieve the stated
goals.

Such inferences from the best explanation are essential to science. Indeed, they may be the single fundamental
form of scientific inference. But it is crucial, in such
arguments, that relevant alternatives be considered. One
relevant alternative is this: quite apart from organizational
forms, basic United States government policy disproportion-
ately tends to serve group interests which conflict with the
achievement of stated goals. There is no discussion of any
policy-area in this long and detailed book in which such an
alternative is considered. In effect, Lowi assumes that the
electoral weight of numbers would guarantee that the interests of most of us would prevail, if we were not (politician
and voter alike) misled by the ideology of interest-group
liberalism. This vigorous, even outraged attack on one
version of pluralist thinking, support for interest-group
bargaining as the best basis for politics, itself operates
wholly within the general framework of pluralist theory.

RULING CLASSES AND POWER ELITES

I have suggested that many critics of pluralism share
its overemphasis on issue-by-issue tallies of success or failure in particular policy debates. This certainly cannot be
said, though, of the major academic alternative to pluralism:

the power-structure studies of Hunter, Mills, and Domhoff.[18] There, the basic question about political power is, in the first instance, concerned with the social setting, not with the power of individuals: "what are the mechanisms, especially the patterns of informal interaction, by which certain social groups exercise disproportionate influence on government?" Claims that such mechanisms exist are part of the thesis that there is a ruling class. However, the question of the extent to which a group is a ruling class also depends on other questions concerning the nature of its interests and the direction of political change in response to crisis. The most detailed description of mechanisms of influence may fail to answer them.

Though their distaste for elitism is often clear enough, power-structure analysts do not investigate in detail whether the interests of a dominant elite conflict with the interests of society at large. No doubt, many of Hunter's Atlanta businesspeople and Domhoff's bankers and corporate lawyers would accept that they have disproportionate influence on government, but claim that this is reasonable and in the public interest, because of their special knowledge, responsibilities, and administrative skills. You can read through **Community Power Structure** and **Who Rules America?** without finding evidence for or against this view-from-the-executive-dining-room.

In addition, knowledge of mechanisms of influence may not tell us the order of power among interconnected the elites. Is the influence of major businesspeople on government a reflection of their basic control over government, or is it a tribute they are forced to pay to the independent power of politicians? Although this sometimes seems to be just the issue separating power-structure theorists from pluralists, it is actually an unintelligible question within the power-structure framework. The determination of the relative power of the influencers and the influenced depends, not on the description of a network of interactions, but on the investigation of what happens when the network is strained or disrupted, of who wins and who loses. To the extent to which the power of big business explains the failure of previously successful politicians, the passing away of

----

[18] For example, see: Floyd Hunter, **Community Power Structure**, Chapel Hill, University of North Carolina Press, 1953; C. Wright Mills, **The Power Elite**, New York, Oxford University Press, 1956; G. William Domhoff, **Who Rules America?**, Englewood Cliffs, NJ, Prentice-Hall, 1967.

a whole style of politics, or even the replacement of one set of political institutions by another, big business has power over the political establishment and approaches the status of a ruling class. By their nature, such efforts to change the personnel, style, or institutions of politics mobilize resources that are not engaged in normal patterns of influence. Obviously, there were many channels of influence running from business to government in the late-nineteenth-century United States. What shows that there was also considerable power of business over government is the unhappy fate of political leaders who stepped out of line: for example, Altgeld in Illinois and the Populist government of South Carolina. In these episodes, business resources were employed which differed in degree from those used in the normal network of influence (e.g., the regimentation of the news became much more absolute) and which sometimes differed in kind (e.g., mobs were organized to attack politicians).

Similarly, the study of actual networks of influence does not tell us how strong is the connection between government action and elite interests. For at any given time, this is a question of what would happen: in particular, of whether the connection would be broken by feasible sorts of activism of kinds protected or, at least, permitted by government. However messy and speculative such claims are, people may need to examine them in a thorough discussion of strategies for change. Suppose we know all there is to know about elite social clubs, conferences, study groups, the constant interchange between the top echelons of business and government, and all the other mechanisms reported in power-structure studies. We still may not know how far things can be changed through a strategy of advocating the election of the less pro-business of the candidates, wherever one exists. At what point would banks refuse to float government bonds? At what point, if any, would the business community sponsor violent rightwing groups or support a military takeover, toppling even conservative politicians of a parliamentary sort? These are questions which must be faced when we ask to what extent there is a ruling class, but not when we study current patterns of influence. The Kucinich fiasco in Cleveland may be a small token of the gap between these questions, the Chilean coup a big one.

FUNCTIONALISM AND SOCIAL INTERESTS

The remaining outlook on political power of major importance in empirical political theory is the structural-functionalism explicit, for example, in Easton's writings and implicit in much of Almond and Verba's analysis of the civic culture. Here, government is assumed to be a means of interpreting and coordinating diverse particular interests, in pursuit of a common interest in stability and efficiency. In effect, the study of political power becomes a study of helps and impediments to the achievement of this common goal. The competing functional alternative according to which the patterns of government action are best explained as due to a function of protecting the interests of a dominant elite is, in effect, dismissed without argument. Thus in **The Civic Culture**, when Mexican and Italian responses to questionnaires display alienation from the political process, this alienation itself, not objective political facts to whch it corresponds, is taken to be the main obstacle to effective democracy.[19] It is interesting that structural-functionalism and pluralism should be the two respectable approaches to political power, in firm intellectual alliance, providing alternate paradigms between which even mildly eclectic theorists unself-conciously shuttle. For in the abstract, the approaches and research methods characteristic of each are radically different, quite as different as between such warring factions as the neoclassical and the institutionalist approaches to economics or the formalist and substantivist wings of economic anthropology. Structural-functionalist theory studies systems of institutions and cultural values, using surveys and large-scale speculative theorizing to discuss how they approach or depart from an ideal in which each subsystem serves to maintain the stability of the whole. Pluralist theory studies processes of political influence and initiative, mapping their course by examining issue-by-issue outcomes, often confined to a few years in a particular city. Here, there is no ideal of long-term equilibrium or even of an enduring pattern in the political life of a society. What is characteristic of the thinking of actual structural-functionalist and pluralist theorists is a common tendency not to take seriously the possible rationality of breaking the rules of the game of a

----

[19] Gabriel A. Almond and Sidney Verba, **The Civic Culture**, Little, Brown, Boston, 1965, pp. 3-7, 308-318, 368-379.

reasonably stable and efficient political system, at least when it is a parliamentary democracy. If such possibilities are dismissed, two natural questions of political power remain: "who wins and who loses as the game is played?" (pluralism); and "what makes the game stable and efficient?" (structural-functionalism). Thus, when political strategies worth considering are confined to the electoral realm, theoretical questions worth considering are correspondingly limited.

THE CHAINS OF METHODOLOGY

While the academic study of politics does not include the question "to what extent is there a ruling class?", it would be misleading to say that the question is simply ignored. Rather, the possibility that there is something like a ruling class in the United States today is believed to be too far-fetched to merit investigation. This general kind of dismissal is not antagonistic to science, but essential to it. The investigation of reality always depends on dismissing some possibilities as too far-fetched. But this particular dismissal is premature, based on biased methods of research and a narrow conception of motivation.

First of all, there is a tendency to adopt methods for investigating power that presuppose the nonexistence of a ruling class. Not surprisingly, investigations guided by such methods often make the hypothesis of a ruling class look utterly implausible, if one forgets that the question has been begged. A prime example is the pluralist proposal to measure political power by determining how often people get what they want in a contested issue on the agenda of an official forum. Thus Dahl, in the central empirical argument of **Who Governs?**, measures "the distribution of influence" by examining official decisions on urban renewal in New Haven. The issues considered are essentially those reflected in the deliberations of the Citizens Action Commission, an advisory group consisting of government officials and businesspeople, including "the heads of large utilities, manufacturing firms, banks and other businesses." Power is measured by determining "which individuals...most often initiated the proposals which were finally adopted, or most often vetoed the proposals of others." When power is measured in this way, the result is a vindication of the dominance of the Mayor and the Development Administrator, as against the Economic Notables, a result that is said to defeat the hypothesis of "the hidden hand of an economic elite."[20]

In fact, the investigator who assumes that wins and losses in official forums measure power cannot defeat the hypothesis that there is a ruling class. He can only assume its falsehood by choosing this measure. For empirical findings such as Dahl's (as distinct from his interpretations) are what one would expect if big business is a ruling class. One would expect political acts that would threaten big business not to be under discussion in official forums. On the other hand, official forums are likely to serve as testing grounds for the feasibility and public acceptability of various options which are all tolerable to big business. Political leaders and top administrators, those most alive to questions of feasibility and acceptability, will most often have the last word.

A rigid methodology may also obscure the connection between government and social interests in another way. Ruling-class hypotheses tend to be identified with implausible conspiracy theories, on account of a basically Weberian preference for subjective reasons, rather than objective interests, as explanations of action. Politicians tell us that they are equally committed to the interests of all. Thus, if the explanation of their behavior should appeal to their own reasons for doing what they do, a ruling-class hypothesis would dictate that they are lying, covering up hidden class-commitments or ties of outright bribery that are their real reasons for their actions.

In fact, the behavior of politicians and major businespeople, in the ruling-class approach, is best seen as guided by objective interests that may diverge from conscious reasons, sincerely stated. You will not find it mysterious if I say that a typical nuclear engineer has an objective interest in viewing himself as a useful professional which leads him to argue, quite sincerely, for the safety of nuclear power plants even when he should know better. It should seem no more mysterious to say that the objective interests of successful United States politicians lead them to promote the distinctive interests of big business, even when they sincerely appeal to the common interest.

A variety of arguments and investigations, power-structure studies among them, would contribute to a psychologically plausible account of how the typical history and typical situation of the successful politician make it possible

---

[20] Dahl, **Who Governs?**, pp. 122-126.

for him to be guided by the interests of big business, while honestly professing commitment to the interests of all. Some important factors reflected in the normal narrative of political success are the need for large campaign expenditures and media support, the sharing of the same personnel at the top echelons of business and public administration, the common school and social ties of those personnel, and the distinctly non-working-class life-style that political success encourages and affords. Corporate executives and politicians are not the only actors in this drama. Labor union leaders, with their impact on campaign funds, and newspaper editors, with their impact on news coverage, are crucially important as well. So are the academics who have given an air of plausibility to such theses as that a twelve-hour workday or the defense of the Diem regime was dictated by the national interest. Thus the tendency to achieve authority in labor unions, newspapers, and universities needs to be investigated as well. That militant union locals are frequently taken over and put into trusteeship is at least as important a fact for politics as the legislated structure of public utilities commissions. Finally, more attention should probably be paid to obvious facts that enormously increase the risks if a political leader should challenge big business. Governments rely on banks and similar institutions for credit. When businesspeople become demoralized about the future, there is a tendency for millions to be thrown out of work. Because of these facts, a serious violation of big-business interests often could not be managed by a head of government who is not the consciously revolutionary leader of a mass movement.

How do we determine whether major political figures are influenced by such interests, as against the democratic commitments they sincerely profess? We resolve the question of interests and principles with them as with anyone else, by looking at what they actually do and at the information in the background of their choices. Suppose that United States Presidents since World War II should have known better than to suppose that support for Diem, Reza Pahlevi, and the Somozas benefits democracy. Suppose that such support does conform to the pithy saying of Kennedy's Secretary of the Treasury: "I speak as an investment banker when I say that the less developed countries are our most important investment resource."[21] That is part, though only part, of a case for supposing that political

----

[21] **Department of State Bulletin,** May 6, 1958.

leaders' interests in serving the social interests of big business dominate United States political life.

So long as we assume that the reasons why someone acted as he did in politics are his reasons for acting as he did, ruling-class hypotheses will seem to be either conspiracy theories or unintelligible appeals to occult, impersonal forces. The development and effectiveness of objective interests in connection with social roles is the link between social structure and the relatively insightful, flexible actions required to maintain that structure in a changing world full of rebellious people. I discuss the logic of reasons, interests, and explanation in more detail elsewhere.[22]

As usual, a diagnosis suggests a cure. If political theorists are to take seriously the question of the extent to which there is a ruling class, they must connect descriptions of political structure with explanations of historical change. They must face the fact that disorder and repression have played an important role in the politics of all the Western democracies and have often been a part of processes leading to useful change. They must become aware of the factual assumptions behind the measurements and interpretations they make, not in order to pursue the chimera of methods independent of factual assumptions, but to avoid begging the question when rival hypotheses need to be compared. In sum, political theory, if concerned with the extent to which there is a ruling class, is more historical, more aware of the role of nonelectoral conflict, and less apt to end disputes over underlying theories on methodological grounds.

The confusions I have tried to expose in this paper have always been barriers to effective theorizing. They have a special practical importance now. Every major political figure is calling on us to help arm, even "reindustrialize" the United States. Here, the differences between Reagan, Carter, Kennedy, and Anderson were differences over tactics and timing, not fundamentals. In short, we are asked to respond to a call to discipline and obedience. How shall we answer? To help us respond, political theory must illuminate, not hide, the question of the extent to which there is a ruling class.

----

[22] See: Miller, "Methodological Individualism and Social Explanation."

POLITICAL THEORY AND POLITICAL SCIENCE:

THE REDISCOVERY AND REINTERPRETATION

OF THE PRAGMATIC TRADITION

Charles W. Anderson

I am not a professional political philosopher, but a political scientist in general practice. For this reason, my response to the question of what political theory should be doing now is different from that of some other contributors to this volume. I am less concerned with the prospects of political theory as a specialized field of study than I am with its contribution to a discipline that is engaged in the study of issues of public concern.

It is the task of theory in any academic profession to provide a sense of direction and a program of inquiry. To be sure, political science has never been notable for the power or coherence of its paradigmatic structure. But today, one feels an unusual sense of drift in the discipline. We are in a period between bright ideas. The grand designs of the behavioral revolution have pretty much run their course; and what is left is tedious methodological refinement, increasingly narrow research, and arcane debates among small clusters of specialists in fields where much of the undertaking's original point has been lost. The so-called behavioral revolution was rich in criticism, but seems to have left very little that a second generation could build upon. Political science seems to have become, once again, a loose and eclectic collection of specialties, with little in the way of common ground or shared inspiration. Even our well-wishers are hard pressed to identify recent achievements of genuine intellectual or social significance.

Political science seems to be between eras. Practicing political scientists are casting about for fresh ideas, and they are looking to political theory to provide them. In searching for themes that might guide future political research, we would do well to reconsider the heritage of the discipline itself, to look to the foundational assumptions that gave political science distinctiveness as a discipline. I have in mind specifically the political thought of American political science and institutional economics in the first decades of the twentieth century. This heritage is still very much alive in the discipline, informing everyday political science research and teaching. To explore the assumptions of this era may refresh our understanding of some customary ways of doing political theory, and it may clarify the implications of some current trends in political philosophy.

Unfortunately, the behavioral movement sought to repudiate this heritage as atheoretical, failing to understand the distinctive conception of theory and inquiry that had informed it. The new political science was to be built on the models and methods of the natural sciences. The role of creative theory in this period was to seek approaches to inquiry from other professions. Methods and models were borrowed from sociology, psychology, economics, cybernetics, physics, and elsewhere. What was absent was an effort to build on the history of political science itself.

One effect of this trend was to sever the connection between political theory and political science as that had been conventionally understood. Political theory itself became increasingly a derivative and specialized field, taking its cues from philosophy. A certain hostility between political theory and political research emerged in the profession. On the one hand, those who aspired to create a positivist science of politics regarded normative political theory as irrelevant to their purposes; on the other, political theorists tended to look upon empirical political science as the grossest philistinism. This divorce of theory from practice was a remarkable phenomenon, perhaps unique to the learned professions. Fortunately, its time is long since past. It may be an **idee fixe** in the minds of some or a form of ritualized combat at some institutions. But what is vital in the life of the profession today is the effort to reestablish the link between political theory, as it is understood in this volume, and the practice of political science.

In any event, the behavioral revolution was never quite complete. A strong residue of continuity remained in the practice of the profession, in the way political scientists were trained, in the dominant ideas of the field. There were few enough who actually tried to construct a pure science of politics or who took the canon of absolute value neutrality seriously. Many of the major theorists of the era (Dahl and Easton notably) understood perfectly well that significant political research had to be informed by distinctively political values, issues, and concepts. Most political scientists went their own ways, pursuing themes that were inherent in an older conception of the discipline as one concerned with problems of public life. Many of the landmark studies of the period, in voting behavior, elections, power structures, interest groups, the performance of representative institutions, took their significance from classic issues of democratic theory. In public administration, comparative politics, and foreign policy, the workaday political scientist tried as before to understand prevailing practice and provide contextual criticism or recommendation. But such efforts became increasingly fragmentary and isolated (atheoretical) as theory came increasingly to be associated with the search for general paradigms or concerned with convoluted philosophic debate. The problem, in many ways, was less that the profession had repudiated its theory than that its theorists had lost touch with the profession.

To ask what political theory should be doing now suggests an occasion for taking stock. Here I consult the longer history of the discipline in an effort to understand both what is expected of political theory in the ongoing activity of the profession and how political theory might be helpful in dealing with some of the intellectual puzzles and quandaries that now beset it.

THE PRAGMATIC FOUNDATIONS OF POLITICAL SCIENCE

Far more than we sometimes realize, political science is the intellectual legatee of the tradition of American pragmatism. The positivist and behavioral ideals of scientific inquiry were superimposed (and relatively recently at that) on more fundamental philosophic foundations. American political science emerged as a separate discipline as part of the "revolt against formalism" in philosophy, law, and social science at the turn of the century.[1] The dominant motifs of its early development, its programs of inquiry, were progressive, institutionalist, reformist, and empiricist, in contrast to the metaphysical abstractionism of late-nineteenth-century social thought. The profession's historians have noted these foundations; Merriam and Lasswell, Bentley and Truman, Dahl and Lindblom, and others acknowledge their debts to the likes of James, Royce, Peirce, and Dewey.[2]

----

[1] Morton White, **Social Thought in America**, Boston, Beacon Press, 1961.

[2] Bernard Crick, **The American Science of Politics**, Berkeley, University of California Press, 1959; Arthur Somit and Joseph Tanenhaus, **The Development of Political Science**,

This tradition continues to inform the discipline's characteristic patterns of inquiry and its method of practical reason: its strategy of decision making and evaluative judgment. The distinctive style of political science is perhaps particularly apparent if contrasted to that of its sister discipline of economics. Economics is now dominated by axiomatic reasoning and formal modeling, very much in the classic tradition of liberal political economy and utilitarianism. To be socialized as a political scientist, however, is to cultivate a certain suspicion of universal models and generalizations. Political institutions are seen in historical and cultural context. Close, empirical, substantive inquiry into institutions and processes establishes "how they work in practice." Prescription takes the form of proposals for reform: indicated adjustments in the going concern. Dominant metaphors are organic, evolutionary, and institutional; not formal, rationalist, and individualist. Theory gravitates to the middle range: limited generalizations based on detailed substantive inquiry. All of this is totally consistent with the basic presuppositions of pragmatic philosophy and the institutionalist, instrumentalist tradition in social thought.

In the pragmatic tradition of political science, theory and empirical research were always seen as intertwined in the process of investigation, and particularly so in coming to grips with practical problems of policy choice and public action. Political theory was not regarded as a specialized field; nor was it perceived as primarily concerned with matters of epistemology, models, and methods. It was simply an integral part of the process of inquiry into problems of public concern.

It is also essential to this pragmatic conception of the discipline that political theory not be divorced from the ongoing political discourse of society. Pragmatic political science takes its projects, problems, and much of its paradigmatic structure from public life. It conceives itself as part of a larger process of investigation, inquiry, and concern. In this respect, pragmatic political science differs fundamentally from the assumptions of both behavioral political science and much contemporary political philosophy. In orthodox behavioralism, the role of the social scientist is that of the detached observer. Similarly, the stance of the political philosopher is that of the stranger studying political life from outside. The political philosopher judges

---

Boston, Allyn and Bacon, 1967.

political values and practices from a standpoint apart from the political order itself. In function, the political philosopher is primarily a social critic.

Philosophic pragmatism contains a political vision that is at once utopian and conservative. The pragmatic political ideal is one of the free person in the free society. Dewey maintained a positive image of freedom that has much in common with Mill or Habermas. His vision of democratic society is more akin to Rousseau than to Locke. Yet it is also essential to the pragmatic conception of method that established practice be regarded as initially valid. It is the product of successful historic adaptations. It provides the context for further exploration and development. The problem is how to build upon that legacy, how to enhance and perfect the institutions and practices inherent in the going concern. This conservative element in pragmatic thought may seem uncongenial or parochial to some, but I think it is worth exploring as an alternate conception of political theory. Social criticism is an important function of political theory, but not its only function. Political theory should also generate proposals and innovations to test against valued continuities, just as it should also point to unexploited possibilities in existing institutions and practices.

In any event, my purpose is to recommend philosophic pragmatism, not as a political doctrine, but as an intellectual legacy which we would do well to consider in contemplating the future of political theory. More than we perhaps realize, our sense of what is significant or problematical in political theory and research can be traced to the assumptions and premises of this tradition. It is the peculiar paradigmatic structure of political science, and it is not like that of any other social science discipline. It is a richer foundational framework than we perhaps suspect: one that we might well build upon.

THE HISTORICAL STUDY OF POLITICAL THOUGHT

In recent years, the study of the tradition of political thought has often been viewed as a remnant of classicism, a humanistic adornment to the curriculum. Easton dismissed the work of Sabine and Dunning as "mere historicism" and thought that the study of the classic texts was an evasion of the essential tasks of political theory.[3] But it may be that the founders of American political science had a more cogent notion of where historical political theory fit into the curriculum of the new discipline. Pragmatism contained elements of idealism and evolutionism. Kant, Hegel, and Darwin had influenced Peirce, James, and Dewey. The pragmatists did not share the passive-mind hypothesis of classic liberalism. They saw the world as theory-driven. From this perspective, the tradition is an ongoing legacy of experiment and adaptation. We examine it to understand how the human mind works in the realm of politics and to appreciate the sources of the working logic that we bring to understanding and appraising everyday political events and practices.

Political science is the last of the social sciences to teach its theory from a standpoint of history. Economists rarely read the classics; and for sociology, history begins with Durkheim and Weber. I have become convinced that the historical approach has certain pedagogic advantages. Social theory taught without this perspective may seem peculiarly timeless and authoritative. Theory, as economists presently teach it, seems more a given than a controversy. One misses the sense of puzzlement and groping, of the search for a fit between context and perennial themes, that attends the creative work of the theorist. Furthermore, it is important that we act as the trustees and guardians of this legacy of thought. If we do not preserve and transmit the tradition, it may die out as part of the common inheritance of the civilization.

Still, the historical study of political thought may have an important role to play in the development of a political science that can move once more beyond social science orthodoxy. Historical political theory can contribute to a political science more normatively informed and thus more pertinent to treating concrete issues of public choice and action. Certain recent studies seem distinctly relevant to this task. J. G. A. Pocock, Quentin Skinner, and Garry Wills explore what Pocock calls the "conceptual vocabularies" of an age and thereby read the classic texts, not for their own sake, but as reflections of the logic of political discourse, the system of practical political reason, of various epochs.[4]

----

[3] David Easton, **The Political System**, New York, Knopf, 1976, pp. 233-265.

Practical political discourse is guided by a limited number of fundamental concepts: ideas of public interest, common good, justice, rights, order, freedom, efficiency, authority, consent, and community. These are defined differently in different ages and contexts. Emphasis is distributed differently among these values, and they are related differently to one another in particular systems of thought. As Pocock and Skinner suggest, one of the tasks of creative political theory may be to give new content to concepts that are part of the common vocabulary of politics or to re-establish the salience of ancient usages. This view is perfectly compatible with the pragmatic conception of political theory. We develop a more adequate (more **useful**) public philosophy by the progressive adapatation of shared values and constructs to new situations and problems.

A THEORY OF PRACTICAL POLITICAL REASON

Such historical studies share much with what is suggestive for political theory about the method of analytical philosophy. Against positivism, analytical philosophy argues that legitimate statements cannot be reduced to either analytic or synthetic propositions. Thus ethical and political discourse is not "meaningless," in the strict sense. Rather, such normative discourse has a "working logic" of its own. Following the later Wittgenstein, we can discover this by examining what we **do** in ethical or political assertion and argument. As Richard Bernstein and others have noted, there is a considerable affinity between post-Wittgensteinian philosophy and pragmatism.[5] Both focus on language as a tool of action through which we carry forward human projects and purposes.

Positivist political science cannot take the vocabularies

----

[4] J. G. A. Pocock, **The Machiavellian Moment**, Princeton, NJ, Princeton University Press, 1975; Quentin Skinner, **The Foundations of Modern Political Thought**, Cambridge, Cambridge University Press, in two volumes, 1978; Garry Wills, **Inventing America**, New York, Random House, 1979; Wills, **Explaining America**, Garden City, NY, Doubleday, 1981.

[5] Richard J. Bernstein, **Praxis and Action**, Philadelphia, University of Pennsylvania Press, 1971, pp. 5-6, 165-304.

of actual politics seriously. For it, value statements are no more than "personal preferences," to be explained by emotional predispositions, background experiences, cultural conditioning, or socio-economic interest. Post-Wittgensteinian philosophy and phenomenology insist that "reasons" count as well as "causes" and that understanding an action requires comprehending its meaning for an individual: the actor's explanation and justification of it. A rigorous post-positivist political theory must come to grips with the structure and logic of political argument: with the processes of political evaluation, judgment, and discourse. This conception of method would be consistent with the fundamental assumptions of the discipline. The creation of such theory could draw on analytical philosophy, a kind of empirical inquiry, and a particular approach to the historical study of political thought.

The analytical political philosopher tries to clarify the meaning of critical terms, to survey their use and possibilities in ordinary political language. This is illustrated by the work of S. I. Benn and R. S. Peters, Brian Barry, Hanna Pitkin, Richard Flathman, and David Miller on such central political values as representation, the public interest, rights, and social justice.[6] Such work is not intended to settle the argument. Rather, it provides an heuristic for thought. We make choices when we invoke fundamental principle in making political recommendations, evaluations, and appeals is to make choices; and the rigorous inventories of potential meaning provided by analytical philosophy can clarify the implications of these choices.

A theory of practical political reason seeks to build on a heritage of shared values in order to provide a framework for political discourse and action. Such a theory requires that we know how our "working logics" of political analysis operate in practice. This calls for a special kind of empirical and theoretical inquiry. We live in a pluralistic universe of political ideas and methods. Even more than

----

[6] S. I. Benn and R. S. Peters, **Social Principles and the Democratic State**, London, Allen and Unwin, 1959; Brian Barry, **Political Argument**, London, Routledge and Kegan Paul, 1965; Hanna Fenichel Pitkin, **The Concept of Representation**, Berkeley, University of California Press, 1967; Richard E. Flathman, **The Public Interest**, New York, Wiley, 1966; Flathman, **The Practice of Rights**, Cambridge, Cambridge University Press, 1976; David Miller, **Social Justice**, Oxford, Oxford University Press, 1976.

major ideologies, the proliferating technical languages of policy analysis and the specialized norms of political cognition and commitment in specific institutions, industries, and subcultures call for skilled commentary. We need to know how the terminologies of modern economics work when applied in political practice, just as we must understand the languages of environmentalism, systems analysis, and recent jurisprudence. We need to know more about the normative structures of business, the professions, and various religious orthodoxies. This task is as much anthropological and sociological as philosophical, but it is necessary for a more adequate political theory.

Even so, our understanding of the distinctive character of Western (and especially American) political reason can also be enhanced through historical investigation. This gives us a sense for the longer continuities. In grappling with complex public problems, pragmatic political science has always insisted on searching for unexploited or forgotten possibilities in the common heritage of ideas and practices. Through historical inquiry, we also come to see how political theory adapts a finite number of basic themes to diverse circumstances and problems. For pragmatic political science, the tradition is an evolving legacy of thought. It is the record of human efforts to deal with the perennial issues of politics under different institutional conditions and in contexts of different cosmological, philosophical, and theological assumptions. One reads the classic works, not as sacred texts, but to understand this distinctive enterprise of human thought.

THE EFFORT TO FORMALIZE LIBERAL THEORY

Pragmatic political science is deeply embedded in the political culture of liberalism. Therefrom it takes its sense for what is significant in political research and what is problematic in the realm of public affairs. Pragmatic political science is not neutral among all possible forms of political cognition. (Of course, neither is modern physics neutral about pre-Copernican physics or astrology. There can be no totally objective paradigm for political inquiry.) While much neo-Marxian analysis, particularly on the structural characteristics of capitalist states, is germane to pragmatic political science, much classical Marxism is not. The latter's epistemological preconceptions simply yield a different kind of political science.

Liberalism, however, has peculiar qualities as a framework for political thought. It is better understood as an arena of argument than as a doctrine or ideology. The characteristic liberal values form a loose configuration. There is no necessary order among such constructs as freedom and equality, equity and efficiency, public interest and private right. Since Locke, Smith, and Bentham, the continuing tasks of liberal political theory have been to suggest systematic relationships among these values and to state conditions, principles, or rules to resolve apparent paradoxes in this scheme of political evaluation.

Represented by Rawls, Nozick, Ackerman, and others, the recent rebirth of formal liberal theory may be understood as an effort to find (or reassert) a kind of rational necessity in liberalism. If its purpose is to end argument, to create a doctrine of liberalism, then this kind of theory would be distinctly contrary to the spirit of pragmatism, which affirms the perennial openness and indeterminacy of the liberal problem of value. But if this formal theory's purpose is to **contribute** to argument, then it suggests much for the future development of political theory. John Rawls has recently provided a restatement of the goal of formal liberal theory, one which seems closer to the temper of pragmatic political science than the contractarianism of his **magnum opus**. "The aim of political philosophy, when it presents itself in the culture of a democratic society, is to articulate and make explicit those shared notions and principles thought to be already latent in common sense; or, as is often the case, if common sense is hesitant and uncertain, and doesn't know what to think, to propose to it certain conceptions and principles congenial to its most essential convictions and historical traditions."[7]

Here the task for the formal theorist is more like that prescribed for analytical philosophy: to clarify ordinary usage in implication and logic. While conventionally, the analytical political philosopher may aim for the meaning of fundamental concepts and values, perhaps the formal theorist can be said to look for their logics of interrelationship. As a purpose of systematic liberal theory, this is suggestive for the further development of pragmatic political thought. We need a framework to bring greater rigor and clarity to public debate; we may even need new ways of

----

[7] John Rawls, "Kantian Constructivism in Moral Theory," **Journal of Philosophy**, 77, 9, September, 1980, pp. 515-572, on p. 518.

looking at the liberal problem of political valuation. The touchstone is not rational necessity but social agreement and coherence. The worth of our effort is tested in practice. Proposed principles of justice, public interest, or liberty are either helpful in defining and resolving public issues or not.

I am urging that we build on the legacy of pragmatic political science, not merely adopt it. The open structure of pragmatic thought may not be suitable for the coming age. The pragmatic sense of politics as experimentation and adaptation provides little sense of limits. Opposed to formalism, it offers little normative guidance to the decision maker or citizen. It applauds the robust pursuit of public purpose, but says little about the integrity of private life. It relies basically on procedural norms, thus offering few substantive criteria of public policy. Still, explorations in formal liberal theory may yet, in the future, give us clearer criteria for public problems and solutions within the normative framework of liberal society. There is every reason to believe that Rawls' is not the last word and that approaches other than the contractarian or utilitarian can help us with this problem. For there are other ways of trying to think systematically about our shared intuitions and values.

THE PARADIGMATIC STRUCTURE OF POLITICAL SCIENCE

The function of theory is to provide a disciplinary program. A generation ago, the theorist's tasks were to advance general propositions about political behavior that could be tested empirically and to propose new approaches, models, and methods toward creating a positive science of politics. In its formative years, however, the discipine's dominant paradigm was more explicitly political. This earlier conception of political inquiry is still vital in the profession; and there is a growing desire to recover, re-examine, and build on it.

Pragmatic political science is predisposed toward the positive state, much as economics is biased in favor of the market. In the first instance, American political science was strongly influenced by the Continental (specifically, Bismarckian) model of the state, which was nativized and legitimated by appeal to democratic process. Philosophically, pragmatism has had little use for metaphysical doctrines of the state or definitions of its essential purposes.

The state is simply regarded as an adaptive mechanism, responsive to a public will which determines its purposes. Allied to the Progressive movement, American political science found the classical Lockean doctrine of the minimal state inadequate to the needs of a growing, complex industrial society. Even the Constitution provided few constraints on the purview of public action. The positive law was envisioned as a "living" instrument: its genius being an ability to adapt to changing needs and circumstances.

These formative predispositions have guided political science well into our own period. The central concern of political science has long been issues of process and procedure rather than the substance of public action. **Responsiveness** of government action to public will is the privileged problem of political science. Significant research addresses this question: perhaps by measuring the discrepancy between legislators' votes and constituents' attitudes, perhaps by evaluating the disparity between "input" and "output" in the cybernetic metaphor for studying public policy.

Far more than we perhaps realize, the pragmatic vision of politics and the state has provided a paradigm for our political inquiry. This is a paradigm in the classic sense: an ideal of order; a standard for measuring what is puzzling, problematic, and worthy of inquiry. Parties, interest groups, and legislative bodies were interesting precisely because of the way they did or did not institutionalize, channel, and manifest the public will in public action. Problems for applied research arose when obstacles appeared to thwart or distort the articulation and aggregation of interests or the implementation of policies based on public intent.

Like any useful paradigm, the pragmatic theory of the positive state served, not only as a vehicle for organizing inquiry, but as a point of departure for criticism and theoretical development. In ordinary science, paradigms provide models for explanation; and their adequacy comes into question when they no longer account for the data. In political science, paradigms are normative as well. They provide ideals not only of natural order but of right order. (Thus in economics, markets provide not only models of expected behavior but standards of evaluation. At equilibrium in a free market, prices are not only natural but also justifiable. Similarly in pluralist politics, the state not only does respond to a configuration of demands but it also should do so.)

The pragmatic model of the flexible, responsive state has provided a basis for criticism. The radical political science of the 1960s argued that American politics could not be shown to be consistent with the ideal that orthodox political science had formulated, nurtured, and celebrated. Democratic pluralism could not be regarded as either an empirical description of the system or a sufficient proxy for Dewey's public, the "community of inquiry" that legitimated the positive state. This revisionist political science was an exercise at once in social criticism and in scientific criticism, questioning the paradigm that had long guided political research. The critics were often well aware of Thomas Kuhn's idea of the nature of scientific revolution. Self-consciously, they made a point both scientific and political. More recently, the pragmatic conception of the positive state has been challenged by neoconservative writers: Bell, Huntington, Lowi, Moynihan, and others.[8] (Significantly, many of them are practicing political scientists.) They argue that this image of the state as problem-solver, virtually unlimited in its scope as an agent of public interest, leads to excessive demands, exaggerates the realm of political competence or even politics generally, and weakens authority structures.

Now that the dust has settled a little, we may want to consider whether we can contrive a more provocative paradigm of the state to guide inquiry in political science. The controversy between the pragmatic positive state and the liberal minimalist state has pretty much run dry as a resource for public discourse and creative scholarship. Theory at that level is mostly a matter of repeating platitudes generations, if not centuries, old. We need not abandon inherited models of the state, nor the discipline's persistent concern for the integrity and vitality of democratic process. But we do need to elaborate these models, giving them new dimensions that suggest new avenues of inquiry.

We need a more differentiated theory of politics and

----

[8] Daniel Bell, **The Cultural Contradictions of Capitalism,** New York, Basic Books, 1976; Samuel P. Huntington, **Political Order in Changing Societies,** New Haven, Yale University Press, 1968; Huntington, "The United States," in Michael Crozier, Huntington, and Joji Watanuki, **The Crisis of Democracy,** New York, New York University Press, 1975, pp. 59-118; Theodore J. Lowi, **The End of Liberalism,** New York, Norton, 1969; Daniel P. Moynihan, **Maximum Feasible Misunderstanding,** New York, Free Press, 1969; Moynihan, **Coping,** New York, Random House, 1973.

the polity, a more elaborate framework to describe and evaluate relationships among the state and other institutions or associations. Public or private; authority versus the market; class, group, and interest: old, reductionist categories cannot do justice to the complex institutional order of the twentieth century. We should reconsider the terms of legitimacy of this political order, lest we encumber political argument with a vocabulary partly irrelevant to the situation. We must ask: what would render the modern corporation legitimate in our eyes? or the private association? or the university? What grounds are appropriate for criticizing the performance of such institutions, and what are not? In answering such questions, we need to move beyond the formulas of Lockean liberalism, Marxism, and pragmatic progressivism.

The search for a more differentiated theory of the polity might suggest a political theory more Aristotelian or medieval in character: emphasizing the particular public functions of different institutions and the terms of their interrelationship. But it may be possible to find the raw materials for such theory closer to home. The social thought of the early twentieth century was much concerned with the evolving institutional structure of industrial America. Indeed, the founders of political science understood pluralism in a more essential sense than we do today. Our "pluralism" primarily as interest-group representation is a pale residue of the more intricate theory, virtually ending with Laski, of a complex polity composed of various institutional loyalties, identities, and functions.

To include the study of private government, of the political order of institutions other than the state, within the scope of political science would revitalize a tradition of inquiry once thought important but since almost abandoned. The careful, empirical study of the historical development of political norms and practices in specific industries, sectors, subcultures, and communities could provide honest work for a generation of researchers. This once was "normal science" in the study of both politics and economics, but now it is nearly forgotten. And lost with it are a detailed understanding of economic and societal operations, plus a sense of the possibilities for reform in carrying out public purposes that remain inherent in the institutional structure of our polity.

These are the lines along which political science can make its contribution to the formulation of a new political economy. In its concern for aggregate phenomena and highly generalized models, economics has virtually lost touch with its tradition of institutional analysis, which paralleled historically the development of pragmatic political science. Yet it is increasingly apparent that political economy cannot ignore the concrete practices and interrelationships of advanced industrial institutions if it is to be an adequate basis for policy. We need to understand what John R. Commons called the "working rules" of the firm, the industry, the sector: the practices, normative understandings, and terms of discourse that structure basic economic relationships and responses of economic actors to public initiatives and incentives.[9] Ordinary political scientists know how to undertake the empirical, historical, comparative, and often simply descriptive inquires now needed. Economists, by and large, have lost the art.

A more differentiated study of the polity provides an agenda for research. But it also sets tasks for theory. Like institutional economics, pragmatic political science was empirically rich at its peak of development. In the end, though, neither generated a theoretical framework of great sophistication, generality, clarity, or power. Perhaps this is part of the reason why they have been superceded by more formal models and modes of analysis. Still, I suspect that the next development of pragmatic theory lies in connecting normative concerns about concepts, working logics, and rules of discourse with empirical and institutionalist interests in operational routines and principles of organizational behavior. The problem now is bridging the gaps and seeing the picture whole.

POLITICAL SCIENCE AS POLICY SCIENCE

American political science has always seen itself partly as an applied science. Its mission includes educating those who would pursue public service careers. In this, too, its approach has been strongly influenced by pragmatic philosophy. Basically, there are two doctrines of systematic policy analysis taught in schools of public affairs today, with more than a little rivalry (even hostility) between them.[10]

----

[9] John R. Commons, **The Legal Foundations of Capitalism,** Madison, University of Wisconsin Press, 1968, pp. 359-371.

[10] Aaron Wildavsky, "The Political Economy of Efficiency," **Public Interest,** 8, Summer, 1967, pp. 30-48.

The first is largely economic and utilitarian in ethos. It stresses highly technical methods of modeling and forecasting; and it culminates in an ideal cost-benefit analysis, taken as an applied equivalent of an aggregate social welfare function. The second is normally associated with political science and emphasizes creative problem formulation; cognitive flexibility in examining evidence, assumptions, and proposals; plus an experimental, incremental approach to public action. It is tough-minded about political feasibility and the perils of passing from intent to impact. Its underlying theories of cognition, inquiry, purposive action, and politics are strikingly reminiscent of Dewey.

Here the prospects for reuniting political theory and political science are particularly promising. Long-established assumptions of policy science are being rethought, much under the influence of philosophy. Today it is a virtual truism that policy analysis cannot be "objective" or "value neutral." There is general dissatisfaction with the ideal of instrumental rationality, by which the analyst's task is presumably confined to seeking efficient measures to realize the purposes of an authoritative decision-maker. Means and ends are recognized to intertwine in analysis, with value judgment inherent in any exercise of public decision-making.

Through a more philosophically informed approach, policy analysis is understood as a process of argument: more like making a case than solving an equation or undertaking a scientific investigation. Policy analysis is part of political and ethical discourse generally. Thus what matters are the grounds or warrants offered for values introduced into argument. Policy theorists have begun to explore post-Wittgensteinian philosophy and phenomenology in quest of rules of discourse to guide rigorous normative analysis. Duncan MacRae, Jr. set the stage by suggesting that the rules of consistency, generality, and clarity which ground scientific communication apply also as tests of ethical assertion.[11] As William Dunn argues, "The growth of knowledge in the policy sciences thus demands open and critical discourse which, in turn, presupposes rules or standards of appraisal that make it possible for committed participants to examine rival ethical claims, but without any one participant dominating the outcome."[12] (Notice here the distinct flavor

----

[11] Duncan MacRae, Jr., **The Social Function of Social Science**, New Haven, Yale University Press, 1976, pp. 77-103.

of Habermas on undistorted communication.) To explore
this connection between the most speculative and the most
practical branches of political science strikes me as an
enticing exercise. For years, political philosophers have
had all too little to say to students of public administration
and policy, and vice versa.   But today, they share an
important interest.

Peculiarly suggestive about such applied normative
theory is its idea of method. Policy science aspires to systematic, yet practical political reason in order to prescribe
techniques and strategies of public decision-making. Policy
analysis sees itself as a craft; and in any craft, one of the
functions of theory is to specify rules of good practice. In
turn, this sets an interesting problem for the political philosopher: to show how studying history, deriving political
principles from ethical assumptions, or analyzing the languages of politics and ethics can be applied in concrete
situations that call for public choice. Like William James,
policy scientists are interested in the "cash value" of philosophical ideas.

This concern for systematic treatment of valuation in
policy science is an attempt to extend and develop the
framework of pragmatic philosophy itself. It represents a
recognition that the classically pragmatic conceptions of
puzzlement, inquiry, exploration, experiment, and discovery
are not sufficient for a doctrine of practical political action.
Pragmatism needs a more rigorous ethical and political
dimension, and policy theorists are now trying to supply it.
This effort may even lead to the development of a kind of
political theory better able to inform the future course of
political science.

A THEORY OF POLITICAL EDUCATION

Most political scientists find some degree of estrangement between their teaching and research interests,
between the materials that advance their purposes in the

----

[12] William N. Dunn, "Introduction: Symposium on Social
Values and Public Policy," **Policy Studies Journal**, 9, Special Issue 2, 1980-1981, pp. 519-521, on p. 519. On this
theme, also see: Frank Fischer, **Politics, Values and Public
Policy**, Boulder, Westview Press, 1980.

classroom and the research product of their specialties.[13] In some fields (notably decision-making and public administration), to be sure, theory and research do derive from a conception of educational mission. But we seldom ask the contribution to our ultimate educational purposes when assessing the worth of scholarship.

My own view is that any philosophy of political education culminates in a method of practical political reason and that every teacher of political science intimates a preferred mode of political cognition, appraisal, and judgment. In the pragmatic tradition, politics is understood primarily as a process of inquiry, and this may be the source of our notion that to think well politically is to think scientifically. Thus we presume the virtues of democratic citizenship can be taught by instilling students with the scientific spirit of objectivity, tentativity, and skepticism. Or we think it our function to "disillusion" our students, to liberate them from economically functional or socially convenient patterns of cognition so that autonomous reason can do its work. Or we conceive education as a marketplace of ideas, presuming it our role to portray all contending perspectives on a given theme and leaving it to students (following the rule of **caveat emptor**) to select personal orientations from the many possibilities. In any event, we talk little about such matters; and we seldom, if ever, attempt to justify the educational implications of our approaches to inquiry.

In the last analysis, the social function of political science is to prescribe a pattern of political cognition, a discipline of practical political reason, for a society. What else can be the point of our endeavor? We may doubt our influence in such matters, but we would be wise to act as if this were the case. Political science is a discipline, with rules of discourse and standards of significance that are, in ways customary to communities of inquiry, enforcible upon its members. Therefore at least to some extent, this must be a collective undertaking. Either we act as preservators of our culture and its values, or as critics. Thus it is an important part of the agenda of political theory to discuss the consequences of various approaches to political inquiry, cognition, and appraisal, understood as philosophies of political education. What if we were taken seriously by those we presume to instruct? This question is congenial to

----

[13] William C. Havard, "Political Education: Who Gets What, When, How and Why," **Journal of Politics**, 42, 4, November, 1980, pp. 934-950.

the pragmatic heritage of the profession. It is a test of the practical implications, the "cash value," of our ideas. But it is also a way to ask about the adequacy of pragmatic philosophy's own presuppositions and methods.

CONCLUSIONS

I have tried herein to specify a few strategic points at which mainstream political science seems ready for a more philosophically informed theory and to identify a few areas where current work in political philosophy seems suggestive for further development of the discipline as a whole. I have emphasized six areas where it would seem profitable to reaffirm or re-examine the legacy of pragmatic political science.

First, let us acknowledge forthrightly that we are the custodians of a tradition of discourse. This legacy may not be the ideal state of public consciousness, but it is what we have. It provides civility and coherence to our culture; many moves are possible within it; and its implications are far from exhausted. Second, we might use post-Wittgensteinian philosophy to begin an examination of the vocabularies of practical political life, as found in various professions, industries, and subcultures. This might provide an antidote to psychological or economic reductionism and enhance the capacity of political science to account for the institutional dynamics of pluralist society. Third, let us see whether the explorations of formal liberal theory can provide pragmatic philosophy with a more acute sense of the value dimensions imperative in public problem-solving. Fourth, let us re-examine the pragmatic conception of the positive state, asking critically whether we want to sustain or to modify this central paradigm for political research. Fifth, let us join the search of the policy sciences for a more adequate, because more normatively informed, sense of practical political reason. Finally, inasmuch as theories must monitor professional rules of discourse, let us ask how to test the significance of inquiry, not only by its contribution to a cumulative body of scientific propositions, but by its pertinence to political education as well.

This agenda for political theory will not be congenial to all. It will not attract those who persist in investing political science with the conceptual abstraction and methodological obscurity of more prestigious social sciences. Still, that vision of high science may be losing some of its lustre; and in the future there may be greater appreciation for socially meaningful research. Furthermore, to begin with the legacy of pragmatic political science is to affirm, not only the basic integrity of its intellectual enterprise, but also the conventions and institutions of democratic civilization. This, too, is controversial; for many practicing political philosophers stand estranged, both from the academic discipline and from the practices of everyday political life.

To be sure, social criticism is essential to the vocation of political theory. Yet there is more to theory than that alone. The kind I have recommended is constructive theory, which works in collaboration with ongoing politics, taking its cues from our puzzles and predicaments. Each project has a place in political theory, like the prophetic and pastoral functions in the life of the church. The task of the prophet is to chastize and criticize, to hold out utopian visions and to judge the affairs of everyday life from ultimate perspectives. But we also need a pastoral political theory, one of stewardship and husbandry, one which seeks to preserve and to build upon the institutions and practices of the going concern.

PART EIGHT

PRACTICES AND PRINCIPLES

EDUCATION FOR POLITICS:

RETHINKING RESEARCH ON

POLITICAL SOCIALIZATION

John S. Nelson

In irregular spasms since the Second World War, political scientists have become dissatisfied with existing programs of research and perplexed about the nature of theory, method, and objectivity in science. Their two general responses account for the contents and contours of much that now passes as scientific theorizing about politics. Some try to apply purportedly authoritative principles from philosophies of inquiry. These abstract conceptions are to be fleshed out: first into operative methods of political science and then into substantive theories of politics. Others try to emulate supposedly successful projects from other scientific disciplines. Then actual (if alien) theories and methods are imported along with broad standards of self-criticism: leaving only adaptation to the topics and purposes of political scientists to be accomplished. Often, of course, the two strategies are pursued in tandem.[1]

Of late, both borrowings have been criticized, even more for conception than execution.[2] The criticisms are impressive, but they easily go too far. For if all such borrowings were to cease, would political scientists retain sufficient resources for self-improvement? Because we have borrowed poorly in the past, does it follow that we should foreswear any further inspiration from other disciplines or

----

[1] Without inspiration from years of discussion with Youlika Kotsovolou Masry, this essay simply would not be. Greg Caldeira, Lane Davis, and Alan Stern also deserve credit for helping me to rethink the many modes and means of research on political socialization. I thank also the University of Iowa for its generous support of my research toward this essay.

[2] See: John G. Gunnell, **Philosophy, Science, and Political Inquiry**, Morristown, NJ, General Learning Press, 1975; Paul F. Kress, "Against Epistemology: Apostate Musings," **Journal of Politics**, 41, 2, May, 1979, pp. 526-542.

philosophies of inquiry? Criticisms of recent research in political science convince me that we cannot afford to forego outside guidance. The trick is to make our borrowing more imaginative and intelligent than before. Hence we must learn better **how to learn** from philosophies and programs of research beyond current political science.

The way to show this is not by abstract argument about principles of inquiry, after the fashion of all too many philosophers of science. Instead, it is by concrete consideration of an actual research project, drawn from the current work of political scientists. For several reasons, to become clear as we continue, I propose to focus on the field of political socialization.

Initiated in the heyday of behavioralism, research on political socialization represents well the conceptions and practices dominating scientific political theory during the past two decades. With many sources contributing to its growth, no field of political science has swelled more swiftly. Lately, however, the question has become whether any source can provide permanent impetus for the field, lending it purpose and coherence. Deep doubts about directions of research have surfaced among its researchers themselves. And their worries of theory, method, and objectivity make times right for reassessing the field: in itself, in its ties to other substantive studies, and in its relationship to philosophies of inquiry.

ARGUMENT

My overarching argument is that the field of political socialization has failed to see, let alone pursue, its true importance. This becomes clear when the field is reconstructed as a broader and deeper inquiry into political education. In turn, that should be reconceived to include not only inquiry into learning about politics but also inquiry into the politics of learning: the politics of inquiry itself.

Thus mine is an argument about what research on political socialization must learn from sound principles of inquiry. Yet part of what the field must learn is how to learn about itself. In turn, that includes what philosophies of inquiry can learn from studies of political socialization.

The field's self-misconception stems from uncritical acceptance of standards and strategies of inquiry hostile to its proper topics and techniques. It apes inapt projects from elsewhere in social science and then fails to adapt them to its own needs. Worse, it imports principles of inquiry from various logical positivisms and empiricisms. Sometimes, these principles are simply wrong; other times, they are inadequate or irrelevant. Either way, the result is ignorance of the field's real problems and promises of research. Both borrowings mislead substantive research on political socialization and continue to make impossible a sound sense of its potential significance.

Especially obnoxious is the field's borrowing from poor philosophies of science. Categories from logical positivism and empiricism cannot even express, let alone legitimate, a central project of research on political socialization: to inform a self-reflective philosophy of political inquiry. Nor can they appreciate the proper scope of such research. For it reaches beyond political socialization strictly construed to embrace all aspects of political learning, education, and inquiry: including those which we call "political science."

This argument spans four steps. The first identifies the biggest single shortcoming of studies in political socialization as their lack of consistent guidance by any theories at once substantive, coherent, and relevant. The second explains how that has led the field to fail in refining appropriate methods of inquiry. The third shows how a resulting mishmash of methods has pushed the field toward naive and self-defeating notions of objectivity, thereby preventing it from becoming constructively self-critical. And the fourth traces how this incapacity for full self-reflection has thus far made the field miss a great opportunity to spur all political research toward more accurate and productive principles and procedures of inquiry.

Research on political socialization has avoided consistent work with any body of theory at once substantive and coherent. "Systems theory" gives little concrete guidance about either politics or socialization. Anchored there, research on political socialization slips easily into ad hoc hypothesizing and confused attempts at testing. Gradual recognition of the need for substantive theory has spurred repeated borrowing of bits from theories established elsewhere, especially in psychology. But there has been little effective effort toward making the resulting patchworks cogent theories in their own right.

Instead of careful and comprehensive adaptation, such foreign theories have been plundered for isolated propositions and uncriticized assumptions. Torn away from their full contents and contexts, these fragments of theory can neither establish nor encourage coherent programs of research. They are easy victims of assaults by the largely alien methods which, far more than sound theories, now determine the field's modes of conjecture and refutation. Close connections of theory to epistemology (and hence to method) now go unnoticed, spawning a mindless succession of methological fads. Thus do theories, methods, and findings in this research fragment into incoherence.

In sum, research on political socialization is troubled by insufficient self-understanding. That traces in turn to lack of a sound philosophy of inquiry. In this condition, the field cannot escape confusion about its own projects. Pursuing a naive notion of objectivity, it overlooks the stronger, more sophisticated standards of self-criticism striving to rise from within. Worse, it even overlooks its own potential significance for the rest of political science and general philosophies of inquiry.

Ideally, studies of political socialization could teach much to philosophers of inquiry. This is because acquisition and transmission of (political) knowledge and error are appropriate topics of epistemology. It is also because recent epistemology suffers self-imposed isolation from substantive research, resulting in ignorance of how we actually inquire in politics, science, or other endeavors. Finally, it is because a few philosophers are now more sensitive to general needs for political skills and sophistication in pursuits of knowledge. For all three reasons, the times are increasingly in tune with such specific studies as the field of political socialization can contribute to general studies and skills of inquiry. Bringing these lessons to light, we can reconstruct research on political socialization in order to help it realize its own implicit principles of inquiry and its full, if surprising, promise.

Rethinking research on political socialization in this way is not meant to replace edicts of logical empiricism (or its political-science cousin of behavioralism) with some other set of alien, a priori, mechanical commands. To the contrary, its aim is to improve substantive studies along with the very philosophies of study which aid that improvement. Nor should a danger of "epistemological anarchism," after the fashion of Paul Feyerabend's philosophy of inquiry, stop us short.[3] Reconceiving rigor in research need not mean that anything goes. Indeed, the recommendations here should turn a sloppy field into one far more (if rather differently) rigorous than before.

----

[3] See: Paul K. Feyerabend, **Against Method**, Atlantic Highlands, NJ, Humanities Press, 1975.

All this requires, not a coup to switch one dictator of research with another, but a true revolution to change the forms for governing everyday investigation in political science. An adequate contextualism neither rejects epistemology altogether nor restricts it to retrospective accounts of substantive research. Instead, it develops dialogue between principles and experiences of inquiry, between abstract epistemology and actual, daily conduct of inquiry, with the idea that neither should be the same again.

In its largest implications, my argument is too adventurous to receive complete support, even in so ample a space as this. Still, the failure of research on political socialization to live up to its promise cannot be comprehended without covering all four steps of the argument. Accordingly, I concentrate here on the sweep of the argument as a whole, providing as much support for each step as I can without stumbling into intractable details.[4] We need to know what went wrong with political socialization research, how to put it right again, and what this implies for relations between philosophies of inquiry and sciences of politics.

THEORY

Two bodies of theory have dominated research on political socialization. At its inception, the field was tied to species of structural functionalism. More recently, it has turned to psychology. But in both cases, flaws of the theories themselves or their uses have left studies of political socialization as close to the behavioralist bete-noire of barefoot empiricism as can be found in current political science. The field has never really understood what theories are or do, despite its special emphasis on standard behavioralist calls for theory and its pride in theoretical sophistication.[5] The absence of actual theories which has stopped

----

[4] Thus I forego innumerable citations to relevant articles and books on political socialization, for they could easily crowd out the argument which warrants them. I likewise limit references to works on epistemology and scientific inquiry. The few citations I do provide are bulging with lists of relevant materials.

the field of political socialization short of "continuous, general comprehension" of itself.

If anything has been calling a tune for research on political socialization, it would be fadish methods adapted from other fields of political science. However much this simply repeats the general pattern of political science, though, research on political socialization labors under two extra burdens: its founding "theories" provide almost no relevant social or political content, but their best replacements run against the grain of behavioralist methods and canons.

Because structural-functionalist "theories" have been almost empty of concepts and propositions aimed specifically at political socialization, researchers have been left largely to their own devices. As a result, the field has had recourse to the full range of ad hoc hypothesizing. Even its turn to psychology for theories of social and political substance has helped little thus far. Instead of careful and comprehensive adaptation, such theories have simply been plundered for isolated propositions, uncriticized assumptions, and fragmented methods. Lumping together claims from different theories for testing in terms of foreign methods looks better on the surface, but actually accomplishes little more than any other ad hoc move. These are the main points to be established by detailed treatment of the field's default from theory to method.

----

[5] See: Jack Dennis, "Major Problems of Political Socialization Research," in Dennis, ed., **Socialization to Politics**, New York, Wiley, 1973, pp. 2-27, on pp. 2-3: "a number of attempts to lay down theoretical foundations for the field or some part of it have been made by such writers as Easton, Hess, Almond, Verba, Greenstein, Mitchell, Froman, Pye and others....Beyond exhibiting vitality these several studies show a serious concern for theory and its uses in directing empirical research. This is a quality that is by no means as apparent in other, better established branches of behavioral political inquiry....Because the political socialization specialists have persistently engaged in these several types of theoretical discourse, there is a relatively good chance of avoiding hyperfactualism; and there are better than average prospects, therefore, for maintaining a continuous, general comprehension of the 'state of the discipline' by its members."

STRUCTURAL FUNCTIONALISM

In the beginning and still today, explicit inspiration for research on political socialization has most often been sought from David Easton's writing on systems and Talcott Parsons' treatment of social action. There are many self-proclaimed systems theories other than Easton's and many approaches to action other than Parsons'. Still, theirs are the two bodies of work holding sway in studies of political socialization.

Why researchers on political socialization were attracted to the work of Easton and Parsons is easy to understand. Of course, Easton himself played a direct part in producing and promoting political socialization as a distinct field of research. But beyond his personal role, the self-professed behavioralists who founded the field of politi-.cal socialization learned from logical positivism and empiricism to see theories as abstract tools of analysis (rather than concrete representations of reality).[6] Easton and Parsons provided the two "theories" most prominent in political science when political socialization coalesced as a field. As that implies, they were also among the most abstract and analytical "theories" available.

Yet the very abstraction prized by students of political socialization has proved the main defect of functionalism as a foundation for their field. Strangely, neither Easton's nor Parsons' functionalism has much to contribute to concrete research in the field. Most commonly, both are accused of covert conservatisms, said to be concealed beneath veneers of value neutrality. This is a standard complaint against most forms of structural functionalism. And indeed, the criticism makes some sense, although more for specific studies than for functionalist strategies of explanation. It is no accident that functionalist inquiries have been obviously, if not overtly, conservative in most cases. Yet the reasons are often more subtle and variable than those cited by critics.[7]

----

[6] Strict abstraction, formalism, and instrumentalism have been rejected as necessary features of theory by many who have rejected logical positivism and empiricism. See: Frederick Suppe, ed., **The Structure of Scientific Theories**, Urbana, University of Illinois Press, 1973.

[7] See: John S. Nelson, "Meaning and Measurement across Paradigms: Metaphor and Irony in Political Inquiry," paper

Insofar as "theories" after the fashion of Easton and Parsons are the focus, though, the remarkable feature of structural functionalism is its absence of specifically political content and implication. This encourages a kind of conservatism but certainly does not require it. Moreover, it is a most peculiar "conservatism," different indeed from what the word usually calls to mind. In supporting these points, I interchange particulars from the "theories" of Easton and Parsons, since they are roughly equivalent as vehicles of structural functionalism in research on political socialization. Both suffer the defects identified here.

After criticisms by C. Wright Mills and many others, the emptiness engendered by the sweeping abstraction of Parsons' action theory should be well known.[8] In its own peculiar way, Parsons' work on **The Social System** probably offers more specifics on politics in general and political socialization in particular than does Easton's approach to **The Political System**.[9] Even Parsons' approach, though, remains far too abstract for unaided direction of detailed research. Moreover, many of its apparently useful particulars manage only precarious connections to the main pillars of Parsons' "theory," thus violating the very rigor for which it was chosen in the first place.

Neither body of work can be considered in great

----

presented to the Annual Meeting of the American Political Science Association, Washington, D. C., September 1-4, 1977. And remember that many Marxists pursue and defend funtionalist theories.

[8] See: C. Wright Mills, **The Sociological Imagination**, New York, Oxford University Press, 1959; Martin Landau, "On the Use of Functionalist Analysis in American Political Science," **Social Research**, 35, 1, Spring, 1968, pp. 48-75; Lewis Lipsitz, "If, as Verba Says, the State Functions as a Religion, What Are We to Do Then to Save Our Souls?" **American Political Science Review**, 62, 2, June, 1968, pp. 527-535. Also see: Irving Louis Horowitz, "Sociology and Politics: The Myth of Functionalism Revisisted," **Journal of Politics**, 25, 2, May, 1963, pp. 248-264; Joan Smith, "The Failure of Functionalism," **Philosophy of the Social Sciences**, 5, 1, March, 1975, pp. 33-42; Anthony Giddens, "Functionalism: Apres la lutte," **Social Research**, 43, 2, Summer, 1976, pp. 325-366; Peter A. Munch, "The Concept of 'Function' and Functional Analysis in Sociology," **Philosophy of the Social Sciences**, 6, 3, September, 1976, pp. 193-213.

detail here.   Hence I shall concentrate on Easton's systems theory.   It duplicates most of the independent contributions to research on political socialization inspired by Parsons' project, and it reveals the commitments of functionalism a little more clearly.   Many who appeal to some form of functionalism as a foundation for studying political socialization have combined the two.   Finally, Easton's version has from the first had a deeper influence in determining the language and orientation of research in the field.

Basically, neither Easton's nor Parsons' functionalism affords a theory of political socialization.   Worse, neither even offers a theory of some matter more or less directly related to political socialization.   There are two sides to such a criticism: whether the main body of either Easton's or Parsons' work should be counted as a theory and whether either has much specific guidance to give research on political socialization.   These functionalisms may fail to be theories at all.   If they are theories, their domain is analysis itself, rather than any particular matter to be analyzed.   As such, they are poor theories of analysis, since they presume a complete split of the forms and techniques of analysis from the contents of analysis.   And in any event, not even a good theory of analysis can either serve as a theory of political socialization or eliminate the need for one.

As these sources imply, most points about Parsons' functionalism apply also to the functionalisms of Robert Merton in sociology, A. R. Radcliffe-Brown in anthropology, and many people in political science: Gabriel Almond, Sidney Verba, Norman Nie, Bingham Powell, and others.   But care is required here, for there are aspects of these functionalisms which do not fit the Parsons mold.   Moreover, there are functionalisms of fully different molds: those of Claude Levi-Strauss and G. A. Cohen, to name but two.

[9]   See: David Easton, **The Political System**, New York, Knopf, (1953), second edition, 1971; Easton and Jack Dennis, **Children in the Political System**, New York, McGraw-Hill, 1969; Talcott Parsons, **The Social System**, New York, Free Press, 1951; Parsons and Neil J. Smelser, **Economy and Society**, New York, Free Press, 1956; Parsons, **Essays in** Sociological Theory@, New york, Free Press, (1949), revised edition, 1954; Parsons and Edward A. Shils, eds., **Toward a General Theory of Action**, New York, Harper and Row, 1951.

In the main, I doubt that either Easton's or Parsons' work deserves to be called a "theory." That accounts for my quotation marks around the word when it designates either body of work. Thus Easton is precisely right to term his contribution **A Framework for Political Analysis**, except that there is no reason to limit his principles of analysis to politics alone.[10] Look at Easton's key concepts: system, environment, response, feedback, input and output, demand and support, unit and boundary, interaction, and so on. Nowhere in this or any more exhaustive list is there much specific to analysis of **politics**, let alone political socialization. By posing it as prior to substantive theorizing about politics, Easton himself implies that such a framework falls short of actual political theory.

Such conceptual frameworks should not be confused with substantive theories.[11] They range from isolated ideal types to mere modes of analysis. But they never achieve the diverse, concrete contents of theories. Their strict formal consistency is gained through extreme abstraction, leading away from specifics which would constitute a theoretical domain. If this functionalism projects theories, they are theories of analysis and classification alone. If Easton presents a theory, it is a theory of systems, of modes of analysis. If Parsons achieved a general theory of action, it is so abstract as to cover not only any kind of action, but almost anything at all. And of course, "theories" that cover almost everything explain almost nothing.

This accounts for the ways in which such "theories" seem so generally applicable and yet also so flexible or even empty. Such functionalism is bereft of substance, in any ordinary sense. This is how it can cover almost any topic and angle of application. Making a virtue of this vice, Easton insists that the units and boundaries of systems of analysis may be drawn any where and way that pleases the social scientist. "Since by definition any set of interactions may be labeled a system, the appropriate question to pose is whether a particular kind of abstracted behavior, to be identified shortly as political, constitutes a scientifically

----

[10] David Easton, **A Framework for Political Analysis**, Englewood Cliffs, NJ, Prentice-hall, 1965.

[11] See: John G. Gunnell, "The Idea of the Conceptual Framework: A Philosophical Critique," **Journal of Comparative Administration**, 1, 2, August, 1969, pp. 140-176.

interesting one."[12] Several critics have targeted precisely this substantive emptiness and arbitrariness of Easton's systems theory.[13] This is one reason that propositions from these "theories" tend to turn into mere tautologies, definitions, or truisms upon testing or any other treatment which requires specifying their unduly general pronouncements. To be sure, such systems of analysis are hardly worthless in social science, where clear thinking has not always been the rule. But they are no substitute for substantive theories.

In addition, the frameworks of Easton and Parsons are suspect because of their predication on the one principle that no adequate theory of analysis can stand. Both suggest that there need be no significant connection between the shape and dynamic of study (on the one side) and the subject of study (on the other). Both are poor theories of analysis precisely because they try implicitly to confine shifting distinctions between form and content, analytic and synthetic, and so on into a single, rigid dichotomy. Unable to succeed at this, they actually do carry some substantive commitments concerning subjects of study. But the commitments are kept covert or even unconscious, suppressed by a strict split between frameworks of analysis and contents of inquiry. Hence the commitments frequently fail to connect well with the matters at hand. And the paradoxical result is unsystematic inquiry and analytically incoherent findings.[14]

Neither "theory" provides natural grounds for plunking systems down here rather than there. Nor can it

----

[12] Easton, **A Framework for Political Analysis**, pp. 44-45.

[13] See: Paul F. Kress, "Self, System, and Significance -- Reflections on Professor Easton's Political Science," **Ethics**, 77, 1, October, 1966, pp. 1-13; Eugene F. Miller, "David Easton's Political Theory," Political Science Reviewer, **1, Fall, 1971, pp. 184-235; David Easton,** "Systems Analysis and Its Classical Critics," **Political Science Reviewer**, 3, Fall, 1973, pp. 269-301; J. S. Sorzano, "David Easton and the Invisible Hand," **American Political Science Review**, 69, 1, March, 1975, pp. 91-106.

[14] Compare my parallel partly argument about some survey research: John S. Nelson, "The Ideological Connection, Parts I and II," **Theory and Society**, 4, 3-4, Fall-Winter, 1977, pp. 421-448 and 574-590.

uncover such grounds, since its very power and neutrality seem to come from sustaining its initial separation from the substance to be analyzed. Implicitly, substance and science are dichotomized.[15] Failure to appreciate the inevitable interaction of form and content, as of analysis and synthesis, prevents such functionalism from fulfilling its promise as a theory of analysis, let alone as a generator of theories about social or political reality.

Still, this is not a failure of all systems theories and certainly not of all theories of analysis. The key point is that, although good theories of analysis may begin as conceptual frameworks for approaching substantive concerns, they end as full-fledged theories of the domains to which they are applied. Or at least, they engender such substantive theories. By constituting substantive domains, these theories open themselves to testing and reshaping in a truly "empirical" way. They become more than mere frameworks of analysis; they become substantive theories of some reality.[16] Such reality involves analysis, because it involves those who analyze. Actual theories of political reality are about analysis, because they account at least partly for their own creators, conditions, and characteristics. But truly political theories are not about analysis alone.

That the systems theories of Easton and Parsons lack accounts of the analyzers, the systematizers, is a major defect from the standpoint of research on political socialization. Such research could and should drive directly toward treatments of political scientists as objects and agents of political socialization. Yet the field has attended little to the latter and not at all to the former. Of course, to admit that research on political socialization is crucial for the self-comprehension of political science is to reject the positivist and empiricist conceptions of scientific objectivity

----

[15] Trade-off between substantive significance and scientific rigor has been a continuing theme of Philip L. Beardsley's work: "Substantive Significance vs. Quantitative Rigor in Political Inquiry: Are the Two Compatible?," **International Interactions**, 1, 1, 1974, pp. 27-40; **Redefining Rigor**, Beverly Hills, Sage, 1980; **Conflicting Ideologies in Political Economy**, Beverly Hills, Sage, 1981.

[16] This suggests a significant sense in which "reality" can be a collective noun, an implicit plural. In this volume, see my essay on "Political Theory as Political Rhetoric."

basic to the field ever since its behavioralist beginnings.

Plainly, political scientists are socialized politically through their discipline as well as other agents. Just as plainly, this is bound to affect findings on political socialization, not to mention other subjects. Yet this very idea affronts the principles of scientific neutrality and method upon which the field of political socialization is founded. To suggest that this connection is a good thing, to be cultivated rather than overcome, is to scandalize both behavioralists and their successors in political science. Their latent, looming crisis of self-comprehension has been avoided about the only way possible: by banishing **overtly political theory** from any important place in studies of political socialization. Substituting conceptual frameworks of functionalism for substantive theories of politics, researchers seek to free themselves from detailed problematics, which might demand self-reflection.

The most obvious feature of these "theories" is their lack of specific content concerning political socialization. Neither provides the details that even a poor theory of political socialization must contain. Easton's "theory" seems to concern problems of political legitimacy. But even there, its contribution lies mostly in a distinction between diffuse and specific support which is itself so diffuse as to be mildly notorious among students of public opinion, representation, and related topics.[17] Impoverished even as a framework for analyzing legitimacy, these concepts plainly fall far short of the rich complex of distinctions actually needed for a theory of legitimacy, let alone political socialization. Nor has Parsons "theory" offered much better. At their most detailed, such forms of structural functionalism amount to little more than logics of role-analysis. Worse, they seldom approach the sophistication of role theories like those of Goffman and Sarbin.[18]

----

[17] See: Jack Dennis, Leon Lindberg, and Donald McCrone, "Support for Nation and Government among English Children," **British Journal of Political Science**, 7, 1, January, 1971, pp. 25-48; Edward N. Muller, "Behavioral Correlates of Political Support," **American Political Science Review**, 71, 2, June, 1977, pp. 454-467; David Easton, "A Re-Assessment of the Concept of Political Support," **British Journal of Political Science**, 5, 4, October, 1975, pp. 435-457.

[18] See: Erving Goffman, **Relations in Public**, New York, Harper and Row, 1971; Goffman, **Frame Analysis**, New

For both Easton and Parsons, systems theory is the scientific alternative to radical dialectic, which is also a framework of analysis and sometimes functionalist to boot. For them, as for other liberals, science means neutrality means replacing substance with procedure. By this bargain, the status of science is purchased at the price of (political) substance. Minimally, theories are reduced from substantive conceptions of reality to neutral instruments of research: mere models at most. Moderately, theories are replaced or confused with methods in guiding research. Maximally, theories are redirected to domains of method (rather than social or political substance). The subtle result is a shift of social science from ontology to epistemology.

Lack of substance is the reason that many allegations of a systematic bias of such functionalism toward conservatism miss the mark. Systems theories are seldom rich enough in political detail to sustain the charge that they are vehicles for smuggling standard kinds of conservatism into the sterile research rooms of social science. Nonetheless, systems theories do evidence an elective affinity for stability. That is, they encourage conservatism in style and sensibility. This can become straightforwardly political conservatism, but its tie to system theories remains loosely symbolical rather than strictly logical.[19] More often than not, therefore, systems theories favor the status quo. And far more often than not, they focus on problems of political

----

York, Harper and Row, 1974; Theodore R. Sarbin, "Role: Psychological Aspects," in David L. Sills, ed., **International Encyclopedia of the Social Sciences**, New York, Macmillan, 1968, Volume 13, pp. 546-552; Sarbin, "Schizophrenic Thinking: A Role-Theoretical Analysis," **Journal of Personality**, 37, 1, June, 1969, pp. 190-206. Also see: Eileen M Loudfoot, "The Concept of Social Role," **Philosophy of the Social Sciences**, 2, 2, June, 1972, pp. 133-145; Evan Fales, "The Ontology of Social Roles," **Philosophy of the Social Sciences**, 7, 2, June, 1977, pp. 139-161.

[19] This line of thought came to me in discussions with Youlika Kotsovolou Masry. It is related to her arguments in: "Un essai d'application du modele d'Easton," **Greek Review of Social Research**, 17, 1873, pp. 99-109; **Political Theory, the Category of the "Whole," and the Psychoanalytic Perspective**, doctoral dissertation, Department of Political Science, University of North Carolina at Chapel Hill, 1981.

stability. This kind of "conservatism" is compatible with a variety of political positions. Indeed, most functionalists have sought to "conserve" political liberalism, the basic ideology of American politics and the science thereof. But there is nothing strictly necessary about this. Some functionalists are even Marxists; and of course, their researches are often at odds with a stability bias. The Marxists, too, tend to be mesmerized by issues of legitimacy, stability, and order. But not even that complex of questions is required by functionalism per se. Still, these "conservative" concerns are very much in the style of functionalism, even if not in its (missing) substance.

Peculiarly flexible and limited, this style of conservatism comes from precisely the lack of political substance which prevents functionalism from being conservative in a more ordinary sense. The elective affinity between systems theories and this conservative style stems from the fact that, without substance, there can be no change. Absent substance and an appreciation of it, systems theories cannot understand change of an actual system. In turn, their ability to understand change in an actual system is limited, since external agents of change can seldom be severed completely from those internal to a system. This problem increases as the units and boundaries of a system become more arbitrary, because reasons for including some factors and excluding others are reduced as the system grows less substantive. The result is a strong, but subtle bias for problems and principles of stability.

Yet this bias can be overridden by substantive interests external to functionalism. Indeed, its very emptiness virtually invites interjection of detailed interests from some external source: the more covert or unconscious, the better. Political socialization was conceived in a climate of concerns about change and legitimacy, for these dominated establishment liberalism in the United States at the time. Beneath the surface of early socialization research is a sense of turmoil, spurring a turn to topics of allegiance and legitimacy.[20] Ever since, the substantive orientation of research on political socialization has come mostly from these secret concerns, rather than any sense of purposes and

----

[20] See: Philip Green and Sanford Levinson, eds., **Power and Community**, New York, Random House, 1969; Peter L. Berger, **Pyramids of Sacrifice**, New York, Basic Books, 1974; Marshall Berman, "Sympathy for the Devil," **American Review**, 19, January, 1974, pp. 23-75.

processes bestowed by the various "theories" of the field. At least until recently, then, research on political socialization has had no substantive theories to guide it. Instead, it has proceeded primarily by ad hoc hypothesizing.

AD HOC HYPOTHESIZING

In studies of political socialization, reliance on ad hoc hypothesizing has hardly been an occasional lapse. On the contrary, the behavioralist principle that research must be directed by theory in order to be scientific and productive has been seldom been practiced. (Of course, it has been preached all the more vigorously for that.) To make up for this absence of substance, researchers have looked outside the field to four main modes or sources of hypotheses: politics, methods, paradigms, and theories about related topics.

POLITICS. Political hypotheses have been drawn from both general events or conditions and personal interests or positions. As these vary, so do researches on political socialization. For the most part, though, their effects on the field are glacial. This probably says less about research on political socialization than political science, academic politics, and American politics (in ascending order of importance). In structuring actual research, implicitly political commitments of method, paradigm, and external theory either interact with or override these more explicitly political sources of ad hoc conjecture. Linked by elective affinities, these other political impulsions are themselves loose and flexible. Thus the pulls and pushes of political influence can be very difficult to sort out, even in individual instances.

Still, the larger point remains that political interests of all kinds can play proper parts in research on socialization or other political topics. Propriety ought to be judged case by case, because what prejudices research here can have a reasonable role there. Thus the problem is not that some hypotheses are politically inspired, but that there is little real theory to provide the criteria and sense of context needed for keeping such hypotheses in place and complementing them with propositions from within the field. Whether its sources are political or otherwise, ad hoc hypothesizing is neither always bad nor altogether avoidable. Still, ad hoc hypotheses ultimately depend on integration into theories within the field. Research does not progress by hypothesizing alone or even largely. This is what the field of political socialization seems to have forgotten.

In research on political socialization, the easiest example of inspiration by general political events and conditions is the proliferation of studies about effects of the Watergate Crisis on postures toward the presidency.[21] There are good reasons to investigate repercussions of apparently important events. But why ape public-opinion polls in noting variation of moods and attitudes from one signal event to the next? To defend this is to note that a plausible theory of political socialization shows such variations to be important politically (as trends) or scientifically (as tests). Mapping reactions to assassinations of the sixties, scandals of the seventies, or events of the eighties easily leads supplants understanding the anatomy and physiology of political socialization with mere monitoring of declarations on the state of the Union. We cannot know whether and how those declarations are significant without a theory to pattern and explain them.

Without substantive theories of political socialization, turning to politics for research inspirations can readily become sheer collection of facts. Along with too many other political scientists, students of political socialization are inclined to confuse regression results with theories. Such correlationism is a far larger danger to the field than any corruption of scientific objectivity from putting the field on a political footing.

METHODS. Without detailed direction from its own theories, research on political socialization is often guided by appropriation of methods from other fields of political science. Methods in mind, researchers shape hypotheses to fit questions which a given means seems able to answer. Worse, researchers choose subjects and angles of study according to methods available, not even projecting any particular hypotheses in advance. Not all good hypotheses precede substantive study, but seldom posing hypotheses prior to mucking in data makes a mockery of scientific procedures endorsed by behavioralists themselves. Philosophies of hypothesis and deduction fall apart when researchers seldom test prior propositions implied by a relevant theory. By these philosophies, at least, there can be no

----

[21] Oddly, the rush to study these effects has resulted in only a few articles, far fewer than initial flurries of questionnaires might have projected. By publication time, political socialization was no longer the hot topic it had been only a few years before. Political science is a fickle and faddish discipline.

true testing of "hypotheses" derived from "testing" itself.

Without theories, how can good questions and plausible answers be identified? Without prior hypotheses, how can good methods be conceived and executed? Political inspiration of hypotheses cannot compensate for theoretical voids. Thus methodism fills the breach, and sheer correlation rules the field. But state-of-the-art statistics are becoming too complex and flexible to use well without substantial theories in the background to inform necessary decisions in applying proper techniques to collecting and processing data. Moreover, patterns projected by various techniques are too vulnerable to vagaries of interpretation to be tackled without theoretical guidance.

The field at hand has compounded these problems by trying to force every fragment of evidence and theory into accord with methods of testing chosen for their familiarity in other fields. Early reliance on surveys (all too similar to those prominent in studying adult attitudes toward politics) has already been rejected by some researchers, although others continue to work in that mode. Even where lessons have been learned from this first folly, however, they have been too limited. Instead of seeing that methods must be shaped to research requirements, not vice versa, the field has simply appealed to other alien methods. At best, it imports new methods for shaping research and then does a decent job of adapting them to tasks mysteriously at hand. (But even adaptations go awry, as I explain later.) Lost in this shuffle is the main lesson. **Methods must follow from theories, not theories from methods.**

PARADIGMS. The largest single source of ad hoc hypotheses in research on political socialization is extant research in this and other fields. In Thomas Kuhn's terms, study cues come from "paradigms" or (more precisely) "exemplars."[22] That some might take this as a compliment merely reveals anew how poorly the nature and need for theories is understood. For however ambiguous "paradigm" might be, it is far from synonymous with "theory." Paradigmatic research need involve no explicit, substantive theories at all. Its basic idea is to emulate a fine piece of research from another area. Thus did early research on the benevolence of American presidents in the eyes of

----

[22] See: Thomas S. Kuhn, **The Structure of Scientific Revolutions**, Chicago, University of Chicago Press, (1962), enlarged edition, 1970; Nelson, "Meaning and Measurement across Paradigms."

schoolchildren prompt similar studies in other locales.[23] The same research strategy produced a famous study of the malevolence of American presidents as seen by schoolchildren in economically throttled Appalachia.[24] More broadly, impetus toward surveys of children came from an impulse to imitate the "success" of such research on adults. Later methods have spread in similar ways.

Such emulation should not be confused with replication of results. Although that receives all the respect a methods text can give, it is seldom tried and little attended. (Ignoring the philosophers for a change, political scientists have come to see that it is usually hard, often impossible, and probably never necessary in their actual inquiries.) Emulation, on the other hand, is almost everywhere. Taking hypotheses from a research literature can involve testing another's ideas in different setting or applying them to a different problem. Either move can be meritorious. Misleadingly, imaginative moves of the former kind are sometimes called "scientific replication," while research bordering on real repetition is termed "trivial." Clever moves of the latter sort are praised as "scientific inspirations," whereas clumsy ones are condemned as "mistaken applications." The key point, though, is that merit must remain difficult to assess until theoretical criteria come on the scene.

Equally ad hoc are hypotheses spurred by a researcher's sense of "holes" left by previous projects. Such research produces highly technical patchwork which enlightens us little, if at all. For there is an infinity of these "gaps" in any paradigm of political research. One thing that a theory does is tell us which holes need filling. It gives research a set of substantive priorities coming from

----

[23] See: Fred I. Greenstein, "The Benevolent Leader: Children's Images of Political Authority," **American Political Science Review**, 54, 4, December, 1960, pp. 934-943; Greenstein, **Children and Politics**, New Haven, Yale University Press, 1965; Greenstein, "The Benevolent Leader Revisited: Children's Images of Political Leaders in Three Democracies," **American Political Science Review**, 69, 4, December, 1975, pp. 1371-1398.

[24] See: Dean Jaros, Herbert Hirsch, and Frederic J. Fleron, Jr., "The Malevolent Leader: Political Socialization in an American Subculture," **American Political Science Review**, 62, 2, June, 1968, pp. 564-575.

a conception of the subject itself. Without theories, research on political socialization has had trouble telling its holes from its findings.

EXTERNAL THEORIES. All along, research on political socialization has carved hypotheses from the corpus of one or another theory outside the field. Implicitly or explicitly, this involves removing propositions from the theoretical context in which they were conceived and through which they should be tested. Typically, the full theory itself is either ignored or repudiatd. Thus have old theories of political education, new theories of social knowledge, and various theories of psychological change been plundered for propositional gems.

This procedure is predicated on the behavioralist conceit that familiar methods are both adequate and required for assessing any serious statements, regardless of context. (Behind this is an insistence on formal models of explanation and operational techniques of testing.) But even on this (discredited) view, the notion of testing propositions apart from their theories makes no sense. For example, a theory tells whether key concepts can be operationalized in particular ways for particular tests (or other purposes). Indeed, although oscillation between atomism of propositions and deductivism of theories sometimes misplaces this point, even the behavioralist insists that scientists test theories, not individual propositions.

As an example, let me cite on of the better projects in the field, for it shows how a good move can be ruined if not pursued appropriately. Most studies of political socialization turn on two principles taken from psychoanalytic theory. The primacy principle states that things learned earliest are learned best and most enduringly, with profound implications for later life. The structuring principle says that general attitudes or orientations shape specific beliefs (and thus, presumably, behaviors) to a significant degree. The first step in testing and refining such principles should be to explicate the theory in which they take shape and from which they take substance. Through spelling out their meaning and significance, sensible methods for assessing them could be identified. But in the standard style of research on political socialization, Donald Searing and several collaborators moved immediately away from psychoanalytic theory, turning toward uses in research at hand. Thus the principles were "tested" through statistical manipulation of survey data on adults, when truly appropriate tests could be conducted only through depth interviews and other psychoanalytic methods seldom deployed by political scientists.[25]

The problem here is that previous research on political socialization affords virtually no context for specifying these principles in any way, not to mention the ways peculiar to psychoanalytic theory itself. When unpacked apart from proper contexts, the two principles are mazes of ambiguity. It is hard to see how such tests of survey research actually touch the psychoanalytic principles presumably at issue. Worse, it is not clear what has been tested, well or otherwise, since no theory lends the context and criteria crucial for answering these questions. In that case, can we even say that a test has taken place? This pernicious paradox is produced repeatedly by untheoretical research. Testing propositions apart from their theories is just another kind of ad hoc hypothesizing.

PSYCHOLOGICAL THEORIES

More than a few students of political socialization have see that their functionalisms are not substantive theories and that ad hoc hypothesizing will not suffice. From anthropology and cybernetics, some are drawing full theories of learning, communication, and acculturation. But most are looking to psychology for theories salient to political socialization.

The result is an emerging tie between the fields of political socialization and political psychology. This is evident in work by Fred Greenstein, Judith Torney-Purta, Richard Mereleman, Dani Thomas, and others.[26] Sometimes

----

[25] See: Donald D. Searing, Joel J. Schwartz, and Alden E. Lind, "The Structuring Principle: Political Socialization and Belief Systems," American Political Science Review, 67, 2, June, 1973, pp. 415-432; Searing, Gerald Wright, and George Rabinowitz, "The Primacy Principle: Attitude Change and Political Socialization," British Journal of Political Science, 6, 1, January, 1976, pp. 83-113; Ronald B. Rapoport, "The Sex Gap in Political Persuading: Where the 'Structuring Principle' Works," American Journal of Political Science, 25, 1, February, 1981, pp. 32-47; Nelson, "The Ideological Connection."

[26] See: Fred I. Greenstein, "A Note on the Ambiguity of 'Political Socialization': Definitions, Criticisms, and Strategies of Inquiry," Journal of Politics, 32, 4, November,

fields are more switched than integrated, but there is a strong drive to synthesize.   The Department of Political Science of the State University of New York at Stony Brook has pioneered laboratory facilities for experiments on political dimensions of psycho-physics and -physiology, plus other areas potentially relevant to political socialization.   No longer is Robert Lane almost the only political scientist skilled in theories and techniques of depth psychology; for he has been joined by Arnold Rogow, Alan Stern, Jane Flax, and others interested in political socialization.[27] Humanist and (especially) cognitivist theories also direct some research.   At last, whole theories figure in research on political socialization.

But for all its new-found theories, psychological and otherwise, the field remains weak.   It is plagued by at least three recurring infections from the old styles of inquiry.   Of course, the contagions carried by eager traders, missionaries, and immigrants from political science may menace the psychological theories more than their new neighbors.   Careless, partial, and sometimes stupid uses of depth psychology already threatens to discredit "psychohistory."   At a minimum, preventive measures are in order. And they surely involve self-critical diagnosis of dangers in working with new theories.

Easiest to identify, if not to cure, is the chronic tendency to plunder propositions rather than adapt new

----

1970, pp. 969-978; Judith V. Torney-Purta, "Children's Social Cognition: Recent Psychological Research and Its Implications for Social and Political Education," **Teaching Political Science**, 8, 3, April, 1981, 297-318; Richard M. Merelman, "The Family and Political Socialization: Toward a Theory of Exchange," **Journal of Politics**, 42, 2, May, 1980, pp. 461-486; Dani B. Thomas, "Psychodynamics, Symbolism, and Socialization: 'Object Relations' Perspectives on Personality, Ideology, and Political Perception," **Political Behavior**, 1, 3, Fall, 1979, pp. 243-268; Richard G. Niemi, ed., **The Politics of Future Citizens**, San Francisco, Jossey Bass, 1974.

[27] See: Robert E. Lane, **Political Thinking and Consciousness**, Chicago, Markham, 1969; Kenneth Keniston, **The Uncommitted**, New York, Dell, 1960; Keniston, **Young Radicals**, New York, Harcourt, Brace and World, 1968; Robert Jay Lifton, **Thought Reform and the Psychology of Totalism**, New York, Norton, 1961.

theories wholly to the field. As explained above, this first syndrome defeats adequate assessment of hypotheses. For only full theories can comprehend the principles, practices, and processes of a complicated phenomenon such as political socialization.

The second syndrome besetting the turn to psychological theories is failure to research the full processes of political socialization projected by any particular theory. One part receives excessive attention; other parts go unstudied. Sadly, it is often hard to comprehended any one part separate from the others. This syndrome plagues research predicated on behaviorist psychologies. To date, study of responses dominates; and stimuli are seldom studied. Thus agents and means of political socialization in schools are neglected in favor (presumed) responses to such stimuli.[28] Yet without substantive study of the stimuli, there is little basis for inferring that specific behaviors (let alone attitudes) are responses of political socialization. According to the very theories invoked, then, any sense of how political socialization proceeds must remain more a matter of supposition than research. In this way, substantive theories lose their value (and validity) in research.

The obvious excuse for unbalanced diets of research is that these theories are relatively new to the maws of political science. But the pattern of disproportionality belies this. Flawed understanding of individual theories and of theory generally is all too evident here. Residual empiricisms and methodisms continue to trouble the field.

Chronic subservience to methods poorly selected and applied is the third ill still besetting the study of political socialization. Even as the field strives for greater sensitivity to substantive theory, methodism manifests itself in at least ill-conceived attempts. First, the field tries to test new theories by old methods of other fields of political science. Second, it tries to take over new psychological methods without adapting them adequately to its new applications. Third, it tries to fit new techniques to old ideas of methodology, left over from the rhetorics of logical positivism and empiricism which dominated the early days of the field. As a general rule, none of these attempts can succeed. They reveal a failure to understand adequate relationships between theories and methods.

----

[28] For an exception, see: Charles Harrington, "Textbooks and Political Socialization: A Multivariate Analysis," **Teaching Political Science**, 7, 4, July, 1980, 481-500.

As a whole, political science has a poor understanding of the nature of theories. Actual theories have been both scarce and suppressed within political science. As a result, the discipline has virtually no appreciation of (scientific) theories as complicated structures of interdependent arguments that invoke rich varieties of evidence. Its conception of what can and should count as "empirical evidence" (a redundancy if ever there were one) is unbelievably narrow, based more on familiarities imparted in training than any imaginative attempt to support an argument persuasively. But then, political science seldom pursues or produces the kinds of extended, detailed arguments characteristic of theoretical work. Instead, members generally "report findings" to the discipline.

These "findings" usually result from applying techniques of regression analysis to bodies of data thought (for reasons often underspecified) to relate to some question unresolved by previous research. Tacitly, the discipline thus expects to progress by building small sets of correlations into "empirical generalizations." Whether intentionally or inadvertently, the latter are typically treated as though they already were theories or will somehow jell into theories when a critical mass is reached. Absent cogent arguments, though, there is no serious danger that such political research will one day explode into theory.

When political scientists are not mistaking correlation for argument or regression for explanation, they still confuse small and restricted sets of arguments with scientific theories. But in this primary sense, theories are usually about broad domains of occurrence and experience. The very idea of "theories" of presidential popularity, state elections, or patterns of political participation ought to strike us as strange. For on its face, each of these domains should seem suspiciously small for sustaining a scientific theory. Historians of science show repeatedly that theories are not nailed together of myriad facts, painstakingly collected and fitted to one another (statistically or otherwise). Instead, an argumentative web of theory is usually stretched wide for gathering facts to test and refine it.

As a field, political socialization has a special opportunity to overturn these unfortunate patterns of political science past and present. By embracing (more than producing) substantive theories from elsewhere, researchers on political socialization are starting to put themselves in a good position to appreciate the characteristics and capacities of theory. Preeminent among them, given the condition of political science, is how theory must help to determine proper principles and mixtures of method. Hence a sense of the three remaining modes of methodism is needed all the more urgently if research on political socialization is to be skillfully reconstructed.

METHOD

My treatment of methods is premised on four principles which find support in recent philosophy of inquiry. First, methods should be constructed according to sound assessment of their subjects of study and according to sound principles of epistemology. Thus second, theories are the sources of assessment of subjects of study. That is because subject of study are constituted by theories as their domains. Third (and less obviously), theories are prime sources of principles of epistemology. Finally (and most radically), both assessment of subject matters and principles of epistemology for any single method must come primarily from the same theory or group of theories (i.e., paradigm).

In other words, for any particular method, the specifics of its subject and the principles of its epistemology are properly determined in large part by the theory which is its object of elaboration and testing. This means that each theory plays a key part in constituting its own methods of research. This also means that the thorough splits between science and metascience which logical positivisms and empiricisms have sought to enforce should be overcome in theory, because they cannot exist in practice. Philosophies of inquiry and practices of inquiry are too tightly intertwined to sustain such splits.[29]

----

[29] For arguments which tend to support not only my four principles of method, but also this general indictment of dichotomizing science and metascience, see: Feyerabend, **Against Method**; Hans-Georg Gadamer, **Truth and Method**, Garret Barden and John Cumming, eds. of trans., New York, Seabury Press, (1965), 1975; Gunnell, **Philosophy, Science, and Political Inquiry**; Kuhn, **The Structure of Scientific Revolutions**; Nelson, "Meaning and Measurement across Paradigms"; Marshall Spector, "Theory and Observation, I and II," **British Journal for the Philosophy of Science**, 17, 1-2, May-August, 1966, pp. 1-20 and 89-104;

Influenced partly by logical empiricism and partly by pseudotheories such as structural funtionalism, students of political socialization have had a hard time facing up to needs for substantive theory. It is no surprise, therefore, that they simply miss or ignore the systematic dependence of method on theory. Without theoretical specification of subject and epistemology, no method of study can be completely warranted. Hence methods of research on political socialization have long lacked adequate justification, for the field had no real theories. But the real trouble here is not an absence of self-conscious reasons for methods practiced. It is rather the result: that research on political socialization has proceeded by poor and inappropriate methods which are seldom able to test what needs testing and learn what needs learning. Even now, unless proper dependence of methods on theories is practiced, newly substantive theories may mean only minimal improvement in the field. Especially on objectivity, epistemologies implicit in some of the theories now being brought into the field are strikingly different from those tied to recent pseudotheories in political science. For the field to miss this chance to reconceive the relationship of theory to method would be awfully unfortunate. Its three remaining methodisms show that this is no idle danger.

Matters of method are enormously complicated, here ruling out anything approaching an exhaustive treatment. Instead, let me touch four key topics in highly abbreviated fashion. First comes some elaboration of my principles on theory, method, and epistemology. Second is a contrast between epistemologies of I-see or I-know and those of I-feel or I-want. The former fit with positivist and deductivist pretensions of behavioralism, whereas the latter arise from cognitivist and depth psychologies new to the field of political socialization. Third follows a summary of epistemological implications of theories from sociology and anthropology relevant to political socialization. And fourth is a survey of the three remnants of methodism in studies of political socialization. Thus this section works toward noting as many particular problems and remedial measures as possible in socialization research.

Throughout, my main concern is for abuses of method. Failing to see how each theory helps to determine

----

Hugh Stretton, **The Political Sciences**, New York, Basic Books, 1969; Frederick Suppe, ed., **The Structure of Scientific Theories**, Urbana, University of Illinois Press, 1973.

its own appropriate methods of research, students of political socialization have mismatched theories, methods, and
epistemologies. Though making a mishmash out of recent
research, these mistakes still can aid in developing better
theories, methods, and principles of inquiry.

THEORY AND EPISTEMOLOGY

Plundering Thomas Kuhn's theory of science for terminology and isolated ideas to use (or misuse) in assessing
current reseach became a favorite pastime of political scientists in the late 1960s. Considerable skirmishing over
Kuhn's work continues to the present day.[30] This contest
is conducted as though principles of epistemology could be
pillaged from abstract philosophies of inquiry, then brought
into a separate arena of substantive science, and there
employed to wage mock war against the projects and principles of other political scientists. Somehow, the sport
inspired by Kuhn has ignored a basic implication of Kuhn's
theory: science must not be dichotomized from the study of
science. Philosophies of inquiry (should) include not only
logics but also histories, sociologies, psychologies, aesthetics, and even politics of inquiry. And never should they
be severed from inquiry itself. If anything is fundamental
to Kuhn's philosophy of paradigms, it is the principle that
theories help to establish the very epistemology by which
they are to be evaluated.

This principle is even more explicit in philosophies of
inquiry posed by Paul Feyerabend, Stanley Cavell, Richard
Rorty, and Michael Polanyi.[31] For all four philosophers,

----

[30] For lists of relevant essays, see: Garry Gutting, ed.,
Paradigms and Revolutions, Notre Dame, IN, University of
Notre Dame Press, 1980; John S. Nelson, "Once More on
Kuhn," **Political Methodology**, 1, 2, Spring, 1974, pp.
73-104.

[31] See: Feyerabend, **Against Method**; Feyerabend, **Science
in a Free Society**, London, NLB, 1978; Stanley Cavell, **The
Claim of Reason**, New York, Oxford University Press, 1979;
Richard Rorty, **Philosophy and the Mirror of Nature**,
Princeton, NJ, Princeton University Press, 1979; Michael
Polanyi, **Personal Knowledge**, New York, Harper and Row,
1958; Polanyi, **Beyond Nihilism**, Cambridge, Cambridge Uni-
versity Press, 1960; Polanyi, **Science, Faith and Society,**

this principle attacks any attempt to fix in advance the particulars of epistemology appropriate to specific projects of
investigation. It is no coincidence that these are among the
most political of recent theorists of inquiry. That is, they
explore mutual implications of inquiry and politics with far
greater self-consciousness and skill than usual. Revolving
around technical debates of "meaning variance" and "incommensurability," their philosophies are recurrently criticized
as relativist and nihilist.   Elsewhere I address these
charges in detail.[32] Here let me simply state that actualities
(and difficulties) of communication across theories and paradigms reveal that phenomena of incommensurability rule out
general, a priori methods for choosing among theories,
which is precisely the point of the principle at stake.
(Rules of thumb may remain, but they are hardly precise
enough to qualify as actual methods.) Moreover, these
same phenomena show that no theory is either properly or
actually the sole and utter determinant of its principles of
testing, which allows room to avoid not only nihilisms but
radical relativisms as well.

Added to the generally accepted dependence of
method on epistemology, this dependence of epistemology on
theory implies that theories should be the prime determi-
nants of their own methods of research. This is what John
Gunnell has called contextualism."[33] Even in theory, it is
impossible to rule all political science by a priori principles
of philosophy. In disciplinary practice, such rhetoric supports enforcement of a few favored methods or even statistics, which are presented as the epitome (if not the full
scope) of Science. But not even logical positivisms or
empiricisms would go that far, producing a peculiar incompatibility between the methodology of behavioralism and its
supposed warrant in philosophy of science.[34]

Chicago, University of Chicago Press, 1964.

[32] See: Nelson, "Meaning and Measurement across Paradigms."

[33] See: John G. Gunnell, "Social Science and Political Reality: The Problem of Explanation," **Social Research**, 35, 1,
Spring, 1968, pp. 159-201; Gunnell, "Deduction, Explanation, and Social Scientific Inquiry," **American Political Science Review**, 63, 4, December, 1969, pp. 1233-1246.

[34] See: Thomas A. Spragens, Jr., **The Dilemma of Con-**

One place where objectivist rhetoric comes home to roost in current research on political socialization is in celebrations of "multiple-method research." To be sure, nothing is wrong with using many methods to learn about politics generally or test some hypothesis particularly. In this sense, good research is often "multiple-method research." But multiplicity of methods is no substitute for self-critical selection of methods according to criteria inspired by the substantive theories structuring research. Both because a single theory can suggest many methods and because several theories can be invoked at once, "multiple-method research" should be the norm. In studies of political socialization, however, piling layer upon layer of miscellaneous methods is sometimes supposed to substitute for for thinking through specific methods compatible with a particular line of inquiry. Moreover, since such methodological thinking is practically inseparable from theoretical argument, only substantive theories are able to project contexts for coordinating methods in pursuit of defensible inferences.

Of course, the fallacy that many methods mean good reseach is reinforced by continuing confusion of statistics with methods. Partly, decisions to plaster data with one statistical technique after another trace to inadequate understanding of the statistics involved. Better training at this level can slowly improve the methodology of the discipline. But these decisions also stem from incapacity or unwillingness to sort out methodological implications of unfamiliar theories. Laying methods on thickly and indiscriminately makes for lumpy, even research which cracks readily and lacks a strong enough structure to house extended research.

Like some loose and faddish talk of "postbehavioralism," invocations of "multiple method research" have served to circumvent serious challenges to old methods and principles of inquiry.[35] Panicked by increased complications in health science, some doctors subject patients to a vast and largely irrelevant battery of tests in order to protect

----

temporary **Political Theory,** New York, Dunellen, 1973; Spragens, **The Irony of Liberal Reason,** Chicago, University of Chicago Press, 1981.

[35] See: Jack Dennis, "Future Work on Political Socialization," in Dennis, ed., **Socialization to Politics,** pp. 492-502, especially on pp. 495-496.

against malpractice suits. Yet the very volume of tests can confuse the intelligent judgment on which proper treatments must depend in the end. Similarly, having many methods and statistics to throw at issues of theory and politics is no replacement for facing up to requirements of imaginative argument and careful judgment in truly theoretical research. Using many methods in research is far from wrong in itself, but it does tempt us to turn our backs on difficult questions that cannot be skirted.

Political socialization is far from the only field of social science now facing a crisis of method. By comparison with other fields, though, it has an advantage of (new) theories which imply self-reflexive principles of inquiry. Properly developed, these could prove fundamental for much political science to come. Epistemologies suggested by several theories now being borrowed by students of political socialization can help overcome the objectivisms which have passed for behavioralism in many parts of political science. Certainly, these objectivisms sit ill with what the field is starting to learn about political learning. Its rich conceptions of symbol and ideology fit ill, if at all, with objectivist tenets and practices of political research. A glimpse of this potential can be gained through a short inventory of principles of inquiry implicit in current cognitive and depth psychologies.

Dynamics of learning are important topics of depth psychologies by Sigmund Freud, Carl Jung, Erik Erikson, Bruno Bettelheim, Otto Kernberg, Melanie Klein, and too many other theorists to mention here. This is also the level at which cognitive psychologies like those of Jean Piaget, Robert Ornstein, and Milton Rokeach make their most direct contributions to research on political socialization. Insights of these theories into perception, desire, self-deception, and belief imply epistemological commitments contrary to behavioralism.[36] Indeed, the psychological theories most relevant to political socialization are precisely the

----

[36] See: Jean Piaget, **Genetic Epistemology**, Eleanor Duckworth, trans., New York, Columbia University Press, 1970; Piaget, **Psychology and Epistemology**, Arnold Rosin, tr., New York, Viking, 1970; Piaget, **The Place of the Sciences of Man in the System of Sciences**, New York, Harper and Row, 1970; Paul Ricoeur, **Freud and Philosophy**, Denis Savage, trans., New Haven, Yale University Press, 1970; Robert Jay Lifton, **Explorations in Psychohistory**, New York, Simon and Schuster, 1974.

ones most antagonistic to the objectivisms on which the field was founded. This is not to say these theories agree completely on epistemology. But even where they disagree, they usually depart dramatically from principles of inquiry standard in research on political socialization. Even within a single theory, there are more angles on inquiry than can be covered here. Let me settle for a synoptic presentation of four which are particularly revealing: symbols, choices, ideologies, and practices. My aim is a decent snapshot of political socialization from each of these angles, not a detailed treatment of individual theories or theorists.

SYMBOLICAL KNOWLEDGE

Central to most depth psychologies and to some cognitive psychologies is the concept of symbols. They are the units of figurative speech, capable of becoming literalist only at a (sometimes heavy) cost in meaning and power: not only of emotion and imagination but also of intellection as well. Symbols are the elements of cognition in its broadest and best sense. What Philip Wheelwright has written of the "tensive symbol" holds for any actual symbol: it "cannot be entirely stipulative, inasmuch as its essential tension draws life from a multiplicity of associations, subtly and for the most part subconsciously interrelated, with which the symbol, or something like it and suggested by it, has been joined in the past, so that there is stored up potential of semantic energy and significance which the symbol, when adroitly used, can tap."[37]

In this sense, a symbol neither comes nor can be unidimensionalized in meaning. Every symbol is a shorthand for a complex of ideas, images, and experiences extending into a rich range of associations. Drawing these together under its rubric, symbol are inherently synthesizing: yet always through connection and comparison, never through reduction. These suggestive, flexible connections of symbols account for many processes of socialization in particular and learning in general. Hence many a good theory of political socialization must be a theory of symbols.[38]

----

[37] Philip Wheelwright, **Metaphor and Reality**, Bloomington, Indiana University Press, 1962, p. 95.

[38] See: Ben Halpern, "The Dynamic Elements of Culture,"

Literalists of all kinds, behavioralists included, are chronically inclined to confuse symbols with signs, which make one-to-one mappings. Thus study of political beliefs and learning has tried repeatedly to reduce symbols to signs, either overtly through operationalizations intended to divide symbols into many discrete dimensions or scales of meaning or covertly through technical usage of terms to the same effect. Less programmatically, similar attempts occur through determined misinterpretation or sheer avoidance of phenomena dense in symbols.

Conceived heavily laden with images, myths, and so on, the field of political socialization is constrained to face up to the presence and importance of symbols. For some time, researchers have rightly been seeking substantive theories which explore learning as a symbolical activity. Since little in politics is not significantly symbolical, another strategic advantage of studies in political socialization is their lead in illuminating this topic for the rest of political inquiry.

Still, a scientifically disastrous reduction of symbols to signs is sadly characteristic of the field. This is especially evident in its reliance on short survey questionnaires almost exclusively. These prevent respondents and researchers alike from tracing subtle ties among images, meanings, beliefs, and actions. Categories are imposed in advance, which is often fatal to eliciting respondents' own symbols and their political significance. The symbolical realities are too intricate and fluid for the analytically fixed concepts of literalist inquiry to comprehend across the many cases needed for statistically significant results. And in any event, considerations of time and expense insure that information generated by such questionnaires is typically too limited for correlational statistics to coax forth patterns complicated to tell us much we did not already know.

Of course, sign-oriented methods make some sense in

Ethics, 65, 4, July, 1955, pp. 235-249; Victor Turner, Dramas, Fields, and Metaphors, Ithaca, NY, Cornell University Press, 1974; Turner, "Process, System, and Symbol: A New Anthopological Synthesis," Daedalus, 106, 3, Summer, 1977, pp. 61-80; David Apter, ed., Ideology and Discontent, New York, Free Press, 1964; Thomas Remington, The Origin of Ideology, Pittsburgh, University Center for International Studies, 1971; Roger W. Cobb, "The Belief Systems Perspective," Journal of Politics, 35, 1, February, 1973, pp. 121-153.

terms of epistemologies of stimulus and response theories, which are virtually the only ones taken seriously by behavioralists. Like the closely related epistemologies of logical positivism and empiricism, these rely on simple correspondence theories of truth, which seek one-to-one correlations between words and atomistic bits of world. Similarly, the related "theories" of psychology readily devolve into various meta- and pseudo-theories which are more groundless rules for language than substantive conceptions of reality.[39] This should warn students of political socialization away from behaviorism in psychology every bit as much as behavioralism in political science. Serious concern for symbols leads away from sign-based epistemologies and theories alike. It leads toward symbolical epistemologies such as those projected by some cognitive and depth psychologies[40]

Signs turn epistemology toward passivism, literalism, and objectivism; symbols toward activism, figurativism, and perspectivism.[41] Sign-oriented, objectivist inquiries favor mechanical, cause-effect modes of explanation; symbol-centered, perspectivist epistemologies encourage patterning, acausal accounts of events. Indeed, symbols could be described as acausal patterns. Much more could be said about symbols and their implications for inquiry, but my purpose here is only to convey a feeling for how different symbol-directed studies of political socialization can and probably should be from the sign-dominated studies to this point.[42]

----

[39] See: Noam Chomsky, "The Case Against B. F. Skinner," **New York Review of Books**, 17, 11, December 30, 1971, pp. 18-24.

[40] See: Susanne K. Langer, **Philosophy in a New Key**, New York, New American Library, 1942; Langer, **Feeling and Form**, New York, Scribner's, 1953; Ernst Cassirer, **The Philosophy of Symbolic Forms**, Ralph Manheim, trans., New Haven, Yale University Press, in three volumes, 1953, 1955, 1957; Paul Ricoeur, **The Rule of Metaphor**, Robert Czerny, trans., Toronto, University of Toronto Press, (1975), 1977.

[41] See my essay on "Political Theory as Political Rhetoric" in this volume.

[42] See: John S. Nelson, "Postmodern Myths of Politics, with Special Reference to Science Fiction," paper presented

The tension between taking symbols seriously and retaining objectivism is nowhere more evident than in the depth psychology of Sigmund Freud, who strained long and unsuccessfully to reconcile objectivist terminology and epistemology with symbolical psychology. Most recent commentary identifies some incompatibility between these two commitments in Freud's work. Saying that they do a disservice to his theories and methods, many followers now repudiate Freud's overt terminology and epistemology. These neo-Freudians celebrate repressed principles of symbolical knowledge which remain evident in Freudian analysis, even after decades of orthodox attempts to appear utterly objectivist.[43] In fact, Freud's work attracts philosophical attention more for its implicit principles of inquiry than any other feature. Controversies over not only "the unconscious" and Freud's functionalism but the symbolical dynamics of perception, conception, and deception account for philosophical interest in Freudian psychoanalysis.

Studying structures and dynamics of desire through the lens of the symbol, Freud and others have reopened epistemology to realms of will, appetite, emotion, and imagination. No longer limited to narrow notions of reason promoted by Modernity (and especially the Enlightenment), epistemology can comprehend not only what we see but also what we want.[44] It can (and thus we should) take into

----

to the Annual Meeting of the Midwest Political Science Association, Milwaukee, April 28-May 1, 1982; Nelson, **Ironic Politics**, doctoral dissertation, University of North Carolina Department of Political Science, 1977, pp. 128-231.

[43] See: Ricoeur, **Freud and Philosophy**; Roy Schafer, **A New Language for Psychoanalysis**, New Haven, Yale University Press, 1976; Philip Rieff, **Freud**, Garden City, NY, Doubleday, 1959; Richard Wollheim, **Sigmund Freud**, New York, Viking Press, 1971; Wollheim, **Freud**, Garden City, NY, Doubleday, 1974. Many works by "ego psychologists" could also be listed in this connection.

[44] See: Max Horkheimer and Theodor W. Adorno, **Dialectic of Enlightenment**, John Cumming, trans., New York, Herder and Herder, 1944; Horkheimer, **Eclipse of Reason**, New York, Seabury Press, 1947; Michel Foucault, **The Order of Things**, New York, Random House, 1970; Jacques Derrida, **Writing and Difference**, Alan Blass, trans., Chicago, University of Chicago Press, (1967), 1978; Rorty, **Philosophy**

account the intricate interplay of knowledge and desire. The point is not that perspectivism must altogether replace objectivism. Rather, it is that inquiry tied to a theory about symbols cannot be conducted defensibly in ignorance of what that theory says about symbols. Further, what many cognitive and depth psychologies say about symbols makes objectivism a poor framework for their projects of inquiry. When such theories are appropriate for studies of political socialization, as they often are, they make objectivist methods poor means to generate data, test hypotheses, and otherwise improve our understanding of the principles, processes, and practices at issue.

RATIONAL KNOWLEDGE

The same conclusion emerges from reconceptions of choice and reason by the cognitive and depth psychologies ready to offer substantive theories about political socialization. From their perspectives, objectivism pushes the field into schizophrenic ideas of choice. This is due to the objectivist dichotomy of reason and emotion.

On one hand, objectivism restricts choice and action to fully "rational" decisions: cool calculations of efficient means to ends ultimately given nonrationally (by situation, socialization, and so on). Then "emotional" decisions are regarded as events, as effects of socialization, not as actual choices and actions. The real actor or chooser is the agent of socialization which caused the socialized to behave in one way or another.

On the other hand, the field of political socialization is said to reveal conditions and dynamics of choice. Hence adequate theories of political socialization should reliably predict (or retrodict) political choices. To be sure, such prediction is usually limited to societal patterns; precise projections about individuals are seldom claimed or required. Still, the result is oscillation between pretending to explain choices and presuming to account for events outside that domain.

Neither side provides adequate conceptions of choice, action, and reason. Walled off from emotionality, etc., rationality is reduced to formalist ideals of analysis. Explicitly or implicitly, it is identified with strict deduction in axiomatic systems. (Otherwise, how can objectivism

----

and the Mirror of Nature.

protect the sanctity of scientific study from the prejudice of passion?) Given this strict separation of reason from emotion, choice can be associated with either category but not both. Connected with reason, choice is controlled by necessitarian dynamics of deduction. Hence any "choice" is utterly determined. Tied to emotion (will, appetite, or other nonrational faculty), choice is controlled by determinist dynamics of causation. Thus the causal sciences which can specify such irrational forces and processes of "choice" are equally necessitarian, again leaving no real room for freedom. Yet if choice is not somehow free, then it departs completely from anything ordinarily designated by that category. Therefore, nothing that we normally know as choice can have been well conceived. Given normal conceptual ties of choice to action and reason, the same goes for them, too.

Many cognitive and depth psychologies lead away from this trap by avoiding dichotomies of reason and emotion. Even Freudian rationalism insists that the reality principle of the Ego arises from the pleasure principle of the Id. This implies an impossibility of treating the two as totally separate compartments, despite Freud's intermittent attempts to do so. Subsequent depth psychologists have cautioned repeatedly against reifying such mental "structures." Cognitive psychologists sometimes insist on avoiding all all faculty psychologies for much the same reason. Accounts of reason as emotion checking emotion, desire righting desire, or feeling balancing feeling are starting to emerge. And rationality is being pluralized as styles or complexes of cognition-cum-emotion.[45] Thus cognitive and depth theories encourage better conceptions of choice, even when action is not a central concern.

Significantly, symbols are sets of connections which make sense, but need not be followed (logically or causally). Symbolically understood, reason can be compatible with freedom and hence with choice, since such flexible connections allow recommending options without requiring them. Notice also that to understand reason symbolically is to comprehend the rational as imaginative, emotive, votive, and perhaps even appetitive; for these are the ways in which symbolical links are usually understood. (Symbols

----

[45] See: Willard Gaylin, **Feelings**, New York, Harper and Row, 1979; Amelie Oksenberg Rorty, ed., **Explaining Emotions**, Berkeley, University of California Press, 1980; Nelson, "Political Theory as Political Rhetoric."

are often defined as complexes of imagination or emotion.)
One reconception of choice along these lines is the notion of
elective affinity.[46] As its component concepts suggest, this
idea attempts to allow leeway for freedom and limitation,
showing in abstractions what we experience in situations:
the interdependence of these two categories.

Indeed, perspectivism generally can be portrayed as a
set of attempts to put science and choice back on speaking
terms. Its purpose is to enable choice (freedom, reason,
action) to be informed by inquiry without being utterly
determined (and thereby destroyed) in the process. Since
research on political socialization seeks to clarify why we
think and act as we do, it must contain more coherent conceptions of choice. Reducing choice to several logical laws
or some mechanical cause cannot encompass the very phenomena which the field is supposed to study.

IDEOLOGICAL KNOWLEDGE

Perspectivism is implied as well by substantive theories imported from sociology. These include symbolic inter-
actionism (e.g., Peter Berger and Thomas Luckmann), neo-
Marxism (Jurgen Habermas), and various phenomenologies
(Harold Garfinkel). Anthropological theories such as the
structuralism of Claude Levi-Strauss and Edmund Leach or
the cultural evolutionism of Clifford Geertz and Marshall
Sahlins might also be mentioned.[47] Here again, my main

----

[46] See: Johann Wolfgang von Goethe, **Elective Affinities**,
Elizabeth Mayer and Louise Brogan, trans., Chicago, Reg-
nery, 1963; Hayden White, **Metahistory**, Baltimore, Johns
Hopkins University Press, 1973; Nelson, "Meaning and
Measurement across Paradigms."

[47] See: Peter L. Berger and Thomas Luckmann, **The Social
Construction of Reality**, Garden City, NY, Doubleday, 1966;
Jurgen Habermas, **Knowledge and Human Interests**, Jeremey
J. Shapiro, trans., Boston, Beacon Press, (1968), 1971;
Harold Garfinkel, **Studies in Ethnomethodology**, Englewood
Cliffs, NJ, Prentice-Hall, 1967; Edmund Leach, @Culture
and **Communication**, Cambrige, Cambridge University Press,
1972; Clifford Geertz, **The Interpretation of Cultures**, New
York, Basic Books, **1973**; **Marshall Sahlins,** Culture and
Practical Reason, **Chicago,** University of Chicago Press,
1976.

point is simply that students of political socialization should not keep trying to appropriate theories without taking seriously their implications for modes and methods of inquiry. And once again, the implications in question require major changes of research strategy.

These theories offer substantive accounts of socialization, acculturation, and education. In so doing, they develop rich and respectful conceptions of symbolism, allowing them to appreciate the ambiguities and choices required by sophisticated accounts of roles. Some of these theories are also tied to principles of inquiry defended here. And most of them echo my concerns about reason and emotion, subverting Modern restrictions of reason to technique, to matters of mere means. They pose purviews and processes of rationality which try to detour or span the Modern split of formal, instrumental reason from substantive reason. For they recognize that the contrast is not only theoretically incoherent but practically dangerous, since it supports a ruinous "rationalization" of human life.[48] The methodisms of political inquiry could be cited as examples of being carried away by technical rationality.

Ideology is a central concern of these theories from sociology and anthropology. They lead toward ideological conceptions of knowledge in something of the same way in which some psychological theories work toward symbolical conceptions of knowledge. (Of course, some theories of psychology share this concern with ideology, just as some theories of sociology and anthropology are interested in symbols.) Ideological projects are usually more self-conscious and explicit about epistemological implications. But in either case, the implications are much the same: opposition to objectivism. Indeed, the very category of ideology conjures up ties to emotion, evaluation, politics, rhetorics, and other things plainly repugnant to objectivism in

----

[48] See: Laurence H. Tribe, "Technology Assessment and the Fourth Discontinuity: The Limits of Instrumental Rationality," **Southern California Law Review**, 46, 3, June, 1973, pp. 617-660; Sheldon S. Wolin, "Max Weber: Legitimation, Method, and the Politics of Theory," **Political Theory**, 9, 3, August, 1981, pp. 401-424; Jacques Ellul, **The Technological Society**, John Wilkinson, trans., New York, Random House, 1964; Herbert Marcuse, **One-Dimensional Man**, Boston, Beacon Press, 1964; Habermas, **Knowledge and Human Interests**. In the book at hand, see the essays by Paul F. Kress and William E. Connolly.

inquiry.

These theories show how the ticklish task of reconceiving rationality is a key to keeping perspectivism from
becoming radical relativism. Just as these theories cannot
dichotomize means and ends or reason and emotion, neither
can they sunder facts from values. (Modern ties between
ends, emotions, and values connect these dichotomies.)
Opposing emotivism, the view that values are mere expressions of emotion and thus are without reason, these theories
promote ideology as a realm where logic, fact, and value
interpenetrate. That is, ideology is where the rational
(analytic), empirical (synthetic), and evaluational (normative) meet and merge.

Seeing knowledge as socially constructed, these theories investigate how rationalities (as sets of interests and
symbols) are created and sustained. They explore how
personal differences in perception, conception, deception,
and choice are socially communicated and challenged, culturally learned and criticized. They study how all this
relates to divisions among myriad groups: ethnic, economic, religious, political, professional, and the like.
These theories explain how such intersubjectively sustained
realities produce various difficulties of discussion and decision, both within and across groups. And they account for
modalities of experience in supporting and opposing established paths of social existence. Such emphasis on ideology
leads readily into appreciating how styles, starting points,
and substances of inquiry can (and should) vary, which is
surely a principle of perspectivism.

Stressing this self-consciously, some theories extend
these concerns into fully developed sociologies of knowledge
or what are unfortunately labeled "ideology critiques."[49]
These are promising directions to push research on political
socialization. The biggest problem with sociologies of

----

[49] See: Werner Stark, **The Sociology of Knowledge**, Lon-
don, Routledge and Kegan Paul, 1958; Philip H. Melanson,
"Bringing the Sociology of Knowledge to Bear on Political
Science," **Polity**, 7, 4, Summer, 1975, pp. 564-574; Richard
M. Merelman, "On Interventionist Behavioralism: An Essay
in the Sociology of Knowledge," **Politics and Society**, 6, 1,
1976, pp. 57-78; Larry D. Spence, **The Politics of Social
Knowledge**, University Park, Pennsylvania State University
Press, 1978; Robin Blackburn, ed., **Ideology in Social Science**, New York, Random House, 1972. Also see this vol-
ume's essays by Terence Ball and Richard Ashcraft.

knowledge has been their tendency to stop far short of full philosophies of inquiry.   Perhaps this is because sociologists of knowledge are still too indulgent toward oppositions of the social to the logical, with the latter purportedly providing the ground for epistemology and principles of inquiry.   Similarly, the largest defect of ideology critiques has been their proclivity for excepting themselves from ideological criticism.   Even so, both branches of ideological knowledge depict conditions and characteristics of political learning with substantial success.   And at their best, both branches are able to apply to themselves the principles of learning which they discern in other endeavors.   This sort of self-reflection on political science as political learning and communication is precisely what the discipline needs. By providing it, the field of political socialization could endow the whole of political science with more critical self-understanding.

Proponents of ideology critique and sociology of knowledge usually say that their projects were inspired by Karl Marx and Karl Mannheim.   Not coincidentally, Marx and Mannheim both equivocated between an old objectivism and an emerging perspectivism.   After the fashion of Freud, they, too, struggled with old concepts and principles in order to generate epistemologies suited to their new theories.[50] In Freud, Marx, and (to a lesser degree) in Mannheim, this struggle is intimately tied to a sensitivity to symbols and the politics of language.   Such a concern for interactions of politics and language should come easily and centrally in studies of political socialization.   For this is mostly a matter of attending to the categories of political learning and the media of political communication: topics no research on political socialization can long ignore.[51] In turn, issues of political communication should lead to

----

[50] See: Shlomo Avineri, **The Social and Political Thought of Karl Marx**, New York, Cambridge University Press, 1971; Edward A. Shills, "**Ideology and Utopia** by Karl Mannheim," **Daedalus**, 103, 1, Winter, 1974, pp. 83-90.

[51] See: David V. J. Bell, **Power, Influence, and Authority**, New York, Oxford University Press, 1975; Claus Mueller, **The Politics of Communication**, New York, Oxford University Press, 1975; Hans Peter Dreitzel, ed., **Recent Sociology No. 2:   Patterns of Communicative Behavior**, New York, Macmillan, 1970; Dreitzel, ed., **Recent Sociology No. 3:   Childhood and Socialization**, New York, Macmillan, 1973.

emphasis on the actual contours and boundaries of political interaction. This is a matter of the various practices which constitute our political world.

PRACTICAL KNOWLEDGE

Inspired by theories from anthropology and sociology, the field of political socialization is slowly coming to appreciate the importance of studying actual practices (as distinct from and in addition to analytical variables or systems of the investigator's devising alone). Increasingly, this field can endow the rest of political science with the sensitivity to practical knowledge long lacking in our discipline. A shift toward studying practices might have at least four dimensions: (1) greater respect for self-understandings of the subjects of research, taken as inside informers on their own practices; (2) greater attention to issues identified as important from within practices; (3) greater skill in locating important phenomena at the level or in the context of whole practices; and (4) greater concern for tensions and adjustments among practices.

"Practical knowledge" has several senses, packing several points into a single phrase. Calling to mind a common American constrast, this term refers to knowledge derived more directly and distinctively from practice than theory. In other words, "practical knowledge" is what we learn from experiencing or practicing something personally instead of observing or theorizing something impersonally (at a distance, as a mere spectator). Partly, then, promoting practical knowledge in political science depends on overcoming the objectivist doctrine that categories and explanations from everyday discourse are necessarily suspect and inferior to academic coinage and technical terms.

In turn, an emphasis on practical knowledge would encourage greater respect for the self-understanding of practitioners of politics, who know their phenomena from inside. This does not mean that self-understandings are always correct or that political scientists have no right to override them. But it does mean that inside conceptions of politics must be explained when accounting for the practices of which they are a part. And it means also that study of political practices would do well to start in many cases with eliciting the practitioners' own ideas of their practices. These self-conceptions deserve attentive, theoretical treatment in the mode of field work and participant observation.

All this presupposes that we know what "a practice"

is, and that brings me to the second sense of "practical knowledge." Echoing vocational (professional, occupational) terms like "the practice of law" or "the practice of medicine," this second sense implies a practice to be any coherent, purposeful, and repeated pattern of complicated activity self-consciously pursued by human beings. In other words, a practice is any enduring complex of human activity guided by rules, pursued through principles and strategies, and understood or judged in terms of reasons.[52]

Thus human life is structured in practices: of worship, of banking, of voting, of lobbying, of socialization to politics, and so on. Like the cultures which they compose, practices often include rites of initiation, transaction, and resignation to mark their major stages and boundaries. Like their encompassing cultures, practices are conducted according to distinctive sets of reasons, perspectives, and incentives such as prudence, obligation, virtue, interest, right, and dignity. Almost every practice is a field for the interaction of several such paradigms of principle. Applied to particular problems or embodied in particular actions, one or more paradigms become shaped into a rationale for a specific set of moves. Insofar as these paradigms of principle apply across a variety of practices, they can even be considered the substantive rationalities of human affairs.

To explain a practice is to trace its history, context (including related practices), overall purposes, subpractices, actors (institutional and individual), rules (formal and informal), and common paradigms of principle (plus their standard appearance in rationales of action). Perhaps we can lay claim to a few theories of practices; but basically, this enterprise is just beginning. Among its early forays are histories of professions, a few attempts by phenomenologists to study contours of individual "life-worlds"

----

[52] I am not now sure which, but I know that many of these ideas I owe to James P. Matsoukas, who may nonetheless disagree with some of what I here do with or to them. Closely related to my notion of practices are the conceptions of: Richard E. Flathman, **Political Obligation**, New York, Atheneum Press, 1972; Flathman, **The Practice of Rights**, New York, Cambridge University, 1976; Flathman, **The Practice of Political Authority**, Chicago, University of Chicago Press, 1980; Pierre Bourdieu, **Outline of a Theory of Practice**, New York, Cambridge University Press, 1977; Alasdair MacIntyre, **After Virtue**, Notre Dame, IN, Notre Dame University Press, 1981, especially p. 175.

(as distinguished from an allegedly all-encompassing "Life-World"), and anthropological inquiries into the dynamics of institutions.

In the first sense, "practical knowledge" is knowledge from practice; in the second sense, it is knowledge of practices. In a third sense, it is inquiry designed to answer questions of (political) practice with greater vigor and intelligence than before, reshaping our conceptions of academic and theoretical knowledge in order to connect better with practical concerns of politics. Recent attempts to revive the field of public policy within political science suggest that times are ripe for practical knowledge of this kind. Significantly, students of public policy have generated most of the second sort of "practical knowledge" now evident in our discipline. One example of knowledge of political practices is William Muir's excellent study of policemen as ."streetcorner politicians."[53] And Robert Goodin's work shows an exquisite sensitivity to interactions among competing paradigms of principle within various practices, as well patterns of interdependence and conflict among entire practices.[54] Such a concern with "practical knowledge" makes a good standpoint for reading Charles Anderson's essay on political theory and public policy, elsewhere in this volume.

The styles of research involved in such practical knowledge seem to derive mostly from anthropology and sociology. Similarly, theories of practices seem likely to parallel recent theories in cultural anthropology and (in attention to rules) cybernetics. Already open to these enterprises for other (if related) reasons, the field of political socialization is in a good position to become a conduit into political science as a whole for various projects of practical knowledge.

In sum, the field's new theories can aid our discipline in reconstructing its conceptions of knowledge, making them more symbolical, rational, ideological, and practical. The preceding survey of unfamiliar modes of knowledge and their implications for the field of political socialization serves four purposes. It clarifies and supports my claims about how theory, method, and epistemology interpenetrate.

----

[53] See: William Ker Muir, Jr., **Police**, Chicago, University of Chicago Press, 1977.

[54] See: Robert E. Goodin, "Making Moral Incentives Pay," **Policy Sciences**, 12, 2, 1980, pp. 131-145; Goodin, **Manipulatory Politics**, New Haven, Yale University Press, 1980.

It specifies some epistemological implications of theories new to the field of political socialization, pointing to new standards of research emerging there. It identifies some conceptual crises and related research opportunities buried barely beneath the surface of the field. And it reinforces my argument that the field can occupy a special place in political science as a whole. Since students of political socialization have themselves started to introduce such new, substantive theories into the field, its main obstacle to progress is its remaining methodism.

THREE MODES OF METHODISM

Methodism is bad for many reasons. It relies on Modern caricatures of reason (formalism, instrumentalism) and epistemology (objectivism, literalism). When method precedes theory, hypotheses tend to be taken ad hoc and their testing is suspect. Then investigation slides toward trivial, technical problems alone. And attempts to account for important events become either superficial or incoherent. Since epistemologies by which specific methods make sense may easily conflict with epistemologies implied by theories subsequently selected, methodism jumbles principles of inquiry, often into incoherence. In short, methodism is no way to run a science.

Three modes of methodism remain in research on political socialization, notwithstanding increased concern with substantive theories. To elaborate and exemplify each mode is to tease out contrasts between methods leftover and methods encouraged by theories new to the field. Along the way, this allows suggestions about good strategies for the field in its next decade or more.

TESTING NEW THEORIES BY OLD METHODS

Surveys have dominated research on political socialization from the very first. Whatever their original warrant, which was weak anyway, survey methods make little sense in working with theories of Piaget, Erikson, Berger, and company. For reasons at least implicit above, such methods are ill-suited to most studies of symbols, ideologies, rationalities, and practices.[55]

Still, some students of political socialization persist in trying to test and refine these new theories by survey methods. Apparently, they never ask how survey methods address key concepts of a new theory, test it, or even generate good data about it. Appeals to new statistical techniques in processing data are about as far as some seem to go beyond the systems style of research.

Worse, some who hold to survey research try to work with substantive theories suited so little to such methods that they are bound to sew more confusion than comprehension of the occurrences at issue. Freud, Jung, and their followers have had reasons deeper than dollars, statistics, and computers for avoiding the least leanings toward survey research. But their reasons are little known and less noted. For it has become acceptable to pull a particular idea from hither or yon without coming to terms with the original contexts required for making good sense of it and without even thinking through the new contexts which could at least invent a decent sense for it.

Seeking science is no excuse for scuttling scholarship; nor is it a reason for refraining from real theorizing of one's own. Thus people who promote theories by Erikson and Piaget appear to ignore not only their work on inquiry (which are theoretically distinguished and practically useful), and not just their methods of inquiry (which are very different from those now familiar to political scientists), but also their full theories of socialization and politics (which are bound to require careful adaptation before they are able to be addressed whole by foreign principles and methods of inquiry). Otherwise laudable, Richard Merelman's work exemplifies such methodism. First, it tries to express the theories of Erikson and Piaget in objectivist terms, showing little sense of the obstacles and objections to such a translation. And then, it tries to test (what remeains of) those theories by standard, but here largely irrelevant, methods of political science.[56] Nonetheless Merelman deserves considerable credit for promoting attention to cognitive and depth theories. When the best in the field fail to think past familiar methods, then the rule of

----

[55] See: Nelson, "The Ideological Connection."

[56] See: Richard M. Merelman, "The Development of Political Ideology," in Dennis, ed., **Socialization to Politics**, pp. 289-319.

methodism is secure.

Plainly, my main recommendation is that students of political socialization consider emulating methods of the fields which supply relevant theories. Let us not rule out innovations in method (or statistics). But let us at least learn first a few of the means which have established their worth in these kinds of inquiry. That way, we can refine our sense of what is appropriate, enabling us to judge new methods more accurately. Although there are many others, the methods from psychology, sociology, and anthropology easiest to contrast with surveys are depth interviews, participant observations, and field studies.[57] By contrast with surveys, these procedures are all more adaptable as a study progresses, more dependent on investigators' personal skills of observation and interpretation, and more demanding of close contact between principal researchers and their subjects. These features allow better immersion in full complexes of symbols, rationalities, ideologies, and practices. Where careful and intelligent detection of intricate connections among various parts of such complexes is required, as in much research on political socialization, methods of inquiry must enable and encourage such immersion.

In fact, most of the best work on political socialization is currently being done outside the professional field. Where in political science is there an equal to the works of Robert Coles, Kenneth Keniston, Robert Jay Lifton, or Milton Rokeach?[58] Although this cites only four people from

----

[57] See: Harry Stack Sullivan, **The Psychiatric Interview**, Helen Swick Perry and Mary Ladd Gawel, eds., New York, Norton, 1954; Erik H. Erikson, "The Nature of Clinical Evidence," in **Insight and Responsibility**, New York, Norton, 1964, pp. 47-80; Y. Michal Bodemann, "A Problem of Sociological Praxis," **Theory and Society**, 5, 3, May, 1978, pp. 387-420; Michael Clarke, "Survival in the Field," **Theory and Society**, 2, 1, Spring, 1975, pp. 95-123; Hortense Powdermaker, **Stranger and Friend**, New York, Norton, 1966; Rosalie H. Wax, **Doing Fieldwork**, Chicago, University of Chicago Press, 1976.

[58] See: Robert Coles, **Children of Crisis**, Boston, Little, Brown, in five volumes; Coles, "What Children Know about Politics," **New York Review of Books**, 22, 2, February 20, 1975, pp. 22-24; Coles, "The Politics of Middle Class Children," **New York Review of Books**, 22, 3, March 6, 1975,

far larger fields of capable researchers, the only comparable political science is probably Robert Lane.[59] Sadly, not
even his research is widely recognized as a contribution to
the study of political socialization, perhaps because his
methods are unorthodox in that field.

All these researchers use many kinds of evidence.
All emphasize symbolical and ideological connections in tracing how, what, and why people learn about politics.   All
are sensitive to the multiplicity of our rationalities and
practices.   All attend to theories in compounding their many
methods.   All are led to special reliance on intensive interviews and some on forms of participant observation.   Their
sensible strategies of research deserve emulation by at least
some political scientists interested in socialization to politics.   Methods should be selected for their pertinence to
current questions (and thus theories) of political socialization, not their past use or present popularity in other
fields of political science.

INADEQUATE ADAPTATION OF NEW METHODS

The field's slow gain in subtlety and strength is
shown by its gradual turn from the first mode of methodism
to two others.   Easiest to expect is uncritical choice of particular methods borrowed from other fields with research
relevant to studies of political socialization.   In the same
broad category is faddish fixation on methods from more
prestigious or familiar fields, which nonetheless have little
to do with current issues in political socialization.   Then
the motive for a method is more its momentary popularity
than its potential contribution to substantive research.   In
either case, the borrowed methods are initially ill-chosen

----

pp. 13-16; Coles, "Children and Politics: Outsiders," **New
York Review of Books**, 22, 4, March 20, 1975, pp. 29-30;
Kenneth Keniston, **Youth and Dissent**, Harcourt Brace
Jovanovich, 1971; Robert Jay Lifton, **History and Human
Survival**, New York, Random House, 1970; Milton Rokeach,
The Open and Closed Mind, New York, Basic Books, 1960;
Rokeach, **Beliefs, Attitudes, and Values**, San Francisco,
Jossey-Bass, 1968.

[59] See: Robert E. Lane, **Political Ideology**, New York,
Free Press, 1962; Lane, **Political Man**, New York, Free
Press, 1972.

and subsequently ill-adapted to (theoretical) needs of their new field. As most political scientists concede (about their colleagues), Abraham Kaplan's principle of the hammer reveals all too much about political research.[60]

Failure to work through the implications of a method connects closely with failure to work through the implications of a theory or even a framework for analysis. I mentioned before the paucity of behaviorist studies of political stimuli to schoolchildren whose socialization responses have been studied in decent detail. In a few cases, questionnaires have been given to teachers as well as students, with little illuminating result because of the theoretical carelessness of the studies. Edgar Litt's work on civic norms is the outstanding exception, principally for its focus on textbooks.[61] Still, even in terms of textbooks, it is plain that political stimuli are broader by far than books on American government. Frances Fitzgerald's recent analysis of the history and social-science texts used in American schools is but one instance of the directions further research might take.[62] Of course, her works departs radically from behavioralist methods and their undergirding principles of objectivism. Again, the need for shaking loose from old methodologies is compellingly clear.

One who tries to do that is Carol Barner-Barry.[63] With methods of observation from ethology, she is producing substantial innovations in the study of political socialization. Even so, some of her efforts still fall under the shade of methodism. From a few ethologists, Barner-Barry takes over views about uninvolved observation and avoiding any

----

[60] Less well remembered is Kaplan's own label, "the law of the instrument." See: Abraham Kaplan, **The Conduct of Inquiry**, Scranton, PA, Chandler, 1964, p. 28.

[61] See: Edgar Litt, "Civic Education, Community Norms, and Political Indoctrination," **American Sociological Review**, 28, 1, February, 1963, pp. 23-36; Litt, **The Public Vocational University**, New York, Holt, Rinehart and Winston, 1969, especially pp. 103-156.

[62] See: Frances FitzGerald, **America Revised**, Boston, Little, Brown, 1979.

[63] See: Carol Barner-Barry, "An Observational Study of Authority in a Preschool Peer Group," **Political Methodology**, 4, 4, 1977, pp. 415-449.

advance structuring of perception which both enjoin remaining atheoretical. Of course, these fit some convictions and even more practices of behavioralism. Laudably, Barner-Barry really does focus on "surface" behavior, which political science should study more amply and imaginatively. Contrary rhetoric notwithstanding, survey researchers seldom manage this, settling instead stimulation and analysis of verbal reports. Less laudably, she shares the objectivism which subverts behavioralism and ethology itself.

Making little effort to adapt ethological methods to studying humans, let alone children, Barner-Barry falls into the same trap as many ethologists. Her observations require a set of categories. Trying to avoid theoretical categories, which she implies would bias observation, she still must have terms for making and expressing descriptions of whatever she observes. Of course, these concepts must come from some place; and any place involves (covert and careless) appeal to tacit theories, since all concepts depend for meaning on such networks. Even if terms are taken from everyday life, they contain an abundance of theoretical commitments on politics, for these are the convictions on which we predicate ordinary actions.

This is all the more tragic because Barner-Barry has to start with something like a theory of authority in order to justify her method of observing authority events. But instead of nurturing that start into a full-fledged network of concepts to guide observation, she tries to forget how observing, categorizing, and theorizing interact. Her observations are coherent because (and insofar as) her covert, everyday categories are reasonably well-coordinated into one or more compatible theories. Yet those theories cannot be carefully tested and refined until they are made explicit. Like so many political scientists, Barner-Barry ends up presenting her "findings" as though they were raw facts now in need of tying together into a (totally new?) theory including hypotheses she just happens to have posed.

Ethologists tend to repress awareness that they proceed by theoretically pregnant categories, without which they could "observe" nothing. This throws their work back on tacit theories of society and politics, often those patchwork theories of everyday endeavor. It is not wrong to appeal to everyday theories; in fact, they need to be scrutinized, tested, and improved. But that is not done by keeping them covert. In the study of animal behavior, such procedures tend to project (unconsciously) the observers' theories of human conduct onto other animals. Inexcusable in the study of other animals, this is disastrous in the study of humans. For here it is even harder to stay self-critical, since it is harder to observe from a distance and otherwise stay uninvolved. Indeed, our very observation is one or another kind of involvement. Hence there is great danger of "finding" what we tacitly thought all along. And the main defense against that danger is careful, self-critical explication of the theories involved.[64]

To Barner-Barry's approach, contrast that of Erik Erikson, who has also studied small children. Erikson's involvement with objects of observation varies greatly, for he deploys many techniques in diagnosing children's troubles. Even when his posture appears as distant as that of Barner-Barry, he structures observation by explicitly psychoanalytic categories. This lets him deal directly and self-consciously with symbolical levels of child behavior.[65] Barner-Barry's concern with authority is equally symbolical, but she lacks theoretical means for fully defensible observation on symbolical levels. Self-consciously and -critically woven within a fabric of theories, Erikson's observations are more informative than Barner-Barry's, even though hers are better than would be possible were her tacitly symbolical treatment of authority not much more sophisticated than the bits to which she admits in a preliminary exposition of her conception of authority. Theories forthright and relatively detailed, Erikson's work is more open to argument than Barner-Barry's theoretically elusive work. Such is the spirit of Karl Popper's famous insistence on falsifiability; for without considerable explication and detail, theories are of little service to science.[66]

Arguments of the Freudian anthropologist George Devereux suggest another important point about Barner-Barry's approach. Devereux explains how the least utilized data in social science are, paradoxically, the most reliable and informative about social phenomena.[67] These are the

----

[64] See: C. H. Waddington, "Mindless Societies," **New York Review of Books**, 22, 13, August 7, 1975, pp. 30-32; Max Gluckman, "A Band Wagonload of Monkeys," **New York Review of Books**, 19, 8, November 16, 1972, pp. 39-41.

[65] See: Erik Erikson, **Childhood and Society**, New York, Norton, second edition, 1963.

[66] See: Karl Popper, **Conjectures and Refutations**, New York, Harper and Row, 1963.

data of self-observation.   Indeed, Devereux urges us to
make use of that relationship of observer to observed which
Freud termed "counter-transference."   By noting our own
reactions to objects of observation, by pinning down subtle
distortions or uncertainties created by our desires as spurred by those objects, we can learn much about human
action.   And we can do this without the further uncertainties introduced by usual the "distance" between the
observer and the observed, since now the main object of
obervation is ourselves.   There remain distortions in these
reflexive relationships, to be sure, but they are different
and (sometimes) less than those between people.

        Such observation of self is no substitute for observa-
tion of others, but the two are necessary complements.
Significantly, such self-observation primarily makes sense in
terms of depth psychologies, which recognize and analyze
personal dances of preference and perception, emotion and
reason, intellect and desire.   Whatever the method, of
course, inquiry must come to terms with reactions of the
observer to the observed, for they are the forms which
observation takes.   This is readily evident in Barner-Barry's description of her own judgments about what happened
in a given interaction among children.

        Indeed, she does this so well that her failure to take
the next step of self-analysis is all the more unfortunate.
After all, what is she or any researcher doing in observation save to seek knowledge about politics?   Since hers is a
study of political socialization and learning, why stop short
of addressing the data available about her own political
learning in the project at hand?   Such extensions could
shift Barner-Barry's commendable moves into harmony with
what appear to be important parts of her implicit theories of
authority and socialization: for example, her sophisticated
work with symbols.   Lacking these needed moves, though,
Barner-Barry's study instances the second mode of methodism.   For it fails to adapt exciting new methods adequately
research with appropriate theories.

MATCHING NEW METHODS TO OLD METHODOLOGIES

        At the moment, the third mode of methodism is the
most worrisome in the field.   Barner-Barry seems to escape

----

[67] See: George Devereux, **From Anxiety to Method in the
Behavioral Sciences**, The Hague, Mouton, 1967.

it mostly because the epistemologies of ethology and behavioralism are similar. Yet too much other research on political socialization tries to match new methods to old methodologies. This third mode of methodism stimulates the worst research of the three. Troubles notwithstanding, Barner-Barry's and other studies in the second mode of methodism can retain considerable value. So can Merelman's and other inquiries in the first mode of methodism. But deploying new techniques to serve old and incompatible principles of inquiry is another matter. Its "findings" and statistics may look adequate, but its arguments are seldom coherent.

A premier cause of this third methodism is the field's inflexible commitment to research relying on many cases. There are many places for such methods, but studies of political socialization are not high on the list. Still, the field has a fetish for "large-N" statistics and strategies of inquiry. This explains some of the field's reluctance to deploy clinical methods such as depth interviews: done right, they take too many resources (and include too many variables) to allow compilation of enough similar cases to warrant the usual statistics. Attempts to accommodate such methods to this mass-study mentality have often produced pretentious and superfluous translations of rich clinical results into statistically inappropriate terms. Sometimes, though, this third methodism ruins not only research reports, but researches themselves.

One example is Fred Greenstein's turn toward projective and semiprojective tests. These psychological methods could make eminent sense in studies of political socialization, depending on the (theoretical) issues. Greenstein and others merit praise for their willingness to learn the skills appropriate to research suggested by their theories.[68] But what has been done to "adapt" these methods to old epistemologies of political science is another matter. Its methodological imperative is to treat many respondents, that popular statistics could be justified for analyzing the data. But this necessitates that researchers zip through the tests, prompting only one of two levels of responses and engaging the respondents in precious little discussion of their replies. Already, there is room to doubt whether

----

[68] See: Fred I. Greenstein and Sidney Tarrow, "Political Orientations of Children: The Use of a Semi-Projective Technique in Three Nations," **Sage Professional Papers in Comparative Politics**, Series 01-009, 1, Beverly Hills, Sage, 1970.

these should count as projective and semiprojective tests at all.

Then the transcripts are turned over to coders for translation into data amenable to the usual statistics. Even on its face, this is hard to defend, since intercoder reliability is seldom high enough to inspire confidence in what is left of the original research. Worse, we have good reason to suspect that only the most superficial and thus misleading aspects of response are tapped. For the theories which encourage projective tests insist on their subtlety, difficulty, and variability of interpretation. Moreover, these theories require that the tests be read against substantial background data gathered in several ways. The resources needed for good background data alone will usually exceed the means of political scientists, where many cases are concerned. Each of these considerations speaks against the feasibility of amplifying projective testing into a form of survey research, but the impulsion of old epistemologies can produce just that. Few have judged the substantive results of such research to be worth the effort, and these criticisms can explain why.

Matching new methods to old methodologies often destroys the subtlety and sophistication of data, encouraging misinterpretations. Clouding the original sense of the data, researchers virtually invite covert projections of significance onto what is left. Worse, this final form of methodism often keeps good data from being gathered and patterned at all. Contrary to expectations of old epistemologies, data collected in line with intact versions of new methods can be both valid and significant. To be sure, no methods may simply be assumed useful for any field, including political socialization. As already noted, however, methods like depth interviews and projective tests are taken from research partly on political socialization. Hence we have more reason to accept these "new" methods (and their epistemologies affinities) as we have to pursue familiar methods. And we have every reason to open the field to new principles of inquiry, since we have every reason to think the old ones inadequate even for old, established methods such as surveys.

Still, how are these new kinds of data useful for political inquiry? To take a hard case, how do data from intensely personal interviews in only a few cases address important issues of public policy? At a minimum, there is reason to wonder whether "large-N" research is especially important to policy or other political inquiry. Students of public policy are turning to broad principles and processes of policymaking, and I have argued here that students of political socialization should do likewise. But principles and processes may as well (and probably better) be studied by a few deep, careful probes rather than massive, surface surveys.

Yes, some representative sampling is valuable for a sense of context, for knowing how common and variable are the principles and processes perceived. Further, it is valuable for a sense of conditions, for knowing limits and occasions of the principles and processes perceived. But useful sampling is not restricted to "large-N" statistics. For centuries, historians and philosophers have brought detailed background knowledge to bear on selection of cases, specifying their status in whole populations or contexts. As Barner-Barry's work shows, we can be confident that cases are representative when reasonably detailed explanation of contexts is provided. In addition, truly substantive theories also help us tell which cases are representative of what phenomena. In several parts of political science, increased experience in surveys and sophistication in theories has led to replacing simple random samples with stratified ones. Yet stratified samples embody exactly the same principle of guidance by context and theory that justifies "small-N" research.

"Large-N" work is fostered also by the latent individualism of behavioralism.[69] In ontology, methodology, morality, politics, and more, political scientists have often assumed that the only basic unit is the individual. The agency and uniqueness of individuals means that all research must reach the level of individuals in order to be utterly sound. Thus attempts to touch base with large numbers of individuals would be defensible and even necessary. Yet theories of socialization are especially good at revealing how groups like societies, economies, and polities can be just as basic a unit of study as individuals, which are neither more nor less agentic or unique than such groups. Moreover, this methodological recognition of groups can be accomplished while respecting a certain moral and political priority for individuals.[70] Finally, precisely

----

[69] See: Heinz Eulau, **The Behavioral Persuasion in Politics**, Stanford, CA, Stanford University Press, 1963; Eulau, ed., **Behavioralism in Political Science**, New York, Atherton Press, 1969; John C. Wahlke, "Pre-Behavioralism in Political Science," **American Political Science Review**, 73, 1, March, 1979, pp. 9-31.

insofar as individual agency and uniqueness are important in politics, there is strong reason to concentrate on more intimate and intensive study of individuals, after the fashion of clinical observation and depth interviews. For they afford fuller pictures of the peculiarities of particular cases than do relatively impersonal and extensive methods of study. Certainly the principles and processes of political socialization cannot be understood without considerable work of both broad kinds.

Through most cases for concentrating on "large-N" research runs the dubious assumption that political science or public policy needs to apportion the population into percentages or pattern it into regressions into order to proceed intelligently. Neither scientific nor practical arguments for this position are persuasive. Much political science operates with very few cases. And on average, such "small-N" research is just as salient for public policy-making. The field of international relations provides an obvious set of examples. In any event, sound understandings of particular policy areas may help more than parceling populations into survey categories restricted to surfaces of public opinion. And this goes not only for the third mode of methodism, but the other two as well.

OBJECTIVITY

Repudiating objectivism, research on political socialization stands to gain greater objectivity. Objectivism reaches for unrealistic and even perverse senses of scientific neutrality. Long conceding that no research is "value-free," some political scientists continue to strive for inquiry that is "value-neutral."[71] Meaning that values need and

----

[70] See: Isaac Levi, "Conflict and Social Agency," **Journal of Philosophy**, 79, 5, May, 1982, pp. 231-247; John S. Nelson, "Recognizing Rights of Groups and Communities," paper presented to the Annual Meeting of the Midwest Political Science Association, Cincinatti, April 15-18, 1981.

[71] See: Donald D. Searing, "Values in Empirical Research: A Behaviorist Response," **Midwest Journal of Political Science**, 14, 1, February, 1970, pp. 71-104; Paul F. Kress, "The Web and the Tree: Metaphors of Reason and Value,"

should not bias inquiry, this view is both valid and compatible with better studies of political socialization. Meaning that values need and should not make a difference in inquiry, this view is both invalid and incompatible with better studies of political socialization. Objectivity is neither merely nor possibly the same as some insignificance of values in either the conduct or the outcome of research. This is a mutual implication of the four principles of symbolical, rational, ideological, and practical knowledge. New theories and epistemologies of political socialization present a good opportunity to push the field and its full discipline toward more practical and accurate senses of objectivity.

The same aguments against dichotomizing reason and emotion apply to attempts to bifurcate fact (or science) and value. Moreover, the very possibility of significant research depends on its having value(s). Were values somehow neutralized in research, then inquiry could not intersect public policymaking or any other practical concern. Contrary to objectivism, perspectivism rejects grand gulfs between facts and values in favor of specific distinctions in particular contexts. Since those vary a great deal, and since many contexts make fact/value splits irrelevant or perverse, perspectivism insists that intertwinings of facts, values, and other components of inquiry be unraveled in diverse ways, depending on the actual angle of inquiry. For many purposes and occasions in political science, no such split will be sensible.[72] Hence, if objectivity is to be achieved in research, it must not be pursued as a matter of keeping values separate so as to neutralize their effects on inquiry.

New theories of political socialization show how emotion, imagination, and other "irrational" factors which objectivists associate with evaluation must affect but need not

----

Midwest Journal of Political Science, 13, 3, August, 1969, pp. 395-414.

[72] See: Bruce Kuklick, "The Analytic-Synthetic and Descriptive-Evaluative Distinctions," Journal of Value Inquiry, 3, 2, Summer, 1969, pp. 91-99; John J. Dowling, "Values and Objectivity," The Human Context, 7, 3, Autumn, 1975, pp. 399-421; J. Donald Moon, "Values and Political Theory," Journal of Politics, 39, 4, November, 1977, pp. 877-903; Gunnell, Philosophy, Science, and Political Inquiry, chapters 7-8. Also see Gunnell's essay in the book at hand.

distort what we perceive and conceive, let alone what we do. Although these theories seldom make the mistake of severing value from what is "rational," their demonstration of its ties to the "nonrational" is enough to establish how value permeates research and structures "findings." All four of the field's new principles of knowledge imply that "value-neutrality" is no less ridiculous an idea than "value-freedom." They also imply that the presence and awareness of value can improve research by improving powers of self-criticism.

All four principles of knowledge suggest that objectivity is a function of theories and communities of inquiry far more than individual methods or any rigor with which they are pursued. Insofar as objectivity is a matter of methods, it is a matter of wielding them well. In turn, that places the burden of objectivity on theories and researchers. Criticizing projects of their own, of others in their community, and (less often) of other communities, researchers create the only real objectivity: clear-sighted and conscientious self-criticism. The great advantage of recent theories of political socialization is that they are partly theories of perception, conception, deception, and expression. (To be about political socialization, they have to include such topics. For in its best and broadest sense, the field studies political learning.) Similarly, these theories concern self-deception, desire, discussion, and many other matters complicating human inquiry. Thus the field can now make our understandings of inquiry more complete, incisive, and realistic than before. Better comprehending good principles of inquiry, we can become better critics and practitioners of political inquiry generally.

The prospect of turning research on political socialization back on itself and political science in order to increase the skill and sophistication of both makes this field especially important to the disipline as a whole. For this field is the logical focus of the full discipline's self-criticism and -improvement. Why, for instance, should Barner-Barry not analyze her own learning along with the political learning of young children? Already, readers receive a highly suggestive account of her steps in deciding what transpires in the play-yard. Far from a digression, this further study of her own processes of political learning is indispensable to her study of children's processes of political learning.

If this is so true, then why have so few political scientists yet accepted it? One reason is objectivism or, more specifically, methodism. But why are political scientists attracted to objectivism, methodism, or the like? So far as

I know, there is no solid research on this question. Hence I can only conjecture, informed by the theories mentioned earlier and casual observation of colleagues (and myself). For the most part, the personal styles of political scientists seem incompatible with highly personalized research of the kinds encouraged by these theories. Of course, those styles are shaped somewhat by disciplinary styles, socially transmitted; but my suspicion is that personal styles explain why some find political science congenial in the first place. Relatedly, many political scientists seem less tolerant of ambiguities, emotional involvements, and personal vulnerabilities produced by these new theories and methods of research. Their greater uncertainties, further turn to feelings, and striking subjectivity of self-analysis may be personally distasteful to the principal sorts of people recruited to become political scientists.

Presumably several avenues of research could (and should) attempt to study and specify this possible phenomenon. The various personality theories recently brought into research on political socialization surely imply processes by which this could occur. My own poor evidence of acquaintances and anecdotes encourages the hypothesis that political scientists very different from those just described tend to cluster in the discipline's few fields where extensive personal contact with subjects of research is cultivated and where methods more akin to depth interviews and participant observations are pursued. Study of the presidency might be one such field. Further, political scientists with personalities highly divergent from those just evoked might be more inclined to choose the more interactive and subjective of methods standard in any given field. For example, among those who study police or legislatures, we should inquire to see whether, why, and how those who proceed by interviews and personal observation differ from those who deal in surveys, budgets, votes, and other comparatively impersonal methods.

Even without such research, it is clear that the professional culture of political science is strongly hostile to the humanities. They are distrusted and deplored for overly soft, subjective, flexible -- in a word, personal -- styles of research and expression. Of course, the archive and the text can be pretty impersonal sources of knowledge; but still, studies of history and literature demand resources of personal sympathy and subjective imagination suspect throughout political science. (Oddly, the discipline's need to interpret data should be calling upon the same sorts of resources and probably is, to an impoverished degree.) Political scientists incessantly enjoin one another to abstract from personal peculiarities into general laws of politics, and these injunctions cry out for a psychoanalytic diagnosis of "overdetermination." For they recur beyond anything necessary or proper in political inquiry, yet they legitimate the personal distance which most political scientists maintain between themselves and their subjects of research.

As a field of political science, then, political socialization may be reluctant to embrace some of its most promising theories and methods because their styles of research are mildly offensive to professional taste. Perhaps the field of political socialization is slow to face up to the significance of its substantive theories because their stress on desire and stylistic commitment makes its practitioners personally uncomfortable. And if these subtleties of image, strategy, and emotion seem to lead to matters of politics within political science, that the field's four principles of knowledge point precisely there. Not only psychology, sociology, and economics of inquiry are involved, but politics of inquiry as well.

One implication of facing this possibility is that the discipline rethink another of its self-imposed limits: keeping the profession as far as possible from political engagement. I do not mean that political scientists must immediately or eventually treat themselves as politicians. Still, the gateless wall between the discipline and its subject should be reconstructed to accept an appropriate and almost inevitable traffic between their two territories. Similarly, the ambivalent oscillation between research relevant to public policy and science unsullied by political styles must be ended by abandoning attempts to transcend all traces of political commitment.

Thus I reiterate a recommendation made by others: **political socialization should be reconceived as political education.**[73] There are many ways to contrast socialization and

----

[73] See: Joseph Tussman, **Obligation and the Body Politic,** New York, Oxford University Press, 1960; Tussman, **Government and the Mind,** New York, Oxford University Press, 1977; Robert J. Pranger, **The Eclipse of Citizenship,** New York, Holt, Rinehart and Winston, 1968; Norman Jacobson, "Political Science and Political Education," **American Political Science Review,** 57, 3, September, 1963, pp. 561-569; Donald W. Hanson, "The Education of Citizens: Reflections on the State of Political Science," **Polity,** 11, 4, Summer, 1979, pp. 457-477.

education.   Let me settle for underscoring the compatibility of political education with political freedom.   Processes of socialization and acculturation are typically presented in the mechanical terms of stimulus and response, input and output, system and feedback.   This encourages treating acquisition of political beliefs as a simple imposition of patterns on people, causing them to behave after the fashion of (poorly) programmed robots.   Thus do accounts of political socialization incline toward an inadequate conception of choice, as I noted before.   Centering on role behavior, they shift attention away from free action.   By contrast, the concept of education promotes decent recognition and comprehension of choice in politics.   It spurs inquiry into conditions, principles, and processes of free action.

A further advantage of this reconception concerns the autonomy of politics and political inquiry.   The notion of socialization derives from frameworks which almost invariably portray politics as a mere function of psyche, society, or economy, so that political science might be reduced to a mere field of psychology, sociology, or economics.   Theoretically, this is unfortunate, since it explains away the distinctive features of politics by reducing them to social interactions or the like.   Morally, this is disastrous, because it implicitly substitutes regulation of human behavior by roles for the true freedom of human action by persons.   Even philosophically, this is dubious, for it misses the historical demarcation of distinct disciplines by their different (and only partly overlapping) theories, methods, and standards of inquiry.   Of course, pseudosubstantive "theories" of systems and functions are especially vulnerable to such insensitivities.[74]

Subsuming politics under society (etc.) both promotes and derives from the postmodern swelling of civil society into mass society.   Private affairs and perspectives seep steadily outward in all directions, gradually swamping the public realms, where politics did abide.[75]   Thus a subtle, but significant reason that the study of political socialization seems paralyzed by problems of order and legitimacy is

----

[74] See: Easton, A Framework for Political Analysis, pp. 35-57.

[75] See: Hannah Arendt, The Human Condition, Garden City, NY, Doubleday, 1958; Sheldon S. Wolin, Politics and Vision, Boston, Little, Brown, 1960; Richard Sennett, The Fall of Public Man, New York, Random House, 1976.

that it lacks an adequately political sensibility. Here is another instance of the revenge of the repressed in research, for the original label of this field carries a myriad of covert implications: many unconscious and most unwelcome if the purpose is to study political education. Indeed, the category of education connects more readily and insistently than that of socialization with the field's defining concerns of learning, inquiry, and science. For research on political education is inquiry into political inquiry itself.

PHILOSOPHY OF INQUIRY

This essay begins with lessons from philosophy of inquiry for research on political socialization. This essay ends with a final lesson from political socialization for philosophy of inquiry. Rethinking research on political socialization leads to reshaping it into comprehension and criticism of political education, of political learning in general. Therefore, philosophy of inquiry can learn much from this substantive field of political science. Put otherwise, the last lesson of this essay is that substantive inquiry and philosophy of inquiry can never be fully distinct from one another. For neither can be complete (or successful) without the other.

This last lesson follows from the principle that theories, methods, and epistemologies interpenetrate and interact. Importantly, this principle has enabled and even required approach by the two seemingly separate lines of analysis which converge to form my main line of argument. On one hand, theories of science and inquiry lead to this lesson; on the other hand, theories of political socialization and education yield it, too. Good philosophy of inquiry is substantive; good research is self-reflective. To articulate this lesson and conclude this essay, let me emphasize four corollaries of the principle of interdependence.

CONCRETE CONTEXTS

John Gunnell argues persuasively that no separate field of philosophy of inquiry can bind other fields to details of epistemology or method. Not even formalist philosophies of inquiry can claim authority over the conduct of inquiry in any substantive field. When political scientists try to draw a precise norm for research from an utterly different discipline, they destroy their own autonomy of inquiry to no gain. Everyday research in any field should be directed by those in the field through judgments on specific issues in their concrete contexts of inquiry. Such judgments are disciplined by the field's own culture of criticism. Hence for Gunnell, philosophy of inquiry should follow inquiry itself, although precisely how and why is less clear.[76]

The principle of interdependence plainly implies some sort of contextualism, putting primary responsibility for methods and standards of inquiry on the people doing concrete research. But philosophy of inquiry can have a more constructive role than Gunnell appears to provide. For theories of inquiry come from and lead back to concrete inquiries. Such physicists as Einstein, Maxwell, and Heisenberg have been worthy philosophers of science. And preserving interaction among branches of inquiry is a principle implicit in the insistence of Kuhn and company on informing philosophy of science with history of science, and vice versa. They and other recent theorists of inquiry practice this principle with some skill. They study past and present work, often in several substantive disciplines. If anything, this is even more true of recent philosophers of social science. Indeed, many of the best philosophers of social science come now from the social sciences themselves. Concern with philosophy of inquiry can push them away from substantive inquiry in their original fields, but it need not and has not always done so. On the contrary, their interest in principles and methods appropriate to inquiry arises from their concrete contexts of research.

The need of philosophy of inquiry for immersion in concrete contexts of inquiry is a need for the cultural, clinical sensitivity celebrated by people such as Clifford Geertz and Erik Erikson. Here the cultures are disciplines and the subcultures are research projects. Without cultural comprehension and "thick description" of inquiries, no philosophy of inquiry can understand what it is talking about. Gunnell's contextualism is right in this respect: **detailed knowledge of a concrete context of research is the first requirement of intelligent conduct of research in that context.** But this should not be the whole story of contextualism, as the second corollary makes clear.

----

[76] See: Gunnell, **Philosophy, Science, and Political Inquiry.** Also see Gunnell's chapter in this volume.

COMPARATIVE CONTEXTS

Strangely, Gunnell ends up implying almost as big a gulf between inquiry and philosophy of inquiry as he criticizes in behavioralism and formalist philosophies of science. For inquiry is presented as though it has no need for philosophy of inquiry, however much philosophy of inquiry may depend on substantive inquiry itself. Why would the field of philosophy of inquiry not be able to claim the same freedom from outside criticism, including that of Gunnell? Indeed, how can Gunnell's position comprehend and criticize itself, let alone speak to alien inquiries on this basis? Denied a forum of self-reflection, Gunnell's principles flirt with the very objectivism and incapacity of self-criticism which Gunnell faults in logical positivism, empiricism, and behavioralism. Rather than propound more paradoxes, though, let me simply ask instead: what can sound philosophy of inquiry contribute to specific, substantive inquiries?

From the sad state of analytical epistemologies, we can infer that the contribution cannot be iron rules, unless they are very vague. Then their surface precision and rigor is misleading, for they are "internally flexible," permitting diverse interpretations and applications. And this is to say that they are principles, aphorisms, maxims, or perspectives rather than rigid rules, specific prescriptions, or precise methods. Still, as this essay seeks to show, such principles are needed in substantive inquiry.

Primarily, epistemological principles are needed for their comparative perspective on inquiry. Substantive research requires such comparison among projects for refining old standards or ideas and inspiring new ones. The great virtue of epistemology is its attempt to learn from foreign projects. In the sense that philosophy of inquiry just is this project of comparison, concrete inquiries would not contain a comparative perspective without it. Thus epistemology is an opportunity and an injunction to pay careful, self-critical attention to the inquiries of others, especially when significantly different from one's own. Indeed, how can concrete contexts of research even be delimited except through such comparison of projects and principles?

Instead of Gunnell's autonomy unto atomism, contextualism should be an autonomy unto interdependence. This means mutual information and reflection across the usual divides of disciplines. Gunnell's contextualism is wrong in this respect: **comparative knowledge of other contexts of research is the second requirement of intelligent research in**

any single context. Neither accidentally nor incidentally, the best researchers time and again turn out to be very interested in a wide variety of fields, from which they learn important principles for improving their own inquiries. Substantive inquiries need philosophies of inquiry, as well as the other way around. And the corollary of comparative contexts says why. A better sense of how is afforded by the third corollary.

EVERYDAY EPISTEMOLOGY

Discomfort with tendencies of political inquiry to transform itself into abstract debate about philosophy of inquiry has led diverse people in political science to urge return to substantive political research. The sentiment is laudable; and so is the proposal, as long as it refrains from turning injunctions against forgetting politics into excuses for forgetting epistemology. Lapses of judgment (or changes of vocation?) have allowed some students of politics to wander into epistemological preoccupations, never to bring back fruits for political research. But it does not follow that epistemology proper is to be avoided. On the contrary, epistemology is the path to meeting the needs of political research for improved principles of inquiry. Hence epistemology must be confronted if political inquiry is to make headway, avoiding the snares of abstract replacements for both substantive research and substantive epistemology.

Arguments against epistemology run afoul of the principle that theory and epistemology are interrelated, unavoidably and very significantly. Unless political theory is (in part) also epistemological theory, it cannot know how to proceed. At a minimum, the epistemological project of any political theory is dialogue with other political theories. But more than that, it is dedication to objectivity (as self-criticism) and discipline (as self-improvement). Most ambitiously, it is attention to philosophy as a concern for inquiries distant from politics. In individual investigators, these projects of epistemology may be intermittent but never abandoned altogether. In whole fields or disciplines, they must be continual yet always coordinated with substantive matters at hand.

Last, arguments against epistemology collapse under the weight of recent political crises. For our political worries are importantly about inquiry, reason, terminology, technique, expertise, and proper claims of social science. In other words, controversies about inquiry are center-

stage in current politics.[77] Here I cannot make a detailed
case for this claim, but the earlier tour through theories of
political education has provided considerable evidence for
it.   Unless political scientists are to flee the study of politics in their own times, then, today's discipline must make
issues of inquiry into major ends, as well as means, of
political research.   And the way to face up to these issues
of inquiry is to **make epistemology an intrinsic part of
everyday inquiry.**   This done, the fourth corollary can follow.

POLITICAL LEARNING

Paying attention to the principles and processes of
political education is necessary in order to achieve more
sophisticated, self-reflective sciences of politics.   The field
of political socialization need not lead the way for political
scientists to have their epistemological consciousness raised,
but it now has a special opportunity to do so.   More mind-
ful and better informed about dynamics of political learning,
the field of political socialization can help the other fields of
political science improve themselves as political inquiries.
This does not mean that research on political socialization should be made over into abstract philosophy of
inquiry by another name.   Nor does it encourage that the
field becomes so consumed in self-reflection that its traditional targets of study be slighted in favor of watching
itself watch other fields of political science in inquiry.   The
political education of children, adults, immigrants, and the
like are most important topics in their own right.
What this does imply is that some reseach on political
education should be more direct studies of disciplined political inquiry, including political scientists at work.   In addition, this projects a new conception of the field as a special
arena in which many principles important to learning about
politics are first specified and tested.   Because of the concern of this field with political communication (conscious and
unconscious, based on signs and symbols), it can teach the
other fields of political inquiry about their own procedures
and effects.   Accordingly, the fourth corollary is that

----

[77] See: Jane Flax, "Why Epistemology Matters: A Reply to
Kress," **Journal of Politics,** 43, 4, November, 1981, pp.
1006-1024; John S. Nelson and Ira L. Strauber, "For Epistemology," unpublished paper.

knowledge of politics is the province of political learning, which is the special concern of research on political education.

Thus does openness to new theories, methods, and epistemologies become all the more mandatory in the field of political education. Rethinking research on political socialization reveals special opportunities and special responsibilities for the field, which faces the first crossroads of its short time in political science. May this reconception continue in the course recommended here.

For related reasons, political inquiry generally faces another of its recurrent crises in self-conception. As before, this crisis is partly epistemological. Also as before, it is not limited to political science, but embraces inquiries throughout the social sciences and humanities. This crisis requires us to come to terms with old aspirations to science and epistemology in new ways. Idols of technique must be torn down; cultures of self-criticism must be nurtured. Philosophy of inquiry cannot be king, even if elected. But neither should it be restricted to mopping up after substantive research. Philosophy of inquiry need not and cannot be fully separate from substantive research. Indeed philosophy of inquiry should proceed apace with inquiry itself. Our goal should be to make epistemology a moment in everyday research, rather than a departure from it. Otherwise, our inquiries, like our theories of inquiry, will continue impoverished.

WHAT DOES IT TAKE TO HAVE A THEORY?

PRINCIPLES IN POLITICAL SCIENCE

William H. Panning

> [E]ven scholars of audacious spirit and fine
> instinct can be hindered in the interpretation of
> facts by philosophical prejudices. The preju-
> dice -- which has by no means disappeared --
> consists in the belief that facts by themselves
> can and should yield scientific knowledge with-
> out free conceptual construction. Such a mis-
> conception is possible only because one does not
> easily become aware of the free choice of such
> concepts, which, through success and long
> usage, appear to be immediately connected with
> the empirical material.
>
> Albert
Einstein

During the past two decades, there appeared a fascinating series of studies by political scientists attempting to
determine whether and to what extent the political stability
of societies is affected by economic equality. Four studies
concerned with land distribution are pertinent here. In the
first, Bruce Russett analyzed data from 47 countries and
found that countries with greater inequality exhibited
greater political instability. Using 1961 census data in a
study of 26 provinces of South Vietnam, however, Edward
Mitchell found just the opposite: the greater the inequality, the greater the political stability. (Admittedly, stability was imperfectly measured by the proportion of a province under Saigon control.) Still later, Anthony Russo
reanalyzed Mitchell's data but found no relationship at all
between inequality and support for revolution. Finally,
analyzing that data yet again, Jack Nagel found a curvilinear relationship between inequality and Vietcong control:
maximum support for revolution occurred at intermediate
levels of inequality of land ownership.[1]

----

[1] See: Bruce M. Russett, "Inequality and Instability: The
Relation of Land Tenure to Inequality," **World Politics**, 16,

I recount this sequence of findings in order to raise an important question that many political scientists will find uncomfortable: how to choose among these disparate results. By purity of method? By appeal to differences in explained variation or in t-ratios? By gathering and analyzing still more data? Or by further, more sophisticated analysis of the old data?

One of many, this example suggests the difficulty (if not the impossibility) of accomplishing what most political scientists take to be the aim of their discipline: developing theory by steadily accumulating empirical generalizations. Although accumulating empirical findings is indeed valuable, alone it cannot lead to establishing scientific theory.

In the second part of this essay, I argue that scientific theory depends on the discovery of explanatory principles that lend coherence to what we know. In part three, I exemplify this by sketching one explanatory principle and my reasons for regarding it as especially appropriate to the study of politics. Finally, I try to clarify the relationship between this kind of political theory and activities in the particular field of political theory as well as in the general discipline of political science.[2]

3, April, 1964, pp. 442-454; Edward J. Mitchell, "Inequality and Insurgency: A Statistical Study of South Vietnam," **World Politics**, 20, 3, April, 1968, pp. 421-438; Anthony J. Russo, Jr., "Economic and Social Correlates of Government Control in South Vietnam," in Ivo K. Feierabend, Rosalind L. Feierabend, and Ted R. Gurr, eds., **Anger, Violence, and Politics**, Englewood Cliffs, New Jersey, Prentice-Hall, 1972, pp. 314-324; Jack H. Nagel, "Inequality and Discontent: A Nonlinear Hypothesis," **World Politics**, 26, 4, July, 1974, pp. 453-472.

[2] Through countless discussions, the critical faculties of my colleagues have rescued me from many errors in these matters. I am especially indebted to John Nelson, G. R. Boynton, and Benjamin Most. They will no doubt find still other errors in what I have written here. Russell Hardin likewise provided helpful and timely advice on portions of my argument. I am also indebted to Herbert A. Simon, Stephen Toulmin, and Friedrich A. Hayek, whose works influence my thinking in more ways than can be adequately acknowledged by references within the text.

THE ORTHODOX PRACTICE OF POLITICAL SCIENCE

> A science is built out of facts just as a house
> is built out of bricks. But a mere collection of
> facts cannot be called a science any more than
> a pile of bricks can be called a house.
>
> Henri
> Poincare

Proliferation of disparate findings is not unusual in political science. Investigators differ in the methods they employ, in the variables they consider relevant, and in the specific measures they construct. Ultimately, though, the problem lies deeper: the world is complex, and data are imperfect. Seldom, if ever, do data reflect only the relationship sought. Observations are affected by numerous other variables, only some of which can be controlled experimentally or statistically. Although these effects are postulated to be random, we cannot know this for sure. Moreover, data also reflect limitations of the measuring instruments used to obtain them: measurements are necessarily imperfect.

Political scientists commonly believe that these two sources of error are the principal obstacles to developing theories. Reduce such error, it is argued, and accumulated empirical findings will result in theories. Natural sciences have progressed rapidly, it is asserted, because they have experimental controls and powerful tools of measurement. Thus political scientists devote much effort to developing new statistical techniques and more refined tools of measurement.

From my own research, I know these tools and techniques to be valuable. Yet I am not at all convinced that reducing error in our data is a sufficient or even a necessary condition for developing theories. Recently, I provided a graduate class with data consisting of twenty values for each of two variables. I designated one as the dependent variable, but did not identify what the two variables were. I assured the class that values of the independent variable were error-free and that error in the dependent variable was normally distributed and homoskedastic. (These are conditions assumed in the use of regression procedures.) Then I posed an ostensibly simple problem: find the true relationship between the two variables. Finding the answer is surprisingly difficult, as the class discovered. Below are some of its results, including those

from a very powerful test of the normality of residuals in
each case:

RELATIONSHIP	ADJUSTED R-SQUARED	RESIDUALS
$Y = A + B*X$	0.99	Normal
$Y = A + B1*X + B2*X**2$	0.99	Normal
$logY = A + B*logX$	0.99	Normal
$logY = A + B*X$	0.99	Normal

One relationship is correct, in the sense that I com-
puted the values of Y from those for X using that relationship and then added a small, random error term to those Y
values. In no case did this error exceed 3% of the true
value of Y; indeed, the average error is about 1% of the
true value of Y.

How could one choose empirically among these four
possible relationships? Is the third or fourth decimal in the
value of R-squared a very persuasive standard for judgment? True, all four are quite accurate predictively; but
choosing the correct relationship is important if the aim is
theoretical understanding. Indeed, this choice was so
important that it assured its maker a prominent place in the
history of astronomy. For the correct equation, the third
listed above, expresses in a linear form Kepler's Third Law
(discovered in 1618): the orbital period of a planet (Y) is
proportional to the 3/2 power of its mean distance from the
sun (X), so that $logY = 0 + (3/2)*logX$.

The point of this exercise is (or should be) familiar.
These data are virtually error-free, yet the true relationship between the variables cannot be determined empirically. "Of course," some may say, "you can't know which
is correct unless you have a theory." And indeed, nearly
every political scientist would agree: to choose among
these alternatives, or among the rival findings about inequality and instability, demonstrate that one relationship is
more plausible theoretically than the others. I agree. But
how are we to do this? What does it take to have a theory?

The "official" answer to this troublesome question is
enshrined in nearly every "scope and methods" text used to
train budding political scientists. It is based firmly on
Carl Hempel's notion of "covering-law" explanations: a
theory is a set of related generalizations.[3] But this answer

----

[3] For example, see: Alan C. Isaak, Scope and Methods of
Political Science, Homewood, Illinois, Dorsey Press, Third

is not very helpful if our aim is to choose among rival findings or relationships, for it presupposes that we have precisely what we are still seeking. Consider again the conflicting studies of inequality and instability. Any theory to which we might appeal must say generally how inequality relates to instability. Yet such a generalization is just what these four studies seek to establish. How, then, could there be a relevant theory to guide our choice? Had prior studies established such a generalization, we would say that these four additional studies undermine its credibility! Our only recourse seems more empirical studies or improved measurements and methods. In the meantime, we base judgments on a thorough and critical analysis of the literature and an intimate knowledge of the problem and the data. Thus we do more and more empirical studies, ascribing their failure to "cumulate" to the complexity of our subject and the deficiencies of our data.

Basically, our difficulty lies neither in the prevalence of conflicting findings, nor in the presence of error in data, nor even in the complexity of political phenomena. Rather, it lies in our conception of what to do as political scientists. Specifically, we labor under an impoverished notion of what it takes to have a theory.

I come recently to this criticism. Much of my formal training and research has been similar to others in our discipline. For the reasons just given, though, I am disquieted by what I see as inherent defects of our present conception of theory-building. And I am encouraged by a sustained avocational study of natural science and its his-

----

edition, 1981, p. 304. In the most quantitative portions of our discipline, however, many political scientists conceive theory as a set of relationships among variables: a set of related multivariate hypotheses that have received empirical support. Yet the two notions are virtually identical. Generalizations have the form: "all entities that have property X have property Y." Statistical generalizations of the form "Y = a + bX" can be restated in the form: "all entities that have an X value consisting of some number x have a Y value consisting of the number a + bx." Both forms state relationships between two variables, differing only in the level at which the variables are measured: nominal versus interval. Hence my argument about our discipline's "generalizations" applies to both these popular conceptions of theory.

tory to think that we can do better.[4] Through a glass, darkly, this study permits a glimpse of a very different conception of what it takes to have a theory. In this essay, I hope to show how this alternative pertains to what we do as political scientists.

SCIENCE AS THE SEARCH

FOR EXPLANATORY PRINCIPLES

> Now in the further development of science, we want more than just a formula. First we have an observation, then we have numbers that we measure, then we have a law which summarizes all the numbers. But the real **glory** of science is that **we can find a way of thinking** such that the law is **evident**.
>
> Richard
> Feynman

What does it take to have a theory? Consider an example. Suppose two people are playing a game. On the table between them lie nine cards, the ace through nine of spades, face up. In turn, each transfers one card to his hand. The aim is to be the first player to "make book," to acquire three cards summing to fifteen. (The ace counts as one.) If, when all nine cards have been drawn, neither player has made book, the outcome is a draw. Now consider two questions. First, what is a good strategy in this game? Second, does the order of play advantage either player?[5] I once posed this problem to some students who, by trying their hand at the game and observing the results, arrived at the following conclusions. First, if a player begins by choosing the five, the other is advantaged by choosing the two, four, six, or eight. Second, if a

----

[4] For reasons of style, I write here of "natural science" and "social science" in the singular. But let me emphasize that each comprises many different activities.

[5] This example, but not my use of it, is from: Herbert A. Simon, **The Sciences of the Artificial**, Cambridge, MA, MIT Press, second edition, 1981, p. 152.

player instead starts with the two, four, six, or eight, then the other's best response is to choose the five. Third, players who select cards of intermediate, rather than extreme, values tend to win. Finally, the game seems to be fair: if both players choose optimally, the most likely outcome is a draw.

Had the object of study been some political phenomenon rather than a contrived game, we might say that these four statements are a crude theory of that phenomenon, for they satisfy our current notion of theory. That is, they comprise a set of related generalizations supported by empirical study (consisting, in this case, of playing the game).

In natural science, though, this would be regarded, not as a theory, but as a start toward developing one. In natural science, theorists aim, not to stockpile generalizations, but to understand how the relationships we find are as they are. Theorists seek to say why phenomena occur as they do, and not otherwise. This requires, not some second-order set of generalizations in more abstract terms, but rather a way of thinking about phenomena that permits us to infer what we have in fact observed. As a consequence of conceiving the phenomena in this way, what has occurred seems evident rather than arbitrary. Our urge is to say, Aha!

What would such a theory be for my hypothetical game? Here is one answer. Imagine the cards arranged this way on the table:

$$8 \quad 3 \quad 4$$
$$1 \quad 5 \quad 9$$
$$6 \quad 7 \quad 2$$

In this particular arrangement, known in recreational mathematics as a "magic square," the numbers in any row, column, or full diagonal sum to fifteen. (To win the game, a player must select three cards that sum to this number.) Whenever the first player picks a card, replace its number in the magic square with an "X." Whenever the second player picks a card, replace its number with an "O." Our thinking of the game in this way is a **representation** of the game. To win, a player must, as it were, place three Xs (or Os) in one of the rows, columns, or diagonals of the square. This is the **principle** for applying our representation in answering the two questions with which we began.

By now, you have no doubt said to yourself, "Aha! Playing the card game is just like playing tic-tac-toe." Precisely. That is what the representation, the new

arrangement of the cards ¬and so on, is intended to convey.
But let me draw your attention to some important features
of this recognition and how it came about.

First, our theoretical understanding was brought
about by discovering, not a generalization, but a new way
of thinking about the game. Indeed, our understanding is
completely different in form from the students' generalizations; and it would be difficult or impossible to express it
as a generalization. Were we to explain our discovery to
someone else, we would first need to show them how to represent the card game as tic-tac-toe. Then we would need
to show them how the same principles of play apply to
both. If you want to understand this card game, we would
say, think of it as a game of tic-tac-toe.

But second, since our new way of thinking about the
game is not a generalization, we could not have discovered
it inductively in the usual sense: by "the basic logical
process of going from a set of individual observations to a
generalization."[6] Although our observations (data) no doubt
facilitated this discovery, our leap to a new conception of
the game was an act of imagination rather than logic in the
standard senses. If induction had a role, it was earlier, in
developing the students' generalizations. Still, these generalizations are themselves puzzling, until understood theoretically. We could not say why most games ended in a
draw or the second player was advantaged by choosing the
five when the first player had chosen an even numbered
card. Making more observations, collecting more data,
might have made these findings more certain, but would not
have made them more understandable. Our new way of
conceiving the game is what makes them comprehensible to
us. Indeed, we accept this view of the game precisely for
that reason.

Third, in addition to accounting for what we had
already observed, this new conception suggests further
relationships that had previously escaped our attention.
For example, we can see from the diagram that if the first
player has chosen either the two and the eight or the six
and the four, and the second player has chosen the five,
he should now choose an odd number to avoid losing. We
can confirm this by observation, by playing the game.
Thus our new way of thinking helps us to find new relationships, and this reinforces our acceptance of it.

Fourth, the new conception may lead us to reject

----

[6] Isaak, **Scope and Methods of Political Science**, p. 301.

some previous conclusions. My students decided that cards with intermediate numbers had greater strategic value than cards with high or low numbers. Indeed, of the four generalizations they discovered, this one seemed the most comprehensible. For they reasoned that numbers of intermediate size could be combined in more ways to produce a total of fifteen than could extreme numbers. The diagram, however, shows that (except for the number five, which is included in four winning combinations) the **even** rather than the middle numbers are strategically important. Each even number is part of three winning combinations, whereas each odd number is part of two only. Again, this can be tested by playing the game.

This point has an important implication that is often stated but seldom heeded in political science. The validity of generalizations depends at least as much on their consistency with our theory, our way of thinking about a phenomenon, as on the accuracy of our data or the sophistication of our statistical procedures in discovering them. Francis Crick, co-discoverer of the structure of DNA, stated this point well:

> The point is that evidence can be unreliable....We have three or four bits of data, we don't know which one is reliable, so we say, now, if we discard that one and assume it's wrong -- even though we have no evidence that it's wrong -- then we can look at the rest of the data and see if we can make sense of **that**. And that's what we do **all the time**. I mean, people don't realize that not only can data be wrong in science, it can be **misleading**. There isn't such a thing as a hard fact when you're trying to discover something. It's only afterwards that the facts become hard. [7]

Murray Gell-Mann, a physicist and likewise a Nobel laureate pointed to the same feature about his new theory of the weak interaction. "There were **nine** experiments that contradicted it -- all wrong. Every one....When you have something simple that agrees with all the rest of physics and really seems to explain what's going on, a few

----

[7] Quoted in: Horace Freeland Judson, **The Eighth Day of Creation**, New York, Simon and Schuster, 1979, pp. 113-114.

experimental data against it are no objection whatever. [They are] almost certain to be wrong."[8]

Of these four features, which characterize not only my example but also scientific theories, the first one is the most important for us as political scientists. Theoretical understanding neither consists in nor comes through accumulating generalizations. Instead, it requires finding new ways of thinking about phenomena, new **explanatory principles**, which are representations together with the principles that govern their use.[9] Explanatory principles are thus metaphors, but metaphors that satisfy two particular requirements.[10] First, they must be able to account for what we have already observed: the generalizations with which we began. Second, they must also be able to suggest new relationships later confirmed by observation; they must be fruitful. Consequently, not just any metaphor will do. If in analyzing the preceding problem, we had applied a different metaphor (of the game as a battle, for example) we would not have been likely to succeed either in understanding the game as we now do or in discovering other new features. Finding an appropriate explanatory principle is, therefore, an act of creative imagination disciplined by the results of empirical inquiry.

Yet the artificiality of the hypothetical game makes coming to understand it different from finding explanatory principles through scientific study of natural or social phenomena. It was unfamiliar, not embedded in our network of common sense understandings of the world. Hence we were

----

[8] Quoted in: Horace Freeland Judson, **The Search for Solutions**, New York, Holt, Rinehart, and Winston, 1980, p. 22.

[9] The terms "representation" and "principle" are drawn from: Heinrich Hertz, **The Principles of Mechanics**, New York, Dover, (1894), 1956, especially pp. 1-41. By "explanatory principle," I mean both taken together, since principles presuppose the representations the use of which they govern. As I explain later, representations without principles are sterile.

[10] On metaphors in science, see: Richard Boyd, "Metaphor and Theory Change: What is 'Metaphor' a Metaphor For?," in Andrew Ortony, ed., **Metaphor and Thought**, Cambridge, Cambridge University Press, 1979, pp. 356-408; and Thomas S. Kuhn, "Metaphor in Science," in ibid., pp. 409-419.

little inhibited in our search for and acceptance of a new way of thinking about it.   By contrast, our familiarity with natural and social phenomena restrains our search for better understandings of them.   Common sense tethers our imagination and blinds us to alternate visions of our world. Indeed, this is why we need to **educate** people to see the natural world with the eyes of a physicist, a chemist, or a biologist.

How hard it must have been for Copernicus to conceive of the earth as a planet, for Darwin to see man as one of many evolving species, for Harvey to consider the heart as a pump, or for Wegener to imagine that whole continents move about.   These metaphors, crucial to scientific progress, are now so firmly accepted that it is difficult for us to appreciate how they once shocked the imagination, how they were once metaphors.   How much harder it is to appreciate how they still are metaphors.[11] To glimpse how these novel conceptions once assailed intellectual sensibilities, consider Marvin Minsky's notion of the brain as a "meat machine." Similar to conceiving the heart as a pump, this view, even in the less graphic form which regards the brain as (like) a computer, today arouses fierce opposition.[12] Arduous as these conceptual advances have been, how difficult must it be for we political scientists to conceive what we study in novel but scientifically useful ways, to say nothing of convincing others to share our visions. As the example of Darwin, especially, reminds us: to succeed in reconceiving reality requires altering the very self-conceptions that we individually and collectively hold dear.

But equally debilitating to us as political scientists is the way our discipline's current conception of theory denies the necessity of any such imaginative leap.   This

----

[11] On the difficulty of recognizing the prevalence of metaphors in our ordinary language and thought, see: George Lakoff and Mark Johnson, **Metaphors of Everyday Life**, Chicago, University of Chicago Press, 1980; Michael J. Reddy, "The Conduit Metaphor," in Andrew Ortony, **Metaphor and Thought**, pp. 284-324.

[12] See: John Searle, "The Myth of the Computer," **New York Review of Books**, 29, 7, April 29, 1982, pp. 3-6. Especially see the subsequent exchange of letters between Searle and Daniel C. Dennett: **New York Review of Books**, 29, 11, June 24, 1982, pp. 56-57.

constricting notion of theory is itself a principal obstacle to our progress as a scientific discipline. My advice is not that we abandon collecting data, devising more accurate measurement procedures, refining statistical techniques, or searching for generalizations. These activities are essential to any scientific enterprise. Rather, I argue that we need to do something more: namely, imagine and elaborate new ways of thinking about politics that both account for what we observe and suggest new relationships. In short, I urge the necessity of scientific political theory, conceived as the search for explanatory principles.

EXPLANATORY PRINCIPLES FOR POLITICAL SCIENCE

Where shall our search begin? Are explanatory principles fruitful for the study of politics already around? Let us consider two candidates.

THE RATIONALITY PRINCIPLE

The principle of rationality is useful in explaining economic phenomena and is often invoked in our discipline as well. It represents individuals as preference orderings (or real-valued utility functions) with respect to alternate actions available. And it states that individuals choose the actions that rank highest in their preference orderings (or for which their utility functions are maximized).[13] In practice, the principle of rationality is supplemented with still other principles, such as the principle of self-interest, which ascribes a particular content to individuals' preference orderings.

The representation presumed by the rationality principle is indeed a metaphor. Because some of the specialized terms used in applying the principle have counterparts in

----

[13] The term "rationality" is used in a wide variety of ways in social science. My characterization of the rationality principle applies only to a subset of them, primarily in economics and to a lesser extent in political science. My remarks do not apply, for example, to work by Herbert Simon, Sidney Winter, James March, Richard Cyert, Oliver Williamson, or Russell Hardin, to name just a few.

our ordinary language, we often fail to note this.   But to think of individuals as acting rationally in this sense is to think of them in a precise and special way.   Consider this principle's ultimate use in economics, as described by Thorstein Veblen.   "A gang of Aleutian Islanders slushing about in the wrack and surf with rakes and magical incantations for the capture of shell-fish are held, in point of taxonomic reality, to be engaged in a feat of hedonistic equilibration in rent, wages, and interest"[14] Delightfully juxtaposed by Veblen, description in ordinary language and representation in scientific terms relate to each other in much the same way that an observed landscape of mountains relates to countour lines drawn on a topographic map.[15]

Our difficulty in recognizing the rationality principle's representation as a metaphor results also from the way that ordinary language and common sense evolve in response to dissemination of scientific conceptions.   Once a striking metaphor, the notion of the heart as a pump is now commonplace.   Is it not difficult to conceive otherwise?   We become captives of our metaphors.

Adherents to the rationality principle are increasingly numerous in our discipline.   Still, there are strong reasons to believe that the principle in its present form has little relevance to many political phenomena.   First, the principle now lacks specific implications for choices under conditions of limited information or uncertainty.   Its adherents distinguish three classes of circumstances or contexts of choice: certainty, risk, and uncertainty.   In conditions of certainty, the consequences of possible actions are definite and known to the decision-maker in advance.   Choice under risk occurs when the consequences of possible actions can be assigned a known probability of occurrence (as in flipping a fair coin).   Finally, conditions of uncertainty hold when the probabilities of some outcomes of possible actions cannot be known exactly, if at all.   Choice under uncertainty is typically explained by thinking of the decision maker as assigning to these possible outcomes exact but **subjective** probabilities.   But silence usually reigns on how such subjective probabilities are assigned.   Thus the rationality principle raises questions about choice under uncertainty to which

----

[14] Thorstein Veblen, **The Portable Veblen**, Max Lerner, ed., New York, Viking Press, 1948, p. 20.

[15] See: Stephen Toulmin, **The Philosophy of Science**, New York, Harper and Row, (1953), 1960, pp. 105-139.

there are as yet no satisfactory answers.

Inviting us to view phenomena in a novel way, explanatory principles account for what we have observed and also urge us to ask new questions about the phenomena. This makes them crucial to scientific progress. Taking the heart as a pump and the blood vessels as a vast circulatory system of pipes led Harvey to ask how blood makes its way from outgoing pipes (the arteries) to incoming ones (the veins). Eventually, this produced discovery of the capillary system. About choices under uncertainty, however, the novel questions raised by the rationality principle have yet to be answered in an equally convincing way.

A second limitation of the principle is its inability to say much about choices contingent on the actions of other individuals. Although developed precisely for this purpose, the theory of games has rigorous implications only for situations well represented as two-person, zero-sum games. Even adherents of game theory admit its inadequacy for situations involving more than two parties or payoffs that do not sum to zero. So elementary and fundamental a game as the Prisoners' Dilemma still yields no consensus on which of a player's two strategies is implied by the rationality principle.[16] Even in economics, where the principle is applied most extensively, the behavior of oligopolies remains problematic. Indeed, general equilibrium theory, which many economists consider the crowning achievement of their discipline, conquers the problem of contingency essentially by dismissing it: assuming buyers and sellers to be so numerous that action by any one has no effect on the prices faced by the others.

A third limitation is that the rationality principle in its present form fails to represent adequately the process by which individuals arrive at their choices. To represent individuals as utility maximizers is to represent them as handling quantities of information which we know, on other grounds, that they do not possess. In economics, this problem is concealed by adopting households and firms as units of analysis. For then both psychology and organization theory can be considered irrelevant. For example, economists conceive firms as increasing output until marginal costs exceed marginal benefits, despite good evidence

----

[16] For an elegant treatment of the Prisoners' Dilemma representation and its applicability to human affairs, see: Russell Hardin, **Collective Action**, Baltimore, Johns Hopkins University Press, 1982.

that businessmen usually cannot in practice ascertain the values of those two variables.   Similarly, political scientists often portray actors as possessing information that in practice could be gathered, if at all, only at a cost far exceeding their resources.[17] These presumptions are excused by the claim that only the choice itself, not the process by which it is made, is the subject of inquiry.   Yet the fact remains that the metaphor of the principle of rationality is starkly inconsistent with what we know about the process of choosing.[18]

These three limitations of the principle of rationality as now formulated bear directly on my main question, for they imply that the principle is unable to explain many important political phenomena.   Seldom do political actors choose under conditions other than limited information and uncertainty.   When can presidents, congressmen, judges, bureaucrats, voters, lobbyists, or other political actors anticipate fully and precisely the probable consequences of choosing one course of action rather than another?   Pertinent information is often prohibitively costly or simply unavailable.   Hence much political strategy consists in concealing or wielding information in order to affect decisions by others.[19]   Indeed, as Anthony Downs noted, this uncertainty and limited information is what enables political actors

----

[17] This point is illustrated and its implications for legislative decisions are elucidated in: William H. Panning, "Rational Choice and Congressional Norms," **Western Political Quarterly**, 35, 2, April, 1982, pp. 193-203.

[18] Each of these limitations of the rationality principle is treated in greater detail by Herbert Simon.   See: Herbert Simon, "Rational Decision Making in Business Organizations," **American Economic Review**, 69, 4, September, 1979, pp. 493-513; Simon, "Rationality as Process and as Product of Thought," **American Economic Review**, 68, 2, May, 1978, pp. 1-16; Simon, "From Substantive to Procedural Rationality," in Spiro J. Latsis, ed., **Method and Appraisal in Economics**, Cambridge, Cambridge University Press, 1976, pp. 129-148; and Herbert A. Simon and Andrew C. Stedry, "Psychology and Economics," in Gardner Lindzey and Elliot Aronson, eds., **The Handbook of Social Psychology**, Vol. 5, Reading, Mass., Addison-Wesley, 1969, pp. 269-314.

[19] See: Richard Harris, **Decision**, New York, Ballantine, 1972.

to influence one another.[20]

Moreover, to label a choice "political" is to imply its contingency on the actual or expected behavior of others. "Until Robinson Crusoe met Friday," I have argued elsewhere, "his world was one of psychology and economics (the allocation of scarce resources among competing uses) but not politics."[21] For the fascination as well as the complexity of politics is a consequence of its vast web of interdependencies which affect actors' choices. Concepts of power and influence have long been popular in political science because they highlight these interdependencies.

Finally, to study politics is to understand not only outcomes of political processes but also the processes themselves. Thus our explanatory principle should account for how decisions are made as well as what decisions are made. Herbert Simon showed long ago that explanatory principles which attend only to outcomes may mislead us about processes. "It is only because individual human beings are limited in knowledge, foresight, skill, and time that organizations are useful instruments for the achievement of human purpose; and it is only because organized groups of human beings are limited in ability to agree on goals, to communicate, and to cooperate that organizing becomes for them a 'problem'."[22] Surely, why individuals organize themselves politically in the ways that they do is something that we political scientists want to understand. But we cannot if we think of individuals as omniscient maximizers. Instead, we must see them as having limited cognitive abilities.

Uncertainty, interdependence, and organization are three features central to understanding politics. Unless amended or extended to encompass them effectively, the principle of rationality must remain unable to explain much political behavior.

----

[20] Anthony Downs, **An Economic Theory of Democracy**, New York, Harper and Row, 1957, pp. 82-95.

[21] William H. Panning, "Blockmodels: From Relations to Configurations," **American Journal of Political Science**, 26, 3, August, 1982, pp. 585-608, on p. 606.

[22] Herbert A. Simon, **Models of Man**, New York, Wiley, 1957, p. 199.

SOCIAL INFORMATION PROCESSING

There is, however, another way of thinking about human behavior. It was originated in political science but has since found its main applications in psychology. I refer to Newell and Simon's conception of man as an information processor, a physical symbol system, who uses heuristic rules or procedures to attain satisfactory outcomes.[23] Here I summarize this representation, extend it, and then present a principle which governs our application of it to some important political phenomena.[24]

Fundamental to this conception is Simon's principle of **bounded rationality**. "The capacity of the human mind for formulating and solving complex problems is very small compared with the size of the problems whose solution is required for objectively rational behavior in the real world -- or even for a reasonable approximation to such objective rationality."[25] This principle denies that the process of individual choice can adequately be represented as utility maximization. Instead, individuals are conceived to possess a repertoire of imperfect but useful rules employed in achieving their objectives. Thus individuals' behavior is explained by showing how it is or could be produced by applying these rules to their (necessarily limited)

----

[23] See: Allen Newell, "Physical Symbol Systems," **Cognitive Science**, 4, 2, April-June, 1980, pp. 135-183; Allen Newell and Herbert A. Simon, **Human Problem Solving**, Englewood Cliffs, NJ, Prentice-Hall, 1972; Newell and Simon, "Computer Science as Empirical Inquiry: Symbols and Search," **Communications of the Association for Computing Machinery**, 19, 3, March, 1976, pp. 113-126; Simon, "Studying Human Intelligence by Creating Artificial Intelligence," **American Scientist**, 69, 3, May-June, 1981, pp. 300-309; Simon, **The Sciences of the Artificial**.

[24] For an early survey of potential uses of this representation in explaining political phenomena, see: Simon, "Political Research: The Decision-Making Framework," in David Easton, ed., **Varieties of Political Theory**, Englewood Cliffs, NJ, Prentice-Hall, 1966, pp. 15-24. General introductions to the field of artificial intelligence, in which this representation plays a fundamental role, include: Bertram Raphael, **The Thinking Computer**, San Francisco, W. H. Freeman, 1976; Philip C. Jackson, **Introduction to Artificial Intelligence**, New York, Petrocelli, 1974; Patrick Henry Winston,

information.

For the principle of bounded rationality to explain individuals' actual behavior, we must specify their (presumed) rules. These decision premises may include personality traits and cultural roles. They are if-then rules, stating what action individuals would take in various circumstances.[26] Further, we must specify individuals' current, relevant information: their perceptions, beliefs, and knowledge. Finally, we must specify the process in which relevant rules are selected by virtue of individuals' information about their circumstances.[27] In psychology, Simon and his colleagues employ this representation to account for ways in which individuals solve problems such as cryptarithmetic puzzles and how to choose good moves in chess.[28]

Still, the pertinence of this work to political studies is limited by its almost exclusive concern with **individual** behavior.[29] Even studying chess, Newell and Simon concentrate on how individual players choose without regard to opponents. They treat chess as essentially no different from solving problems in logic or mathematics, where no other individuals are involved. Thus overall patterns or sequences of moves generated by interdependent choices of **both** players are seldom studied. To be sure, Simon's work in political science and economics implies ways to adapt this

----

Artificial Intelligence, Reading, MA, Addison-Wesley, 1977. An early but still useful collection is: Edward A. Feigenbaum and Julian Feldman, eds., **Computers and Thought**, New York, McGraw-Hill, 1963. Pertinent philosophical issues are discussed in: Margaret A. Boden, **Minds and Mechanisms**, Ithaca, NY, Cornell University Press, 1981; Boden, **Artificial Intelligence and Natural Man**, New York, Basic Books, 1977; John Haugeland, ed., **Mind Design**, Montgomery, VT, Bradford Books, 1981. For current work, see: the journals **Artificial Intelligence** and **Cognitive Science**.

[25] Simon, **Models of Man**, p. 198. Also see: Simon, "Theories of Bounded Rationality," in C. B. McGuire and Roy Radner, eds., **Decision and Organization**, Amsterdam, North Holland, 1972, pp. 161-176.

[26] This representation is radically antipositivist, for its language is irreducibly intentional. See: Boden, **Minds and Mechanisms**, chapters 1-3.

principle to political phenomena.[30] But no concrete program of research based on representing man as a physical symbol system has yet emerged in political science.

The key to developing such a research program is clear: shift the focus from individual choices to the **overall patterns of behavior** generated by **multiple** actors who are interdependent. This requires: first, specifying the set of actors involved; second, specifying their (attributed) rules of behavior; third, specifying those rules so that at least some concern actions contingent on information given by other actors or on knowledge of others' actions; and fourth, specifying kinds of information transmitted among the actors and networks of its transmission. Since each actor is represented as an information processor, and since the overall pattern of behavior results from interaction of the individuals' behavioral rules with the information transmitted among them, such a network may be termed a system of **social-information processing.**[31]

How should we use this representation to account for political phenomena? To answer particular questions posed in its terms. First, ask what rules of behavior and channels of information could produce an observed pattern of behavior or aggregate-level phenomenon. Lewis Richardson attempted to account for the occurrence of arms races by

----

[27] See: Newell and Simon, **Human Information Processing.** For a brief introduction to the relevant procedures, see the discussion of "production systems" in: Avron Barr and Edward A. Feigenbaum, eds., **The Handbook of Artificial Intelligence**, vol. 1, Los Altos, CA, William Kaufmann, 1981, pp. 190-199. For a more advanced treatment, see: D. A. Waterman and Frederick Hayes-Roth, eds., **Pattern-Directed Inference Systems**, New York, Academic Press, 1978.

[28] See: Herbert A. Simon, **Models of Thought**, New Haven, Yale University Press, 1979; Newell and Simon, **Human Information Processing.**

[29] Of course, not all political scientists now see that understanding politics takes more than psychology. See: William H. Panning, "Blockmodels of Legislative Data," pp. 585-586.

[30] See: Herbert A. Simon, **Administrative Behavior**, New York, Free Press, (1947), third edition, 1976; James G. March and Simon, **Organizations**, New York, Wiley, 1958.

specifying behavioral rules of the nations involved.[32] Similar in intent, although different in style and execution, is Banfield's account of the cultural pattern he calls amoral familism in terms of a single rule of individual behavior adequate to produce it.[33] Second, ask what overall pattern of behavior could be expected to occur **given** specifically observed behavioral rules and information channels. Thus Schelling experimented with individual rules for choosing neighbors, discovering that, under some conditions, quite innocuous rules can produce marked racial segregation.[34] Another example is my own attempt to determine the consequences for political campaigns if individual contributors adhered to the rule of minimax regret.[35]

Both theory and empirical study have appropriate roles in addressing these two questions.[36] For the first, theoretical explanations will be acceptable to the degree that their behavioral rules and information channels are consistent with independent evidence. For the second, theoretical accounts will be acceptable to the degree that their predictions of overall patterns are borne out under the specified conditions.

None of the studies noted above use the representation proposed here, but they do show the political relevance of the questions it raises. Ross Ashby provides an

----

[31] The level of abstraction or detail for specifying these rules depends on our purposes. If the aim is to account for a few, limited features of some overall pattern of behavior within a group or organization, then a highly simple and approximate representation of actors' rules may suffice. (The actors may be entities other than humans.) Understanding the behavior of a system at one level depends on "only a very approximate, simplified characterization of the system at the level next beneath." See: Simon, **The Sciences of the Artificial**, p. 20. This representation parallels one in research on cellular automata. See: Jackson, **Introduction to Artificial Intelligence**, pp. 345ff; Arthur W. Burks, ed., **Essays on Cellular Automata**, Urbana, University of Illinois Press, 1970; M. L. Tsetlin, **Automaton Theory and Modeling of Biological Systems**, New York, Academic Press, 1973; W. Ross Ashby, **An Introduction to Cybernetics**, London, Chapman and Hall, 1956. From this perspective, what I call information possessed by the actors corresponds their internal states.

[32] See: Lewis F. Richardson, **Arms and Insecurity**, Pitts-

amusing but instructive example in which the second question is posed in terms of this representation. The actors
are a husband and wife, each in direct communication with
the other. The husband's personality traits (rules of
behavior) are:

(a) If startled, he is apt to jump and knock
the ash-tray to the floor.

(b) If asked to take a woman out to a dance he
always says yes.

(c) If he feels sorry for a woman he takes a
bunch of flowers to her.

(d) Going to a dance makes him feel good-natured and affectionate.

(e) If he is given burnt food he always points
out the fault.

(f) When he sees a woman in tears he feels
sorry for her.

(g) If anyone admits their incompetence to him
he replies that they ought to be ashamed
of themselves.

(h) He thinks anyone in an irritated state is
best cured by being told to control his
temper.

----

burgh, Boxwood Press, 1960.

[33] See: Edward C. Banfield, **The Moral Basis of a Backward Society**, New York, Free Press, 1958.

[34] See: Thomas C. Schelling, "Dynamic Models of Segregation," **Journal of Mathematical Sociology**, 1, 2, July, 1971,
pp. 143-186.

[35] See: William H. Panning, "Uncertainty and Political Participation," **Political Behavior**, 4, 1, Spring, 1982, pp.
69-81.

[36] These two general questions are considered in detail by
Friedrich Hayek. See: **Law, Legislation, and Liberty:
Volume I, Rules and Order**, Chicago, University of Chicago
Press, 1973, chapters 1-2; **Studies in Philosophy, Politics,
and Economics**, Chicago, University of Chicago Press, 1967,
chapters 1-4. Hayek also addresses a third question: how
do actors' rules and overall patterns of order evolve?
Applying to this question a representation similar to mine in

(i)   If anyone should throw things at him he would hit back.

(j)   He thinks a wife who could leave her husband is hopelessly bad and should be told so.

The wife's personality traits (rules of behavior) are:

(a)   Going to a dance makes her feel good-natured and affectionate.

(b)   If a fault in her cooking is pointed out she admits to being an incompetent cook.

(c)   The sight of tobacco ash on the floor irritates her.

(d)   When flowers are given to her, her response is "Let's go out to a dance."

(e)   To be told that she ought to be ashamed of herself would make her burst into tears.

(f)   Being told to control her temper makes her really mad.

(g)   She could never live with a man who thought her hopelessly bad.

(h)   When she gets really mad she throws things at whatever annoys her.

(i)   If her husband were to hit her she would go back to her mother.

Given these actors, what would result from either of these events?

(1)   She comes in unexpectedly while he is smoking and startles him.

(2)   The dinner she has prepared proves to be burnt.[37]

----

the text is: Robert Axelrod, "The Emergence of Cooperation among Egoists," **American Political Science Review**, 75, 2, June, 1981, pp. 306-318; Axelrod, "Effective Choice in the Prisoner's Dilemma," **Journal of Conflict Resolution**, 24, 1, March, 1980, pp. 3-25; Axelrod, "More Effective Choice in the Prisoner's Dilemma," **Journal of Conflict Resolution**, 24, 3, September, 1980, 370-403.   Axelrod's work also embodies several of the methods of theorizing that I recommend here.

[37] See: Roger Conant, ed., **Mechanisms of Intelligence,**

Working through this example, you can discover the consequence of either initial condition. You could account for each outcome by showing how it results from an initial event and the actors' rules of behavior. This example demonstrates how representing political phenomena as social processing of information provides explicit and systematic patterns of explanation for guiding research. Furthermore, it facilitates applying to political phenomena the procedures of theorizing already worked out in cognitive science and artificial intelligence. Hence this representation gives a good basis for the kind of theorizing proposed earlier in this essay.

THE SOCIAL COMPARISON PRINCIPLE

To apply this representation to explaining political phenomena, the crucial step is to specify each of its components: the actors, their rules, and their channels of information. Without specification, the representation is abstract: it offers only a form, a language, for saying what we know. To say, "think of the card game as tic-tac-toe" is to convey no insight or understanding, unless we then **show how** thinking this way clarifies the game. Thus we rearrange the cards, note their correspondence with tic-tac-toe squares, explain how taking a card is like marking an X or O, and so on. Only then can listeners use what they already know about tic-tac-toe to understand the card game. These demonstrations give our advice specific content. And similar demonstrations are needed for my representation of political phenomena to gain content.

But thinking of the card game as tic-tac-toe and thinking of interdependent political actors as a system of social-information processing are different in one crucial respect: we already know about tic-tac-toe and how it is played, but we are not already familiar with my representation of political phenomena. Once we see the card game as tic-tac-toe, our questions about it are easy to answer. Yet someone from a culture not including tic-tac-toe (as was one of the students to whom I posed the problem) would not be helped by understanding the correspondence of the card game to tic-tac-toe, since would not know the principles of

----

Seaside, CA, Intersystems Publications, 1981, p. 365. For a longer example about an international dispute, see: **ibid.**, pp. 367-369.

playing tic-tac-toe.   These principles of play are our accumulated knowledge that (and perhaps why) particular lines of play succeed and other strategies fail.   Representing the card game as tic-tac-toe is useful because we already know (some of) the principles that govern its useful application.

For a scientific representation, principles of productive application must likewise be learned.   We discover them by trying to use it to account for phenomena and by learning from others' experiences in doing so.   Indeed, the history of atomic theory from Lucretius to Heisenberg consists of learning how representing matter in terms of elementary particles can explain physical events.   Similarly, the history of political thought, including political science, has concerned how to represent politics in terms of mechanisms, organisms, systems, etc. and how to apply these representations.   Unfortunately, self-conscious study of such metaphors for politics has largely been abandoned by political science, due to our discipline's misleading conception of theories as generalizations.

In sum, representations are not enough for theories, which also require principles to govern the application of their representations.   Little is gained by representing individuals as real-valued utility functions unless principles show how to apply it (e.g., individuals choose so as to maximize personal utility) and unless other principles ascribe an overall pattern or content to it (e.g., maximizing votes for politicians, maximizing budgets for bureaucrats, or maximizing profit for firms).   By itself, to represent a set of actors as a system of social-information processing explains nothing.   A principle is needed to apply that representation to concrete phenomena.[38]

Are there any such principles?   That of bounded rationality helps little at this level, because it applies to actors rather than interactions among them.   Yet it remains important, for seeing individuals as a social information processing system makes little sense **except** in its light. The point is that it needs supplementing by another principle pertinent to relationships among actors.

One such principle is that of social comparison.   Its

----

[38] The conspicuous absence of such principles accounts for the barrenness of many "conceptual schemes" in our discipline.   To say this is not to dismiss rival representations but merely to insist that they, too, require principles of application.

earliest statement, of which I am aware, was by Leon Festinger. "To the extent that objective, non-social means are
not available, people evaluate their opinions and abilities by
comparison respectively with the opinions and abilities of
others."[39] March and Simon give a different formulation.
"The vast bulk of our knowledge of fact is not gained
through direct perception but through the second-hand,
third-hand, and nth-hand reports of the perceptions of
others, transmitted through the channels of social communication."[40] Both statements say that much of what we know
is learned from others rather than from our own direct
experience. A more general formulation of the principle of
social comparison is appropriate here: actors compare their
information and rules with those inferred of other actors
and revise them accordingly.[41]

This principle is important because it helps to specify
how actors in a system of social-information processing can
be interdependent. To apply it in substantive contexts
requires choosing among its several modes of interdependence. Although the general principle can itself be specified much more precisely than I have here, that would take
a lengthy digression. Instead, let me demonstrate two of
its applications to political phenomena.

The first involves Nagel's study of inequality and

----

[39] Leon Festinger, "A Theory of Social Comparison Processes," in Herbert H. Hyman and Eleanor Singer, eds.,
Readings in Reference Group Theory and Research, New
York, Free Press, 1968, pp. 123-146. Also see: Festinger, "Informal Social Communication," in Dorwin Cart-
wright and Alvin Zander, eds., **Group Dynamics**, New
York, Harper and Row, (1953), third edition, 1968, pp.
182-191; other essays in the Hyman and Singer anthology;
and Jerry M. Suls and Richard L. Miller, **Social Comparison
Processes**, Washington, Hemisphere, 1977.

[40] March and Simon, **Organizations**, p. 153.

[41] Because we cannot observe another's information (including beliefs and opinions) or rules of behavior directly, we
must infer them from the other's behavior: what the other
says or does. This makes deception possible. See: Erving Goffman, **Strategic Interaction**, Philadelphia, University
of Pennsylvania Press, 1969. Ability to revise rules of
behavior allows individuals to adapt to their environments.
See: D. A. Waterman, "Generalization Learning Techniques

discontent, one of four noted in the introduction. To derive the relationship between these two varaibles from the principle of social comparison, Nagel specifies: the content of beliefs about which comparisons are made, here the individual's relative economic well-being; the relationship between comparisons and the resulting evaluations; and the set of individuals compared. Nagel postulates that, in any two-person comparison, the discontent (relative deprivation) of the poorer is a linear function of the difference in wealth.[42] But studies by Festinger and W. G. Runciman lead Nagel to postulate also that any person's probability of comparing wealth with another varies inversely with their difference in wealth.[43]

As Nagel demonstrates, these two postulates imply that the poorer's expected discontent is a curvilinear function of the difference in wealth. Expected discontent is greatest when the difference in wealth is moderate, rather than large or small. Nagel conjectures that the same curvilinear relationship holds also at the aggregate level, for the n-person case. He confirms this by finding, through analysis of the Vietnam data, that inequality of landholdings in each province (as measured by the Gini coefficient) and discontent (as measured by the proportion of each province controlled by the Viet Cong) are related curvilinearly.

What Nagel has done, represented in terms of social-information processing, is to specify the relevant actors (residents of each province), the overall structure of communication among them (their probability of comparison), the kind of information transmitted among actors (about relative wealth), and their rules of behavior. The first rule

----

for Automating the Learning of Heuristics," **Artificial Intelligence**, 1, 1-2, Spring, 1970, pp. 121-170; Y. Anzai and H. A. Simon, "The Theory of Learning by Doing," **Psychological Review**, 86, 2, January, 1979, pp. 124-140. On adaptation at the system level, see: Michael D. Cohen, "The Power of Parallel Thinking," Discussion Paper No. 157, Institute of Public Policy Studies, University of Michigan, (October, 1980) revised version, May, 1981.

[42] Nagel, "Inequality and Discontent," p. 454.

[43] **Ibid.**, p. 455. Also see: W. G. Runciman, **Relative Deprivation and Social Justice**, London, Routledge and Kegan Paul, 1966; Festinger, "A Theory of Social Comparison Processes."

relates actors' information about the wealth of others to their levels of discontent. The second rule, which is implicit in Nagel's empirical analysis, relates actors' levels of discontent to their support for the Viet Cong.

Nagel's analysis can be extended by deriving the relationship between inequality and discontent for the n-person case.[44] Three conclusions follow from this. First, Nagel's curvilinear relationship is contingent on a negative correlation between the mean wealth and the inequality of wealth among social units (e.g., provinces). Second, if this correlation is zero or positive, then the relationship of discontent to inequality is linear or curvilinear upward, respectively. This conclusion fits Russett's cross-national analysis, also noted in my introduction, and may account for Nagel's difficulty in replicating his finding with cross-national data.[45] Third, in both cases, redistributing wealth within a social unit so as to reduce inequality also reduces the level of discontent.

Here the social comparison principle is important because it makes coherent the apparently conflicting results obtained by Nagel and Russett. Their contrasting conclusions can now be seen to result from contrasting conditions, removing at least part of our initial puzzlement.

The principle's second application is in studies of congressional voting by Kingdon, Matthews, and Stimson, who never mention the principle itself.[46] Here the issue is the relationship of the two options available on a roll call (voting Yea or Nay) to the achievement of a congressman's goals (e.g., pleasing supporters so as to facilitate his re-election). These studies conclude that, coping with limits on pertinent information and reducing consequent uncertainty about how to vote leads a legislator to base his

----

[44] See: William H. Panning, "Inequality, Social Comparison, and Relative Deprivation," unpublished paper, 1982.

[45] See: Nagel, "Inequality and Discontent," pp. 464-469; Russett, "Inequality and Instability."

[46] See: John W. Kingdon, **Congressmen's Voting Decisions**, New York, Harper and Row, (1973), second edition, 1981; Donald R. Matthews and James A. Stimson, "Decision-making by U. S. Representatives: A Preliminary Model," in S. Sidney Ulmer, ed., **Political Decision-Making**, New York, Van Nostrand, 1970; Matthews and Stimson, **Yeas and Nays**, New York, Wiley, 1975.

decision on information concerning the votes of his colleagues with goals and constituencies similar to his own. But these studies lack a precise specification of the rule by which legislators' votes relate to the information received through these comparisons. They also lack a precise specification of legislators' information channels. By developing this application of the principle of social comparison, it is possible to supply both.[47] If imperfectly, these two applications illustrate the political usefulness of representation in terms of social-information processing, applied in terms of the principle of social comparison. Three features are especially important. Unlike the rationality principle, that of social comparison addresses directly the process by which individuals give content to their beliefs and opinions. Thus it also suggests a whole family of processes by which individuals choose under conditions of imperfect information and uncertainty, as in legislative voting. And inherent in these processes is interdependence between beliefs, and therefore actions, of different individuals. These three characteristics make the principle of social comparison significant for phenomena where the rationality principle now is not.

Moreover, these two applications exemplify an important property of explanatory principles. They are useful, not only because they can be applied to particular phenomena, but also because they can lend coherence to whole classes of phenomena that would otherwise appear utterly diverse. Because the same explanatory principle can be applied to both the generation of discontent and the decision of legislatures, they can now be seen as parts of a large family of political phenomena. It ranges from the influence of reference groups, to the consequences of

----

[47] See: William H. Panning, "Information Flow and Party Influence: Theory, Measurement, and Policy Consequences," paper presented to the Annual Meeting of the Midwest Political Science Association, Milwaukee, April 28-May 1, 1982. A method for determining major channels of information among legislators is described in: Panning, "Blockmodels of Legislative Data." It is extended in: Panning, "Fitting Blockmodels to Data," Social Networks, 4, 1982, forthcoming. These studies are an empirical counterpart to my current work: a theoretical exploration, by means of computer simulation, of the general properties of systems of social-information processing in which actors follow rules consistent with the social comparison principle.

status inconsistency, to the dynamics of racism.   For all these have been explained, at least in part, by the social comparison principle.   We can now see each of them as part of a larger (dare I say, more general?) pattern.

This is the most fundamental aim of scientific inquiry: to discover explanatory principles that establish and specify coherent relationships among phenomena which we had previously thought unrelated.   That is, the most basic goal of science is intellectual coherence, not factual knowledge per se.   Newton's **Principia** was a milestone of science, not because it presented new facts or experimental results, nor because it presented methods for making more accurate predictions, but because it proposed a set of explanatory principles (embodied in Newton's three laws) which made diverse phenomena coherent and intelligible.   These principles not only wove together the astronomical discoveries of Newton's predecessors, but also provided for the first time a uniform conception of terrestrial and celestial motion.   The "Newtonian synthesis" is aptly named.

Thus progress in science consists in substituting new and more powerful explanatory principles for old ones or in extending the range of phenomena encompassed by present principles.   Such principles coordinate our assembly of facts and generalizations into coherent structures.   To be sure, they require components to assemble; and the assembly must be thoroughly tested.   But surely it is the edifice, not merely the collection of materials for its construction, that must be the ultimate object of our endeavors.

WHAT SHOULD POLITICAL THEORY BE NOW?

For those people who insist that the only thing that is important is that the theory agrees with experiment, I would like to imagine a discussion between a Mayan astronomer and his student. The Mayans were able to calculate with great precision predictions, for example, for eclipses and for the position of the moon in the sky, the position of Venus, etc. It was all done by arithmetic. They counted a certain number and subtracted some numbers, and so on. There was no discussion of what the moon was. There was no discussion even of the idea that it went around. They just calculated the time when there would be an eclipse, or when the moon would rise at the full, and so on. Suppose that a young man went to the astronomer and said, "I have an idea. Maybe those things are going around, and there are balls of something like rocks out there, and we could calculate how they move in a completely different way from just calculating what time they appear in the sky." "Yes," says the astronomer, "and how accurately can you predict eclipses?" He says, "I haven't developed the thing very far yet." Then says the astronomer, "Well, we can calculate eclipses more accurately than you can with your model, so you must not pay any attention to your idea because obviously the mathematical scheme is better."

Richard
Feynman

Early in this essay, I argued that political science needs a conception of theory considerably different from the one now dominant in our discipline. Not just a set of generalizations or statistical relationships, a theory is a new way of thinking about phenomena. Thus it makes sense of the generalizations and relationships which we already have and helps us to discover new ones. Later, I presented my own views, still developing, of what one such theory in political science might become. If these views are a recipe for making progress, they are no substitute for the pudding: namely, a series of convincing applications of the principle of social comparison and the representation of social-information processing it presumes. Yet by detailing two applications of this principle, I have attempted to give good reasons for trying out the recipe.

Of my two arguments, the first is the more important: we need a different notion of what a theory is. This claim stands apart from however convincing my own attempt to theorize might be. I do not urge that we abandon what we have been doing as political scientists. The point is rather to recognize that our empirical generalizations and statistical relationships are not sufficient for theoretical understanding of politics. We need something more: a self-conscious search for explanatory principles. In short, my plea is that there be theorizing in political science.

This means according a measure of autonomy to theorizing, just as we accord partial autonomy to refining our measurement procedures, developing new statistical techniques, and describing political phenomena. Each of these activities is ultimately judged by its contribution to the overall progress of our discipline. But in the short run, each is conducted and evaluated by criteria importantly its own. For this is a condition of useful division of labor in the discipline. Thus if there is to be theory in a scientific sense, there must be an opportunity to concentrate on it and to evaluate it by principally theoretical criteria. Reflecting on the evolution of scientific ideas, Stephen Toulmin insists that:

> science has included, and must include, much a priori study of possible forms of theory, developed without immediate regard to the particular facts of Nature. Unless these possible forms of theory are eventually applied to explain the actual course of events, our a priori studies will of course bear no positive scientific fruit. Yet they are a part, and a legitimate part, of scientific enquiry now as in previous centuries. [48]

This, I take it, is likewise the moral of Feynman's tale.

A CONCLUDING UNSCIENTIFIC POSTSCRIPT:

POLITICAL THEORY AND "POLITICAL THEORY"

What I propose is a different way of thinking about theorizing and the aim of scientific inquiry into politics. But it has implications as well for the way we conceive "political theory" as a field within our broader discipline.

First, this conception of theory is closer in principle to the aims and achievements of "great political theorists" than is the notion now dominant in our discipline. The history of political thought is partly a history of great metaphors intended to induce new ways of thinking about politics, in order to explain the principal features of the times and thus to guide political action. For example, seeing politics as the expression of a "social contract" makes it

----

[48] Stephen Toulmin, **Foresight and Understanding,** New York, Harper and Row, (1961), second edition, 1963, p. 108.

understandable in a new way. Like seeing the card game as tic-tac-toe, it provides a guide to intelligent action.

Second, the particular issues I pose for political theorizing are closer in principle to questions in the field of "political theory," past and present, than are questions now prominent in other fields of political inquiry. We should ask what overall pattern of behavior can be expected to occur **given** specific rules of behavior and channels of information. And we should inquire what rules of behavior and channels of information can produce a **given** pattern of overall behavior. Cast in terms of social-information processing, scientific theories in answer to either question must try to identify relationships between behavioral rules or information channels and overall patterns of behavior. As a field, "political theory" has been centrally concerned with similar questions, sometimes couched in different language. One example is the study of ties between human nature and political order: **given** the nature of man, one strand of traditional theory has asked what kind of political order must follow; **given** a kind of political order, another strand of traditional theory has inquired what man must be for it to exist.

Beyond differences in terms, though, these similar inquiries reveal a most important split between scientific political theory and the traditional field of "political theory." In the latter, these questions are frequently posed for a purpose other than scientific explanation: namely, for counterfactual speculation. If people were different in this way or that, what sort of political order would result? What would people have to be in order to bring about this or that political system? These questions are aimed, not at explaining what we observe, but at exploring alternatives to it. They seek to elucidate possibilities.

I believe such speculation to be a useful and necessary counterpart to scientific explanation of politics. By conceiving people and their polities to be different than they are, it holds out the possibility that they may become different than they are. To see the world in a particular way encourages us to see some possibilities but inhibits us from seeing others, especially those inconsistent with current conceptions. Of course, this is as true in natural as in social science. Today, we routinely rely on inventions inconceivable to scientists living less than a century ago. But in social science, current ways of thinking constrain us all the more powerfully because scientific metaphors become central to our self-conceptions. Darwin had to see differently not only the world but himself as well. This makes change more difficult in social science, and it limits the possibility of social change as well.

Natural science in the twentieth century accepts that individuals and groups will and must challenge the reigning scientific consensus. In his later years, Einstein refused to concede the probabilistic formulation of the quantum theory. Fred Hoyle has stoutly defended the steady-state theory in cosmology. Francis Crick proposes a panspermian theory of life's origin on earth. So also in social science, there is an inevitable and invaluable place for those who challenge scientific conceptions of self, society, and politics.

But if speculative conceptions are to be made believable or otherwise affect our science creatively, then speculators must accept the obligations of their place and project. Like Darwin, Einstein, Crick, and Hoyle, they must construct ways of thinking about the world that can challenge orthodoxy by ultimately meeting the same basic criteria of acceptability, of persuasiveness. Thus these rival conceptions must be not only different but better: more illuminating and inclusive. They must have implications concerning not only a world that might be but also the world that is. Only thus can they make good the traditional claim of the field of "political theory" (which is also the scientific aim of the discipline of political theory) to explain the ultimate meaning of our own conduct.

PART NINE

SUMMONS AND SUMMARY

ONE STEP BACKWARD, TWO STEPS FORWARD:

REFLECTIONS UPON

CONTEMPORARY POLITICAL THEORY

Richard Ashcraft

As political theory students in the 1950s, most of us were conscripted as raw recruits into the war against behavioralism, positivism, and historicism: an unholy triple alliance which, at the time, threatened political theory with total extinction. Or, at least, so we were led to believe. We fought in this war dutifully, though perhaps without a great deal of enthusiasm. Behavioralism, it must be said, proved to be an elusive enemy. Its partisans seemingly wandered freely in all directions, gathering information with very little concern for adopting a defensive posture around an agreed upon intellectual core. Behavioralism's defeat, therefore, was always more likely to occur as the consequence of its imperialistic but utopian designs leading to a growing disillusionment within its own ranks than as the result of any well-mounted attack from political theory.

Still, there was one citadel, the Popper-Hempel castle, which served as a last refuge for any behavioralist who found himself suddenly exposed to fire in the marshlands of epistemology. Naturally, this castle was a prime target of attacks for political theorists; though rather curiously, most fighting was done at long range, with a few artillery shells being fired from ancient canons now and then. Hand to hand combat was precluded by the propensity of the castle's inhabitants to raise the drawbridge of falsifiability at any time, thus cutting themselves off from all potential attacking forces outside the castle.

We political theorists, who (at best) constituted a guerrilla army, retreated to the mountain peaks of great books, where a few of us actually lived in caves. There we kept alive the tradition of freedom, truth, and knowledge, or so we were told by our teachers. And so time passed, with no decisive battles, no long march, just seemingly endless skirmishes interspersed with ritual homages paid to long-dead heroes. Eventually, some of us turned away from that struggle in order to fight against another war with more immediate and politically disastrous consequences. What we learned from our participation in that conflict and from the unsettling disclosures of others about the nature of political society had a profound impact upon us and upon our conception of political theory. After that, things were never again quite the same; it just seemed pointless to return to our pre-war preoccupations. And in any event, the behavioralists had never managed to conquer any territory worth recapturing.

Looking back upon the whole affair, one might be tempted to place the blame for our misconceptions about political theory upon our philosophically-minded generals. They indeed bear much of the responsibility for the useless waste of mindpower of a generation of political theorists. On the other hand, they claimed only to be fighting a defensive battle against the positivists who had initiated the attack on political theory; and there was certainly some truth in this accusation. Now, at this distance in time, perhaps we are in a position to view that struggle from a different perspective. More importantly, if we intend to move forward as political theorists, we really have no alternative but to ask ourselves how we have come to be where we are and what, if anything, we are prepared to leave behind as part of the past.

I

The issues of concern to political theorists in the 1950s can be stated in several forms or languages because, to borrow Wittgenstein's phrase, they bear a certain family resemblance to each other. Roughly speaking, therefore, the terrain of the battlefield looked something like this. A theory of epistemology, closely tied to the procedures of a particular model of science, had gained sufficient prominence that it could, on the one hand, advance a claim to serve as the arbiter of problems of meaning and language usage, and, on the other hand, present itself as the foundation for the methodology of the social sciences. Both claims were reinforced by a powerful and widely-held consensus on a distinction between facts and values. Since this dichotomy was accepted as a given even by many of those political theorists who opposed various specific arguments advanced by their "scientific" opponents, it is important to recognize that the structure of the debate, viewed as a whole, was profoundly shaped by this consensual proposition and its corollaries. Certainly the most important of these was the belief that values could be identified as the subjectively-held beliefs of the individual.

Most of the propositions which comprised the scientific position in this debate were, of course, not in themselves new; they and their supporting arguments had been around for quite some time. Much of American social science, for example, was deeply indebted to Max Weber for its methodological self-conception, as Leo Strauss noted in his counter-attack upon positivist social science.[1] The epistemological issues in the debate could claim an even more ancient ancestry. David Easton's **The Political System** was only one of the numerous works written in the fifties which fused these various streams of thought into a sustained critique of traditional political theory.[2] Simultaneously, there appeared a flurry of journal articles, some of them written by political theorists, lamenting the decline of political theory.[3] Much could be said for the view that political theory had adopted a posture of retreat long before this and that when the attack finally came, it merely hastened the demise of an old and decaying structure. Indeed, it is partly for this reason that it is difficult to explain all that happened with respect to political theory in the fifties and sixties in terms of the arguments advanced by both sides. Though formidable, these arguments were far from compelling and contained not a few fundamental weaknesses.

I do not propose to review all the points at issue in this debate; some arguments which have recently been restated in the critiques directed against the new history approach to political theory are discussed below. Here I wish to focus attention on those areas and problems which both sides in this debate tried to avoid. For in my view, the questions which this controversy did **not** ask and the issues which it did **not** pursue are of far greater importance to the future of current political theory than the respective positions adopted by its participants on the issues they did

----

[1] Leo Strauss, **Natural Right and History**, Chicago, University of Chicago Press, 1953, pp. 38ff.

[2] See: David Easton, **The Political System**, New York, Knopf, 1953.

[3] See: Leo Strauss, "What Is Political Philosophy?," **Journal of Politics**, 19, 3, August, 1957, pp. 343-368; Alfred Cobban, "The Decline of Political Theory," **Political Science Quarterly**, 68, 3, September, 1953, pp. 321-337; David Easton, "The Decline of Modern Political Theory," **Journal of Politics**, 13, 1, February, 1951, pp. 36-58.

discuss.

In the first place, it was wondrously implausible to suppose that "values" pertained not to collective social practices, but were held as a kind of inviolate private property by individuals qua individuals. Such an atomistic picture of the value-constituted universe ("a chaos of existential judgments," as Weber put it) was never more than a social myth, and one, moreover, without support from any body of empirical evidence. Indeed, this point was repeatedly demonstrated by the behavioralists themselves in their documentation of the persistent patterns of social and political attitudes. Yet if the "practical value interests" of individuals were rooted in social groupings (or more precisely, in the activities engaged in by social groups), then the problem of the divestiture of values held by the social scientist could hardly be resolved by supposing that the latter's conscious recognition of values effectively "neutralized" their practical influence. On the contrary, what was required was some understanding of the social practices and institutions which supplied these particular values with their contextual meaning and of the relationship between these values-in-context and the kinds of questions asked or commitments held by the social scientist. The problem of meaning as applied to "values," in other words, is improperly conceived as the expression of the individual's subjective will. Nor for that matter, can it be viewed in terms of definitional warrants issued by philosophers. Rather, it is a sociological problem to be investigated empirically. On this level of research, however, the analytical distinction between facts and values collapses. And as the perimeters of that research are concentrically extended to include larger and larger areas of social life, such a distinction becomes decreasingly useful as part of an explanatory account of social action.

The point can be stated in more specific and self-referential terms, applicable to those political theorists, behavioral and traditionalist, in the fifties who accepted the fact/value distinction. Why such an analytical distinction had to be made, a question which bears upon both the sociological origins of the significance attached to making such a distinction as well as upon the latter's practical social utility (i.e., as a means of providing a solution to political problems), seems never to have been addressed. The distinction was simply incorporated as part of the general epistemological justification offered on behalf of a particular model of science. However, if the adoption of a set of methodological rules, whether derived from a model of scientific behavior or from some other example of a social activity performed by another social group, had been viewed as a sociological problem to be investigated, the separation of facts from values would have appeared merely as part of a set of beliefs subscribed to by a specific social group for specific purposes. From this standpoint, such rules and beliefs could never have been mistaken for a more grandiose claim about the nature of "reality," "truth," or "meaning" as such.

Instead of pursuing this avenue of inquiry, traditional political theorists responded with Pavlovian predictability, asserting as a kind of divine right their entitlement to make normative value judgments. Political theorists, in other words, defended the individualism of their subjectively-held values against the behavioral juggernaut of "objectivity." They were not about to be fitted into anyone else's social context, nor were they inclined to offer one of their own. If some larger dimension was needed to defend the traditionalists' conception of political theory (beyond the individual theorists's self-justifying claim to "epic vision"), it sufficed to maintain that we political theorists represented, after all, the last line of defense for a "meditative culture" against the behavioralists' attempts to "mechanize human behavior."[4] I confess that such views now seem to me to be mildly humorous, not to mention that, as responses, they were blown out of all proportion to what might have emerged from a serious analysis of the events and problems which had given rise to the controversy in the first place. But traditional political theory was not interested in exploring this issue, which would have meant forging an alliance with sociology. In its preoccupation with combatting positivism, which it frequently took to be synonymous with social science, political theory wholly identified itself as a branch of moral philosophy, apparently on the presumption that only the uncompromising assertion of "values" by individual theorists could counter a fact-minded empiricism.[5]

----

[4] See: Sheldon S. Wolin, "Political Theory as a Vocation," **American Political Science Review,** 63, 4, December, 1969, pp. 1062-1082, on pp. 1073, 1076-1077.

[5] See: Sheldon S. Wolin, "Political Theory: Trends and Goals," in David L. Sills, ed., **International Encyclopedia of the Social Sciences,** New York, Macmillan, 1968, vol. 12, pp. 318-330, especially p. 329; Herbert J. Storing, ed., **Essays on the Scientific Study of Politics,** New York, Holt,

In fact, most traditional political theorists actually asserted these values in the courses they taught and in the books they wrote through the medium of presenting a history of political theory. This activity, too, was carried out with a minimal amount of self-critical awareness as to what, exactly, a historical account of political thought meant. Had this question received the attention it deserved, texts purporting to introduce the student to the history of political theory could not have been written on the assumption that "political theory is a body of philosophical and scientific knowledge...regardless of when and where it was originally written." Hence the ideas of political theorists could be discussed "without attention to the particular conditions which surrounded them at the time they wrote."[6] "History" written in this fashion became, for a whole generation of political theorists, little more than a metaphor designed to mask the undefended assumptions of an author so eager to protect philosophy from its critics that little time or effort could be devoted to ascertaining the importance of mere historical details. Thus a "tradition" of political theory was established by authority or convention, defended as a body of philosophical knowledge, and presented under the heading of history.[7]

What is worse, the residual, though not always realized, egalitarianism of empiricism (the behavioralists claims that anyone could be a good social scientist, given the proper method) was countered with an authoritarianism according to which a defense of political theory was made to appear as the equivalent of a defense of individual genius, epic vision, creativity, the true philosopher, and a good deal of outright charlatanism besides. It is hardly surprising that some Baconian critics railed against the scholasticism of political theory, imbued as it then was with certain cultist (and a few occultist) tendencies.

Nevertheless, behavioralists often seemed incapable of grasping the point that an effort to understand the relationship between "Lockean" political ideas and a political movement in seventeenth-century England or the

----

Rinehart and Winston, 1961.

[6] Andrew Hacker, **Political Theory**, New York, Macmillan, 1961, p. 12.

[7] See: John G. Gunnell, **Political Theory**, Cambridge, MA, Winthrop, 1979.

determination of the relevance of Plato's ideas to the political culture of Athenian democracy were not, in principle, different from the attempts by political scientists to study a current revolutionary movement in Africa or Latin America or to present an account of the "civic culture" in a modern society. Their "scientific" interest in history, as applied to political theory, was limited to viewing the latter as a storehouse for potentially testable hypotheses which could be applied to current empirical research. It is not merely that such a viewpoint reflected and perpetuated the impoverishment of our cultural consciousness, a critical point scored against the behavioralists by traditional political theorists, but also that behavioralism obscured, through its uncritical acceptance of certain methodological presuppositions, the depth of the problems involved in formulating an empirically-grounded interpretation of social action or political ideas. A recognition of these problems might well have served as a bridge for the definition of a "scientific" approach to political theory, past and present.

If it is true that behavioralists had little use for history, it was hardly their fault that the history of political theory being offered them was bad history. To say that we political theorists replied to the behavioralists' charges of being unscientific by being unhistorical is captured by the comic effect of two people carrying on different conversations simultaneously. It might have been possible to lay aside the blanket condemnations of empiricism we leveled against our fact-minded behavioralist critics if we, as political theorists, had ourselves been more interested in and had attached more importance to getting the facts right with respect to the empirical (historical) context within which the political theories we studied were formulated. We appreciated all the difficulties of accomplishing this objective, from the standpoint of a detached skepticism about the outcome in terms of any claims to "knowledge" or "truth," without having to submit ourselves to the laborious effort of actually trying to come to terms with an empirically-grounded conception of reality or, in this case, of political theory.

Instead of adopting an exclusionary attitude or what amounted in theoretical terms to a break in diplomatic relations with the work of the behavioralists, political theorists could have taught their students to take an inclusionary perspective, incorporating the empirical research into better formulated theoretical frameworks than those offered by the researchers themselves. Occasionally, one heard some talk about doing this; but in fact, nothing much came of it, and it certainly received little official encouragement from the defenders of political theory.

If either side in the debate had tried to view its perspective in relation to the social-historical context in which
that debate had emerged, we might have seen our way past
the immediacy of an exchange of oppositional viewpoints
much sooner than some of us did. In the process of establishing those contextual connections, we could have learned
something important about ourselves and our society.
Instead, as students of political theory, we were expected
simply to accept the controversy as a given and to orient
ourselves with respect to our side in the dispute. If some
explanation was offered, say, for the decline of political
theory, it scarcely went further than the assignation of
blame to the rise of positivism or behavioral science, to the
spread of a belief in the relativism of values, or to the
replacement of "the political" by "the social," as if these
phenomena had been visited upon us, like plagues, by some
angered deity. Behavioralists, for their part, looked upon
political theorists as deafmutes who did not understand the
language of science and who therefore could not be reasoned with. That they nevertheless had to associate themselves with such unfortunates under the general rubric of
political science was a condition inflicted upon them which
provoked, alternately, responses of anger and pity. In
any event, there was underlying this debate something akin
to a "devil theory" explanation which did little to encourage
a historical-sociological approach to understanding the activity of political theorizing, including that which occurred
during the fifties and sixties.

Both sides in this debate agreed not to venture into
the murky regions of ideology. Behavioralists did so in
order to preserve the ark of objectivity from unclean
hands. Political theorists avoided the subject of ideology
because they could not discover the word in their Holy
Writ. As a result, political theory ceased being a form of
communication based upon the recognition of practical needs
and activities; it became something "finer" and more elevated in stature. By definition, it was forbidden to think
of ideology as a system of intersubjective communication in
which reference is made to empirical evidence, cogent reasons are presented, changes and modifications in beliefs
occur over time, and so forth. If these characteristics
were accepted, how would one then be able to distinguish
between "social science" or "political theory" and "ideology?" Although this attack was mounted against a historically definite form of ideology, Marxism, political theory in
its traditional form had also lost much of its appeal and
appeared to be a victim of the same conditions which

accounted for the decline of ideology. As Robert Dahl observed in the late fifties, "in the English-speaking world, where so many of the interesting political problems have been solved (at least superficially), political theory is dead."[8] Writing three years later, another commentator drew the connection even more clearly.

> One obvious reason for the current impression that classical political theory is in decay is that...[there] now prevails in England and the United States and in several other Western-type democracies a quite unusual degree of political relaxation and consensus...[which] obviously embraces the fundamental constitution of the liberal-democratic order....[It] is plausible to suppose that this consensus...is the main factor affecting the character of contemporary political theory.[9]

While the implications of this ideological hegemony were not particularly disturbing to the behavioralists, many of whom were quite content to accept the demise of political theory as we understood it in exchange for the triumph of liberal democracy, this consensus placed political theorists in a more precarious position. Were all the great issues really dead, as an article in **The American Political Science Review** asked at the time?[10] If current political theory was ever to recover from its "decline," the presupposition underlying such an assertion would have to be challenged. But how?

As students, we had been told by Sabine, Wolin, and others that there was some kind of correlation between historical periods of serious social conflict and the production of "great" political theories. Yet what, if anything, did we

----

[8] Robert Dahl, "Political Theory: Truth and Consequences," **World Politics**, 11, 1, October, 1958, pp. 89-102, on p. 89.

[9] P. H. Partridge, "Politics, Philosophy, Ideology," **Political Studies**, 9, 3, October, 1961, pp. 217-235, on p. 222.

[10] See: Arnold A. Rogow, "Comment on Smith and Apter: Or, Whatever Happened to the Great Issues?" **American Political Science Review**, 51, 3, September, 1957, pp. 763-775.

actually learn about the nature of these social conflicts and their relationship to political theory that could have helped us to analyze the condition of political theory in our own society?   There were vague references to "stresses" and "strains" or "systematic derangements" in society which were supposed to prompt the man of vision to theorize.[11] Were we then to conclude that there were no stresses and strains or merely no visionaries in our society?   Even to pose the issues in this manner discloses the depths of social ignorance which such abstract correlations attempted to conceal.   For all that we were taught about the specific connections that might be drawn between political theorizing and class conflict, social movements, or political parties, and the practical dimensions of a political theory shaped by its emergence under such conditions, we might just as well have postulated a correlation between earthquakes and the production of political theory.

Years later, with the experience of a large-scale anti-Vietnam War movement before us, many political theorists came to understand something about the relevance of establishing such connections.   Suddenly, in the midst of this social and political conflict, there was a rebirth of political theory, and earlier obituaries were adjudged to have been premature.   Now we could see how dependent political theory in the fifties had been upon the consensus which made the definitions advanced by analytical philosophers appear to be self-evident; we could see the importance of the compartmentalization of thought to the narrowness of the problems of concern to the political theorist, the extent to which the political stability of society was a function of continuous economic growth, and so on.   It is possible that without the experience of Vietnam, most of us would not have gained these and other insights.   What is true is that nothing we did learn about social analysis in courses on political theory prepared us to formulate an adequate response to Dahl's remarks about the status of political theory.   To a considerable degree, this, too, was a casualty of the general consensus on "the end of ideology" and of a negative attitude towards Marx's political theory in particular.

----

[11] See: George Sabine, "What Is Political Theory?," **Journal of Politics**, 1, 1, February, 1939, pp. 1-16, on p. 3; Sheldon S. Wolin, **Politics and Vision**, Boston, Little, Brown, 1960, p. 8; Wolin, "Political Theory as a Vocation," p. 1080.

Within the limitations imposed by the traditional approach to the history of political theory, there was little we could have learned about the ideological character of political theory in postwar America. The tools necessary for conducting such an analysis were available in Marx's thought; but on the whole, it remained unexplored territory for political theory students in the fifties. As a political theorist, Marx was, of course, a subject of interest to historians of political thought. Yet his perspective presented traditionalists with an interpretive dilemma. If one extracted from Marx's writings a "theory of human nature" or "philosophy of man," then he could be added to the list of great political philosophers, provided that political revolution as a plausible outcome of a study of his political theory was proscribed. On the other hand, if one focused attention upon the practical consequences of Marx's ideas, viewing Marxism as a social-historical phenomenon, then Marx's political theory was not only an ideology to be opposed but also a contributory cause in the explanatory account offered for the decline of great political theory. Thus if one abstracted "politics" and political action from Marx's political theory, his ideas could be integrated into a conception of political **philosophy** defined in terms of timeless issues and perennial questions. But if the politics of Marx's political theory received the emphasis, then the latter lost all of its philosophical interest.

These were the parameters within which we read Marx in the 1950s, if, indeed, we read him at all. For the liberal consensus was a practical reality within the universities, as well as within the country at large. There were then fewer than a handful of Marxists teaching in American universities. The McCarthy era was just ending, and the cold war was in full force, when we began our studies of political theory. If we were expected to view ideology as some form of near fatal disease, that can hardly appear surprising in light of the prevailing political and intellectual atmosphere of that period. The fact that "high" conceptual reasons for this avoidance of contact with ideology were put forward more often than "low" political ones was itself a reflection of the pervasive fear of granting priority to political commitments which was a part of this atmosphere.

Behavioral social science had set aside ideology as a form of frictional interference with technological development and economic expansion. The other side of its dismissal of ideology as a characteristic of political theory was its fascination with technology as a generative source for the new political theory it envisioned.[12] From this standpoint, political problems were transformed into technical problems, a viewpoint which in its most dangerous manifestation persisted throughout the Vietnam War. At the time, this attitude appeared to most of us theorists as empiricism run rampant, not to say, rabid; and so, in a certain sense, it was. Later, after the tide of ideological critiques of this perspective had subsided, and some balance had been restored to our conception of social science, it became clear that empiricism, as distinct from positivism, could be a liberating force, especially if it was directed against the scholastic tendencies within traditional political theory.

One of the most scathing attacks leveled by Easton and other behavioralists against traditional political theory was directed at the latter's apparent indifference towards the resolution of those political problems which were of immediate practical importance to Americans in the 1950s. Reviewing the response of American political theorists to "the distribution of social power" in their society, Easton declared that "there has been a pronounced inclination in political research to assume the stability of the basic power pattern....[P]olitical science has viewed the fundamental patterns of influence as given and has sought largely to trace the way in which the political process functions within this pattern."[13] A preoccupation with the history of political theory was thus viewed by the behavioralists as a retreat from relevance and practicality, and they proclaimed themselves ready to set matters right in this regard. Twenty years later, as numerous critics pointed out and as some of the behavioralists themselves admitted, their record in addressing the "real" political problems of American society was a rather poor one.[14] Indeed, as the course of

----

[12] For a discussion of one way in which these commitments affected the behavioralists' conception of political theory, see: Richard Ashcraft, "Economic Metaphors, Behavioralism, and Political Theory: Some Observations on the Ideological Uses of Language," **Western Political Quarterly**, 30, 3, September, 1977, pp. 313-328.

[13] Easton, **The Political System**, p. 41.

[14] See: Charles A. McCoy and John Playford, eds., **Apolitical Politics**, New York, Crowell, 1967; Karl W. Deutsch, "On Political Theory and Political Action," **American Political Science Review**, 64, 1, March, 1971, pp. 11-27, on p. 12.

events proved, not a few traditional political theorists were in the front lines of the political struggles for civil rights or in opposition to the Vietnam War, while many behavioralists did their best to ignore these immediate political problems.

Fear of ideological contamination and their own proximity to financial institutions and government agencies which underwrite the costs of most of their empirical research have kept the scholarly work of the behavioralists within very narrow, politically-defined boundaries. The task of doing the kind of "bold" research which the behavioralists in the 1950s hoped would lead to new theoretical perspectives about American political life is, paradoxically, more likely to be performed by political scientists whose political views are much less closely identified with the prevailing liberal-democratic consensus than are those of the behavioralists. As much as the traditionalists, behavioral political scientists grossly underestimated the importance of ideology as a structural element in the process of political theorizing.

I have suggested in these reflections that certain assumptions dominated our educational training as students of political theory in the fifties and sixties. If we are to move beyond the confines of the postwar debate, we must be prepared to confront the limitations that inheritance placed upon our conception of political theory. I have briefly alluded to some of the uncritically accepted presuppositions and the unexplored areas of that controversy in order to point out the direction in which a project of self-critical reevaluation ought to move. Already, there are encouraging signs that this movement is well under way.

Viewing some of the developments in political theory which have occurred in the last decade, it is noteworthy that the problems these theorists have chosen to explore are those which lay outside the parameters of the 1950s' debate about political theory. That is, there have been attempts to view political theory within its historical context, to relate the problem of interpretation as applied to textual analysis to the general problem of interpreting the meaning of social action, to restore a sociology of knowledge approach to a place of prominence in the formulation of a methodology for the social sciences, and to understand "social science" or "political theory" in terms of ideology, rather than vice versa. These developments represent, in my view, a step foreward for political theory. Nevertheless, a defense of these advances seems appropriate, not only because they have recently come under attack, but also because there are implications attached to these revisionary tendencies which require further elaboration. That a new perspective, especially one forged in combat with the prevailing viewpoints, should provoke a counterattack, is hardly surprising. Some of these criticisms, however, incorporate presuppositions from the 1950s' debate, which, if they are retained, are likely to send students of political theory back into the jungle of that controversy from which we have only recently escaped.

II

Simultaneously to the ideological critique of political theory, traditionalist and behavioralist, formulated within political science by those whose political commitments placed them in opposition to the dominant conceptions of political theory, an attack upon the latter was launched from within philosophy. Initially, the ground of this attack was the history of political thought, but since the general framework employed by the critics gave prominence to the problem of meaning and the consequent need to develop standards of interpretation, it also supplied the basis for a critique of positivist social science, a point to which I will return later in the essay. Broadly speaking, the critics maintained that a history of political theory forfeited its claim to historicity if it did not treat the political theorist as a historical individual whose political ideas derived much of their meaning from their embodiment as a set of beliefs and arguments shared by his contemporaries and, also, from their relationship to the activity of theorizing as a specific social action performed by the theorist.

Of the three challenges to this view which I shall consider, two question the validity of defining political theory in the terms set forth by the "new-history" approach, while the third (at least ostensibly) focuses upon the practicality of realizing the latter's objectives. The first objection asserts that the history of political theory has little or nothing to do either with political theory or with current political problems. The second argues that the new history not only raises the specter of relativism (and its adjunct, historicism) but actually incorporates these premises into its definition of political theory. Finally, it is suggested that the new historians' project of recovering the author's intended meaning as a necessary element of a historical approach to political theory is incapable of being fulfilled in practice and that, as a consequence, at least some of the assumptions underlying this approach ought to be abandoned.   Following a discussion of these criticisms, I will turn to an examination of the issues raised by the new historians as part of a critique of a positivist model of social science methodology and of the implications this critique has for the future development of political theory.

Recently, it has been asserted that "the vocation of the historian of political theory has little to do with understanding contemporary politics." Moreover, it is charged that the interpretation of past political theory "has become a surrogate for political theory."[15] The history of political theory as an intellectual pursuit, therefore, appears on this view to be an obstacle in the path of doing political theory or understanding current political problems.   If we read these statements simply as a call for some political theorists to devote their attention to a discussion of current issues, they would become both innocuous and superfluous, given that the overwhelming majority of political scientists are already engaged in research on and theorizing about these matters.   If, however, their meaning is that current political theorists should stop doing the history of political theory and do something else instead, something more relevant to the political present, then they do indeed function as part of a critique of a particular type of activity.   But while the polemical intent of these remarks might be clear, the basis of the critique itself remains unclear so long as its operative assumptions are not articulated and defended.

In the absence of such a defense, it is difficult to formulate a response which does not fall into the trap of recreating one's opponent as a straw man.   For the statements cited above could represent an attack upon any attempt to include the history of political theory within one's conception of politics or political theory, or they might refer only to specific limitations inherent in the new-history approach.   In the former case, the reductionism underlying the assertions seems too strident to merit serious consideration.   To take merely the most obvious examples, the meanings of notions such as property, individual rights, or socialism not only possess historical roots as a general feature of their contemporary significance, but they are so closely identified with the ideas and arguments

----

[15] See: John G. Gunnell, "Philosophy and Political Theory," **Government and Opposition**, 14, 2, Spring, 1979, pp. 198-216, on pp. 206-207.

of one or a few past political theories that a critical attack upon a generally accepted meaning of those concepts, even if it presented itself in the form of a commentary upon these ideas as they appeared in the writings of those theorists, could easily become an important part of the political conflict within current society.

More generally, to argue that one's adversary is acting on the basis of outmoded or irrelevant ideas and assumptions has a distinctly unsettling effect upon the holder of such beliefs and, insofar as the arguments are accepted as valid, upon the efficacy of the action itself. One of the primary means by which such an argument defends these critical assertions is through an appeal to historical evidence. Sufficient care has not always been taken by the critics in order to maintain a distinction between a critique of the ahistorical manner in which "the tradition" of political theory was defined by political theorists in the 1950s and the fact that the notion of a tradition has a justifiable place in an account of the transmission of cultural ideas over time, whether those ideas relate to literature, philosophy, or politics.[16] That it is not necessary for everyone, or even a majority, to be conscious of the historical origins or the connections associated with certain ideas which possess cultural significance for members of that society should not be confused with the fact that it is necessary that some individuals and institutions in society preserve the historical dimensions of the cultural consciousness of its members. The specific role played by political theory and by historians of political theory in this process of the transmission of cultural values in a particular society is an empirically determinable matter. It is certainly not a question whose answer can be decided a priori according to some definition of political theory which, from the outset, arbitrarily excludes from its domain the historical status of political ideas.

If we suppose that a more limited criticism is meant, one directed against the new history as a particular historical approach to political thought, then the burden rests with the critics to demonstrate wherein it fails in attaining its historical objectives. This was, of course, precisely what Quentin Skinner set out to do in his critique of the traditional historians of political theory.[17] Thus far, critics

----

[16] See: Gunnell, **Political Theory**.

[17] See: Quentin Skinner, "Meaning and Understanding in

of the new history have not established their claims to have a better understanding of "history" by providing examples of the kind of detailed historical work which might lend support to such claims. Instead, by phrasing their objections in an abstract form, these critics have made it appear, intentionally or unintentionally, that they are rejecting all claims to the study of the historical meaning of political ideas as part of a conception of political theory, thus reinstating in one form or another the presuppositions which prevailed during the 1950s' debate: namely, either "history" is irrelevant to political theory (behavioralists), or it is relevant only if it appears as philosophy (traditionalists).

If we move from the question of the relevance of history to political theory to the related issue of what role, if any, in one's conception of political theory should be allotted to the interpretation of past political theory, here, too, we need to recognize the serious deficiencies of the definition of political theory which informs much of the recent criticism of the new history. It is simply not true, as an empirical generalization about political theorists, that they have displayed little interest in interpreting the ideas of their predecessors. One has only to think of the extensive commentaries of Augustine on Cicero, Aquinas on Aristotle, Machiavelli on Livy, Locke on Filmer, Marx on Hegel, not to mention the countless political theories preoccupied with the interpretation of the Bible. In many intances, what we recognize as the political theory of a particular individual comes to us in the form of a critique or interpretation of a past political theory.

Even when detailed consideration of a text is not at issue, political theorists have shown themselves to be cognizant of the political importance exercised by traditions of thought within their own societies. They have, accordingly, quite consciously aligned themselves with and/or directed their attacks against such traditions. Hence the deployment by countless political theorists in seventeenth-century England of remarks for or against the ideas, influence, and political commitments which were held to follow from an identification with the "Platonic" or "Aristotelian" traditions of political thought. As I have argued elsewhere, the debate between Locke and Filmer is certainly, in

----

the History of Ideas," **History and Theory**, 8, 1, 1969, pp. 3-53; Skinner, "The Limits of Historical Explanation," **Philosophy**, 41, 157, July, 1966, pp. 199-215.

one sense, a debate about the meaning of Aristotelian political theory for English politics.[18] Many other examples could
be cited to show that competing interpretations of traditions
of political thought were very much a part of past theorists'
understanding of contemporary political problems in their
societies: the interpretation of the Republican tradition by
the American revolutionaries or J. S. Mill's interpretation of
Bentham's thought as part of the political conflict about
"immediate" political problems.   The point hardly requires
much emphasis if one reflects upon the effects various
interpretations of Marx's political thought have upon our
understanding of current politics in Marxist and non-Marx-
ist countries.   In short, an interpretation of past political
theory is an integral part of one's political theory.   And
this important aspect of theorizing should not be sacrificed
to a demand for the greater relevance of political theory to
the problems of the present; although in itself, there is
nothing unreasonable about this orientation towards political
theory.   Otherwise, we shall find ourselves merely repeating the errors of the behavioralists by refusing to recognize the legitimate claims of history and an interpretation of
the political ideas of the past.

In the 1950s' debate, each side accused the other of
adopting a relativist and historicist position.   These
charges have reemerged in the critical literature directed
against the new-history approach to political theory.
Bhikhu Parekh and R. N. Berki, for example, in their critique of Skinner, refer to "the lurking dangers of atomism," which they find in his conception of political theory.
"The picture here presented is of a world consisting of an
infinite variety of self-sufficient little worlds, each with its
own petty problems....If Skinner were to be consistent, he
would have to argue that every utterance and every action
is unique".[19] Since such an atomistic and relativistic picture would literally make nonsense of human experience,

---

[18] See: Richard Ashcraft, **The Two Treatises and the
Exclusion Crisis,** Los Angeles, William Andrews Clark
Library Seminar Series, 1980, pp. 58ff.   Also see: Felix
Raab, **The English Face of Machiavelli,** London, Routledge
and Kegan Paul, 1965.

[19] B. C. Parekh and R. N. Berki, "The History of Political
Ideas: A Critique of Quentin Skinner's Methodology,"
Journal of the History of Ideas, 34, 2, April-June, 1973,
pp. 163-184, on pp. 177, 180.

Parekh and Berki take this criticism as a conclusive basis for rejecting Skinner's approach to political theory.

In order to assess the validity of this criticism, however, we need to know just what kind of "problem" is presented by relativism and what type of evidence could be cited against the accusation. What, in other words, constitutes the grounds for the charge of relativism? It might be argued that the author (in this instance, Skinner) intends to promulgate a doctrine of relativism. The criticism would then be premised upon a reading of the theorist's subjectively intended meaning. In fact, this is almost never the case; those accused of espousing an atomistic relativism not only deny the charge, but they have frequently identified themselves as critics of that view.

Karl Mannheim, for example, against whose argument in **Ideology and Utopia** the accusation was most often made, not only denied that he had **said** what his critics imputed to him but maintained that he had in fact argued against relativism as a viable position. Despite this disclaimer and the lack of textual evidence to support the charge, Mannheim's critics continued to accuse him of defending an atomistic, relativistic view of social reality.[20] Clearly, they were not resting their case upon an attempt to recover Mannheim's intended meaning in **Ideology and Utopia**.

It might be supposed that, quite apart from the author's conscious intentions, relativism presents itself as a problem with respect to its practical consequences within the everyday social-life world. That is, if such a viewpoint ever came to be accepted as a portrayal of social reality as it actually exists, this belief would prove to be both socially disruptive and theoretically self-refuting. However valid this objection may be against relativism in its atomistic form, it does not address itself to the real empirical problem; nor does it provide support for the adoption of an absolutist position as the dichotomous alternative. What we experience in our daily lives is not a random or atomistic flux of viewpoints or social activities. Rather, we find ourselves in situations of structural diversity, confronted by a limited number of objective possibilities, whether these appear as theoretical alternatives or as practical actions to

----

[20] For a further discussion of this point, see: Richard Ashcraft, "Political Theory and Political Action in Karl Mannheim's Thought: Reflections upon Ideology and Utopia and its Critics," **Comparative Studies in Society and History**, 23, 1, January, 1981, pp. 23-50.

be taken. How, under these circumstances, we come to make the choices we do is, of course, a problem. Its resolution depends upon our possessing a great deal of specific empirical information pertaining to the social situation within which this problem presents itself to us.

But this is not the problem the critics have in mind. What they presuppose is the logical necessity of assuming the existence of an absolute standpoint in order to make sense out of the diversity of viewpoints one encounters in the social life-world. Since there is a partial truth contained in this reply, it should not be dismissed with an abstract denial, which only insures that the debate will remain on the level of transcendental philosophy. Rather, what needs to be demonstrated are the empirical limitations upon this explanatory framework of the meaning of social action. This point raises some difficult and complicated philosophical issues whose elucidation extends beyond the scope of this essay; but I will try, at least, to make my meaning clear.

Let us suppose that we wish to define "rationality" in terms of certain ontological conditions. We postulate, that is, the existence of individual human beings in possession of consciousness, speech, perhaps a certain social sympathy which is expressed in their interaction with each other, and so forth. Let us further imagine two such ontologically-endowed beings engaging in some specific form of social interaction, say, a discussion. From this activity, we may abstract a few methodological assumptions, rules of behavior to be followed by the actors, in order for the activity of "discussion" to remain within the generally recognized boundaries of meaning which define what a "discussion" is for members of a particular society. Now let us imagine that, for the sake of argument, we conclude that in order for the social activity of a discussion between two rational beings to continue, it is necessary for each participant in the discussion to presuppose the existence of some "truth" in an absolutist sense which may be taken as a possible outcome of the exchange of views in a "discussion." Finally, leaving aside all the objections one might raise if these structuring assumptions were critically examined, we have arrived at a model of "rationality" in which the presupposition of absolute truth claims the status of a logical necessity, i.e., as a built-in element of the definition of rational behavior.

Of course, we can restate the above suppositions in a highly abstract and philosophical form, with no particular reference to any social activity or any contextually stated conditions whatsoever. This is, in fact, how such discussions of the issues raised by the problem of relativism are generally conducted.   This is hardly surprising, since these discussions are usually carried on by philosophers, who, as a group, have a distinct propensity for considering problems in a manner that does not relate them to the con- textual activities which comprise the social life-world for individuals.   And really, this is the point, i.e., what is at the heart of the dispute.   For the partiality of the truth claim attached to the absolutist critique of relativism can be recognized when the philosophical argument is restated in sociological language.   That is, when we recognize that the proposition possesses a meaning, not as an ontological pre- supposition about human existence under all conditions, but as a practical convention conjoined to certain types of social activities or practices, e.g., a discussion in a classroom seminar.   Even if we extend the range of examples, we can from this perspective immediately recognize the limitations of such a model of "rationality," were it to be employed as an explanatory account of all social action.

Now, those who confront the problem of relativism within the framework of a sociological perspective (e.g., Mannheim) perceive the existence of conflicting theoretical or interpretive viewpoints.   Their truth claims cannot nec- essarily be established as valid within the confines of a model of "rationality" embedded in the social activity of dis- cussion.[21] Hence when seen from the standpoint of that model, "irrational" elements enter into one's explanatory account of the meaning of the arguments and concepts employed by the theorist whose ideas are being interpreted. The historical or sociological investigator who accepts the empirical dimension of these differences in viewpoint as "given," i.e., as a structural feature of the sociological conditions under which the ideas or texts make their appearance, thereby endorses relativism, according to the philosophical absolutist.   In fact, what has happened is that an abstract philosophical problem has been transformed into a concrete sociological problem.   As a result, the latter not only assumes a different form, but the evidence required in order to understand its dimensions, and the practical action necessary for its resolution are also radically altered.

----

[21] The significance of a "discussion" model of "rationality" for the tradition of liberal political thought, as well as for Mannheim's own conception of political theory is considered at length in: Ashcraft, "Political Theory and Political Action in Karl Mannheim's Thought."

The point I have been making can perhaps be illustrated through an examination of a specific criticism directed against the new-history approach to political theory. It is implausible, Charles Tarlton asserts, to ascertain the intended meaning of a political theorist and its relationship to the social conventions of meaning prominent in his society because there are a "bewildering number of purposes to which political thought itself can be put."[22] What, then, is an interpreter to do in the face of this apparent infinitude of referential meanings? Tarlton's answer throws the interpreter back into his own subjective, self-contained world. For "interpretation," Tarlton maintains, is nothing more than the sheer manipulation of textual material for our own purposes, which, viewed generally, are just as "bewildering" in their scope and diversity as are those of the original author. Thus our intepretations of past political theory "are not interpretations of the meaning of the texts, but interpretations of **our manipulations** in the presence of the text."[23] It follows for Tarlton that one interpretation of a text is just as "forced" or "manipulative" as another.[24] Here, indeed, is a picture of atomistic relativism. Beginning, in the words of Parekh and Berki, with an ontological reality of "an infinite variety of self-sufficient little worlds," within which a work of political theory may be placed, we arrive at the conclusion that interpretation is totally subjective, such that there can be no grounds for distinguishing between "forced" or reasonable, "manipulative" or nonmanipulative, interpretations.

Quite apart from the fact that such a viewpoint challenges the validity of **all** knowledge claims within the social sciences, it is not at all useful as an empirical generalization about the real problems which confront an interpreter of political theory. If one faces the practical problem of interpreting the **Leviathan** or Locke's **Two Treatises of Government**, what one discovers is decidedly not "an infinite

----

[22] Charles D. Tarlton, "Historicity, Meaning, and Revisionism in the Study of Political Thought," History and Theory, 12, 3, 1973, pp. 307-328, p. 326.

[23] Charles D. Tarlton, "From Theory to Method and Practice: Work and Skepticism in the Historical Study of Political Thought," paper presented to the Annual Meeting of the American Political Science Association, 1979, p. 23.

[24] Ibid., p. 18.

variety" or even a "bewildering" number of extant interpretations.   Rather, even the most scrupulous survey of the
secondary literature on either author will disclose only a
handful of interpretive viewpoints which have emerged during the last three centuries.   Indeed, repetition of earlier
opinions is such a common occurrence that some interpretations which appear to have a distinctive quality are, when
put in historical perspective, seen to be modern restate-
ments of older interpretive positions.   Moreover, if historical evidence is introduced into consideration, not all of the
existing interpretations will be assessed as being equally
plausible, as Skinner demonstrated in a series of articles on
Hobbes.[25] In practice, therefore, any interpreter who seeks
a comprehensive understanding of a particular work in political theory will find himself distributing the emphasis with
respect to accuracy or truth claims unevenly amongst the
existing interpretations of that work.   There is no reason
to suppose that the basis for this distribution of emphasis
must necessarily be purely arbitrary and subjective, and a
considerable amount of historical evidence suggests that this
supposition is false.   In other words, philosophical relativism functions as a justification for not examining the actual
historical and social context within which the problem of
interpreting a particular text assumes a definite practical
meaning.   The assumptions underlying a "forced" subjectivism are neither heuristically useful as a part of the activity
of interpretation nor are they descriptively accurate in relation to the reality they presuppose exists "out there."
They are, however, meaningful as part of a polemical critique of a historical-sociological approach to the problem of
interpretation.
    The other side of this philosophically relativist attack
on the new history is, paradoxically, a positivist argument
against its project of recovering the author's subjectively
intended meaning.   This project is impossible of fulfillment,
the critics assert, because no interpretation can establish
the absolute certainty of its claims regarding the intended
meaning of a text.   Thus "we are left brooding over an
inscrutable intention."   Since "Skinner is unable to ascribe

----

[25] See: Quentin Skinner, "Hobbes's **Leviathan**," **Historical
Journal**, 7, 2, 1964, pp. 321-333; Skinner, "The Ideological
Context of Hobbes's Political Thought," **Historical Journal**,
9, 3, 1966, pp. 286-317; Skinner, "Thomas Hobbes and His
Disciples in France and England," **Comparative Sudies in
Society and History**, 8, 2, 1965-66, pp. 153-167.

certain intentions" to a political theorist, "all he can do is to infer **possible** intentions". But these possible intentions, the critics maintain, cannot claim validity according to the Popperian standards of falsifiability.[26] Both as a reading of Skinner's work and as an argument about interpretation, this critique is seriously deficient.

In the first place, Skinner never maintained that a political theorist writes with only a single intention in mind; rather, like most activities, writing a work of political theory expresses "a complex set of intentions" held by the actor.[27] As an empirically realistic goal of interpretation, therefore, recovering **the** intention of the author could almost never be the interpreter's objective, since this would presuppose the kind of relationship between intention and action which is a relatively rare occurrence in our social experience. Hence from the outset, Skinner argued in terms of searching for empirically plausible intentions. A charge that the certain intention of an author is not recoverable is not only not a critique of his approach, it is a presupposition of that approach.

Secondly, the critics seem not to be conscious of the context in which their own criticism is formulated. That is, the problem of interpretation only arises in a situation in which more than one meaning is possible. It arises, in short, because the "objective" text does not speak for itself (any more than "facts" do), because the meaning of an argument is not self-evident (in the form, 2 + 2 = 4), and because there is not one single certain intention of the author to be recovered. (This last point, however, is an empirical generalization which could, perhaps, in certain

----

[26] Lotte Mulligan, Judith Richards, and John Graham, "Intentions and Conventions: A Critique of Quentin Skinner's Method for the Study of the History of Ideas," **Political Studies**, 27, 1, March, 1979, pp. 84-98, on pp. 87-89, 97. Parekh and Berki accused Skinner of assuming that each action had only one intention; see: "The History of Political of Political Ideas," p. 169.

[27] See: Quentin Skinner, "'Social Meaning' and the Explanation of Social Action," in Peter Laslett, W. G. Runciman, and Quentin Skinner, eds., **Philosophy, Politics and Society**, Fourth Series, Oxford, Basil Blackwell, 1972, pp. 136-157, on p. 142; Skinner, "Some Problems in the Analysis of Political Thought and Action," **Political Theory**, 2, 3, August, 1974, pp. 277-303, on p. 283.

specific circumstances be shown not to be true.) The context of interpretion, therefore, presupposes that more than one reading of a text or an action is possible. The only questions raised by Skinner within this general context are whether there are any empirical constraints imposed upon the "possible" interpretations and, especially, whether these constraints relate to the political theorist's use of language such that: (1) in terms of what we can discover from a knowledge of his behavior, correspondence, and other historical sources, as well as from the text, we can offer an interpretation of the meaning of the latter which is supported by a plausible argument as to the author's intention in writing the work; and (2) we can relate this intention and our interpretation of the political theory to a knowledge of the kinds of social conventions and practices pertaining to specific concepts or arguments contained in the text which were "culturally significant" with respect to the formulation of political theories within the theorist's society. If there are no such empirical constraints, as some of Skinner's critics claim, then we are left with only subjectivism and manipulation as interpretive standards. If there are such constraints, then only an empirically grounded methodology is in any position to discover what they are. This, however, returns us to the specific question of how that historical research is to be carried out, a question to which none of Skinner's critics have thus far addressed themselves.

But if the critics are inclined to ignore the theoretical context within which the problem of interpretation arises, they are no less neglectful of the historical context within which the new history arose as a particular response to the traditional approach to the history of political thought. For interpreters of political theory do not approach a text without some assumptions as to what the author meant by the use of this or that concept or argument. Just as there is no "presuppositionless" social science methodology, so there are no presuppositionless readings of the **Leviathan**. But on what basis does one **ascribe** to Hobbes a specific intended meaning? What grounds are there for imputing a particular intention to the author, and can this imputation be supported by empirical evidence?

Whatever the difficulties posed by Skinner's attempt to deal with these problems, the fact is that traditional historians of political thought rarely even recognized the existence of such problems, let alone suggested any means by which they might be solved. John Plamenatz, for example, who eschews a knowledge of the historical context in which the political theories he interprets were formulated,

nevertheless repeatedly claims that Machiavelli must have
meant this or Locke must have meant that in making such
and such an argument.[28] We are offered no evidence in
support of these suppositions about meaning, which apparently must depend upon the reader's acceptance of the
authority of Plamenatz as an interpreter. No recognition is
given to the problematic nature of the author's intentions.
No attempt is made to establish the contextual meanings for
the theorist's argument. No attention is paid to what specific opponents of the theorist were saying or to their reasons for opposing his position. In short, whatever the
nature of the historical evidence underlying Plamenatz's
judgment, it is not made available to the reader who wishes
to assess **Plamenatz's** interpretation of Machiavelli or Hobbes
in relation to such evidence. Instead, we are simply
expected to accept his interpration as -- what? self-evident? "following" logically from any intelligent reading of
the text? his authoritative reading? It hardly seems worthwhile to endorse **these** methodological presuppositions in the
name of Popperian "science."

     What, then, are the alternatives? If not "certainty"
or "subjectivism" (and if the latter, what counts as "evidence"?), we are left with plausible readings of the text,
grounded in empirical evidence, including the text as an
empirical document. In these circumstances, the compre-
hensiveness of the theoretical framework in relation to the
empirical evidence presented becomes one of the important
criteria for assessing the value of competing plausible
interpretations. In other words, if the text is recognized
to be a problematic object, an expression of a complex set
of the author's intentions, and a legitimating source for
competing plausible interpretations which seek to recover
one (or more) of those intentions, then from the standpoint
of providing evidential support for any one of those interpretations, there is absolutely nothing to be gained from
limiting the scope of the argument to the literal text itself
and much to be gained, in terms of choosing between nar-
rower and more comprehensive interpretations, by including
empirical evidence relating to the historical context.

     The last point, of course, raises the problem of his-
toricism. Each side in the 1950s' debate accused the other
of subscribing to this doctrine, and much attention was
devoted to its refutation. Recently, the accusation has

----

[28] See: John Plamenatz, **Man and Society**, New York,
McGraw-Hill, in two volumes, 1963.

been resuscitated for use against the new historians. The "radical implication of an historical approach" to the interpretation of political theory, according to Margaret Leslie, is that it will lead to the severance of any connection between the past and the present. As historians of political theory, we will be forced to "renounce the attempt to make connections with the present" because we will come to realize that since previous political theorists "were writing in a particular situation and tradition, addressing their arguments for particular purposes to a particular audience," they cannot be supposed to have anything to say to us living in the present.[29] As a historicist approach, therefore, the new history will send students of political theory into the past from which they can then never hope to escape. This criticism conveniently overlooks the fact that one of the objectives of the new history was to discover why and how political theorists were able to draw upon particular past traditions of thought in order to "see" the specific political problems in their own societies from a certain vantage point. It is obvious that, in order to deal with this question, the interpreter must confront the problem of the transmission of ideas and cultural values over time, perhaps centuries. Therefore, a basic presupposition of this approach that connections between past and present political theories not only can be made, but that, historically, they have been made by political theorists. Moreover, it is equally apparent that this problem must be faced by current political theorists, with respect to the kinds of traditions and cultural practices which supply the meaning for political ideas in their societies, in terms of which the political problems of the present are deemed to "make sense."

It is odd that Leslie should have supposed that the new history was unconcerned with discovering the links between the past and the present, since the older alternate view to which she refers merely assumed the timelessness of political concepts and thus begged altogether the question of how one could establish connections between the past and the present. What is precisely not demonstrated by the holders of this view is why some issues (e.g., individual liberty) are timeless and others (e.g., divine right of kings) are not, why **these** specific timeless issues and not others happen to be significant in terms of our political

----

[29] Margaret Leslie, "In Defense of Anachronism," **Political Studies**, 18, 4, December, 1970, pp. 433-447, on pp. 434-435.

problems, why different timeless issues appear differently to different societies or to members of the same society in different historical periods, and so on.   If connections are to be made between past and present political ideas, the connections must stand on the same empirical (historical) ground as the ideas themselves; pulling a transcendental notion of "human nature" out of the air or assuming the existence of an ever-present fogbank of timeless concepts from which one may suddenly withdraw "rights" or "justice" is no substitute for an argument explaining how and why these particular connections have been made.

The definition of historicism which portrays every event as unique and therefore specifically tied to its historical origins is merely another form of atomistic relativism which serves to disavow the possibility of even making "connections" between historical phenomena.   Indeed, this Hobbesian chaos appears to have no other function than to serve as a foil for the advocacy of an absolutist position, which is assumed to be the only possible alternative to relativism so defined.   In fact, from neither perspective is it possible to present a "historical" account of phenomena. Only a position which frames its argument in terms of the relative significance of certain tendencies or patterns of action over time is capable of establishing the empirically grounded connections between the political theories of the past and those of the present.

Finally, I want to consider briefly some of the arguments advanced by the new historians which, in my view, comprise part of a general endeavor within philosophy and the social sciences to encourage a revision in our conception of "social science."   Sociology, Weber wrote, "is a science which attempts the interpretive understanding of social action," where the latter refers to "all human behavior when and in so far as the acting individual attaches a subjective meaning to it."[30] Clearly, the effort to recover the political theorist's subjectively intended meaning falls within the province of this view of social science.   Moreover, Weber maintained that the interpreter's perspective, as well as that of the original theorist, were shaped by "the practical value interests" of these individuals and by the value-constitutive ideas which "dominate the investigator and his age."[31] Now, if we possessed a detailed account of how

----

[30] Max Weber, **The Theory of Social and Economic Organization**, Toronto, Collier-Macmillan, 1964, p. 88.

these "practical value interests" are organized, how certain evaluative ideas become "dominant" within a culture, and how these relationships change over time, we might be able to provide some substantive meaning for these methodological assertions. We would then be in a position to draw the connections between the subjective meaning of the actor and the objective possibilities supplied by the conventions of meaning which are culturally significant for members of his society. A particular political theory could thus be related both to these conventions of meaning and to the organization of practical interests which, together, comprise the social context. The interpretation of the meaning of a social action (including political theorizing as a social activity) is, therefore, implicitly or explicitly, made in terms of a theory about social relationships: i.e., how society is structured.[32] Such a theory supplies the ultimate referential context within which a particular social action can be said to convey a meaningful form of intersubjective communication between its participants.

As I suggested earlier, one consequence of the new history's association of the interpretation of texts with the problems of interpreting social action (of which, writing a work of political is an instance) is to place the problem of meaning within a sociological context. Intersubjective meanings, that is, are not "contained" in propositional statements or concepts "as such." They are embedded in social practices.[33] To know whether certain practices are politically prevalent or whether certain values are dominant in society is precisely a type of knowledge one cannot deduce from a consideration of a particular statement contained in a specific text written by an individual theorist. For the new historians, a theory of meaning is inextricably tied to a theory about the social uses of language in relation to social

----

[31] Max Weber, **Methodology of the Social Sciences**, Glencoe, IL, Free Press, 1949, pp. 76-85.

[32] All intentional explanations presuppose a given social context, which, at a minimum, supplies the rules and criteria for making judgments about intentionality. See: Brian Fay, **Social Theory and Political Practice**, London, Allen and Unwin, 1975, pp. 74-75.

[33] See: Charles Taylor, "Interpretation and the Sciences of Man," **Review of Metaphysics**, 25, 1, September, 1971, pp. 3-51.

action.   Sooner or later, therefore, this approach was bound to lead the interpreter of political theory onto the terrain of ideology.[34]

For a variety of reasons, there has been considerable resistance, outside of the Marxist tradition, to the formulation of such a theory, despite the fact that its basic ingredients are provided by the presuppositions of Weberian social science.   Such a theory is needed not only in order to place the activity of theorizing in a definite relationship to other social activities, but also, more generally, in order to offer a sociological account of how people have organized themselves and their thinking in an effort to realize specific practical objectives.   In the 1950s, this avenue of investigation was methodologically blocked by the reliance of social scientists upon a set of analytical distinctions which separated "science" or "rational discourse" from "ideology" or emotional commitments.[35]   The more these distinctions are challenged on empirical grounds for the inadequacy of the view they present of actual social behavior, the more the lines between science and ideology tend to disappear altogether.

Another reason why the problem of ideology has remained an unexplored topic for political theorists is that, according to a widely-accepted view, the identification of political theory with ideology necessarily entails a "reductionist" conception of political thought: one, that is, which portrays ideas as mere "reflections" of some nonideational "material reality."[36]   Since it cannot be denied that some Marxists have occasionally written about ideology in a manner that lends some substance to this charge, it is important to distinguish the position I wish to defend (and, I believe, the view held by the new historians) from this reductionist standpoint.

Let us, therefore, approach the issue carefully, if

----

[34] See: Quentin Skinner, "Preface," **The Foundations of Modern Political Thought**, Cambridge, Cambridge University Press, in two volumes, 1978, pp. ix-xv.   Also see the essays by Skinner cited in previous footnotes.

[35] For example, see: David Apter, ed., **Ideology and Discontent**, Glencoe, IL, Free Press, 1964.

[36]   Tarlton, "Historicity, Meaning, and Revisionism," p. 313; Parekh and Berki, "The History of Political Ideas," p. 177.

somewhat obliquely, by reconsidering the problems of interpreting the meaning of social action, viewed in the context
of everyday social experience. I will incorporate into this
discussion an earlier point regarding intentionality:
namely, that in executing a particular action, the agent has
in mind "a complex set of intentions." Or to state the
problem from the standpoint of the interpreter, we can say
that there are reasonable grounds for supposing that more
than one of the agent's possible intentions may be cited as
the basis for a plausible interpretation of the subjectively
intended meaning of that action. The multiplicity of possible intentions may or may not be a matter of practical
importance to us.

The beggar who receives alms from a passerby does
not care whether this action expresses the latter's conscious
desire for his betterment, a form of therapeutic relief for
the giver's bad conscience, or some other possible intention
on the part of the giver. In other situations, however, a
determination as to which of the possible meanings an action
might have is of crucial practical importance. I enter a
room and see a stranger with a knife in his hand. Generally speaking, I would rely upon my knowledge of the context, especially in the case of strangers, to supply a meaning for this action. It might be a butcher in his shop, a
doctor in a hospital, a sculptor in his studio, and so on.
If, on the other hand, the context provides little assistance
(e.g., it is an ordinary hotel room), I must "interpret" his
intentions. Is he: examining the knife as an ancient relic?
about to scrape the mud off his boots? sharpening pencils?
Since one possibility is that he intends to use the knife as
a weapon against me, what kind of action I decide to take
in this situation will certainly depend upon my interpretation of his intention.

These kinds of situational decisions, under less dramatic circumstances, occur all the time as a feature of our
everyday social activity. Through the use of such illustrations, what I wish to argue with respect to political theory
is that the problem of interpretation presents itself in the
context of social relationships where the indeterminacy of
outcomes (possible meanings for the action) and the practical importance of the interpreter's choosing one of them are
structural characteristics of this "problem." There are, I
suggest, sufficient grounds, in the form of an empirical
generalization, for viewing the production of political theory
within this framework. Political theories exist in two
worlds: they are suppliers of possible meanings for certain
social actions, and they are a constitutive element in the
process of organizing practical interests. The latter,

however, is not only itself a "meaning-determined" series of actions; it is also capable of bringing about a restructuring of the range of objectively possible meanings. From this standpoint, in other words, the social role of a political theory cannot be explained in reductionist terminology.

A political theory may possess considerable social significance as a structured set of meanings, although its directives for practical action are not executed by any specific social group. Alternately, it may happen that the meaning of a political theory undergoes striking changes as it becomes an integral aspect of the social practices of different social groups. The nature of the social composition of the theory's "audience" will, in turn, affect the types of arguments, evidence, authorities, concepts, etc. employed by the theory's defenders. The **theoretically** interesting question, I am arguing, is how, in a particular historical-social context, including the present, these tensions which describe what a political theory is (for us) manifest themselves. This theoretical issue is bound up with the problematic relationship I have described. It is a quality which is precisely lost as soon as a particular set of ideas is identified with the members of a particular social group and this identification is offered as an account of the social meaning of those ideas. Such a procedure, at a minimum, neglects the importance of that political theory as a **possible** framework of meanings for social actions, and its importance in shaping the concrete choices for members of other social groups.

When we are asked as political theorists to provide some interpretive standard for explaining how people organize their thinking and activities when they are confronted with a situation in which various possible political actions can be taken, there are several ways in which we might respond. We could undertake an analysis of how social groups in the present have mobilized themselves with respect to achieving certain political goals. We might, however, formulate such a standard through the use of historical examples, drawn from an interpretation of past political theories (seen in their social contexts), especially if these examples are ones that illustrate the importance of specific institutions or traditions of thought which claim a significant place in the social consciousness of our contemporaries.

In one sense, what I have described as the task of the political theorist is not so far removed from what the traditionalists attempted to do during the fifties and sixties. Leo Strauss, for example, constructed his view of contemporary political theory by building upon the assertions that

"the politicization of philosophy" in the seventeenth century, the spread of a belief in the relativism of values in
the seventeenth and eighteenth centuries, and the rise of
positivism and historicism in the nineteenth century, have
brought about "the decline of political philosophy."[37] Now
these appear to be historical suppositions about changes in
social consciousness in Western societies. But what historical evidence is actually presented in support of such global
assertions? And what theory of social change, applicable to
these changes of social consciousness, guides us through
these shifts in world-historical thought spread over four
centuries and two continents? In some simple but unex-
plained manner, we are left to assume that the ideas of
Machiavelli and Hobbes (as interpreted by Strauss, but not
necessarily as they were actually read by anyone else)
merely "flowed" into the mainstream of social conciousness
for "the West."

Similarly, Wolin and Arendt have written of "the
decline of the political" and its replacement by "the social."
And other theorists tell us of the rise of economic consciousness, the secularization of political theory, and so
forth, as if the historical-sociological basis and evidence in
support of these sweeping generalizations were perfectly
self-evident. Yet if one did not grant the **historical** plausibility of these presuppositions, the interpretaions offered
us by Strauss, Wolin, Dante Germino, and others would lose
both their internal-logical and their social-political significance. Nevertheless, it is far from clear why we should
take seriously these assertions about historical and social
changes in our society when so little evidence is presented
relating to the structure of society: viz., the interrela-
tions between various social groups, the relationship
between the political theorists discussed and these social
groups, changes in these relationships and in the meaning
of political ideas over time, and many other such questions.

In other words, what needs to be demonstrated is
simply assumed at the expense of supplying evidence which
would reconstruct the social-historical context for the "theoretical" propositions being advanced by these theorists.
As a consequence, a whole range of difficult theoretical
problems are simply not considered in their writings.
Despite this, however, and paradoxically, some theory of

----

[37] Strauss, **Natural Right and History**, pp. 13, 16, 34, 78.
Also see: Strauss, "What Is Political Philosophy?," **Journal
of Politics**, 19, 3, August, 1957, pp. 343-368.

historical change and social structure is being presupposed by them as the contextual guarantor for the meaning of the assertions they make. But this theory of historical development and social structure, a theory of ideology, is not itself articulated and defended as part of the evidence for the argument they are advancing.

In the 1950s, this approach to political theory rested on a number of assumptions: a preference for philosophy over history, an elitist conception of philosophy, an absolutist epistemological position, a belief in the subjectivity of moral and political commitments, a view of ideology as a reductionist treatment of ideas, and so on. All of these have, in the last decade, come under sharp attack by a diverse group of political theorists and social scientists. The point I wish to emphasize in this essay is not that the problems raised by this discussion have been solved, but rather that students of political theory ought to be encouraged to think about these issues and to recognize their importance to the future development of political theory. For it has been the conscious intention of the new historians of political theory and others to redirect the attention of political theorists towards those problems which were ignored by the participants in the 1950s' debate about the nature of political theory. It is in that context that I have tried to suggest why a step backward might prove helpful in gaining some perspective on the present state of political theory.

DOES POLITICAL THEORY HAVE A FUTURE?

Robert Booth Fowler

"What Should Political Theory Be Now?" is the kind of question that sounds innocent enough at first hearing, but is hardly that. I wonder today if it is not really a cry of anxiety (or at least a cry of confusion) which fairly begs for analysis as to its origin at least as much as to its answer. This may not be the first time we have heard it, but it is certainly loud in our times. In this essay, I intend to argue speculatively, addressing several questions.[1] First, I will contend that political theory is in some serious trouble within political science, while also noting its health, especially outside our profession. I will suggest that this strong other life of political theory is the behavioral balm to an intellectual sore. Second, I want to explore some good and some less good reasons which motivate the current concern over the condition of political theory in political science. Then I want to argue that even if we break down the "ghetto" of political philosophy, there will be no welcome mat from within political science. We should not be naive and chase (or consider chasing) an ever-retreating hare. Finally, I intend to argue that political philosophy must move toward more commitment to doing political theory engaged with politics and the world. Only then will it really survive and flourish in and out of political science.

This is an essay in counter-analysis and counter-argument, a plea that there is reason to worry about political theory at home, but not abroad. It is also a plea against the perpetual problem of political philosophers taking themselves and their enterprise so seriously that they sometimes don't get around to doing it. Political theory deserves admiration for its successful practitioners, of whom there are many. More emulation off their practice and less hand-wringing or rusading to smash our "ghetto" seems appropriate, despite the warning signs about the health of the political theory subfield.

Before I begin, a few introductory words are in order. First, for some souls we could not discuss political

----

[1] Many people graciously read earlier drafts. I thank them all, but especially David McConnell and John Nelson.

theory without a definition of it. And there are many candidates for "the" proper definition of the field. But I
think that providing a definition is necessarily a political
act, and one which alienates some as it will attract others.
This is not an essay on the nature of political theory, but
on its future. I prefer to get on with it and simply
describe political theory in terms of those who are in the
subfield, as self-proclaimed theorists and outside observers
see them and their work. "Theory" is for the purposes of
this paper as theory is perceived and named: the most
inclusive and general of definitions.

Second, in what follows I often talk of political science. There is such an entity, similarly defined phenomenologically, but nothing in what follows implies that it is
without its own divisions. It has no monolithic unity; and
of course, it has a lot of tensions: over methodology, over
subject, over professionalism, over much else. Yet I think
it is fair to say that, as a whole, it is in tension with political philosophy, and vice versa; and in this sense it has
some, though hardly perfect, coherence. It is in this
sense that I speak of political science.

I

I begin by asking why there is so much interest in
the "Future of Political Theory," the topic of a 1980 panel
at the annual meeting of the American Political Science
Association, a 1981 conference at the University of Iowa,
and so many conversations among political philosophers --
and why, in that context, there is so much concern as to
whether political theory is isolated from political science,
stuck in a "ghetto." What is in the air, or wherever, that
activates this urge in us? The mysteries of the Zeitgeist
are beyond me, and most of us, just now. Perhaps another
day, it will all seem obvious; and this concern will fall in
with a great many events to form a picture which now is
only an unpainted canvass. So I do not plumb the universe
for an answer. I will tentatively (but without shame) suggest four reasons of a more earthly nature. One points out
marginality in our profession. Another suggests that the
very survival of our subfield within political science hangs
in the balance. Another insists that political theorists have
no impact on the larger world. A fourth argues that
theory is mostly lost in an "alienated" world, counting its
toes and too little else. I share the complaints that all four

embody and agree with them also that political philosophy within political science is trouble.

My first reason is not pleasant or painless, but it must be faced. It does not stand alone, but it is there; it tells us something about contemporary political theory; and it points to what some consider to be a frightening future. It frankly ignores for the moment the intellectual case for closing the gap between political theory and political science. This reason is arguably the not very secret heart of today's concern, and it is far more mundane and practical than it is philosophical. It starts from the concrete situation of the political theorist presently in the world of political science and in political science departments -- with the existential situation, so to say, of political philosophers. Here I do not mean the few who have well-known names, the jet-setters; but the ordinary political philosophers, the vast majority.

Many political theorists clearly feel they face difficult situations at home. For them, the crisis of political theory is something they confront every working day. They know they are often intellectually lonely there; they know they are often isolated; they know they are often powerless in departmental decisions. These complaints are very widespread. Though there are no studies confirming or denying this situation, theorists take these facts as part of life. If we don't experience them ourselves, we have spent many hours listening to colleagues who do.

Let me just mention one straw in the wind. At the last political science convention, I went out to dinner with a hefty group of political theorists I know and love. Once we sat down, we talked about the condition of political philosophy today. I was surprised at the alacrity at which we jumped at this opportunity. What followed was a torrent of complaints about the treatment of political theory. There was acute sensitivity (and often pessimism) about how the theory subfield was doing in college and university after college and university. Again and again, complaints about little influence and large intellectual loneliness came up. I had the latter reemphasized when several of these friends saw me later at the convention, and we talked about how valuable it was to have a "serious" dinner topic instead of gossip or silence. We had a hunger to talk about theory, a hunger few of us could fulfill at home.

We could engage in some possibly interesting speculation as to why it bothers many political philosophers to be partly or greatly isolated. For some, it is a matter of simple human need to be respected, a need denied by the notorious fact that the still-dominant behavioral generations

within political science do not offer such respect. For others, it is partly a matter of political ideology, endorsing a
communitarianism they see so missing in their workplace.
For still others, it is surely a desire to contribute to their
profession as a whole, a desire which is now so hard to fulfill.

I think it is clear that this isolation does exist in
many cases. It does describe the situation of many political
theorists. Yes, it is true that we cannot be sure how
many. Nor is it wrong to note that there have been similar
"crises" before, in which theory was under fire and theorists were lonely. The crisis of the 1950s attracted Isaiah
Berlin, Sheldon Wolin, and the like. If that crisis really
existed, it was a crisis of the intellectual role and purpose
of political philosophy. It was not an existential and survival crisis. Of course, there are other reasons for the
sense of isolation. One is natural division of labor: how
many methodologists or students of Indonesia feel isolated in
their departments, too? Moreover, much of the problem
may result from an intellectual choice: theorists self-consciously taking themselves from the world, which I discuss
more below. Finally, we pursue our work in a context that
often ensures we will feel isolated. The abstraction which
attracts many philosophers in our subfield almost guarantees
isolation. So does the self-conscious disdain for political
science which animates many theorists.

In any case, the isolation is there in many cases.
There is a good deal of this situation in my own department, a basically benevolent world -- and much, much more
in many other places, where things are often far from
benevolence. As a result, what political philosopher doesn't
in a weak moment wonder how much better life would be if
he or she were "with it" and in public administration?

A second reason involves even more objective signs of
trouble. Rumors that there are no jobs in political theory
often have unsavory origins and do not describe the truth.
But some ominous statistics in PS should not be cavalierly
ignored. First, look at the poor fit of candidate numbers
and placements. This situation is grim. According to the
latest (Winter, 1980) figures, there are more candidates for
jobs available in political theory than in any other subfield.
Only 54.5% of political philosophy candidates got jobs in the
1978 and 1979 placement years. Placements in international
relations and comparative politics fell toward 60%; and the
rest of the subfields reported success rates over 70%, some
much over. There are simply too many people who want to
be political theorists, perhaps we should say too many doctorates in theory receiving training that they cannot use in

the academy.

Second, look at whether there are or likely will be many theory jobs. Over the last two years of hiring in political science (for which we have figures), only 10.5% of the jobs were in political theory. Although from reading the professional placement newsletter, it is sometimes easy to expect the imminent and total disappearance of political theory, this percentage suggests that such predictions are just a bit premature. Theory may have too many candidates for the jobs available, but there are some jobs. Indeed, for these two recent years, there were more jobs in theory than in public policy or methodology. On the other hand, when it comes to the total number of jobs, political theory is now a very distant cousin not just to American government, but to comparative politics and international relations as well. Political theory has become a small subfield of political science, though not one about to disappear as yet.

My analysis here is deliberately (if modestly) empirical because, in talking about political theory as so much else, we open our softest side to our political-science colleagues when we refuse to make even the most minimal effort to sustain our empirical claims. But the picture cannot be completed in empirical terms. For there is also a mood, hard to capture and as yet little-studied empirically, which is very real in phenomenological terms. It is the mood of depression that can precipitate after a glance at the latest placement newsletter. It is the mood of dejection that has affected more than a few graduate professors surrounded by students who may be placed after a struggle, if at all. And it is the mood of discouragement that sets in when one compares the tremendous interest in political-theory panels at the American Political Science Association meetings -- where in 1978-1980, they once again attracted the most people and had the highest mean attendance -- with the ten-plus percent of new jobs that are in theory or with the realization that many of those graduate students at the panels will never teach political philosophy. No wonder several graduate theory professors I know are out of the placement business. They experience too much present pain and intimate too grim a future to go on in the old way.

Again, it is possible to wonder if the present situation is so different from the past. Within this century, the time span of political science, has political theory been in any different situation? Haven't we always had too many candidates and too few openings? Haven't we always been a small subfield? The histories do not answer the first question; as for the second, they clearly suggest that theory is in great decline. Just how many schools require every political-science graduate student to take one or two semesters of theory, something still common in the 1950s? Very few, if any. That world is gone. Perhaps it is true that the problem seems so acute because of a decline from the prosperous and then conflictual 1960s, which helped theory regain its balance after the blows of the behavioral revolution. It looks, however, like the curve has once again resumed its downward direction. Here, as elsewhere, the 1960s appear as an age of exception.

Overall, the facts are these. Political theory is not dead within political science as of this time. Interest is there: no doubt of that. Theory, however, is fading. There are not that many jobs, and there is no mood of hope.

For those who see matters such as marginality as too personal and job statistics as too vulgar, there is a third reason for crisis. It derives from the embarrassing but undeniable fact that political theorists within the political-science profession simply have little or no impact on the larger world. This, too, is an unpleasant fact. It is one, however, which must be faced squarely and not ignored in the conversation or argument at political theory panels or conferences. Who would put one of our political theorists on a list of leading intellectuals in the United States? Who would put one on a list of the most significant political thinkers in America? Who can identify a book by one of our political thinkers which has had wide intellectual, not even to think of political, impact? Maybe Michael Walzer and his work would be an exception here; but when the names roll down -- the Bells, the Rawls, the Friedmans, and more -- they are not from political science. There are scant signs of influence.

Now it is possible that this is a commentary on the world at large, on the United States, on something or other besides political theory. I doubt, though, that very many of us would offer such an excuse. Nor is it all a matter of luck, capitalism, or the constellations in the sky. I reflect on the possible reasons in a moment. For now, the matter is that impact is not there; and I suspect that precious few of us think that it is. We are talking to ourselves and, more important, our students. That is about it. This isn't a matter of anything so appalling as whether we are selling ourselves at "retail" or even "wholesale." It is a question of whether others beyond our hermetic borders see anything of use within our world. If they don't, surely that is a warning sign, even an alarm bell.

Lastly, political philosophy is in crisis because, in its political-science version, it is sadly detached, not just from larger intellectual influences, but all too often from the politics around us, even as a subject matter. It is not removed from politics of the past, of Hobbes' or Plato's day, to be sure. But frequently, **our** politics barely seems to exist. Perhaps it is an embarrassment to many theorists. What does exist is a subfield which is increasingly arcane and hermetic in its interests and publications. One need not be reduced to "vulgar" utilitarianism to be uncomfortable about such corrupting and fruitless insularity and abstractness. Political theory need not be under the gun of relevance all the time (no real worry with our subfield); but in this time of crisis in our history, it is legitimate to ask why this activity of humans proceeds so often, so far outside of history. It is also legitimate to ask if such abstract thinking produces theory good by standards other than assisting others. Is it good in itself? Can any theory be insightful, can it provide illumination, when it is lost in itself and so far away from ordinary human experience?

We should applaud and cheer John Gunnell and his powerful attack on this "alienated" political theory. He is right to note that much of political philosophy is remarkably and often self-consciously remote from politics, politics in the historical world we know and experience. Gunnell has not really articulated an alternative; but he has identified the problem, found a label for it, and raised searching questions of purpose in the most direct way possible. His contribution is great.

That too many modes of political theory within political science display such alienation is clear. It includes repetitious discussions of yet another side of a traditional theorist in complete abstraction from our time, and often his; highly formal analytic and normative essays far, far away from politics; unspeakably boring discussions of metatheory; dated contests between Marxist and liberal ideologies; and interminable (and often hopeless) forays into epistemology.

The concept of "alienated" theory has its problems, to be sure. In some hands, it goes in directions that merit pause. It can be a weapon used, usually too quickly, to dismiss all sorts of theory and other persuasions in political theory. It can be the banner of a movement; and then what might start as an articulation of direction can become a force for monism. And it can be a fashionable way of expressing pessimism and little else: political theory is alienated; political theorists can't help themselves, and they can't help us; they cannot get out of their academic chairs and into politics and history enough to produce good theory. So it is all hopeless.

Such monism or pessimism is, however, not at all necessarily connected with the protest against "alienated theory." Focusing on reducing the amount of "alienated theory" mandates nothing about maintaining other traditional roles, such as museum-keeping. Moreover, there is no real reason to be so pessimistic, unless one considers academics or political philosophers hopeless as a group.

II

There is every sign that political theorists recognize their situation. After all, conferences on the Future of Political Theory don't occur every year. What have our responses been? They have been varied, though not necessarily always as impressive as one might wish. Each in its way is a portrait of part of our world of political theory and perhaps deserves some respect as a response to a painful situation. It is impossible to review every reaction. But several can scarcely be ignored.

One, which I suspect is quite self-conscious, is to hunker down. Yes, things are not good. The worthy are not welcomed and are far less welcomed than they once were. Nonetheless, we can and should carry on in the old ways. What else can we do? We are more or less helpless; and besides, we like what we do. Maybe such a view alarms crisis-mongers, but we are merely embracing reality.

The hunker-down approach, of course, also ratifies isolation. Yet this fact does not seem to lessen its appeal to a good many political theorists. This is, I think suggested by many of the theory articles which appear in political-science journals, particularly in **The American Political Science Review**. It is also, we should note, characteristic of most of what appears in **Political Theory**. The overwhelmingly traditional nature of these articles is striking and suggests that business as usual, or much fiddling, is going on.

This is not at all to repudiate traditional approaches to political philosophy. There is nothing wrong, though by this time there is rarely anything illuminating, about the endless articles on Rousseau, Locke, and the rest. The point, rather, is that they go on being produced and published as if there had been no developments in political theory in hundreds of years and certainly as if there were

no "crisis" in political theory.   Perhaps such a hunker-
down approach makes life easier, but it is doubtful that
self-chosen isolation will help the problem go away.

We should note that the hunker-down approach apparently also appeals to many political scientists.   This should
cause no wonder.   It nicely ensures that political philosophy will not be a serious factor in the discipline.   It also
confirms the widespread belief among political scientists that
theorists are merely museum-keepers.   As one who teaches
both theory and American politics, I regret this assumption;
but I am convinced that the hunker-down strategy only
confirms it.   Being quiet and being good converts no one.

Another common response has been breastbeating and
anger of a kind that we all know well and in which some of
us have often engaged.   Sometimes it is private.   When the
door closes in the political philosopher's office, with the
other theorist(s) there after the department meeting, the
talk can turn quickly to how "they" ignore "us," how
"they" never accept "our" perspectives.   And sometimes it
gets bitter.   The complaints continue at conventions and
anywhere else theorists meet.

At some times, in some departments, and in some
articles and books, these feelings burst forth into public.
The sense of marginality, in some cases the perception of
what one political scientist recently described to me as the
"contempt" some political scientists feel for their philosopher
colleagues, activates anger which can hardly be confined to
quiet moments.   The anger is human, it even makes sense;
but it does not help theory (though it may help theorists'
psychological survival).   Perhaps the calling and holding of
conferences and panels on political philosophy is a sophisticated version of breastbeating.   Yet there is the important
difference that such conferences or panels can include much
that is intellectually positive.   They need not be studies in
whining or anger (whatever the therapeutic uses).   They
can be studies in reflection, in analysis, even in stimulating
creative introspection.   However, they also provide plenty
of opportunity for handwringing, complaining about marginality, and (yes, still) bemoaning positivism's influence in
political science.   I don't want to sound pious here.   I do
all of these things, sometimes with great relish.   It is a
matter of balance.

The same point applies to political theorists' hopeless
love of arguments over epistemology and metatheory.   A lot
of serious learning can occur in these contexts.   Yet after
a while, these discussions in and out of print are too obviously a substitute for doing theory, indeed for doing
theory in a realistic context regarding its intradisciplinary

prospects.

The epistemology dead-end is apparent by now to almost everyone, and it is good news that impatience with it is on the rise. The recent article in **The Journal of Politics** by Paul Kress makes part of the case in eloquent and telling fashion. Epistemology in political science has more and more turned into a self-focused entity churning out essays and articles with little light to complement their considerable (but self-contained) heat. There are creative exceptions, of course, but the epistemology detour is indeed an escape from political theory. Not that some reflections on epistemology cannot assist us. They can, but enough is enough. Paul Kress is right: it is time to make sure impatience no longer deserves being described as "apostate musings."

We also seem to find inexhaustible energy for arguing about exactly what political philosophy should be. And we know very well that many political theorists would be busy doing that on the deck of the sinking Titanic. They take us on the endless ride from one "true belief" about political theory to another. One tells us that political thought should really be psychoanalytic interpretation; another tells us that it should be the "true" (as opposed to the apparent) meaning of the great texts; another claims that it is really normative policy analysis; yet another that it is the investigation of class relations and politics; one more that it must be the development of a phenomenological approach to politics; and on and

Of course, there is nothing particularly wrong with an ongoing process of discussion of one's intellectual mission. It is a legitimate, if tiring, activity which by no means is necessarily correlated with the "decline" of political theory. At the present time, however, such emphasis on it seems to be not only a diversion, but a rather pointless battle, a fight over the petals of a wilting rose. I see no reason to think that political philosophy would be more loved if it were more "relevant," or psychoanalytical, or Marxist, or formalist, or whatever. Nor do I think that it is likely to get better, the more we spar over these topics. Does anyone? We might be a happier profession, on the other hand, if we fought less with ourselves. Maybe we should turn away from our internecine struggles and take a hard look at the overall condition of political theory. Maybe that is where our attention belongs just now -- rather than worrying about the purity of the disorganized, but perhaps wonderful reality that is political philosophy in political science.

Another approach goes in quite a different direction, though its origins also lie in confusion, this time the confusion of our age, or even the universe. Theorists of this expansive disposition cannot possibly address questions of the future of political theory, at least in political science. They are much more concerned with the lonely individual, the loss of community and thus of politics, the absence of meaning, the presence of angst or even nihilism. From their perspective -- on the one hand, cosmic, on the other hand, deeply personal and individualistic -- much of political philosophy and most of the questions about its future miss the mark and (worse) are embarrassingly trivial as well.

They have a point. Worrying about political philosophy's fate in political science is hardly a great question of this or any age. A better brief might be constructed for concern with political theory as a more inclusive enterprise. My complaint here, however, remains: nervous painting in existential hues, or far more pessimistic colors, usually means no political theory at all. Angst and nihilism are not fruitful breeding grounds for any kind of philosophy (despite Sartre or Kierkegaard). They usually announce its death and don't feel able to try a revival. Some things can be scratched out of this earth (look at the achievement of Glenn Tinder). Nonetheless, proponents and critics of this approach agree that it has an agenda which goes its own way. And (perhaps admirably), it could care less about how political theory is doing in narrow professional confines.

More than a lot of theorists, I sympathize with this inclination. Yet I also concede the critics' perspective: for all their frequent concern with the concrete person, many of these theorists are so involved with fundamental concerns of epistemology, metaphysics, and religion as to leave the world of politics very far away. When such treatments of the individual human being turn philosophical or nihilistic, the skeptics have a strong point.

In the guise of explicating some of the responses that theorists make to their survival problem in political science, this series of complaints illustrates yet another way in which we come to terms with our declining condition. This is our affinity for masochism. Somehow it is said to be the fault of theory that we hunker down, waste time fighting over epistemology, love anger, or indulge in nihilism. And to this general complaint, we must add those particular accusations enunciated by and against one or another faction of political philosophers. Some say (though rarely for the record) that Straussians give theory a bad name. They insist that Straussians are cultists, hostile to mainstream political science, with a reputation for contentiousness and irrelevance to political life. Others fault the emergence of Marxism in our subfield for confirming the contradictory caricature that has us simultaneously stirring the waters and stuck in the past (here, on issues of the nineteenth-century West). And there are other indictments, including our attitude toward political science: to put it gently, our often ill-disguised lack of respect.

The tendency to blame ourselves so often and so much -- regardless of the varying substance of the complaints -- is the issue here. Seldom is it said quite this way, though this is what it can and frequently does amount to. Of course, it is rarely you and I who hurt political theory, so much as it is they and the others. Yet it still comes down to faulting the subfield as a whole. Since we do have sins in abundance, it is not so outrageous to note them; but once in a while we ought to share the blame: with an uncomprehending political science or with the stars, if need be. Political theory has a lot to be proud of, too; and (within political science), it suffers a shortage of friends. We should speak up about our good sides once in a while, most of all to ourselves. And, anyway, what does masochism get us?

III

Another reaction to the lack of health of philosophy within political science appears as the counsel and practice of what I call "integration": moving political theory and the larger discipline together as rapidly as possible. The obvious hope here is that in integration there will be life, even comfort, and certainly not death.

I do not mean integration on the terms of theory's sometime affection for the queen-bee syndrome. Yes, there are still a few theorists who yearn for a political science led or guided by philosophy and philosophers, despite the impossibility of this "ideal." There never has been such a time in the eighty-odd-year history of our profession; but the aspiration has been around for a long, long time. It is in eclipse now, and the present situation is rapidly erasing its few remaining proponents. Even its most obdurate advocates must recognize in their hearts that the queen bee will have no hive in political science.

I have in mind another (and growing) school of integrationists. They have far less demanding, but perhaps not less ambitious terms. They aspire to unite theory and science in our profession by giving theory a different focus and different modes and rules of trade with political science. These enthusiasts -- and they are often exactly that -- reject pessimism about our future. They do not necessarily deny the portents, but insist that our future can be different, if we are willing to change. There is a way, they sometimes suggest, which will ensure that present fears will never come true. Give us political philosophers involved with the world of political science. Then we will be taken seriously. Then we will make a genuine contribution to an integrated discipline. The "ghetto" walls will fall; political theory will survive, maybe even grow. And it will deserve to grow, because it will be contributing.

Let me be clear. The integrationists (examples follow) propose integration not just (nor primarily) to save political theory, but because they believe it can make genuinely important and lasting gifts to political science. Because these gifts will be worthy, they will obtain recognition. This is a statement of faith; and integrationists do frankly believe in political theory, political science, and what they can do together. This is an authentic hope for them, and cynics who damn these people as water carriers and apple-polishers miss the point; sincerity is not the issue.

It is not possible, fortunately, to classify everyone who proposes such a view. There are, however, at least four modes of this optimistic focus on redemption through political science. By no means are all their practitioners "optimists," but there are more hopeful sorts among them than among others in our subfield. The modes are: analytical theory, philosophy of social science, structural theory, and normatively oriented policy theory.

There is considerable agreement in principle that analytical and linguistic theory can help clarify terms and concepts. Such theory often goes down the all too well-travelled road of ridiculous quibbling and/or arid conceptualizing, but it does not have to. It can be useful for anyone and any discipline. Those who believe it can be an important bridge between theory and political science as a whole, however, enter a more problematic realm.

These hopeful souls like to note, as we would expect, the considerable praise from political scientists far from the world of theory that sometimes has fallen on Hanna Pitkin or Brian Barry. Yet we need to be careful concerning what about Pitkin or Barry obtains such praise. Is it Pitkin's brilliant discussions of obligation and justice, or her less original models of legitimacy? And who in political science really uses (not merely cites) Barry's work? Is his work on Rawls used? Is his considerable effort to fashion categories of political analysis admired by a test of practice? Well, then, we might ask: how about the work by William Connolly on language and politics? It is admirable, often exciting. Who, however, sees the slightest sign that Connolly's explorations of the paradoxes of political language and their frequent ideological overtones has had any impact on ordinary political science? The truth is, I suspect, that some political scientists may want analytic political theory to help them with terms and concepts. Yet if they do, then the practice before us suggests that most do not want theorists -- the Pitkins, the Barrys, the Connollys; they want underlaborers, which is something else again.[2]

Sometimes optimists latch onto another approach that can be related to the direct servicing of other political scientists. This is the philosophy of social science. Surely, a few suggest, this could (or should) be the terrain (or a terrain) for political theorists. It would link us with the larger science and the larger discipline. In some places, political philosophers do this task and do it well. After all, political theorists can play a significant role here, one very much needed. They can bring to methodology, if not freedom from bias, at least freedom from the reigning biases. They can often make contact with students from whom they would never get a hearing otherwise and so accomplish considerable mind-expanding, while at the same time helping political science. There is, in short, a real need for theorists who, at least for part of their time, are willing to serve, if not as methodologists, then as philosophers of social science.

On the other hand, increasingly political theorists are not wanted in this mission. More and more, the most quantitatively oriented political scientists handle all concern with methodology and philosophy of social science. They hold on tightly, I have observed, because they are confident of their knowledge. No doubt also, they have full awareness that these courses can be crucial recruiting grounds. In two universities where I have taught recently, the highly quantitative souls controlled methodology and most of what

----

[2] See: Hanna Fenichel Pitkin, **Wittgenstein and Justice**, Berkeley, University of California Press, 1972; Brian Barry, **The Liberal Theory of Justice**, New York, Oxford University Press, 1973; William E. Connolly, **The Terms of Political Discourse**, Lexington, MA, D. C. Heath, 1974.

philosophy of social science there is.   This is quite typical.
In one of them, there is no relief; and in the other, this
domination is abridged only by the presence of an "empirical theorist" who readily admits that he faces suspicion.

A third area which has attracted some political theorists, often from untraditional starting places, is what I
would call "structural theory."   Its band of practitioners
are convinced that they have much to offer political science.   In **Size and Democracy**, which exemplifies this enterprise, Robert Dahl and Edward Tufte nicely describe its
mission: "to develop new theory which will offer useful
guidance about the appropriate relation among units."[3]
Structural theorists do not call for the development of
empirical theory alone.   Empirical theory is on the agenda
of most research-oriented political scientists, and they do
not expect political philosophers to lead the way there.
What people like Dahl and Tufte seek, rather, is the development of structural answers to current problems, such as
the institutional requirements for a healthy business-state
interaction or the primary system that should replace the
present one.   The agenda here is normative, let there be
no mistake about it, but it concentrates largely on improvement of institutions.   It assumes that great normative principles are not at issue and, sometimes, not even relevant.
It expects that issues will be resolved very much within the
boundaries of empirical, situational, and value terms as we
know and experience them; nothing less, but also nothing
more.   It is a search for pragmatic structural answers, not
"Utopian" ones.

Despite calls for this kind of theoretical enterprise,
even from such luminaries as Dahl, there have been surprisingly few answers from political theorists.   Perhaps the
activity seems to be too mundane or exceedingly modest,
despite the examples of the "great" political theorists, who
often dipped into structural theory.   In any event, this
project is clearly unattractive to most political theorists to
produce an overall integration of their subfield into political
science as a whole.

Certainly the project I would term "normative policy
theory" is far more ambitious than that.   Its advocates hold
that there is a need for a political theory that can assist
political science in facing the realm of normative policy

----

[3] Robert A. Dahl and Edward R. Tufte, **Size and Democracy**, Stanford, CA, Stanford University Press, 1973, p.
20.

choice.   Such theory is now gaining currency among some postbehavioral policy analysts, political economists, and experts in public administration.   In one sense, their mounting interest in it is an exciting development from the perspective of political philosophy.   This represents an opening to normative analysis in political science and other circles at least twenty-five years past their last-known enthusiasm for political theory.

Normative policy theory is far from a fully articulated, coherent position.   It also has a long way to go before it gains wide acceptance.   Charles Anderson is particularly notable among those who have led the advance here, and he deserves praise.   He has sought to articulate standards for a legitimate approach in terms of coherence, logic, and normativity.[4]   It is not easy work, but surely it is the work of a political theorist.   It is significant that Anderson, and not he alone, comes to this task from outside the subfield of theory.   Moreover, he has found only mixed support from the "official" political philosophers at his institutional home.   They are rather unaccustomed to having someone around who is a theorist and at the same time is recognized as "relevant" by at least a few of his colleagues.

This is surely an approach whose focus on the pragmatic side is obvious.   It is careful to steer away from general claims and sweeping judgments.   It is not at all uncomfortable in taking specific positions within particular circumstances and one political ideology (American liberalism).   This is probably just what is necessary to be of help to contemporary political science, though there is really little evidence that this approach has caught the imagination of many political scientists.   There has been some interest; whether it will go beyond that is merely speculation at this time.

In short, there is a reason to remain skeptical of the strength and general attractiveness of many of these purported bridges.   Neither political scientists nor ordinary political theorists seem to be hurrying to give them their blessing.   Maybe it is a matter of time only.   Or maybe the tensions and suspicions go much deeper than some of our optimistic brothers and sisters think.   Exactly what would bridge-builders say to political philosophers who believe

----

[4] See: Charles W. Anderson, "The Place of Principles in Policy Analysis," **American Political Science Review**, 73, 3, September, 1979, pp. 711-723.

that these ideas will mean a surrender of the profound normative and historical concerns that have always been political theory?   Exactly what do they say to those political scientists who stubbornly continue to insist (how often have we heard it said?) that all forms of political theory belong in either the philosophy or the history department?

The truth is that there is little interest as yet on either side of the "ghetto."   Ordinary political philosophy continues to have few aspirations to assist political science, and little pretense that it does.   And the feeling is mutual. The gap is huge in practice, and I can discover no evidence which suggests most political scientists and political theorists are not prepared to live with it.   I don't say that it is a comfortable decision, especially for political philosophers.   Their isolation and other discontents exact too high a cost for that.   I do say that it is a fact and perhaps one with some sense.   Political science and political theory are extremely diverse.   Maybe they would be wise to abandon worry and let each other alone in respective diversity, allowing creativity to poke its head up where it will.

Certainly we should not kid ourselves that there is much sign of interest in normative analysis by political scientists in general.   True, they often engage in it; but they notoriously refuse to see this.   Nor is there sympathy for political theory in its historical dimension on the part of a discipline still astoundingly ahistorical.

On the other side, meanwhile, political theorists often resist the integrationists.   Sometimes we can recognize pride at work.   The suspicion is strong that closing the gap means relegating political theory to underlaborer status.   This is unlikely to be an attractive prospect to a field whose image of selfworth has often gone in the opposite, queen-bee direction.   Still, we should resist the call of pride.   It cannot be the issue; contribution must be.   What political theory can contribute and how: this remains our agenda.

We must ask, outside the natural but corrupting realm of pride, why the integrationist route is not the secure path.   There are three reasons that strike me most forcefully.   First, we need to reflect on what might be the intellectual losses.   Do we have any reason to be confident that theorists could expand their insight into things political by snuggling tightly into the political-science nest?   Wouldn't the considerable contribution to human understanding and change which some political philosophers have provided (and no doubt will continue to provide) by raising fundamental questions about the world as it is surely decrease?   It would have to, since all these bridges operate firmly within the existent (however loosely defined) paradigm of the political world. In a Mannheimian sense, we must ask if we want political theory to give up its utopian role (whether pursued through broadly normative or historical study)?

For example, I welcome the advent of normative policy analysis.   Still,   I   have   strong   reservations   about   any wholesale move by theorists in that direction.   It is not clear how we can know beforehand how to balance the putative gains of this fashion in policy study against the benefits of an often stumbling, but hardly dead, political theory, including both its skeptical and its utopian roles. The performance of the latter today is clearly mixed.   This we know; but we should recognize that, at best, many of the siren calls of the integrationists are as yet only the most ethereal of promises.

Second, all the enthusiasm for integration and getting out of our ghetto suggests a sharply less diverse political philosophy.   It is not certain that this would be the result. Maybe a fuller engagement with political science -- which is itself more diverse than some of its critics realize -- would work to make political theory yet more diverse, open, and congenial.   Don't count on it, however; not at all.   Moreover, we should recognize that some integrationists actively yearn to reduce diversity by marriage with political science -- and thus reduce our marginality, which they believe is founded in our intellectual separation from political science. Insofar as such a thought is in any of our minds, it seems strange to me.   Theorists should seek more diversity and so should scientists, if I am to be allowed to affirm my Millian confidence in the intellectual benefits of openness. This may not mean political science should open its doors to those who predict political events on the basis of sunspots (though I would like to see a disproof of this hypothesis). But on the other hand, it would not be too corrupting to let a few "strange and irrelevant" political theorists wander around.   They might even promote some new ideas.   Too many of us appear to hold to the integrated, paradigmatic model of science, even though its enthusiasts never explain why it is so attractive to them.   Yet this model is largely illusory.   Has it existed in the creative periods of any science?   Pluralism still seems a better bet for creativity in political theory and political science.

Third, it is doubtful just how many political philosophers could contribute, at least to structural or policy tasks. As many a political scientist could tell you, there is an army of political theorists who are so lost in history that they would be of no use. One of the University of Chicago's (considerable) number of unemployed theory doctorates works as a policymaker in the Department of Local Government in one of our states. He laughs at how much he had to learn when he turned from his dissertation on John Milton (was he a pre-Straussian or an early Hobbesian?) to town planning. This is no great shock. The enterprises are different. Most of us know it and are not particularly enthusiastic about changing that fact.

We should not even count on positive results when (if) theory reorients itself toward tasks of policy and structure as part of the kingdom of political science. A friend of mine who was let go at an "upwardly mobile" university in the South was informed that his work on harm was just not relevant to the mainstream of political science. He had tried integration and worked to demonstrate the considerable policy implications of exploring harm. Attempting to "integrate," he discovered that the lingering suspicion -- no, the very active suspicion -- which many political scientists have for a political theorist regardless of his stripe still flourishes. It may turn out to be a painful and short-lived embrace. The lure of marriage to political science is great, but there is considerable reason to suspect that both spouses will soon prove cold and disappointing.

And yet the subject is not finally done. For the "crisis" remains -- factually and, indeed, intellectually. In fact, political theory in political science is declining; and in intellect, it is drifting in disarray. Maybe the integration thesis deserves a second look. Maybe several ideas do. Is there some way to inch political theory into not so much political science, but the world of politics? Is there some way to edge it toward a less "alienated" condition, both increasing its contribution to the larger world (which wouldn't take much) and facilitating better relations with political science? This is the goal.

IV

To search for this goal actively is to decide that there are possibilities other than naivete or unhappy coping. It constitutes a statement of optimism that maybe there is a route that will get us to a place where we are still diverse but bold and determined to strive for political knowledge and argument as of old. It will lead us away from worry over political science or any established discipline; it will focus us on doing political theory well and having impact on the world. On the other hand, maybe such a path, such an aspiration, is beyond us more than I want to admit. Obviously, I don't know. Yet I have a view about what this direction for political theory should be. It suggests perspective and urges practice, and is my statement of hope.

I make only two points. First, I urge that we stop fussing about the fate of political theory. Yes, we should acknowledge the crisis in fact and in spirit with a clear nod. At the same time, we should recognize that the political theory in political science is not yet a corpse and that, outside of our narrow precincts, it booms. And second, we should get on with doing theory, in as "unalienated" a fashion as possible. If we do not do so, then we cannot produce good theory; and we cannot have a beneficial impact on our world.

Like everybody else, I have heard the complaints from theorists, not to mention others, about our subfield. And I've expressed my skepticism that such strategies as hunkering down or marrying quickly (if ever so solemnly) with political science will solve them. I know the cries about the absurd and unending deluge of articles on remote thinkers of the past, the earnest search for another unlikely twist to yet one more obscure Platonic dialogue, the arid formalism of endless discussions of liberty or justice, the idolization of intellectual history, the confusion of ideology with argument, and much else.

This is, however, only a part of the story, just as the few jobs are only part. There are other sides which are worth celebrating. The process of introducing students to aspects of political theory goes on in hundreds of classrooms every week. With it, often comes the excitement and the illumination that we theorists remember when we first encountered political philosophy. And then there is evidence that many people are doing theory which is excellent from all sorts of angles and perspectives. No Great List is appropriate or possible, because there are simply too many people actively contributing for that. As a sampler to illustrate the diversity which abounds, consider: Robert Dahl on democratic theory, John Gunnell on the "tradition" of political philosophy, Patrick Riley and Judith Shklar on the social-contract tradition, John Schaar and Wilson Carey McWilliams on loyalty and fraternity, Hanna Pitkin on obligation, Straussians on American political thought, Jean Elshtain on feminism, Michael Walzer on war, and on and on.[5]

----

[5] See: Robert A. Dahl, **A Preface to Democratic Theory,**

There is simply too much going on in the subfield of political philosophy for unqualified gloom. Intellectual vitality does not replace lost jobs, but it probably does cut losses. And I think that vitality gets some small recognition. The success of the entire group of political-theory panels at the APSA year after year in attracting far more people than any other group suggests a continuing appeal; the presence of political-theory panels among almost all of the alternative groups at the APSA convention is another sign; so is the emergence of **Political Theory** as an important journal in political science; and there are others.

These intimations of a future do not prove anything, and they are not meant to do so. None of them confirms that the death of political theory in any traditional sense may not lie ahead. Perhaps it is not unreasonable, though, to draw a measure of optimism and suggest that the "crisis" may be exaggerated. It is not exaggerated in terms of the lack of jobs and what that implies. It may be exaggerated if we assume that political theory as a whole proceeds in a fruitless manner, doing obeisance to antique traditions which yield little theory and less impact. This description fits a good many of us at least partly. Yet we know that it doesn't describe a good many of us in the slightest. We know that our subfield is very much alive, if far from what it can be. There may be a serious crisis, then, in terms of numbers; and there may be another in terms of concrete

----

Chicago, University of Chicago Press, 1956; John G. Gunnell, **Political Theory**, Cambridge, MA, Winthrop, 1979; Patrick Riley, "How Coherent Is the Social Contract Tradition?," **Journal of the History of Ideas**, 34, 4, October-December, 1973, pp. 543-562; Judith N. Shklar, **Men and Citizens**, Cambridge, Cambridge University Press, 1969; John H. Schaar, **Loyalty in America**, Berkeley, University of California Press, 1957; Wilson Carey McWilliams, **The Idea of Faternity in America**, Berkeley, University of California Press, 1973; Hanna Fenichel Pitkin, "Obligation and Consent, I-II," **American Political Science Review**, 59, 1, December, 1965, pp. 990-999, and 60, 1, March, 1966, pp. 39-52; Robert H. Horwitz, ed., **The Moral Foundations of the American Republic**, Charlottesville, University Press of Virginia, 1977; Jean Bethke Elshtain, **Public Man, Private Woman**, Princeton, NJ, Princeton University Press, 1981; Michael Walzer, **Just and Unjust Wars**, New York, Basic Books, 1977; Walzer, **Obligations**, Cambridge, MA, Harvard University Press, 1970.

impact. There may even be an intellectual crisis, but we should not proclaim political philosophy a desert. We can do a lot better, but we are hardly hopeless.

Moreover, some of us (including myself) could do with a little perspective. Whatever the vigor of political theory in political science, it is in an enormous growth phase in other areas of American intellectual life. This is an important observation to make, not least because several thoughtful foreign observers I know suggest that there is no difference in the "crisis" theory forces in or out of political science: the treatment of political philosophy wherever practiced in the USA is merely another example of the non-intellectual and nonphilosophical approach perennial in so many areas of American culture. The implication here, of course, is that the American mind is practical and matter-of-fact at best, and anti-intellectual and hopelessly insular at worst. While I don't pretend to enter the now ancient struggle between the United States and Europe or probe the sources of European intellectual hostility toward America, this particular negative hypothesis doesn't describe our age. There is a sharply different pattern between the health of political philosophy in and out of political science. Indeed, in the larger American intellectual world, these are flood times for theory. It is in a lush state of activity almost everywhere.

To grant the fact that much of the political philosophy with wider currency today does not come from within our little terrain may depress some souls. Should it? When did popular or potent political philosophy ever come from within political science in particular or academia in general? Moreover, we can look at all this in quite a different way. It is at least as reasonable to draw considerable consolation from this situation. It shows that, in broad perspective, political theory is doing just fine and is likely to continue to do so. As illustrations of the robust health of political theory outside of political science, six areas come immediately to mind, though the number could be much larger. It is not an unfamiliar list; but put together, it is impressive. A brief look will explain my enthusiasm.

(1) While political and social philosophy are hardly at the center of modern philosophy, nonetheless philosophers have contributed significantly to every major realm of current political theory. John Rawls, however much or little one responds to his work, is the premier political philosopher of our time. **A Theory of Justice** ("alienated" or not) is a major work of political philosophy by any standard. The remarkable Rawls industry spawned in several fields -- economics, law, social science in general, and even political

science in particular -- suggests Rawls' influence. From discussions of liberalism and anarchism to pursuit of Kant, Robert Paul Wolff is another valuable contributor from the discipline of philosophy. Consider, too, Ronald Dworkin, whose **Taking Rights Seriously** is the most significant work of legal philosophy in decades. And then there is Robert Nozick, Rawls' sometime colleague at Emerson Hall. According to his admirers, he is every bit Rawls' equal as a political thinker. Further, there are the more analytical thinkers such as Gerald MacCallum, known for his work on freedom. Undoubtedly, there is a lot of political theory in philosophy.[6]

(2) This is increasingly true also in the world of economics, a world which more and more seems to be at the center of social science. For a long time, of course, John Kenneth Galbraith has operated from this home. From **The Affluent Society** to **The New Industrial State**, his books are widely discussed essays in political thought. The current cult of laissez-faire economics brings us to Milton Friedman, who once again is a best-selling thinker, a role he began with his serious **Capitalism and Freedom**. At a less public, but certainly not less serious level, we encounter the efforts of a host of other economists deeply engaged in political theory. One example is the work by Marxist economists and structuralists at the University of Massachusetts at Amherst and elsewhere. In controversial fashion, they have explored the role of the state, the proper educational system, and (of course) the relationship between economics and politics. Special mention must be made of Charles Lindblom for his meshing of political and economic analysis with political theory. His latest foray, **Politics and Markets**, is intriguing and challenging and has received fittingly strong reviews from political scientists. Clearly, he is not easily classified as either economist or philosopher;

----

[6] See: John Rawls, **A Theory of Justice**, Cambridge, MA, Harvard University Press, 1971; Robert Paul Wolff, **The Poverty of Liberalism**, Boston, Beacon Press, 1968; Wolff, **In Defense of Anarchism**, New York, Harper and Row, 1970; Wolff, **The Autonomy of Reason**, New York, Harper and Row, 1973; Ronald Dworkin, **Taking Rights Seriously**, Cambridge, MA, Harvard University Press, 1977; Robert Nozick, **Anarchy, State, and Utopia**, New York, Basic Books, 1974; Gerald C. MacCallum, Jr., "Negative and Positive Freedom," **Philosophical Review**, 76, 3, July, 1967, pp. 312-334.

he is both and more.[7]

(3) Another world where political theory notably flourishes today is that of grand (and not so grand) social philosophy. This is often undertaken by "neoconservatives," whatever their formal home disciplines. Robert Nisbet is one. He has written some of the most thoughtful books on the political ideas of the West -- from **The Twilight of Authority** to his recent, overpraised **History of the Idea of Progress**. Daniel Bell, of course, is another. Bell alone has done more theorizing about the United States than any political theorist I know. The most-discussed of his recent books is **The Cultural Contradictions of Capitalism**; but as we all know, there have been many more. And consider such journals as **The Public Interest** or **Commentary**, organs of the neoconservative movement. For any recent year, it would not be hard to show that they offered more significant (if sometimes distasteful) political theory than did **The American Political Science Review**, indeed than did **Political Theory**. From a "neo-Marxist" perspective, **there are the essays of** Michael Harrington, whose vision of democratic socialism and explorations of public policy range from "big-picture" adventures in political thought to influential indictments of poverty in America and the Third World.[8]

(4) Another realm where political theory is alive, growing, and prosperous is futurism. It may not be fully distinct from several other arenas already mentioned, but it

----

[7] See: John Kenneth Galbraith, **The Affluent Society**, Boston, Houghton Mifflin, 1958; Galbraith, **The New Industrial State**, New York, New American Library, 1967; Milton Friedman, **Capitalism and Freedom**, Chicago, University of Chicago Press, 1962; Michael H. Best and William E. Connolly, **The Politicized Economy**, Lexington, MA, D. C. Heath, 1976; Charles Lindblom, **Politics and Markets**, New York, Basic Books, 1977.

[8] See: Robert Nisbet, **Twilight of Authority**, New York, Oxford University Press, 1975; Nisbet, **History of the Idea of Progress**, New York, Basic Books, 1979; Daniel Bell, **The Cultural Contradictions of Capitalism**, New York, Basic Books, 1976; Michael Harrington, **Socialism**, New York, Saturday Review Press, 1972; Harrington, **The Twilight of Capitalism**, New York, Simon and Schuster, 1976; Harrington, **The Other America**, Baltimore, Penguin Books, revised edition, 1971; Harrington, **The Vast Majority**, New York, Simon and Schuster, 1977.

is a particular focus where political thought is respectable and indeed welcome. Prophets are as frequent today as the disasters that they imagine or see in our future. Robert Heilbroner qualifies with **An Inquiry into the Human Prospect** and several of his other books, raising disturbing problems for world political order and making challenging arguments toward their resolution. Or consider Barry Commoner. Leave aside his polemical style and his ill-fated presidential campaign. What is left is political thought: written with intelligence, directed toward our future, our planet, and our common political life. While Commoner is notoriously pessimistic, there have been and are other futurists more optimistic. Buckminster Fuller comes to mind. In such influential books as **Operating Manual for Spaceship Earth**, he proposed a utopian political theory and suggested that it is not at all beyond our grasp. [9]

   (5) As always, history continues to be a fertile ground for contemporary political thought. Just take the work being done on American political thought, most of which has the author's norms expertly woven throughout each book. Consider Daniel Boorstin and his multivolumed **The Americans**. This is one of the cleverest and most tightly orchestrated arguments that I've read in political theory. Or consider the plethora of books on the subject of the American revolution, the Constitution, and the figures and ideas of that time. Most of them are essays in political argument. Some examples come from people outside the formal discipline of history, for instance (philosopher) Morton White in **The Philosophy of the American Revolution** and (journalist) Garry Wills in **Inventing America** and more recently in **Explaining America**. Other works in political theory are by professional historians, such as Gordon Wood and Bernard Bailyn, both widely admired for their insight regarding the beginnings of American political thinking. Even so, looking at the world of historical exploration and argument about American political thought only scratches the surface of the relevant activity within history. There are so many other examples which deserve notice: Peter Gay's lifelong argument for Enlightenment liberalism and

----

[9] See: Robert L. Heibroner, **An Inquiry into the Human Prospect**, New York, Norton, revised edition, 1975; Barry Commoner, **The Closing Circle**, New York, Knopf, 1971; Commoner, **The Poverty of Power**, New York, Knopf, 1976; R. Buckminster Fuller, **Operating Manual for Spaceship Earth**, New York, Simon and Schuster, 1970.

Frank and Fritzie Manuel's tour de force on **Utopian Thought in the Western World** among them. This is as rich a lode for political theory as one can find.[10]

(6) Finally, there are other areas, too. B. F. Skinner, most recently in **Beyond Freedom and Dignity**, is only the most famous of many from within the world of psychology and psychiatry (discretely, I will pass by pop psychology) who present themselves as thinkers with considerable political vision. There is also theory generated within the enormous and growing religious culture in the United States, which many political philosophers know little about. Within that world, there are a number of insightful and contributing political theorists. Three who come to mind immediately are: Harvey Cox in **The Secular City, Turning East**, and other books; James Wall in editorials for the leading liberal-protestant weekly, **The Christian Century**; and Jim Wallis in **Sojourners** magazine. Each is intensely concerned with developing and arguing a political philosophy grounded in religion, and each is good at doing so.[11]

And I could go on. The fact is that political theory is doing just fine. A hundred -- and more -- flowers are blooming. Yes, we could argue forever whether all these people deserve the name "theorist;" or whether "philosopher," "theorist," and "thinker" represent different levels of accomplishment or insight or something. None of this is to the point. What we should admit is that there is no reason to worry that political theory's general condition has anything whatsoever to do with its situation in political science. It doesn't.

----

[10] See: Daniel Boorstin, **The Americans**, New York, Random House, in three volumes, 1958, 1965, 1973; Morton White, **The Philosophy of the American Revolution**, New York, Oxford University Press, 1978; Garry Wills, **Inventing America**, New York, Random House, 1978; Wills, **Explaining America**, Garden City, NY, 1981; Peter Gay, **The Enlightenment**, New York, Random House, in two volumes, 1966, 1969; Frank E. and Fritzie P. Manual, **Utopian Thought in the Western World**, Cambridge, MA, Harvard University Press, 1979.

[11] See: B. F. Skinner, **Beyond Freedom and Dignity**, New York, Bantam Books, 1971; Harvey Cox, **The Secular City**, New York, Macmillan, revised edition, 1965; Cox, **Turning East**, New York, Simon and Schuster, 1977.

V

My second suggestion follows from my first and from the rest of this paper. We should get on with political theory. This is supposedly what we are about. If so, then let us proceed: not in a spirit of hunkering down and pretending; but in a wide-awake manner, knowing the situation, yet still wanting to do theory. Action, even intellectual action, is not the end of the world; but short of a cult in its name, it can address many aspects of our crisis as nothing else can. But I do not want to be disingenuous. I do not think that just anything people could or have called "theory" or "philosophy" is what we require right now. I think we need "unalienated" theory which will both help us in the world and, in fact, be better theory.

I am not entirely comfortable, to be honest, in recommending such a direction for political theory. Partly, this is because I recognize that what I suggest will have scant effect on the magnificent freedom which political philosophy and its practitioners will exercise far from what I urge. I don't fool myself here; but I don't feel badly about this fact either, although it does suggest that there is a tinge of the absurd in plowing ahead. Partly, this is a matter of my own affection for the current world of political theory in political science. I see the crisis, I have the frustrations; but the affection is there, perhaps especially for the pluralism. We may be in our fall, so to say, but the colors of the leaves are many and sometimes beautiful. Directions can become paradigms, which look like limiters of creativity to me. We need more creativity in political theory, not less. And besides, paradigms are so terribly boring.

On the other hand, I insist that it is time we take the step and unashamedly get back in touch with politics. As a subfield, political theory has a good deal of ground to travel before it can make that rendevous. There are four reasons why I think we need (perhaps desperately) to move away from theory which ignores or hates or cannot find politics. There is no inherent logic to their order below, but I am comfortable with it.

First, the result would be a political philosophy which makes a much greater contribution to the public realm. I have no faith that political theory can save us. But the contribution of political theory to public affairs is now so extremely slight that such a shift is bound to make a modest improvement. It is obvious to us all that we are struggling as citizens and as people now, late in the twentieth century.   Political philosophy can help us in this struggle; and there is little doubt that we need help.

I have no neat program, but I do have a question. It is one that I would like all political theorists to ask of themselves and their work from time to time. It is a simple and hardly very restrictive query. We might ask in our classroom and in our studies whether our activity involves any engagement with the world, seeks any connection of theory and practice? Perhaps we should pose this query in the proverbial still, small hours of the night. We need to be honest with ourselves. I don't doubt that most theorists could respond affirmatively. If so, good; yet again, there is a need to be honest. In the process, I believe we should keep in mind that there can be no formula for how engagement does and can take place. The future easily escapes our formulas. Moreover, the need for normative, historical, and analytical insight is too great for anyone to be too strict.

Second, I am confident that, as a result, we could produce better political theory on its own terms. Somehow the idea is afoot that a political theory in touch with the world is a vulgar, cheap, and trivial theory. In some cases, certainly; but let's look around today or any day: a lot could be excellent. This is not entirely a statement of faith. Theory would be more interesting in large part because it would interact with the world. In this sense, it would be open and not closed, reaching out and not in. Its current condition of hermetic asphixiation would cease. It would also be better because it would be disciplined by the world: not necessarily overwhelmed by it, as skeptics worry; but disciplined. This means almost instant decline in the utterly irrelevant, the mere games for journal refer- ences or articles, the new interpretations of a thinker twice or thrice overdetermined already. The result would be far more energy available and in contact with the world, a base for more theory of quality.

Third, such a subfield would turn out to have some things to offer political science after all. Interacting with the world, it could interact with that (possibly diminishing) proportion of political science that is in touch with the world. It could look at common problems, events, and phe- nomena in order to offer its insights: normative, analyt- ical, and (even) empirical. Perhaps it could also help polit- ical science by showing one of its usually undoubted strengths: a taste and a talent for argument.

There are reasons for hope. There are a good many people doing unalienated theory in our subfield: no doubt many more in their classrooms than on paper, but a good number either way. What is needed is for others to take up the mantel. Some examples are in order. There is the impressive illustration of Michael Walzer. His way of probing through cases of obligation or acts of war unites theory and practice in a self-conscious and successful way. It is with good reason that he is admired in political theory and is perhaps the only political philosopher linked with political science who has a considerable intellectual reputation outside our discipline. Or consider Brian Barry. When he is connecting his analytical explorations with the larger world, he is at his most successful and suggests exciting possibilities for analytical work focused this side of Absolute Abstraction. Then there is Robert Dahl, whose work in empirical theory is an obviously accomplished dance between theory and practice. Or there is the new work in political economy and policy studies, already mentioned. Its practitioners may be the most consistent and determined adherents of nonalienated theory today. Their home may not always, or even often, be political science. When it is, however, they deserve encouragement.

But is there really a need to list just several of many who are venturing (or have ventured) into the world of unalienated theory? The answer is yes, just to show they are there. These people and their approaches exist. The larger goal, though, is not to name pioneers or stars, but to encourage less museum-keeping or seminars in existential angst and more work in political theory which looks down to earth as well as up to the heavens. There are times when I think that the answer is a political science which has abolished all fields called "political theory," "political philosophy," and the like. That would surely force theorists to take stock at once. In truth, in the long run, this is the way to go. Perhaps it would happen naturally, so to say, like the falling of the proverbial ripe fruit, if theorists turned to politics.

I don't mean that I expect magical embraces. This is not likely to happen, even if my advice were followed. We well know that political science is no simple universe of monolithic opinions or ideas, either. Yet theory and science would move closer together this way, and this might ease some tension, even improve the root health of theory within political science. Granted, I would not bet on this. But in this essay, there is room for optimism.

This would not, however, imply integration in the senses in which I have referred to before; not at all. This would not be integration so much as partial, self-chosen congruence. The difference matters a great deal. This would not be political theory rushing to "help" political science or to work in its field or paradigms. This would be political philosophy largely unconcerned with political science and certainly not devoted to helping it or always speaking in its tongues. This would be political theory closing the gap with at least some political scientists by rediscovering the political (as I've suggested, some political scientists might do the same). And in that rediscovery, theorists would join with others concerned with the political in the many ways that exist or might exist to illuminate it. Moreover, this would be alliance on terms chosen by theory -- or rather, by individual theorists -- which is not always the case with some of what the integrationists urge. That last difference over choice of terms matters a lot. It is not merely a matter of pride again. It is also a matter of how to do what we do best.

Are there possible paths toward a less alienated political theory which might be both especially useful and interesting and maybe particularly close to political science? Again, I hesitate; but let me underline at least a few of many possible hopes.

(1) We require normative analysis desperately. There is justifiable concern among many normative theorists that their efforts garner no respect. They suspect this is true within political science because they are taken to be expressing mere "opinions" and within political theory for reasons that reduce to the same dismissal. Beyond respect, normative theory needs outlets, especially those that don't follow one of several well-known party lines. **Philosophy and Public Affairs** is more and more the province of philosophers and less and less a journal for political theorists; nor is **Political Theory** the answer, either: though both are a good deal more than nothing. Moreover, the mainstream political-science journals continue to confuse political philosophy with the study of "the greats." This is especially true of **The American Political Science Review**.

One might assume that normative theory would be the ideal for nonalienated thinking in our age, but this is not necessarily so. Normative theory can easily soar far beyond the realm of human politics or turn into a self-conscious activity that is governed by strict rules which become more important than the process of thinking or illumination itself. It is not just analytic theory which sometimes has (and deserves) the reputation for arid and formalized theory.

(2) In this context, I think we should applaud those who seek to connect policy and theory. They produce intriguing examples of one way in which normative theory might make contact with the political world. The danger

here, and it is a real danger, is that normative policy
theory will simply surrender to those in policy studies who
reject any normative side or who routinely confuse endorsing the status quo with normative argument.

(3) And then, we come to analytical theory. Obviously, exploration of the central concepts, terms, and linguistic assumptions that underly our political life is praise-
worthy, even essential. We all know the impressive work
done in this area by political philosophers in recent years;
and we should welcome more, not less, of it. At the same
time, we are increasingly inundated with impossibly turgid,
abstract analyses and distinctions -- far, far from politics.
They are worthy only of philosophy in its worst analytical
mood.

(4) Even history can play a valuable role. But it is
a question of what kind of history. If it is history which
probes thinkers for their current and permanent illumination
for our time or for all time, then let us welcome it. If it
helps us to think about politics, let us encourage it. And
yes, if it helps us to explore our civilization, let us
embrace it. On the other hand, the alienated history now
so prominent is more problematic. There is a great deal of
room for the wideranging activities our subfield calls "the
history of political thought." Yet we should draw back
from history as abstract study of thinkers just because
they are "great," or we like to solve the puzzle of their
meaning, or this is the way we were taught in graduate
school. We should draw back from the huge proportion of
theory which is repeated investigation of past thinkers who
have been explored almost until (our) death. If we are
honest, we know that much of this activity exists solely for
its own sake and wholly in a world of its own. (Was Locke
really Hobbes, or Hobbes really Locke; and what is the
"true" interpretation of Machiavelli?).

(5) Last, there is experimental theory. We need to
appreciate that, in moving toward the political, there will
be all kinds of avenues to follow. We need to encourage
each other to take risks with approaches, ideas, and experiments that might be nonalienated theory, however unconventional. This is the way that political theory will grow
and develop as an enterprise, if I may slip into the language of our time. Instead of protecting our turf and mut-
tering further incantations over Plato, Hobbes, or Marx, we
should open ourselves up to many souls, as long as they
seek to think systematically about politics in the world.
When I look hard at political-theory books and journals, I
see less pluralism than a list of approaches and foci would
suggest. We have our different paths, yes, but they are

well-trod. We need to open our doors: to let ourselves
get needed fresh air.   In more concrete terms, this means
more gentleness in judging each other, more thoughtful
encouragement of nonalienated theory, and more openness to
many definitions of engagement.   We should also strive to
provide support for good, younger men and women coming
along in the profession.   The cold realities are that such
support will encourage experimentation but its absence will
encourage carefulness.   "Careful as an assistant professor":
that is a term which has real meaning, much more than it
should.

All of this sounds marginal, maybe even accommoda-
tionist (heaven forbid!) to the more freewheeling anti-tra-
ditionalist reformers of political theory.   They hold the
gospel of nonalienated theory impatiently and can be harsh.
They can go too far -- and anyway are not going in quite
the appropriate way to follow.   They might err and reject
the impressive sections of theory which are "lost" in Plato,
Rawls, or Jefferson; but they are correct to urge us on to
more engagement.   They might well remind us that connecting politics and political theory was exactly what the classic
philosophers did.   Their aim was intensely political and
this-worldly, a fact as true of Plato as of Marx.

In this process, we will be doing theory -- connecting with and maybe helping the world -- in an atmosphere
of considerable purpose yet pluralism.   Then we will do
better, more useful theory; and then perhaps our subfield's
crisis of future existence and intellectual integrity may
ease.   Certainly, we will worry less about whether or not
we serve political science.   After all, we know that political
science is not a discipline of great importance or accomplishment.   My guess is that only when we recognize this
will relations improve and theory be of more help to political
science.

The strange fact is that political science can't quite
do without us; and I think it realizes this, in a modest
way.   It should continue to do so as long as we are confident of our future outside and even inside the discipline
and convinced that we should not marry into political science.   It should do so more if we act as a concerned,
always nonalienated, and sometimes irritating lover.   In this
day and age, we should know that not everyone has to
marry anymore.

INDEX